EDITORIAL ADVISORY BOARD

POLICY STUDIES

STUDIES

REVIEW

ANNUAL

1979   Volume 3

Edited by
Robert H. Haveman
and
B. Bruce Zellner

SAGE
PUBLICATIONS

Beverly Hills   London

H
1
P73
vol. 3

Copyright © 1979 by Sage Publications, Inc.

For information address:

SAGE PUBLICATIONS, INC.
275 South Beverly Drive
Beverly Hills, California 90212

SAGE PUBLICATIONS LTD
28 Banner Street
London EC1Y 8QE, England

Printed in the United States of America

International Standard Book Number 0-8039-1183-1

Library of Congress Catalog Card No. 77-72938

International Standard Series Number 0163-108X

BT 2857-81   10/17/80

FIRST PRINTING

CONTENTS

INTRODUCTION

Robert H. Haveman and B. Bruce Zellner

Every editor of the *Policy Studies Review Annual* brings a unique perspective to bear in selecting articles to be included. This perspective reflects varying methodological and disciplinary judgments, varying judgments on what the field of policy studies or policy analysis is and where it should be going, and varying judgments regarding the quality of articles which are or claim to be in the field. Because it is the objective to assemble a set of essays which are both interesting and topical, there will be varying perspectives on these matters as well.

The volume clearly reflects our perspectives. Here we will be explicit about these judgments and perspectives, and then let the content of the volume speak for itself. First, we are both economists. As a result, the general topics selected and the articles chosen under each topic tend to emphasize economics more than the other disciplines involved in the field of policy studies—sociology, psychology, political science, law, and so on. This emphasis is clearly seen by comparing the contents of volume I (edited by Stuart Nagel, a political scientist) and volume II (edited by Howard Freeman, a sociologist) with that of this volume.

Second, we have a particular view of what policy studies or policy analysis is. That view has several aspects. In the first place, we feel that the field of policy studies or policy analysis must define itself, and this definition will develop as researchers do just what the title of the field says—study or analyze policies. A corollary of this view is that we place a low weight on papers which discuss the policy process or reforms in policy-making, relative to papers which analyze a policy, a policy proposal, or a problem which leads to calls for policy action.

Moreover, by "studying or analyzing policies" we also mean something fairly specific. Numerous problems exist which generate calls for collective action. Many of these problems have a basis in some failure on the part of the private economy to achieve an efficient allocation of resources or to yield a distribution of income which meets the standards of equity held by the society. Others have to do with the failure of some institution other than the market economy to serve accepted social goals. Identifying the nature of market or institutional failure leads to the specification of the objectives which policy actions should be designed to achieve. In any given case, numerous policy options can be defined, each of which contribute to the attainment of the objectives in some degree.

It is in this context that policy analyses and studies can claim to make a contribution. Such studies contribute to the identification and understanding of the efficiency, equity, or broader social or institutional problems motivating calls for policy action. Such analyses contribute to the identification of well-defined objectives which policy action should be designed to achieve, as well as the trade-offs among these objectives. They both identify and design specific policy actions which contribute to the attainment of the objectives. And, finally, policy analyses evaluate the extent to which alternative policies or policy proposals contribute to these objectives, and identify side effects which such alternatives might entail. By and large, the studies we have chosen for volume III of *Policy Studies Review Annual* are consistent with this view of the field.

A third judgment concerns the quality of the analyses which are to be included. The judgment lying behind this volume is that the essays must meet accepted research standards in the scholarly community. To this end, our search for studies proceeded along three primary lines. First, we made a search of the primary journals in the social science disciplines, and the major policy analysis journals which have grown in number and circulation in recent years. These sources have been identified in the introductory essay by Stuart Nagel in volume I of *Policy Studies Review Annual.* Second, letters were sent to the directors of the primary policy research institutes or centers (private, university based, and government related), soliciting articles which could be considered for inclusion. This resulted in the submission of a large number of essays, many of which we would not have otherwise discovered. Finally, we relied on the suggestions of the Editorial Board, many of whom are included in this volume. Clearly, a large number of articles had to be screened and only a limited number could be included.

There are a final set of judgments which any editor must make in assembling a collection such as this. These concern the need to construct a volume which potential readers—with diverse interests and backgrounds—will find interesting. These judgments may well (and did) conflict with judgments on quality and with the consistency of our view of the field of policy analysis. We gave this objective fairly high priority. Our primary means of accomplishing this was to identify those issues most central to the policy debate in the federal government. As a result, inflation, energy, regulation, taxation, and welfare are highlighted in this volume. We also looked to debates in the literature in each of these areas, and attempted to include two or more essays which presented alternative views or evidence on a particular issue. Consequently, this volume covers fewer issues than its predecessor, but includes more studies dealing with each issue.

Section I deals with the most pressing policy problem in 1978—*inflation.* And in the 1978 policy debate over effective anti-inflation policy, many other, traditionally separate, policy areas—regulation, energy, and employment— became joined with the more conventional macroeconomic policy measures. And joining with these approaches was the strategy of direct wage and price controls. Henry Aaron's article in this section sketches the recent failure of what had become conventional wisdom regarding the relation between inflation and the labor market. The existence of a stable trade-off between higher rates of inflation and lower rates of unemployment—often referred to as the Phillips curve—has been challenged both by recent research and experience. Aaron concentrates on the implications of this new skepticism for employment and—by implication—inflation policy. One clear implication is that traditional monetary and fiscal measures are not adequate by themselves.

Among the new anti-inflation tools to emerge from this changing perspective on the problem of inflation and the unemployment-inflation relation is one known as "Tax-based Income Policy" (TIP). Sidney Weintraub's contribution presents the empirical and intellectual basis for the anti-inflation policy dilemma which TIP is designed to solve. Weintraub then describes some of the alternative forms of a TIP strategy and the ways in which they could be implemented.

The essay by Albert Rees should be read with the Weintraub selection. Rees sees numerous drawbacks to the implementation of either a TIP or a deregulation strategy as antiinflation measures. Many of these difficulties are of an administrative, or measurement, sort.

The third selection is by Herbert Stein, who was the Chairman of the Council of Economic Advisors in the Nixon Administration. His article introduces a quite different anti-inflation strategy into the discussion—wage and price controls. In his analysis, Stein reviews the U.S. experience with direct controls during the 1971-1974 period. He finds this strategy to have been a failure in the effort to control wage and price increases, and discusses the primary reasons for this conclusion.

The final article is by Karl Brunner, a prominent critic of conventional fiscal policy measures. In Brunner's view, none of the anti-inflation strategies now being debated—from the current administration's program to TIP strategies to deregulation to wage-price controls—confront the basic, long-run, underlying cause of inflation, namely, an excessive growth rate in the money supply. The implications of this view for the behavior of the monetary authorities are drawn clearly.

The lack of agreement among these essays characterizes the current state of the economics profession regarding short-run anti-inflation policy. The debate is as unsettled as the problem is important.

The issue of *economic regulation*—or, more accurately, *deregulation*—was a close runner-up to inflation in terms of policy debate at the level of the federal government in 1978. Unlike inflation, there is something of a consensus in this area. Increasingly, both analysts and policy-makers agree that many of the rigidities and inefficiencies in the private sector are attributable to what Albert Rees has called "old-style regulation"—the comprehensive regulation of an entire industry by a single regulatory authority with broad powers.

The first two articles in this section both concern the regulation of the trucking industry by the Interstate Commerce Commission. In the first, John R. Felton describes the nature of federal regulation in this area, and attempts to measure the benefits and the costs of this governmental activity. Using the economist's benefit-cost analysis framework, he concludes that federal trucking regulation generates net social costs of about $5 billion annually. In a companion article, Thomas Gale Moore also examines the economic effects of trucking regulation, concluding that organized labor in the trucking industry experiences substantial economic gains from regulatory decisions. The losers, of course, are those who purchase goods that rely on regulated trucking for transportation. Because of his finding and his judgment regarding the political power of the Teamsters Union, Moore concludes that deregulation of trucking is unlikely.

The pessimistic tone of the Moore article has a contrast in the selection by Alfred Kahn, former Chairman of the Civil Aeronautics Board and now head of President Carter's antiinflation program. In his analysis, Kahn presents the theoretical economic basis for deregulation, reports on the successful deregulation of the airline industry, and analyzes the problems which confront the economy and particular industries during the transition from regulation to free competition.

The discussion of regulation-deregulation leads naturally to the next topic in the volume—*energy policy*. Perhaps no other policy area is so heavily burdened by regulations and controls, particularly the petroleum industry.

The articles by V. Kerry Smith and Walter Mead provide the natural bridge between regulation and energy policy. Both Smith and Mead analyse and critique the National Energy Plan (NEP) of the Carter Administration. Using a review of the objectives of governmental energy regulation and the economics of the market allocation process for exhaustible natural resources (like crude petroleum) as a background, Smith concludes that NEP opposes the principles of efficient regulation which he has outlined, and hence is "misdirected." He attributes much of this misdirection to the failures of past regulation. And it is the failures of past energy regulation which are the concern of the Mead essay. Like Smith, he too sees the NEP as an effort to elude the misguided policy measures of the past. Because it is difficult to extract government from a complex web of regulatory controls built up over a half-century, he too foresees serious problems for NEP.

The two other pieces included in this section are summaries of analyses, but not the studies themselves. Lying behind both are lengthy and more technical analyses which are available from the two sponsoring organizations—the RAND Corporation and the Congressional Budget Office (CBO). The RAND study, by Charles Phelps and Rodney Smith, analyzes the economic impacts of price controls on the oil industry, and the effects of price decontrol. Contrary to most analyses, Phelps and Smith conclude that existing controls have not reduced the price of refined petroleum products, while they have caused the U.S. to increase its imports of oil. This contrary conclusion is based on an analysis of the economics of price determination in both the crude and refined products segments of the industry. The primary effect of the controls and entitlements has been to transfer billions of dollars of profits among various levels of the industry, and to increase these profits.

The CBO analysis is more specific and focuses on President Carter's most recent version of his energy plan—decontrol with a windfall profits tax. After describing the current system of controls and the President's proposal, this study presents estimates of the price, production, consumption, and balance of payments effects of the proposed decontrol. It also addresses the effect of the proposals on the poor. Similar estimates are also presented for modifications and alternatives to the President's proposals.

The debate on *pollution control policy* in the United States in 1978 had many common elements with the debate over deregulation and energy policy. The first two articles in this section deal with an alternative to the direct regulatory nature of existing air and water quality policy. This alternative involves levying an "effluent charge" on waste generators, thereby discouraging the emission of discharges and encouraging the installation of pollution control equipment. In his essay, Clifford Russell analyzes what can and cannot be expected from publicly determined prices such as effluent charges. While indicating the importance of pricing the use of the environment on technological changes designed to economize on the use of the environment for waste disposal services, Russell notes serious problems with such a strategy. These problems involve information, legal, and administrative problems, as well as the difficulty of establishing a simple charges system which will achieve efficiency goals in a complex, interrelated, and diverse environmental context. The article by Thomas Teitenberg addresses one of the complexities noted by Russell—the spatially differentiated nature of the pollution problem. In analyzing the economic, administrative, and legal aspects of spatially differentiated effluent charges in the air pollution area, Teitenberg reaches a somewhat more optimistic conclusion than does Russell. In his words, the charges system would "offer the nation a realistic opportunity to achieve its air pollution goals at significantly lower costs."

While both Russell and Teitenberg examine the economic efficiency and administrative aspects of a pollution control strategy, the article by Henry Peskin concerns the distribution of the benefits and costs of air pollution policy. Peskin estimates that the losers from existing policy exceed the gainers, and speculates on the reasons why, if this is so, the policy appears to be supported politically. He emphasizes the important role which distributional considerations should and will play in any proposed revision of environmental policy.

With President Carter's introduction of the Program for Better Jobs and Income in 1977, it is difficult to discuss separately *income support policy and labor market policy*. The Carter proposal reflects the judgment that welfare and poverty problems are interdependent with inadequacies in the structure and performance of the labor market. Hence, effective income support policy must involve simultaneous changes in labor market policy. Our section reflects that same judgment, and we placed the relevant studies in one large section.

Each of the first four articles on welfare policy empirically addresses an important policy issue. Martin Rein and Lee Rainwater examine one of the most persistent questions raised regarding welfare policy and the welfare system: "Is there a 'welfare class' and is it growing?" "Does the growth of the welfare class account for rising welfare costs?" Using a recent national sample of families which have been interviewed annually for a decade, the authors find that, of the welfare recipients in any year, only a small proportion heavily depend on welfare for long periods. They conclude that policy reforms should emphasize universal rather than income-tested programs if the objective is to best meet the needs of both the working and nonworking poor.

Sheldon Danziger and Robert Plotnick treat the question of whether welfare reform measures, such as the proposal of the Carter Administration, can eliminate income poverty. After reviewing both the current welfare system and the progress against poverty made in the last decade, the authors focus on what might be called residual poverty. Because of the demographic characteristics of the current poor population, they conclude that no welfare reform plan with acceptable budgetary consequences will eliminate income poverty. They undertake this analysis with particular reference to President Carter's Program for Better Jobs and Income, and conclude that the elimination of poverty requires a redirection of policy away from means tested programs, toward both universal and employment oriented measures. This conclusion complements that of Rein and Rainwater.

A third question regarding welfare policy concerns the seriousness of the residual poverty problem in the U.S. Increasingly, the official measure of poverty has been criticized because it inadequately indicates the level and trend of U.S. poverty. In his essay, Timothy Smeeding addresses one of the main shortcomings of the official measure—its failure to count in-kind transfers as income or an income substitute. He demonstrates that the level of poverty is halved when the cash-equivalent value of food, housing, and medical care transfers are included in the income definition. His results also show that in-kind transfers are relatively inefficient measures of reducing income poverty. His conclusions have implications for both welfare policy and for more fundamental policies relating to the definition and measurement of poverty.

The final essay, by Michael Keeley et al., makes the tie between welfare and labor market policy explicit. It reports on the major Seattle-Denver Income Maintenance experiment; in particular, on the measured effect of alternative Negative Income Tax plans on work effort. The study is important for both its methodology and its results. The labor supply functions estimated exploit the experimental nature of the data, while making progress in avoiding some of the difficult econometric problems inherent in data from social experiments. The empirical results indicate that labor supply does indeed respond to the incentive implicit in income transfer and welfare policies, and that for certain types of problems the expected reduction in work effort could be substantial. An implicit lesson again relates to the limits of income-tested policies, relative to the possibilites for universal and employment-oriented measures.

The second group of articles in this section concerns the labor market and policies related to employment and earnings. Daniel Hamermesh presents a discussion of the empirical issues surrounding the Unemployment Insurance program and the effects of the Unemployment Insurance program on the duration and frequency of unemployment. The incentives implicit in the income transfer that unemployment insurance represents, according to Hamermesh, are likely to raise the unemployment rate by .71 percentage points—mostly by increasing the duration of spells of unemployment.

Embodied in both federal and state law, the minimum wage has become an established feature of the U.S. labor market. Like the Unemployment Insurance program, it has been viewed as a serious impediment to the efficient operation of the labor market. Finis Welch outlines the economics of the minimum wage and reviews the major empirical work on the effect of the minimum wage on employment. His concise analysis makes it clear that the effects of the minimum wage depend on the responses of employers, consumers, and labor suppliers. Both the analysis and empirical review indicate that many of these responses have not worked to benefit low wage labor. Welch concludes that "the minimum wage was one of our earliest forays into a national welfare program. It was a misguided idea then. But the world of welfare of 1938 is not the world of today, and after 40 years of evidence of adversity, it would seem that the time for mandated minimum wages has passed."

One group that is adversely affected by the minimum wage are workers in their late teens and early twenties. For this group, the role of the military as an employer and as a means to gain experience and maturity has become important. Richard V. L. Cooper explores this aspect of the military and its effect on youth unemployment. Cooper includes a special section on unemployment. For black youths, he finds that the military is an important source of employment and has a larger effect on the black youth civilian labor supply than on any other.

With the decline in the reliability of macro-policy as a tool to affect labor market conditions, a new view of the problem of unemployment is gaining prominence. Unemployment is most often described by the unemployment rate—a ratio of the number of unemployed to the total labor force at a point in time. However, unemployment hits hardest and with a more severe impact on specific groups within our society: low-income youth, handicapped workers, the undereducated, and the unskilled. Although increasing the general level of employment through macro-policies benefits persons in these groups, a more direct approach involving selective employment subsidies has been put forward as an effective anti-poverty tool and as a partial substitute for the conventional tools of aggregate, monetary, and fiscal policy. The article by John Bishop and Robert H. Haveman describes how selective employment subsidies work and explores their macro-impact. More specifically, Okun's Law—which describes the relation between the unemployment rate and changes in GNP—depends implicitly on the institutional and aggregate behavioral characteristics of the labor market. Bishop and Haveman show how selective employment subsidies tend to alter these aggregate characteristics, thus removing the constraint on employment policy implied by Okun's Law. They go on to estimate the effect of the New Jobs Tax Credit program, a form of employment subsidy which was in effect from 1977 to 1979. Their preliminary investigation indicates that a significant increase in employment growth in the industries included in their study can be attributed to the program.

With the rise in *health care* costs, the financing and distribution of health care services has, over the past few years, become an increasingly heated policy issue. And with the expectation of a proposal for national health insurance from the Carter Administration, 1978 was no exception. The federal and state role in the medical care sector was greatly expanded with the introduction of the Medicare and Medicaid programs in 1967 and has continued to grow with the expansion of these and other programs and with rising health care costs.

Karen Davis and Cathy Schoen's article revises some of the evidence on health benefits and the improved distribution of medical care services attributable to the expansion of the public sector's role in the medical care system.

The essay by Laurence S. Seidman presents one option for extending the government's role in health care financing through a particular form of National Health Insurance. Related to these two articles, that by Robert B. Helms presents the argument that market forces do operate in the health care system and can be strengthened by making consumers bear a larger share of the cost of the medical care they receive. Helms sees a competitive health services market as an alternative to regulation.

William Schwartz and Neil Komesar address the issue of medical malpractice from the perspective of providing physicians with an incentive to avoid mistakes. In their article, they argue that, as an incentive system, current malpractice insurance fails to penalize the negligent physician in a systematic fashion. No-fault malpractice insurance, they point out, would further reduce the incentive for physicians to avoid error.

One of the most publicized policy issues in 1978 was *taxation policy* and *public sector limits*. Concern with the taxpayer revolt peaked with the passage of California's Proposition 13. The main question which that referendum raised was: Has there been a basic shift in voter attitudes towards government and is the level and structure of taxation a cause of that shift?

William H. Oakland examines the fiscal circumstances in California leading up to the time of the referendum on Proposition 13 and analyzes some of the likely effects of its passage. He concludes that California property taxpayers faced a fiscal situation that was not characteristic of that in other states, and that the impact of the referendum on the level of public services enjoyed by California's citizens will not be substantial.

The four articles following Oakland's analysis explore the meaning of Proposition 13 from a variety of perspectives. Milton Friedman, arguing from the point of view that shrinking the size of government is desirable economic policy, concludes that partial tax limitation measures such as Proposition 13 are likely to provide inefficient and only partial solutions to the problem of government spending. This theme is taken up by Daniel Orr, who evaluates the effect of Proposition 13 in a complex system of fiscal federalism. He concludes that Proposition 13 by itself will shift political power from local to state and federal governments. Along with Friedman, Orr contends that controlling government spending by piecemeal tax reforms may be ineffective, and he advocates a constitutional amendment to reduce the scope of federal activity and spending.

The possibility that Proposition 13 does not represent any basic shift in voter attitudes is interestingly explored by James Buchanan. Buchanan puts forth the proposition that voters will favor any proposal whose benefits they receive directly and whose costs are diffuse. Passage of Proposition 13 may have been assured only because of the way the choice was presented to voters. Only if voters approve generalized tax or spending limits can a case be made that a shift in voter attitudes has occurred.

Robert J. Lampman's study views Proposition 13 in the context of our present distribution of tax burdens and public benefits among income classes. Rather than expressing a fundamental shift in voter attitudes toward government, Lampman suggests that voters may be expressing a concern with how benefits of government programs are distributed.

One reason for concern with the nature of the tax system is explored in articles by Martin Anderson and W. Lee Hansen. Both of these essays deal with the widely fluctuating pattern of marginal income tax rates over the income distribution due to the combined effect of tax measures on the state and federal level. Anderson analyses this irregular pattern for California, concluding it is most serious for low income families. Hansen, using Wisconsin's income tax and property tax relief programs, finds a pattern of irregular marginal rates and alternating regressive-progressive burdens in that state which are at least as great as in California. This inequity produced by the lack of integration among state and federal tax systems suggests one reason for voter concern.

The discussion of taxation and the taxpayer revolt was closely related to the debate over *education policy* in 1978. As David Breneman states in his section of the Brookings Institution's, *Setting National Priorities, The 1979 Budget*, "One issue dominated higher education discussion last year—the financial squeeze facing middle income families with children in college." In his article, which is the first presented in the education section, Breneman describes the primary bills (including the Carter Administration's direct student aid proposal), mainly for education tax allowances, introduced in 1978 to provide relief for college expenses. In discussing the efficiency and equity effects of the various options, the effect of the tax credit proposals on parental decisions regarding private and public school choices is cited as a key issue in this debate.

The debate over education tax credits is pursued in the three following essays by E. G. West, Thomas Sowell, and Walter Williams. They present a somewhat more favorable analysis of the consequences of the Packwood-Moynihan tuition tax credit bill—a focal point in the debate. They also discuss some of the legal and constitutional issues which surround debate on the tax credit approach.

The two remaining articles in this section deal with another important educational issue in 1978—school desegregation. Both are concerned with the effects of desegregation policy, the first on demographic behavior (white flight), and the second on the school achievement of black students. These essays review the evidence existing on these issues, and emphasize the difficulties in resolving the debates. The study by Karl Taeuber and Franklin Wilson analyses the difficulties of statistically identifying the effect of school desegregation on white flight when a large number of other variables affect the movement of whites in urban areas. Their analysis employs data from Louisiana parishes to illustrate their suggestions for alternative data sources and analytical methods which might end the "battle of the sociological experts" occurring in the nation's courts.

The article by Robert Crain and Rita Mahard addresses another major question—how has school desegregation affected black achievement? After reviewing seventy-three studies, they concluded that, while a majority of the studies (and especially the stronger ones) found desegregation to have had a favorable effect, the effect of the policy varies substantially by site. In particular, the positive result of desegregation appears to be related to the age level of the students when it is introduced and the voluntary vs. mandatory nature of its introduction.

While *crime policy and the criminal justice system* were not among the most widely debated policy issues of 1978, a number of important policy analyses appeared during the year. The first article, by Philip Cook, sheds empirical light on the gun control debate. As part of his testimony before the House Committee on the Judiciary, Cook presents his cross-section regression analysis of the relation of gun availability to both robbery, and murders associated with robbery. His findings support his testimony on the desirability of federal hand gun restrictions.

The remaining essay in this section concerns the criminal justice system. Stuart Nagel, Marian Neef, and Nancy Munshaw examine the problem of delay in handling civil and criminal court cases. In the authors' view, the techniques of management science can be used to reduce delays while, simultaneously, providing insights into the workings of the judicial system. They discuss the principles of, and possibilites for, six of these techniques, including queuing theory and Markov chain analysis. In an accompanying comment, John Paul Ryan describes the efforts of the Orange County court in implementing one of these techniques, concluding that the answers given by such approaches are both too simple and value laden, and may well have unintended costs "related to larger questions of citizen access to courts."

Section

I

Anti-Inflation Policy

1

UNEMPLOYMENT AND INFLATION

Henry J. Aaron

Unlike popular and academic ideas about the effect of education on future earnings, which were vague and at least partly correct, views of political leaders and academics in the early 1960s about unemployment and the labor market were more precise and turned out to be demonstrably false in many important respects.

The unemployed, like the poor, were viewed as definable groups. The problem of "hard-core unemployment" absorbed political, journalistic, and intellectual attention, and training programs were designed to solve it. Widespread concern about the impact of automation and structural unemployment caused many government officials and some academics to stress the difficulty of reducing unemployment much below the 5 to 6 percent range that prevailed from the mid-1950s through 1964. Improved training, education, and relocation of workers or regional development were viewed as necessary by some and, with enough aggregate demand, sufficient to reduce the unemployment rate to 4 percent and eventually even lower. In a review of economic policy during the 1960s, one scholar asserted that the attitude among at least some economists "was that within wide limits the norm of 'full employment' was what the nation wished to make it."[1] The penalty for low unemployment would be inflation, but it was anticipated by many to be modest and by some as subject to attenuation through a variety of policies, including training programs to improve the match between the skills workers possessed and those demanded by employers, presidential exhortation, and such informal devices as wage-price guideposts.

With the passage of time, these views were modified or rejected. It became clear that fears about the impact of automation were fantasy; equally exaggerated but opposite fears about the end of economic growth from exhaustion of natural resources and pollution replaced concern over automation. The national significance of the hard-core unemployed was seen to be minor compared to the difficulties encountered by the "soft-core employed," the millions of workers who had no difficulty finding jobs of sorts but could not land or keep jobs that held out the prospect of promotion and a decent wage. The idea that unemployment could be reduced to 4 percent or even less if the nation would only tolerate an increase in prices of a few percent a year lost much academic respectability and political support. New theories about the operation of labor markets competed with the old view that labor markets in a rough way recognized and rewarded the inherent skills of workers. In the late 1960s reformers, concerned that workers lacked the skills to perform the increasingly demanding tasks a modern economy required, had urged sympathetic administrations and Congress to introduce programs to accelerate the acquisition of such skills. In the early 1970s they were calling for government programs to upgrade the content, to increase the pay, and to speed the elimination of low-skill, low-wage jobs whose disappearance had in the 1960s been held partly responsible for unemployment. Unfortunately, no generally accepted view of labor markets now exists with which to explain the problem of wage inflation or upon which to base policies to reduce unemployment.

A Backward Glance

In academic and political discussions during the 1960s unemployment, like Gaul, was commonly divided into three parts—cyclical, frictional, and structural—according to whether the unemployment was due to a lack of aggregate demand, to normal labor turnover, or to automation or other technological change, shifts in the composition of demand, or foreign competition.[2] But other categorizations were common; a survey of the "definitions and terminology describing the major types of unemployment (cyclical, structural, frictional, seasonal, etc.)" prepared for the Joint Economic Committee in 1961 contained a glossary with fifty-eight different terms used in various combinations for describing unemployment.[3] The common characteristic of all such categories was that they would enable all workers without jobs to be classified as cyclically, structurally, or frictionally unemployed.

One could also classify the unemployed into those who could be expected to find work promptly, whether the cause of unemployment was cyclical, structural, or frictional, and those who could not. Certain people —notably white prime-age males in economically prosperous areas—fell into the former category; others—notably women and especially blacks of both sexes and all inhabitants of depressed areas—tended to fall into the latter group, often labeled the hard-core unemployed. Not all women or blacks or residents of depressed areas, of course, were unemployed; but once out of a job, it was perceived that members of these groups tended to experience much longer than average spells of unemployment. As a report of the Chamber of Commerce put it: "Some people are chronically unemployed. Apart from those too old, too sick, or too disabled to work, these people are unemployed primarily because (1) they lack the qualifications needed for available jobs, and/or (2) they lack the basic abilities—such as reading and writing—to qualify for training for jobs"; and the solution for such unemployment followed directly from its description: "To devise solutions for such chronically unemployed people, priority should be given to programs that offer education and skill training that will lead to jobs in the competitive markets."[4]

To abolish cyclical unemployment, it was thought necessary only to ensure sufficient aggregate demand through fiscal and monetary policies. To eliminate structural unemployment, it was necessary to ensure the best possible match between the skills workers possessed and those employers demanded. A variety of government policies would be required to achieve this goal, including education, training, regional development, and measures to protect workers against job loss due to foreign competition. Frictional unemployment was viewed as necessary in a free labor market in which workers shopped for the jobs that best fitted their skills, locational preferences, and tastes among pay, fringe benefits, and working conditions; its reduction below some necessary minimum would lower economic efficiency and work to the long-run detriment of both employers and workers themselves. Its elimination was viewed as impossible because some labor market entrants always would be seeking their first jobs and other labor force participants would be seeking new jobs after having quit or been fired.

Government fiscal and monetary policies could generate sufficient demand to create enough jobs for all who wanted to work, economists proclaimed, but aggregate policies could not ensure that the jobs would be in the right places or require the available skills of workers seeking employment. Consequently, as the unemployment rate declined, it became increasingly likely that the demand for workers in certain areas or with particular skills might exceed supply at going wage rates. First, wages in such areas or for such skills would be increased; then the prices of commodities those workers produced would begin to rise and the effects would spread to other sectors, causing a general increase in prices and wages. The extent and size of such an increase would be greater, the closer the economy was to general full employment. In short, there would be an inverse relationship between the rate of unemployment and the rate at which prices and wages would increase. Research on data for the United States and Great Britain seemed to confirm the existence of such a relationship. This relationship came to be known as the Phillips curve, after the economist who postulated it. It suggested that the United States could have price stability, but only if unemployment was sufficiently high—around 5 to 6 percent— to prevent excessive demand for labor from occurring often or intensely. Conversely, lower unemployment could be achieved, but, as a result, labor markets would be so tight that wages would rise faster than productivity; the result, sooner (if profit margins were maintained) or later (if profits were squeezed), would be inflation.

The facts were unsettling. After postwar demobilization, unemployment had averaged 4.3 percent from 1948 to 1957, but during the succeeding seven years, from 1958 to 1964, unemployment averaged 5.8 percent. Except for the runup in prices during the consumer binges immediately after World War II and at the onset of the Korean War, prices remained remarkably stable, rising only 1.5 percent per year at an annual rate from 1948 to 1956. But inflation, set loose during the mid-1950s, persisted until unemployment had remained at uncustomarily high rates from 1957 to 1959. The trade-off between unemployment and inflation was not precise, but it was disturbing.

To improve what then seemed a rather dismal trade-off, the government could take a number of steps to reduce structural unemployment—that due to the imbalance between available skills and the needs of employers. Where the supply of potential workers was excessive, programs to encourage regional development were advocated and enacted, first focused on Appalachia, later diffused more broadly under the aegis of the Area Redevelopment Administration. Other proposals, such as relocation allowances to help unemployed workers move from areas of high unemployment, received considerable academic and administration support, but foundered on political objections best summarized by the remark of one member of Congress: "Sir, are you asking *me* to vote for appropriations to help *my* constituents move to some *other* district?" To increase the supply of needed skills, numerous programs were proposed and, it seems, almost as many were enacted under which the federal government trained workers or paid for their training. The first major program along these lines was the Manpower Development and Training Act of 1962, but it was followed by a torrent of similar legislation subsumed under the War on Poverty or the Great Society.[5]

Some observers felt that the problem of structural unemployment could be solved only at enormous cost, if at all. Among these pessimists were only a few academic economists but a goodly number of lawyers, sociologists, and other nonspecialists who were impressed with the computer and the technological breakthroughs it seemed to make possible. The problem, as this group perceived it, was that technological change had accelerated or changed in character, causing large numbers of workers to become essentially redundant and unemployable. New words were applied to the phenomenon; cybernation referred to the development of machines to control other machines, automation to the fact that tasks previously performed by people were now performed automatically by machines. In fact, both developments had been occurring since the onset of the industrial revolution (indeed, since the bow and arrow), and the rate of technological advancement as measured by worker productivity had not increased recently.

But in the view of such groups as the Ad Hoc Committee on the Triple Revolution, something new, worthy of being designated as a revolution, was happening, something that invalidated the entire basis of distribution that had until then served to allocate goods among consumers. According to this group, unlimited production was around the corner and there was no way that all previously employed workers could be fruitfully employed.[6]

A less extreme position was taken by economist Charles Killingsworth, who argued only that automation and cybernetics were qualitatively different and quantitatively greater than previous technological change and that they had made structural unemployment more intractable. Moreover, structural unemployment, Killingsworth maintained, would grow in the future as automation proceeded.[7] In fact, adherents of the view that structural unemployment was bad and getting worse were later characterized as "a fairly odd assortment of bed fellows," ranging from the Ad Hoc Committee on the Triple Revolution, through labor market economists concerned about displacement, to conservatives disturbed at the fiscal stimulus advocated by the Council of Economic Advisers and other academic economists.[8]

Professional economists responded to this challenge by inquiring whether there was evidence that structural unemployment had increased during the preceding decade. If it had not, then there was no obvious reason why unemployment rates of 4 percent or less, common in the first postwar decade, could not be achieved again—for example, by tax cuts that would increase private spending. A study by the Joint Economic Committee in 1961 suggested that the increase in unemployment was more likely to have been due to inadequate demand than to an increase in structural unemployment.[9] In 1964, a leading labor economist summarized the views of professional economists with the comment that "to submit the rise-in-structural-unemployment hypothesis to yet another test may strike some as pretty much like subjecting an apparently dead horse to one last thumping."[10] With singular lack of caution, *New York Times* economics reporter Edwin L. Dale, Jr., predicted that "with no new training programs, with no shortening of the work week, with no special manpower policies, with no radical measures like paying people who do not work, this country will get full employment by expansion of demand alone."[11] This view and that of most economists was founded on the belief that with sufficient demand employers would train workers for available jobs or redesign jobs for available workers. Furthermore, the intuition that workers were in the wrong place or lacked the right skills for available jobs was repeatedly refuted by analysis.[12]

With the declaration of the War on Poverty, however, the issue was transformed. The question was not whether structural unemployment had increased, but how to combat it. There was little disagreement that the problem was serious. Unemployment rates of different demographic groups varied widely. White prime-age males enjoyed the lowest rates; blacks, women, and the young all suffered from substantially more unemployment. Cutting across all of these groups, those who lacked education and training suffered higher than average unemployment. Writing from their perspectives in the research office at the Office of Economic Opportunity, Joseph Kershaw and Robert Levine asked for an end to debate between those who stressed structural causes of unemployment and those who stressed demand: "Our thesis . . . is that the disagreement between the structural and aggregate demand theories of unemployment is largely an illusory one; that both increased demand and structural change are necessary support for one another in solving the labor market portion of the poverty problem."[13]

In the rhetoric of the War on Poverty, structural changes primarily meant additions to human capital through education and training, not changes in the demand for low-wage workers or in the composition of jobs. Improved education was necessary to provide new entrants to the labor force with the necessary abilities to read and write and the ability to acquire job-related skills. One observer labeled federal grants to school districts with poor children under the Elementary and Secondary Education Act of 1965 as "the most important manpower policy of all."[14] But a large number of programs, directed to training adults or young people or to encouraging them to remain in school by providing part-time jobs, followed in rapid succession: Job Corps, to provide basic remedial education and training in live-in centers; Neighborhood Youth Corps, to provide money and jobs to adolescents and young adults while schooling continued or after it terminated; job opportunities in the business sector; the concentrated employment program; the work incentive (WIN) program for welfare recipients; and many others. Whether these programs were necessary to permit the unemployment rate to decline below about 5 percent without inflation, as the structuralists suggested, or 4 percent, as maintained by those who stressed the importance of sufficient demand, was clearly less important than that both groups viewed them as necessary to permit full use of economic resources, as important for the prevention of inflation, and as essential for equality of economic opportunity.

The fact of the matter was that enactment of the 1964 tax cut and the later increase in military expenditures associated with the Vietnam War drove unemployment below 4 percent even before the programs of the War on Poverty and the Great Society were fully under way. Inflation rose almost immediately, but concern that it would continue to rise was limited. The various training programs were directed at structural problems in the labor market. The academic and journalistic debate between demand and structural strategies to deal with unemployment was made moot by the political pursuit of both.

New Facts, New Theories, New Policies

No more than five years later, most economists had concluded that the goal of a 4 percent unemployment rate without excessive and perhaps accelerating inflation was unachievable. However, explanations emphasized not the diagnosis initially advanced by the "structuralists," but rather changes in the composition of the labor force and new theories of the relationship between inflation and unemployment. The political goal of 4 percent unemployment, regarded as only a modest interim target when first put forward in the Kennedy administration, had been abandoned because few observers of the labor market thought that an unemployment rate below 5 percent could be achieved in the foreseeable future without triggering rapid inflation; many doubted whether even 5 percent was possible. Moreover, the conviction that training programs or education would bring a more ambitious target within reach seemed to have vanished. One reason for this turnabout was that evaluators had dealt as harshly with government-sponsored training programs as they had with efforts to use education to improve economic opportunities for the poor. As will become clear, these evaluations suffered from many of the same shortcomings. A second reason was that events had invalidated all previous estimates of a simple trade-off between inflation and unemployment. A third reason was the development of a better understanding of the nature of unemployment.

Character of Unemployment

The categories into which unemployment had been classified were intuitively satisfying; it was easy to understand that unemployment could be caused by recession, depressed regions, or job switching. Unfortunately, these causes help little in interpreting the actual experience of the overwhelming majority of the unemployed.[15] Except at very high rates of unemployment, nearly all unemployed workers appear to find jobs after a relatively brief period of joblessness whether they are unemployed because of a cyclical decline in economic activity, because an obsolete factory has closed, because of recent migration to a new city, or because of recently entering the labor market. This seems to be true whatever the initial cause of joblessness and whatever the person's sex, age, or race. A small fraction of the unemployed experience protracted unemployment. Furthermore, members of some groups find it easier to find jobs than do others; the average period out of a job is slightly longer for blacks than for whites, for example. But the difference is nowhere near sufficient to account for the fact that black unemployment rates are about twice white unemployment rates. Young workers of both races and sexes seem to be able to find jobs after shorter spells of unemployment than do older workers, in sharp and paradoxical contrast to the fact that young workers' unemployment typically is manyfold greater than that of prime-age workers.

The large difference in unemployment rates instead seems to be due to two factors that do not fit neatly within the old categories. First, there are enormous differences among demographic groups in the probability of losing a job. White teenage boys, for example, are more than four times more likely than white prime-age males to lose a job either voluntarily or involuntarily; black prime-age males are nearly two times more likely than white prime-age males to lose a job. Women, black or white, are less likely than men of the same race to lose a job, although blacks are more likely than whites of each sex to lose a job. Second, and even more important, there are large differences among demographic groups in the probability of workers who enter the labor force remaining unemployed after the temporarily unsuccessful search for a job.

As a result, most of the differences between unemployment rates of blacks and whites, men and women, young and prime-age workers, can be attributed to the frequency of unemployment; very little is attributable to differences in the duration of unemployment. Teenage nonwhite females, for example, are nearly sixteen times as likely to be unemployed as are white prime-age males. A sizable fraction of the unemployed are temporarily laid off with a fixed date of recall; that is, they have a job but have been furloughed without pay. Many such workers, as well as many who are indefinitely laid off, do not actively search for work.

The picture that emerges is one of a massive lottery, in which people at any given time are in one of three states—employed, unemployed, or not in the labor force. The chances of moving from unemployment into a job differs, but by only a little, from one demographic group to another. But the chances of moving from employment either into unemployment or out of the labor force altogether differ greatly and account for almost all of the differences among demographic groups in unemployment.

These facts are quite inconsistent with the belief, widely held in the 1960s, that the high unemployment rates of blacks, youths, or females were due to the inability to find jobs. Most of the difference seems to be frictional, if one of the formerly popular categories must be used. Something seems to be wrong either with the jobs to which these groups can gain access or with the habits of these groups that cause them to leave employment so often.

These facts should not be construed as suggesting that long-term unemployment does not exist, that those who experience long-term unemployment may not suffer from important disabilities or lack skills, or that the unemployed do not include disproportionate numbers of blacks and other minorities. Indeed, clear-cut evidence demonstrates that the chance of finding a job diminishes the longer a worker is unemployed and that a disproportionate fraction of those unemployed longer than twenty-six weeks are black. The personal catastrophe that protracted unemployment can inflict is beyond question. Both because those with the fewest problems find jobs first, on the average, and because protracted unemployment creates and exacerbates existing problems, the long-term unemployed are more likely than other groups to require assistance in finding and keeping a job.

The point is that long-term unemployment accounts for a very small part of the difference in unemployment rates among demographic groups, and eliminating protracted unemployment completely would reduce total unemployment negligibly. If no unemployment in 1976 had lasted longer than twenty-six weeks, the unemployment rate would have been 6.3 percent rather than 7.7 percent; in 1973, a year of relative prosperity, the elimination of unemployment lasting more than twenty-six weeks would have reduced the overall unemployment rate from 4.9 percent to 4.5 percent.[16] The newly discovered facts, of course, do not indicate whether high turnover rates are due to job characteristics that lead to layoffs or quitting or to worker characteristics that lead to the same results. A recent attempt to determine which cause of high turnover was more important produced inconclusive results.[17] But the stress on these facts marks the end of the neat distinction between the "unemployed" and the "employed."[18]

Another pillar of the old structural unemployment hypothesis crumbled as evidence accumulated that technological change has not accelerated. In fact, it has slowed. Productivity, measured as output per unit of input, rose 2.3 percent a year between 1948 and 1955, but rose only 2.1 percent a year between 1955 and 1969.[19] The computer has not revolutionized the economy, however significant it has been for particular industries. Automation and cybernation, the modish fears of an earlier age, have been replaced by concern over the exhaustion of resources or pollution, which is thought by some to herald the end of economic growth and, in some versions, mass starvation, diminishing worldwide living standards, and other terrestrial disasters. Actual developments will no doubt be less dramatic than the fears of doom through stagnation so extravagantly expressed today, just as they were considerably less drastic than the predictions of doom through technological progress expressed a decade or more ago.

Unemployment and Inflation

Although the reasoning advanced by the structuralists in support of the proposition that an unemployment rate of 4 percent or less could not be achieved without creating inflation has been contradicted by events, the proposition itself has been accepted. It is now generally agreed that unless something else is done to keep prices in check, any attempt to reduce unemployment through aggregate fiscal and monetary policy to levels thought attainable in the 1960s will cause excessive and possibly accelerating inflation. The reasons for this belief are quite diverse and no consensus seems emergent.

According to one line of reasoning, the 4 percent target for unemployment was reasonable when it was advanced in the early 1960s, but it is unattainable today. Conditions are now less favorable, it is alleged, because the composition of the labor force has changed. In particular, the proportion of the labor force composed of women, teenagers, and other young workers has increased.[20] These groups are less productive than are prime-age males, as signified by their low wages. Furthermore, young workers and women change jobs and move in and out of the labor force more often than do men. They generate more unemployment in the process because they spend some time classified as unemployed while they seek work. For both reasons, it is argued, a given number of unemployed workers represents less unemployed productivity and exercises less drag on wage increases than did the same percentage of unemployed workers a decade ago.

To the extent that unemployment, measured in terms of productivity, retards wage increases, a given level of unemployment, measured conventionally, corresponds to a tighter and more inflationary labor market today than was the case a decade ago. Consequently, according to this view, the trade-off between inflation and unemployment is less favorable today than in the past. The wage inflation associated with about 5 percent unemployment is about the same as the wage inflation that was associated with 4 percent unemployment in the past. From the standpoint of inflation, it is argued, the definition of full employment should be revised. Furthermore, experience with inflation at palpable rates during the past decade seems to have made both workers and their employers more sensitive and resulting wage and price decisions more responsive to labor market conditions.[21]

The view that full employment corresponds to a higher rate of unemployment than in the past does not imply that in a social sense the unemployment of women or young workers is less serious than that of prime-age males, although some people support this quite independent proposition. The deprivation caused by the unemployment of a low-wage worker and the damage caused by unfortunate initial contacts with the labor market may be as harmful as that caused by the unemployment of a prime-age male. The point is simply that the change in the composition of unemployment may have one effect on wage stability and quite another on social stability.[22]

This argument can be turned around, however. During the postwar decades, the educational attainment of the labor force has increased markedly. Since unemployment rates for the relatively well-educated are lower than those of the little-educated, this change in the demographic composition of the labor force should have made the attainment of ever-lower rates of unemployment feasible.[23] An obvious, but unsatisfactory, rejoinder to this argument—that the education-specific unemployment rates may have increased, thereby negating the supposedly beneficial effects on unemployment of increased education—raises a troublesome question for those who point to the changing age-sex mix of the labor force to explain why low unemployment has become increasingly difficult to achieve. Why were unemployment rates of the young and of women, already higher absolutely than those of prime-age males in the 1960s, even higher in the 1970s? Why had employers not altered the mix of jobs to take advantage of the available supply of workers? If they did not react to this shift in supply, why would they react to other shifts in supply—such as the growing stock of well-educated workers—by altering the mix of available jobs?

The view that there is a stable trade-off between inflation and unemployment has fallen on hard times. First, no estimated relationship has successfully forecast combinations of unemployment and inflation for very long.[24] Second, although each estimate is rather sensitive to the pattern of wage increases contained in union contracts, the pattern assumed in all studies is arbitrary and not necessarily consistent with fragmentary available evidence.[25]

The view that there is any *stable* trade-off between unemployment and the rate at which wages increase has come in for more basic criticism from those who deny that *any* long-run trade-off exists. The criticism now comes from two directions. One group holds that only at an equilibrium rate of unemployment can stable prices be maintained: at lower unemployment rates wage increases will accelerate and, eventually, so will price increases; at higher-than-equilibrium unemployment rates, prices and wages will decline at ever faster rates.[26] If workers are able to obtain wage increases that exceed productivity growth, prices will begin to rise. Once workers and employers come to expect inflation, all negotiations will take such increases for granted and start there. If labor markets are tight enough to generate wage increases greater than increases in productivity, such increases will be in addition to the commonly expected rate of inflation. Such wage bargains will necessitate ever larger price increases, which then come to be expected, and so on.

The other group holds that the relation between unemployment and wage inflation exists only in the fevered imaginings of economists. Unemployment, it is argued, is determined by overall economic conditions generated by fiscal and monetary policy. Wage increases are institutionally determined by businessmen and workers, who are heavily influenced by customary relative wages. When special events disturb these wage contours, attempts to restore them can trigger protracted wage inflation.[27]

Throughout the history of the Phillips curve, its advocates have been bedeviled by difficulty in explaining the failure of previously estimated statistical relations to forecast accurately the rate of wage inflation associated with any level of unemployment. During the early 1960s, the problem was that wages persistently rose *less* than previously estimated statistical relations suggested. Various explanations were put forward: the alleged success of the wage-price guideposts employed by the Kennedy and Johnson administrations from 1962 to 1966;[28] faulty statistics on unemployment that understated the pool of workers potentially available for work;[29] or, as at least one analyst suggested, both.[30] Labor economists, in fact, were surprised by the size of the increase in the labor force during the period 1961–69 when unemployment more or less steadily declined from 6.7 percent to 3.5 percent.[31] But both of these explanations of the better-than-anticipated performance of the economy accepted the reality of a trade-off between inflation and unemployment.

In the early 1970s, a combination of high unemployment and rapid increase in wages and prices completely defied previously estimated relations. Both adherents and critics of the idea that there was a trade-off between inflation and unemployment tried to assimilate these developments. Adherents pointed to the devaluation of the dollar, which raised the price of imports, to the world food inflation, which boosted food costs at home and stimulated demands by labor for higher wages, and to the tripling of fuel prices triggered by the Organization of Petroleum Exporting Countries as special factors that created an inflationary environment. Faced with these inflationary events, governments tried to fight inflation by curtailing demand, but went far enough only to increase unemployment, not to snuff out the inflation.[32] Unfortunately, this after-the-fact explanation sounded to many like a rationalization of a discredited theory.

These facts were also assimilated by critics of the Phillips curve. Those who held that there exists some natural rate of unemployment viewed the inflation and high unemployment of the early 1970s as the inevitable consequence of attempting for too long to keep unemployment too low. The result was a bad case of accelerating inflation, which only an extended period of economic slack could cure; high unemployment was a regrettable side effect that the economy would have to endure, possibly for a few years, to ensure a complete remission of the disease of inflation. Those who denied that there was any long-run trade-off between unemployment and inflation simply pointed to the facts and let them speak for themselves.

Which of these views turns out to be closest to the truth hinges on the resolution of several analytical questions. How much does previous inflation affect current wage increases? How much do wage increases in one economic sector affect those in another? When inflation has persisted for some time, will both employers and employees assume the continuation of inflation when they bargain for wages and set prices? What events must occur to change those expectations and how long will it take for those events to change inflationary expectations?

On one issue proponents of the Phillips curve have given considerable ground to those who contend that there is a natural rate of unemployment. If a 1 percent increase in prices in a previous period is associated with a less than 1 percent increase in current wages, then a trade-off between unemployment and inflation exists. In that event, a particular rate of unemployment and attendant labor market conditions lead to some estimated increase in wages. If this wage inflation exceeds the growth of productivity, then eventually prices will rise by the difference between the increase in wages and the growth of productivity. As long as this price increase is not fully translated into higher wages, the increase in both wages and prices will settle down to some stable rate. If, however, a rise in prices sooner or later causes the rate of change in wages to increase by the same proportion as prices, then unemployment below some critical level cannot be sustained. Empirical estimates of the proportion of any increase in prices that is translated into wage increases have steadily risen. Initial estimates suggested that wages rise about another 4 percent for every 10 percent increase in prices. As time passed, these estimates rose until wages were calculated to rise about 8 to 9 additional percent for each 10 percent increase in prices; if wages rise a full 10 percent for each 10 percent increase in prices, there is no long-term trade-off between inflation and unemployment.[33] It is apparent that the statistical differences between many of those who insist on a trade-off between inflation and unemployment and those who deny it have become quite narrow. The crucial question—whether these statistical estimates can be used for accurate forecasts—remains unanswered.

Events following the great recession of 1974 were unkind to both views. Wage and price increases both declined markedly from levels reached in 1974 in the face of unemployment that reached 9.0 percent in May 1975. Wages, which had risen 9.4 percent during 1974, rose at an annual rate of only 7.5 percent during the last half of 1975. Prices, which had risen 11.0 percent during 1974, rose at an annual rate of only 7.1 percent during the last half of 1975. But the rate of increase in both prices and wages did not diminish much further in 1976 and 1977 and was forecast to decline only slightly in 1977 and 1978, despite the persistence into 1977 of unemployment rates higher than any that had prevailed in earlier postwar recessions and that exceeded all earlier estimates of the natural rate of unemployment. Why wage and price inflation did not diminish further became a major puzzle for both models of the economic process. History had already posed a similar puzzle. During the depression unemployment rates had exceeded 10 percent for more than a decade and 20 percent for years. Nevertheless, average hourly earnings, which fell from 1930 to 1933, did not fall during the rest of the 1930s.[34] These facts are difficult to reconcile with either the Phillips curve or the natural rate hypotheses.

Manpower Training

Manpower training programs proliferated and expanded in a hectic and confusing fashion during the 1960s. They were intended to help increase economic growth by removing shortages of critical skills, to reduce the threat of inflation by improving the balance between the demand for and the supply of all skills, to assist depressed areas in regaining economic health, and to combat poverty by endowing the poor with skills that would enable them to earn adequate wages. Programs were operated through schools, factories, and community agencies. The result, in the words of one sympathetic critic, was that "few programs were able to operate as efficiently as one might otherwise have expected . . . especially . . . where there were competing programs in the same locality, with each being run on a small and inefficient scale."[35]

Federal management of most training programs enacted during the 1960s has been terminated. State and local governments still operate many of them, supported in large measure by federal funds provided through the Comprehensive Employment and Training Act (CETA), first enacted under the Nixon administration to replace a wide variety of narrowly defined federal grant-in-aid programs with broad categorical grants that would increase state and local discretion and diminish federal control. The debate about this transfer covered many issues: the political pros and cons of federal attempts to achieve narrowly defined objectives that might differ from the desires of state and local governments; the relative solicitude for problems of the poor and of minorities by different levels of government; and the general desirability of having the federal government transfer funds to state and local governments with few or no strings attached. Participants in this political debate cited evidence about the effectiveness of the many federal training programs.

This evidence consisted of the results of many economic studies of the effectiveness of these programs. Government agencies performed some of these studies; private consulting and research organizations carried out most of them.

The results of these studies fall into two categories. First, no perceptible nationwide effect of the training programs on employment or productivity could be discerned, perhaps because the programs were too small in the aggregate.[36] Nor is it clear how training can reduce unemployment unless it causes the substitution of less productive, lower-wage workers for more productive, higher-wage workers or the substitution of labor for capital. Substitution of low-skill for high-skill labor would be desirable, however, because it would delay the appearance of inflationary pressures in the labor markets for skilled workers, where labor shortages first appear during booms, and because it would improve the trade-off between inflation and unemployment. If training programs did improve the trade-off, this effect was overwhelmed by other events, for the trade-off did not in fact improve. Nor did the differences between the unemployment of blacks and that of whites narrow.[37]

Second, many analysts studied the effect of training programs on individual workers. These studies fall into a pattern familiar to consumers of educational research. A few of the programs were unambiguous failures. The work incentive program, for example, an effort to help families off the welfare rolls by offering adults basic instruction on how to get and keep jobs, was later described as misnamed because the welfare system "constituted a notorious disincentive" to gainful employment.[38] For the major training programs, however—those authorized by the Manpower Development and Training Act and the Job Corps, for example—the results were favorable and mixed, respectively. In some studies, under certain criteria, and for some groups the programs were successes; in others, they were failures.[39]

The absence of unambiguous conclusions about the effectiveness of the major training programs has many sources. First, evaluators could choose among various criteria of success, such as higher earnings or reduced unemployment; they could observe the effects of training for a relatively brief period—six months or so—or they could follow the training recipient for a longer time; they could include among the benefits of the program declines in public expenditures on behalf of the trainee, such as reduced unemployment insurance or welfare payments, or they could ignore them; they could attempt to measure, and possibly to assign a cash value to, noneconomic consequences of the training, such as changes in arrests or improvement in family stability. A program that was successful by one criterion might fail by another.

The most difficult problem in evaluating training programs, however, was deciding how to measure their effects. Should the post-training earnings of the trainee be compared with his own earnings before training or with the earnings of similar workers who had not gone through the training program? The first course was obviously unsatisfactory because trainees were never randomly selected and, in any case, the state of the economy of local labor markets, and other circumstances certain to affect job opportunities, were bound to change over time; consequently, one would never know whether the difference in earnings before and after training was due to the special characteristics or circumstances that led to the selection of the particular trainees or to the training. A worker, threatened with the loss of a job using the only skills he possessed, might seek out training, acquire new skills, and obtain a new job. His earnings might go up, down, or stay the same; but any change in earnings would be unlikely to provide an accurate guide to the value of the training.

The second course, the comparison of the change in earnings of the trainees with those of similar workers, was the mark of superior studies. It suffered from similar problems because applicants could not be assigned randomly to training or to a control group. But even if random assignment were possible, evaluations of the impact of training on individuals might fail to detect any effects if employers relied on such gross characteristics of workers as age, race, sex, or level of schooling to categorize workers into groups acceptable or unacceptable for particular jobs. An effective training program would increase the skills of a small proportion of the groups to which trainees belonged; but unless the training caused employers to change these rules-of-thumb, the training would improve earnings of the trainee no more than it would affect earnings of otherwise similar members of the same groups. The trainee might experience some short-run benefits if job placement services were part of the package of benefits that trainees receive. And, indeed, some studies found that employment and earnings increased immediately after completion of training but atrophied until, a year or eighteen months after completion, little or no difference could be observed between the earnings of the trainee and those of members of the control group. Whether these results are due to the widespread use of gross characteristics by employers in hiring or to another explanation—that training is ineffective in raising skills but helpful in finding one a job—cannot now be determined.

Thus, someone convinced of the effectiveness of training programs could argue that the apparent failure of the programs was due to their smallness. He could attribute the failure of evaluations to find higher earnings for trainees than for controls to the use by employers of gross characteristics in hiring; he could cite studies that revealed higher earnings for trainees than for controls as instances where such rules-of-thumb were not so strong as to obscure the presumed beneficent effects of training. One who lacked such faith could claim that training programs, like various educational interventions, were not consistently effective and would not have succeeded even if they had been larger. The crucial point is that there was, and still is, no practical way to determine which of these two explanations of the "facts" is correct. For this reason, decisions about whether to continue training programs and, if so, under which governmental auspices have had to be settled on grounds other than "scientific" evaluation of their effectiveness.

The Labor Market

Economists have carried on a lengthy debate among themselves about the pervasiveness of "rational, maximizing behavior." During the 1940s the debate focused on the behavior of businesses; the issue was whether they maximized profits by setting prices so that the additional revenue from selling one more unit was at least as great as the additional cost of producing one more unit. The technical argument concerned whether businesses were aware of their "marginal cost" and "marginal revenue" curves, the graphs that depicted the mathematical relations from which additional revenues and costs could be calculated. Some held that firms were aware of the extra income and expenditure that producing one more unit would entail. Others held that as a practical matter businesses could not have such detailed information, but in the long run acted *as if* they did, because firms that maximized profits would eventually drive less profitable firms from the marketplace. Still others maintained a variety of competing propositions: that businesses sought to sell as much as they could as long as their profits were satisfactory, for example, or that firms had a multiplicity of objectives among which high profits was only one.

The debate was never settled. The view that businesses maximize profits remained at the core of economic theory for a variety of reasons, one of the more important of which was that it enabled economic theorists to employ the powerful mathematical tool of calculus in drawing inferences that were subtle and suggestive and that were only on occasion conspicuously refuted. The other views have remained alive on the periphery of the profession.

A similar, long-smoldering debate concerning the operation of labor markets flared up during the late 1960s and still rages. The issues bear considerable resemblance to those in the debate over profit maximization. According to the conventional view, workers possess a set of skills determined by genetic endowment, other social and economic influences (such as parental education, religion, or income), education, on-the-job training, and experience. Their productivity in any job depends on these characteristics, and their earnings depend on this productivity. Workers find their way into the job in which their productivity, and hence their real earnings (including not only pay but also working conditions and perquisites), are as high as possible, thus ensuring that the labor force is allocated optimally among available jobs. An excess of workers with a particular set of skills will depress their wages until the demand for workers with those skills equals the supply. In planning what profession to enter and what education and training to acquire, workers are guided by the real earnings they can expect to receive.

A slight variant of this view admits that young people planning careers and older workers contemplating job changes or the acquisition of new skills lack detailed information about the various rates of return but nevertheless act *as if* they had such information. In both variants, however, the labor market operates smoothly, with wages and the number of workers in various occupations adjusting with reasonable speed to prevent persistent shortages or gluts (i.e., extended unemployment) of workers.

This view is supported by indirect, but little direct, evidence. Writing in 1966, Charles Killingsworth observed that "one of the most basic assumptions of the . . . aggregate-demand school . . . remain[ed] essentially unverified," that "when the supply of more desirable kinds of workers gets tight, employers will greatly increase their hiring of teenagers, older workers, nonwhites, and less educated workers and will concurrently engage in wholesale retraining and job redesign programs. . . . There has been virtually no empirical investigation of how employers will respond under present-day conditions to moderate increases in demand; and there haven't even been guesses as to how much private retraining programs and job design might add to unit labor costs and prices."[40] Later work by Okun and Vroman found that tight labor markets have.a modest effect on job structure.[41] Michael Piore reported in a study of how industrial plants are designed and processes modified that, in the words of one engineer, "plants 'mold men to jobs, not jobs to men.' " Nevertheless, he concluded that the observed insensitivity of engineers to the supply of various kinds of workers and to their relative wages was probably consistent with cost minimization, because it was just too costly to tailor jobs to the available labor force.[42]

The view that labor markets adjust to available skills has direct bearing on what policies should be adopted to solve the problems of unemployment and low wages for workers now in the job market. If such adjustment occurs, policy should aim to improve the skills of the low-wage workers. If it occurs sluggishly or not at all, policy must increase the demand for occupations for which low-wage workers qualify or can be trained.

Critics of the view that labor markets adjust promptly to changes in the supply of skills, like those of the theory of profit maximization, hold that the world is too complex to permit such nice calculations of the value of individual workers. Instead, the labor market is encrusted with custom and habit, which impede, if they do not block, the processes described in the conventional view. According to this alternative view, the way jobs are structured, the relative wages different classes of workers receive, hiring practices, promotions, tenure and seniority, all are governed by customary behavior that prevents workers from being paid according to their marginal productivity, except by coincidence. Employers find it costly or impossible to measure the actual productivity of individual workers in most jobs; in governments and nonprofit institutions the concept of marginal productivity is hard to define. Workers in government or nonprofit institutions may produce something measurable, but it generally has no clear market value; how much, for instance, is the processing of an application for social security worth? Furthermore, finding and training new workers is costly for employers, and finding and learning new jobs is costly and upsetting for workers. As a result, employees and employers, as if guided by an invisible hand, throw up barriers to minimize these costs of job mobility and, by doing so, make indeterminate the exact wage that they will negotiate.[43] To put it another way, if workers and employers have a long-term, but imprecise, commitment to one another, the worker's marginal value to the firm may be measured over a day, a week, a year, or more, and is probably impossible to estimate precisely.[44]

Critics of the conventional view of labor markets also tend to stress the importance of the job in determining or altering the productivity of the worker. According to one variant, a good part of differences in productivity inhere in jobs that a broad cross-section of the labor force could perform about equally well. According to another, the attributes that jobs require their holders to exhibit are eventually inculcated in the worker. Jobs that require punctuality, precision, and dependability produce punctual, precise, dependable workers. Jobs that permit slack habits produce slack workers who, eventually, are rendered incapable of holding responsible and demanding employment. In either case, productivity is not something workers bring to a job; rather, the job teaches productivity to the worker or confers it on him.

Adherents of the view that businessmen maximize profits have recourse to an argument that adherents of the conventional view of labor markets cannot employ. Firms that do not pursue maximum profits in a competitive market can eventually be driven out of business by aggressive competitors that do. The profit-maximizing firm will exploit cost-reducing opportunities and cut prices in order to enlarge its share of the market. The slack firm will be unable to meet competitive prices and still make a profit and will be forced out of business. But the worker who fails to find a job in which his earnings are as high as possible will not be forced out of business. He will simply get a lower wage than he might be capable of earning.

The crucial question adherents of the conventional view of the labor market had to answer was how workers could be assured of finding the best-paying jobs. If information was hard and costly to obtain, if hiring was dominated by customary procedures that limited access to many jobs, if the wage structure was heavily influenced by differences among jobs that time had rendered legitimate, natural competitive pressures could not be relied upon to direct workers to the best-paying jobs. Workers could not be driven out of business. But they might be trapped in jobs less demanding and less rewarding than those they might perform; the structure of jobs might not respond, or might respond only with considerable delay, to surpluses or shortages of workers with various capacities. Furthermore, it is difficult to reconcile the view that wages adjust promptly and that workers move smoothly into occupations where they have the highest productivity with the palpable facts that, in the aggregate, real wages do not in general decline in the face of high unemployment, and that protracted unemployment of workers with particular skills or in different regions can coexist with labor shortages in other occupations or places. When economists forecast unemployment with econometric models, they typically assume that money wages do not fall if labor is in excess supply—that is, if there is unemployment. When they theorize about labor markets, economists typically assume that real wages adjust to clear the market. These theories are not consistent unless inflation always occurs when unemployment is high, and neither theory readily accommodates the possibility that patterns of relative wages are a dominant influence on wage changes.[45]

The seeming inconsistency among these various perspectives on how labor markets operate may be more apparent than real. The institutional rules and wage rigidity thought by many to be inconsistent with the operation of competitive labor markets may instead be the form competition takes when it is costly for both workers and employers to obtain good information about available skills and job opportunities, when it is costly to find and train new workers, and when switching jobs requires costly adjustments.[46] Job ladders and internal labor markets probably economize on training costs, and seniority provisions are important in securing the cooperation of existing employees in providing on-the-job training to new workers. In the face of variations in demand, the maintenance of rigid wages with fluctuating employment may be preferred by both workers and employers to the maintenance of full employment with fluctuating wages.[47] In the former situation, uncertainty affects only a minority of workers, in the latter, all; and, as previously noted, unemployment typically is briefer than many analysts have supposed.

A number of radical critics have gone beyond suggesting that the failure to consider institutional imperfections mars conventional analysis of labor markets. They hold that wages are not determined and jobs are not allotted on the basis of productivity, but rather to increase the power and wealth of a narrow group of economic and political oligarchs, often identified as monopoly capitalists. They argue that the asserted stability of the income distribution and such problems as discrimination by race and sex, poverty, and, especially, their recalcitrance, can only be explained by the existence of a dominant class pursuing its economic and political interests to the detriment of the powerless.[48]

Although radicals cite many of the same characteristics of labor markets as do other critics of the conventional view of labor markets, they draw conclusions for policy quite different from those of nonradical critics. The radicals hold that there is no hope of reforming the capitalist system because the interests of the dominant capitalist class will ultimately prevail, while other critics share with adherents of the conventional view the perception that incremental reform in labor markets can succeed in improving the fairness and efficiency with which labor markets operate, although they disagree about the desirability of various reforms. The flavor of this difference was keenly perceived by Paul M. Sweezy, who wrote,

What [radical] writers . . . have in common is a total rejection of the whole capitalist-imperialist system and a profound lack of interest in schemes or efforts to reform it (except as they may be related to revolutionary tactics). . . . it should be clear that what is involved here is not really an old-new dichotomy but rather a radical-reformist dichotomy. . . . [Radicals] see the present as the frightful outcome of some four centuries of the history of capitalism, a system the very heart of which is exploitation and inequality and which is now careening out of control toward its final crises and catastrophes. Wars and revolutions are not a matter of preference or choice: they are the inevitable outcome of capitalism's inner contradictions, and the question is not whether they will happen but whether they will finally do away with the system that breeds them. To speak of reforming capitalism is either naïveté or deception.[49]

Both the strength and the weakness of the radical view flow from its emphasis on historic regularities and patterns in the economic system. By stressing such regularities, radicals can draw inferential support for an interpretation that stresses immutable class interests. By downplaying as insignificant changes in economic relations that others regard as profoundly significant, radicals can claim that only superficial characteristics of capitalism have been modified. Thus, the development of the welfare state, the emerging political and economic role of women and of blacks, and the development of trade unionism are all downplayed as tactical concessions by the dominant class to maintain power. The obvious weakness of such a view is that these developments have transformed the lives of most people. To dismiss these changes as insignificant strikes most people as palpably absurd.

Policy Alternatives

Whether or not the alternative nonradical views about the operation of labor markets can be reconciled with the conventional view, it is apparent that such a reconciliation has not yet occurred. As a result, the prescriptions for improving the earnings of low-income workers and for permitting a reduction in overall unemployment without inflation that enjoyed widespread acceptance during the 1960s now face a number of competing prescriptions.

It is relatively easy to design a training program for a worker who is presumed to suffer bouts of protracted unemployment or for groups that have above-average unemployment rates because of a lack of education or skills. But if one holds that the job market is governed by customary relations and that the structure of relative wages depends on the character of the jobs rather than of the individuals who fill them, policies that change people but leave the labor market as it is will do nothing except ensure that those who hold jobs without futures and from which they will soon be laid off have superfluous and irrelevant skills. And from a radical perspective, training programs are certain to fail; they are opiates that deaden their recipients to a recognition of the exploitative nature of the economic system.

The change in perceptions about how the labor market operates and how to characterize the problem of unemployment has led to proposals that government directly alter the demand for low-skill workers, and has caused many to condemn government-sponsored training programs for focusing on the inadequacies of workers who, if anything, are more than adequate for the jobs that are available to them. New proposals include wage subsidies payable to low-income workers or to their employers, public service employment, bonus payments to employers who retain specified people on their payrolls for longer than minimum periods of time, increases in minimum wages, and sheltered workshops.

Minimum Wages

The evolution of attitudes among economists toward minimum wages illustrates the play of these alternative views of the labor market. The general popularity of minimum wages among union officials and members, the general public, and political leaders contrasts with their almost universal condemnation by most traditional economists. Analysts critical of the conventional view are more likely to embrace aggressive use of minimum wages to improve the earnings of low-wage workers. According to the traditional view of labor markets, minimum wages may increase wages for some workers, but force other workers to accept lower wages in other occupations, to leave the labor market, or to suffer unemployment. Wages depend on the value of the skills workers possess; an employer simply will not hire workers whose value to the firm is less than the wage they must be paid. Minimum wage laws can thus injure low-wage workers, the very group they are designed to serve.[50]

Only a slight modification in this view of labor markets is necessary to see minimum wage laws as a potentially useful device for helping low-wage workers. If workers are imperfect substitutes for one another, then employers will respond to minimum wages by trying to replace formerly low-wage workers with other workers possessing different skills. As a result, they will hire fewer low-wage workers, but those whom they continue to employ will receive more pay—fewer of the formerly low-wage workers will be employed, but those who work will be paid more. In that event, total wages paid to workers who earned less than the minimum wage before may increase. This increase may come at the expense of other workers or out of profits. Whether the remaining employees receive more or less pay as a result of an increase in minimum wages will depend on whether the reduction in employment in such jobs is proportionately greater or smaller than the increase in wage rates. In general, the higher the minimum wage relative to the wage that would have prevailed in its absence, the less the chance that workers whose jobs are directly affected by minimum wages will benefit. In addition, of course, workers who lose jobs because minimum wages make it unprofitable for their former employers to retain them may qualify for unemployment insurance benefits and have a significant chance of finding alternative employment.

Some evidence suggests that current minimum wage laws serve to increase the total wages paid to adults who normally hold low-wage jobs (because the wage-increasing effect is proportionately greater than the job-reducing effect) but to reduce the total wages paid to teenagers (because the job-reducing effect exceeds the wage-increasing effect).[51] Advocates argue that minimum wage laws have considerable potential for improving the earnings prospects of low-wage workers. Whether one believes that workers are competing for jobs that they can all perform about as well as one another with sufficient training, or that the structure of jobs and wages is governed more by custom and convention than finely calculated profit maximization, minimum wages may be an effective device for shaking the wage and job structure into a new configuration within which formerly low-wage workers are paid more, and one that is not significantly less productive than the former arrangement.

Public Service Employment

The growing advocacy of federally sponsored programs of public employment reflects a similar change in attitudes. After being used extensively during the Great Depression to provide jobs for the unemployed in the most direct way possible, public employment lost political acceptability and acquired the image of useless make-work. While public employment has come back into favor, the definitions are far from clear. Public employment can consist of direct hiring by the federal government, federal subsidies for state and local hiring (as is done under the Comprehensive Employment and Training Act), or sheltered workshops for those unable to find or keep employment in the private sector. The reasons for the renewed appeal of public employment are also diverse. Some advocates of improved public services look upon publicly employed workers, who might otherwise be collecting unemployment insurance or welfare, as a cheap way of securing some services for payments that would be made in any case. Some view assistance through work as better for the recipient than cash transfer payments. In part, hazy memories of how public employment operated during the depression have been revised; one can as easily reason from the numerous, enduring public works constructed by the Work Projects Administration as from the leaf-raking of the Civilian Conservation Corps. In part, the refusal by many economists and others to accept the conventional view of labor markets has made attempts directly to alter the demand for low-wage workers an appealing alternative, or a necessary complement, to training programs designed to transform low-wage workers themselves.

Unfortunately, the way public employment programs should be designed has received insufficient attention.[52] Should public employment temporarily serve workers who have suffered extended unemployment or should it be a permanent guarantee of a job? Should wage subsidies be paid to low-wage workers? Should wage bill subsidies be paid to employers to induce them to hire low-wage workers? Only after such questions are answered is it possible to decide whether the number of public service jobs should be small or large, limited in number and duration or open-ended, and whether the wages paid on public service employment should be low enough to discourage all but those who held the worst jobs or no job at all from applying or high enough to enable a worker to support a spouse and two children at something above the officially defined poverty standard. Even if wages are set around the minimum wage, millions of workers, who now earn less than the minimum wage, may apply, unless eligibility is limited in some other way; but if such workers are the sole support of even moderate-sized families, they will remain in poverty. If wages are set high enough to enable one earner to support a family of four above the poverty threshold—about 15 percent above the minimum wage—the wage would induce millions of workers who now earn less to switch from private to public employment.

If jobs were temporary, they might reinforce the pattern of repeated bouts of brief employment without chance of progression, the syndrome that recent data on unemployment suggest principally afflicts workers in groups suffering from higher-than-average unemployment. If jobs were permanent, it would be necessary to find a sufficient number of useful jobs for the very large number of potential applicants. Skepticism about the effectiveness of public employment in improving the kinds of jobs to which low-wage workers have access is based on such concerns.[53] Unless public employment shifts the demand for labor toward low-skill workers, it will do nothing to reduce the unemployment rate that can be achieved without causing excessive price increases; without such a reduction the effects of public employment on job opportunities for low-wage workers would not differ from those of tax cuts or other increases in public expenditures.[54]

Conclusions

During the early 1960s a vague consensus marked views about how labor markets work and about the problem of unemployment. The consensus encompassed policies to improve job opportunities for the low-wage worker and, simultaneously, to lower the rate of unemployment that could be sustained without excessively rapid inflation. A certain amount of unemployment—a frictional minimum—was viewed as necessary to ensure both that workers could find the jobs for which they were best suited and that employers could find the workers who could best perform available jobs. Cyclical unemployment was a useless waste that sound management of the economy would terminate. Structural unemployment, the problem found especially in depressed areas and among disadvantaged groups, could be corrected by training and other manpower policies. These programs would bring into the labor force workers who, in effect, were excluded from it by some kind of personal disability.

The seeming failure of training programs to reduce the amount of structural unemployment was signaled by the continuing higher-than-average unemployment rates of blacks (even after one adjusts for educational differences between blacks and whites) and by the inability of the economy to tolerate unemployment rates of 4 percent or less without the onset of severe wage and price inflation; and the failure was certified by the ambiguous and conflicting results of evaluative studies of training programs. The prospects of achieving low unemployment waned; the threat of inflation waxed. In the face of these frustrations, the conventional theory of how labor markets operate was criticized and alternatives were proposed. New information about the frequency and duration of unemployment made clear that the old distinctions among various kinds of unemployment were hard to make when one looked at the actual experience of the unemployed.

As a result of this intellectual turmoil, advocates of a wide range of alternative programs have found support. Those who emphasize training can turn to conventional analysis of labor markets. They can accommodate the new data on duration and frequency of unemployment by claiming that workers with few skills are limited to short-term jobs or ones that hold out no prospects for promotion. But they can only express a faith that if and when low-wage workers acquire skills, the short-term or dead-end jobs they had formerly held would promptly disappear; there is negligible evidence to support (or to refute) such a faith. This same faith— that employers would alter the mix of skills and types of workers they sought to hire to match the available supply—underlay the conviction in the 1960s that adequate aggregate demand would suffice to keep unemployment low without producing unacceptable inflation. Those who emphasize direct job creation can find support in a variety of alternative views of the labor market that cannot be refuted by available evidence.

To keep inflation in bounds, some hold that unemployment would have to exceed the "natural rate" variously estimated at 5 to 6 percent of the labor force. But there is disagreement whether lower unemployment would cause inflation to rise and remain at a higher rate or to accelerate without limit. Still others advocate a variety of measures to reduce inflationary pressures; these measures include a return to something much like the Kennedy-Johnson guideposts,[55] investment incentives, limits on the power of unions, and free use of antitrust, tariff, tax, and regulatory policies to make wage increases that exceed productivity growth unattractive under labor market conditions where such increases now would seem profitable.[56]

Those responsible for economic policy must proceed with this cacophonous intellectual chorus in the background. Milton Friedman has often stated that differences in recommendations for policy among economists stem far more from a lack of knowledge about how the economy works than from disagreement about objectives. It is now apparent that disagreements about values often masquerade as disputes about facts. Friedman's statement is certainly false for the nonexpert, who must decide what policies to support and who inevitably must depend on his own values. Policies to reduce unemployment, to train the unskilled, to change the structure of jobs and wages, and to limit inflation must reflect to varying degrees the strength of commitment to these objectives as well as the analytical conclusions of professional economists.

Notes

1. Edmund S. Phelps, "Economic Policy and Unemployment in the 1960's," *Public Interest*, no. 34 (Winter 1974), p. 31 (emphasis deleted).

2. See Albert Rees, "Dimensions of the Employment Problem," in Arthur M. Okun, ed., *The Battle Against Unemployment* (Norton, 1965), p. 25, for these categories and definitions of them. This three-way division was often increased to four with the addition of "seasonal" unemployment, such as experienced by the northern construction worker in February, the cannery worker between harvests, and so on.

3. *Unemployment: Terminology, Measurement, and Analysis,* Prepared for the Subcommittee on Economic Statistics of the Joint Economic Committee, 87:1 (Government Printing Office, 1961). The quotation appears on p. 3.

4. *The Disadvantaged Poor: Education and Employment,* Third Report of the Task Force on Economic Growth and Opportunity (Chamber of Commerce of the United States, 1966), p. 86.

5. Once again, one should keep in mind that although the number of laws enacted was large and the rhetoric lavished in their support extravagant, the budget expenditures to which they gave rise were modest. See chapter 1.

6. Ad Hoc Committee on the Triple Revolution, *The Triple Revolution* (Santa Barbara: Ad Hoc Committee, 1964). Lest any readers swept up in the

current concern about scarcity think that this description of attitudes in the early 1960s is an exaggeration, the following quotations may persuade them. "The fundamental problem posed by the cybernation revolution in the U.S. is that it invalidates the general mechanism so far employed to undergird people's rights as consumers. Up to this time economic resources have been distributed on the basis of contributions to production, with machines and men competing for employment on somewhat equal terms. In the developing cybernated system, potentially unlimited output can be achieved by systems of machines which will require little cooperation from human beings. As machines take over production from men, they absorb an increasing proportion of resources while the men who are displaced become dependent on minimal and unrelated government measures—unemployment insurance, social security, welfare payments" (ibid., p. 6). And later, in a flight of almost unparalleled idiocy, "Cybernation raises the level of the skills of the machine. . . . [T]he machines being produced today have, on the average, skills·equivalent to a high school diploma. If a human being is to compete with such machines, therefore, he must at least possess a high school diploma" (ibid., p. 9).

7. See, for example, Charles C. Killingsworth, "Three Myths of Automation," *Nation,* vol. 191 (December 17, 1960), pp. 467–70; Killingsworth's testimony in *Unemployment Problems,* Hearings before the Senate Special Committee on Unemployment Problems, 86:1 (GPO, 1960), pt. 3, pp. 1144–54; and Killingsworth, "The Bottleneck in Labor Skills," in Okun, ed., *The Battle Against Unemployment,* pp. 32–36.

8. Lloyd Ulman, "The Uses and Limits of Manpower Policy," *Public Interest,* no. 34 (Winter 1974), pp. 87–88.

9. This study received popular coverage through James W. Knowles, "Why Unemployment Stays Up," *New Republic,* vol. 147 (October 20, 1962), pp. 18–19. While he denied that structural unemployment was more of a problem in the early 1960s than it had been in previous years, he put in a plug for programs to train and relocate workers, asserting that expenditures on such programs "will . . . pay large dividends in higher average per capita incomes, a higher growth rate and a reduction in human misery" (p. 19).

10. N. J. Simler, "Long-term Unemployment, the Structural Hypothesis, and Public Policy," *American Economic Review,* vol. 54 (December 1964), p. 985.

11. "The Great Unemployment Fallacy," *New Republic,* vol. 151 (September 5, 1964), p. 10.

12. Simler cites numerous studies that seemed to dispose of one variant or another of the structural hypothesis. See "Long-Term Unemployment, the Structural Hypothesis, and Public Policy," pp. 985–87.

13. Joseph A. Kershaw and Robert A. Levine, "Poverty, Aggregate Demand, and Economic Structure," *Journal of Human Resources,* vol. 1 (Summer 1966), p. 67.

14. Albert Rees, "Economic Expansion and Persisting Unemployment: An Overview," in Robert Aaron Gordon and Margaret S. Gordon, eds., *Prosperity and Unemployment* (Wiley, 1966), p. 345.

15. This section draws on recent research on the nature and causes of unemployment, most notably: Stephen T. Marston, "Employment Instability and High Unemployment Rates," *Brookings Papers on Economic Activity, 1:1976,* pp. 169–203; George L. Perry, "Unemployment Flows in the U.S. Labor Market," *Brookings Papers on Economic Activity, 2:1972,* pp. 245–78; Nancy S. Barrett and Richard D. Morgenstern, "Why Do Blacks and Women Have High Unemployment Rates?" *Journal of Human Resources,* vol. 9 (Fall 1974), pp. 452–64; Martin S. Feldstein, "The Importance of Temporary Layoffs: An Empirical Analysis," *Brookings Papers on Economic Activity, 3:1975,* pp. 725–44; Robert E. Hall, "Why Is the Unemployment Rate So High at Full Employment?" *Brookings Papers on Economic Activity, 3:1970,* pp. 369–409. For a precursor of this view of unemployment, see Edward D. Kalachek, "The Composition of Unemployment and Public Policy," in Gordon and Gordon, eds., *Prosperity and Unemployment,* pp. 227–45.

16. The 6.3 percent and 4.5 percent were derived by subtracting the number of persons unemployed twenty-seven weeks and over from the total number unemployed and dividing by the total civilian labor force. (*Economic Report of the President, January 1977,* pp. 218, 221, 222.) This assumes that jobs are found after twenty-six weeks of unemployment so that the total labor force remains unchanged.

17. Stephen Marston found that personal variables such as race, family status, education, age, and sex were correlated more closely with movements from jobs into unemployment than were job characteristics such as industry of employment, occupation, and part-time work. See "Employment Instability and High Unemployment Rates." Such a statistical exercise cannot settle the question, because much of the collective influence of these variables cannot be assigned uniquely to either set of variables. More basically, however, it is not clear whether Marston's job breakdown is sufficiently fine grained so that given occupation-industry categories can be characterized as good or bad jobs.

18. Robert E. Hall observed that one could "no longer speak of the employed and the unemployed as if they were distinct groups over time, although this mistake still appears in popular accounts of unemployment." "Turnover in the Labor Force," *Brookings Papers on Economic Activity, 3:1972,* p. 710.

19. Edward F. Denison, *Accounting for United States Economic Growth, 1929–1969* (Brookings Institution, 1974), p. 62.

20. This view achieved popular acceptance following an influential paper by George L. Perry, "Changing Labor Markets and Inflation," *Brookings Papers on Economic Activity, 3:1970,* pp. 411–41. The same idea had been advanced a decade earlier as a forecast rather than a description in Harold Demsetz, "Structural Unemployment: A· Reconsideration of the Evidence," *Journal of Law and Economics,* vol. 4 (October 1961), pp. 80–92; "Committee Issues Unemployment Recommendations," *Congressional Quarterly Weekly Report,* vol. 18 (April 1, 1960), p. 594; and Thomas Dernberg and Kenneth Strand, "Hidden Unemployment 1953–62: A Quantitative Analysis by Age and Sex," *American Economic Review,* vol. 56 (March 1966), pp. 71–95.

21. Michael L. Wachter, "The Changing Cyclical Responsiveness of Wage Inflation," *Brookings Papers on Economic Activity, 1:1976*, pp. 115–59.

22. See Perry, "Changing Labor Markets and Inflation," p. 438.

23. This argument was put forward by Edgar L. Feige, "The 1972 Report of the President's Council of Economic Advisers: Inflation and Unemployment," *American Economic Review*, vol. 62 (September 1972), p. 512.

24. The succession of articles amending previous estimates in the *Brookings Papers on Economic Activity* forms the most accessible compendium of such revisions.

25. J. C. R. Rowley and D. A. Wilton, "The Sensitivity of Quarterly Models of Wage Determination to Aggregation Assumptions," *Quarterly Journal of Economics*, vol. 88 (November 1974), pp. 671–80.

26. Milton Friedman, "The Role of Monetary Policy," *American Economic Review*, vol. 58 (March 1968), pp. 1–17; and Edmund S. Phelps and others, *The Microeconomic Foundations of Employment and Inflation Theory* (Norton, 1970).

27. John T. Dunlop, *Wage Determination Under Trade Unions* (Macmillan, 1944), pp. 147–48.

28. Gail Pierson, "The Effect of Union Strength on the U.S. 'Phillips Curve,' " *American Economic Review*, vol. 58 (June 1968), pp. 456–67; George L. Perry, "Wages and the Guideposts," *American Economic Review*, vol. 57 (September 1967), pp. 897–904, and comments on this article and Perry's reply in *American Economic Review*, vol. 59 (June 1969), pp. 351–70.

The effectiveness of the guideposts was challenged from the outset, principally by those who believed that market forces, too powerful to be controlled by human actions, determined both wages and prices. For a lucid statement of this view in the context of a critique of the 1972 Report of the Council of Economic Advisers, see Reuben A. Kessel, "The 1972 Report of the President's Council of Economic Advisers: Inflation and Controls," *American Economic Review*, vol. 62 (September 1972), pp. 527–32. Kessel writes, "Precisely how inflation is caused by price and wage increases that are unjustified by competitive market conditions is unspecified. How does monopoly pricing in wage and product markets cause inflation? One will search in vain for an answer to this question in the Report" (p. 528).

29. N. J. Simler and Alfred Tella, "Labor Reserves and the Phillips Curve," *Review of Economics and Statistics*, vol. 50 (February 1968), pp. 32–49. Official statistics excluded those who enter the labor force when job opportunities are plentiful but who remain out of the labor force, and hence are not counted as unemployed, when jobs are scarce.

30. Wayne Vroman, "Manufacturing Wage Behavior with Special Reference to the Period 1962–1966," *Review of Economics and Statistics*, vol. 52 (May 1970), pp. 160–67.

31. Albert Rees, writing in 1966, conceded that "we cannot quarrel with the conclusion that the elasticity of labor supply in response to demand fluctuations is far greater than we suspected a decade ago." "Economic Expansion and Persisting Unemployment," p. 331.

32. Precisely such a relationship was estimated by Nancy S. Barrett, Geral-

dine Gerardi, and Thomas P. Hart, who wrote, "Evidence of short-run compensatory pricing implies that measures to reduce aggregate demand tend to worsen the inflation-unemployment trade-off. But unlike the accelerationist view, our results suggest that the inflationary process will be dampened in the longer run once higher unemployment rates are established." "A Factor Analysis of Quarterly Price and Wage Behavior for U.S. Manufacturing," *Quarterly Journal of Economics*, vol. 88 (August 1974), p. 408.

33. Robert Solow, in commenting on a paper by Robert J. Gordon, had observed that "the accelerationist idea of inflation gets essentially no support from the data. . . . I would suggest that we leave that theoretical question out of our discussion unless somebody has something new to offer." *Brookings Papers on Economic Activity, 1:1970*, p. 42. Two years later Gordon had new results to offer that were much closer to the accelerationist position; see Robert J. Gordon, "Wage-Price Controls and the Shifting Phillips Curve," *Brookings Papers on Economic Activity, 2:1972*, pp. 385–421. Two years later Robert Hall embraced the accelerationist position; see Robert E. Hall, "The Process of Inflation in the Labor Market," *Brookings Papers on Economic Activity, 2:1974*, pp. 343–93.

34. Michael R. Darby has recomputed official unemployment rates for the 1930s and found them to be lower than previously believed; "Three and a Half Million U.S. Employees Have Been Mislaid: Or, an Explanation of Unemployment, 1934–1941," *Journal of Political Economy*, vol. 84 (February 1976), pp. 1–16. Average hourly earnings (which are not the same as average hourly wage rates) fell from 56 cents in 1929 to 44 cents in 1933, but rose to 66 cents in 1940, despite slack labor markets.

35. Ulman, "The Uses and Limits of Manpower Policy," p. 95.

36. Albert Rees estimated that training under the Manpower Development and Training Act and the Area Redevelopment Act had reduced unemployment by only 84,000 by the end of 1964. "Economic Expansion and Persisting Unemployment," p. 343.

37. See Phelps, "Economic Policy and Unemployment," p. 43.

38. Ulman, "The Uses and Limits of Manpower Policy," p. 100.

39. Orley Ashenfelter, "Estimating the Effect of Training Programs on Earnings with Longitudinal Data," and Nicholas M. Kiefer, "The Economic Benefits of Four Manpower Training Programs" (papers presented at the Conference on Evaluating Manpower Training Programs, Princeton University, Industrial Relations Section, May 6 and 7, 1976; processed).

40. "Discussion" [Gertrude Bancroft paper] in Gordon and Gordon, eds., *Prosperity and Unemployment*, p. 252.

41. Arthur M. Okun, "Upward Mobility in a High-pressure Economy," *Brookings Papers on Economic Activity, 1:1973*, pp. 207–52; and Wayne Vroman, "Worker Upgrading and the Business Cycle," *Brookings Papers on Economic Activity, 1:1977*, pp. 229–50.

42. Michael J. Piore, "The Impact of the Labor Market upon the Design and Selection of Productive Techniques within the Manufacturing Plant," *Quarterly Journal of Economics*, vol. 82 (November 1968), p. 619.

43. Peter B. Doeringer and Michael J. Piore, *Internal Labor Markets and*

Manpower Analysis (Heath, 1971), pp. 74–76; Michael J. Piore, "Fragments of a 'Sociological' Theory of Wages," *American Economic Review,* vol. 63 (May 1973, *Papers and Proceedings, 1972*), pp. 377–84.

44. See Lester C. Thurow, *Generating Inequality: Mechanisms of Distribution in the U.S. Economy* (Basic Books, 1975), app. A.

45. The difficulty of reconciling these three processes of wage determination is stressed by Thurow, ibid., pp. 51–54.

46. This possibility is admitted by Michael L. Wachter, "Primary and Secondary Labor Markets: A Critique of the Dual Approach," *Brookings Papers on Economic Activity, 3:1974,* p. 646.

47. See, for example, Donald F. Gordon, "A Neo-Classical Theory of Keynesian Unemployment," *Economic Inquiry,* vol. 12 (December 1974), pp. 431–59; Martin Neil Baily, "Wages and Employment under Uncertain Demand," *Review of Economic Studies,* vol. 41 (January 1974), pp. 37–50; Oliver E. Williamson, Michael L. Wachter, and Jeffrey E. Harris, "Understanding the Employment Relation: The Analysis of Idiosyncratic Exchange," *Bell Journal of Economics,* vol. 6 (Spring 1975), pp. 250–78; and Costas Azariadis, "Implicit Contracts and Underemployment Equilibria," *Journal of Political Economy,* vol. 83 (December 1975), pp. 1183–1202.

48. See David M. Gordon, *Theories of Poverty and Underemployment: Orthodox, Radical, and Dual Labor Market Perspectives* (Heath, 1972); and Samuel Bowles and Herbert Gintis, *Schooling in Capitalist America: Educational Reform and the Contradictions of Economic Life* (Basic Books, 1976). For a sharply critical, but not unsympathetic, examination of radical contributions to the economics of labor markets, see Glen G. Cain, "The Challenge of Dual and Radical Theories of the Labor Market to Orthodox Theory," discussion paper 255–75 (University of Wisconsin–Madison, Institute for Research on Poverty, 1975; processed).

49. Paul M. Sweezy, "Comment," prepared for a Symposium on the Economics of the New Left, *Quarterly Journal of Economics,* vol. 86 (November 1972), pp. 658–60.

50. Numerous studies have been undertaken to measure the reduction in jobs for low-skilled workers caused by minimum wages. See Douglas K. Adie, "Teen-Age Unemployment and Real Federal Minimum Wages," *Journal of Political Economy,* vol. 81 (March–April 1973), pp. 435–41; Marvin Kosters and Finis Welch, "The Effects of Minimum Wages on the Distribution of Changes in Aggregate Employment," *American Economic Review,* vol. 62 (June 1972), pp. 323–32; Thomas Gale Moore, "The Effect of Minimum Wages on Teenage Unemployment Rates," *Journal of Political Economy,* vol. 79 (July–August 1971), pp. 897–902; and Finis Welch, "Minimum Wage Legislation in the United States," *Economic Inquiry,* vol. 12 (September 1974), pp. 285–318.

51. Edward M. Gramlich, "Impact of Minimum Wages on Other Wages, Employment, and Family Incomes," *Brookings Papers on Economic Activity, 2:1976,* pp. 409–51.

52. This lack is being reduced by a study of alternative approaches to em-

ployment programs in progress for the Brookings Institution by John Palmer and Michael Barth.

53. Doeringer and Piore observe, "Public employment programs are likely to expand the demand for low-wage labor in the secondary labor market, which already behaves like a tight labor market, without initiating any corrective mechanisms necessary to overcome instability and to upgrade workers to primary employment. Moreover, a guarantee of work may even aggravate instability on the supply side of the market. Unless such upgrading can be assured, programs directly tied to opening primary employment are preferable." *Internal Labor Markets and Manpower Analysis,* p. 206.

54. Robert E. Hall, "Prospects for Shifting the Phillips Curve through Manpower Policy," *Brookings Papers on Economic Activity, 3:1971,* pp. 692–94.

55. Gardner Ackley, "An Incomes Policy for the 1970's," *Review of Economics and Statistics,* vol. 54 (August 1972), pp. 218–23; and Barrett, Gerardi, and Hart, "A Factor Analysis."

56. Hendrik S. Houthakker, "Are Controls the Answer?" *Review of Economics and Statistics,* vol. 54 (August 1972), pp. 231–34; and George L. Perry, "Stabilization Policy and Inflation," in Henry Owen and Charles L. Schultze, eds., *Setting National Priorities: The Next Ten Years* (Brookings Institution, 1976), pp. 271–321.

2

TIP FOR INFLATION
Why and How

Sidney Weintraub

Our credibility as a nation has been jeopardized by inflation and aggravated by the accompanying unemployment. Every age faces setbacks to test its resolve for historical evolutionary survival. The 1930s grappled with unemployment, and the not unrelated march of dictators. The 1940s saw the war, peacetime conversion, and the Cold War. Subsequent traumatic episodes, as the Cuban missile crisis, Vietnam, and Watergate can be cited. Energy and inflation, or inflation and energy now appear paramount. Blot out the inflation blight and, barring nuclear war miscalculations, we should again be able to resume the free world leadership that our military might compels and our economic power commends.

My position remains that (except by happenstance) a stable price level and minimal unemployment will elude us on traditional monetary policies, or on the less efficient fiscal policy except in extraordinary circumstances such as the 1930s. At the moment, it would entail some digression to develop this. To those who see monetary policy as ample for the desired price and job stability, and in a relatively noninterventionist framework, I hope my own proposals will be assessed as at least a necessary *supplement* to monetary policy. I would even go further: on the assumption that an effective and largely nonbureaucratic tax-based incomes policy (TIP) is adopted, I would see no difficulty, for the most part, in subscribing to the steady money growth rule foreshadowed in the 100 per cent money of Irving Fisher, or the Simons-Hayek-Robertson discussions of the 1930s, or by modern exponents. The difference between us, as I see it, is whether steady money emissions per annum can perform the stable price feat or whether a TIP-type incomes policy is essential as a prior condition for the real output control mechanics implicit in steady money growth.

I dwell on this because it would be a curious misreading of my position to allege that I deny the potency of money supplies.[1] It has been the efficacy of money control as an inflation instrument that has drawn the criticism, never its

Dr. Weintraub is Professor of Economics at the University of Pennsylvania.

From Sidney Weintraub, "TIP for Inflation: Why and How," in Center for the Study of American Business, *Alternative Policies to Combat Inflation* (1978). Reprinted by permission of the Center for the Study of American Business at Washington University in St. Louis.

potency. It has, too often, been simply too potent, chopping jobs and production rather than subduing the price level. Money retains its majesty in financing output and funding jobs.

Subsequent discussion will strike on literally three planes, with first some general views to establish a position; next, to deal with some slightly more technical issues; and finally, a statement of my own proposals for inflation policy followed by an evaluation of the evolving Carter price level package of October 24.

STAGFLATION: THE IMPOSSIBLE HAS HAPPENED

For perspective, the formidable importance of inflation is sketched so that discrepancies in assessing the issue can emerge sharply.

Inflation: The Number One Problem

Concurring with the various polls, inflation remains our number one economic problem. It is "the one in many" that mars our economic performance, suppressing actual accomplishments well short of our potential. It impedes full employment; it engenders income inequities and anguish, social unrest and political turbulence; it contributes powerfully to the international dollar decline and raises import prices; it occasions stock market jitters, bearish bond markets, historic high interest rates, and unstable financial markets; it visibly upsets government and private budgets; and it deflects allocational and expenditure decisions from patterns (presumably more rational) ensuing under a more stable price order. The stop-go of minor skirmishes and major failures in combating inflation has repercussions on the housing and construction industry, with multiplier ramifications through the economy.

Subdue inflation and our other national problems should fall into place. Continuing our past stumbles and fumbles leads to a cumulating agenda of unfulfilled objectives, whether envisioned as new ventures for government or as designs to eliminate areas of intervention and alter the scope of the private and public sector.

The Great Intellectual Distraction

Not least, the alarms over inflation and its acceleration constitute a great intellectual distraction. Constantly discussed, new issues are shoved into the background. In the competition for the limited attention span devoted to public issues, a Gresham's law is at work: the familiar diverts reflection from the more novel phenomena. An undue amount of professional skills, moreover, are preoccupied with the chronic economic ill. Yet despite the concerted focus of intellectual resources, the number of original ideas to arrest the inflation stalemate are conspicuously few.

The Stagflation Ordeal: The Impossible Has Happened

The last decade has witnessed the *simultaneous* distress of too much inflation and too much unemployment, with the odd couple constituting the stagflation ordeal. The debacle in the United Kingdom has at times been more severe, as output fell amid a chaotic price level surge, giving currency to the *slumpflation* term. The price of this enrichment of the language was a more total disorientation of the economy.

In the older boom-bust cycles, prices and output rose during the upswing and unemployment rates fell; the reverse pattern marked the recession fallback. Either inflation *or* higher unemployment rates prevailed. Now, the see-saw has yielded to the buzz-saw: we have simultaneous bad economic tidings. Instead of a single disorder one at a time, we suffer the double trauma. What used to happen in banana republics, or in bizarre comic operas where everything went wrong at once, creating havoc in all directions, has happened to us, and to other affluent, politically mature, and sophisticated economies endowed with all the prescribed sophisticated stabilization techniques.

The "impossible," or "inconceivable," has thus happened. Older economists would have been appalled at the juxtaposition of events. Manifestly, the double-trouble attests to some failure of ideas, and their reenforcement in policy. It is especially perplexing that in an age where economics has become mathematized, fascinated with econometrics and obsessed with the computer devouring piles of data, the main tangible result is a sequel that previous generations of economists averted, namely, the stagflation malaise. Buried under the enriched technical avalanche, progress in ideas for the smooth functioning of the economy has been impaired.

THE KEYNESIAN-MONETARIST DIALOGUE

Passing reference must be made to the prescriptive versions of the dominant Keynesian and monetarist dialogue filtered over from professional to popular consciousness.

Over the stagflation decade monetarists have generally alleged that central bank policy has been too lax, with the money spill culminating in inflation. They usually advocate annual money increases in the three to five per cent range. In more inadvertent renditions, a steady money pace seems to be the virtue, rather than the two-pronged rule of steadiness at a rate consonant with longer run production growth. The objective remains, to abort inflation on the premise that the steady percentage rule will restore a stable, full employment economy.

Keynesians, with minds riveted on past unemployment episodes and, until a late day, less mindful of the inflation burden and inequities, have usually targeted their money supply recipes on alleviating job distress. Their money supply advocacy has more frequently, over the dour decade, seized on annual money growth rates in the seven to ten per cent zone.

Dialogue has often been at cross-purposes, and misspent; much of the debate has been over whether the glass of water is half empty or half full. Nonetheless, each has called attention to part of the problem, the monetarists to the Keynesian inflation neglect and the Keynesians clinging to implant the dire past unemployment memories.

As a long-time critic of the fashionable brands of Keynesianism, even while not derogating the potency of monetary policy, it is possible to deprecate its efficacy against inflation. Monetary policy scores its hardest direct blows on jobs and production, being particularly destructive to the housing industry when it is severely restrictive. By creating enough unemployment—as under good Phillips curve doctrine—it can *indirectly* slow up the average wage and salary ascent and thus contain the price level. Effectually, by inflicting unemployment distress, it can mitigate the inflation disorder: it supplants the unwanted for the undesirable. For it to win against inflation, there is a precondition, namely, that labor must acquiesce in moderating its wage demands. When labor grows more adamant despite unemployment, insisting on higher pay despite jumping unemployment rates, the double-trouble of stagflation or slumpflation occurs.

The monetary cure against inflation thus partakes of the same dubious policy attributes that Pigou long ago noted for wage cuts as an automatic route to full employment (*Lapses from Full Employment*); through the "real-balance" effect the ensuing price deflation remedy might be more devastating than the original disease. Pigou might be chided for understating the social, political, and economic plight ensuing from fairly universal bankruptcy.

My conviction thus remains, that over both the near future and the long haul, monetary policy is destined to be inefficient in establishing a stable economy. I offer this as a reluctant conclusion; I would prefer being mistaken, for my analysis suggests that new institutions must be organized to cope with the systematic contradiction. In error, the sole result would be that these skeptical views would be demolished by events and we could go on as before—a very small price to pay for the maintenance of an orderly and venerable economic system.

The Incomplete Fed

The Fed has been fighting inflation over most of its sixty-four years. The dismal inflation history is a result not of the lack of will on the part of the Fed officials, but of a lack of tools for a direct attack on the price problem without dumping us in the unemployment ditch and, over the last decade, without discernible inflation surcease. The last two chairmen of the system were dedicated and implacable inflation foes, yet both left office with prices over fifty per cent higher than at the start of their incumbency. Even as they reminded us of their zeal and the Fed's eternal vigilance, they would intone the lugubrious price statistics. As in the military communiques, they would always see light at the end of the tunnel crowning their valor, yet always the victory has been beyond reach.

After sixty-four years of retreat, and cumulating distress, we would long ago have altered military strategy and probed whether the weaponry was ample for the task. My conclusion has been that an unaided monetary policy cannot usher in a sidewise price trend, at least not without a catastrophic cost in unemployment and festering social and political conflict with irreparable damage to the market economy. Where alternatives compatible with the functioning of a market economy are available, in blocking mild reforms, the friends of the relatively free economy who want it to succeed join unwittingly with enemies who prefer that it fail.

Mischievous Phillips Curve Doctrine

Monetarists nonetheless insist that their tight money medicine, pursued long and relentlessly enough, will stop inflation. *How long,* and *how relentlessly,* are subjects too often left vague. Too, circumstances under which they might abandon the pressure are seldom revealed; alternatives, if the policy failed to operate on schedule, are not drafted. In the military, there is at least a contingency plan in case the battle goes awry.

More candid espousal of monetarist recipes acknowledge that the policy can spell unemployment. This is good Phillips curve doctrine but it embeds some bad theory and dubious policy, dangerous to the viability of the market system.

There is no need to dwell on the intricacies of Phillips curves, or their wayward patterns of recent years, or the transformation of what was originally hailed as a *predictive* law into a less edifying *post-mortem* on why events misbehaved. The case might be made that the Phillips curve lacks even the staying power of the law of demand in consumer markets under the *ceteris paribus* proviso.

Most dejecting is the advocacy of a policy that aims to replace one dismemberment with another disfiguration, or to supplant the inflation woes with the unemployment morass. To me it is simply immoral, let alone uneconomic, to recomment unemployment for other people, usually to menace the least adaptable members of our economy with the indignity of a loss of jobs and income. I have said on occasion that advocates of these policies should resign, join the ranks of the unemployed, and become the great inflation fighters. If unemployment is good policy, they should be first to enlist in the battle.

Too, the policy is spurious. It is as if a doctor advises a patient that he can cure him of a coronary ailment by inducing kidney troubles (iatrogenic is the medical word, as Hyman Minsky, Professor of Economics at Washington University, has enlightened us). Most of us would seek a new physician. Medicine aims to eradicate all debilitating ailments, and not to substitute a pernicious malaise for a terminable affliction. In economics, however, we seem less concerned with restoring total health, preferring some impenetrable, often mystic, talk of trade-offs.

The Phillips curve, even when well-behaved, reports relations in labor markets as organized in the past. Not inconceivably, by adopting innovating policies compatible with the market economy, or involving acceptable departures, money wage and salary movements may be moderated to much less inflationary sights without bending too much from the goal of jobs for all who are willing to work at prevailing real wages.

The Destroy-To-Revive Fantasy

Monetary policy, as practiced, entails a curious "destroy-to-revive" fantasy that would stir incredulity in wanderers not steeped in the conventional wisdom.

Every time the economy approaches full employment, we are warned of the danger of inflation ahead and cautioned against the economy "overheating." The sequel involves a tightening of the money screws, and deliberate retardation of the growth rate and job access. Sighting the Promised Land, a bugle call to retreat is sounded.

This is bewildering. Every time we show signs of robust economic health we are coerced into iatrogenic sickness, with the economy dropped into a recession tailspin. After the repressive process runs on for a time, we gather our courage to denounce government for stop-go tactics, and to sound some clarion calls (by Keynesians) for renewing the march to the fuller employment gates. Money policy is eased, to build the economic patient to better health—not to complete vigor but, for his own good, this is presumed to make him susceptible to later illness. Only the worst symptoms of joblessness are mitigated.

Thus we are perennially trapped below our best performance, and *deliberately* so condemned. We are compelled to adopt a posture of dedicated underachievement at best, and significant frustration at worst. Systemic masochism earns the more euphemistic name of "fighting inflation."

Despite this "destroy-to-revive" tactic, we have not dislodged the price spiral. (Currently, another tight money venture is in process). We have, however, sponsored a sputtering economy, rather than a market system riding smoothly at peak efficiency. Monetary policy, despite good intentions, has mired us in an abject outcome compared to an optimal and presumably attainable goal.

THE ASSAULT ON THE LAWS OF ARITHMETIC

Over the last decade especially, we have been engaged in a mad assault on the laws of arithmetic. Average productivity over the longer term has been inching ahead by two to three per cent per annum; money income—with money wages and salaries comprising the seventy-five per cent bulk of the total—has been leaping by eight, ten, twelve . . . per cent or more. In the United Kingdom and Australia, to name but two countries, the more herculean feat was essayed in 1974 and 1975, with pay increases approaching a twenty-five per cent annual pace. Consternation ensued when prices vaulted in concert.

A Basic Truism

A price level surge is imperative whenever a sharp discrepancy occurs between average income and average productivity. Our inability to apprehend this homely truth is amazing for the results *must* follow:

(1) $PQ = Y$, where P = average price, Q = aggregate real output,

$$Y = income$$

$$\therefore P = (Y/Q) = (Y/N)/(Q/N) = (y/A), \text{ where } N = \text{employment,}$$
$$y = \text{per employee income,}$$
$$A = \text{average product} =$$
$$Q/N.$$

Regardless of what the Fed does, so long as average income[2] including wages, salaries, profits, rent, depreciation, etc. per employee runs faster than average productivity, the private sector price level is bound to fill the gap.

Futility of Monetary Policy Under Outsized Pay Increases

To make average money wages and salaries stand out more prominently in the price equation, from $PQ = Y - kwN$, then:

(2) $P = kw/A$, where k = average price markup

(or the reciprocal of the wage share, from $k = PQ/wN$).

Year-to-year, k is reasonably constant, showing slight downward drift over time. Since about 1950, on the score of the k-factor P should show about twelve per pent lower! P is thus bound up with the flex in unit labor costs (w/A), climbing almost exactly in unison.

Some may characterize this as a "wage-push" theory of inflation. This is a cultivated error: money wages and salaries are simultaneously the chief ingredients of costs, on the supply side of the price equation, and the mainspring of consumer demand, responsible for about eighty-five per cent of consumer purchases. "Cost-push" and "demand-pull," rather than being disparate phenomena, are simultaneous strings in consumer markets emanating from the same money wage phenomena.

Neither in (1) nor (2) are there any separate terms for money, to link money quantities to the price level. Money plays an indirect role in affecting output and jobs, and thus (as under Phillips curve doctrine) through unemployment levels it can deflect the money wage trend. Tight money, presumably, will rein in the $w(t)$ path over time and thereby work a meliorating price level impact, at least where Phillips curves are well-behaved so that labor militancy does not impair the relations. Tight money, however, by retarding investment, may defer plant modernization and thereby contain the $A(t)$ course. Through this channel tighter money may be (mildly) inflationary.

Instant Billionaires?

The general theory must be correct. Otherwise we could raise average money wage and salary incomes not by two or three per cent per annum for a steady price level, or the eight, ten, twelve per cent figures of recent years, or the egregious twenty-five per cent numbers of the United Kingdom and Australia, but by a thousand or millionfold: why not make everyone an instant billionaire? Why oppose the fulfillment of instant happiness? After all, if money incomes have nothing to do with inflation, and money control by the Fed can inhibit the price level excrescences regardless of wage increases, there should be no objection; there need never be any strikes by people unhappy over their money income lot if price levels are not upset by outsized general pay upheavals.

In concurring that there is a "right," or optimal, pace of average money wage gains, we are assenting to the ubiquity of incomes policy. Too, there is implicit a recognition that money policy, unaided by a supplemental conscious—or fortuitous—gearing of w's and A's, cannot usher in a flat P-trend.

Productivity and Costly Regulations

The productivity term A stands prominently in the price level equation. Historically, productivity growth was measured at two or three per cent per annum, with three per cent leaning to the high side. The 1970s estimates disclose a shade below two per cent.

Tight money, it was observed, by impeding plant modernization may have had a (mild) inflationary bias. Recent ecological concerns, with pollution and safety drum-beats, have fostered enactment of new regulations and stricter enforcement of old ones. In terms of (1) and (2), insofar as a steel mill has to install scrubbing devices, say, it deflects capital sums from steel-making equipment, indirectly reining A. Likewise, in hiring personnel to clean up the air or to conform to safety rules, the number of employees per ton of steel tends to depress the A-term. Regulatory consequences can thus retard productivity growth rate.

It is easy to oppose sin—or excessive cost raising, or superfluous productivity-depressing, health and safety regulations. Others will be better informed to cite particulars. Largely, however, their removal contributes a one-shot productivity booster, conceivably with delayed impacts. Big irresistible productivity gains are more likely to follow fresh innovations and technological triumphs.

OTHER INFLATION THEORIES

Many would fault big business for excessive price markups as the decade's inflation source: the available evidence invalidates this view. Others indict the federal deficit. Yet the last fifty budget years have seen only nine years of surplus, often of piddling size and yet, until the last decade the price level performed reasonably well. In 1933, with a deficit of about fifty-five per cent, the price level actually *fell*. Deficits are hardly the indomitable inflation-maker despite the popular rhetoric. More detailed analysis would reveal the deficit theory, when undraped, as a crypto-money theory of inflation amenable to a monetary remedy.

Government Debt and Expenditure

Government debt, comprising the residual cumulation of deficits, also gets its share of inflation calumny. Fact: since 1945 private debt has plunged far faster. Until recent years, the big public debt lurch occurred between 1930 and 1945, in a period when the price level behaved "orderly," again by modern standards. Relative to GNP the federal debt has declined sharply over the last generation.

Bombed by Proposition 13, though never really out of season, current onus is directed to government expenditure, especially the federal government though its aggregates are outpaced at the state and local level in recent years. The projected $500 billions federal outlays for fiscal 1979 would, in 1963 prices, be about $240 billions. Government outlays under even unaltered programs cost more as a *consequence* of inflation: when defense hardware prices go up, when civil servant pay climbs to match private sector trends, budget outlays inevitably advance. Relative to GNP, federal absorption of output has not been making greater inroads on the recent aggregates.

Although it braves heresy to say so, if government expenditure "causes" inflation, then other forms of expenditure must also be included, especially insofar as government outlay has not gone up disproportionately. All this, however, presumes that stagflation is a story in excess real demand—a view which I reject. One would presume, however, that our people would oppose wasteful government outlay in inflation season or out.

More difficult to fathom is the conviction that taxes be chopped with a meat axe while government outlay cuts are evaded, or trimming ordered without assessing military or social consequences. Tax slashes without outlay containment would feed larger deficits, with implications for monetary theories of inflation.

To illustrate the penchant for concentrating on the less significant while the substantial slips away, total employee compensation now amounts to $1.4 trillion. At compound rates of 10 percent, in just over three years the mere augmentation will overshadow the $500 billion federal 1979 outlay. At an eight per cent annual escalation, the feat will take under five years. Containment of the wage and salary climb, and thus civil service pay and the price of government procurement, would appear to be the best route to repressing government expenditures.

SOME ASPECTS OF MONETARY THEORY

Emphasis here on the wage-productivity nexus as the price level-maker make remarks on where money fits in obligatory. Discussion inevitably must be brief.[3]

Modern quantity theory doctrines link money supplies primarily to money incomes, finding the connection of money supplies to prices and to output variations more perplexing. In the symbols of the old income equation of exchange of $MV = PQ$, implied is:

(3) $m(\Delta M/M) = (\Delta P/P) + (\Delta Q/Q)$,

where $m = [1 + (\Delta V/V)/(\Delta M/M)] = (\Delta Y/Y)/(\Delta M/M)$

Murkiness—or indeterminateness—enshrouds whether money supply changes affect primarily the P's or the Q's, the latter welcomed and the former ordinarily rejected in economic policy. In adumbrating the steady money rule of, say, three per cent annual money increments, there is an implicit proviso that the money swell will sustain the $(\Delta Q/Q)$ increment rather than spill over to generate a ΔP splurge.

From the wage-cost markup equation (WCM) of $P = kw/A$, or from $MV = PA = kwN$, it follows:

(4) $m(\Delta M/M) = (\Delta k/k) + (\Delta w/w) + (\Delta N/N)$

If we neglect k in (4), as with $\Delta k = 0$, and if money wage jumps are excessive, and taking m (= the money income elasticity at values conjectured in monetarist studies) nearly constant, then a failure of money supplies to balance money wage hikes will have impacts on employment, ΔN. In (4) the potency of money policy for WCM theorizing emerges, with Q and N being hit by the Fed's slingshot, instead of P being brought directly to hand.

From the WCM:

(5) $(\Delta P/P) = (\Delta k/k) + (\Delta w/w) - (\Delta A/A)$

By-passing k, P reflects a tug of war between w and A. From (5), determinateness is imparted to (3) with $(\Delta P/P)$ resolved by the WCM elements and $(\Delta Q/Q)$ a resultant of money supplies.

The Potency of Monetary Policy

Monetary policy thus retains its clout in WCM theory. With reasonable constancy in m, whether money policy is expansive, neutral, or constrictive depends on $m(\Delta M/M) = (\Delta P/P) \gtreqless (\Delta w/w) - (\Delta A/A)$.

Table 1 indicates the variety of potential economic situations. Whether the economy lands in row 1, 2, or 3 depends, in WCM arguments, on the wage-productivity nexus. Whether column 1, 2, or 3 is our lot rests on monetary policy. Others may elect different names for the circumstances which fill the matrix. To make separate provision for unemployment, a twenty-seven cell, or three dimensional table, testing our facility for devising names, would have to be erected.

INCOME GEARING: THE TIP PROPOSALS

All economic systems that pay out money incomes, whether a capitalist or a collectivist model, must adopt some method of gearing money incomes to output flows. The market economy has hitherto relied on an *indirect* tie, namely, the control over money supplies in the thought that the MV aggregate, equal to Y, money income, can thereby be managed. My remarks have assayed the imperfections in the system, or the effect in $Y = kwN$, on the N variable when Δw has flounced disproportionately; too, when unemployment has grown politically intolerable, the ΔM variations have invariably had to be relaxed.

TABLE 1
The ΔP and ΔQ Matrix Pursuant to ΔM Action

ΔP \ ΔQ	+	0	-
+	Growthflation	Stagflation	Slumpflation
0	Growth at Constant Prices	Stationary State	Recession
-	Deflationary Growth	Steady State Deflation	Depression

My thoughts then have gone to ways to gear average money incomes more closely to productivity developments, and in a manner compatible with the enterprise economy. With P(t) reasonably flat over time, monetary policy should then be able to stablize the Q's and N's in the acceptable incomes policy, monetary policy should be able to pursue, more or less, the steady money rule. In this sense monetary and incomes policies can be mutually reenforcing.

Opposition to Price and Wage Controls

Those of us who have preferred market-oriented incomes policy have been concerned with what we contend are modest institutional reforms to protect, to improve, to salvage, to restore, and to perpetuate the market system; the aim is to embed measures to enable it to realize its maximum potential. It is the market system that the policies intend to preserve, rather than to devise grandiose, impractical, and futile plans to supplant it. But the system admits of improvement, notoriously in respect of jobs and inflation.

To dispel any confusion on the matter, mandatory wage and price controls are neither contemplated nor advocated; the quest is for noninterventionist policies. Controls are anathema to the market system: they are bureaucratic, dilatory, harassing, costly to administer and for business to abide; they are apt to be politicized; they induct an army of snoopers and enforcers; they breed a new type of crime engaged in consensual transactions, they thereby erode freedom; they erect a forum for legal histrionics to clog court calendars; they support a retinue of court attendants and jailers; and they outrage vexed citizens.

Nothing advanced here can be remotely interpreted as an espousal of mandatory price and wage controls. My own support for controls would extend only for a brief interlude while measures to be outlined are being legislatively contemplated prior to enactment; for example the Nixon 90 day price and wage freeze in

1971 operated with tolerable effectiveness—which implies mainly that the economy can stand practically anything for a few months.

The image of Captain Queeg tyrannizing over the theft of a plate of strawberries must not be elevated as the prototype in lieu of private decision making under traditional (or modified techniques) of monetary and fiscal policy, harmoniously meshed with incomes policy in a market system altered in an acceptable evolutionary way to obviate the inflation blight. Private decision making under the corporate income tax is a commonplace, erecting incentives and deterrents to enterprise conduct. Incomes policy can build on this characteristic.

The Wallich-Weintraub TIP

The Wallich-Weintraub TIP (for tax-based incomes policy) is reasonably familiar. Briefly, it is intended to subject firms to an extra corporate penalty income tax if they violate an *average* money wage and salary norm of, say, five per cent per annum.[4] The TIP object, however, is *not* to collect taxes but to deter inflationary money income conduct. Firms could surpass the norm, but at a price; like all good legislation that takes account of special cases, therefore, there is an escape valve for those who cannot conform or who prefer to overshoot the target. The analogy is to a posted speed limit which can be transgressed, subject to a penalty. Obviously, a very steep penalty scale builds an almost absolute prohibition, while a modest rate structure entails a less formidable obstacle. On the progressivity of the penalty schedule, differences of judgment can abound.

As the object is not to collect taxes, the normal corporate income tax rates could be reduced so that the estimated treasury tax-take is held constant, or reduced. Inasmuch as monetary and fiscal policy could work more closely toward full employment under less inflationary pay conduct, on balance it should be possible to lower the corporate tax rates. TIP could not be fairly indicted with eroding internal corporate venture capital.

TIP could be confined to about the largest one thousand firms, covering about fifty-five per cent of GBP, or the largest two thousand firms responsible, according to available estimates, for about eighty-seven per cent of business output. Legislation could specify firms employing over five hundred, or five thousand employees, etc., or reporting a sales volume of over $5,000,000, or $50,000,000, or whatever numbers judgment condones as reasonable and feasible. As about one half dozen extra lines on a corporate income tax form are entailed (involving known information on the wage and salary bill and number of employees), presumably one auditor should be able to examine ten forms per week or about five hundred per annum. For two thousand firms the administrative personnel directly involved would be nominal, and a trifling cost considering the full employment prize at stake, involving $50 to $150 billions in lost output in recent years. The tradeoff of administrative outlay as against economy gains is overwhelmingly favorable.

TIP Supplements

Labor bargaining would not be precluded under TIP though settlement terms are bound to be more restrained on the principle that firms would not go far to trespass the norms, and unions could not expect to win huge gains. Blue Collar labor could secure more than, say, five per cent if other employees obtained less than the stipulated average. Bargaining would be centered in a dispute over *relative* pay scales, rather than all pay moving along synchronously, after minor or longer time lags, so that in the end all run faster and all occupy practically the same position in the pay pack.

To strengthen TIP, at least in its early implementation, for firms that agree to pay, for instance, at least one percentage point over the stipulated norm, several corollary features can be devised. The following are illustrative; others will be able to provide better ideas. For example, some firms may face bankruptcy if their offer is rejected and unions strike. These firms may be candidates for temporary loan guarantees to cover payment of fixed costs; the provisions would have to be hedged to prevent collusion, obviously. Likewise, some NLRB penalties may be levied on unions for rejecting the norm-plus contract. Labor and business specialists may be able to prescribe more workable provisions to forestall gross violations of the TIP objective. Prospective supplementary stiffening of TIP reflects the versatility of the approach.

Widening the TIP Settlement Band

The conclusion that the TIP norm, say, of five per cent, would become the *minimum* settlement figure, need not follow. For example, firms could be allowed a two percent reduction in the "normal" income tax for settlement, say, at from three to five per cent over the previous year's average pay levels. Some have suggested even widening the band, leading to a perverse conclusion that firms which *cut* average pay would win a sharp tax break.

Obviously, any provision of this sort would arouse labor's ire for fostering "slave" labor. The intention is to block price ascent, not to foster a price level decline! So, some stop on the lower end of the pay band would be critical, to provide for firms that could not match the average five per cent pay norm, but would still qualify for tax benefits with a settlement in the three to five per cent range. (All numbers are purely illustrative though they represent reasonable magnitudes.)

TIP-CAP

The illustrative five per cent annual pay increase, on the presumption that productivity trends of three per cent per annum are resumed, would mean an annual price trend in the two per cent range. By recent standards this would be noninflationary indeed. A flat price level would entail about a three per cent norm and, if future productivity improvements because of higher energy costs are more nearly zero, a more stringent incomes policy will be imperative. In the retrogressive economy, average money incomes would have to fall to realize a steady price level.

Economy-wide productivity is the proper guide for establishing the pay norm, rather than firm or plant productivity. In my early writings on TIP, the basic calculation for the penalty tax was a simple pay average.[5] In my collaboration with Federal Reserve Governor Henry Wallich, a weighted pay average was recommended in order to avert some possible fudging by firms that raised executive pay excessively and then hired many superflous low paid employees to reduce the average for TIP calculations.

My colleague, Dr. Lawrence Seidman, who has written extensively on the subject, has persuaded me that any wage-padding could only be advantageous on a short term look at the matter: after the first year, the firms would be saddled with a too-costly work force for no possible tax benefit or, in making layoffs, they would encounter the same penalty prospects.

Weighting clearly introduces extra complexities and invites endless controversy on the "right" weights. To immunize some pay grants above the norm, and to evade the weighting aspects while encouraging productivity improvements, firms might be permitted to compute a simple productivity average for TIP reporting, and then to correct the value-added figure per employee by any of a variety of price level indexes to eliminate distorting price changes. If the corrected average productivity (CAP) surpassed the economy-wide productivity growth, employees could share in the special gains. For example, if the firm's productivity calculation was nine per cent or six per cent above the economy-wide figure, the average pay increase could be equal to the norm of five per cent, plus one-third of the six per cent productivity bounty, lifting the wage and salary norm in that firm to seven per cent without penalty.[6]

Labor could thus be an immediate beneficiary of superior productivity performance, with a direct stake in improvements. By and large, however, superior productivity improvements should translate into relative price drops. Firm or plant productivity figures cannot be fully allotted to the firm's employees as a bonus without erecting a discriminatory pay scale through the economy, and blocking output advances by maintaining costs and prices in sectors of even spectacular productivity triumphs.

TIP can thus be fortified in TIP-CAP, with the extra productivity attachment going some way toward dismantling outmoded feather-bedding restrictions.

CAIP: Government Construction and Procurement

TIP or TIP-CAP, because of the tax aspects, would have to clear tax committees of Congress where it is certain to be misconstrued as a tax measure, and subjected to misdirected debate. Faster progress in income gearing or incomes policy might be made on other lines.

Under the Davis-Bacon Act the government mandates that on government construction, or government assisted construction, prevailing wages must be paid, usually interpreted generously as the highest in the vicinity. Effectively,

Davis-Bacon nails a high floor on government-related construction, and inserts a high pay underpinning for the industry. Without general cognizance under Davis-Bacon, and Walsh-Healey which covers minimum wages, the government is effectively imposing an incomes policy; the idea of incomes policy, therefore, is nothing new in our legislative annals.

As matters stand, labor often lobbies with business for construction contracts which mean jobs, and at good pay. After the sums are voted come strikes for still higher pay. It should be possible to limit pay grants, over the life of the contract to an annual increase of five per cent, as well as to cover executive and managerial pay. Pay aggrandizement at government expense and raids on the treasury might be aborted thereby. Penalties could take the form of disallowing magnanimous pay settlements as costs in computing income tax profits; disallowance of cost overruns in contract negotiations; or closing off bids by offending contractors on other government jobs for a period of years.

The idea could be extended to military procurement and government purchases generally. Inasmuch as the veritable Who's Who in American enterprise engage in sales to government, CAIP (Contractual Award Incomes Policy) could blanket from twenty-five per cent or so of the business sector, and could do something to suppress the wayward pay explosion.

The Okun Variants of TIP

Arthur Okun, in a more recent variant of the original TIP proposal, has tried to hide the "stick" and dangle a "carrot."[7] While his proposal has not been spelled in detail, he endeavored to build foremost on a principle of "voluntarism."

Union employees who agreed to a pay increase of about seven per cent per annum would qualify for a tax credit of about $225 per annum, amounting to about two per cent of a $12,000 income and enlarging their pay increase to about nine per cent. Firms that abided by the norm would also realize a two percentage point or so corporate tax reward.

It is possible to be dubious of the "voluntarism" feature, except as a tactical debating wedge. Too, the exclusion of nonunionized employees from a tax benefit would be an inequality. A fairer method would inscribe a three per cent tax credit for all those with employee compensation (or all taxpayers?) of, say, under $12,000, and two per cent for those above this figure, with a $200 minimum and $300 maximum credit.

This feature adopted from Okun could impart real income protection to labor, and make a TIP program more attractive, especially as labor leaders have shown little willingness to analyze the proposal while plunging headlong into advocacy of mandatory price and wage controls.

Nonetheless, the Okun "voluntarism" will not do. Militant labor leaders could aim for fifteen per cent gains while others accepted seven per cent, with the former deriding the latter as "weak" sisters: why accept a $200 tax credit when maybe this much extra can be grabbed off per month by an exercise of muscle and power?

Likewise, a two percentage point corporate tax cut appears too limited to induce firms to stand against extravagant pay demands. By accepting the Okun tax cut for subscribing to the pay norm (or settling slightly below), and invoking a penalty for transgressing the norm, the effective tax stimuli and deterrent can be widened to make pay excesses more costly.

Government Employees and Anti-Trust

Government employees could be held to an annual five per cent pay increase. For conformable state and local pay behavior, federal grants could be made contingent upon compatible pay norms. To prevent government pay scales from trailing private sector trends, government pay scales could be corrected every two or three years to ensure reasonable correspondence.

To counter labor protests that prices are not touched, and to avoid debate over the issue, the FTC might be required to report quarterly on trends in profit margins of firms covered by TIP. Where margins rise unduly, data for reasonable review would be on hand. According to the evidence, however, we can be confident that price margins will not be inflationary so long as wages and salaries are reasonably aligned to productivity.

THE CARTER INFLATION MEASURES

The Carter measures of recent days to subdue inflation provoke comment. On October 24, after twenty-two months of incumbency, and thus about eighteen months late, the President announced a program which, in principle, was based on the theory that motivates TIP proposals. Meeting negative reaction in foreign exchange markets and Wall Street impelled the President on November 1 to impose a fairly drastic set of measures typically described as monetary persuasion.

Let's consider the latter first. There was the almost unprecedented full percentage-point tick in the rediscount rate, effectuated by the Federal Reserve. There was also, a two percentage point jump in reserve requirements against certificates of deposit of $100,000 or more. A foreign exchange stabilization fund of $30 billion was organized to discourage the frenzied wave of speculative attacks against the dollar, whose prolonged sinking spell brought soaring import prices. A steeper pace of gold sales was put on the agenda.

Shock impacts were uniformly and dramatically unfavorable. The dollar rose instantly in Tokyo, Frankfurt, and Basel. The stock market, in splendid euphoria, rebounded by thirty-five points in the Dow Jones for the largest single day flourish ever.

Assessments are that the tighter money curbs will, over time, rein in the economy and yield a harvest of recessionary tendencies, especially in the housing industry, with multiplier ramifications through the economy. Prediction of a lagged downturn are thus rife. It may be, however, that as the rest of the President's program falls into place, monetary policy can be eased and that a serious fall-back can be evaded. Time, the great hindsight prophet, will reveal the answers.

The President's non-monetary program, disregarding the inevitable born-again homilies opposing government waste to take the edge off political adversaries, contained three main features:

(1) First, a summons to labor to hold pay demands on new contracts to seven per cent per annum.

(2) In reciprocity, the President pledged to ask Congress to provide tax "rebates" insofar as price rises exceeded seven per cent. This embeds the Okun "real income insurance" to make the seven per cent norm more palatable to labor. Calculations by the press and economists tended to magnify the possible tax loss though, if the program is successful and prices rise by less than seven per cent, "rebates" will be nil.

The President's description of the rebates was vague. They probably will take the form of tax credits, with rebates only for those who have overpaid withholding taxes. As noted above, it seems to me that this protection should be universal, and not confined to unions volunteering to abide by the program. Too, it can be interpreted as a gesture to advocates of indexing of income tax rates.

To many, the seven per cent norm is too high. For 1980, a six per cent number is in the wings—designed more to shave the inflation rate than to stop inflation. The pace reflects a concession to opinion that inflation must wind down "gradually," to avoid damage to expectations from a sharp price deescalation. The United Kingdom has dumped its inflation rate from twenty-five per cent to under ten per cent in short order, with benefit rather than deterioration. Under the gradual time-table, nobody will get hurt, according to exponents, except those who have been basely ravaged already.

(3) Business firms are to hold their annual price increases to five and three-quarter per cent per annum, or one-half per cent below the pace of the previous year. Sanctions on firms that fail to comply will consist of denying government procurement to them, or removing import protection, or subsidies, or other forms of penalty as yet unspecified. News releases indicate that the price policies of four hundred of the largest firms are to be monitored.

The denial of procurement is a "stock" lifted from a country-cousin of TIP that Chancellor of the Exchequer, Dennis Healey in the United Kingdom, is readying for parliamentary enactment.

While applauding the President for a "better late than never" commitment to subdue inflation, the present program is too bureaucratic for my tastes; monitoring prices and costs smacks of price controls. Too, it is likely to engender bureaucratic hassles when for example, the Department of Defense wants essential component purchases and encounters opposition from the price overseers. The air will be filled with "yes, they did; no, they didn't; and what difference does it make." Snarling is likely to create new headline excitement, but not much surcease from the eternal and infernal immersion in minor aspects of the inflation torment.

Future Prospects?

Contemplating the wage contracts already in the pipeline for 1979, the President's men expect a price eruption of six to six and one half per cent, a miniscule improvement after three Carter years. The 1978 figure should come in at above eight per cent so we are supposed to cheer the snail's progress.

The AFL-CIO George Meany has already voiced displeasure at the package, expressing skepticism of its "fairness" to labor. He has, instead, pronounced his support for mandatory price and wage controls. Some business spokesmen express fears over the price ceilings as a prelude to controls. While opposition has not crystallized, enthusiasm for the measures appears underwhelming.

Still, the President has taken a first step on a necessary journey to bring about a mete of rationality into the wage-price shuffles that have plagued us in generating inflation and evoking the tighter money stagflation response. This I find encouraging. Considering the lack of alternatives, we may have to come to some closer kin of TIP, in lieu of the bureaucratic structure that seems to be in motion.

While such events are seldom predictable, the rocky climb may yet be diverted to mandatory controls, postponing a more rational TIP to the longer future.

NOTES

1. Cf. my *Capitalism's Inflation and Unemployment Crisis* (Addison-Wesley, 1978), and *Keynes, Keynesians, and Monetarists* (University of Pennsylvania, 1978) for further elaboration.

2. I generally use Gross Business Product (GBP) for the income concept.

3. Further elaboration appears in my *Capitalism's Crisis* and *Keynes, Keynesians and Monetarists*.

4. For a recent statement see my "Proposal for an Anti-Inflation Package," *Challenge* (Sept. 1978).

5. The essays are reprinted in *Keynes, Keynesians, and Monetarists.*

6. For detailed elaboration, see *Capitalism's Crisis.*

7. Cf. "Innovative Policies to Slow Inflation," Special Issue *Brookings Papers on Economic Activity,* Number 2, 1978.

3

NEW POLICIES TO FIGHT INFLATION
Sources of Skepticism

Albert Rees

A NUMBER of proposals for new methods to fight inflation are being opposed, especially by labor organizations and the business community. Included among the old methods to fight inflation are restrictive monetary and fiscal policies, wage and price controls, and exhortation or "jawboning," all of which have been used in the United States at various times in the past thirty years. Among the new methods are reductions in excise, sales, and payroll taxes; tax-based incomes policies (TIPs); and deregulation, or the elimination of "sacred cows." This paper explores possible reasons for opposition to these more recent proposals, with major attention devoted to TIPs.

The existence of opposition is well known, but little explanation for it has appeared on the record. When considering objections to a proposed policy, it is important to keep in mind that not all objections are consistent with one another. For example, some emphasize reasons why a proposed policy might not work, and others point out possible adverse consequences if it does work. These two kinds of objections cannot be valid simultaneously, but it might not be possible to determine in advance which to take more seriously.

It is far easier to list objections to a proposed policy than it is to advance a better one. For this reason I do not attempt to distinguish between two alternative purposes of the objections discussed. They can be viewed either as grounds for rejecting a policy altogether or as points to be considered in trying to improve the proposals under discussion and make them more workable.

Note: I am indebted to Daniel Quinn Mills and participants of the Brookings Panel for helpful comments on an earlier version of this paper.

0007-2303/78/0002-0453/$00.25/0 © *Brookings Institution*

Excise and Payroll Tax Reduction

Sales and excise taxes, unlike income taxes, enter directly into the measurement of consumer prices. A reduction in these taxes therefore produces a one-time reduction in the price level.[1] Although this will not offset a continuing source of inflation such as an overly expansive monetary policy, it has an effect opposite to that of the unique events that have helped to raise the price level in recent years, such as the formation of the oil cartel by the Organization of Petroleum Exporting Countries.

Unlike some of the policies discussed below, reductions in excise taxes should be highly acceptable to both business and labor. For example, the reduction in the excise tax on telephone service proposed by President Carter in January 1978 is clearly directly beneficial to the telephone companies, their employees, and the communication workers' union. Even if the reduction were entirely passed on to consumers through lower rates, it would increase the quantity of telephone services demanded and therefore the demand for labor in the telephone industry.

The support of such tax reductions by business and labor should also extend beyond the industries directly affected. The labor movement generally regards income taxes as more equitable than excise taxes because they are progressive rather than regressive. Businessmen often favor cutting taxes whenever possible in the hope that this will eventually result in a corresponding restraint on government expenditures, much of which they may regard as wasteful.

The reduction of excise taxes to lower prices raises a number of problems. The federal government has few excise taxes remaining that can be reduced, and the important ones (gasoline, liquor, and tobacco) can all be defended on special grounds. An alternative proposal is to induce states and localities to reduce sales taxes by replacing the lost revenues with federal funds. The problems of this proposal lie in the area of intergovernmental relations rather than in relations between the government and private sectors—an area that will not be explored here.

---

1. By one-time changes in prices I do not mean to suggest that the events that give rise to them have no secondary effects. A reduction in excise taxes could have secondary effects through the operation of cost-of-living escalator provisions or through a moderating influence on newly negotiated wage settlements. The term "one-time" is intended to mean that such secondary effects will have a tendency to diminish in amplitude and eventually will die out. For a more precise statement of the effect of a one-time reduction in prices on the subsequent rate of inflation, see the comments on the Crandall paper in this volume by Edward Gramlich.

A reduction in payroll taxes will also tend to produce a one-time reduction in the price level to the extent that the costs of payroll taxes are passed forward in the price of products, and this pass-through is probably substantial. A modest proposal of this sort was made by President Carter in January 1977 when he proposed a small reduction in the federal payroll tax for unemployment insurance. Much more ambitious proposals have been introduced in Congress, which would shift the financing of the Medicare and disability insurance programs from payroll taxes to general revenues. These proposals are favorable to the economic interests of unions and corporations and to most low-income individual taxpayers for whom payroll taxes are more important than personal income taxes. However, unless the cost of the programs being financed is reduced, the proposals will either require an increase in personal income taxes or a smaller decrease than would otherwise be possible. It is difficult to predict the reaction of business leaders to proposals that would benefit their corporations at some possible cost to them as individual taxpayers. The cost may be small, inasmuch as current proposals for reducing individual income taxes do not greatly affect those in high tax brackets.

It is not obvious that it would be possible to lower the price level by reducing payroll taxes and to restore the lost revenue by increasing corporate income taxes or by decreasing them less. Corporate taxes may also be passed forward to consumers to a considerable extent, and not enough is known about tax incidence to predict how much different the pass-through to prices is for the corporate tax and for the payroll tax.

Tax-Based Incomes Policies

Tax-based incomes policies (TIPs) have been discussed for a number of years, but recently have received wider attention and support. The earliest and most prominent among these policies is the Wallich-Weintraub proposal to increase the corporate income tax rate for corporations whose wage increases exceed a specified guideline.[2] More recent proposals differ from Wallich-Weintraub by suggesting tax incentives for compliance with

2. See Henry C. Wallich and Sidney Weintraub, "A Tax-Based Incomes Policy," *Journal of Economic Issues*, vol. 5 (June 1971), pp. 1–19. Similar proposals previously had been advanced by the two authors separately. See Wallich, "Can We Stop Inflation without a Recession?" *Newsweek*, vol. 68 (September 5, 1966), pp. 72–73, and Weintraub, "An Incomes Policy to Stop Inflation," *Lloyds Bank Review*, no. 99 (January 1971), pp. 1–12.

both price and wage guidelines and by suggesting tax reductions to corporations and workers in place of or in addition to tax increases. Some of these proposals were considered by Wallich and Weintraub, who regarded them as less desirable than their own.

The general attitude of business and labor toward the TIP proposals reminds one of the famous *New Yorker* cartoon in which a mother is trying to persuade a small girl to eat her broccoli, and the girl replies, "I say it's spinach and to hell with it." Business and labor are now firmly opposed to wage and price controls, and they consider TIP as another form of control. In the sections that follow, I explore some of the similarities and differences between TIPs and controls from the perspective of labor and management.

SCOPE AND COVERAGE

The Wallich-Weintraub proposal would apply to all corporations paying corporate income tax, with a possible exemption for small corporations. This is a far narrower scope than that of the wage controls in effect during the period 1971–74; those controls covered partnerships and proprietorships, state and local governments, and nonprofit institutions. The last two of these have been areas of rapid growth of unionism and collective bargaining in recent years. It is quite possible that in the future strong pressures for wage increases could originate in the unions of the public sector. This appears to have happened in Canada in recent years; the level of wage settlements there has exceeded that in the United States, despite the fact that workers in the private sector in the two countries are largely represented by the same set of unions.

The exemption for small firms and the exclusion of unincorporated business would exclude from coverage many firms in construction and trucking, which are industries with both high wages and strong unions. Wallich has suggested that special policies to restrain wages might be needed for these industries. Unfortunately, he has not stated what these policies would be. The exclusion of trucking would be especially important because the International Brotherhood of Teamsters is the largest and one of the strongest unions in the United States, and its master freight agreement has an important pattern-setting influence beyond trucking, especially in food wholesaling and retailing. More generally, the exemption for small firms could lead to spillovers of wage increases from small firms to larger ones, or could lead to distortions of relative wages.

One supporter of TIP, Laurence Seidman, has proposed an exemption for "very low-paid" workers, without specifying how those workers would be defined.[3] Past experience shows that such an exemption would have strong support in Congress, but could seriously diminish the effectiveness of TIP. For example, the 1973 extension of the Economic Stabilization Act exempted low-wage workers from wage controls effective May 1, 1973, and defined them as those earning less than $3.50 an hour.[4] In May 1973, all production and nonsupervisory workers in private nonagricultural employment were receiving average hourly earnings of $3.85, so that almost half of this group was excluded from wage controls by this exemption.

It should also be recognized that TIP would not apply to those large private corporations that have no tax liability because they are not profitable in a particular year or because they carry forward tax credits. A union such as the retail clerks or the meatcutters negotiating under TIP with several supermarket chains in the same geographical area might choose to make a pattern-setting agreement with an unprofitable chain, which has no tax disincentive applicable to wage increases above the guideline and has the least financial ability to resist a strike. The union could then confront the profitable chains with a newly established wage rate, and it would be difficult for them not to match it.

Some advocates of TIP may feel that the concentration of penalties on profitable firms is desirable because high profits encourage large wage increases. Little solid evidence exists to support this view, however. In such industries as railroads and shipping, unions have bargained for and won high wages and costly manning requirements not only from unprofitable firms, but even from bankrupt ones.

The scope of the Wallich-Weintraub proposal could be greatly extended by applying the tax penalty to payroll taxes rather than to corporate income taxes. It would then include unincorporated businesses, corporations with no tax liability, nonprofit institutions, and those state and local governments that participate in the social security system.

Wallich and Weintraub argue against the use of payroll taxes for TIP on the ground that those taxes are more likely to be passed forward in prices than are corporate income taxes. It is easier for me to agree that

3. Laurence S. Seidman, "To Fight Inflation," *New York Times*, December 22, 1976, p. 29.

4. U.S. Department of the Treasury, Office of Economic Stabilization, *Historical Working Papers on the Economic Stabilization Program, August 15, 1971 to April 30, 1974* (Government Printing Office, 1974), pt. 1, p. 347.

payroll taxes are passed forward than to accept the view that corporate income taxes are not. If one corporation in a competitive industry negotiated a wage increase above the guideline established by TIP and paid the resulting corporate income tax penalty, the firm would have difficulty passing the penalty forward because its competitors would have both lower wage costs and lower taxes. In some cases, however, wage agreements are negotiated with entire industries, such as basic steel. In others, such as automobiles, an agreement reached with one major producer is extended to the others with little or no change. If in such cases one firm reaches a wage agreement that exceeds the guideline and results in tax penalties, it might set higher prices to restore in large part the previous rate of return on capital after taxes. Both the wage increase and the price increase would then probably be followed by other firms in the industry. Indeed, in industries where demand for a product is relatively inelastic, the only major barrier to such an outcome would seem to be foreign competition. For TIP to be effective in industries characterized both by price leadership and by industry-wide bargaining or pattern-following in wages, guidelines and penalties would be required for excessive price increases. Such proposals are discussed below.

Another difference between the use of corporate income taxes and payroll taxes as a base for TIP is that the penalty rates of payroll taxes would augment the effect of higher wages in inducing the substitution of capital for labor. The use of corporate income taxes would presumably not induce factor substitution or, if anything, would cause substitution of labor for capital.

The Wallich-Weintraub proposal is limited to wages because its proponents believe that markups of prices over unit labor costs are historically quite stable. In Weintraub's words, TIP "presupposes that the wage-productivity nexus is crucial in inflation."[5] Thus, in Weintraub's view, postwar inflation has been essentially wage-push inflation. Needless to say, the unions (among others) vigorously disagree with this view; they would point to the rises in prices of raw agricultural commodities and imported petroleum and to the devaluation of the dollar since 1971 as contributors to inflation for which they bear no responsibility. They regard the Wallich-Weintraub proposal as completely one-sided and therefore unfair to labor. Although unions are opposed to any kind of incomes

5. Sidney Weintraub, "Incomes Policy: Completing the Stabilization Triangle," *Journal of Economic Issues*, vol. 6 (December 1972), p. 119.

policy, they are most strongly opposed to one that focuses exclusively on wages. They would fight its enactment by the Congress with as much force as an aroused labor movement can muster, which is considerable.

The view that price inflation merely mirrors wage inflation has been somewhat shaken by the events of recent years. From 1973 to 1974 the consumer price index rose 11.0 percent, while average hourly earnings in private nonagricultural industry rose only 8.2 percent, producing a decline of 2.5 percent in real hourly earnings. Although the events of 1974 were highly unusual, the labor movement certainly cannot be blamed for wanting insurance against their repetition (which is not to say that they necessarily should have it).[6]

ESTABLISHING THE GUIDELINE

The problem of establishing an appropriate wage guideline is not much different under TIP than it is under wage controls, but this does not mean that it is unimportant. Perhaps the principal difference is that TIP necessarily involves an explicit guideline, while wage controls do not. The Construction Industry Stabilization Committee, the most successful of the wage-control bodies of the 1971–74 period, operated without an explicit wage guideline throughout its existence.

Labor unions oppose a wage guideline in part because they fear that it might be unfairly set or that it would not be appropriately modified to changing conditions. Both concerns are based on past experience.

Wallich and Weintraub suggest a wage guideline that could be established at some point between a minimum equal to the trend of output per labor hour and a maximum equal to this trend plus the initial rate of inflation.[7] Their minimum is the same as the wage guideline established by the Kennedy administration in 1962, and could be used in a situation in which the initial rate of inflation was zero or close to it. Even under these circumstances, this guideline is not acceptable to the labor movement. It is well known that increasing wages in proportion to output per labor hour will keep constant the labor and nonlabor shares of output and income. In other words, this guideline freezes the functional distribution of income. Historically, however, there has been a tendency for labor's

6. Some analysts would prefer to use compensation per hour of labor in the private sector for this kind of analysis. However, the unions focus on the hourly earnings of production and nonsupervisory workers because they have few members in the private sector who are salaried employees.

7. "A Tax-Based Incomes Policy," p. 12.

share of income to rise gradually through time, even after adjustment for the decline in self-employment.[8] Understandably, labor does not want this historical trend that is favorable to its constituents brought to a halt, not even temporarily.

A rough check on whether guidelines actually had this effect on labor's share is afforded by computing the compensation of employees as a percentage of national income for selected years. This figure was 71.6 in 1961 before the Kennedy guidelines and 70.6 in 1966; it was 76.3 in 1970 before the Nixon controls and 75.1 in 1973. I would ascribe the declines in labor's share during the periods of guidelines and controls to the business cycle rather than to incomes policy. However, the sharp rise in labor's share during the intervening period when there was no incomes policy is also noteworthy. In any event, the labor movement is not likely to draw favorable conclusions about guidelines from these figures.

The opposite extreme in the range of possible wage guidelines of the Wallich-Weintraub proposal would surely not be acceptable to business. To allow wages to increase by the trend of productivity plus a full allowance for inflation is to allow labor larger gains than it has been able to win in the period since mid-1974, when there have been no guidelines. If we accept 2 percent as a rough estimate of the trend of productivity, *real* hourly earnings of all employees in the private nonagricultural sector have not risen as much as this trend since 1972. A guideline of productivity plus a full allowance for inflation therefore seem more likely to accelerate wage increases than to retard them.

Intermediate positions, such as the trend of productivity plus half the rate of inflation, seem superior to the extremes, but even these have substantial difficulties. If the initial rate of inflation were 6 percent and the trend of productivity 2 percent, a wage guideline of 5 percent would result. If such a guideline were enforced, real output per labor hour could rise at a rate of 2 percent a year, and real wages would initially fall 1 percent a year—an outcome totally unacceptable to the unions. Eventually the rate of inflation should decline to 3 percent if the program is successful, but the unions might not be patient enough to wait for this. Moreover, at this point the wage guideline would be reduced to 3.5 percent, again producing a real wage gain much lower than the trend of productivity. Only

8. See Irving B. Kravis, "Income Distribution: Functional Share," in David L. Sills, ed., *International Encyclopedia of the Social Sciences,* vol. 7 (Macmillan, 1968), pp. 132–45.

in some final equilibrium where prices are not rising at all do real wages rise with the productivity trend.

I conclude that if there is to be a wage guideline acceptable to unions, it cannot include a constant allowance for ongoing inflation, but may need to adjust that allowance each year. Formulas based on theoretical considerations may be inferior to more arbitrary ones based on simple deceleration from existing rates of increase in compensation. For the guideline to be acceptable and fair, it must allow for growth in real wages. For the guideline to have any effect in restraining inflation,, it must be less than the wage increases that would occur in its absence. It is not clear that a number always exists that meets both of these constraints; indeed, it is not even clear that one exists at present.

Labor's fear that a guideline might become less favorable to the interests of workers over time is supported by the events of both 1962–67 and 1971–74. When the Kennedy administration adopted wage guidelines based on productivity in 1962, the trend of productivity change was substantially above the rise in consumer prices, so that a guideline based solely on productivity provided for considerable growth in real wages. By 1966, the guideline had become a specific number—3.2 percent a year. During 1966, as the Council of Economic Advisers noted in its January 1967 report, consumer prices rose 3.3 percent. Adherence to the guidelines therefore implied a slight fall in real wages. The council nevertheless did not change the guideline number.[9]

A second aspect of the 1966–67 guidelines was also disturbing to the labor movement. The 3.2 percent figure that became the wage guideline was the latest average of the increase in output per labor hour in the private sector for the five-year periods ending in 1963 and in 1964, as measured at the end of those years. For the five years ending in 1965, the corresponding figure was 3.4 percent. In its January 1966 report the council did not accept this higher figure as a basis for revising the guide-

9. See *Economic Report of the President, January 1967*, pp. 127–29. Because the position of the council was somewhat ambiguous, a direct quotation may be helpful: "The Council recognizes that the recent rise in living costs makes it unlikely that most collective bargaining settlements in 1967 will fully conform to the trend increase of productivity. But it sees no useful purpose to be served by suggesting some higher standard for wage increases, even on a temporary basis.

"The only valid and noninflationary standard for wage advances is the productivity principle. If price stability is eventually to be restored and maintained in a high-employment U.S. economy, wage settlements must once again conform to that standard" (p. 128).

line on the ground that five consecutive years of economic expansion had created a productivity gain that was above the long-term trend.[10] Although this belated recognition that five years is too short a period to establish a trend was probably correct, the unions were offended because the rules had been changed in the middle of the game. Their sense of grievance, oddly enough, existed although—according to knowledgeable observers of collective bargaining—the guidelines had little or no effect in restraining negotiated wage settlements.[11]

The 1962–66 experience was repeated in 1971–74. In November 1971 the Pay Board set the general pay standard for the new wage control program at 5.5 percent. This was widely interpreted as based on a combination of the long-run productivity trend and a portion of the current increase in consumer prices. The productivity trend was then about 3 percent a year, and the controls program was expected to reduce the rate of inflation to 2.5 percent by the end of 1972. A 5.5 percent wage standard minus a 3.0 percent productivity trend implies a 2.5 percent rate of increase of unit labor costs, which is consistent with an equal increase in prices. By 1973, however, the rate of increase of the consumer price index (December 1972 to December 1973) was 8.8 percent. Nevertheless, the 5.5 percent wage standard was never formally abandoned during the controls programs, though exceptions to it became more and more numerous.

Those proponents of TIP who advocate tax penalties or bonuses based on both price increases and wage increases usually select a pair of guidelines that differ by the trend of output per labor hour. If this trend were 2 percent, they might propose a wage guideline of 6 percent and a price guideline of 4 percent.[12] Such a pair of guidelines is consistent, on average across all industries, with unit labor costs rising as fast as the price guidelines.

The problems of establishing a price guideline, however, are much more formidable than those of setting a wage guideline. Okun suggests a "dollar-and-cents pass-through of any increases in costs of materials and supplies."[13] These costs would presumably differ according to the prod-

10. *Economic Report of the President, January 1966*, p. 92.

11. See John T. Dunlop, "Guideposts, Wages, and Collective Bargaining," in George P. Shultz and Robert Z. Aliber, eds., *Guidelines, Informal Controls, and the Market Place: Policy Choices in a Full Employment Economy* (University of Chicago Press, 1966), p. 84.

12. See Arthur M. Okun, "The Great Stagflation Swamp," *Challenge*, vol. 20 (November/December 1977), p. 13.

13. Ibid.

uct, which would make departures from the price guideline difficult to detect. Moreover, the term "materials and supplies" may be overly narrow. Are corporations to absorb all increases above 4 percent in the costs of purchased services, such as legal and accounting fees, travel costs, and so on? But even if there were no increases in the costs of materials, supplies, and purchased services, a uniform price guideline would be unfair because the productivity trends of individual industries differ dramatically from that of the economy as a whole. It is reasonable to state that workers doing the same work in different industries should receive roughly the same pay regardless of industry differences in productivity, but it is altogether unreasonable to assume that the prices of the products of industries with different productivity trends should move together.

For the period 1970–75 the average growth in output per production worker hour in the industries for which separate measures are published by the Bureau of Labor Statistics ranged from an increase of 9.2 percent in candy and other confectionery products to a decrease of 4.8 percent in bituminous coal and lignite mining.[14] An industry that experiences no change in productivity and has a 6 percent increase in wages will be forced to raise prices at close to 6 percent unless it uses little labor. An industry whose productivity is rising at 8 percent should be reducing product prices unless its nonlabor costs are rising rapidly. A price-control agency with discretionary authority can take such circumstances into account to the extent that available data permit, but it is almost impossible to write them into the Internal Revenue Code.

COLLECTIVE BARGAINING AND INDUSTRIAL DISPUTES

The proposal to tax corporations on excessive wage increases must consider the differences between tax units and collective bargaining units. A corporation might treat all its domestic operations as one entity for corporate tax purposes, but within this entity it might have many different collective bargaining units, often represented by several different unions, as well as a large number of nonunion employees.

Weintraub attempts to convert this problem into an asset, in my opinion unsuccessfully. He writes, "A not inconsiderable virtue [of TIP] is that unions can bargain for sums in excess of.the productivity norm and perhaps succeed in redistributing some income from profits and mana-

14. U.S. Bureau of Labor Statistics, *Productivity Indexes for Selected Industries, 1976 Edition,* bulletin 1938 (Government Printing Office, 1977), table 1.

gerial employees."[15] This is a clear statement of why business might oppose TIP.

Even if the goal of policy were to redistribute income by differential changes in compensation to create greater equality, it could not be achieved by the route that Weintraub suggests. Nonunion employees are not all managers. In most firms, the majority of nonunion employees are clerical workers, and they generally receive lower wages than unionized production workers. Suppose that a firm had equal numbers of union and nonunion employees, that the wage norm was 6 percent, and that the union succeeded in obtaining a wage increase of 8 percent. To avoid a tax penalty, the firm would have to hold its nonunion employees to a 4 percent wage increase. If firms chose to do this, there would be an increase in union-nonunion wage differentials, which are already large; many economists might say they are too large. However, in my judgment few employers would risk such a policy. To provide nonunion workers with only half the wage increase of union workers would lower morale and perhaps decrease productivity or invite the unionization of the nonunion group. Most firms would prefer to pay the tax penalty. But if they did, the effectiveness of TIP would be reduced. The unions, however, could and probably would use Weintraub's argument as grounds for not adhering to the wage norm.

The same kind of problem arises when a company bargains with two unions of unequal strength. If the stronger union negotiated first, it might insist on a settlement in excess of the guideline, and the employer would have to decide whether to pay the tax penalty or to try to reach a settlement below the guideline with the weaker union. However, the existence of a wage guideline makes it more difficult for a weak union to accept a settlement below the guideline.

The general strategy of the Wallich-Weintraub proposal is to "stiffen the backbone" of employers in wage bargaining—that is, to encourage employers to resist excessive union wage demands. It seems logical that this will increase both the frequency and the duration of strikes, and the Wallich-Weintraub analysis explicitly suggests the latter effect. In the diagram below, which is a slight simplification of a similar one used by Wallich and Weintraub, the horizontal axis measures time, and the vertical axis measures the rate of change of money wages. Point D is the union's original wage demand, and the line labeled U represents the union's modification of its wage demands through time. The line E shows

15. "Incomes Policy: Completing the Stabilization Triangle," p. 119.

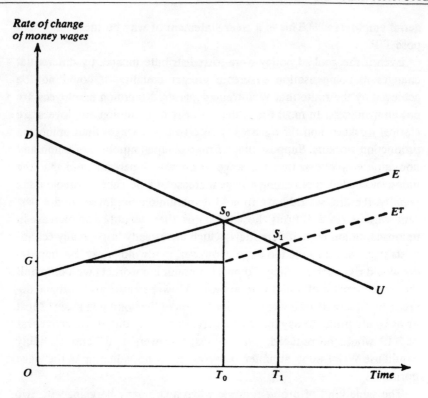

the improvement of the employer's wage offer through time without TIP. The introduction of such a policy, with the wage guideline established at point G, shifts the righthand portion of the employer's offer curve to E^T. Without TIP, settlement is reached at point S_0 at time T_0; after the introduction of TIP, settlement is reached at point S_1 at time T_1. Wallich and Weintraub do not divide their time scale into two segments representing negotiations before and negotiations during a strike. However, if a strike began before T_0, it would be prolonged by the time between T_0 and T_1. Presumably some strikes would also begin in this interval.

Business and labor generally prefer to avoid strikes whenever possible because of the losses they bring to both parties. This aspect of TIP gives them additional reason to oppose the policy. Strikes also impose losses on the general public, and the shortages that result from them can lower productivity and raise prices.

In this respect, TIP is inferior to wage controls, which actually reduce strikes. Days idle resulting from work stoppages were 0.15 percent of total working time in 1972 and 0.14 percent in 1973, the two years in the past decade in which wage controls were in effect throughout the year. These figures are below those for any other years in this decade, including the recession year, 1975. It is easy to understand why controls deter strikes—there is not much point in a union placing economic pressure on an employer to make wage concessions if the government will not permit these concessions to go into effect.

It is crucial to the Wallich-Weintraub analysis that union demands decline consistently through time, although it is by no means obvious that they will. The union may have some minimum demand for which it is prepared to bargain to the point of impasse or even to strike for a protracted period. In the diagram this would be shown by a horizontal segment of U. If this horizontal segment began at or to the left of S_0, TIP would increase the frequency or length of strikes without any reduction in the wage increase at which they were settled. Wallich and Weintraub recognize this possibility, but argue that a union that fails to take account of TIP in its demands is not maximizing benefits for its members.

I know of no evidence that industrial disputes arise from or are settled by maximizing behavior by both parties, any more than are international or religious disputes. It is not unknown for a strike to be settled for more than the union's original demand when a strong union is determined to teach management a lesson and recoup some of the losses suffered during a strike. When the union has the power to win a long strike, it does little good to strengthen management's backbone. There will certainly be some cases in which the TIP guideline would cause the size of the eventual settlement to be smaller. But this would not be true of every settlement, and it is an open question whether the gains would be worth the costs.

One advantage claimed for TIP is that it is automatic and thus easy to administer. The opposite side of this coin is that TIP does not enable its administrators to help in the settlement of actual or potential disputes in collective bargaining or in the improvement of collective bargaining structures. There have been cases in which the administration of wage controls accomplished this in the past, and this has been one of the mitigating aspects of wage-control programs.

If TIP does lead to more strikes, it could also lead to more government intervention to settle those strikes. Such intervention usually brings pressure on management to offer more generous terms because there may be no way in which the government can bring effective pressure on union members. The federal government would then either have to work at cross-purposes with its own TIP or suspend the TIP to help settle emergency disputes.

ADMINISTRATIVE PROBLEMS: WAGES[16]

As I noted earlier, one of the principal claims made for the TIP proposals is that they do not involve substantial administrative costs. Laurence Seidman, in his letter to the *New York Times* of December 22, 1976, lists as TIP's first advantage over controls that "no new bureaucracy is required." Critics of the TIP proposals have been skeptical of this claim. Gardner Ackley has commented, "From my experience in designing and administering price controls during World War II, and again, in a policy role, during the Korean War, I retain keen, and sometimes bitter, memories of great ideas about ways to restrain wage and price increases for which the fine print could never be written—or if it could be written, filled endless volumes of the *Federal Register* with constant revisions, exceptions, and adjustments necessary to cover special situations that could never have been dreamed of in advance by the most imaginative economists, accountants, and lawyers."[17] This section explores the basis for these diverging views.

The difficulty of administering wage guidelines depends in part on how increases in compensation are defined. Originally, Wallich and Weintraub proposed four possibilities: (1) total wages, salaries, bonuses, and fringe benefits divided by the number of employees on a given date; (2) total wage and related payments divided by the daily average number of employees; (3) total wage and related payments divided by employee hours worked (that is, compensation per employee hour); and (4) total wage and related payments in each job classification and grade divided by the number of man-hours worked, combined into a weighted index of wage increases.[18]

Wallich and Weintraub recognized that the first three of these proposals were subject to possible manipulation by the employer or could result in windfall gains and losses through changes in the skill mix. For example, an employer could increase wages by more than the guideline in every occupation, yet escape penalty taxes because employment or hours had increased most in the low-paid occupations. By March 1972, Wallich was writing that these proposals "probably will not do at all."[19] Yet Wal-

16. Some of the problems raised in this and the following section are considered in more detail in the paper in this volume by Larry L. Dildine and Emil M. Sunley.

17. Gardner Ackley, "Okun's New Tax-Based Incomes-Policy Proposal," *Economic Outlook, USA*, vol. 5 (Winter 1978), p. 8.

18. Condensed from "A Tax-Based Incomes Policy," pp. 13–14.

19. Henry C. Wallich, "Phase II and the Proposal for a Tax-Oriented Incomes Policy," *Review of Social Economy*, vol. 30 (March 1972), p. 8.

lich and Weintraub also recognize that the fourth proposal involves substantial difficulties of computation for large firms with many establishments and hundreds of different job titles. Firms do not now ordinarily maintain weighted indexes of wage increases, and even the Bureau of Labor Statistics has only begun such an index in the past decade. Average hourly earnings are easily obtained by accountants from payroll records; weighted indexes of wage changes must be computed by statisticians. Neither the typical corporate employer nor the Internal Revenue Service has the capabilities of the Bureau of Labor Statistics in this area. Specifying the proper computation of a weighted index of compensation increases in TIP is a task that gives rise to the kind of fears that Ackley has expressed.

An area of difficulty in the administration of wage controls that would also be present in TIP is the treatment of fringe benefits. Costs of fringe benefits are easy to compute when employers make contributions of cents per hour to a benefit fund, as they do in the construction industry. They are difficult to estimate, however, when a collective bargaining agreement or an employer benefit plan specifies future pension or health benefits rather than current contributions. Translating such benefits into current costs requires complicated calculations about which competent actuaries can disagree. The Internal Revenue Service already faces these difficulties in auditing employer costs of fringe benefits claimed on tax returns.

Past wage-control programs have controlled benefits more loosely than wages and salaries. This can be justified if fringe benefits are believed to be too low as a proportion of total compensation, which may have been true during World War II and the Korean War. It could also be justified during a demand-pull inflation on the ground that future pensions and health benefits, unlike current wages, do not add to aggregate demand. However, the theory underlying TIP assumes that the problem is cost-push, not demand-pull inflation. To be consistent with this theory, TIP advocates must fully include fringe benefits in their compensation measure.

The costs of fringe benefits can rise not only because benefit levels are improved, but also because inflation raises the cost of maintaining existing benefit levels. Such increased costs have been exempted from previous wage-control programs, but it is not at all clear that this could be permitted in a future incomes policy without seriously weakening the policy.[20]

20. For an elaboration of this view, see Daniel Quinn Mills, *Government, Labor, and Inflation: Wage Stabilization in the United States* (University of Chicago Press, 1975), pp. 202–05.

Another area of administrative difficulty is the implementation of incentive pay programs. In most of these programs, an increase in pay resulting from higher output would nevertheless reduce unit labor costs. Because the main purpose of TIP is to contain the cost of labor per unit, this suggests that increases in amounts received as incentive pay under existing schemes should be excluded from the proposed wage index. However, past wage-control programs have regulated the introduction of new incentive pay schemes on the ground that a large loophole might be created if regulations were absent. Special consideration needs to be given to incentive programs for executives based on corporate and divisional profits rather than on output. None of these problems is by any means insurmountable, but addressing them requires regulations and administrative machinery.

The negotiation of cost-of-living escalator provisions will create an area of increased uncertainty for management under TIP; more than half of all major collective bargaining agreements now contain such provisions. Any tax penalties arising from escalator provisions can be levied after the fact on the basis of wages actually paid. When negotiating the agreement, management must predict the future rate of inflation, as it does now. However, the possibility of a tax penalty will increase the cost of underprediction. This could restrain the spread of escalator provisions, but those managements already using them will not welcome the added risk.

Attention must also be paid to problems of wage inequities. During the wage-control program of 1971–74, the base date for calculating wage increases was November 14, 1971. Collective bargaining agreements reached before that date were allowed to operate as negotiated unless challenged. Those reached afterward required approval if they exceeded the pay standard, and were often cut back. Situations then arose in which two groups of workers in the same local union who had always received the same wage rate would have different rates because one employer had signed an agreement on November 13 and another had signed an identical agreement on November 15; such differences created great unrest among union members and strong political pressures on union leaders. Some of these inequities were later remedied by awards of retroactive pay to the aggrieved workers. This solution was most distasteful to management, which had not included the originally disallowed wage increases in prices, and viewed retroactive payments as impinging directly on the bottom line of the profit and loss statement.

From a union's viewpoint, TIP is preferable to controls in preventing wage inequities from arising when the program is first instituted. By actual or threatened strikes, unions could compel most managements to follow the traditional patterns established in previously negotiated settlements, even at the cost of tax penalties. However, the inequity is shifted to the firm: the employer who follows patterns pays penalty taxes; the one who sets patterns does not. Again, regulations could be written and administered to address such problems, but not without the usual bureaucratic costs.

Multiyear agreements negotiated before the inauguration of a TIP give rise to a problem even if they do not cause wage inequities. If wage increases in the second and third years of such agreements exceed the guideline, employers could be liable for tax penalties that were unanticipated when they entered into the agreements. To avoid this effect, prior agreements could be exempted from TIP, but this would mean that TIP would need three years to become fully effective.

Not all distortion in wage structure arises from the operation of incomes policies. Some comes from the sequential nature of collective bargaining and wage determination in the private sector. Wage settlements elsewhere and changes in labor market conditions can create situations in which some wages in a firm are inequitably low or are different from prevailing rates in the area or industry. Wage-control programs have always included provisions for dealing with such inequity problems, usually administered by staff with experience in industrial relations. Such exceptions are less necessary under TIP than under wage controls because an employer can remedy inequities and pay the tax penalty without obtaining previous permission and without violating the law. However, if no exceptions were permitted, some employers would probably pay tax penalties resulting from circumstances essentially beyond their control.

The most difficult question for unions in past wage-control programs has been whether or not to participate in the administration of the program. If union leaders did not participate, they feared that the program would be administered in ways that were adverse to the interests of their members. If they did participate, they could be criticized by rivals within the union for holding wages down when they were being paid to raise them. The resulting ambivalence is shown by the several cases in which union leaders have walked out of wage stabilization boards—and sometimes have been persuaded to return by changes in the program. The best option that union leaders have at present is to try to prevent TIP from going into effect.

The threats to incumbent union leaders from rivals within their own unions have increased greatly in both frequency and force since the enactment of the Landrum-Griffin act in 1959. It is public policy, and in my view correct public policy, to encourage democracy in trade unions. However, one disadvantage of the act is that it makes labor leaders less willing to cooperate, in the name of the "public interest," when economic policies are adverse to the interests of their members.

The most difficult union attitude to predict is the reaction to possible tax incentives payable to workers when wage settlements are below guidelines. This carrot approach to the TIP proposal can substitute tax benefits for wage benefits won by a union. Although the individual worker may be unaffected, the benefits are not attributable to the union as an organization and do not win support for union leaders. For this reason, if support of such a plan were voluntary, I would expect that many unions would not participate.

ADMINISTRATIVE PROBLEMS: PRICES

The Okun proposal is less explicit on the price side than is the Wallich-Weintraub proposal. In general, Okun proposes that each firm would have to maintain a price index for its domestic products. Many large firms do so now for internal use, though the methods used must be far from uniform and would have to be prescribed. However, the problems of constructing adequate price indexes are far more difficult than those of constructing adequate wage indexes. Most of these problems are well known, and need only to be mentioned briefly. Regulations would be needed to specify how to handle changes in discounts, delivery charges, extras, and similar components of the final price to the buyer. For some products, such as clothing, problems would arise from changes in style. In other cases, such as computers, there would be problems of measuring quality change. Indeed, computers are currently not included in the wholesale price index.

All the difficulties of devising useful price indexes are now dealt with by the Bureau of Labor Statistics in the computation of the consumer and the wholesale price indexes, which is to say that they are generally not insuperable, although few corporations have the statistical competence and resources of the Bureau of Labor Statistics. Moreover, in the absence of a TIP or a price control program, differences of opinion about how to measure prices will not generally give rise to judicial or administrative proceedings; if TIP were in effect, they undoubtedly would.

The agencies that administered price controls had great discretion to omit some products from control by regulation if they did not seem to be important contributors to price increases. This probably could not be done in a TIP that depends on the average price increase of a corporation's products. If exceptions were not possible, the program would have broader price coverage than that of past control programs.

The Okun proposal also calls for a "dollar-and-cents pass-through" of any increases in costs of materials and supplies. This would again entail additional recordkeeping if firms did not maintain separate aggregate measures of the quantity and price of materials purchased. However, the administrative problems are small compared to the inequities mentioned earlier arising from the application of uniform price guidelines in the face of sharply divergent productivity trends among industries. The answer might be different price guidelines at the industry level, at least where there are adequate industry measures of productivity, but again this could not be done without administrative machinery.

The claim that TIP requires no new bureaucracy may be true in the sense that it would not require a new government agency. However, it might require the Internal Revenue Service to expand its staff and to recruit personnel with the skills of those at such agencies as the former Cost of Living Council.

One important reason for the strong opposition of business to wage and price controls is that the administrative problems they created absorbed much of the time of corporate officers and required large additional expenditures on legal and accounting services, both internal and external. TIP would probably have similar costs. It is entirely legitimate for TIP proponents to argue that the benefits would exceed these costs, but it is unconvincing to pretend that the costs would not exist.

Deregulation

The third nontraditional way in which economists have recently proposed to fight inflation is to repeal or modify some government regulations that raise prices or increase costs without creating corresponding benefits. A modest program to seek such changes in regulation was enacted as part of the Council on Wage and Price Stability Act of 1974 and has been in effect for more than three years. However, the success of these efforts has been limited.

Cost-reducing changes in regulations, like cuts in excise taxes, should have a one-time effect in lowering the price level, with gradually diminishing effects on the subsequent rate of change. Such regulatory reform has wide support among economists: those economists who believe that inflation is largely or entirely a monetary phenomenon support deregulation because it would improve the allocation of resources or reduce unnecessary government intervention in the economy.

The business and labor view of deregulation differs sharply from case to case. Any proposal for deregulation is likely to create both groups that gain and groups that lose among business firms and employees. To identify these gainers and losers it is useful to distinguish two major styles of regulation, which I call old and new.

OLD-STYLE REGULATION

By old-style regulation, I mean the kind of regulation exemplified by the Interstate Commerce Commission, which has broad power to set rates or prices and control the entry of firms in a sharply limited industry or set of industries. Many of the agencies that make and administer such regulations are independent commissions outside the cabinet departments. With a few notable exceptions, the general effect of this regulation has been to set prices or rates higher than they would have been without regulation and to limit entry into the regulated industries. In such cases, relaxing the regulation generally tends to lower prices or rates and to increase the quantity of the service supplied.

Proposals for deregulation can be expected to have a mixed reception by business, depending on how a particular enterprise is affected. A few examples will make the conflict of interests apparent.

Some provisions of the 1936 Robinson-Patman act, administered by the Federal Trade Commission, and certain regulations of the Interstate Commerce Commission prevent private carriers of freight from achieving cost savings by carrying freight on return trips, or backhauls.[21] For example, retailers and wholesalers of food would like to have these restrictions on backhauls removed so that when they make deliveries to food stores they can save freight charges by using their own empty trucks to bring back to the warehouse products manufactured near the destination

---

21. Private carriers are truck fleets owned or leased by companies that are not certificated common carriers; these trucks carry goods belonging to the company using the fleet.

of the delivery. They understandably complain that empty backhauls waste resources and raise costs. Their efforts are vigorously opposed by the certificated common carriers, who would lose revenue traffic if the restrictions were lifted. These efforts at deregulation are also opposed by some manufacturers of brand-name grocery products who prefer to sell at delivered prices.

In this case, the union representing the affected workers (International Brotherhood of Teamsters) represents drivers for both private carriers and common carriers and thus may not have a large stake in the outcome. However, the union cannot be expected to support a proposal that might reduce the total employment of its members.

Regulated passenger airlines offer another example of a division between firms now protected and those excluded from regulation. For many years all domestic, regulated carriers opposed deregulation, as did the Air Line Pilots Association. Commuter airlines and charter flight operators favored it, presumably because it would give them access to markets from which they are now excluded.[22] Recently some reductions in airline fares have been taking place under regulation. This reflects both the pressures created by proposed changes in legislation and the appointment of two economists to membership on the Civil Aeronautics Board.

Domestic interstate natural gas is a leading case in which industry-specific regulation has kept prices below the level that would exist without regulation. In this case, it is the protected industry that seeks deregulation, and the consumer groups that oppose it. Unions generally view deregulation of natural gas from the standpoint of their members as consumers. Deregulation of natural gas would raise price indexes in the short run, but could lower them eventually if the supply response were sufficient to reduce the need to import natural gas.

The events of the last few years suggest that some improvement can be made in those aspects of old-style regulation that raise prices and costs, but progress will come slowly. Regulation that has substantial effects creates large benefits for some segments of the economy. Those segments that receive benefits will naturally fight harder to preserve regulation than the diffuse losers will fight to reform it.

22. Among the many anomalies of present airline regulation, I note here that United Airlines is required to serve the eastern Nevada towns of Elko and Ely. In 1970, Elko had a population of 7,621 and Ely 4,176. These locations are served by the smallest plane in the United Airline fleet, a Boeing 737 jet. For a recent discussion of some of the issues raised by air passenger regulation, see Paul W. MacAvoy and John W. Snow, eds., _Regulation of Passenger Fares and Competition among the Airlines_ (American Enterprise Institute, 1977).

NEW-STYLE REGULATION

New-style regulation, as exemplified by such agencies as the Environmental Protection Agency, tends to have a narrow focus of concern but a broad coverage of industries. Other examples include the Occupational Safety and Health Administration, the Consumer Product Safety Commission, and (with somewhat narrower industry coverage) the National Highway Traffic Safety Administration. Many such agencies are within cabinet departments.

There are many instances in which the costs of new-style regulation seem to exceed their benefits, or where the benefits are not obtained in the least costly way. Again, the reactions of industry and labor to proposals to reduce the cost of regulation depend largely on the particular regulation in question. The automobile industry and the United Automobile Workers have joined in opposing certain costly motor vehicle emission standards. The automobile industry has opposed the mandatory use of air bags to protect the occupants of automobiles in accidents, while the casualty insurance industry has favored it. Industry frequently criticizes OSHA regulations for being too costly, while labor may criticize the same regulations for being too lax.

There is little general understanding of economists' approach to such questions through benefit-cost analysis. The public and legislators frequently argue that life, health, and safety are priceless, and that no cost is too high to pay for them. This is, of course, nonsense, but appealing nonsense. Decisions are made everyday that implicitly place a less than infinite value on life and health—for example, in permitting the use of cigarettes or in constructing a two-lane rather than a four-lane highway. However, opposition to the excessive cost of some new-style regulation is easily depicted as opposition to its worthy purposes.

Better economic analysis could perhaps reduce the cost of new-style regulation without sacrificing desirable objectives. Nevertheless, the aggregate costs of such regulation and its effects on measured prices will probably continue to rise. Perhaps the most that can be accomplished is a deceleration of the rate of increase.

Concluding Comments

If business and labor oppose some of the new proposals for fighting inflation, particularly the TIP proposals, it is proper to ask whether they would prefer the alternatives. This is not a question they will be eager to answer; it is similar to asking whether one prefers to die by shooting or by hanging. Some guesses about the answer are nevertheless possible.

It seems clear that labor would prefer TIP to wage and price controls, especially if TIP covered prices. Wage controls are a binding constraint on wages, and unions may pay part of the penalties for deliberate violation of them. In contrast, strong unions might feel confident that under TIP they could exert influence through militant strikes, and that management would take the consequences. By the same token, management might choose wage and price controls as the lesser evil because in return for their costs they might effectively restrain strong unions.

Both unions and management might prefer the use of monetary and fiscal policy to either TIP or controls. A probable exception on both sides of the bargaining table is the construction industry and its suppliers, which under present institutional arrangements in financial markets are particularly vulnerable to increases in interest rates.

The labor movement is on record as being opposed to tight money and high interest rates and as favoring an expansionary fiscal policy. But these policies do not impinge as directly as TIP on the central function of the trade union, which is wage determination. Moreover, labor's view is less crucial to the outcome in this area because the use of monetary and fiscal policy does not require new legislation.

Management would clearly favor the use of tighter monetary and fiscal policies. Although management is now generally willing to concede the need for budget deficits in a recession, it would prefer the budget to be balanced over the full business cycle and strongly questions the need for large deficits in the third year of a recovery.

Business support for tight monetary policy rests both on opposition to inflation and on acceptance of monetarist rather than Keynesian macroeconomic theory. An analysis of the reasons for these views is beyond the scope of this paper, but their strength is not open to question. One element of the explanation may be that business believes neither that the economy is far from full employment at present, nor that there are now large gains in output to be achieved from increased monetary and fiscal stimulus. Keynes did not persuade the business community to abandon the old-time religion, and I doubt that Wallich and Weintraub will be any more successful.

4

PRICE-FIXING AS SEEN BY A PRICE-FIXER
Part II

Herbert Stein

Summary

Despite official disavowals of an intention to impose mandatory price and wage controls, the possibility of such controls hangs over the American economy. This is partly because such controls were adopted in 1971 despite similar disavowals. This paper considers how the country reached the point at which mandatory controls were imposed, even though almost all responsible public leaders, in and out of government, had been saying for years that they didn't want them. It also examines the proposition that the generally recognized failure of the 1971–1974 controls is not evidence of the basic ineffectiveness of such a policy, but was due to special factors, notably the Nixon administration's distaste for such measures.

Four main factors seem to have contributed to the imposition of mandatory, comprehensive, and long-lasting controls despite the "leadership" opposition to them.

(1) Congress gave the President blank-check, standby authority to impose controls, not because the Congress wanted controls but in order to embarrass a President who had vowed never to use them. The existence of this authority generated a strong temptation and demand to use it.

(2) Unrealistic predictions, mainly emanating from the administration, led the public to expect that conventional measures of fiscal and monetary restraint would work quickly and with minimum increase of unemployment. When these predictions proved incorrect, the whole conventional, gradualist approach was discredited, and the public demanded more radical measures.

(3) Influential leaders of public opinion, mainly outside the administration, while denying any desire for mandatory controls, argued

From Herbert Stein, "Price-Fixing as Seen by a Price-Fixer," pp. 113-135 in William Fellner (ed.) *Contemporary Economic Problems.* Copyright 1978 by the American Enterprise Institute for Public Policy Research.

continually for "voluntary" incomes policies, which were, in fact and in public perception, close to mandatory controls, in the sense that they implied the ability of the government to determine the "right" amount of wage or price increase, not only in general but also in specific cases, and the responsibility of government to try to induce conformity to these "right" price and wage increases. Once this is accepted as a legitimate role for government, it is only a small step to accepting the legitimacy of mandatory controls.

(4) The establishment of the controls, which were intended to be very short-lived in any comprehensive form, generated public expectations which made their early termination politically and psychologically impossible.

Despite their determination not to make price and wage controls a permanent feature of the American economy, the officials of the Nixon administration had every incentive to seek the success of the controls while they were in force. Moreover, the management of the controls was largely in the hands of people who did not entirely share the aversion of the White House to them. If it is accepted that the controls were to be temporary, and that the requirements of the control system were not to override all other objectives of economic policy, it is hard to ascribe the failures of the controls to inadequacies of their management. The one charge most commonly made against the management of the 1971–1974 controls is that decontrol came too early. However, there were substantial reasons for the timing of the movement to decontrol, and there is little reason to think that delay would have done any permanent good.

Two lessons of this history are relevant today.

- *Do not think that we can flirt with controls and not get them.*

- *Do not think that the ineffectiveness of controls, which has roots deep in the American economic and political system, can be overcome by sufficiently enthusiastic operators.*

Introduction

Some readers will recognize that "Price-Fixing as Seen by a Price-Fixer" is the title of an article by Frank W. Taussig that appeared in the *Quarterly Journal of Economics* in February 1919. I hope they will not think it presumptuous of me to borrow the title. I do so because it describes precisely what I am setting out to write and because it has a certain nostalgic interest for me. When I was an undergraduate I wrote a senior essay on "Government Price Policy in the United States during the

World War" (I didn't have the foresight to say World War I). Taussig's article was the most professional writing on the subject available.

There are several striking things about Taussig's article when it is looked at from today's perspective. The economic analysis seems archaic, and I suspect that it was crude even from the standpoint of 1918. Most of the discussion is premised on taking as marginal cost the average cost of the bulk-line producer—the producer whose output embraces about the eighty-fifth percentile of all output when producers are ranked by average costs. But, despite the lower level of sophistication in the theory with which Taussig and his colleagues worked, what they actually did was not inferior to what we have recently done or would do now. Our advance in theory since World War I has not been matched by an advance in data or in operating procedures. It should be recognized, however, that the World War I price control was largely confined to the easier cases of standardized commodities. If they had tried to cover a larger part of the economy the inferiority of their capability as compared with ours would have been obvious.

Taussig's detachment about price-fixing is something that few who have been through it recently can equal. The whole area of price control has become "hot." Some participants write about their experience with pride and exuberance, some write to rationalize their failures or put them off onto others, some write to apologize for having been in a place like that at all. Taussig, although he entitles his article ". . . as Seen by a Price-Fixer," hardly lets us know that he was a responsible participant. Indeed, only a footnote on the second page of the article, which lists the members of the Price Fixing Committee, tells the reader what Taussig's role was. He writes with knowledge, but the kind of knowledge that an economist sitting in the corner observing but not participating might have had. He writes as a traveler just returned from a strange country with which he has no emotional connection and which he never expects to revisit, informing his friends but not advising them whether to go there or not.

Taussig's conclusions about the World War I price-fixing experience are moderate and common-sensical. He believes that the controls worked, in the sense of holding down prices, but not much—but, then, they weren't expected to do much. He gently chides his colleagues in the academic practice of economics for thinking that prices are precisely determined by demand, supply, and the quantity of money. These determinations are approximate only, and that leaves room for controls to affect prices without having to contend with strong market pressures or creating shortages.

These conclusions are unsupported by any statistics, let alone econometrics. Probably the basic fact about World War I price control is that there wasn't much of it, either in coverage or in duration, and that contributed to the appearance of effectiveness, especially if attention is confined to the area and period of coverage. Much of the World War I inflation came after the war and the controls were over, and even after Taussig's article was written.

Taussig's paper on price controls did not deal with the question whether we should have the controls again, any more than people writing in 1918 about World War I felt it necessary to deal with the question whether we should have another war. To the economists of 1919 those controls were an unusual experience which might throw some light on economic questions even if the experience were never to be repeated, just as an earthquake would be instructive to geologists aside from the question whether it would, let alone should, be repeated.

Today's situation is different. We live under the shadow of the possibility that the controls will be reimposed. Just as it is necessary for the Jews to reread every year the story of their enslavement under the Pharaohs and their subsequent deliverance, it is necessary to repeat the story of our 1971–1974 price control experience, so that subsequent policy makers, even those who come only four years later, will bear it in mind.

What needs to be retold is not primarily the failure of the 1971–1974 controls. Perhaps that part of the story will have to be repeated for later generations, but every adult now alive must know that the controls did not check the inflation. It is hard to imagine a scenario in which the present price level or inflation rate would have been higher if the controls had not been imposed. When we went into the controls in August 1971 the unemployment rate was 6 percent and the inflation rate about 5 percent. As this is being written the unemployment rate is again 6 percent and the inflation rate is 6 to 7 percent. In the interim (1971 to 1977) the consumer price index has risen 50 percent, or at an annual average rate of 7 percent. The controls repressed inflation in the latter part of 1971 and in 1972, but whatever effect they may have had was washed away by the inflationary surge of 1973–1974.[1]

Not only is our most recent controls experience universally recognized to have been ineffective, but also the administration now in power and everyone else with any authority expresses an immovable determination not to resort to controls. Why, then, does the fear of the restoration of controls hover over the economy, as evidenced by the decline of the stock market whenever the word is breathed?

---

[1] For a systematic evaluation of the effect of controls, see Marvin H. Kosters, *Controls and Inflation: The Economic Stabilization Program in Retrospect* (Washington, D.C.: American Enterprise Institute, 1975).

There are two reasons. One is the memory that the controls were imposed by a government that was in principle deeply opposed to them and that had made promises not to use them at least as strong as those made by the Carter administration. We have learned how quickly and unexpectedly an administration can change its mind on this subject. The second reason for the continuing fear, perhaps less important than the first but reinforcing it, is the belief in some quarters that the failure of the 1971–1974 controls was not inherent in controls but resulted from inadequacies in their management. Thus, there is the possibility that the government will move to controls, despite its vows not to do so, and that it will rationalize this action by saying, and believing, that it will run the controls differently from the way they were run before.

These two reasons lead to two questions. First, how did an administration that was almost religiously opposed to controls come to resort to them? Second, were there deficiencies in the management of controls which caused a failure that could have been averted if they had been managed differently, or by other people?

In the remainder of this paper I will offer the observations of a participant in those controls on some points that are relevant to these two questions.[2]

On the Menace of Standby Authority

Mandatory wage and price controls cannot be imposed in the United States without legislative authority. This authority does not ordinarily exist, and does not exist now.

Mr. Nixon had no specific authority to impose price and wage controls when he came into office. The Vietnam War was under way, and he might conceivably have been able to interpret controls as falling within the President's war powers. He had no desire in those days to impose controls. But even if he had wanted to do so, reliance upon inherent war powers would have been very difficult for him. The war was exceedingly unpopular, his conduct of it was already considered by many to be high-handed, if not illegal, and there would probably have been a furious reaction, in and out of Congress, if he had assumed power over the domestic economy in the name of that war.

As it turned out, the President was given authority by Congress

---

[2] I was first a member and then chairman of the President's Council of Economic Advisers from January 1969 through August 1974, when controls were debated, imposed, redefined, and finally terminated. I was chairman of a committee of the Cost of Living Council, charged with developing plans for Phase II of the controls, and vice chairman of the Cost of Living Council from January 1, 1972, until its extinction on April 30, 1974.

against his will and as a result of a political accident. In August 1970, Congress passed the Defense Stabilization Act, authorizing the President to control prices and wages. The act was a blank check, specifying no standards except that controls imposed under the act should be applied in a nondiscriminatory way. There was no attempt to conceal the fact that the authority was being given to the President to embarrass him. The economy was not in a crisis. The unemployment rate was 5 percent and the inflation rate 6 percent. Hardly anyone wanted mandatory controls imposed at that time. To test this, Representative Benjamin B. Blackburn (Republican, Georgia) introduced an amendment to the bill which would have imposed the controls immediately, rather than giving the President authority to do so. Only five congressmen voted for the amendment. Some members may have wanted controls then, without wanting to take the responsibility for imposing them, but they were probably few. President Nixon said that he would have vetoed the bill if it had not been an amendment to the extension of the Defense Production Act.

The act was passed in the firm belief that the President would not use the price control authority, and the Democratic Congress could place the responsibility for the continuation of the inflation exclusively on the back of the President. This strategy did not depend on any belief by congressmen that controls were an effective or desirable way to stop inflation. It only required the belief that there were a certain number of citizens in the country who did believe that, and who would accept the idea that the President was withholding the sure and painless remedy for inflation. Confidence that the President would not impose controls also relieved the Congress of the necessity of being specific about what was to be covered and what the criteria for establishing maximum permitted prices and wages were to be. If anyone had thought that the authority would be used, the Congress would have been deluged with demands for exemption or for favorable treatment of particular cases.

Although the administration resisted the enactment of the authority, it did not regard passage of the act as marking any significant change in its basic anticontrols stance. Events then moved with what now seems amazing speed. In February 1971, six months after the authority was given, it was used, in the case of the construction industry. The President had asked for voluntary restraint by the construction unions in raising wages. However, national union leaders were afraid of being undercut by rivals within the movement if they accepted wage limitations voluntarily. Their problem was solved by formally invoking the price-wage control authority, which gave the impression that the union leaders had been compelled to agree to the wage restraints. The reliance on the legal authority was only on paper; in fact, everything was done by negotiation. No one in the administration felt that they had crossed the Rubicon to mandatory controls. But still a line had been crossed.

In March the new secretary of the treasury, John Connally, testified in favor of the extension of the control authority. Since the authority was going to be there anyway, he did not want the administration to seem so timid in its anti-inflation policy that it was afraid to have the ultimate weapon in its arsenal. At the same time he assured everyone that the administration had no intention of imposing controls. But still another line had been crossed.

On August 15, 1971, the President, using the authority given him by the Economic Stabilization Act, imposed a total freeze on wages and prices, implementing a decision to which he had been gradually coming during the spring and summer.

If there had been no authority there would have been no controls. Perhaps the President would have obtained the authority even if Congress had not forced it upon him in the politically motivated way it did. He might have asked for the authority, and Congress might have given it to him. But that course of events would have encountered a number of obstacles that might not have been overcome. The President would have had to do much more explaining of his radical change of position about controls. Moreover, the psychological and political aspects of asking Congress for authority would have been quite different from coming down from Camp David and with a single thunderclap putting an end to the inflation. In the latter case he established himself immediately, although not permanently, as a national hero and savior of the economy. In the former he would have entered into a struggle with an opposing and hostile Congress, from which he might not emerge a winner, even if he got the authority. That is, the authority might be so encumbered with restrictions that the President would be left only with the power to anger everyone and please no one. If Congress had believed that the President meant to impose controls it could have become so embroiled in conflict over the terms of the authority that no legislation would emerge. Faced with these prospects there is a strong probability that the President would never have asked for authority, at least unless the economic situation had become more critical than it ever did.

Of course, this is all speculation. But there seems little doubt that the enactment of the authority greatly increased the probability that there would be controls, and that the enactment was not intended by its authors to have that effect. The political situation of 1970 does not exist today. The Democratic Congress is unlikely to give a Democratic President price control authority for the sake of embarrassing him. But the experience is relevant to the idea which arises repeatedly that the President should be given standby authority to impose controls, either as a way of inducing "voluntary" restraint by business and labor, or as a preparation for quick action in some situation that is not present and not expected but is possible, or merely as a means of showing the public that the government is sincerely concerned about inflation.

The lesson of that experience is not to play political games with lethal economic instruments. Chekhov said that a dramatist should not put a gun on the wall in the first act unless he intends it to be fired in the last act. Congress should not provide authority for controls unless it intends them to be used. Probably the greatest assurance we have today against a return to controls is the absence of authority. That condition should be preserved.

On the Importance of Realistic Expectations

The fact that he had authority did not, of course, require the President to use it, although it leaned in that direction. In 1971, when the controls were imposed, Milton Friedman explained them by saying that if 75 percent of the American people believe in witchcraft it is difficult for the President not to practice witchcraft. This is a generous interpretation, and most of the people involved would probably settle for it. However, it deserves to be pushed a little further. What was it the American people believed that made the controls hard to avoid, and why did they believe it?

The belief had two parts. One was that the course of the economy demonstrated that the "natural" solutions—essentially fiscal and monetary policy—had not worked and would not work. The other part was that "supernatural" solutions—some version of wage and price controls—would work.

Certainly by the middle of 1971 there was a general belief in the country that the conventional policy of reducing inflation by fiscal and monetary restraint which would sustain a good deal of slack in the economy was not working. Of course, there were many people who never believed that it would work. The idea that the rate of inflation is influenced by demand is a strange idea, except in the most runaway situations, like all-out war, to the man in the street, and even to fairly sophisticated men in the street. The head of one of this country's largest retail establishments once told me that he never knew a price to be raised because the demand for a product was strong.

But still there had been a common view, beginning in 1968, that slowing down the expansion of the economy, which would involve some increase of the unemployment rate, was the proper way to check the inflation, and would work. This was the rationale behind the enactment of the temporary tax surcharge and ceiling on federal expenditures in 1968 and the policy of gradualism, meaning gradual restraint, preached and followed by the Nixon team in 1969.

Many people who had held this view in 1968 and 1969 were disillusioned by the experience of 1970 and the early part of 1971 and came to believe that the policy of demand restraint would not work. The unemployment rate, which had been 3.3 percent at the end of 1968, had risen to 6 percent, and the rate of inflation, which had briefly touched 6 percent in the early part of 1969, was still around 5 percent, and it was by no means certain that the rate would stay that low. This seemed to many obvious evidence of the failure of the conventional strategy. But it was only obvious if the strategy had implied that the inflation rate would have declined more than that with a smaller rise of unemployment or in a shorter time.

If the commonly held expectation had been that significant reduction of the inflation rate would take three or four years and might involve an increase of the unemployment rate to, say, 7 percent, the policy would not have seemed a failure—at least, not by 1971—and the pressure to move to another solution would have been less. Possibly knowing how long the gradual process of disinflation would take might have convinced some people even earlier of the need to move to controls. But that does not seem to be the most likely reaction. In fact, the country was not suffering any severe injury from the process of gradualism. What soured people on gradualism was not that it took such a long time but that forecasts of what it would deliver in the way of lower inflation were repeatedly disappointed, and this gave rise to the belief that gradualism would never work.

The fault was therefore in large part not in the performance of the economy but in the unrealistic expectations against which the performance was measured.

These expectations came from various sources, but the government was probably the most important. From the time the inflation began to speed up, in 1966, the government repeatedly underestimated the time that would be required to check the inflation. President Johnson's last economic report, published in January 1969, predicted that a brief slowdown of the economy, lasting only until mid-1969, would suffice to get the inflation rate under control. The first statements of the Nixon administration discounted this forecast somewhat, but not much, implying that an economic slowdown lasting throughout the year would be necessary. In January 1970 the Nixon Council of Economic Advisers took the position that an economic decline lasting until the middle of that year, followed by a slow rise, would suffice to get the inflation rate on a downward path. A year later, in January 1971, they said that in view of the slack that then existed in the economy a fairly vigorous recovery during the year would still be consistent with a significant reduction of the inflation rate.

These forecasts all proved to be wrong, and this seriously reduced the credibility of the idea that a continuation of moderate slack in the economy would in time get the inflation rate down, even though this idea might have been, and in my opinion was, correct. The credibility of the idea was reduced for some people in the government, as well as for many outside. These forecasts were based on what seemed at the time a reasonable interpretation of the evidence, including a continuous adaptation to the fact that earlier forecasts had been wrong. With hindsight a number of reasons can be adduced for these errors.[3] What is more relevant today is that even with the forecasts it made, the government should have been more aware of the margin of error that was around them and of the consequences of the expectations that it was generating with these forecasts. If the government had given early warning of the possibility that the disinflation process would be long drawn out there might have been less impatience when that turned out to be the case and less demand for abandoning the policy.

This situation has its counterpart today. Government forecasts are creating the expectation that the inflation rate can be stabilized, that is, kept from accelerating, with what it calls a moderate rate of expansion, which would involve about 4½ percent real growth per annum during 1978 and 1979. It is also fostering the view that if this real growth is not achieved the nation will pay a great price in lost production and excessive unemployment. In this way it is laying the base for a great disappointment with the "moderate" policy and a public demand for stronger and more direct action to hold wages and prices down in order to permit a more expansive policy to be followed.

On the Slippery Slope

For the man in the street it was perfectly natural to think that the most effective way to stop inflation was for the government to tell businesses and unions not to raise prices. The man in the street could not be expected to make much of the distinction between trying to restrain the rise in the average level of prices and trying to restrain increases of particular prices. Neither could he be expected to be a stickler for the distinction between voluntary and mandatory government influence over particular prices.

---

[3] The model of the inflationary process presented in Phillip Cagan's essay in this volume would, I think, have led to more realistic forecasts.

But the demand for controls did not arise spontaneously from the men in the street. It was stimulated and legitimized by the national leadership—the political leadership, the intellectual leadership, and the media leadership. Almost everyone in a leadership position maintained—up to the time mandatory controls were imposed, and in many cases afterwards—that he was against mandatory controls. But the words and actions of these leaders during 1970 and the first half of 1971 were paving the way for mandatory controls.

The grant of authority to impose mandatory controls, which we have already described, is a clear example of this unintended but important miseducation of the public. Even though the congressmen who granted the authority in 1970 said that they did not want controls, their action could not be interpreted as reflecting a conviction that they regarded mandatory controls as beyond the pale, to be ruled out forever. When the President used the authority in the case of the construction industry, even though all the parties regarded that action as window-dressing, outside observers must have gotten the impression that the executive branch considered mandatory controls a respectable anti-inflation instrument. And this idea was enhanced when Secretary Connally testified in favor of extending the authority to impose controls, while denying any intent to use the authority.

The call from respected opinion makers for "some kind of incomes policy"—whether guideposts, a wage-price review board, or whatever—became louder and louder as we went through 1970 and 1971, and was probably even more influential in making the idea of mandatory controls acceptable. These people all insisted that they did not want mandatory controls, but they were relying on a fine and indefensible distinction between mandatory and voluntary. The critical question is whether the government knows best—better than the market—what particular prices and wages should be, from the standpoint of economic efficiency, fairness, or some other criterion. The proponents of incomes policy were saying that the government does know best. Once this is said, it is not convincing to say that it makes a great deal of difference whether the government achieves its preferred prices by mandatory or voluntary means, or that it should not use mandatory means if voluntary means fail. In fact, the distinction between mandatory and voluntary systems in this field is quite loose. The "voluntary" systems can involve a good deal of coercion—in the form of threats of exposure to public calumny, loss of government contracts, or other sanctions—whereas the mandatory systems always have a considerable voluntary element, because they cannot work without the cooperation, or at least the agreement, of the parties.

The largest part of the argument for voluntary incomes policies was also an argument for mandatory controls and helped to create the impression that mandatory controls were an admissible policy. The administration's strategy was to try to appease the mounting demand for incomes policies by making concessions to it, in the hope that the inflation would be checked before the demand escalated into irresistible pressure for mandatory controls. Thus we got the inflation alerts, the National Commission on Productivity, the Government Regulation and Purchasing Review Board, the jawboning of the steel industry, and the Construction Industry Stabilization Committee. These moves did not have the desired effect of slowing down the demand for incomes policy. In fact, they may have intensified that demand, since they were a concession by the administration that to some degree the solution to the inflation problem could be found in the box of government guidance of private price and wage decisions. This was probably true despite the limited scope of the administration's moves and the free price rhetoric with which they were accompanied.

By mid-1971 the President had concluded that further small steps within the area of "voluntary" policies would not satisfy the demands in the country for stronger measures, would not silence his critics, and would not reduce inflation but might accelerate it by inducing people to try to get big price or wage increases before the door was finally slammed shut by mandatory controls. The possibility of avoiding mandatory controls might have been greater if the President had rejected any moves in the direction of "incomes policy" rather than taking homeopathic doses which encouraged the popular belief that the medicine might be of value if taken in larger amounts. The possibility of avoiding mandatory controls would have been still greater if the private leaders of public opinion who were demanding an incomes policy but foreswearing any desire for mandatory controls had paid more attention to the kind of education they were giving the public.

A similar process of public miseducation is going on in the country today. The President and many others are teaching the public that the inflation can be controlled and the operation of the economy improved if leaders of business and labor would follow standards specified by the government, rather than make wage and price decisions in the light of their own conditions as they see them. At the same time the President and most others insist that they do not want to *require* the private parties to abide by these standards. They only want the government to point out what proper behavior is, and persuade the private parties to follow their lead. They sometimes describe inflation as if it were a bad habit, which only needs to be pointed out to be overcome, to the great relief of its former practitioners and of the country at large. But this is simply telling the public that the government knows best, and leaves no convincing answer to the question why the government should not require that people do what is best, for themselves and the country.

The currently favored version of incomes policy, among academics and editorial writers, is the tax-based incomes policy, or TIP. The basic notion is that if an economic unit raises its wages, or prices, by less than some amount which the government specifies it should get a tax reduction, or, alternatively, if the increase is more than the standard it should incur a tax penalty. This is much closer to mandatory controls than most other suggested incomes policies are. It requires legislative authorization. It requires quite precise specification of standards, of a kind that would stand up in court, and does not leave the room for negotiation between the government and private parties that exists in less formal incomes policy. And the TIP would probably have to be of universal coverage, whereas most other kinds of incomes policy are operationally applied only to large economic units. If there is to be a tax benefit for not getting a wage increase in excess of, say, 6 percent, that benefit has to be available to the shoeshine boy in a three chair barber shop as well as to the members of the United Steel Workers.

TIP is mandatory price and wage control in which no one goes to prison. The government would establish standards of price and wage behavior and a financial penalty, in the form of additional tax imposed or tax relief forgone, for failure to conform. Presumably the penalty would be set so as to be powerful.

TIP is, in my opinion, less likely to be adopted than mandatory controls of the conventional sort. However, its proponents feel able to argue for it while denying that they are in favor of mandatory controls. And the argument for TIP is a large part of the argument for controls of the conventional sort.

Proponents of TIP (and other incomes policies) say something like this: The country would be better off if the average of wages, which we will call capital W, rises by 6 percent rather than 8 percent. Therefore let us give a benefit to everyone whose wage rises by less than 6 percent, or impose a penalty on everyone whose wage rises by more than 6 percent. But at this point they have slipped from talking about W to talking about all the hundreds of thousands of little w's which are the specific wages for specific jobs in specific industries and locations. And while it may be correct that W should rise by 6 percent it is by no means correct that all the little w's should rise by 6 percent. In fact, it is neither efficient nor fair that they should. Once the effort is made to specify how much each of the little w's should rise, TIP loses its initial appeal. But if the argument for TIP convinces people either that the government knows how much each little w should rise, or that it doesn't matter how much each of them rises, then much of the argument against mandatory controls is undercut.

The Momentum of Controls

The talk about incomes policy, and the small steps taken in that area, in 1970 and 1971, helped to lead the country to a point that almost everyone had said he didn't want to reach—mandatory controls. Once the controls were adopted they also turned out to have a momentum to lead us in a direction that no one had wanted or foreseen.

When the decision was made, in August 1971, to freeze prices, wages, and rents for a period up to ninety days, there was no clear idea of what would follow the ninety days. However, the quite tentative discussion of that question among the government officials who met at Camp David on the weekend of August 13 suggested a radical reduction in the scope and rigor of controls. Most of the ideas discussed were of the order of the establishment of a Wage-Price Review Board, to examine and form opinions about actions of the largest corporations and unions, possibly with mandatory authority but possibly not.

The initial examination of options for policy to follow the freeze covered a wide range of possibilities, from total decontrol to continuation of something very close to the freeze itself. But it soon became clear that the more far-reaching moves back to the free market were not really possible. The freeze had instantly become the most popular economic action of government that anyone could remember. There was a widespread public rejoicing that at last the government was protecting the people. And it was not, or not only, General Motors and U.S. Steel from whom the public was being protected but also the landlord and the corner grocer. The freeze was a powerful piece of economic education. It taught the people that the government could stop inflation in its tracks. It was not possible to turn people back to the tender mercies of their landlords and merchants. This was not only politically impossible. It was psychologically impossible; the general disappointment at the sudden loss of this new-found protector would have been too wrenching. The danger that this new-found protector might become a nuisance, if not an enemy, referred to a future that most people did not foresee or weigh very heavily.

This became clearest in the case of rent control. This was the area in which the managers of the program were most convinced of the economic folly of continuing the freeze. It was also the area in which the administrative difficulties were the greatest. But it was also an area in which the public—that is, the tenants—most valued having government on their side.

In the end the Phase II program was quite comprehensive and, in principle, entirely mandatory, although it could not literally be enforced on every small economic unit in the country but depended in considerable part on voluntary compliance. This went far beyond any of the possibilities that had been thought of when the freeze was first imposed. And the other options that were most seriously considered when the Phase II decision was made were even more freeze-like than the system that was actually adopted.

This experience is a vivid example of the importance of asking, "What next?" when any step is taken in this field. Every step closes some options.

The Management of Controls

There are, as I have said earlier, some people who deny the value of the 1971–1974 experience as evidence of the ineffectiveness of controls, on the ground that the controls at that time were not properly managed. Among those who think that, the most common argument is not to refer to a specific deficiency of the controls system but to point out that the controls were run by people who did not "believe" in them, as if that contributed to their failure.

I shall indicate later what I think were the reasons for the failure of the controls. My list does not include the fact that they were run by people who didn't believe in them. I recognize that I am not an entirely objective witness on that point, but I will put down some observations which may help others to judge what there is in it.

When it is said that the people who ran the controls did not believe in them, the reference is primarily to Mr. Nixon and to George Shultz, who was chairman of the Cost of Living Council during most of the period. The list probably includes me, since I was vice-chairman of the Cost of Living Council, and have more writing and speeches against controls on the record than anyone else in the government at that time. The questions are, What were our attitudes to the controls, and In what sense did we run the controls?

A distinction must be made between liking the controls and believing in them. Given that there is a controls program to run, there is no advantage in having it run by people who like controls, any more than there is advantage in having surgery performed by surgeons who like to cut or wars commanded by generals who like to bomb. Liking controls can warp judgments and lead to excesses which overstrain the control system as well as interfere with economic efficiency, growth, and other objectives.

It is easy to come to like the controls if one has a position of authority in the system. The price controller has a sense of great power as the heads of large corporations file through his office asking for exemptions or increases in their ceilings. Anyone who has seen J. K. Galbraith on television describing his experience as a price controller in World War II can see the relish with which he still recalls his power over the captains of industry. I observed this attitude in the 1971–1974 period, but we who then ran the controls did not share it.

We not only didn't like controls but we would have preferred not to be in them and we felt that we had gotten there only as a result of strong external pressure. But being there, we believed strongly in trying to use the controls to help effect a transition to a permanently lower inflation rate at high employment.

We did not believe that controls should be permanent. We did not believe that the requirements of the control system should take precedence over all other objectives of economic policy—including the increase of output and employment, and the reduction of unemployment; a high rate of investment, which would contribute to future output; and efficiency in production and distribution. We did not want to establish a huge bureaucracy and enforcement apparatus. We valued economic freedom, including freedom of collective bargaining, highly, not only because of its economic benefits but also because of the underpinning it provides for personal and political freedom. In other words, we did not want to create a permanently and totally managed economy in the United States, and did not believe that the American people expected us to do that.

If those qualifications are not accepted, then the management of the 1971–1974 controls must seem unduly weak. But if these qualifications are accepted, it is difficult to see that the management of the system was inhibited by the ideology of those who were running it. As already noted, the Phase II controls system was much more comprehensive and mandatory than the administration or any one else had expected it to be. Also, the system was kept in operation for a relatively long time. Decontrol during Phase II was quite gradual. Although the move to Phase III in January 1973 had been criticized, I shall argue below that it was a necessary and prudent step. When, nevertheless, inflation accelerated in 1973 the administration made a strenuous, although unsuccessful, attempt to check it by tightening up the system again.

Moreover, in very important respects the price-wage control system was managed by people who did not share the ideological inhibitions of the President and his chief economic officials. During Phase II, the standards and procedures were established, and case-by-case decisions made, by the Price Commission and the Pay Board, and their staffs. In Phase III and IV these functions were largely carried out by the executive director of the Cost of Living Council and his staff, much of which had formerly been Price Commission and Pay Board staff. In December 1973 control over prices of petroleum and its products was shifted to the newly created Federal Energy Administration.

These other agencies were naturally more single-minded in their determination to hold down prices and wages by controls than were the officials with more general responsibilities for economic policy. This was not only, or even mainly, because of the ideologies of the more general officials. The latter had to be more concerned with output, employment, growth, efficiency, and good international economic relations than were the agencies that concentrated exclusively on controlling wages and prices. Moreover, the general officials had to be concerned with what would happen when the controls and the controllers were gone.

There were disagreements between the general officials and the price-wage controllers. However, these disagreements were not usually over matters that were crucial for the success of the program, and the price controllers most frequently had their way with respect to the control standards and their implementation and the administration of the system. The administration recognized the value of leaving a large degree of responsibility for the operation of the controls in bodies that were independent of and somewhat removed from the White House, and it respected that independence.

The Move to Phase III

Insofar as the charge that the 1971–1974 controls were badly run has any content, aside from the complaint that they were run by people who did not believe in them, the content refers to the relaxation of controls in January 1973, when Phase II was followed by Phase III. The rate of price increase began to accelerate sharply in the early part of 1973, and there were many people who believed then, and there probably are some who still believe, that this was the result of the relaxation of controls. Some conclude from this that if the relaxation had not come when it did not only would there have been less inflation in early 1973 but also the whole subsequent course of the inflation would have been different.

Of course, it makes a difference whether one considers the wisdom of relaxation in January 1973 in the context of a policy in which it is possible to have controls forever or in the context of a policy where permanent controls are not accepted as possible or desirable. If, as is almost universally accepted in this country, comprehensive controls are not to last forever, one must ask whether there would have been some better, later, date for taking the step toward decontrol. This question calls for a great deal of speculation, but even in retrospect it is hard to see a better time. Perhaps it would have been wise to keep the controls in their Phase II form until the recession of 1975, when the inflationary pressure of demand would have been less. But this possibility runs into the counterpossibility that prolonging the controls in the Phase II form would have so depressed business investment as to make the recession come sooner than it did. In any case, in January 1973 no one was foreseeing the 1975 recession. And while it is always prudent to expect that there will be a recession within the next few years, the prospect at the beginning of 1973 was that the economy would go through more tightness and demand pressure on inflation before it reached the next recession.

Given a determination to end the controls sometime, the step taken in January 1973 seemed timely and moderate. There were several reasons for acting then:

(1) Some relaxation of the Phase II wage standard was a necessary condition for restoring participation of the labor leadership in the program. The labor members had walked off the Pay Board in April 1972, and while labor had continued to comply with the standards, the absence of the labor leadership seemed a risky condition. Establishment of a new Labor-Management Advisory Committee was a key element in Phase III, and this required movement to a more flexible and negotiated wage-determination process.

(2) Continuation of the Phase II profits limitation as part of the price control system was a threat to business investment. A new standard was desired, which would relax the profit limitation while retaining a fairly firm limit on price increases. Since for most corporations the profit limit was applied on a calendar year basis, it was desirable to announce the new standard early in the year.

(3) As economic activity rose, the price control system was running into an increasing number of cases where the price ceilings were an impediment to production or efficient allocation of output. Revision of the rules to allow more room for adjustment in those cases was in order.

(4) The price control authority would expire on April 30, 1973. There was an advantage in having the new rules in force so that Congress would understand them before it acted on extension of the authority, so that the Congress would not inadvertently make changes in the

authority which would interfere with the new system but would have a chance to modify the system deliberately if it wished to do so.

The changes made in the shift from Phase II to Phase III were not radical. The pricing standards were altered only marginally. The wage standard was made ambiguous, with the idea of case-by-case decisions in the foreground and the Phase II standard of a 5.5 percent limit on increases in the background. Companies were relieved of the requirement to notify the Cost of Living Council of price increases in advance, but they were required to file quarterly reports. The Cost of Living Council asserted its readiness to adopt tougher standards and procedures if necessary.

The rate of inflation was expected not to accelerate significantly in 1973, and not to be visibly greater with the Phase III system than it would have been with the Phase II system. Although the rate of unemployment had come down to 5 percent at the end of 1972, this was thought to signify that there was still a good deal of slack in the economy, even though there would be some cases of shortages at the existing prices. There was confidence that the relations among wages in different unions and sectors had reached a condition of balance in which there would not be a strong drive from any quarter for exceeding the recent pattern of wage increases. The shift from the 5.5 percent wage standard to a more flexible standard was considered to be more formal than real—a concession to the desire of the labor leaders to get credit for wage increases rather than to the desire for larger wage increases. The shift from requiring businesses to notify the government of price increases in advance to requiring reporting after the fact was not expected to change business behavior. Agricultural prices would continue to rise, as they had done in 1972, but this was estimated not to exceed an amount that could be accommodated within an overall price increase of about 3 percent.

Of course, the inflation turned out to be much greater in 1973 than was envisaged when the decision was made to go to Phase III. This unforeseen increase in the inflation rate was not, however, the result of the changes in the standards or procedures of the controls system. The estimate that wage increases would be moderate turned out to be correct. Also, the increase in profit margins was small. The big surge of inflation came in two sectors that had not been under control in Phase II and that are not usually covered by price control systems. These are raw agricultural products and imports. They are typically excluded from controls because price ceilings in these fields have a quick supply response and lead promptly to shortages. The price effects of low food supplies, especially of meat, had been seriously underestimated. So had the effect of the boom in the United States and in the rest of the world on the prices of internationally traded raw materials. The effect on prices of the decline in the exchange rate of the dollar during the first half of 1973 was also underestimated. But the inflationary surge of the first half of 1973 could not have been prevented by the retention of the Phase II controls, as is suggested by the failure of the extreme tightening of the controls in the summer of 1973.

In the middle of 1973 I was asked at a congressional hearing whether, in view of the big rise of the inflation rate, I thought it would have been wise not to shift to Phase III. I replied that I did not think so, except for the fact that by our action in January 1973 we had given decontrol a bad name. There might have been a tactical advantage in not making the shift to Phase III and therefore not taking the blame for the rise of the inflation rate, but that would not have kept the rate from rising.

From the vantage point of 1978 what seems the main problem with the decontrol process was not that it came so soon but that it was incomplete. The system of ceiling prices on domestically produced crude oil established during the controls period remains in effect today, under special price control authority that was enacted before the general authority to control prices expired. The two-tier method, holding down the price of "old" oil and allowing "new" oil to be free, was established in 1973 and is still basically in operation. Even the ceiling price of $5.25 a barrel set in December 1973 for old oil is still in effect. The responsible officials recognized in 1973 that this system was holding back domestic oil production, since the regulatory distinction between old oil and new oil was not identical with an economic distinction between oil that would be produced at the ceiling and oil that would not be produced at that price. Moreover, freeing the domestic oil price after the oil embargo would have eliminated the need for allocations, would have discouraged oil consumption, and would have reduced oil imports. However, the officials feared the immediate effect on the price level if oil was decontrolled and worried about the example that might be set for other prices and the possible reaction of wages to a rise of energy costs. Also there was a strong sentiment in the country and in the Congress against any increase in oil prices.

The oil case illustrates the great tendency of price controllers to be obsessed with this week's price numbers and the inability of anyone to imagine and give adequate weight to the longer-run consequences of today's decisions. It also illustrates the danger that price controls will leave behind a residue which pollutes the economic environment for a long time. The leading example of this danger used to be the rent controls which persisted in many cities around the world after the 1914–1918 war and interfered for decades with the construction of new housing and the efficient use of old housing. But the continuation of oil price controls after other price controls were terminated in the United States in 1974 is probably a more serious example of the residual damage left behind by controls. Possibly we would have had oil price controls if there had not been general price controls, but that is quite uncertain. And if we had never had oil price controls, the economic history of the United States would have been quite different from what it was.

Why Controls Failed

The controls obviously failed in the sense that there was an acceleration of the inflation rate before they ended and an even greater acceleration afterwards. They failed for a number of reasons, some of which are common to most price control experiments, and some of which may have been unusual although not unique.

(1) The underlying rationale of the controls was faulty. If there is to be less inflation after a temporary price control system than before it, something must have changed during the controls period. The post-controls situation must be less inflationary than the precontrols situation was. The argument for the 1971–1974 controls was that they would exorcise the expectation of inflation and lead people to make smaller price and wage increases than they would otherwise have made in similar conditions. This is the rationale that is now being used to explain a temporary incomes policy. But in fact the controls and the incomes policy do not have that effect. They only create the expectation that when the controls, or the incomes policy, end prices will rise more rapidly.

(2) The controls were accompanied by a strongly expansionary fiscal and monetary policy, and in fact probably helped to make that policy more expansionary than it would otherwise have been. The economic officials of the time were aware of the fact that this had been the cause of the breakdown of controls and incomes policy systems in the past. Being aware of it, they thought they would avoid at least that error. But they did not. They were misled by the apparent success of the controls in their early months into thinking that there was more room for noninflationary expansion than there actually was.

Perhaps this is not an inherent defect of controls. But it has been encountered so often as to suggest that it is in fact an inescapable concomitant of controls, even if not a logical necessity. A government does not ordinarily get into controls in peacetime unless it feels a strong desire to pump up demand close to the inflationary danger point. And when prices are under control it becomes difficult to tell when the danger point is being neared.

(3) Prices began to rise sharply in two important sectors where controls are hardest to maintain even for a short while—raw agricultural products and imports. When these prices began to rise sharply it became very difficult to keep the rest of the price structure steady. Any practicable price control system will allow for the pass-through of cost increases, and wage controls will have to respond to the cost of living, so it is quite possible to have a cost-price spiral within the controls system if a few key prices go into motion exogenously. It may be said that the poor crops and the booming world markets were unfortunate accidents which need not have occurred, but they are the kinds of accidents that occur frequently.

(4) The controls failed because they were basically in conflict with the way the American public, or at least powerful forces within it, want the political economic system to work. This is true despite the majority that is commonly revealed by public opinion polls to be in favor of price and wage controls. Once the first flush of enthusiasm has passed, and controls became a matter of continuing regulation that is increasingly detailed, labor and business become more and more resentful and resistant, and a larger and more irritating bureaucratic machine is required in an effort to achieve compliance. This was most obvious in the case of the labor organizations. Although there never was any union defiance of the system, the labor leadership clearly felt that the controls had displaced them from their role as the source of wage increases for their members, and their continued cooperation could be obtained even for a while only by a significant relaxation of the controls. Also businesses were becoming more determined and skillful in trying to find their way through ambiguities and gaps in the regulations. An attempt to make the controls work in those conditions would have required the exercise of government power over the economy on a scale which hardly anyone wanted.

•   •   •

The history of 1971–1974 is not recounted as conclusive evidence that price and wage controls can never work in a beneficial way. To prove that would require much more historical evidence and analysis than is presented here.

The conclusions I draw from this history are much narrower. The first is that incautious actions and talk did a great deal to lead the country to a policy which hardly anyone had wanted—namely, mandatory controls. The actions included irresponsible provision of legal authority for controls and mild steps in the direction of incomes policy, which were intended to stave off demands for controls, but only sharpened the appetite for them. The talk consisted in part of overly optimistic predictions of the speed and ease with which inflation would be controlled, leading to disappointment with conventional policies when the predictions turned out to be wrong. The talk also included a flood of argument for nonmandatory incomes policy, which turned out to convince the public of the need for controls of some kind—the degree of coercion involved being a secondary consideration.

The second conclusion is that the generally acknowledged failure of the controls in 1971–1974 cannot be convincingly attributed to the lack of enthusiasm of those who ran the control system or other easily remediable deficiencies in the management of the system.

These conclusions suggest two lessons for today. We should not evaluate the possible use of controls under the impression that the difficulties previously experienced will be escaped if the controls are managed by different people or in a different way. More important, all steps taken in this field or words uttered should be carefully considered in the light of the expectations they will arouse, the options they will close, and the momentum they will generate in directions that are unintended.

5

THE COMMITMENT TO PERMANENT INFLATION

Karl Brunner

THE DRIFT INTO FINANCIAL MISMANAGEMENT

A period of remarkable economic stability ended in 1965. The United States experienced over twenty years a solid expansion of output and employment, in contrast to the gloomy predictions made at the end of the second world war. Bursts of inflation in 1951-1952 and 1955-57 were successfully contained by comparatively cautious financial policies. This heritage of a determined anti-inflationary policy was reenforced under the Kennedy Administration by an essentially modest and stable course of monetary and fiscal affairs. The price level remained practically constant and interest rates reflected the absence of inflation. The prime rate stayed around 4.5 per cent until the middle of the 1960s.

A new era opened beyond 1965. The United States entered the age of permanent inflation previously confined to the Latin-American scene. Our economy suffered in the last thirteen years four waves of inflation with increasing duration or magnitude (1965/66, 1967/69, 1972/74, 1976/?). On four occasions our monetary authorities (1966, 1969, 1971, 1974) substantially lowered monetary growth by design or accident. On each occasion the attempt at an anti-inflationary course in our policy was abandoned. Political pressures or serious misconceptions deeply embedded in the Fed's policy making procedures induced a reversal in policies. These reversals ended in every case the gradual decline of inflation and initiated a new surge of prices with a deeper commitment to permanent inflation. Our policies contributed in this manner to the emergence of a positive association, observed in the average over many years, between rising unemployment and inflation. The consequences of an essentially political failure to maintain an anti-inflationary monetary course over a substantial time horizon were increasingly interpreted as signs of an intractable inflationary process "anchored in our social structure."

Dr. Brunner is Director of the Center for Research in Government Policy and Business at the University of Rochester.

From Karl Brunner, "The Commitment to Permanent Inflation," in Center for the Study of American Business, *Alternative Policies to Combat Inflation* (1978). Reprinted by permission of the Center for the Study of American Business at Washington University in St. Louis.

At the time the Carter team shaped its policy programs in the fall of 1976 the rate of inflation had drifted to a level of about 4.5 per cent per annum and the dollar held firm on the foreign exchange markets. There appeared a growing chance of sustaining a rising hope that the prevailing course in our financial affairs would produce further reductions of inflation, halt the intermittent fall of the dollar and prevent a new surge of the (nominal) rates of interest on credit markets. But the Carter Administration wasted this opportunity. A persistent acceleration of monetary growth, contrasting (as usual) with the official rhetoric of the Federal Reserve authorities, and large uncertainties bearing on the magnitude of the budget and the deficit lowered the confidence in the U.S. dollar and unleashed new inflationary forces. Until the fall of 1978, the rate of inflation had almost doubled compared to its lowest level in 1976, and the debacle of the dollar on exchange markets evolved into a political embarrassment. The disarray in the financial affairs of the United States imposed serious burdens on foreign economies and produced pervasive uncertainties about U.S. policies and future U. S. postures. The international repercussions confronted economies with a bitter choice between large real burdens due to adjustments suffered by the export industries or the social costs associated with new waves of inflation produced by persistent and large scale interventions on exchange markets. The financial disarray was also reflected by the stagnation of the stock market. The signs of the Carter Administration's financial mismanagement thus multiplied. They eventually forced the attention of the White House to cope more directly with the persistent threat of inflation. The advisory huddle in the White House eventually produced an "anti-inflation program" announced by the President on October 24, 1978.

PRESIDENT CARTER'S ANTI-INFLATION
AND DOLLAR SUPPORT PROGRAMS

This announcement contained four parts with very different significance. It promised first to lower the increase in government expenditures and secondly to reduce the budget deficit. A third strand addresses a variety of measures designed to raise the efficiency of our resource-utilization patterns and to increase the growth rate of labor productivity. These measures are essentially directed to raise the competitive level of the U.S. economy, to lower the extent and magnitude of monopolistic shelters granted by a wide diversity of governmental arrangements and to remove governmental impositions enforcing an increasingly wasteful use of our resources. The last strand introduces "voluntary" guidelines for wage and price increases. These guidelines are linked with an expectation that Congress will legislate a subsidy to all workers (or employees?) accepting the limit of 7 per cent on their wage increases while suffering a higher rate of price inflation.

The announcement was not really a "non-event." Things did happen, but all the wrong way. The stock market responded with a drop in prices and the dollar slipped on the foreign exchanges. The only markets available to register voter reactions and public appraisals signaled a vote of "no confidence" to the White House. Their behavior revealed in the most unmistakable fashion that the President obtained and accepted bad advice in crucial matters of economic policy. A second huddle assembled hurriedly and produced an additional array of measures designed to "tighten money" and to reverse the drift of the dollar. A substantial increase by 1 percentage point in the discount rate and a supplementary reserve requirement on certificates of deposit, with large denominations impounding about $3 billion of bank reserves into required reserves, should convey the idea of a determined anti-inflationary shift in domestic monetary policy. These internal actions were reenforced with measures and operations directed to the exchange market. The Swap lines with the German, Japanese and Swiss Central Banks were dramatically extended. The U.S. Treasury envisaged borrowing foreign currency by the sale of special drawing rights. President Carter also announced substantially accelerated sales of gold from the Treasury's stocks and possible issues of U.S. debt instruments denominated in foreign currency. These "external measures" are designed to provide the foreign currency required for massive intervention on the foreign exchange market.

AN EVALUATION OF THE PROGRAM

The European response to the second White House huddle appeared remarkably positive. It seems generally conceded that the announcement on November 1 reveals, at long last, a major shift in the attitude and financial policy of the U.S. government. The bond market also signaled a positive evaluation. A consensus emerged over the subsequent days that the change in policies was significant enough to produce a recession next year with falling interest rates and a retardation in the momentum of price movements. This evaluation of President Carter's two packages is unfortunately somewhat erroneous and suffers from serious misconceptions about the events and the situation. I will argue that some measures misleadingly convey the impression of an anti-inflationary turn in monetary policy when actually no real evidence supports, so far (December 11), this contention. I will argue furthermore that the external measures exert, without a generally recognized and credible action by the Fed to maintain a lower rate of monetary growth, at most a temporary effect. Lastly, the domestic non-monetary approach to contain inflation is essentially irrelevant with respect to inflation and threatens us, in the absence of monetary control, with expanding controls over prices and wages, lowered welfare and a further loss of freedom.

Among the first lessons of economic analysis looms the recognition that the best intentions of policy programs yield no guarantee for their realization. The most adroit invocations with all the appropriate "McLuhanery" offers us no assurance that the explicitly described public goals are even roughly approximated in reality. Economic policy seems particularly prone to the negative association between intentions and outcome. It may suffice here to note the rhetoric and the facts bearing on the minimum wage legislation or the noteworthy and traditionally negative association between the Federal Reserve's words and actions.[1] The anti-inflation program presented by the President to the American public on October 24 and on November 1 thus deserves some careful examination.

Lower the Deficit

A persistent reduction in the budget deficit would certainly yield major benefits for our economy. The direct effect on inflation is however a negligible component of these benefits. Neither Keynesian nor monetarist analysis implies any significant impact on the ongoing *rates* of inflation. The encouragement to capital accumulation in the private sector seems the major gain obtained from a lower deficit. It reduces "crowding out" and shifts, over the longer horizon, the public's portfolio balance towards investments representing productive resources. The higher level of real growth associated with the expanded productive facilities raises over time our welfare but lowers the inflation rate by a negligible margin. An *indirect* effect of smaller deficits mediated by the Federal Reserve's traditional approach in terms of money market conditions may actually be more important with respect to inflation. A smaller deficit lowers pressures on interest rates and dampens political incentives to "monetize" portions of the Treasury's borrowing requirement. This mechanism, linking budget deficits and monetary growth, could inadvertently, without the Fed's deliberate intention and design, produce the crucial condition, i.e., a falling rate of monetary growth, causing a lasting and persistent decline of the rate of inflation. A non-inflationary control over monetary growth appears increasingly improbable as large deficits persist into the future. A reduction in the deficit does not assure, however, the required decline of monetary growth. Immediate and direct attention to monetary growth, so carefully avoided with great circumspection by President Carter, is still the best and most relevant guarantee of a truly anti-inflationary policy. Still, a determined decline in the deficit alleviates at least the political pressures of "accommodating monetization" and lessens the likelihood of rising monetary expansion.

And Budget Expenditures

The President's fiscal proposals foresee, beyond the compression of the deficit, moderation in the rate of increase of government expenditures. We obtain some sense in the matter with an appropriate modification of an old relation between money, expenditures and the value of output. We write for our purposes

$$MV + G = PY$$

where M denotes the money stock, V is the circuit velocity based on private sector expenditures, G expresses government outlay on goods and services in the national income account sense. The right side represents the value of output as a product of price level P and output Y.

Government expenditures are measured as a proportion g of private absorption of total output. We may thus write the approximation

$$\Delta \log M + \Delta \log V + \Delta g - \Delta \log Y = \Delta \log P$$

i.e., over the longer run the rate of inflation, $\Delta \log P$, equals the sum of monetary growth, the velocity trend, the trend in the proportion of government absorption minus normal output growth. A positive value of Δg thus raises the basic rate of inflation beyond the level determined by the rate of increase in private expenditures. A negative Δg on the other hand lowers the prevailing rate of inflation below the level adjusted to the expansion of private expenditures.

Consider, however, some further aspects in this matter. A single percentage point decline of g produces in the average a corresponding decline in log P. But this percentage point decline in g implies a reduction of approximately 4 percentage points in the rate of increase of government expenditures on goods and services below the rate determined by a constant g. In order to produce even a small effect on inflation, a substantial reduction of the government sector's real absorption would be required.

The President's plan foresees (possibly?) a total reduction of g by approximately 2 percentage points distributed over several years. This would lower by itself the average inflation rate at the very most by 1 percentage point per annum over this time period. But this negative Δg will occur as an essentially temporary event in the hope of confining the government sector's absorption to a lower proportion. Once this desired level of g is achieved Δg centers on zero and the temporary reduction of inflation evaporates. It seems quite unlikely that a negative Δg would prevail for many years. It seems also highly unlikely that any negative Δg would be (numerically) large enough to moderate the inherited inflation by any relevant fraction. The likelihood of a negative Δg could thus be expected under the best circumstances to lower the price level by less than 1 percentage point per annum over a few years. The President's emphasis on government expenditure is indeed most appropriate with respect to a more productive use of our resources and a correspondingly higher real income. But it seems an ineffective and cumbersome approach to curtail inflation.[2]

The most rapidly expanding component of budgetary expenditures has not been considered thus far. Transfer payments need particular attention. Their explosion affects the normal rate of unemployment; the incentive to work, and to invest in human and non-human capital; and in this manner they influence the average rate of output growth over the longer run. They do not affect per se the rate of monetary growth or the trend in velocity. A revision of the trend in transfer payments may thus importantly shape our longer run social welfare, but we cannot rationally expect from a lower expansion rate of social transfers any significant reduction of inflation. Any effect on inflation emerges as a counterpart to the increase in the long term growth of output produced by a revision of the transfer system. The cumulative impact on our general welfare may be substantial, however, even with a vanishing effect on the rate of inflation. This particular combination of events occurs in case the revision of the transfer system essentially induces a once-and-for-all effect on the productive use of our human and non-human resources.

Regulation, Competition and Productivity

The need to remove the many constraints imposed by government on the efficient use of our resources has attracted increasing attention in recent years. A new magazine addressed to the financial world recently argued that government regulation is the dominant cause of inflation in the United States: "The costs that have been imposed on private business, labor and agriculture under the rules of government regulation are a fundamental cause—conceivably the fundamental cause—of inflation."[3] The President and his adviser also seem to believe that measures designed to raise competitive levels and increase productivity by removing obstructive regulations and wasteful impositions effectively lowers inflation. But this approach to cope with our inflationary experiences is again futile. It fails to distinguish between once-and-for-all consequences on the price level and persistent effects on the rate of inflation. It fails moreover to assess adequately the relevant orders of magnitude. A successful removal of obstacles to productivity would probably raise both the *level* of productivity and the longer run *rate* of growth in productivity. The level effect permanently lowers the price level relative to any given monetary stock and appears in form of a *temporary* decline of the inflation rate. The longer run effect lowers on the other hand the prevailing rate of inflation by an amount equal to the increase in the normal growth rate of output. It appears in my judgment highly unlikely that the President's plan would lower inflation via this route by anything even approximating 1 percentage point. But the welfare implications produced by an "opening of the economy" to more efficient production processes exceed by a wide margin the negligible impact on inflation. The once-and-for-all level effect supplemented by the long run effect on productivity growth would raise real income over the years substantially beyond the level otherwise achieved.

The Guidelines

But what about the "non-control" guidelines imposed on price and wage setting of the private sector? Political processes exhibit an inherent propensity to respond to inflationary waves with an array of specific political institutions recorded under a shifting set of names (controls, income policy, guideline, etc.). This disposition is particularly remarkable as no evidence would seriously support the contention that "income policies" ever exhibited much success measured in terms of the anti-inflationary intentions or rhetoric in the absence of adequate monetary controls. Controls over prices and wages by themselves never moderated the rate of inflation beyond a shorter period without unleashing over time rising social costs and a loss of freedom. The experience accumulated with controls from diverse historical conditions overwhelmingly establishes their ineffectiveness as anti-inflationary instruments and their dangers to our welfare. The impairment of welfare follows from their effect on the use of our resources. The more stringent and "effective," at least in intention, the controls are designed, the greater loom losses in welfare associated with the resulting distortions in resource utilization patterns. Controls systematically obstruct the adjustment of relevant prices and costs to underlying market conditions. This obstruction distorts the pattern of resource utilization away from the optimal usages approached by the operation of open markets.

Stringent controls create moreover socially undesirable short and long run incentives on the supply side. A persistent inability to adjust prices to the realities of the market place fosters implicit rationing schemes. Personal idiosyncracies, personal and political connections, political weight, and the skill to manipulate non-market institutions or non-market relations tend to determine under the circumstances the suppliers' rationing behavior. The "controlled" price raises in particular the cost of search and transacting exchanges to the consumer. The resulting arrangements imply a shift from wealth maximizing behavior by business firms (executives) to behavior more attentive to the executives' utility-maximization. This involves a redistribution of wealth from owners and employers to the management level and selected customer groups. This redistribution offers no incentives for productive applications of resources.

This effect is reenforced by repercussions affecting shorter run supply patterns bearing on quantity and quality. The constraints on price adjustments direct attention to costs of production and the nature of the production process. Adjustments are thus concentrated on lowering the quality of the product. There also emerges under the circumstances a strong incentive to invest in political activities designed to influence the political institutions surrounding or representing the control apparatus. Such investments produce at a positive *social* cost, a positive (expected) *private* gain but actually yield a vanishing *social* product. We obtain thus a classic case of negative externalities and "market failures" imposed by policy arrangements. The nature of this externality reflects the loss of welfare associated with a socially wasteful use of resources induced by the political institution. The political reality surrounding the control apparatus increasingly exploits these arrangements for purposes of a politically manipulated redistribution of wealth with little concern or interest for the initial and official purpose of "inflation controls." The social cost of "political investments" tend to be reenforced by pervasive incentives to search for means circumventing the prevailing mode of controls via adjustments in product classifications, production operations or marketing and exchange arrangements. But such adjustments require the investment of valuable resources and impose a social cost. Controls also lower the incentive to invest and explore new productive opportunities. Evaluations of investment projects involve returns and costs over a larger horizon. The administration of controls unavoidably produces a diffuse uncertainty and a pronounced instability pertaining to the rules of the game confronting the private sector. The assessment of future returns and costs associated with any given project becomes substantially more risky. Business will be increasingly more hesitant under the circumstances to commit resources for projects with longer horizons. The volume of investments enlarging our productive potential thus stagnates and the rate of normal growth declines. We note in summary that the consequences of an anti-inflationary approach based on controls essentially threatens to offset any gains potentially achievable by attempts to raise efficiency and productivity via "deregulation." The reality of controls will suffocate the promise to raise the competitive edge and to improve the use of our resources.[4]

Three aspects associated with the current control program should also be noted in this context. The program was presented as a voluntary exercise in self-restraint addressed to the private sector. This emphasis suffers however under the fraudulent language pervading the political market place.[5] The legal form and legal basis of the controls is of comparatively minor importance in this context. The relevant conditions confronting the producers in the private sector are reflected by the actual cost of non-compliance. Business firms failing to cooperate and comply may expect "attentive treatment" by a wide range of federal agencies well beyond any procurement offices. It seems most likely under the present circumstances that "voluntary controls" or guidelines really involve substantial cost of non-compliance for large and well-known corporations.[6] Smaller and particularly non-corporate business or agricultural producers will hardly be seriously troubled by the guidelines. The cost of non-compliance is probably sufficient for most of the large corporations to assure some measure of careful cooperation. For this group in our economy guidelines are for all practical purposes essentially similar to mandatory controls. It follows therefore that the consequences of controls traced in a previous paragraph would gradually appear with the lapse of time in this range of our economy. But the effect on inflation still remains quite negligible. The inflation, represented by *general* price movements, continues in accordance with the momentum of private expenditures dominated by the monetary growth produced by our Federal Reserve authorities. Obstructions on price adjustments in the controlled corporate subsector lower the *relative* prices of this subsector without significantly modifying the *general* movement. Prices in non-controlled sectors respond with a correspondingly greater speed and magnitude as expenditures shift from the controlled to the non-controlled sector. The current program thus imposes social costs to no avail with respect to our crucial malady.

The subsidy proposal included in the President's program deserves some passing attention. Suppose monetary growth continues to raise the level of inflation substantially beyond 7 per cent per annum. The proposal currently provides about $9 billion worth of subsidies to employees for every percentage point that the rate of inflation exceeds the benchmark. At a rate of inflation of 9 per cent per annum, government expenditures would rise by roughly $18 billion. The effect on the budget deficit seems obvious.

The Rationale of Ineffectual Anti-Inflation Policies

The remarkable irrelevance of the President's explicit proposals and argument as an anti-inflation program requires some examination. The explanation lies probably with a mixture of various beliefs about the nature of the inflation process combined with a specific perception of the White House team concerning the comparative political advantages associated with different policy options.

The President's presentation of the anti-inflation program on television contained a noteworthy imputation of responsibilities. He claimed credit for his Administration having raised the level of employment and lowered the rate of unemployment. The responsibility for inflation was subtly assigned to the private sector. There appeared some acknowledgment that government may contribute to inflation only via purchases, public employee wage settlements, higher taxes, and the Federal Reserve push on interest rates. But the context and tone of the presentation clearly conveyed to the listeners that the private sector dominates the mass of transactions unfolding in the economy, and consequently bears the crucial responsibility for the evolving price-wage patterns. Inflation, in the President's view of the world, forms a social problem essentially caused by the private sector independent of monetary policy and just marginally related to the government's fiscal affairs expressed by the direct impact on output and labor markets. This vision of the inflation problem naturally produces a program assigning some *minor* significance to the budget, *no* significance and *no* attention to monetary policy, with *most* of the attention expressing the "Moses syndrome," i.e., exhibiting a disposition to wave a stick to make the surrounding world behave according to one's enlightened insights. Controls of one sort or another are the natural consequence of this vision. The prevalent semi-socialist conceptions cultivated by members of the Carter team on operational levels in various departments influence moreover the direction of controls and their concentration on the "corporate sector" of the economy.[7] This concentration is reenforced by administrative advantages of the procedure. Lastly, the governing perception explains the ingrained failure to appreciate the real effects of controls occurring in various disguises.

The view from the White House overlaps with the "sociological conception" of inflation extensively used by the intelligentsia (exemplified by the *New York Times),* cultivated by sociologists, and argued by large groups of economists in Europe and even in the United States. Inflation appears in this vision as the necessary outcome of social factors and processes deeply embedded in the contemporary social structure. Inflation is governed according to this conception by an autonomous social process essentially independent of monetary and fiscal policy.[8] Lower monetary growth is useless under the circumstances and harmful in terms of our welfare. It lowers employment, raises unemployment and forces output into stagnation without lowering inflation. The only solution lies in a re-form of the social structure associated with a new array of political institutions controlling price and wage setting. Such a view would support the President's guidelines and confirm a policy of mandatory controls, but hardly approve or find relevant the proposals bearing on the budget. Some versions of the "socio-logical approach," however, seem to offer support for a shot-gun approach to the inflation problem. A diffuse social process with pervasive and uncertain ramifications in all directions may suggest that random combinations of larger and larger programs raise the likelihood of "doing the right thing."[9]

There is a third and distinct view vaguely centered around the Brookings Institution, which also provides an intellectual basis for the President's anti-inflation program. This view recognizes that in the long run monetary growth dominates the average rate of price movements via the momentum of private ex-penditures. The relevant time horizon seems to involve, according to this view, an extended calendar time reaching probably up to ten years. Within this extended time horizon price levels move for appearances in autonomous fashion. Prices move over the shorter run, so it appears, independently of monetary evolution. General price movements are controlled by an inertial process subject to inter-mittent explosions. It is fully acknowledged that a lower monetary growth would *eventually* reduce the prevailing rate of inflation. But the time required is judged to be *very* long and certainly *beyond* any "realistic political considerations." The responsiveness of inflation to lower monetary growth is not conditioned in this view by the history of inflationary policies and the credibility of anti-inflationary policies. Any attempt to combat inflation with lowered monetary growth pro-duces under the circumstances a serious and persistent loss of output, a fall in employment and a heavy burden of unemployment. An anti-inflationary policy executed via control over monetary growth implies a protracted recession with a heavy loss of welfare. The argument concludes that a wiser course avoids mone-tary contraction or fiscal restrictions. A policy of permanent inflation supple-mented with an array of political institutions shaping, guiding, supervising, "con-trolling" or "advising" the private sector's price-wage behavior appears therefore more appealing. This recommendation is moreover supported by the claim that the social cost of a policy of permanent inflation is really quite negligible.

A Critique of Some Views of the Inflation Process

The three views summarized in previous paragraphs are fundamentally flawed. The first two conceptions are in conflict with the best established parts of economic analysis. The claim to a total autonomy of price movements independ-ent of monetary growth is substantially disconfirmed by evidence from many different countries or historical episodes, based on data generated under widely different institutional arrangements. We note in particular that upon careful examination most of these views yield no explanation of relative magnitude or direction of inflationary movement. They offer essentially untestable *ex post facto* interpretations which fail to satisfy basic requirements of a relevant scientific hypothesis.[10]

Attempts to explain inflation in terms of money wages offer some instructive material in this respect. Both wages and prices respond to underlying real and nominal shocks. With real shocks dominated by nominal shocks wages and prices jointly and simultaneously reflect the dominant monetary impulse. Occasional perturbations in real conditions produce, on the other hand, as the French episode of 1968 vividly protrayed, a wedge between price and wage movements. It follows thus that in either case, i.e., in situations accompanied by real shocks, or in states experiencing overwhelming nominal impulses, money wages yield no satisfactory explanation of the inflation phenomenon. The correlation between wages and prices substantially breaks down in the first case. This failure of correlation reveals the causal irrelevance of wages per se and reflects the prevailing pressures of nominal impulses on price movements.[11] It also reveals that the solid correlation between wages and prices observed in the second case simply results from the simultaneous adjustments of these variables to the driving causal force expressed by the nominal impulse.

Some major observation patterns cannot be reconciled with the sociological approach without adjustments destroying all relevant content. We observe for instance in all countries major surges of accelerating price movements and extended phases of substantial retardations. We also observe large variations in observed inflation across time between countries. Any procedure which reduces this variety, in the absence of real perturbations, to wages or unit labor costs is essentially equivalent to an explanation of inflation in terms of inflation. We are thus offered words with essentially no explanatory power. The sweeping array of "sociological ideas" fares not much better. It fails to cope with the observed patterns for a simple but basic reason: The occurrence and magnitude of inflation is essentially random with respect to any of the social entities ever adduced in this context. Inflationary experiences are on the other hand *not* randomly associated with the evolution of monetary growth. In particular, no inflation ever emerged without prior monetary acceleration and no inflation was ever curbed without a lower level of monetary growth. We should note in a similar vein that the variations in the rate of inflation across and over time are not randomly related to corresponding differences in monetary evolution.

The third view requires separate examination. It suffers from a faulty perception of the shorter run aspects of the inflation processes and the failure to link the alleged shorter run autonomy of price movements with the longer run conditioning by monetary growth. It fails lastly with a thoroughly inadequate analysis of the social costs associated with a policy of permanent inflation.

The first two failures follow from an inadequate analysis of the private sector's price and wage setting practices. These practices occur in a social context conditioned by systematic evaluations on the part of economic agents of the policy regime prevailing in the future. It follows that the responsiveness of inflation to variations in monetary growth depends on the length and magnitude of observed inflation, the frequency of aborted anti-inflationary policies and the magnitude or speed of experienced reversals in policy to a renewed inflationary course. The responsiveness of inflation to a lower monetary growth depends thus in general on the inferences made by economic agents pertaining to the prevailing inter- action of transitory and permanent real and nominal shocks operating on the economy. This inference is influenced by the observations noted above and other information signalling the nature of a policy regime. This analysis implies that the course of our policies, followed over thirteen years, systematically *weakened* the responsiveness of inflation to a *lower* monetary growth. It also *accelerated* the responsiveness of inflation to *rising* monetary growth. The increasing ap- pearance of relative shorter run autonomy of price movements with respect to monetary evolution should be recognized as the rational outcome of a policy implicitly committed to permanent inflation expressed by a long run pattern of monetary accelerations, interrupted by intermittent phases of retardation. This argument implies furthermore that the social cost of an effective anti-inflationary policy persistently rises over time with the accrual of information confirming the commitment to permanent inflation. This social cost is not a constant deter- mined by an autonomous social structure. It is largely the consequence of the policies pursued over a longer horizon. These policies, however, also affect the other side of the ledger. A commitment to permanent inflation also raises over time the social cost of this commitment. Advocates of permanent inflation typically assign comparatively small significance to such costs. We are told that "many Harberger triangles cover a single Okun gap." The social cost caused by permanent inflation is thus attributed purely to the welfare loss associated with smaller real balances.[12] But the welfare loss of a steady and fully anticipated infla- tion forms just one component of the total loss of an actual state of permanent inflation. The welfare loss derived from lower real balances is supplemented by cost components associated with an erratic and unpredictable pattern of infla- tionary policies.

An accommodating policy of persistent inflation introduces pervasive incen- tives into the social system to explore opportunities for accelerating wage and price setting as a means of competitive wealth transfers. A policy of permanent inflation encourages general expectations that the emerging price-wage patterns will be validated in the average. Such explorations in price-wage policies exploit the political process to produce under appropriate pressures an accommodating stance in financial policies. It follows under the circumstances that a permanent policy of accommodating inflation will experience repeated waves of increased inflation. Every surge in price movements introduces new political opportunities and raises political rewards for the supply of "leadership in the fight against inflation." This pattern has been observed on repeated occasions and all over the world. The resulting shifts in financial policies unleash unavoidable retardations of economic activity expressed by a decline in output and rising unemployment. A policy of permanent inflation produces, therefore, sequences of substantially accelerated price movements interrupted by retardations with declines in output and higher unemployment. An accommodating inflation policy may thus easily produce two or three recessions, combined with continued inflation, over a span of ten to fifteen years. The current value of the costs determined by the future series of recessions forms an important component in the relevant social cost of permanent inflation. This series may already balance the social cost of a determined policy designed to lower monetary growth gradually and predictably over four to five years.[13]

The erratic course of monetary policy characteristically associated with a regime of permanent inflation raises the level of uncertainty in the economy. The penumbra of risk associated at any moment with future returns and costs resulting from longer range projects substantially increases under the circumstances. The basic uncertainty operating on the social system as a result of the real shocks unleashed by nature, including the tastes and propensities of people revealed on the market, are augmented by additional uncertainties attributable to the behavior of specific socio-political institutions centered on the Central Bank. The higher level of risk affects investment and lowers capital accumulation and retards the expansion of productive capacity. This disincentive effect may be reenforced by the expectation of a systematic increase in the marginal effective tax rate produced by permanent inflation.

Another dimension of uncertainty produced by a regime of permanent inflation deserves some attention. Some recent work indicates a positive association between the dispersion of individual prices and the general rate of inflation. But the greater dispersion generated by larger inflation lowers the information level of economic agents and raises the cost of acquiring given information levels about market conditions. Households will find it advisable to invest more time, effort and resources to search and sample their potential opportunities. The larger shifts in relative prices expressed by an increasing price dispersion also induces more social tension and a greater disposition for social conflicts. More rapidly or more widely shifting relative prices involve a quick decay of accumulated information capital and impose heavier and unexpected adjustments on various social groups. The widening price dispersion means substantial wealth transfers between shifting social groups. The social tensions fostered by this process are not based on systematic transfers between broad groups, e.g., "labor" and "capital." The transfers are almost randomly distributed between many smaller and changing groups. This random impact is particularly prone to encouraging diffuse social unrest and tension.

The permissive regime of permanent inflation may also contribute to raise the average (i.e., normal) rate of unemployment. A pattern of accommodating policies unleashes incentives fostering aggressive wage setting policies. With given expectations about monetary accommodations, aggressive wage settlements become an instrument of shorter run wealth transfers. Organized suppliers are systematically induced to overestimate the most probable degree of accommodation and risk some measure of additional unemployment. The possible wealth transfer still affects a large majority of the organized suppliers and the social cost of the unemployed minority is shifted via the welfare system to the rest of the community.

The social costs resulting from an open inflation do not exhaust the problem. The discussion, presented in a previous section, of the real effects associated with controls over prices and wages circumscribes the nature of the additional costs. These costs emerge in summary as a consequence of the distortions in the utilization of resources, augmented by the effect on the short run supply of output in terms of quality and quantity, reenforced by the allocation of resources of the political process involving a (socially) negative sum game of redistributive conflicts, and lastly, supplemented by the effect on the longer run growth of output.

The social cost of permanent inflation follows thus from two major facts: first, the observed variability of inflation and monetary growth produced by the nature of the political process, and secondly, the observed disposition of the political process to respond to intermittent accelerations of price movements with controls. These facts appear to be disregarded by the advocates of permanent inflation and the omission explains their casual treatment of the social cost emanating from their policies. It would appear that decades of Keynesian macrotheory clogged the vision with respect to the consequences on the supply side caused by persistent or even intermittent controls. My argument thus tentatively suggests that the comparison of a modest "Harberger triangle" with a yawning Okun gap misses the crucial point. The relevant juxtaposition seems more appropriately between a single Okun gap associated with a determined non-inflationary policy of stable monetary growth on the one side and a multiplicity of Okun gaps augmented with other social costs on the other side.

We should note lastly that in a policy regime governed by a mixture of the three views presented above, policy makers increasingly lock their economies into a pattern of permanent inflation. There emerges an apparent intractability "deeply anchored in a complex social nexus beyond the reach of shallow (or superficial) financial manipulation." But this intractability is not imposed by an autonomous social fate. It is produced by the policy regime and can be broken by a determined and credible return to a well-controlled monetary growth. And whatever the level to which the social cost of anti-inflationary policies drift as a result of the previous long-time mismanagement, the social cost of permanent inflation probably drifts even higher. But the selective myopia fostered by the incentive system prevailing in the political process, so clearly represented by the Carter team, discounts heavily the future cost accruing from the permanent inflation and concentrates on avoidance of the contemporary short run cost of an effective anti-inflationary policy. This vision influences the "program" offered by the President, a program disregarding monetary policy and offering the appearance of judicious and concerned leadership. Once the unavoidable failure of such a program becomes generally acknowledged on the public scene the President may safely invoke either one of the first two views of the inflation process and accuse the private sector of "social betrayal" or "inadequate cooperation" in the government's attempt to cope with inflation. Mandatory controls supplemented probably with controls over interest rates and bank credit will be imposed under the circumstances and possibly presented at the time as the "moral equivalent of war" (or the "energy crisis"). And so we would gradually sink ever deeper into the Latin-American swamp.

What About the Discount Rate and Reserve Requirements?

Some readers may object and insist that a turn in the trend of monetary policy has been clearly signaled. The discount rate was raised by a whole percentage point and supplementary reserve requirements on certificates of deposit with large denominations were introduced. The change in the discount rate was indeed large by historical standards and the reserve policy action lowers the monetary base (by itself alone) by about $3 billion. These measures mean unfortunately very little by themselves. The growth rate in the monetary base could still move in any direction and even accelerate very sharply. Large shifts of Treasury funds from the Federal Reserve Banks to commercial banks or substantial open market purchases could raise the growth of the base in spite of the revised discount rate. They could furthermore easily overwhelm and more than offset the action bearing on reserve requirements. There is no real indication at this time (December 15, 1978) that the Federal Reserve shifted gears to a lower trend in the monetary base. Such a change is not impossible and appropriate evidence may emerge by the end of this year. The lower monetary growth would produce a recession reaching into the year 1980 with initially small effect on inflation. The longer the Fed delays in effective control over monetary growth, the more probably the consequences of the resulting recession threaten to determine the climate of the Presidential election in 1980. The probability of moderating monetary growth thus declines as the winter of 1978/79 progresses. In case the Fed actually reduces monetary growth, however, contrary to all the impressions conveyed by the Carter team, then all the available evidence from history and the nature of the policy institution suggests that policy will be reversed to an inflationary course within three quarters under the increasing pressure of political apprehension fostered by the incipient recession.

The Fed's traditional interpretation of monetary affairs justifies some reservations pertaining to the emergence of any significant action lowering monetary growth. This interpretation was usually geared to the level of short term interest rates. Low interest rates were always understood to reveal substantially expansionary policies. More expansionary policies were generally indicated by lower rates. The Federal Reserve authorities thus concluded in 1930 that a highly expansionary policy had actually been initiated to counteract the cyclic decline. The same behavior and interpretation persisted over the decades into this year. The Federal Reserve authorities reenforced in the spring and summer of 1978 the media's impression that monetary policy moved on a comparatively restrictive course. The facts were unfortunately just the opposite of the traditional interpretation. During 1930 monetary growth receded and revealed a weakening monetary thrust in a downward sliding economy. A similar pattern occurred in 1960, whereas in the current year, monetary growth accelerated when policy was claimed to have become more restrictive. Our experience demonstrates moreover that monetary accelerations yield a much closer approximation to the monetary thrust exerted on the economy than the level of interest rates. But the Federal Reserve authorities still believe at the moment that they shifted to a cautiously moderated policy in early November. The rapid increase in short term rates in October and early November is, however, quite consistent with even an accelerated monetary thrust expressed by a rising trend in the growth of the monetary base. We note here in passing the consensus appearing among financial analysts. This consensus accepts the Fed's accustomed interpretation and expects therefore that the economy will slide during 1979 into a recession irrespective of monetary evolutions. This perspective is however fundamentally faulty.[14]

The External Measures and the Support of the Dollar

The reservations noted in previous sections with respect to the domestic program announced on October 24 seem well correlated with the "voting responses" on dollar and stock market. This positive correlation does not extend to the range of external measures announced on November 1 and addressed to the support of the dollar on the exchange markets. Whatever the detailed differences in the technical execution of the various measures, they all share a common strand. They are uniformly addressed to modify the relative stock demand for and stock supply of foreign currencies in terms of dollars. The common strand may also be stated as a means to influence the relative stock demand for and stock supply of dollars. This modification of relative demand and supply is executed in order to offset market induced shifts on relative demand (or relative supply) and thus to contain the resulting price movements.

The case of the Swap arrangements may be used to elaborate the point. The monetary base and the money stock expand in Germany whenever the Fed draws on its Swap line at the Bundesbank. The monetary base in the United States remains on the other hand unaffected under the standard procedure. This result offsets the experienced increase in the world demand for D-Mark, and the dollar price of D-Marks is held near the inherited level. The use of an IMF loan would actually reenforce the relative shifts in stock supplies, as the operation per se would simultaneously raise foreign money stocks and lower the U.S. monetary aggregates. Similar patterns hold for selling special drawing rights, gold or the issue of U.S. debt denominated in foreign currency.

The crucial aspect of these operations is their essentially transitory character. They could be accepted as rational procedures under two circumstances. We may suspect that the exchange markets suffered a transitory shock since the fall of 1977, raising for a short period the relative demand for foreign currency (or lowering the relative demand for dollars). One would rationally expect in this case that the pressure on the dollar vanishes in due course. The external measures initiated by the U.S. government express in this case the determination of an official speculator to stabilize the price over the transitory shock. Official counterspeculation is particulary designed under the circumstances to penalize the private speculators producing or magnifying the transitory pressures. An entirely different situation prevails on the other hand in case exchange markets reflect a permanent drift conditioned by underlying nominal or real shocks. The operations executed under the external measures are designed under the circumstances to prevent a further fall in the price of the dollar in the *expectation* that suitable policies modify the underlying conditions causing the drift. In particular, this would mean that monetary growth and the budget deficit be permanently lowered in the United States, or that other countries (most particularly Germany, Japan and Switzerland) *permanently raise* their money growth and budget deficits. Such modification in the basic conditions shaping the "permanent drift" of exchange markets affects the dollar probably with some delays. Market participants would hardly change portfolio commitments without some credible signals bearing on the change in circumstances in the United States or abroad. The external measures offer thus an opportunity to shift the eventual outcome on the dollar market forward in time. The *expected* change in relevant policy conditions converts the *current* pressure into a *transitory* deviation rationally offset by the external measures.

The crucial question bears of course on the nature of the underlying forces shaping the drift in the exchange markets. Unfortunately, we do not possess any firm knowledge in this matter. We have no evidence or relevant information suggesting that we should assign substantial credence only to the assumption of a transitory shock requiring no further adjustments in our financial policies. A rational course should attend under the circumstances of diffuse uncertainty to the control of monetary growth and the budget deficit in the United States. As the winter passes and no relevant signals of the necessary revisions in U.S. financial affairs emerge, the dollar market will reveal a new wave of doubt. This development will raise the domestic political pressure in West Germany, Japan and Switzerland, encouraging the return to the inflationary course imposed by the U.S. government on the world. The dollar may ultimately be "saved" by a concurrent and general policy of inflation and *not* by the "leadership of November 1."

FINAL REMARKS

In the days following the second package announced on November 1, officials of the Carter Administration assured the public that their anti-inflation program is the "only way." The alternatives are either recession or mandatory and sweeping controls. This line is fraudulent or illusionary. The juxtaposition between "recession or guideline programs" misleads attention. There is indeed only one way to lower inflation and that is to lower monetary growth over a long time. This instrument of an effective anti-inflationary policy unfortunately induces a temporary recession. But a policy of permanent inflation supplemented with incantations and partially mandatory and unpredictable controls (i.e., guidelines) yields the social costs associated with erratic inflation, sluggish output and higher normal unemployment. The promise of permanent inflation at a negligible social cost is a dangerous illusion or an irresponsible fraud committed on the public.

The juxtaposition between voluntary guidelines and mandatory controls also obscures the relevant issues. It obscures the fact that guidelines are in reality *selectively* applied *mandatory* controls. Moreover, these guidelines will fail in a context of permanent inflation policies. Such failure leads unavoidably, as a result of the persistent refusal to adjust our financial affairs to the requirements of a noninflationary course, to *sweeping* mandatory controls. We should hope that the American public eventually rebels against the persistent irresponsibility of our financial policies which endanger our economic welfare and ultimately our basic freedom.

NOTES

1. The reader is referred for a detailed documentation of this point to the study jointly prepared in 1964 with Allan H. Meltzer on "Federal Reserve Monetary Policy-Making." The study was published by the Committee on Currency and Banking, U.S. House of Representatives.

2. It may be that the anti-inflationary rhetoric is considered a useful means to overcome the political opposition to "budget tightening."

3. Louis Kohlmeier, "New Analysis of Regulation as Fundamental Inflation Cause," *Financier,* September 19, 1978. The thesis advanced makes little sense. It means that regulations simply raise nominal costs, i.e., prices of inputs, without change in the real cost of production. "Regulation inflation" is then simply a special case of "cost-push inflation." But this is hardly the relevant issue. The range of government activities alluded to actually does raise real costs and this implies a fall in the level and growth rate of normal output. The effect *raises* the *price level* in proportion to the fall in the level of normal output and also raises the *rate* of inflation according to the lower rate of real growth.

4. Marxist or socialist intellectuals occasionally claim that inflation reflects the "inherent contradictions and the basic vulnerability" of capitalism. Socialist economies experience either, as in the case of Yugoslavia, a permanent inflation at a rate exceeding the corresponding magnitude in most Western countries, or suffer from all the symptoms of severely repressed inflation. An excellent article in the *Neue Zurcher Zeitung* from December 9, 1978 summarizes the state prevailing in Eastern Europe with the following points.

    i) There occurs a substantial volume of "forced savings." Price controls imply that portions of the income cannot be used to acquire goods. The marginal price becomes "infinite."
    ii) Large differences between unregulated prices (e.g., on the "peasant markets") and regulated prices
    iii) The pervasive existence of long queues
    iv) Prepayments with long waiting periods for durable goods
    v) A pervasive occurrence of side payments
    vi) Special supplies in special stores for privileged groups

5. A revealing event occurred in early December on some television program. A commentator discussed judiciously and earnestly the difficulties encountered with the *enforcement* of *voluntary* controls. At least in terms of "newspeak" we are proceeding well on our Orwellian time schedule.

6. A useful description of the political mechanism governing the cost of non-compliance can be found in an article published in the *Wall Street Journal* on November 29, 1978, by Congressman Clarence J. Brown on "The Servility of Business." We note in particular: "The excuse for such

pusillanimity (by the business sector) is that the 15 foot shelf of Federal regulations passed by Congress has put a vast arsenal of weapons for punishment in any administration's hand."

7. Senator McGovern argued in the late fall of 1978 on television that the Democratic Party should make inflation its own issue. He proposed in particular that mandatory controls be imposed on the "corporate sector." We encounter here a remarkable example of how the political scene favoring "some anti-inflationary" action can be exploited for substantial changes of the "system."

8. Mr. Kahn seems to advance such a view: "Mr. Kahn sees inflation as a fundamental social problem. . . ." "'Inflation is a symptom and a reflection of a society that is . . . in a state of dissolution. . . .'" *Wall Street Journal,* December 11, 1978.

9. This position seems to describe Robert Nathan's view when he pleaded in the discussion that the President's program should be given a chance.

10. The reader will find a more detailed argument in my forthcoming paper "The Political Economy of Inflation: A Critique of the Sociological Approach to Inflation." The fact that many of these ideas and formulations yield no propositions about the very phenomenon under consideration is particularly noteworthy.

11. It is occasionally argued that "correlation does not establish causation." Indeed, but it seems overlooked that every causal hypothesis implies the occurrence of specific correlation patterns. The observed absence of such correlation patterns thus disconfirms quite unambiguously the causal hypothesis. The reader is also referred to the Carnegie-Rochester Volume 9 on Public Policy. The chapter on the French inflation is particularly instructive in this context.

12. Martin Feldstein recently objected in an unpublished paper that the traditional computation overlooks that the welfare loss should be considered as a stream over time and should be properly discounted. The relevant net discount factor is the time discount minus the rate of real growth. Feldstein thus concludes that the traditional argument severely underestimates the resulting welfare loss of a steady and fully anticipated inflation.

13. One may object that the comparison is incomplete. Fluctuations in output and unemployment under permanent inflation should be compared with similar fluctuations emerging in the absence of inflation. This is, however, not the relevant comparison. We need to compare the real fluctuations produced by shifting nominal impulses typically associated with the alternative policy regimes. The crucial point emphasized in the text is the comparatively higher variance of monetary growth under a regime of permanent inflation. The almost explicit refusal by the Federal Reserve authorities to consider monetary control or implement appropriate control procedure, combined with the Fed bureaucracy's traditional notions, will most probably produce an erratic course of permanent inflation.

14. The institutional innovations of the recent past lower substantially the information content of the traditionally measured monetary aggregates M_1 and M_2. The evolution of "overnight-repos" between banks and corporations and the development of NOW accounts or AFT accounts obscures the significance of some published data. The monetary base is, however, not affected by these developments. But rational policy making would require a thorough overhaul of the Fed's concepts and measurement procedures.

Section

II

Regulation
and
Deregulation

6

THE COSTS AND BENEFITS
OF MOTOR TRUCK REGULATION

John R. Felton

It is no secret that government regulation is not generally held in high esteem by the business community. There is one kind of regulation, however, which has earned the dogged support of at least one segment of that community. Specifically, the regulated highway carriers of freight are ardent proponents of continued economic regulation of the trucking industry. Virtually every issue of *Transport Topics,* the weekly news publication of the American Trucking Associations, contains one or more accounts of the activities of the "deregulators" who seek to plunge the industry into chaos and confusion.

There are a number of reasons for believing that economic regulation of the trucking industry increases the social costs of freight transport while conferring meager benefits in the process. This article explores the rationale for such a prediction and endeavors to measure the costs and benefits attributable to the regulation of the trucking industry in the United States.

THE COSTS OF TRUCK REGULATION: A PRIORI CONSIDERATIONS

A priori reasoning would suggest that inefficiencies engendered by economic regulation of motor freight transport have their genesis in entry controls, rate regulation, and limitations on the activities of exempt agricultural and private carriers. Each of these sources of prospective cost enhancement will be considered in turn.

Entry Controls

To engage in the interstate highway transportation of freight, other than unmanufactured agricultural commodities, a prospective for-hire highway carrier requires the prior approval of the Interstate Commerce Commission. There is little reason to believe, however, that limitation upon entrance into the industry, without more, would increase carrier costs or even the rates for carrier services. First, there are some 16,000 interstate common carriers in the United States [1, p. 16]. Second, despite extensive market segmentation by

From John R. Felton, "The Costs and Benefits of Motor Truck Regulation," 2(18) *Quarterly Review of Economics and Business*, pp. 7-20 (Summer 1978). Copyright 1978 by the Bureau of Economic and Business Research. Reprinted by permission.

commodity and origin-destination pairs, trucking company resources are inherently very mobile; the unspecialized nature of a large percentage of the vehicles plus their geographic mobility make intermarket transference an ever present possibility. Third, unlike highway carrier regulation in some European countries, American regulation does not limit individual firm investment; therefore, an increase in the size of existing firms is an alternative to the entrance of new firms. Fourth, empirical studies, almost without exception, have concluded that highway freight transportation is an industry of constant returns to scale. As a consequence, the growth of existing firms should not occasion higher costs.

In order for economic regulation to attenuate highway carrier competition, then, it must supplement restrictions on entrance into the industry with restrictions on entrance into particular markets. This it accomplishes by limiting the commodities which a carrier may transport; the points, terminal and intermediate, which it may serve; and the route or routes which it may traverse. An unintended side effect, however, is to increase carrier costs by reducing the average number of tons per load and increasing the circuity of truck movements.

Rate Regulation

As if entry controls were insufficient to curtail the inherent competitiveness of the trucking industry, Congress also saw fit to legalize motor carrier rate bureaus, as well as to confer upon the Interstate Commerce Commission the authority to establish the minimum rates which the carriers might charge for the performance of transport services. While such cartellization, in conjunction with entry controls, may generate some monopoly profits for the holders of operating authority, it is even more likely to promote nonprice competition in the form of more frequent scheduling of truck departures. This, of course, will exacerbate further the problem of inefficient truck utilization.

RESTRICTIONS ON EXEMPT AGRICULTURAL AND PRIVATE CARRIERS

Economic regulation may also increase highway freight transport costs by virtue of the restrictions on for-hire carriage by exempt agricultural and private trucks. Pursuant to regulations of the Interstate Commerce Commission, these exempt and private carriers are foreclosed from the transportation of regulated commodities on a for-hire basis. As a matter of fact, a company may not even transport commodities for a wholly owned subsidiary if the latter is a legally separate corporation.

The predictable result of such restrictions on the operations of exempt and private carriers is a greatly reduced ability to secure balanced two-way traffic. This is precisely what Edward Miller [13] found in his study of the effect of regulation on the ability of private carriers to obtain backhauls. Thus, he points out that, "if the private vehicles [of the closed, unrefrigerated van type] could be brought up to the level of performance of the ICC regulated vehicles, it would be possible to obtain an increase in total loaded vehicle miles of 17.1 percent without any significant increase in line haul costs" [13, p. 10].

THE COSTS OF TRUCK REGULATION: EFFECT ON RATES

The first step in the estimation of the costs induced by the regulation of truck transportation is the determination of the effecs of regulation on for-hire carrier rates. To the extent that higher rates are attributable to monopoly profits, however, it will be necessary to deduct such income transfers in computing the cost increase. On the other hand, it will also be necessary to add the costs which regulation imposes on private and exempt carriers, as well as the direct costs incurred by the regulatory authority.

A number of attempts have been made to measure the impact of economic regulation on highway carrier rates. In the wake of two US Supreme Court decisions holding fresh and frozen poultry and frozen fruits and vegetables to be exempt agricultural commodities, the Department of Agriculture made several "before and after" studies of truck rates [20 and 21]. Following deregulation, fresh poultry rates declined by an average of 33 percent and frozen poultry rates, by an average of 36 percent. While the rates on frozen fruits and vegetables declined less extensively, an average of 19 percent, there was a contemporaneous increase in rail rates on frozen fruits and vegetables of 6 to 14 percent. At the same time, "stop off" charges of $5 to $15 per stop which were common prior to deregulation were either eliminated entirely or substantially reduced [12, pp. 4–5].

In contrast to the "before and after deregulation" study of the USDA, Richard N. Farmer [7] undertook a cross-sectional analysis of the costs and revenues of 25 exempt agricultural carriers in comparison with 171 common and contract carriers. The regulated carriers' costs and revenues exceeded those of exempt carriers by 66⅔ percent or more. A part of the explanation presumably resided in the 40 percent or more greater average tonnage of the exempt carriers.

James Sloss [19] endeavored to measure the effect of regulation on rates by comparing Canadian provinces which regulated truck rates with those which did not. After having isolated the regulatory effect, he proceeded to compute average revenue per ton-mile disparities between the two groups of provinces. To accomplish this he incorporated into his multiple-regression equations average length of haul, average net weight per loaded vehicle, average fuel tax per gallon, average license cost per truck or per tractor per year, and average annual wage per employee. The obvious difficulty with this methodology is that two of these variables, namely, average length of haul and average net weight per load, may themselves be adversely affected by regulation. Thus, the residual rate differences may understate significantly the effect of regulation on truck rates. Perhaps this explains why Sloss found that regulation in Canadian provinces raised rates by only 6.7 percent [19, p. 351], a value several orders of magnitude lower than the USDA and Richard Farmer estimates.

Finally, Thomas Gale Moore [15] made a comparative study of trucking regulation in five European countries to develop a rough measure of the effect of regulation on truck rates in the United States. He found that truck rates per ton-mile in West Germany, where the stringency of truck regulation rivals that of the United States, were about on a par with our own. On the other hand, the rates in Great Britain, Belgium, the Netherlands, and Sweden, countries with substantially less highway carrier regulation than the United States, were approximately 43 percent lower [15, p. 10]. Admittedly, labor costs are somewhat higher in the United States than in Europe, but this is probably offset by the higher fuel costs and generally less satisfactory operating conditions present in Europe.

On the basis of these studies it would not be unreasonable to conclude that economic regulation of for-hire truck transportation in the United States had increased rates by at least one-third and, conceivably, by one-half or more. Inasmuch as the operating revenues of Class I and Class II ICC-regulated trucking firms in 1976 totalled some $22 billion [23, p. S8], it follows that regulation of entry and rates of interstate for-hire highway carriers of freight may have increased the freight bill by $5½ billion to $7⅓ billion per year.

Though it would be inappropriate to maintain that the foregoing studies provide a definitive measure of the impact of economic regulation on highway carrier rates, all of them indicate that the effect is more than de minimis, and the USDA, Farmer, and Moore studies suggest that regulation has occasioned a very sizable increase in truck rates. Furthermore, even though there may be some dissimilarities in the inherent structural and operational characteristics of agricultural and nonagricultural carriers for which these analyses do not account, both the USDA and Farmer studies incorporate a downward bias of the effect of regulation on rates. This arises from the inability of agricultural carriers to transport nonagricultural commodities in backhaul. Obviously, this disability tends to increase the cost of exempt commodity transport and to understate the reduction in rates which would occur with deregulation.

Moore's method of measuring the extent to which regulation had increased rates in the United States also tends to underestimate regulatory effects. By considering trucking in Great Britain, the Netherlands, Belgium, and Sweden as "unregulated" because the regulation in these countries was less extensive than in Germany and the United States, his work may well have understated the impact of regulation on highway carrier rates.

It is difficult to determine to what extent the foregoing estimates of regulatory effects are equally applicable to all segments of the regulated trucking industry. Thus, to the extent that carriers utilize highly specialized equipment, backhaul opportunities decline and deregulation may not yield a reduction in rates comparable with that possible in the transportation of general freight by ordinary vans. Despite the fact that regulation of specialized carriers may nonetheless increase rates through service competition, circuitous routing, and inability to serve intermediate points, a *very conservative* estimate of the impact of deregulation on truck rates would exclude specialized and household carriers from the calculation. Thus, only common carriers of general freight have been included in the ensuing social cost calculations.

In 1976, Class I and Class II common carriers of general freight had revenues of $14,030.2 million [23, p. S3]. If regulation increased the rates of these carriers by one-third to one-half, then the rates were from $3½ billion to $4⅔ billion higher than they would have been in the absence of regulation.

THE COSTS OF REGULATION: OTHER EFFECTS

To the extent that economic regulation has succeeded in generating monopoly profits for trucking companies, then it has induced a greater increase in rates than in costs. Since monopoly profits are transfer payments, rather than social costs, they should be subtracted from the estimated increase in truck rates in any final assessment of the costs of regulation.

Class I and Class II carriers of general freight had intangible assets of $525.9 million in 1976 [10, pp. 11 and 28]. These assets represented payments to the previous certificate holders by the acquiring firms. On the reasonable assumption that such assets constitute the capitalization of the monopoly profits accruing to the holders of certificates which restrict the entry of potential competitors, a rough estimate can be made of monopoly profits in the regulated trucking industry. If monopoly profits are capitalized at, say, 15 percent, then intangible assets of $525.9 million would presuppose monopoly profits of $78.9 million per year. For a number of reasons this estimate is probably low. First, some carriers' operating rights date from the passage of the Motor Carrier Act of 1935, so there has never been any occasion to incorporate intangible asset values into their balance sheets. Second, some transfers of operating authority certainly occurred some time ago, so that the present value of operating rights may exceed, by some substantial margin, the transfer price. Third, some intangible asset values may have been written off. Thus, Moore estimates that trucking companies have probably amortized about 20 percent of their intangible asset values [14, pp. 60–61]. Fourth and finally, the appropriate capitalization rate might be somewhat more than the 15 percent rate assumed in these calculations.

It is also possible that monopoly profits have been dissipated, at least to some extent, in the form of higher wages. If the Teamsters Union has been able to divert to its members some of the excess profits generated by regulation, the sum transferred from truck owners to teamsters, as well as residual excess profits, should be deducted from the increase in truck rates attributable to regulation to calculate the true social costs. Thus James E. Annable has contended [2, p. 44] that the Teamsters Union "has been able to expropriate the excess profits which accrue to the cartel."

Neither the theoretical nor the empirical basis of this proposition is very convincing. The teamsters would be able to "expropriate the excess profits" only if the ICC was unwilling to permit carrier rate increases in the face of wage increases achieved by the union. As for the general association of monopoly and wage rates, David Schwartzman, who compared "average annual earnings in Canadian monopolistic industries with those in matched United States industries which are competitive, or less monopolistic" [18, p. 428], discovered "little ground for believing that monopolistic firms either exploit their employees or distribute excess profits to them" [18, p. 438]. Furthermore, Annable himself concedes that "a dual wage structure, that is, a rate in for-hire motor carriage higher than exists in the private segment of the industry in the same area . . . is not employed in motor freight" [2, p. 41].

If, on the other hand, higher wage rates resulting from the bargaining activities of the Teamsters Union are passed on to shippers and receivers, it does not follow that the teamsters would be any less successful in organizing and raising wages in an unregulated trucking industry. If so, no additional deductions need be made from regulated carrier revenues in calculating the social costs of regulation.

The fact that the teamsters are strong supporters of continued government regulation is not convincing proof that wages would be lower or even that the teamsters believe they would be lower after deregulation. Even though the teamsters could achieve equally high wage rates in a competitive trucking industry, there might, as Moore [14, p. 62] has pointed out, be fewer jobs because of greater efficiency. Also, deregulation might lead to an influx of owner-operators and, thus, to a substitution of entrepreneurs for employees.

Even if the estimated $78.9 million of monopoly profits is too small by a factor of two, the deduction from the social costs of truck regulation is very small. If economic regulation has increased truck rates by at least 3½ billion per year, $79 million is a 2¼ percent deduction and even $158 million is only 4½ percent.

Costs of Reduced Volume of Regulated Truck Freight

While regulation may well have increased the costs of transporting the current volume of general freight traffic by some $3½ or more billion, it has also imposed some additional costs by reducing the volume of traffic transported. On the very reasonable assumption that motor freight transportation is a constant-cost industry and that Haskel G. Benishay and Gilbert R. Whitaker's estimate of −1.15 [4, p. 251] is the best available for the elasticity of demand for truck transportation,[1] the calculation of welfare loss is quite straightforward. In 1976, Class I and Class II common carriers of general freight accomplished

98 billion ton-miles of transportation and earned $14 billion in operating revenues or average revenue of 14.3¢ per ton-mile. If regulation increases rates by ⅓ or more, average revenue in the absence of regulation would have been at least 3.5 cents per ton-mile lower.[2] With a linear demand curve and an arc elasticity of demand of −1.15, a reduction of rates to an average of 10.7 cents per ton-mile (14.3 cents − 3.6 cents) would have generated an additional 15 billion ton-miles of traffic or a welfare gain of $270 million.[3] See the chart. This must be added to the costs of regulation.

Costs of Underutilizing Private Trucks

In any complete reckoning of the social costs of truck regulation, it is also necessary to consider the impact of regulation on private carriers. Inasmuch as private carriers may not legally engage in for-hire transportation of any commodity other than an unmanufactured agricultural one, their costs per ton-mile will increase owing to their inability, typically, to obtain balanced two-way loads. A 1969 survey by Comsis Corporation revealed that privately owned and operated tractor-trailer vans were empty 31.4 percent of the time, implying an

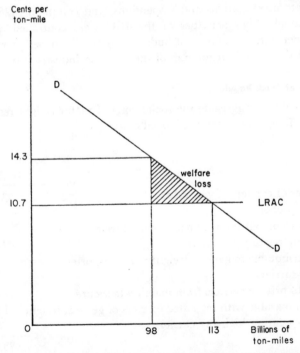

WELFARE LOSS FROM REDUCTION IN THE NUMBER OF TON-MILES OF COMMODITIES TRANSPORTED BY ICC-REGULATED CLASS I AND CLASS II COMMON CARRIERS OF GENERAL FREIGHT FROM 98 TO 113 BILLION TON-MILES IN 1976, OCCASIONED BY REGULATORY INDUCED INCREASE IN RATES FROM 10.7 CENTS PER TON-MILE TO 14.3 CENTS PER TON-MILE.

empty backhaul 62.8 percent of the time, while similar vehicles transporting regulated commodities were empty 19 percent of the time, equivalent to a 38 percent empty return experience [13, p. 11].

Private vans produced some 8,095 million truck miles in 1972 [25, Table 2, p. 2; Table 11, p. 16; and Table 29, p. 4]. If they had been able to achieve the same utilization as regulated ones, private trucks could have accomplished the same volume of traffic in 1972 with 1,435 million fewer vehicle miles.[4]

The value of this saving, of course, is dependent upon private carrier costs per vehicle mile. In 1975, common carriers of general freight earned revenues of $1.77 per intercity vehicle-mile [1, p. 8]. If economic regulation elevated rates as much as 50 percent over social costs, then private carrier costs of transporting general freight must have been at least $1.18 per vehicle mile. For 1,435 million vehicle-miles, the cost comes to $1,693 million.

Direct Costs of Regulatory Agency Activities

Finally, there are the costs incurred by the Interstate Commerce Commission, itself, in regulating the trucking industry. Fully 90 percent of the workload of the ICC is accounted for by cases involving motor carrier operating authority, finance, rate investigations and suspensions, and complaints [26, pp. 100–101]. Even though other activities of the ICC were continued, presumably much, say 50 percent, of the present budget of $50 million per year [26, p. 92] could be saved if economic regulation of the trucking industry were eliminated.

Aggregate Costs of Truck Regulation

It is now possible to aggregate the social costs of motor freight regulation by considering the foregoing elements of social cost:

Item	Social cost estimate (millions)
Increase in rates of carriers of general freight	$3,481
Less monopoly profits	158
Added social costs of existing volume of general freight transported by regulated carriers	$3,323
Welfare loss attributable to general freight not transported by regulated carriers	270
Increased cost to private carriers from inability to secure backhauls comparable with regulated carriers of general freight	1,693
ICC costs of regulating highway carriers	25
	$5,311

An annual saving of $5.3 billion constituted 0.4 percent of the 1976 national income of $1,348 billion or $25 per year for every man, woman, and child in the United States. Furthermore, there are several reasons for believing this estimate to be on the low side: (1) each constituent of total social cost was conservatively estimated; (2) regulated carriers other than ICC-regulated Class I and Class II common carriers of general freight and trucks other than general-purpose vans were excluded from the computation;[5] and (3) exempt carriers, although they face much the same difficulties as private carriers in obtaining backhauls, were also omitted from the estimates of regulation-induced costs.

THE BENEFITS OF TRUCK REGULATION

The monopoly profits generated by truck regulation are only a "benefit" if a redistribution of income from final consumers to the owners of regulated trucking firms is deemed to enhance economic welfare. There are probably very few individuals outside the regulated trucking industry who would give assent to such a proposition.

The ICC's Estimate of Benefits

The only comprehensive, quantitative assessment of the benefits of trucking industry regulation was completed recently by the Bureau of Economics of the Interstate Commerce Commission [6]. The bureau notes that, if motor carrier rates had risen to the same extent between 1969 and 1975 as wholesale prices generally, motor carrier revenues would have been higher in 1975 by some $3,735 million [6, pp. 23–24]. It is the bureau's contention that this suppression of rate increases is a direct benefit of regulation. Such a "post hoc, ergo propter hoc" argument does not merit serious consideration.

In addition to the benefits attributable to rate-level suppression, the bureau contends that additional benefits accrue from the increased efficiency of the industry in a regulated environment. Based on Daryl Wyckoff's finding that, after deregulation, truckload rates in Great Britain declined by 10 percent while less-than-truckload rates rose by 40 percent, the bureau [6, p. 7] maintains that a similar impact in the United States would increase the total highway carrier freight bill by some 20 percent or $3.8 billion in 1975 prices.[6]

While the bureau might reasonably contend that the reported increase in motor carrier rates in Great Britain after deregulation confirms the bureau's estimate of the extent to which regulation suppressed rates in the United States, the bureau treats the "costs" of deregulation and the "gains" of regulation as additive. It is certainly difficult to avoid the conclusion that the bureau is engaged in double-counting.

In addition to the foregoing "benefits," the bureau [6, pp. 16–20] calculates that regulation has reduced carrier financing costs by some $25 million per year (more double-counting) and consignee inventory costs by another $59 million. All together, the bureau concludes that economic regulation of the trucking industry has conferred benefits of some $7,634 million. Inasmuch as both the costs of regulation, discussed earlier, and the bureau's computation of the benefits of regulation depend for their validity upon the presumed effect of regulation upon truck rates, clearly they cannot both be correct.

Service Benefits

Perhaps the most frequently alleged benefit of truck regulation is that it improves the quality of service, especially for rural and other isolated shippers and for those who wish to ship relatively small loads. The argument is that regulation, by allowing truck revenues in excess of costs on some traffic, permits the subsidization of small shipments and the provision of service to areas of low traffic density. As T. B. Alfriend [5, p. 50], a consultant to a number of motor freight rate bureaus, has declared,

It is necessary to subsidize the traffic of shippers and receivers located at points that do not generate sufficient traffic to make adequate service economically feasible at rates they can afford to pay. Otherwise those shippers and receivers would not have adequate service and the growth and dispersion of industry throughout the nation would be drastically retarded.

Regardless of the merits of the policy of subsidizing small and isolated shippers so as to promote geographic dispersion of economic activity, it is doubtful that the existing regulatory process contributes to that objective. In the first place, the mere fact that regulation permits carriers to secure monopoly profits in the transportation of some commodities, in some quantities, and to and from some locations does not motivate them to dissipate those profits by serving small, isolated shippers at a loss. It could be argued, of course, that, whatever their motivation, regulated trucking companies are required to serve such shippers by virtue of their common carrier status. The truth seems to be, however, that where there is a will, there is a way to avoid these obligations. As Gilbert L. Gifford [9, p. 19] has observed,

A growing number of motor carriers, seeking to avoid shipments they consider to be unprofitable, resort to the curtailment or abandonment of service by embargoes, rate increases, insistence upon more expensive packaging, and/or by tariff restrictions. The most serious threat to maintenance of adequate small shipments service appears to be the increasing tendency of interlining carriers to cancel through route-joint rate agreements, and their refusal to participate in new agreements.

Second, the commodity, route, and intermediate point restrictions imposed on regulated carriers restrict their ability to provide that flexibility of service which would benefit small and isolated shippers, in particular. In order to overcome some of the limitations on operating authority, growth through merger is a widespread phenomenon in the regulated motor freight industry. Unfortunately, whatever gains in flexibility may accrue to a carrier by virtue of some expansion of operating authority may be more than offset by the inflexibility associated with increasing firm size. As R. L. Banks and Associates

[3, p. 5] concluded after a study of nine Class I and Class II common carriers serving primarily small communities,

The overwhelming impression after interviews with carrier management, as somewhat supported by comparative data, is that small carriers succeed because they are specialists in serving markets requiring the kind of attention which appears to be uneconomical for large carriers to offer. In essence, small carriers appear to be better equipped to handle shipments in small markets because their pickup-and-delivery service, as well as terminal operations, are geared for small LTL shipments, their managements maintain close relations with customers, tight control over their organizations and pay close attention to changing market conditions.

Third, regulation makes private transport a less feasible alternative for small than for large shippers. Despite the inability of private carriers to transport nonagricultural commodities, the large shipper may be able to achieve sufficiently high utilization to justify resort to operation of his own fleet. Small shippers, however, are more likely to find that their shipment sizes are too small, their shipment schedules are too irregular, and their shipment destinations are too scattered to warrant private carriage in the absence of an opportunity to engage in supplemental for-hire transport.

Fourth, isolated areas whose principal exports are agricultural in nature are handicapped by the inability of exempt haulers of agricultural commodities to transport nonagricultural commodities in backhaul. The fact that inbound regulated carriers may transport agricultural commodities as a backhaul from the rural area may well prove an inadequate alternative.

All in all, the proposition that regulation is the sine qua non of adequate truck service to small shippers and out-of-the-way locations is unconvincing. As a matter of fact, the increase in the social costs of motor freight transportation which appears to be occasioned by the existing regulatory process is so great that it is difficult to imagine that even internal subsidization of the magnitude alleged by the supporters of regulation would offset the higher costs affecting, to some greater or lesser extent, all users of truck transportation.

CONCLUSION

The Bureau of Economics of the Interstate Commerce Commission may have identified one benefit from economic regulation of the trucking industry. If rate regulation promotes nonprice competition in the form of more frequent scheduling, it is possible that some inventory savings may accrue to consignees. Such an outcome is not certain, however, since the greater flexibility and carrier utilization possible in an unregulated highway transport market might produce equally frequent and speedy service. Even if the full $59 million in inventory savings estimated by the Bureau of Economics is realized, however, this is a meager benefit to counteract a $5.3 billion additional social cost attributable to the continuation of economic regulation.

NOTES

1. Other studies have suggested substantially higher values for the price elasticity of demand for truck transportation. Eugene D. Perle [17, p. 43] placed the overall elasticity coefficient at -2.0223 and Alexander L. Morton [16, p. 53], at -1.841. Not only does the Benishay and Whitaker estimate produce the most conservative welfare loss, but also, more important, their methodology seems clearly to be superior. They employ a longer span of years, and they include population, urbanization, industrial production, and time trend in their regression equation.

2. This implies that, in the absence of regulation, the rates of common carriers of general freight would have been reduced to a competitive level, namely, long-run average costs. Some question has arisen, however, as to the applicability of the competitive model to all phases of the trucking industry. J. C. Spychalski, for example, has pointed out that "the supply characteristics of LTL-oriented truckers, coupled with the fact that aggregate amounts of LTL traffic moving and potentially movable between many if not a majority of origin-destination point pairs can be accommodated by relatively few carriers, suggest that tendencies toward concentration would exist in this sector of trucking even in the absence of institutionally imposed constraints" [22, p. 18]. While such concentration might render the competitive *model* less applicable to the LTL segment of the common carriage of general freight, it does not negate a competitive *outcome*. E. S. Mason observed long ago that while a "substantial degree of concentration is a necessary condition to the exercise of monopoly power ... it is not a sufficient condition" [11, p. 34]. In the trucking industry, the potential competition of firms not currently transporting commodities between particular origin-destination pairs is the primary reason that concentration is not a sufficient condition for the exercise of monopoly power. As I have commented elsewhere [8],

"To count only those firms actually engaged in transporting a particular commodity between two points during any short time span may convey an erroneous impression of market concentration. The reason is that the non-specialized nature of many trucks, together with the geographic mobility which they exhibit, makes inter-market transference a relatively simple phenomenon even in the short run."

· 3. The welfare gain can be calculated as [($.143 $-$ $.107) $\times$ 113 billion ton-miles $-$ 98 billion ton-miles]/2 = ($.036 $\times$ 15 billion ton-miles) /2 = $270 million.

4. This "private capacity shortfall," as Moore [14, p. 63] has called it, is calculated as (.81 regulated van utilization $-$ .688 private van utilization) /.688 private van utilization = .1773 $\times$ 8.095 million private van-miles = 1,435 million van-miles of private capacity shortfall. This is a conservative estimate of the effect of regulation on private truck utilization, since regulated carriers themselves would probably be able to reduce their empty backhauls were it not for limitations on their routes, commodities, and intermediate points served.

5. While the inclusion of other regulated carriers and other vehicle types would have increased somewhat the estimate of social costs, common carriers of general freight are the most important single constituent of the regulated trucking industry. Furthermore, the ordinary van, the truck type providing the greatest opportunity for backhauls because of its unspecialized nature, tends to overshadow in numerical importance all other truck types engaged in intercity freight transport.

6. Since Wyckoff's findings were the subject of an oral presentation rather than published writings, the evidence on which he based them is unknown to me. At any rate, the findings are in direct conflict with those of Moore [15]. He notes, first of all, that "historical data on industry revenues, profits, and the return on investment

[in Great Britain] do not exist" (p. 35). Furthermore, he cites several instances in which real rates fell in 1972 and 1973 (pp. 37–38), that is, subsequent to deregulation. Finally, Moore points out that "in the small-consignment market several companies offer premium service at premium prices, but the largest firms do not" (p. 38). It may well be that Wyckoff had reference to this little used service when he noted a 40 percent increase in LTL rates following deregulation.

REFERENCES

1. *American Trucking Trends, 1976 Statistical Supplement* (Washington: American Trucking Associations, 1976).

2. James E. Annable, Jr., "The ICC, the IBT, and the Cartelization of the American Trucking Industry," *Quarterly Review of Economics and Business,* Vol. 13 (Summer 1973), pp. 33–47.

3. R. L. Banks and Associates, *Economic Analysis and Regulatory Implications of Motor Carrier Service to Predominantly Small Communities, A Final Report to the U.S. Department of Transportation* (Washington, 24 June 1976).

4. Haskel G. Benishay and Gilbert R. Whitaker, Jr., "Supply and Demand in Freight Transportation," *Journal of Industrial Economics,* Vol. 14 (July 1966), pp. 243–62.

5. *The Case Against Deregulation* (Washington: American Trucking Associations, undated).

6. *A Cost and Benefit Evaluation of Surface Transport Regulation* (Washington: Interstate Commerce Commission, Bureau of Economics, 1976).

7. Richard N. Farmer, "The Case for Unregulated Truck Transportation," *Journal of Farm Economics,* Vol. 46 (May 1974), pp. 389–409.

8. J. R. Felton, "The Inherent Structure, Behavior and Performance of the Motor Freight Industry," *International Journal of Transport Economics,* forthcoming.

9. Gilbert L. Gifford, "The Small Shipments Problem," *Transportation Journal,* Vol. 10 (Fall 1970), pp. 17–27.

10. Stephen Hannahs and Joseph Tune, *1977 Financial Analysis of the Motor Carrier Industry* (Union Oil Company, Union 76 Division, undated).

11. E. S. Mason, *Economic Concentration and the Monopoly Problem* (Cambridge: Harvard University Press, 1959).

12. Walter Miklius, *Economic Performance of Motor Carriers Operating under the Agricultural Exemption,* Marketing Research Report No. 838 (Washington: US Department of Agriculture, 1969).

13. Edward Miller, "Effects of Regulation on Truck Utilization," *Transportation Journal,* Vol. 13 (Fall 1973), pp. 5–14.

14. Thomas Gale Moore, "Deregulating Surface Transportation," in Almarin Phillips, ed., *Promoting Competition in Regulated Markets* (Washington: Brookings, 1975), pp. 55–98.

15. ———, *Trucking Regulation: Lessons from Europe* (Washington: American Enterprise Institute, 1976).

16. Alexander L. Morton, "A Statistical Sketch of Intercity Freight Demand," *Highway Research Record,* Number 296, Highway Pricing (Washington: Highway Research Board, 1969), pp. 47–65.

17. Eugene D. Perle, *The Demand for Transportation* (Chicago: University of Chicago, Department of Geography, 1964).

18. David Schwartzman, "Monopoly and Wages," *Canadian Journal of Economics and Political Science,* Vol. 26 (August 1969), pp. 428–38.

19. James Sloss, "Regulation of Motor Freight Transportation: A Quantitative Evaluation of Policy," *Bell Journal of Economics and Management Science,* Vol. 1 (Autumn 1970) , pp. 327–56.

20. J. R. Snitzler and R. J. Byrne, *Interstate Trucking of Fresh and Frozen Poultry under Agricultural Exemption,* Marketing Research Report No. 224 (Washington: US Department of Agriculture, 1958) .

21. ――――, *Interstate Trucking of Frozen Fruits and Vegetables under Agricultural Exemption,* Marketing Research Report No. 316 (Washington: US Department of Agriculture, 1959) .

22. J. C. Spychalski, "Criticisms of Regulated Transport: Do Economists' Perceptions Conform with Institutional Realities?" *Transportation Journal,* Vol. 15 (Spring 1975) , pp. 5–17.

23. *Transportation Facts and Trends,* 13th ed. (Washington: Transportation Association of America, July 1977) .

24. *Trinc's Blue Book of the Trucking Industry* (Trinc Transportation Consultants, September 1977) .

25. US Bureau of the Census, *1972 Census of Transportation,* Truck Inventory and Use Survey, Vol. II (1973) .

26. US Interstate Commerce Commission, *89th Annual Report* (Washington, 1975) .

7

THE BENEFICIARIES OF TRUCKING REGULATION

Thomas Gale Moore

A SERIES of studies which have been published in recent years indicate that a major impact of Interstate Commerce Commission (ICC) regulation of the trucking industry has been to raise freight rates.[1] James Sloss, for example, found that average revenue per ton-mile was 6.73 per cent lower in "unregulated" Canadian provinces compared to average revenue in regulated Canadian provinces and in the United States.[2] His study underestimates the impact on rates for a number of reasons that I have spelled out elsewhere.[3] Suffice it to note that his regulated provinces would be relatively unregulated by U.S. standards.

During the 1950s we witnessed what might almost be considered a controlled experiment. Some products—fresh and frozen poultry—that had been carried only by regulated carriers were declared by the courts to be exempt commodities under the Interstate Commerce Act. There is no reason to believe that regulated trucking rates on these commodities were significantly higher relative to costs than were those of any other commodity. As a result of these court decisions, prices declined substantially: 12 to 59 per cent in particular markets with an unweighted average of 33 per cent for fresh poultry and 36 per cent for frozen.[4] The weighted average decline for frozen fruits and vegetables was 19 per cent.[5]

* I would like to thank George Stigler, James C. Miller III, John Snow, and especially H. Gregg Lewis for their thoughtful comments and suggestions.

[1] Thomas G. Moore, Trucking Regulation: Lessons From Europe (Am. Enterprise Inst.—Hoover Policy Studies, 1975); James Sloss, Regulation of Motor Freight Transportation: A Quantitative Evaluation of Policy, 1 Bell J. Econ. & Management Sci. 32 (1970); James R. Snitzler & Robert J. Byrne, Interstate Trucking of Fresh and Frozen Poultry Under Agricultural Exemption (U.S. Dep't of Agriculture, 1958) (Marketing Research Rept. No. 224); id., Interstate Trucking of Frozen Fruits and Vegetables Under Agricultural Exemption (U.S. Dep't of Agriculture, 1959) (Marketing Research Rept. No. 316); Transportation Act of 1972, Hearings on H.R. 11824, H.R. 11826, and H.R. 11207 Before the Subcomm. on Transportation of the House Comm. on Interstate and Foreign Commerce, 92nd Cong., 2nd Sess., 1434 (pts. 1-3, 1972) [hereinafter cited as Transportation Hearings].

[2] James Sloss, *supra* note 1.

[3] Thomas G. Moore, *supra* note 1.

[4] James R. Snitzler & Robert J. Byrnes, Interstate Trucking of Fresh and Frozen Poultry Under Agricultural Exemption, *supra* note 1.

[5] *Id.*, Interstate Trucking of Frozen Fruits and Vegetables Under Agricultural Exemption, *supra* note 1.

From Thomas Gale Moore, "The Beneficiaries of Trucking Regulation," 21(2) *Journal of Law and Economics* 327-343 (October 1978). Copyright 1978 by the University of Chicago Law School.

More recently a study of trucking regulation in Europe showed that some countries in Europe have no or little regulation of trucking; others such as West Germany regulate rates and entry very strictly. Comparisons of rates between countries—which admittedly is always difficult because of the unclarity of the appropriate exchange rate—show that rates in countries with no or little regulation were 43 per cent lower than rates in West Germany and the United States.[6]

Another piece of evidence on the level of rates comes from a survey by the National Broiler Council of its members. The member firms ship fresh poultry by exempt carriers and cooked poultry by regulated carriers. In comparing rates for the same routes between the same points, they found that on average unregulated rates were some 33 per cent less than the rates on regulated carriers of cooked poultry.[7]

It would seem that regulation has substantially raised rates in the trucking industry. This is not surprising; the Interstate Commerce Act appears to have been designed mainly to cartelize the industry. Trucking firms are encouraged to join rate bureaus to agree on charges for particular shipments. Changes in rates by independent truckers, including price cuts, must be filed thirty days before they are to be effective with the ICC and be open to inspection. Upon protest, the ICC may and often does suspend such lower rates, a procedure that obviously inhibits competition.

Moreover, the ICC restricts entry into the trucking industry. Every carrier must have either a certificate of public convenience and necessity or a permit (contract carriers). Certificates or permits are not lightly given out. Upon application, the commission considers any objection by other carriers that the new entrant might divert traffic. The commission has asserted that:

It has been consistently held that existing carriers should be afforded the opportunity to transport all the traffic which they can handle adequately, economically and efficiently in the territory they serve before a new service is authorized.[8]

In practice, the ICC granted 207 property certificates and 232 permits to new firms without previous authority in fiscal year 1975.[9] Table 1 presents an analysis of a sample drawn from this list. As can be seen, in a large majority of cases the authority is to serve only one shipper and no opposition is recorded. In the minority of cases where opposition is expressed, the commission structures the grant so that no business of existing carriers can

[6] Thomas G. Moore, *supra* note 1.

[7] Transportation Hearings, *supra* note 1.

[8] J.H. Rose Truck Line Inc., 110 M.C.C. 180, 184-85 (1969).

[9] Robert S. Burk, Acting General Counsel of the Interstate Commerce Commission, provided me with a list prepared by the staff of new carriers covering fiscal year 1975.

TABLE 1

SAMPLE OF NEW ICC GRANTS OF AUTHORITY, FISCAL YEAR 1975

Authority	Total Cases	No. Oppo-sitions	No. Backhaul Authority	Serving Only One Shipper	Operated Previously	Protested by Other Truckers	Increased Competition for Existing Carriers
Passengers	3	3			1		
Common Carrier							
General Commerce	2	8	6	6	2	2	1[a]
Special Commerce	10	7	6	12	8	3	0
Contract Carriers	12			18	3	5	0
Total Property	24	15	12	18	13	10	1[a]

[a] Competition increase is de minimus. Requested authority to serve two areas, Montgomery Township, New Jersey, population 6,353 and Mercer County, New Jersey, population 303,968 from Newark Airport. Received authority in competition with existing carrier only for Montgomery Township. MC-138863 Sub. 1.

Source: This sample of motor carrier dockets was collected from a list of new carriers with no previous authority located in the docket room of the Interstate Commerce Commission in Washington, D.C.

be carried by the new firm. The one exception is described in the table and is minimal.

As a general rule, therefore, new service is authorized only where a new shipper need has developed and in particular where the new service will not divert traffic from existing carriers.

It would appear that regulation has raised rates and prevented new firms from competing away the monopoly rents. Profit maximizing should lead existing certificated firms to compete for traffic. Since rates are set through rate bureaus and price competition made unprofitable, nonprice competition should lead to reduced rents for trucking firms, as each firm equates the marginal cost of nonprice competition with the marginal revenue. Thus firms will schedule more frequent service and have better equipment than they would in a free market. If the elasticity of demand with respect to this nonprice service variable is significantly less than infinity, average revenue will be appreciably above marginal revenue and marginal cost. Unless there are increasing returns to scale in trucking, average costs cannot be larger than marginal costs. Therefore, rents are likely to be earned in trucking even with nonprice competition.

The objective of this paper is to identify and measure the beneficiaries and benefits from trucking regulation. In an earlier study, I estimated the costs of ICC regulation of common carrier trucking in 1968 to be between $1.4 and $1.9 billion.[10] In that study I made some crude estimates of the rents secured by trucking firms from regulation. I also assumed that none of the benefits from regulation were passed on to factors of production. This paper is a further examination of this issue and, in particular, a partial refutation of the earlier work.

A useful approach to the subject of the beneficiaries of ICC regulation can be derived from Sam Peltzman's "Toward a More General Theory of Regulation."[11] In this paper Peltzman points out that regulation is likely to confer benefits on several politically influential groups and that as a consequence cartelization will always be incomplete. Thus some customers, some factor owners, some suppliers, and perhaps other related groups are likely to receive benefits.

To particularize his model to trucking regulation is quite straightforward. Cartelization will confer some rents on the owners of a certificate of public convenience and necessity and on the permit owners. Other groups that might benefit would include organized labor, other suppliers to the industry,

[10] Thomas G. Moore, Deregulating Surface Freight Transportation, in Promoting Competition in Regulated Markets 55, 60-61 (Almarin Phillips ed. 1975) (Brookings Inst.).

[11] Sam Peltzman, Toward a More General Theory of Regulation, 19 J. Law & Econ. 211 (1976).

and some shipper groups. This paper develops evidence on the benefits accruing to two groups: organized labor and the owners of operating rights.

BENEFITS TO LABOR

It is clear that truck drivers benefit from the additional mileage driven as a result of circuity and as a result of the nonprice competition, but of course the higher rates discourage traffic which reduces the demand for their services. On net, miles driven may be greater or smaller under regulation, but the impact is likely to be small.

Regulation does appear to have increased wages significantly. James Annable has argued that most if not all of the cartel gains stemming from ICC regulation were captured by the International Brotherhood of Teamsters.[12] He claims that cartelization could be expected to raise profits over time, and if the Teamsters could capture part or all of the profits trucking wages should rise relative to other wages during the postwar period. The difficulty with this position is that there is no economic theory or other reason to believe that cartelization should raise profits over time. Presumably a cartel would aim at achieving a monopoly profit-maximizing position. Once that level of prices is achieved (which could take some time), there should be no further increase in relative profits or prices. Actually, one would usually expect the cartel profits to be eroded over time as substitutes develop. Moreover, a finding that wage rates in trucking increased more rapidly than in other industries is consistent with many hypotheses (for example, the income elasticity of demand for employment at home is positive, skill levels have increased, and the supply curve of truck drivers is positively sloped).

Nevertheless, in naturally competitive industries regulation may strengthen organized labor by making nonunionized competition less effective. Management will be less unwilling to agree to higher wages knowing that the ICC will not only permit higher rates but enforce them on any nonunionized competition. Moreover, regulation prevents new nonunionized firms from entering the industry and competing for the traffic carried by the unionized firms. Regulation therefore lowers the cost of agreeing to higher wages and, *ceteris paribus,* thus should increase the wages earned by Teamsters.

In particular, the ICC bases its rate regulation on the average operating ratio for a region of the country defined as the ratio of operating costs to total revenue. Rate increases for a region of the country can and must be justified by showing that, on average, operating ratios are above a given level. Thus an increase in Teamster wages usually triggers ICC approval of a rate increase. Since over 60 per cent of operating costs are labor expenditures, a

---

[12] James E. Annable, Jr., The ICC, the IBT, and the Cartelization of the American Trucking Industry, 13 Q. Rev. Econ. & Bus. 33 (1973).

simple extension of the Averch-Johnson hypothesis[13] implies that more labor or higher wages for the industry as a whole may actually increase total profits. Of course since the rates are exogenous to each firm, any single firm has an incentive to reduce its costs but the industry which does bargain collectively may be able to increase total industry profits by increasing over-all operating costs. Thus in such a regulated environment, the industry will not object as strongly to wage increases or demands for more employment by unions.

To see this take a very simple model where there is only one truck rate P based on ton-miles Q. The industry acting in concert to maximize:

$$\pi = PQ - wL - rK,$$

subject to the constraint that

$$wL/PQ \geq R^*,$$

and where w is wages, L is the hours of work, r is the cost of capital, K is the quantity of capital, π is profit, and R^* minimum average allowed operating ratio. We are assuming that only labor costs are involved in calculating the operating ratio. After setting up the Lagrangian and taking the partials we have:

$$(1 - \lambda R^*) \left(P + Q\frac{\partial P}{\partial Q} \right) \frac{\partial Q}{\partial L} - (1 - \lambda)w \leq 0, \tag{1}$$

$$(1 - \lambda R^*) \left(P + Q\frac{\partial P}{\partial Q} \right) \frac{\partial Q}{\partial K} - r \leq 0, \tag{2}$$

and dividing (1) by (2) gives:

$$\frac{\partial Q}{\partial L} \Big/ \frac{\partial Q}{\partial K} \leq \frac{(1 - \lambda)w}{r}.$$

If $\lambda = 0$, then R^* is not binding and the industry maximizes profits. Assuming $\lambda > 0$, it is clear that if $\lambda = 1$ then $R^* = 1$, which implies no profit. Since $R^* < 1$, $1 > \lambda > 0$ and cost minimization implies

$$\frac{\partial Q}{\partial L} \Big/ \frac{\partial Q}{\partial K} = \frac{w}{r},$$

there will be too much labor used or the wage rate will be inflated.

Thus we can conclude that regulation will tend to increase wages through two effects. It will strengthen union power by eliminating or reducing the competition of nonunion firms. In addition, operating ratio regulation will

[13] Harvey Averch & Leland Johnson, Behavior of the Firm Under Regulatory Constraint, 52 Am. Econ. Rev. 1053 (1962).

either make it more profitable to pay higher wages or, at worst, make it less unprofitable to do so.[14]

Data do not permit a direct test of the hypothesis that truck drivers receive major benefits from regulation. While the Department of Labor has collected data on wages paid union truck drivers, no figures exist on wages paid in the unregulated unorganized sector. However, the Census Bureau has collected some figures on unregulated trucking.[15] According to the census there are some 6,871 non-ICC regulated trucking establishments operating that were not local operations in 1972. Most of these firms haul exempt agricultural products and generated well over one billion dollars in revenue from trucking alone that year.[16] There were 164 establishments with annual revenues of over one million dollars each, which would make them Class I carriers if regulated by the ICC. It is obvious, however, that the bulk of unregulated carriers are small firms; just as 74 per cent of regulated carriers are Class III (under $300,000 a year revenue).

Table 2 compares average compensation paid by regulated and unregu-

TABLE 2

AVERAGE ANNUAL EMPLOYEES COMPENSATION IN REGULATED
AND UNREGULATED TRUCKING (1972)

	Regulated	Unregulated	Percentage of Regulated over Unregulated
All Class I—Property	$12,299	$8,504	44.6
Class I—Property (Revenue $1 million— $5 billion)	11,099	8,504	30.5
Class II—Property	10,033	7,566	32.6

Source: 1 U.S. Bureau of the Census, SC 72-S-7, 1972 Census of Selected Service Industries, tab. 3, at 17 (1975); ICC Transport Statistics in the United States, releases 2 & 3 (pt. 7, 1972).

[14] Wallace Hendricks, Regulation and Labor Earnings, 8 Bell J. Econ. & Management Sci. 483 (1977), concluded that for a single firm individually regulated, the cost of agreeing to higher wages depended on the profit level of the firm and the "toughness" of the regulatory commission. His evidence was focused on the electric utility industry. There are several reasons to believe that his model is not applicable to trucking. Trucking is an inherently competitive industry where even under regulation, several firms are usually competing for the same traffic. Rate regulation is not firm specific but industry specific with rates being set by rate bureaus and upward movements of average rates being a function of high average operating ratios. Rates therefore, unlike those in the electric utility industry, are based on operating costs, not capital costs. It may also be relevant that a strike in trucking will close down the industry, whereas in the electrical power industry a strike will usually not result in an immediate interruption of service.

[15] 1 U.S. Bureau of the Census, SC 72-S-7, 1972 Census of Selected Service Industries (1976).

[16] *Id.* at tab. 4.

lated carriers for 1972. Since average compensation rises with the size of the carrier, the largest unregulated carriers are compared both with all Class I carriers of property regulated by the ICC and with those with a revenue between $1 million and $5 million. The average revenue for nonregulated carriers with receipts over $1 million was approximately $1,750,000 in 1972, so a more appropriate comparison would probably be between regulated carriers with receipts of $1 million to $5 million and all unregulated firms with receipts over $1 million. As Table 2 shows, this comparison indicates that regulated carriers are paying more than 30 per cent higher compensation than the unregulated. Published data show that truck drivers on intercity routes are paid the highest wage of any group of employees in a trucking company except for a very small group of owners, officers, and sales managers.[17] Thus, the higher wages paid in the regulated sector probably are due mainly to drivers' wages.

Table 2 also compares regulated and unregulated Class II carriers (receipts falling between $300,000 and $1,000,000 per year). In this category in 1972, there were 760 unregulated firms and 2,202 regulated ones, with regulated firms on average paying 32.6 per cent more compensation per worker than unregulated.

While there is no reason to believe that cartel profits should rise relatively over time and therefore lead to increasing relative wages over time, the institution of regulation in 1935 could be expected to raise wages. Such a rise would not likely be immediate, especially since many benefits would come through strengthening the position of the union. Thus, it would take time for a union to organize a basically competitive industry, and quite a few years might elapse before the union had fully exploited the situation. Table 3 presents data on the average compensation and changes in the relative earnings of employees of Class I motor carriers of property. Data on compensation for platform workers goes back only to 1946 but follows a similar pattern to drivers from 1946 to 1972. As can be seen, drivers and helpers made slightly less than other trucking firm employees prior to the Second World War, although they did seem to be catching up. The first year the ICC collected data on trucking was 1938. Actually the commission was still deciding "grandfather" applications well into 1940. By 1950 drivers and helpers were earning more than other employees, and the differential has continued to grow up to the present.

Table 3 also indicates that drivers' and helpers' wages have grown relative to the average weekly earnings in manufacturing. There are of course a multitude of factors that might produce this result that have nothing to do

---

[17] Interstate Commerce Commission (ICC), *Transport Statistics in the United States* pt. 7, release 1, at tab. 12 (1972).

TABLE 3
RELATIVE EARNINGS OF CLASS I MOTOR CARRIER (PROPERTY) EMPLOYEES

Year	1 Drivers & Helpers	2 Average Annual Compensation All Other Employees	3 All Employees	Ratio of Columns 1 to Average Weekly Earnings in Manufacturing*	2	3
1938	$ 1,366[a]	$ 1,502	$ 1,433	1.19	1.31	1.25
1939	1,476[b]	1,588	1,506	1.20	1.29	1.23
1940	1,565[b]	1,630	1,597	1.21	1.26	1.23
1950	4,037[c]	3,538	3,813	1.33	1.17	1.26
1960	7,080[c]	5,886	6,439	1.52	1.26	1.38
1970	11,056[c]	8,980	9,819	1.59	1.29	1.41
1972	14,120[c]	11,317	12,295	1.76	1.31	1.53

[a] Average for all motor carriers of property.
[b] Average for intercity motor carriers of property.
[c] Average for common carriers of general freight engaged in intercity transportation.
* Assuming a 52-week year for truckers.
Source: ICC, Transport Statistics in the United States, Motor Carriers (various years); and Economic Report of the President (various years).

with regulation. Hours of work during the year might have changed for a variety of factors.[18] Column 2 shows, however, that the gain in relative wages in the trucking industry is virtually entirely due to the rise in wages of drivers and helpers—the heart of the Teamster Union.

Let us put the data together to estimate how much regulation and unionization have increased wages of drivers, helpers, and platform workers. We can define average compensation C^r of employees of regulated firms:

$$C^r = a^r w_D{}^r + (1 - a^r) w^r{}_o,$$

where $w_D{}^r$ is the average compensation of drivers, helpers, and platform workers. And $w_o{}^r$ is the average compensation of other employees and a^r is the proportion of drivers to all employees. Similarly, the average compensation C of nonregulated firms can be defined:

$$C = a w_D + (1 - a) w_o.$$

Now the proportion of drivers and helpers to all employees has averaged around .47 since 1938 with no apparent trend but some small fluctuation from year to year. Since the Second World War, the number of drivers, helpers, and platform workers has totaled about two-thirds of all employees. Note from Table 3 that the average compensation of all other employees has

[18] Since 1950 paid hours of work per truck driver have declined 6.7% (1950-1972). See ICC, *supra* note 17 (various years).

moved almost exactly with the average for all manufacturing up to 1970. Therefore, let us assume that

$$a^r = a$$

and

$$w_o{}^r = w_o.$$

In other words, we assume that regulation and unionization have neither changed the relative number of truckers and platform workers needed nor have they affected the wages of other employees.[19] Then we want to estimate the impact $(1 + \alpha)$ of regulation-unionization on wages of drivers, helpers, and platform workers, where $(1 + \alpha)$ is defined in:

$$w_D{}^r = (1 + \alpha)w_D.$$

We have estimated that $C^r = (1.33)C$ approximately. From this it is trivial to calculate that

$$(1 + \alpha) = 1.33 + .16\frac{w_o}{w_D}. \tag{3}$$

Now assuming that $w_o/w_D = .93$, which is approximately what it was prior to World War II, regulation-unionization has increased the wages of drivers, helpers, and platform employees approximately 50 per cent. To the extent that other employees such as mechanics and clerical workers are organized, this estimate overstates the impact of regulation-unionization on earnings of drivers and helpers.

Table 3 indicates also that drivers' and helpers' wages are 48 per cent higher than they would have been if they had simply paralleled compensation in manufacturing. But not all drivers and helpers are unionized, and therefore the wages of unionized drivers and helpers must be more than 48 per cent higher than they would have been. Average compensation in non-regulated trucking (Table 1–Class I firms) is only 6 per cent above the average in manufacturing. In 1938 the average in regulated trucking was 19 per cent (Table 2) above the average in manufacturing. If the data from 1938 are taken as reasonable estimates of relative wages prior to regulation, un-regulated truckers have suffered a 13 per cent point decline in relative wages. Adding this decline to the 48 per cent increase over manufacturing

---

[19] If unionization has raised the relative wages of truckers and platform workers, firms can be expected to have substituted other factors for these workers. Thus, the relative proportion of unionized workers should have declined. In this case our procedure would underestimate the gain going to labor.

wages for regulated-unionized firms indicates a total impact of over 61 per cent.

Another approach to the impact of regulation-unionization would be to assume that in its absence the wages of drivers and helpers would have paralleled all other employees, some of whom are also unionized. In that case Table 3 shows that drivers' and helpers' wages are 37 per cent higher than they would have been with no regulation-unionization. Actually, since not all drivers and wages are unionized and since at least some other workers (for example, platform workers) belong to the Teamsters, the effect of unionization must be greater than 37 per cent.

According to Teamster officials, about 400,000 union members work for trucking firms. In 1972 there were approximately 600,000 nonsupervisory employees of Class I and II carriers (local and intercity).[20] Thus about 73 per cent of such employees are union members. It should be noted that the 400,000 estimate by the Teamster official is crude, and several newspaper reports have indicated that the number might be as high as 450,000. On the other hand, these estimates relate to 1976 while the data on number of nonsupervisory workers are for 1972.

A 1965 Labor Department study reported that some 62 per cent of non-supervisory employees in trucking work for firms where a majority of such employees are covered by union contracts.[21] This same study reported that wages of employees, where a majority were covered by bargaining units, earned 55 per cent more per hour than employees in other firms.[22]

Daryl Wychoff and David Maister calculate that an owner-operator (unregulated and not represented by a union) would earn about $11,125 working a 250-day year and expecting a return of 15 per cent of his investment.[23] In 1973 the average compensation of a driver of an ICC regulated Class I common carrier of general freight engaged in intercity service earned $17,249 or some 55 per cent more than Wychoff's owner-operator.[24]

From the 1967 Survey of Economic Opportunity Research Computer file,[25] one other piece of evidence on the effect of unionization can be derived. This sample contained 30,000 households which included 209 truck

---

[20] Calculated from ICC, *supra* note 17, release 3, at tab. 1, on the assumption that the ratio of nonsupervisory employees to total employees was the same for all Class I and II firms as the ratio calculated for common carriers of general freight. (*Id.* release 1, at tab. 12).

[21] U.S. Dep't of Labor, Bureau of Labor Statistics, Trucking, 1965 (Rpt. 335-11 1965).

[22] *Id.* at tab. 2.

[23] D. Daryl Wychoff & David H. Maister, The Owner-Operator: Independent Trucker 36 (1975).

[24] ICC, Transport Statistics in the United States (1973).

[25] Survey of Economic Opportunity Research Computer file (1967), conducted by the Bureau of the Census for the Office of Economic Opportunity to supplement the Current Population Surveys.

drivers employed in the trucking industry. Of these 38 were self-employed and 100 were unionized. There were 53 nonwhite workers and 181 who worked 40 to 52 weeks during 1966.

To measure the impact of unionization, annual income (wages plus self-employed income), weekly earnings, and hourly wages were regressed on education, age, race, region of country, size of metropolitan region, regular employment, wage and salary or self-employed, and of course unionization. Only education, race, regular employment, and unionization were significant.

The regression results are presented in Table 4. The dependent variables are in logs and all the independent variables are dummy variables as follows:

$x_1 = 1$ if less than eighth grade education
$x_2 = 1$ if had 8 years of education
$x_3 = 1$ if had 12 years of education
$x_4 = 1$ if had 13 or more years of education

TABLE 4
OLS ESTIMATES OF EARNING FUNCTIONS

Independent Variable	Log of Annual Income (1966)	Log of Weekly Earnings (1967)	Log of Hourly Wages (1967)
C	5.999**	3.430**	4.977**
	(0.261)	(0.335)	(.281)
X_1	−0.247*	−0.377**	− .338**
	(.123)	(0.130)	(.109)
X_2	−0.222*	−0.098	−0.167*
	(.115)	(0.112)	(0.094)
X_3	−0.020	0.073	0.035
	(.099)	(0.093)	(0.078)
X_4	−0.120	−0.043	0.065
	(.167)	(0.174)	(0.146)
X_5	0.623**	0.258**	0.123*
	(0.067)	(0.083)	(0.070)
X_6	0.424**	0.323**	0.391**
	(0.092)	(0.084)	(0.070)
X_7	−0.259**	−0.240**	−0.208**
	(0.090)	(0.089)	(0.075)
X_8	0.206**	0.273*	0.030
	(0.097)	(0.122)	(.102)
R^2	.549	0.362	.375
F	30.44	9.13	9.59
N	209	138	137

Note: Standard errors in parentheses.
* Significant at 10 per cent level.
** Significant at 1 per cent level.
Source: Based on data from Office of Economic Opportunity Research Computer File.

x_5 = 4 if worked more than 39 weeks during 1966
    = 3 if worked more than 26 weeks but less than 40 weeks during 1966
    = 2 if worked more than 13 weeks but less than 27 weeks during 1966
    = 1 if worked less than 14 weeks
x_6 = 1 if belonged to a union
x_7 = 1 if nonwhite
x_8 = 1 if truck driving is usual job.

Table 5 gives the estimated income for 1966 and weekly earnings and

TABLE 5

EFFECT OF UNIONIZATION ON INCOME, WEEKLY EARNINGS, AND HOURLY
WAGE RATES, 1966 AND 1967, FOR WHITE TRUCKERS
WITH A 9-11TH GRADE EDUCATION

	Annual Income 1966	Weekly Earnings 1967	Hourly Wages 1967
Nonunion	$5,985	112.97	2.38
Union	9,150	156.05	3.51
Percentage increase	52.9%	38.1%	47.9%

Source: Table 4 *supra.*

hourly wages for white, regular drivers with a ninth through eleventh grade education. As Table 5 shows, income in 1966 was 53 per cent higher for unionized workers. Weekly earnings and hourly wage rates were some 38 and 48 per cent higher.

In summary then there are two pieces of evidence dealing with regulated versus unregulated labor: the 1972 census data and the Wychoff and Maister study of owner-operators. They both indicate gains for regulated drivers over unregulated of some 50 to 55 per cent. The ICC time series comparisons with manufacturing and other trucking employees (which include unionized workers) indicate unionization gains over 37 to 48 per cent. The 1965 Department of Labor study shows unionized rates 55 per cent higher than nonunion, and an analysis of the 1967 Office of Economic Opportunity survey data indicates effects of 48 per cent on wage rates and 53 per cent on annual income.

A conservative estimate of the impact regulation-unionization has on wages of truckers, helpers, and platform workers would therefore be about 50 per cent. Some of the evidence suggests the gain could be as large as 55 per cent; the most conservative estimate is 37 per cent. This implies that the gains to Teamster members would have been between $1 billion and $1.3 billion in 1972.

CERTIFICATE HOLDERS

The other major beneficiary of ICC regulation of trucking is the original owners of certificates of public convenience and necessity. After the Motor Carrier Act of 1935[26] became law, the Interstate Commerce Commission "grandfathered" in existing carriers. Out of some 89,000 "grandfather" applications, the commission approved only about 27,000.[27] Any firm that could show evidence it was carrying commodities was licensed to carry the type of commodities it had been handling between the points it had been servicing. Since that time, as was pointed out above, the commission has been very reluctant to grant new competitive authority. Moreover, mergers and failures of existing trucking firms have reduced the number of such firms from over 25,000 in 1939 to 14,648 in 1974. At the same time, the tons shipped by regulated trucks in intercity service have increased from 25.5 million in 1938 to 698.1 million in 1972: a 27-fold increase.[28]

The growth in traffic, the decline in number of firms, and the discouragement of rate competition by rate bureaus and ICC practices have increased the value of certificates considerably. The value of certificates should be equal to the discounted present value of the future rents generated from having the license—these rents being measured as the return above the cost of capital and other resources invested in the trucking industry.

According to a brief submitted to the Financial Accounting Standards Board of the Financial Accounting Foundation by the American Trucking Associations, Inc., the investment in operating rights grew at an annual rate of 16 per cent over the ten-year period from 1962 to 1972.[29] The American Trucking Associations also claimed that "Recent acquisitions in the motor carrier industry indicate that amounts paid for operating authorities are approximately 15 per cent to 20 per cent of the annual revenue produced by those authorities."

The value of certificates as carried on the books of carriers is a poor guide to their actual market value. For certificates that have never been sold, the book value is usually zero. Sometimes the certificate is valued at the legal cost incurred in acquiring it. If the certificate has been bought, however, the acquiring firm may list it at the initial acquisition price. Moreover, at times trucking firms have been permitted or required to amortize the value over

---

[26] Motor Carrier Act of 1935, 49 U.S.C. 301-27 (1939).

[27] ICC, Annual Report (1940).

[28] ICC, *supra* note 17, at releases 2 & 16.

[29] American Trucking Associations, Inc., Accounting for Motor Carrier Operating Rights: Brief and Petition Before the Financial Accounting Standards Board of the Financial Accounting Foundation 6 (1974).

some period. In general it can be safely concluded that the book value is a gross underestimate of the true value of certificates.

Accordin̄g to Section 312 (b) of the Interstate Commerce Act, "Any certificate or permit may be transferred, pursuant to such rules and regulations as the Commission may prescribe."[30] However, the commission must weigh the effect of the proposed transaction and determine whether it is in the public's interest. In interpreting this section, the commission has permitted the sale or lease of operating rights for bona fide business reasons but has frowned on "traffiking" in rights. Thus, if a firm is going out of business because of financial trouble or because the owner is retiring, its certificates can be sold. However, the ICC is generally unwilling to permit a carrier that acquires duplicate rights to sell the duplicate authority.

To investigate the value of these rights, a sample of financial cases involving attempts to purchase certificates or contract-carrier permits was selected by taking all the listings of proposed acquisitions of operating authority from *Traffic World* for several months in 1975 and 1976. Data were collected on over 40 proposed transactions. In the great majority of cases, the selling company claimed either financial difficulty or that the owner was old and sick. In virtually all cases, a protest by another carrier to the proposed transaction was filed, often on the grounds that at least part of the rights had been abandoned and were unused.

From 23 dockets where only rights were being purchased, the contracted price, the estimated revenue, and the estimated before-tax profits that were to be secured from the rights were collected. The estimated revenue and before-tax profits were taken from the "giving-effect" reports filed with the finance application. These "giving-effect" statements report what the purchaser believed would have been the effect if he had owned the certificate in the period immediately prior to the purchase approval.

For the sample of 23 contracts with data on projected revenue, the prices to be paid for the rights were regressed on annual revenue. The regression coefficient was 0.152 with a standard error of .016 and an R^2 of .91. This result turns out to be very robust; elimination of five large observations (the expected revenue ranged from $15,000 to $5,025,000 and the price to be paid for the rights from $3,500 to $800,000 with only three observations of expected revenue over $500,000) produced a regression coefficient of 0.149 with a standard error of 0.025 and an R^2 of .69. It should be noted that these estimates indicate that buyers were on average paying about 15 per cent of the expected annual revenue for the rights being purchased—a figure which is consistent with the estimates made by the American Trucking Associations. In fact, with 90 per cent confidence we can be sure that the true

[30] Interstate Commerce Act, 49 U.S.C. §312(b) (1970).

relationship lies between 12.5 and 17.9 per cent of operating revenues. Since total operating revenue for all Class I and Class II carriers in 1972 was $16.8 billion,[31] we can estimate that the value of certificates and permits outstanding for these carriers were worth between $2.1 billion and $3 billion.

To estimate the rate of return generated annually from the certificates, the projected before-tax profits were regressed on the price paid for rights. The regression coefficient was 0.568 with standard error 0.080 and the R^2 of 70 with 23 observations. This indicates that the true rate of return lies between 43 and 70.6 per cent with 90 per cent confidence—a high rate of return.

Estimating directly the relationship of gross revenue to before-tax profits to measure the gross rents generated indicates that profits were 10.7 per cent of revenue ($R^2 = .877$) with a standard error of 0.87 per cent. This implies that the rents generated from Class I and II certificates and permits in 1972 were between $1.5 billion and $2.0 billion with 90 per cent confidence.

Adding the estimates of the rents to union members of between $1.0 and $1.3 billion and the rents to the owners of certificates and permits of $1.5 to $2.0 billion gives a total of income transfer of between $2.5 and $3.3 billion. As mentioned in the introduction, the price decline that would take place in the absence of regulation would be substantial, and I have used 20 per cent as a conservative figure elsewhere.[32] If we apply 20 per cent to the revenue in 1972, the reduced revenue would be $3.4 billion of which between 74 per cent and 97 per cent were rents to capital and labor. The rest would reflect more efficient operations, less circuity, higher load factors, and less nonprice competition.

CONCLUSION

These figures indicate that three-quarters or more of the cost to shippers and ultimately to consumers of trucking regulation take the form of income transfers to labor and capital involved in trucking. Trucking firms that have bought rights, however, get no real gain from the regulation, since the amount they paid covered the discounted present value of the earnings for the rights. But organized labor continues to receive considerable gains and continues to support the ICC vigorously. It seems likely that some of these gains to labor are dissipated in efforts to secure union jobs in the trucking industry so the net gain may be substantially smaller.

The magnitude of the benefits from regulation make fashioning a deregulation package difficult. To secure the acquiescence of the Teamsters' union

[31] ICC, *supra* note 17, release 3, at tab. 1.

[32] Alexander L. Morton, A Statistical Sketch of Intercity Freight Demand, [No. 296] Highway Research Record 47 (1969).

and the trucking industry would require buying them out at a very large cost. It seems unlikely that Congress would be willing to pay each Teamster truck driver the present value of his gain—a total amount that would be in the billions. Nor would Congress be willing to buy out the owners of certificates and permits for the $2.1 to $3.0 billion estimated above as their present value. Thus any deregulation package is going to face the vigorous opposition of both labor and management.

8

DEREGULATION OF AIR TRANSPORTATION— GETTING FROM HERE TO THERE

Alfred E. Kahn

CAB regulation of the airline industry. Suggested methods of transition to deregulation and increased competition. Free market entry. Price regulation: discount fares and the adjustment of airline revenues. The elasticity of industry demands. Scheduled v. standby service. Price discriminatory practices— discount and standby rates.

This paper will report on a fascinating venture in applied economics—the current efforts at the Civil Aeronautics Board (CAB) to deregulate the airline industry and to restore it as much as possible to the rule of competition. My emphasis will not be on the case for and against deregulation. but rather on the problems of transition, especially on the problem of getting a clear intellectual grasp of what a rational policy for the transition would be. Yet I must begin with the case for deregulation. since it has a strong bearing on the course we are following.

From Alfred E. Kahn, "Deregulation of Air Transportation—Getting from Here to There," pp. 37-59 in Institute for Contemporary Studies (ed.) *Regulating Business: The Search for an Optimum.* Copyright 1978 by the Institute for Contemporary Studies. Reprinted by permission.

THE CASE FOR DEREGULATION, AND A FIRST AREA OF UNCERTAINTY

Fundamentally, this industry is structurally suited to effective competition. Economies of scale are evidently quite limited, and—but for the Federal Aviation Act and the CAB itself— barriers to entry are relatively low. This is true of entry into the industry itself *de novo,* but even more of the entry by existing carriers into new markets, since the principal physical plant is itself mobile.

A second strand in the case for deregulation is that there is no reason to fear that competition in this industry would be destructive. Most city pair markets will support only one carrier, and most of the traffic is concentrated in markets that will support only a few, so oligopolistic restraint is far more likely than cutthroat price rivalry.

The prime requisite for destructive competition is that capital, once sunk in an industry, be immobile, so that under intense rivalry it may have to remain in a depressed industry, while earning subnormal returns for long periods of time. But in this respect the airline industry is almost unique, in that its physical plant, which is only moderately long-lived, can move from one market to another, including to an active second-hand market.

With relatively easy entry, relatively small economies of scale, and mobility of its capital equipment, the technology of aviation seems ideally suited to exactly the flexible adaptation of supply to dynamic market conditions that a market system, if unimpeded by government restrictions, can efficiently accomplish.

There are also the familiar defects of regulation as practiced in the last four years: its heavily protectionist character, the tight limitations on entry, the clogged lineup of applicants for new entry, the restrictions on carrier operations and price competiton. And while it would be quite wrong not to appreciate the quality of service that the airline industry provides, it is possible to see in its performance the consequences of this governmentally imposed cartelization: the tendency for service—and especially scheduling—competition to adjust costs upward to meet the price rather than the reverse, the limited availability of low price and cost options to travelers and shippers, and the inefficiencies and inflexibilities forced on carriers by the persuasive, protectionist restrictions to which they are subject.

My major residual uncertainty concerns the phenomenon of scheduled service. The untutored observer may think that what the airlines provide is simply seats on moving objects, and that one seat is pretty much the same as any other. But an important aspect of the service is availability—the reasonable probability that a passenger can get a ticket by a simple telephone call, on relatively short notice, and for a conveniently scheduled flight, with no penalty if he fails to show up at the flight time. Thus, when average load factors begin to get above 60 or 65 percent, the quality of that particular service begins to deteriorate markedly.

This means that the equilibrium price for this particular, regularly scheduled service has to be high enough to cover unit costs with planes less than, say, 65 percent full; and that means, in turn, that the typical situation is one in which the short-run marginal costs of taking on additional passengers is less than average total costs.

The implications of this are not entirely clear. When marginal costs are close to zero, destructive competition becomes possible because of the strong temptation for sellers to compete in trying to fill those seats at prices far below average cost.

This situation suggests the desirability of a complicated, differentiated scheme of different prices for different packages or kinds of service associated with a seat on a plane. The most obvious, of course, is standby service; but other variations are conceivable, such as truly firm reservations—at some sort of premium, particularly as long as penalties for no-shows are infeasible. Other possibilities include conditional reservations, to account for the necessity of deliberate overbooking in order to maintain load factors and the consequent probability of having to bump overbooked passengers, and various possible auction schemes to minimize the social costs of overbooking by ensuring that passengers who are bumped accept that fate voluntarily because they are suitably compensated. A variety of peak-load pricing schemes is also possible, with standbys being only one kind; other kinds would involve probabilistic calculations in advance of the relationship of demand to capacity at different times and on different flights, along with suitable variations in price (this is the purported basis for such discount fares as Super-Saver, Budget, Apex, and Super-Apex); yet another variation is charter service, with restrictions—advance ticket purchases, cancellation penalties, and acceptance of the risk that the flight will be cancelled if too few seats are subscribed—designed to assure the high load factors that are essential to the economics of the charter operation.

It would seem that the optimum competitive solution would be to offer these various packages of services with only such restrictions on each as are required to make certain that its price is related to the cost of providing it, permitting travelers a free choice among them. While this is indeed my disposition, I confess to a lingering uncertainty about the beneficial effects of the outcome—again, because of the peculiar nature of scheduled service.[1]

THE PROBLEMS OF GRADUALISM

There are really two possible approaches to the goal of transferring this industry from governance by the CAB to the competitive market. One, which is intellectually attractive, is the big-bang method: total freedom of entry and total freedom of pricing at some pre-announced time in the future. That is one that I can genuinely understand, and a reasonably well-developed body of economic theory exists to predict its consequences.

But there is no realistic hope of getting such an act of faith by Congress, and it is impossible to be convinced of its desirability. This is an industry that has grown up in a hothouse, that gives good service, and that has to be financially healthy if it is to continue to give good service in the future. Yet this industry, exposed as it is to critical fluctuations, has one of the highest debt-to-equity ratios in the economy, has only a 2.6 times coverage of its fixed charges, and earned only about 11 percent on equity last year on its trunk lines. Investors obviously agree, since market values of airline equities are averaging only about two-thirds of book value.

So we are inevitably committed to gradualism — necessarily, if there is no change in the statute, but almost certainly even if there is. The problem, however, is that there really is no blueprint for a gradual transition, no organized body of theory by which to plan and monitor it.

Second-Best Options

On the contrary, we are left with the theory of second best. This theory tells us that if we want to go from point A, which is here, to point C, which is there, it is not necessarily socially efficient to go part way in that direction, from A to B.

One lesson we have learned from the history of airlines is that, in the absence of price competition, rivalry among carriers tends to take the form instead of costly improvements in service. And the evidence seems quite clear that an increase in the number of carriers in a particular market appears to be correlated with a decline in load factors—an increase, in other words, in cost-inflating service rivalry.

These applications, therefore, confront me regularly with the vexing question of whether in fact I want to substitute a less efficient duopoly or oligopoly for a more efficient monopoly. This is not to deprecate the value of service competition: in view of the kinds of needs that scheduled service is intended to satisfy, load factors can be too high as well as too low. The difficulty is that if passengers are presented with no alternative, higher load factor/lower fare options, there is no effective market determination of whether service is too good, in a sense of being costlier than consumers would be willing to accept if given a choice.

Although, therefore, two sellers are closer than is one seller to many, and the change may increase the likelihood of effective competition in second-best terms, going part way (or, in the more familiar application of second best, all the way in one part of the economy) may be worse than not moving at all.

I am reasonably persuaded that if we are to make genuine progress toward effective competition, we have to institute some system of automatic, discretionary entry into markets—some reliable promise to all the carriers that they will at some certain date, or according to some predetermined time schedule, be free to start entering new markets, and, by the same token, be subject to penetration of their markets by others, without CAB permission.

The virtue of such an arrangement is that it will force each of the carriers to start figuring out now what services it can provide best, and what kinds it had better leave to its competitors; to start planning a rationalization of its route structures in order to improve its ability to compete; to start examining the services it now offers and effecting such improvements as it can, with an eye to forestalling competitive entry.

But if the process—of entry, rationalization, and exit—is to be gradual and limited, we have reason to be worried about the beneficence and effectiveness of the competition that is likely to ensue.

It is unlikely that the resulting competition can be on the basis of relative efficiency alone. From past practice, the main determinant of relative carrier costs is not the quality of management, but the route structures—long haul or short, in thin markets or thick. The ability of carrier A to compete successfully over a particular route with carrier B will be heavily influenced not by its efficiency, but by the nature of the carriers' respective feed-in and beyond routes. Competition is based on whether business goes to seller A in preference to seller B because A has customers available from its own feeder routes, or because it has rights to routes beyond that enable only A to offer single-plane service to travelers to these beyond points.

This last distortion raises questions about the ultimate feasibility of competition in this industry, not simply about the feasibility of a gradual transition. I am, I regret to say, unable as yet to assess its significance. In part, it seems to describe a genuine service advantage of integration, to the extent that multistop carriage by a single airline reduces the need to change planes. But where transfer between planes is involved, the advantage enjoyed by a single airline is merely tactical: if a single carrier handled all the traffic in and out of O'Hare airport, it is difficult to see how the average walk between planes could be reduced, unless the monopolist reduced flight schedules.

My tentative resolution of these dilemmas—the danger of transforming efficient monopolies into inefficient duopolies, competing only in cost-inflating services, and the dangers of unequal competition because of differential route restrictions and handicaps—is along the following lines:

First, we must be as receptive and as liberal as possible in permitting existing carriers to realign their routes and to slough off the restrictions that limit their operating flexibility and force inefficiencies on them.

Second, more and more of the certificated authority that we grant must be made *permissive* and *nonexclusive*. If two carriers are applying for a particular route—the traffic on which appears to be large enough to justify only one—I suggest that we should carefully consider *permitting both* but *requiring neither*. At present, applications are too often essentially preclusive in their motivation: a carrier applies for a certificate for a particular market because it wants to prevent a competitor from getting the award, and because also, since the license is exclusive, it is salable. These considerations, it may feel, are valuable enough to justify its undertaking the minimum service required to keep the authority, even if it is uneconomic.

Making the grants nonexclusive and permissive in these circumstances should:

(a) cut down on the applications that are justified only on the expectation that the certificates granted will be few, and that if X gets it, Y will not;

(b) cut down on the offer of uneconomic service, merely in order to hold an authority;

(c) keep a competitor or competitors with unexercised authority standing by at the edge of the market and in a position to enter without further permission from us, if service is too poor or rates too high;

(d) and so, perhaps, put a limit on cost-inflating, nonprice competition.

Third, we should be particularly receptive to proposed new services with a low price dimension. I refer here not to the mere verbal promises of low fares, but to the offer of a plan that backs up that promise with a credible expectation of low-cost operations with high break-even load factors. Such entry is the most effective device for holding cost-inflating service rivalry in check.

And fourth, we must extend freedom of entry as widely as possible. This, paradoxically, is the only answer I can think of to the contention that free entry will permit the bigger airlines, with ample feeder and beyond operations, to funnel intermediate traffic into its own aircraft, making it impossible for smaller, more specialized carriers to compete. For if there are either genuine economies or merely tactical advantages of linking routes together in this way, there are also powerful economies of specialization.

So far as I know there is no objective basis for deciding where the integrated, typically larger carrier can out-compete more specialized rivals, and where the specialized carrier will have a clear advantage. Since there will undoubtedly be situations of both kinds, we may conclude that under a competitive regime these various market situations will sift themselves out automatically, with various kinds of suppliers emerging successful on the basis of their respective advantages and handicaps in each kind of market situation. Hence my prescription of free entry.

PRICING

The task of trying to regulate price in a period of transition is proving even more difficult than regulating entry.

Price Ceilings

First is the question of whether carriers should be free to raise their rates. In principle, obviously they should: the introduction of more competition surely means that some prices will have to go up just as others will go down.

But there is still a great deal of monopoly power in this industry. To extend to carriers the freedom to increase prices more rapidly than the increase in effective competition is to assure exploitation of customers. Introduction of the former must be synchronized with the latter, and specifically with freedom of entry, if we are not going to follow the big-bang approach.

So I don't see how we can soon give up control over rate levels or cease to set rate ceilings. In fact, we have scarcely begun to confront the question of whether we can ever totally deregulate price in the majority of markets that can support only a single carrier.

Rate Reductions

The question of whether we need to limit the freedom to cut prices, and if so, how, is the most complicated of all.

At first blush, it would seem that we must be able to set price floors so long as we must also fix ceilings. In a system that is part competitive and part monopolistic, price reductions are likely to be selective and discriminatory—directed at particular markets or at particular categories of travelers, and framed to deny the benefits to customers whose demands are comparatively inelastic. This is not necessarily bad in a situation in which marginal costs are below average, and in which, therefore, the cost of picking up additional customers may be very low. But in contrast with the regulation of traditional public utilities, where, at least in principle, the regulatory commission can permit such selective price reductions only when they produce additional net revenues which can be passed on to all customers, there is no way the CAB can permit unrestricted price competition and have that kind of assurance. On the contrary, if we do not intervene in one way or another, the clear danger is that selective price reductions producing declines in net revenues will lead automatically to requests for general rate increases—with the probable result of accenting the discrimination between the customers who get the cuts and the ones who are forced to bear the increases.

In regulated markets, there is ordinarily no reason for concern about this kind of recoupment: there is usually no reason why a price cut in one market would change the profit-maximizing price in another. But if price regulation is at all effective, it prevents the full exploitation of monopoly power, so that recoupment of net revenue losses is not only possible but, in a sense, obligatory under the 5th and 14th amendments to the Constitution!

Partly for this reason, the CAB has typically judged proposed discount fares in terms of whether they would be mainly "diversionary" or "generative" of new traffic. In so doing, the board was actually deciding whether the reduction was in the interest of the carrier that proposed it. But the board also seems to have attempted to serve as a grand monopolist, permitting only price decreases that would be profitable for the industry as a whole. So, for example, it traditionally opposed rate cuts by small suppliers, on the ground that the increased sales would be mainly at the expense of their competitors. Of course, it is precisely the greater elasticity in the demand for the services of the individual competitor—and particularly the individual competitor with a small stake in the market—that of the market as a whole that makes competition work; and it is precisely in the nature of a monopoly or an effective cartel to permit only price decreases that are justified in terms of the elasticity of total industry demand.

It is not clear to me, however, that this kind of close CAB scrutiny of proposed discount fares is necessary to protect regular fare-paying customers from the burden of recoupment. We make our calculations of industry cost of service, and therefore of the presence or absence of revenue deficiencies such as are required to justify general rate increases, on an industry-wide basis; and, even more pertinent, for the last several years we have, in making these calculations, applied an adjustment of industry revenues for the traffic moving under discount fares. The purpose of this adjustment is to assure that revenue deficiencies resulting from discount fares do not in fact justify fare increases.

To understand this discount fare adjustment, one must begin with the board's decision in the early 1970s, in its Domestic Passenger Fare Investigation, to establish a load factor standard—which it set at 55 percent—in order to shelter passengers from having to bear the costs of excessive unused capacity. Under that adjustment, when the carriers come to us with a request for fare increases, we remove from consideration a share of capacity-related costs equivalent to the number of percentage points by which the percentage of seats occupied falls short of the standard. In principle, this adjustment makes 55 percent the break-even load factor for the industry as a whole. If the companies acquire equipment and schedule flights beyond the levels that will permit a 55 percent use of capacity, they will earn less than their nominally permitted rate of return.

But this adjustment alone does not say anything about how those permitted revenues will be obtained from the various classes of customers; specifically, it does not protect the regular fare-paying customer from the burdens of nonremunerative discount fares. The more the 55 percent standard load factor is achieved with discount-fare passengers, the higher the regular fares will have to be. For this reason, the board has introduced its discount fare adjustment, the essential purpose and consequence of which is to set the fares for regular service at the *average* cost of service with the standard load factor.

This means that if carriers charge some passengers less than this fare, they will either suffer shortfalls in their rate of return *or* will have to operate at a higher than 55 percent load factor. The adjustment, therefore, increases the break-even load factor above 55 percent in proportion to the discount fares offered. Thus, the carriers as a group will be motivated on the one hand to control their scheduling, and on the other to offer only such discount fares as generate enough additional traffic to compensate for the reduced average yield.

I began this discussion by expressing doubt that, in view of the discount fare adjustment, it is necessary for the CAB to evaluate and consider disallowing proposed discount fares in order to protect regular fare-paying customers from having their rates increased to compensate for any resultant net revenue deficiencies. There might, however, be three residual bases to justify the CAB continuing to pass on discount offerings. First, they might be predatory. Second is the possibility that competition in the industry, in price and/or scheduling, tends to be destructive—i.e., tends chronically to induce companies to offer discounts that cover marginal but not average costs and that generate insufficient additional traffic to compensate for the reduced yields; and/or to schedule flights in such volume as to make the industry as a whole fail to achieve its break-even load factor. These fears are not necessarily ridiculous, when the typical situation is one in which (a) flights go out with large numbers of empty seats, and (b) seats are not auctioned off to the highest bidders when the demand for reservations exceeds the number available, but must instead be sold at average costs.

The third possible reason for CAB review of proposed price cuts would be a desire to protect the regular fare-paying customer, the threat to whom is not only that his fares may be raised—something that the discount adjustment presumably prevents—but that the quality of the service provided may deteriorate. If the various discount fares have the effect of filling planes, they clearly could diminish the ability of regular fare-paying customers to make reservations on flights of their choice on relatively short notice. Such customers can obviously be injured just as much by increases in load factors above 55 percent—with a consequent decline in the quality of the service they get, while continuing to pay fares set at the cost of giving them 55 percent load factor service—as by having the fares themselves increased to recover net revenue losses from discount fares. I am told it was Louis Engman who coined the aphorism that the businessman who has an empty seat next to him to put his hat on would probably be less pleased if he realized he was paying the fare for the hat too; but he would presumably be even less pleased if he continued to pay for the hat, but the empty seat was now filled with a discount fare-paying passenger!

The Question of Discrimination

As this last consideration suggests, we cannot ignore the question of whether discount fares of various kinds are, as the statute puts it, unduly discriminatory.

The first question is, are they discriminatory? The answer is neither obvious nor simple.

A reduced fare for genuine standby service is obviously in itself not discriminatory: the passenger is buying a distinct (and inferior) service, with a marginal cost anywhere down from the regular fare to zero.[2]

But, you may remonstrate, if a plane would otherwise go out with seats empty, isn't the marginal cost below the regular fare for all the passengers, rather than just for those who happened to opt for standby service? Wouldn't the only non-discriminatory price be the one that cleared the entire market—i.e., equated the total number of seats on the plane with the number demanded—on every flight just before departure time?

One answer is that the regular passenger buys an advance assurance of a seat, at a fixed price, as well as some reasonable possibility of being able to make reservations in advance on a flight of his choice; he is also paying for the privilege of not having to pay a penalty if he does not show up at flight time. All of these aspects of the service have a higher marginal cost than does standby service. Scheduled service is marginally responsible for a carrier's incurring capacity costs; standby, which corresponds to sales of gas or electricity on an incompatible basis, is not.

Lower rates for charters, similarly, are not in themselves discriminatory. In charter service, the unit of sale is the entire plane, at an implicit price per seat equal to the average total cost of a flight 100 percent full. The risk of a lower load factor is transferred to the tour operator, and through him, in large measure, to the ultimate passenger; the latter bears the burden of guaranteeing the operator a sale in advance, with a heavy penalty for no-shows, and a risk that if the load factor falls far enough below 100 percent, the plane will not depart. Both the short-run and the long-run marginal cost of this kind of service is clearly far below that of regular scheduled service.

On the other hand, there can be no question that many of the restrictions imposed on charter flights go far beyond what is necessary to assure the kind of risk shifting I have just described and the low marginal costs it entails, and are therefore clearly discriminatory. The most obvious case is the historic attempt to confine the privilege of flying on charters to affinity groups. But also the long advance-purchase requirements, the minimum stay (this blatant discrimination obviously prevails on scheduled service as well: there is absolutely no inherent reason why the marginal or average cost of providing service to travelers who stay, say, 22 to 45 days is in any way less than for passengers whose trips must be much briefer); the prohibition of fill-ups (which, in fact, contribute positively to the likelihood of securing the high load factors that make charters cost-justified); the requirement that the traveler purchase various ground packages; the minimum group sizes; the limits on the substitution; and the obligation to return with the group. All of these restrictions were clearly designed for protectionist reasons, to confine these lower fares to the presumably demand-elastic customers, to prevent leakage into that market of the demand-inelastic customers, and to protect the scheduled carriers against excessive loss of traffic. They are, in short, designed to effect the separation of markets that is necessary for price discrimination to be practiced; in the process, they clearly harass and confuse passengers, and unnecessarily degrade the quality of service they receive.

The most interesting and difficult cases are the discount fares that we have been receiving in great profusion during the last year from the scheduled carriers. These provide advance reservation of guaranteed seats on regularly scheduled flights at low rates, subject to such restrictions as the need for advance reservation, advance ticket purchase, a penalty for no-shows or cancellations, and minimum stay requirements. In the case of Budget fares, some uncertainty about the particular day and time of departure exists until as little as a week before flight time; in the case of part charters and charter transfers, the same restrictions are applied as those of the charters themselves, with the transfer being at the option of the carrier; and, in all cases, a carrier sets limits, varying with the day of the week and season of the year, on the number of seats made available at these rates.

The theory is, of course, that these fares will be used only to fill seats that would otherwise go empty. They therefore represent a form of peak-load pricing, and—paradoxically, in view of the fact that the reservation must be made many weeks in advance—they partake of the character of standbys, anticipatory standbys, as it were, with the carriers estimating the number of seats that they can safely offer at these low rates. The carriers say they can make these advance commitments without later having to deny regular fare-paying customers reservations because of the accuracy of their forecasting techniques and their conservation in determining the number of seats they will offer at these fares.

In many ways, therefore, the marginal costs of this business, both long- and short-run—including the opportunity cost of denying places to other passengers—is less than those of regular service, for the same reasons as apply to standbys: these are off-peak rates, and the limitation on the number of seats made available at these low prices is a form of interruptibility, such as is frequently practiced in the distribution of gas and electricity. The passenger who calls for a regular reservation has a greater likelihood of obtaining a seat; the greater that likelihood, the more it costs in the long run to provide. The purchaser of the Super-Apex stands a greater chance of being told that the number of seats available has been exhausted.

But, in contrast with ordinary standbys, these fares also embody very substantial elements of discrimination. Many of the restrictions on their availability, closely resembling the ones imposed on charter passengers, are clearly aimed at confining them to demand-elastic customers. Indeed, the discrimination is even more blatant here than in the case of charters, since these tickets are on regularly scheduled flights, and since—apart from the rather mild penalty for cancellation (and some of the timing uncertainties of Budget service)—the customer gets the same assured reservation, far in advance, as the normal fare-payer.

Moreover, if the availability of seats is correctly calculated so that these are truly anticipatory standbys, with the result that the short-run marginal cost is very low, then it is just as clearly very low for the regular fare-payer, who may call on the very same day to make a reservation on the very same flight but, if he fails to utter the magic words "Super-Apex," pays twice as much.

The question of whether these fares—and particularly the last group—are discriminatory is thus a fairly easy one. But an affirmative answer to that question is not a sufficient basis for prohibiting this kind of pricing on either economic or legal grounds. The economic case for price discrimination in situations in which the marginal costs are below average is a familiar one: so long as the lower-fare traffic covers its marginal cost, it is economically efficient to take it on; and so long as the demand for the lower-fare services is sufficiently elastic that the discounts will bring in additional net revenues, the customers discriminated against cannot be injured and may actually be benefited. How do these fares measure up against these two conditions?

Do These Fares Cover Marginal Costs?

There are three dimensions or components of the short-run marginal cost (SRMC) of a service like Super-Saver or Super-Apex.

1. One is the costs, such as ticketing, check-ins, baggage handling, and meals, that vary with the number of customers. If the only seats made available are seats that would otherwise go out empty, these would be the only marginal costs imposed on the supplier.
2. Since the number of seats made available at the discount fares is restricted, there is a possibility that the supply on a particular profit will fall short of the number demanded, with the rationing accomplished on a first-come-first-served basis. In these circumstances, the measure of SRMC would be the opportunity cost involved in A getting the seat·in preference to B—specifically, the value of the trip to the one who would have been the highest unsuccessful bidder if the seats had been auctioned off.
3. Finally, there are what we might regard as the external costs— the effect of filling these seats in advance on the ability of regular fare-paying customers to get reservations, and the diminution in the comfort those customers experience when planes are fuller than the 55 percent load factor, the average cost of which their fares are intended to cover.

I do not see any reason to believe the carriers would ordinarily set these fares below SRMC, measured in any of these ways, except possibly for predatory reasons.

For the first component, it would clearly be irrational for them not to cover the out-of-pocket customer costs. As for the second aspect, it is difficult to see why the carriers would intentionally set the prices of the restricted number of seats they offer at a level below what would clear the particular market. On the contrary, one would expect them to try to maximize their net return over customer costs, even if that meant letting some of the seats remain empty. In point of fact, their range of discretion is probably quite limited. These fares are set within range of such alternatives as charters and the Laker Skytrain, with adjustments for differences in the quality of service; because of the expected high cross-elasticity of demand among these competing services, there seems little reason to expect carriers to set these fares significantly below their short-run marginal opportunity costs, as I have defined them. The main purposes of the capacity limitations would seem not so much to ration demand at prices below the market-clearing levels as to minimize the adverse impact on the availability of reservations for regular service, and to placate regulatory authorities who may be concerned about an impact.

This is *not* to say it would be reasonable to expect the third component of marginal cost—the value of these seats to any would-be normal fare-paying customers foreclosed from getting them by the discount traffic (and the marginal discomfort imposed because of the congestion they cause)—to be held to zero. On the contrary, I would expect carriers, if they were free to pursue their interests, to offer these discount seats up to the point at which their marginal costs, measured in this way, equal the fares. It would pay a carrier to offer these seats at, say, $100 (above customer costs) until the point that the expected loss of passengers at the normal fare of $200 (above customer costs) reached 0.5. What I would *not* expect them to do would be to charge *less* than those short-run marginal opportunity costs—i.e., the value of the seats to the displaced regular fare-paying customers, multiplied by the probability of such displacement at the margin. There is no reason to expect a carrier to take on a $100 discount customer when there is *more* than 0.5 probability of displacing a $200 one—i.e., when the mean expected result would be to lose $101.

So, still confining our attention to SRMC (and ignoring the possibility of predatory motives), I believe these fares are probably economically efficient. If a carrier prefers to take on two discount customers at $100 each (above customer costs) at a mean expected loss of one regular fare at $198, that is socially efficient: the value of the service to the marginal customer who travels is $100, the marginal social opportunity cost $99.

Long-Run Incremental Costs (LRIC)

The Civil Aeronautics Board has objected in the past to discount fares, however—only a few years ago, in its Discount Passenger Fares Investigation (DPFI), it adopted the rule that it would permit them only temporarily, and in times of general excess capacity—on the ground that in the long run the marginal cost of discount traffic is no less than that of regular traffic.

There were two bases for this conclusion: first, the apparent absence of economies of scale in the airline industry, and second, the belief that additional discount traffic in the long run leads to additional scheduling in the same way as regular traffic. These two premises, taken together, compel the conclusion that any additional traffic generated by discount fares has the same LRIC as regular traffic, with both being equal to average, fully allocated costs.

The second of these assumptions is, I think, incredible, in the presence of the board's discount fare adjustment. It would be irrational for a carrier to count a half-fare paying passenger more than half as much as a full-fare customer (as always, I refer to fares in excess of customer costs) in inducing it to acquire additional planes or to schedule additional flights. The break-even load factor—which is the point at which adding capacity becomes marginally profitable—of a plane with a large number of discount customers will obviously be higher than if all paid the full fare.

This would not be so in the absence of the discount fare adjustment. If a carrier can recoup any net revenue losses from discount traffic by raising regular fares, with the result that its *average* net yield per passenger is unchanged, the break-even load factor and the point of adding capacity would obviously remain constant. This is perhaps part of the explanation of the historical stability of load factors in the face of spreading discount fares in the past to which opponents of these fares have often pointed.

This reasoning has the interesting consequences of making the LRIC of a particular class of customers dependent on the price they are charged—the lower the fare, the less the individual sale contributes causally to additional scheduling. But of course it is rational for a supplier to vary output so as to equate marginal cost with prices; and that is what I am predicting here.[3]

In short, then, I see these troublesome fares as almost certainly covering both their SRMC and LRIC; in these circumstances, it seems it would almost always be economically efficient to permit them.

The Impact on the Regular Fare-Payer

There is a strong regulatory tradition, however, that discriminatory discounts should be permitted to certain classes of customers only up to the point that maximizes the benefit to the customers discriminated against; that tradition would not contemplate with equanimity an actual injury to the latter. But, although our discount fare adjustment protects regular fare-paying customers from recoupment in the form of higher money prices, it does not protect them against an effective increase in price when the quality of service declines.

Increasing the average load factor to, say, 75 percent by the sale of "anticipatory standbys" does not necessarily diminish the ability of regular fare-paying customers to get reservations. If carriers had perfect foresight, they could theoretically get even 100 percent load factors without having that effect. But, as I have already observed, it appears carriers would have to go beyond 75 percent, because two birds in hand at half fare are worth up to one in the bush at full fare, even though the telephone call from the one in the bush were 100 percent predictable. And there remains the fact also that a full plane is less comfortable to ride in than one that is half full.

The regulator under injunction to avoid "undue discrimination" will continue to be uneasy with discriminatory discounts, therefore, even if persuaded they are economically efficient, until he can figure out some way of having the regular fare-paying customer get some benefit from them as well. Perhaps they do benefit automatically. The possibility of scheduled carriers offering these special rates to fill empty seats improves the financial viability of their service—recall my earlier expression of concern about the possible attrition of scheduled service if travelers have free access to low-cost charters, and my suggestion that one way of preserving the former option is to encourage the scheduled carriers to offer a variety of price/quality options in order to fill more of their seats. Indeed, the additional traffic they are able to attract in this way could justify additional scheduling, and in this way confer positive benefits on their regular fare-paying patrons.

It is worth considering the possibility of a direct recompense as well. Possibly regular fare-paying customers should be entitled to rebates when load factors on a particular flight get above a certain level—forcing the carriers to share with them some of the benefits from the higher load factors that also adulterate the quality of the service they receive. One drawback of such a scheme would be that the rebates would go partially to the wrong people—to the ones who get on the high load factor flights rather than to those who call vainly for reservations on them.

THE PROPER FOCUS OF REGULATORY CONCERN

Although we spend a great deal of time evaluating these special rates and trying to devise standards by which to judge them, the overriding responsibility and concern of regulators must ultimately be to preserve and accentuate the competitiveness of this industry's market structure as the principal means of protecting the interest of passengers. This means not only that we must be alert to possibly predatory price cuts—to which I have alluded only in passing—as we obviously were in dealing with the transatlantic fares that purported to be responses to the Laker Skytrain. Much more important, we must liberalize the conditions of entry and exit, leaving those decisions to the unfettered discretion of management. This is the best possible protection for passengers, regular fare-payers, and discount passengers alike.

This means, among other things, that we should be constantly considering how we can loosen the fetters we now impose upon different segments of the industry. Here, as in the case of entry, if we are not to take the big-bang approach, we must try to introduce the liberalizations as much in step as possible, in the interest of preserving equality of competitive opportunities—loosening the restrictions on the incumbents as well as new entrants, on supplementals, tour operators, and the scheduled carriers, on the combination carriers of freight and the all-cargo carriers, on the airlines traditionally restricted to international traffic as well as to domestic routes, and to foreign carriers as well as to domestic.

During the next several years—in a regime less hostile to rate cuts, selective or general, and more hospitable to entry—I look to a more variegated airline industry structure, in which the traditional rigid geographic and functional boundaries between different carriers and categories become blurred and governmentally protected spheres of influence less distinct, a structure that offers the maximum possible assurance of continuation of the competitive spur and that offers exciting new opportunities for managerial enterprise. And I look for a corresponding and increasingly variegated set of price and service options, competitively offered to passengers and shippers.

COMMENT

RAYMOND F. O'BRIEN
President, Consolidated Freightways, Inc.
The two basic regulatory features which are the chief targets of the
[motor carrier] deregulators are control of entry and collective
ratemaking. Congress believed these provisions were necessary to
ensure a healthy and stable transportation industry. Those who advocate removal or substantial weakening of those provisions believe
it would mean more competition, lower rates, and presumably, better service.

The trucking industry—or most 'of it—thinks it would result in
rate and service discrimination against small shippers and small
towns, a deterioration in the quality of service, and general distress,
if not chaos, in much of the industry—all without accomplishing
the stated goals except for a few big shippers. . . .

Judging by the nervousness of . . . lenders and investors, the
current pressure for deregulation seems to be a bit stronger than in
the past. . . . [It] also reflects the growing public distrust of both
big government and big business, and the popularity of words like
"reform.". . . If you're going to reform something, you have to
change it. Governmentally speaking, that generally translates into
more regulation of what is perceived as too free, and more freedom
for what seems too regulated. Some of the same people who advocate deregulating the trucking industry to provide more competition
and lower prices seem to think we should regulate the oil industry
to provide more competition and lower prices. . . .

The director of the ICC's Bureau of Economics, Ernest R. Ol-
son, recently commented on the lack of adequate information. He
said the ICC knows little about such problems as traffic flow, commodities hauled, authorities used, industry structure, service factors, and the infrastructure of trucking. If this makes it hard to
regulate, it should also make us leery of academics who claim to
have all the answers. So my first question is: What is the problem? . . . There are remarkably few facts on which there is any
general agreement. Most of the statements are made by people who
really know very little about the trucking business, or about any
business, for that matter. . . .

When I hear someone say there should be more competition, I
think they must be talking about some other business. Investors in
some of the well-known companies which have gone bankrupt in
the past few years . . . would have to laugh at that idea if it didn't
hurt so much. A Department of Transportation study found that 85

percent of shippers surveyed thought there was enough competition in trucking. That's about as close to a consensus as you're likely to get on any subject. . . .

Who wants a change? . . . We find a strong push coming from educators, economists, and government officials, many of whom consider themselves spokesmen for and defenders of the public interest. They deal mainly in theories, and they have plenty of colleagues who disagree on all counts. I, for one, do not agree that Ralph Nader and his associates necessarily represent the public interest 100 percent of the time.

Another group which generally favors partial or total deregulation is the independent operator, the man who owns his own truck and either operates under lease to a certified carrier or handles unregulated commodities. Either way, he often has difficulty lining up return loads, and assumes that he could do better if he were permitted to haul anything for anybody. I agree that he has problems, stemming largely from the steep rise in fuel costs and the 55-mile speed limit. But letting him haul common carrier freight would only shift the problem, not cure it. . . . Deregulation would not create any new freight to haul. It would only redistribute it somewhat.

Why do they want a change? . . . The world is full of people who want to change things, and other people who want to leave things as they are. Some feel a need to justify their education by tinkering with the system. They are full of solutions and looking for problems.

It is often charged that the regulators have become more concerned with the well-being of those they are regulating than with the public interest . . . but after all, the National Transportation Policy as enacted by Congress clearly requires the regulators to "foster sound economic conditions in . . . and among the several carriers." Regulatory tradition calls for an adversary relationship, but a realistic view of the problems of large portions of our transportation system indicates that a cooperative approach may be needed. . . .

Suppose we allow freedom of entry. As Mr. Kahn has stated, effective competition and simple equity would require that carriers be given freedom of exit as well as entry. When I count the number of motor carriers with whom we compete in every sizable market, I feel we already have all the freedom of entry we need. . . . In California, which has an easy entry policy, the "in and out" turnover rate is already estimated at 2,500 small carriers per year. It's hard to see how such a situation can result in the kind of stability needed to foster sound business relationships.

Finally . . . from a purely selfish standpoint, Consolidated Freightways should probably favor total deregulation of trucking. I believe we would eventually operate more profitably, and that we have little to fear. . . . The fact that there is no regulation of an industry does not mean there is complete freedom of entry. In today's world, most industries require substantial capital investment to compete successfully, let alone start from scratch. There are many fields in which there is seldom if ever a new competitor to contend with, yet there is generally plenty of competition.

I recently read a letter to the chairman of the Interstate Commerce Commission, Dan O'Neal, from John Wagner, president of the Local and Short Haul Carriers National Conference . . . outlining the serious effects which commission actions and proposals have had and would have on members of the conference. His letter makes the following statement: "Deregulation—by big government action—is, after all, really pro-big business. Easier entry into trucking, for example, is ultimately a hollow thing, an empty promise, because the economic forces are already so heavily weighted in favor of existing big carriers." I think Mr. Wagner has a point, and that there are economies of scale in trucking despite Mr. Shenefield's contrary opinion. . . .

The need to assure efficient service to the public at reasonable rates, and without discrimination as to people or places, is what tips the scales in favor of ICC-type regulation, in our opinion.

To close with another quotation, the report on National Transportation Policy prepared in 1961 for the Senate Committee on Interstate and Foreign Commerce remarked that, "There appears to be no chance of unregulated competition operating in the national interest until the Golden Rule becomes the universally accepted law of business relations." It would seem a lot of people think the millenium is already upon us.

JORDAN JAY HILLMAN
Professor of Law, Northwestern University

Having made room for the future in our total calculus, we have to shift our mental gears again by recognizing that an established system of regulation inevitably engenders its own adaptive responses and nurtured expectations. We simply can't sweep away the investments which have been made under the rules as they are known today, whether those rules be economically rational or not. . . .

Like any broker representing all parties to a transaction, who would like to continue in the job, Congress often finds equivocation a prudent substitute for clear-cut decisions. . . . In the Transportation Act of 1958 . . . Congress provided a first-rate demonstration of how to make major changes in the language of the law while keeping its substance intact. I note the possibility of a similar occurrence in the 1976 Quad-R Act. While seeming to establish the reasonableness of competitive rates productive of revenues in excess of relevant variable costs, Congress nevertheless declared as unlawful, not only any competitive practice which is "unfair, destructive or predatory," but also those which "otherwise undermine competition which is necessary in the public interest." The opportunity to find rates illegal on the basis of this amorphous phrase again gives to a regulatory agency which remains hostile to the basic statutory standard a potentially powerful weapon with which to subvert that standard. . . .

It is not hard to entice Congress into using boards and commissions as dumping grounds for hard decisions. It is an especially dangerous practice, however, when the effort is to force new rules and the administrative agency, in its heart, remains wedded to the old rules.

Section

III

Energy
Policy

9

REGULATING ENERGY
Indicative Planning or Creeping Nationalization?

V. KERRY SMITH

Rationale for government intervention. Efficiency motives—
micro and macro. The three Ps of regulation: principles, procedures, and practice. Private market allocation of exhaustible
resources. The old policy and the NEP. Price control inefficiencies. NEP misconceptions and implications for the future.

INTRODUCTION

The president's recent energy proposals are based on the
premise that energy is a unique resource, requiring continuous governmental regulation.[1] The allocation of energy resources therefore offers an appropriate case study for those
interested in the uses and abuses of regulation. Moreover, our
newly formulated National Energy Plan (NEP) is an excellent
starting point. It proposes national consumption goals, outlines government policies which are admittedly incapable of

*Thanks are due J. Alterman, E. N. Castle, R. Kopp, M. Russell, E. Seskin, S. P.
Smith, and P. Smith for most helpful discussions of these issues. The views expressed, however, are entirely those of the author.

achievement without complementary efforts, acknowledges that further mandatory controls will be undertaken if these goals are not realized, and extols the virtues of voluntary private market solutions to the energy problem.

Large-scale government intervention in the extractive sector does not begin with the proposed NEP. Its origins can be found in the 1913 provisions of early income tax legislation. Differential treatment of these industries has increased historically, partly by accident, partly by design. In this paper, however, I will argue that our current policy proposals represent a new, potentially ill-fated approach to remedy problems induced, in part, by the failures of past government intervention.[2] Assuming that "a price is enough," current proposals seek simultaneously to: (a) achieve the microefficiency goals traditionally associated with regulatory programs, (b) "do no harm" to the overall economy, and (c) determine the quantity, mix, and ultimate consumers of our energy resources — all under the banner of "indicative planning."[3]

While this appraisal may seem too roughshod and therefore unfair, the history of intervention in this area suggests that our current energy problems are closely linked to the failures of government policies, particularly since 1973. Rather than reform the process of intervention completely, the newly proposed measures merely "add on" further controls, potentially compounding past errors.

Let's begin by considering whether our energy problems are the direct result of OAPEC actions in 1973.[4] In my judgment, the dramatic increase in world prices that occurred at that time only accentuated a process initiated by earlier regulation of the industry. The most basic problem is that regulation has served to give *different* signals to consumers and producers of energy resources, with corresponding differences in their responses.

Figure 1: Real Price Trends for Energy to Consumers

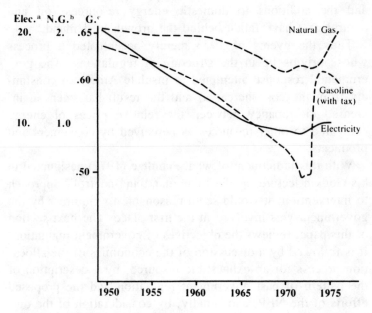

Elec.[a] N.G.[b] G.[c]

aDollars per million BTU.
aDollars per million BTU.
cCents per gallon.

Source: Russell 1977*a*

Figure 1 illustrates the movements in the real prices of three primary sources of energy for U.S. consumers from 1950 to 1976. In all cases the prices, in constant dollars, are lower in 1976 than they were twenty-five years earlier. The unsurprising result was the substantial increase in energy consumption.[5] At the same time, however, the real prices received by producers remained relatively stable until 1973, and the additions to domestic energy resources (oil and natural gas) have fallen behind the growth in demand.[6]

Thus the events of 1973 merely accentuated a process whose origins lie in the structure of regulations. The governmental response attempted to insulate American consumers from the cost increases, and the result has been an increased discrepancy between the relative prices of energy compared to other resources as perceived by consumers and producers.

With this indictment of what Schultze (1977) designated in his Godkin lectures as the "command-and-control" approach to intervention, it would seem reasonable to inquire why the government gets involved in the first place. The next section of this paper reviews the objectives of government regulation. It is followed by a discussion of the economics of the allocation process for an exhaustible resource, by a description of the pattern of past government regulation and the proposed efforts of the NEP, and, finally, by consideration of the outlook for energy regulation and prospects for the use of private markets in the future allocation of energy resources.

WHY REGULATE?

Under ideal conditions, private markets represent a rather unique form of social interaction. Through the process of exchange, those who demand products and those who supply them reveal their respective marginal valuations and costs, and this interaction assures that resources are allocated to their highest valued uses. Unfortunately, these circumstances are idealized, and there are a number of cases when the production or consumption of a good or service has special attributes not reflected by market prices.[7] Therefore, if these characteristics affect resource allocation, intervention is often warranted on grounds of efficiency.

In discussing efficiency as a motive for intervention, it is important to distinguish the concepts of micro and macro efficiency. The former relates to the allocation of resources to their highest valued uses—in general terms, a gauge of the manner in which an allocation process meets the material needs of consumers. Macro efficiency relates to stabilization policy, to the overall use of society's resources, and thus to the aggregate outcomes of micro processes, such as unemployment and price stability.

Within the general category of micro efficiency, it is possible to identify the source of resource misallocations to be corrected through intervention. In most cases these are associated with impediments to the process of market-based social interaction. For example, ownership rights for the resources exchanged must be clearly defined. In addition, if there are side effects of the production or use of the goods involved whose implications are not, or cannot be, adequately reflected in the transactions, then the idealized conditions for efficient interaction are violated.[8] Finally, the transaction costs and/or informational requirements for the functioning of a market may be prohibitive. The most apparent examples of this last problem can be found in the issue of the safety of a wide array of consumer products. It would seem to be impossible (certainly very costly) for an individual to acquire the information required to appreciate the full effects of all the goods and services he may utilize. Regulations offer one means of conveying this information.

Apart from efficiency objectives, social intervention is also motivated by the desire to assure a certain threshold level of access to all, or to a particular subset of material goods and services by all individuals. While we can logically distinguish efficiency and equity objectives, all resolutions of efficiency-related problems have corresponding equity implications. In fact, several prominent economists contend that failure of the economics profession to promote effective intervention processes can be tied to their unwillingness to deal, in a substantive way, with the equity implications of policies designed to promote efficiency.[9]

All of these concepts relate to the first of the three Ps of regulation, namely the *principles* that form the initial rationale for intervention.[10] In evaluating existing regulations such as our national energy policies, it is necessary also to consider the *procedures* used to redress apparent inefficiencies (or inequities in resource allocations), and ultimately the actual *practice* of intervention. Schultze focuses on procedures, and calls for marketlike incentives rather than the command-and-control approach to achieve policy objectives.[11] Evaluation of intervention programs requires consideration of all dimensions of regulation; therefore it would be incomplete to concentrate on any one aspect—principles, procedures, or practice.[12] Energy policies are particularly difficult to evaluate within this framework, since they have been designed to respond to multiple objectives, including several we have not considered. With this limitation in mind, we will discuss the general principles for private market allocation of an exhaustible resource as a means of identifying the conventional motives for intervening in the allocation of energy resources.

PRIVATE MARKET ALLOCATION OF EXHAUSTIBLE RESOURCES

One of the central propositions underlying the National Energy Plan is that the world is running out of crude oil and natural gas. Despite the incomplete evidence available, policymakers have chosen to assume that world production of these resources will peak before the end of this century, and then decline. If this assumption is correct, the principle of micro efficiency as discussed in the previous section leaves no role for social intervention. Referring to issues paralleling this case, Stiglitz (1978:25) recently observed that:

the existence of a natural resource problem has no immediate implications:it is neither a necessary nor a sufficient condition for governmental intervention in the markets for natural resources. The market could be doing as well as could be done—and the economy could still be facing a doomsday; and the market could be doing a quite bad job of resource allocation and yet there might be no doomsday in store. . . . A pattern of growth which left our grandchildren with few resources might be efficient, yet very undesirable.

The prospects of exhaustion for a particular natural resource do not in themselves imply micro inefficiency in allocation among economic agents at either a given point of time or over time.[13] Stiglitz suggests, rather, that these resources or their existing markets may have characteristics which would warrant government intervention on the grounds of micro efficiency.

For exhaustible resources, four attributes of their allocation process have been suggested as grounds for intervention to improve efficiency of allocation, aside from the existing pattern of government policy. They are (a) structure of the market, (b) absence of futures markets, (c) absence of risk markets, and (d) common property problems. The first issue, which concerns the possibility of monopoly power, has received great attention in regulatory literature. In the case of exhaustible energy resources, market structure is not necessarily sufficient to change extraction patterns over time. Competitive firms and a monopoly may yield identical patterns of extraction.[14] Moreover, this has *not* been the basis for past or current energy policies concerning petroleum or natural gas. Despite some debate over monopoly control and market power of the major oil companies, most policymakers seem to agree that there is "workable competition."[15] For this reason policies have not been designed to reduce the market position of energy firms (particularly the large petroleum firms).

On the remaining issues there is scope for judgment. Organized futures markets for future delivery of resources do not exist.[16] The same is true for risk markets. The question is whether their absence is important to resource allocation. Regarding futures markets, the issue is whether investors can make systematic, persistent errors in guessing future prices. While market incentives exist to discover such systematic mistakes, great variation in expectations can nonetheless cause market instability.[17] Similar difficulties arise from the absence of insurance (risk) markets, as owners of the exhaustible resource must bear all risks arising with price instability, new technologies, and other unforeseen events.

Different analysts evaluate these imperfections with different conclusions. Stiglitz observed that, .without futures markets, indicative planning may be a useful role for government as an aid to forecasting demand and supplies, but that it should avoid direct allocation of resources themselves. Regarding risk markets, he is less convinced (Stiglitz 1978:35):

Uncertainty undoubtedly has an effect on the intertemporal allocation, but for some purposes this is not as important as the question of what policy implication this has. . . . The risks associated with uncertain future supplies and demands borne by private individuals in imperfect risk markets are real "costs"; and the fact that under some idealized world in which these risks are not borne by these individuals the intertemporal allocation of oil would be different is of interest, but of no direct policy import. An appropriate question to ask, for instance, is whether a Pareto optimal improvement could be made within our market structure by taxing or subsidizing the return to holding oil; . . . The answer, in general is no.

In contrast, William Nordhaus (a current member of the Council of Economic Advisors), in a paper published shortly after the OPEC cartel's 1973 actions, concluded that the market mechanism in the U.S. was an "unreliable means of pricing and allocating exhaustible appropriable natural resources," with energy serving as his prime example (Nordhaus (1973:537). He urged the use of indicative planning as a policy alternative.[18] Under this approach, the government would determine a complete set of spot and future prices implied by an efficient allocation of energy resources (Nordhaus 1973:538).

The last problem—the common property or common pool nature of oil and natural gas—yields more consistent recommendations on the appropriate intervention. Difficulties arise when one or more independent producers simultaneously seek to extract resources (i.e., oil) from a common pool. Under a single producer (i.e., where the property rights are clearly defined), individuals can forego consumption today and know that it will be available in the future. But when many producers have access to the same source, these circumstances are not maintained; therefore a decision by a producer not to extract today offers no guarantee of future availability. Since other producers may extract it, there are incentives for an excessively rapid extraction.[19] One way to avoid this problem is to establish a single managerial unit for the pool. Compulsory field unitization accomplishes this.

Macro-Efficiency Motives

Turning to the equity and macro-efficiency motives for intervention, the arguments are again not clear-cut. The crux of the debate on equity concerns the treatment of future generations. When judging how a particular extraction pattern for an exhaustible resource affects different generations, most analysts urge that consideration be given to the levels of technology and physical capital that are transferred to future generations.[20] Of course, their conclusions assume that the resource in question has ready substitutes, and that its production and consumption do not result in harm to environmental common property.[21] In any case, current policy does not seem to have intertemporal equity objectives.[22]

This discussion suggests that, based on the principles stated earlier, there may be a place for government involvement in the allocation of energy resources. But the rationale does not arise from the exhaustibility of energy. It comes, rather, from the market failures we noted at the outset *and* their importance to efficient allocations in markets for exhaustible resources.[23]

These conclusions do not necessarily imply that regulatory intervention will improve (in a Pareto sense) the allocation of oil or natural gas. In fact, Stiglitz's views may be interpreted as a judgment on the ability of conventional *procedures* for intervention to achieve such an improvement.[24]

The question of macro efficiency has not been considered in theoretical models for the allocation patterns of exhaustible resources. It has, however, played an important role in much current and proposed energy regulation, and for that reason I will now discuss the problem, along with a review and evaluation of past interventions in the market allocation of oil and the NEP in terms of the criteria we have discussed.

ENERGY POLICY: THE OLD AND THE NEW

Any brief summary of sixty years of government intervention in a market is bound to be oversimplified, and the present account is no exception. To keep manageable the scope of our inquiry, we will focus on crude oil to highlight the relationship, if any, between past policies, the general goals of regulation, and the special features of the markets for exhaustible resources.

The Old

The first column of Table 1 summarizes the primary components of past intervention in the domestic crude-oil market. It is clear that the effects on prices and on incentives for new supplies are quite mixed. The percentage depletion allowance and favorable treatment of intangible costs both promote investment into oil (and gas) exploration and production, since the former is similar to a negative excise tax, and the latter directly reduces tax liability. In the absence of constraints on entry of foreign crude to the United States, the third policy would also encourage exploration to other parts of the world. Thus, on balance, we would expect the first three actions to reduce prices. The next two measures, however, seem to move in the opposite direction. Both prorationing[25] and the oil import-quota system tend to increase prices by restricting the supply of oil.

None of these measures can be related directly to the objectives of intervention, and they cast doubt on the prospects for any well-designed intervention in this sector. This view is supported by Walter Mead (1977:341), who recently concluded: "This record does not lead one to be confident that the public interest will be served by additional government intervention. This record should surprise no one. Congress and the Administration must respond to dominant organized pressures." These comments may be more relevant to the pre-1971 period than to more recent government policies. Items 6 through 8 in Table 1 do seem to serve, at least in part, the objectives of macro efficiency and intratemporal equity.

In hopes of controlling inflationary price increases, Phase IV of the Nixon administration's Economic Stabilization Program and the Emergency Petroleum Allocation Act of 1973 introduced extensive price controls which finally produced a two-tier price system for domestic crude oil. Oil produced from a property at roughly 1972 levels or less was "old" (first tier) oil, with prices controlled at slightly above pre-embargo domestic wellhead levels. Production above these levels from the same property was "new" oil, and its price was uncontrolled. In addition, each barrel of "new" oil produced released one barrel of "old" oil from price controls — thus giving those refineries with greatest access to "old" oil a definite cost advantage. The price of "old" oil averaged

Table 1

Overview of Government Regulation of Petroleum[a]

Past Intervention	NEP[b]
1. Percentage depletion allowance at a rate of 27.5 percent (from 1926 to 1969)	1. Crude-oil equalization tax to bring prices to world levels in 1980
2. Favorable treatment of intangibles (i.e., non-salvageable drilling costs)	2. Price of newly discovered oil to rise to 1977 world price (adjusted for inflation) in three years; newly covered > 2.5 miles from onshore well or 1,000 ft. deeper, and offshore oil discovered after 20 May 1977
3. Foreign tax credit	3. Users[2] tax beginning at $0.50 per barrel in 1979, rising to $3.00 per barrel in 1985 for industrial users; utilities taxed at $1.50 per barrel beginning in 1983; exemption for consumption under 90,000 barrels per year, and for fertilizer manufacturers and certain agricultural uses
4. Market demand prorationing: producers permitted to produce only at a specified percentage of maximum efficient rate (ended in 1972)	
5. Mandatory Oil Import Quota System: limit amount of crude oil and petroleum products to enter U.S. (ended in 1973)	

4. Tax rebates equal to year's oil or gas tax for investment in coal conversion
5. No new gas-burning boilers; possible prohibition of oil-burning if capable of burning coal
6. Best available technology for all coal-burning plants; scrubbers mandatory regardless of coal type burned
7. Eliminate entitlements program
8. Liberalize tax treatment of intangibles
9. Expansion of strategic petroleum reserve

6. Phase IV of Economic Stabilization Program and Emergency Petroleum Allocation Act (1973):
   a. Crude oil price controls (two-tier pricing)
   b. Crude oil cost equalization (entitlements) program
   c. Petroleum product price controls
   d. Mandatory petroleum product allocation program
7. Energy Policy and Conservation Act of 1975: continued price controls for crude and petroleum products (phased out controls on latter except gasoline and jet fuel in 1976)
8. Energy Conservation and Production Act (1976): oil-pricing policy changed to reflect reassessment of macroeconomic conditions; greater increases in crude prices to allow for tertiary recovery

[a]Summary based on discussion in Congressional Budget Office (1977), Zarb and MacAvoy (1976), Mead (1977), and Montgomery (1977).
[b]The "gas-guzzler" and standby gasoline taxes have been ignored, since legislative action on them was unclear at the time this paper was prepared.

about $5.00 a barrel, while the uncontrolled price was about $12.00 a barrel after the OAPEC price increases.

To insure that all U.S. refineries paid the same average cost for crude oil, the cost equalization or entitlements program was instituted, giving monthly entitlements to each refiner, based on the national proportion of "old" oil to total domestic production. For each refiner, entitlements to use price-controlled oil must equal the quantities of "old" oil in production—and therefore individual refiners would buy or sell entitlements to maintain the balance. This practice is a rationing scheme, which gives each producer equal access to a scarce commodity—oil with a controlled price.

In addition, price controls and allocation schemes were imposed on refinery products, and they remain in effect on gasoline and jet fuel. These actions imposed direct control over the markets, maintaining artificially low prices below world levels, and constraining market adjustments.[26]

Do these actions bear any relation to the objectives discussed earlier? Montgomery (1977:25) notes that two reasons were cited for the price controls in the discussion that accompanies the Energy Policy and Conservation Act (EPCA) of 1975: ". . . protection of low and middle income consumers from the impact of energy price increases and mitigation of the macro economic impact of a sudden increase in energy prices." EPCA thus kept upper-tier ("new") oil below the world price, with entitlements allocating both first-tier ("old") and second-tier ("new") oil—again requiring that the average cost of crude to refiners, including imported oil, be equalized. The EPCA of 1976 continued controls, but permitted greater domestic crude-oil price increases than under the earlier legislation.

The net result of the price controls was to prevent the domestic market for crude oil from reaching equilibrium. At the controlled prices, the quantity demanded would always exceed domestic production. Without the ability to import, rationing would have been essential; imports allowed the market to clear. Unfortunately, the policy effects do not end with this imbalance; the dynamic incentives that result are at least as important as the static consequences.

Government policies since 1973 may be explained with the use of a stylized example. Consider the implications of holding the market price below equilibrium (i.e., below the point at which demand would equal supply). In equilibrium, the last unit of demand is priced at the willingness-to-pay for that unit—which, in turn, exactly equals the marginal cost of providing it. When price is maintained artificially below that point, demand will exceed supply. Without an external supply source (in addition to the market supply schedule) to meet this excess demand, the available supply must be rationed in some way among users. (For a more technical discussion of these arguments, see Appendix.) These conditions are important for two reasons. First, price controls introduce inefficiencies in resource allocation at the time when they are imposed. Second, and equally important, they can accentuate the imbalance in demand and supply over time by influencing expectations. This example is one simple way of understanding both the effects of the price controls initiated under the Economic Stabilization Program and the role of imports of crude oil since 1973. This foreign supply has served the role of meeting a growing excess of U.S. domestic demand over domestic supply at controlled prices.

Table 2 lists the individual regulatory programs in the Federal Energy Administration's (FEA) Office of Regulatory Programs. Private compliance with these mandates required an estimated 200,976 forms per year for the FEA to evaluate (Zarb and MacAvoy 1976: Appendix L, p. 2). The public cost of overseeing these programs in the FEA Office of Regulatory Programs and the General Counsel's Office will amount to an estimated $47 million in FY 1977.[27] Thus it is not surprising that the Presidential Task Force on Reform of Federal Energy Administration Regulations concluded (Zarb and MacAvoy 1976:20):

The cost of current FEA regulations outweighs their benefits.
a. FEA product pricing and allocation regulations, the crude oil buy/sell program and supplier/purchaser freeze are unnecessary in present supply conditions.
b. The current regulatory structure will not work in a future shortage.
c. FEA regulations impose substantial costs on the business community, taxpayers, and consumers.
d. Continuation of present controls will result in long-run inefficiencies.

Table 2

Regulatory Functions of FEA's Office of Regulatory Programs

Program	Status
Crude Oil Entitlements Program	Current
Domestic Crude Oil Allocation Program (buy/sell)	Current
Canadian Crude Oil Allocation Program	Current
Refinery Yield Program	Current
Mandatory Oil Imports Program	Current
Propane/Butane and Other Products Allocation Program	Current
Motor Gasoline Allocation Program	Phase out under EPCA
Middle Distillate Allocation Program	Phase out under EPCA
Aviation Fuels Allocation Program	Phase out under EPCA
Residual Fuels Allocation Program (utilities)	Phase out under EPCA
Residual Fuels Allocation Program (nonutilities)	Phase out under EPCA
Regional Assistance Program	Phase out under EPCA

Source: Zarb and MacAvoy (1976).

Faced with these conclusions, the regulatory response which emerges in our new energy plan is an *increase* in the scope of control on the allocation of energy resources.

The National Energy Plan

The second column of Table 1 highlights principal aspects of the proposed National Energy Plan (NEP),[28] a dominant feature of which seeks to curtail the growth of domestic consumption of oil (and natural gas). This objective rests on two assumptions. The first is that domestic petroleum production will not greatly increase, regardless of price increases. Further increases in consumption thus will increase U.S. vulnerability to foreign supply interruptions, since most of the increased demand for crude oil must be met with imports. The second assumption is that world production of petroleum will decline before the end of this century; therefore, a beginning must be made to adjust to the end of crude oil as a dominant energy source. Curiously, the plan attempts to command and control the character of responses to these factors rather than to permit market adjustment.

In principle, it is possible to classify the impact of past regulations on the supply of crude oil and its domestic price. Problems arose, in large part, because demand factors were free to respond to the perceived opportunity costs for petroleum—that is, its value in alternative uses. And the result was a pattern of progressive increases in excess demand for crude oil and corresponding increases in imports, from 6.3 million barrels per day in 1973 to an estimated 9 million in 1977.

It seems reasonable to assume that meeting domestic demand for crude from domestic sources of supply alone would require a price in excess of the current world price. Thus, price adjustment to the world price levels will reduce but not eliminate the excess domestic demand (i.e., the difference between domestic demand and domestic supply). The NEP assumes that (a) complete price adjustment to achieve zero excess domestic demand is not feasible for policy purposes; and therefore, (b) excess demand must be reduced so that imports and consumption correspond to predefined targets at the plan's posted prices. Within our simple diagram, the only option available to achieve these targets, given the imposed constraints, is further control on the market by restrictions on *demand*. Thus, items 3 through 5 in Table 1 may be interpreted as direct attempts to control the derived demand for crude oil by the manufacturing sector and public utilities.[29]

The NEP does nothing to change regulatory control over supply. Prices are proposed to rise to the current world prices of crude oil (in real terms) by 1980. However, the complex and arbitrary pricing tiers for "old," "new" (designated "previously discovered oil"), and yet another category — "newly discovered oil" — are retained, with taxes raising the effective costs to refiners to the world price level. By equalizing the average costs of crude to all refiners, these taxes eliminate the need for the entitlements program. While it is apparently assumed that these prices will induce efficient responses by demanders and suppliers, a price in itself will not assure this response. Free adjustment must be permitted. Moreover, the price must result from the interaction of all economic agents. Even Meade's (1972) indicative planning called for a balancing of demands and supplies. If regulatory measures establish a single price, without controls both demanders and suppliers can be expected to respond to it efficiently. This efficient response must be interpreted as conditional to the established price. That is, it is possible that the reshuffling of resources which would arise from the imposition of a new price would yield an improvement in the well-being of all involved.

Thus, on efficiency grounds, it is difficult to justify the users' tax on petroleum, initiated at different times for different types of users, and with built-in exceptions for a consumption of less than 90,000 barrels of oil.[30] Moreover, restrictions on the use of multiple fuel boilers, and the acquisition of boilers designed for specific fuels (petroleum and natural gas), restrict the nature and timing of private sector responses. Finally, the mandates of BAT air pollution control technology, regardless of the sulphur content of the coal used, eliminates yet another avenue for adjustment. All these aspects of the plan seem to represent attempts to "second guess" market adjustment processes. Similar observations could be made on the pricing provisions, users' taxes, and boiler restrictions imposed on consumers of natural gas.

For these reasons, the NEP does not correspond to either the Stiglitz or Nordhaus conception of indicative planning. It assumes that prices and adjustment controls can direct economic behavior as a market would. More specifically, the NEP document observed that (Executive Office of the President 1977:93):

Achievements of the goals and strategy of the National Energy Plan could demonstrate the benefits of indicative planning. If private decision makers voluntarily act within the framework proposed in the plan, the United States could achieve its energy and economic goals with relatively little direct Government regulation of economic activity.

Unfortunately, little discretion is left for voluntarism; intervention is both direct and comprehensive.

The post-1971 pattern of intervention into energy markets appears to be based in concerns for equity and macro efficiency (i.e., price stabilization). These objectives were achieved at the cost of substantial losses in micro efficiency and in the resulting misallocation of energy resources. By contrast, the NEP proposes to achieve arbitrarily defined levels of consumption of energy resources while "doing no harm" to existing equity and macro-efficiency considerations. Energy resources thus are to be effectively removed from the market, and the micro efficiency of the resulting allocation pattern is ignored.

IMPLICATIONS

Most analysts of the NEP have argued that the proposed targets for the domestic consumption of crude oil, natural gas, and coal, as well as for the imports of oil, are unrealistic.[31] In all cases, the targets reflect an optimistic appraisal of outcomes which cannot be expected on the basis of the plan's incentive structure *alone*. The prospects for further controls thus seem assured, if the targets are to be maintained.

It seems logical, then, to ask why. Why must the rate of domestic consumption of crude oil and natural gas, imports of oil, and use of coal correspond to the specified mandates? The expanded Strategic Petroleum Reserve is designed to insure against the threat of supply interruptions, so that insecurity of supply from foreign sources cannot be the sole basis. One reason might be that policymakers feel we cannot afford the reserves required by an effective insurance program. It seems reasonable, however, that those responsible for imposing the risk of disruption should bear the costs of adequate insurance, and that the prices paid for crude oil should include the costs of this insurance.

An alternative justification for the plan's artificial limitations stems from the need to speed the process of adjustment to new energy sources. Past policies, however, provide ample evidence that intervention can retard adjustment mechanisms, and this is particularly true of the post-1973 policies. On the other hand, imposed adjustments can also come too quickly. Nordhaus's empirical demonstration of the role of his brand of indicative planning for energy resources, while admittedly a numerical exercise to illustrate the outcomes dictated under "efficient" allocation programs, concludes that (Nordhaus 1973:567):

As a long-run policy it would be unwise to jack up the prices of energy products in the interests of preserving energy resources. Nor does a more drastic policy of permanent rationing of energy make sense. As long as investment yields about 10 percent, it seems best to use the cheap resources now and to put the real resources thereby saved to work on producing synthetic fuels later.

Several years and a direct role in policymaking have intervened since he made these observations. The overall intent of the recommendation, however, is to call for energy use patterns that reflect relative costs of the resources involved as well as the costs of adjustment, and not for a mandated schedule of fuel switching.

Of course, Nordhaus's simplified schedules assume that smooth substitutions are fully possible. New energy sources must be available as the price rises with the exhaustion of the type in use. The circumstances are not so clear-cut today. The NEP recognizes some of these uncertainties in formulating its policies toward nuclear power, but not for increased coal production. Increases in coal use may *not* be possible in the presence of an effective BAT pollution-control policy. Moreover, some pollutants which are not currently subject to control, such as carbon dioxide, have been ignored; yet they have the potential for serious climatological impacts. Finally, international wealth transfers may be the central concern for some policy measures, but these cannot be the sole basis for domestic energy policies.

The National Energy Plan set forth policies which will effectively remove energy resources from the market allocation process in order to achieve mandated price *and* quantity targets simultaneously. These policies are in direct opposition to the principles outlined early in this paper. In part, this policy drift results from failures in the procedures and practices of past regulations. In part, the trend reflects an increase in the number of objectives to be subjected to control. Since no basis exists for accepting all of these objectives, we must conclude that the policies are misdirected.[32]

APPENDIX

Consider a simple demand and supply diagram as given in Figure 1A.

Figure 1A: Effects of price regulation on excess demand.

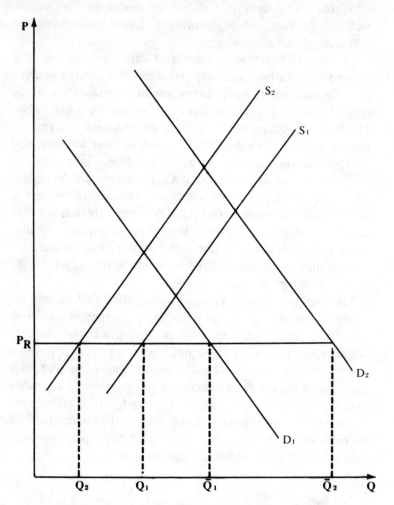

D_1 is the demand in period one and S_1 the domestic supply of crude oil. The government policies since 1973 have served to maintain prices at P_R—below the market equilibrium for domestic demand and supply, with an excess demand of

$Q_1\overline{Q}_1$. This excess demand was met through petroleum imports at world prices. Since domestic producers faced controlled prices for domestically produced oil and uncertainty as to whether (if ever) the government would allow them to rise to world prices, it seems reasonable to assert that there would be reduced incentives for additions to domestic supplies. To illustrate these effects, suppose supply in period two is S_2. Domestic demand also responds to an artificially low price by shifting to D_2 in period two (through consumers' choices of energy-using durables). The result is an increase in the extent of excess demand to $Q_2\overline{Q}_2$. Though obviously simple, this diagram serves to illustrate the incentive structure. In order to maintain the artificial condition in the markets for both crude and refinery products, government allocation schemes (see Table 2 in the text for a listing) were necessary. These measures serve to reduce the adjustments possible underlying a market supply relation, and *ceteris paribus* decrease its elasticity.

10

THE USE OF TAXES, REGULATION
AND PRICE CONTROLS IN THE ENERGY SECTOR

Walter J. Mead

I. The Record of the Past

THE purpose of this paper is to analyze the use of taxes, regulation and price controls by the Federal Government to alter the pattern of resource allocation in the energy sector. Where these devices are used, the pattern of resource allocation that is being rejected is the pattern which would occur in response to private decisionmakers in pursuit of private gain, constrained by the extent of prevailing competition. Our concern will be limited entirely to intervention in the energy markets. In order to judge the probable effect of future uses of taxes, regulation and price controls, we will examine the record of past intervention in energy markets. We will consider only major energy policies adopted by the Federal Government over the past half-century.

Under ideal conditions, optimum allocation of scarce resources over time would maximize the present value of the stock of resources. Following McDonald, we will define an optimum allocation of resources as a condition in which

No increase in net satisfactions could be obtained by increasing or decreasing the employment of any resource, by increasing the output of one good at the expense of another, or by shifting some consumption in either direction between present and future. These conditions, in turn, mean that the marginal sacrifice of employing more or less of any resource is exactly equal to the marginal gain of satisfactions, that marginal net satisfactions per dollar of expenditure are the same for all goods, and that the marginal rate of return on both investment and postponement of natural resource use is equal to the marginal rate of time preference. The last condition further means that the present worth, expressed in terms of net satisfactions, of both capital assets and natural resources is maximized, given the marginal rate of time preference.[1]

In short, optimum resource allocation occurs when the time distribution of resource use maximizes the present value of the flow of expected net revenue throughout all time.

The foregoing definitions also define the term "conservation" from an economic perspective. But this term, as currently used in Congress and the Administration, is implicitly defined in two words as "use less." The use of the term has no theoretical content. Whatever level of present resource use is attained, this definition always requires further reductions in current consumption. This devolves in an infinite regression to another two-word expression—use none.

The naive "use less" version of conservation is found throughout such prestigious studies as the Ford Foundation, Energy Policy Project report.[2] To reduce consumption of one resource normally involves accelerated use of another. One resource is substituted for another. For example, residential insulation may reduce direct energy consumption at the expense of additional use of fiberglass, energy in its production, labor, etc.

Government intervention may be justified under conditions of market failure. Two such contributing conditions may be suggested. First, where significant externalities exist, the pattern of resource allocation may be improved by government intervention through taxes, subsidies, regulation, or price controls.

Second, market failure also prevails when competition is not effective. Optimum resource allocation requires that inputs be purchased and products be sold in competitive markets. Where monopoly

From Walter J. Mead, "The Use of Taxes, Regulation and Price Controls in the Energy Sector," 21(3) *National Tax Journal* 229-238 (September 1978). Copyright 1978 by the National Tax Association-Tax Institute of America.

power exists, product output may be restricted below competitive levels with the result that prices are artificially high and consumption of the monopolized product is artificially constrained. Because products normally have substitutes, under-consumption of the monopolized product leads to over-consumption of its substitutes.

A third major cause of resource misallocation, but not properly described as market failure, is the frequently observed instance of government interference that is not supported by a showing of net externalities or monopoly power. Thus, while instances of market failure may require government intervention for their correction, intervention in itself is also frequently a major cause of resource misallocation. Illustrations will be provided below.

Before recommending an extension of government controls in the energy sector, it would surely be useful to examine the record of past intervention. We will examine this record, touching only on the major landmarks of taxation, regulation and price controls.

(1) Special Tax Arrangements for Oil and Gas.

The system of percentage depletion allowance for oil and gas was developed shortly after the income tax was adopted in the United States. In 1926, percentage depletion allowance rules were established permitting oil and gas producers and royalty owners to receive tax-free 27.5 percent of the wellhead value of oil and gas production, subject to a limit that tax-free revenue could not exceed 50 percent of the net income from each property. These rules remained in effect until 1969 when tax-free income was reduced to 22 percent. Then the Tax Reduction Act of 1975 almost entirely eliminated percentage depletion for major integrated producers of oil and gas and provided for phased reductions of the extent of tax freedom for smaller producers. For 1984 and beyond, the applicable rate of percentage depletion is reduced to 15 percent from its current 22 percent, and the depletable quantity of oil on which tax freedom is granted is reduced to 1,000 barrels per day (6 million cubic feet of gas per day). This extent of tax freedom is limited to independent producers, defined as producers who neither have a retail outlet nor refine more than 50,000 barrels of oil per day.

A companion tax provision permits the immediate expensing of intangible drilling costs incurred in oil and gas exploration and development. The first effect of these two policies together was to make exploration and production more profitable for producers and royalty owners, on an after-tax basis. But higher after-tax profitability led to increased capital flows into oil and gas exploration and production. This capital flow led to additional production which, in turn, led to lower oil and gas prices. The tax subsidies initially increased profitability, but the consequent additional production and lower prices quickly reestablished normal (competitive) profitability from oil and gas production. These tax subsidies contributed to the historic low price policy in the United States and led to extravagant consumption habits. A recent rigorous analysis of the effect of percentage depletion allowances on the conservation question concluded that this tax provision stimulated "over-extraction of resources at the present time at the expense of future feasible extractions rates."[3]

Other energy sources such as coal, geothermal, oil shale, and uranium have received substantially lower effective tax subsidies.[4] Solar energy development has received no Federal tax subsidy until recently. Consequently, the tax subsidies for oil and gas have led to resource misallocation. Development of oil and gas was stimulated, both at the expense of alternative energy sources, and at the expense of future oil and gas production. These two landmark features of energy tax policy have been counter-productive of resource conservation goals.

(2) Market Demand Prorationing.

The two tax incentives discussed above apparently performed their functions well. Large new oil discoveries were found and, given intense competition within the oil industry, prices were depressed to levels unacceptable to the oil industry. The industry resorted to political action which produced the Interstate Oil Compact Commission and the Connally "Hot Oil Act" in the 1930's. The former Federal legislation authorised states to limit all production within their borders, making no mention of the obvious price effects of this output control. The latter legislation was the enforcement mechanism. The Connally act denied any producer the right to sell his product in interstate commerce in violation of state prorationing laws.

The crude oil production industry in the United States has been composed of from eight to ten thousand producers. This industrial structure makes private collusion impossible. The market demand prorationing legislation was an effective use of Federal Government power to monopolize on behalf of an industry that could not monopolize without the power of government.

From 1960 through 1965 the annual average of monthly market demand factors, as administered by the Texas Railroad Commission in Texas, varied from 27 to 29 percent of the basic maximum allowable rate of production by well. The effect of market demand prorationing on price and output was precisely the opposite of that produced by the tax arrangements described above. Market demand prorationing restricted output and thereby caused price increases. In a sense, the tax policies described above led to output restriction policies. Whether the price and output effects of one were offset by the other is unknown.

(3) Oil Import Quotas.

Market demand prorationing supported domestic oil prices at levels that substantially exceeded the landed price of imports from abroad. By 1959 imports of crude oil and products amounted to 18 percent of domestic production. With rising imports, the restrictions of the market demand prorationing program were becoming increasingly difficult for domestic producers to bear. Political pressure was brought on Congress and the Administration during the middle and late 1950's. In 1959 President Eisenhower, by proclamation, imposed mandatory oil import quotas.

Political pressure for quotas came almost entirely from independent domestic producers joined by coal producers. The latter objected to competition from foreign residual fuel oil. The major international oil companies voiced strong opposition to import restrictions. For example, the president of Standard Oil Company of California testified at the Office of Defense Mobilization hearings concerned with oil import restrictions in 1956 as follows: "It is our own carefully considered opinion that the contention of injury to the domestic industry is without substance."[5] He further testified that "There is a serious question in my mind that the economic well-being and strength of this country—the bases of our national security—would be promoted by controls set up to permit a greater dependence on increasingly costly domestic reserves. To the contrary, consideration seems to be warranted for a gradual increase in the proportion of imports to domestic requirements."

The imposition of import quotas in 1959 led to more rapid exploitation of domestic oil reserves than would have occurred in the absence of regulation. But the consequent rapid depletion of this non-renewable resource led to the fall of the quota system itself. Effective May 1, 1973 President Nixon was compelled to remove restrictions on oil imports. The system became impossible to administer.

Having stimulated production by more than half a century of tax subsidies and further stimulated domestic production by import quotas, low cost, easy to find domestic crude oil reserves were simply no longer available. Past policies led to increased dependence on foreign oil sources and to the widely publicized "energy crisis" of the 1970's. By August 1977, imports of petroleum and petroleum products amounted to 45 percent of total consumption.

(4) The Record of Price Controls.

A. *Natural gas price controls.* In 1938, Congress enacted legislation governing tariffs for transporting natural gas in interstate commerce. In 1954, a Supreme Court decision determined that Congress intended those controls to cover the wellhead price of natural gas flowing in interstate commerce, as well as the act of transporting such gas. Thus, since 1954 the wellhead price of interstate gas has been subject to control by the Federal Power Commission (FPC). Prices set by the FPC were lower than the prices that would have been determined by the interaction of supply and demand. As a consequence, shortages developed and increased over time. The average price of natural gas moving in interstate commerce as of August 1977 was 71.1 cents per thousand cubic feet (Mcf). This translates into a crude oil price of about $4.25 per barrel, a price substantially below market values for crude oil or for any petroleum product that is a direct substitute for natural gas. At these artificially low prices, natural gas is a bargain, and there is an enormous natural gas shortage. But, unlike the situation with crude oil, not enough natural gas can be imported to fill the gap. Consequently, a large regulation-induced shortage persists. Those users without sufficient political power are either temporarily or permanently cut off from gas supplies. In many areas of the country, new residential hook-ups are not permitted. However, for most residential consumers, gas supplies are available virtually without limit. Wasteful consumption of this low priced but non-renewable resource is widespread. In addition, the policy is inequitable·in that some consumers obtain gas at bargain prices, while others cannot buy it at any price.

Given the shortage of natural gas, consumers have sought out substitute supplies of energy. For many consumers, the primary substitute is oil products. Thus, price controls on natural gas have led to increased demand for crude oil, which in turn has led to increased oil imports and added balance of payments problems.

In order to relieve part of the shortage, government policy is moving toward liquefied natural gas (LNG) imports. For example, arrangements are currently being made by the Pacific Indonesia LNG Company to import LNG into the West Coast. However, the import price on a regasified basis will be $3.42 per million Btu.[6] This translates into a price of $3.93 per Mcf—more than five times the 71.1 cents allowed for domestic producers of gas sold in interstate commerce.

The cost of developing pipeline quality synthetic gas, using the Lurgi process and based on $22 per ton coal with costs

expressed in 1974 prices, is estimated at $2.74 per million Btu.[7]

The cost of Prudhoe Bay gas delivered to markets in the lower forty-eight states, using 1975 prices, has been estimated by the Federal Power Commission at $2.62 per Mcf.[8] The record of past construction projects of a size similar to that of the proposed Northwest Alcan Pipeline project shows that large scale cost overruns must be expected.[9] Accordingly, this price for Prudhoe Bay gas appears to be underestimated.

The prevailing pricing system used by the federal regulatory agencies permits "rolling in," a method of average-cost pricing which conceals high social costs of energy, including natural gas. Thus, the high-cost gas supplies listed above would be concealed from the consumer.

The current natural gas price control system leads to less domestic production than would occur in the absence of controls. Where the definition of conservation is in terms of "use less," the price control policy would appear to be effective. However, in an economic sense, low priced gas is used wastefully by those who are favored with supplies. Others are forced to use substitutes. As a consequence, energy sources other than gas are used excessively. In both respects the broader goals of conservation are not served by the price control policy.

(5) Oil Price Controls.

As domestic reserves of oil and gas peaked and then started their descent, reflecting the exhaustion of low-cost domestic supplies, the growing power of OPEC, and finally the oil embargo, oil prices moved up sharply. General wage and price controls were introduced by President Nixon on August 15, 1971. In successive phases, price controls were dropped on all products except oil and natural gas.

With oil prices held below the level of import prices, demand for crude oil became artificially stimulated, and supply artificially restrained. The consequent shortage was filled by increased imports. Thus, price controls on crude oil led directly to higher imports and consequent balance of payments problems, which have contributed to a severe decline in the value of the dollar in foreign exchange markets. In addition, crude oil price controls have been the justification for, first, crude oil allocations, and second, the entitlements program. The latter has been described by President Carter in his National Energy Plan as "an administrative nightmare." As soon as the government fixes low prices on various classes of domestically produced crude oil and the nation must import at the world price, a problem is immediately created. Which buyers are to be favored with rights to purchase the artificially low priced domestic supplies? And who must pay a series of higher prices? In order to "equalize" the cost of crude oil among different refiners, the entitlements system was established by the Federal Energy Administration. Under this system, those refiners with access to more than the average amount of low priced domestic oil must transfer money to other refiners who have less than the average access. This program has become an extremely expensive program to administer and even more expensive for oil company compliance. It is a burden on the public and produces no useable products. It draws away talented resources from otherwise productive employment and is therefore a contributing element in the present inflation.

Among economists specialized in the area of energy economics, there is a close to unanimous agreement that price controls in both oil and gas should be phased out as quickly as possible. The problem of eliminating price controls is largely political. There are two major political arguments against decontrol—(1) the "impact on the poor" and (2) "windfall profits."

The "impact on the poor" argument is powerful in a political framework. As an economic argument it is faulty for the following reasons:

First, many poor people have no natural gas hook-up. Consequently artificially low prices are of no value to them and allowing prices to rise to market clearing level would have no direct impact on them.

Second, in the Southwest a major consumer use of natural gas is for swimming pool heating. Relatively few poor people have swimming pools.

Third, in the summer months gas powered air conditioners are a significant element in the demand for gas. Again, poor people do not generally have air conditioned homes.

Fourth, in the winter months the major residential use of natural gas is for space heating. The larger the house, the greater the use of gas for this purpose. Poor people generally do not have large houses.

Fifth, if the public wishes to increase its subsidies to the poor a direct subsidy in the form of a negative income tax would be much more efficient. From an economics point of view it is unwise to adopt policies which have major resource misallocation effects in order to indirectly accomplish income redistribution objectives.

The "windfall profits" argument is also powerful in a political framework. Economic analysis suggests that the argument is faulty for the following reasons:

First, the windfall argument itself was created by price controls. If price controls on natural gas had not been instituted in 1954, and if oil had been decontrolled along with other products in 1972 and early 1973, then these two energy products would have increased in price with relatively little fanfare as in the case of coal and uranium (yellow cake). Prices for the latter two energy sources have increased approximately four-fold in tandem with crude oil, but they are not subject to price controls and the windfall charge. Similarly, timber prices, and residential housing in Santa Barbara, California, have increased four-fold within the last decade without giving rise to the windfall profits issue.

Second, oil companies are almost never owners of natural gas and oil resources. Oil companies are lessees. They normally pay the resource owners a royalty which is usually a function of wellhead value and is calculated on gross rather than net income. Consequently, a large part of any windfall gain would flow to the resource owner. But the resource owner in most cases is the Federal Government. In declining positions of importance are state governments, native American groups, railroads, and private individuals, primarily ranchers and farmers.

Third, in all new leases negotiated after higher oil and gas prices have been acknowledged, the landowner will capture approximately 100 percent of the economic rent. In the case of the Outer Continental Shelf, which represents the major source of new oil and gas production for the United States, competitive bonus bid lease sales take place periodically. Analysis of this record shows that competition for such leases is intense and the rate of return earned by lessees is relatively low.[10] As a consequence, one may infer that the Federal Government captures approximately all of the economic rent to which it is entitled. Thus, windfall profits from higher oil and gas prices on new Federal leases would be transferred to the Federal Government. The same applies to the other categories of landowners listed above.

Fourth, the windfall profits concept itself depends entirely on what time-period one uses. Crude oil prices increased sharply beginning with the Arab boycott. Over a period of about four years prices increased from approximately $3.50 to $14.00 per barrel. A windfall profit by definition is an unexpected gain. But oil producers have been expecting the price of crude oil to rise for many years. Their expectations were not realized until the early 1970's. During the 1950's and 1960's prices fluctuated up and down but were approximately constant over this period of two decades. The domestic price of crude oil in 1950 averaged $3.07 per barrel and rose to $14.00 for imported crude in 1977. After adjusting for inflation, this amounts to a compound annual rate of increase of 3.3 percent per year. It seems reasonable to assume that someone holding crude oil reserves for the future might have reasonably expected to earn a competitive real rate of return of approximately three percent per year. The gain achieved from holding oil resources corresponds closely with this competitive real rate of return. The problem is that the entire increase

came in a four year period and gave rise to what in the longer framework is a windfall profits illusion.

Fifth, any gain achieved by oil companies is subject to corporate income taxation. Currently, as indicated above, integrated oil companies no longer receive percentage depletion allowance tax benefits from oil and gas production. Their corporate income tax rates for oil and gas produced since 1965 must approach the 48 percent statutory tax rate. Therefore approximately half of any windfall profits accruing to larger oil companies would immediately flow to the Federal Government. State taxes would take an additional share which varies from state to state.

Sixth, over time the problem of windfall gains would disappear if price controls are removed. Old oil production is subject to decline rates amounting to approximately 10 percent per year. For new oil production, the economic rents accruing from higher prices would be captured by the landowner as shown above.

(6) Summary of the Record.

We have reviewed five landmark areas of government taxation, regulation, and price controls in the energy area. These five policies constitute major energy policies of the federal government over the last half-century. If these policies are judged in terms of allocative efficiency (which is equivalent to resource conservation from an economics point of view) one must conclude that the policies have been counter-productive. There is widespread agreement among academic energy economists that government interference in the energy sector is the primary cause of the energy crisis. Erickson and Spann wrote that "The energy crisis has been policy-induced and is not a result of market power."[11] Mancke similarly concluded that "Current energy policies have failed to alleviate any of our four energy problems. . . . In fact, they have actually worsened each of these problems."[12] In view of this record one cannot be optimistic that future federal energy policies will suddenly become productive of the general welfare. Indeed, an analysis of past policy leads to the forecast that more government interference in the energy market will simply produce more resource mis-allocation. The resource cost will be in a lower standard of living than might otherwise be obtainable for the American people. The money cost will be paid by consumers and taxpayers.

II. Use of Taxation, Regulations and Price Controls in President Carter's National Energy Plan

Early in his NEP the President enunciates a set of principles. The first principle is as follows: "We can have an effective and comprehensive policy only if the government takes responsibility for it. . . ."[13] The essence of the President's energy message implements this first principle. Price controls for both oil and gas are not only extended to cover previously exempt areas, such as intrastate gas, but are also offered as "permanent institutions." The use of tax subsidies is vastly expanded. New regulations, largely in the name of conservation interpreted as "use less," are extended. The President's proposals have been reviewed by the author elsewhere.[14]

A major improvement is represented by the President's proposal to permit prices paid for crude oil and petroleum products to rise toward the world price. However, this is only half of the market solution which would allow both demand price and supply price to be set by the market rather than by the government. The President stated that "if users pay yesterday's prices for tomorrow's energy, U.S. resources will be rapidly exhausted. If producers were to receive tomorrow's prices for yesterday's discoveries, there would be an inequitable transfer of income from the American people to the producers, whose profits would be excessive and would bear little relation to the actual economic contribution."[15] Therein lies the dilemma facing the President. In order to avoid wasteful consumption of nonrenewable energy resources, he is willing to permit energy prices to rise toward world levels. However, the specter of "windfall profits" is politically unacceptable in Washington. He attempts to avoid the horns of this dilemma through an elaborate and extensive system of producer taxes, particularly on crude oil. The President proposes four tiers of oil price controls. First, the present price of $5.25 per barrel for "old oil" is to be continued. Second, it is proposed that the present fixed price of $11.28 per barrel be continued. The price category has included what has been called "new oil." The designation now proposed by the President is "previously discovered oil." This new label creates a credibility problem for the government. If producers are to be encouraged to explore for new oil under the stimulus of free market prices, but a stroke of the pen can cause new oil to be downgraded to "previously discovered old oil," those who finance exploration and production will surely be skeptical of "new oil" incentives. If so, exploration will be retarded.

Third, another price category to be called "newly discovered oil" is to be given a fixed "current world price." All three tiers are subject to general inflationary price increases. As a fourth tier, incremental tertiary (not including secondary) recovery and stripper oil production is to be free of controls. This provision, viewed alone, is welcome. However, as part of a four tier producer pricing system, it is difficult and expensive to administer. Administration requires a large government bureaucracy and an even larger bureaucracy in complying industry.

With respect to natural gas, the President correctly observed that natural gas, "is now the Nation's most underpriced and oversold fuel." One would expect, following this observation, that the President would call for decontrol of new natural gas supplies. Instead, he recommends the opposite, that wellhead price control be extended to include intrastate gas. Incredibly, this policy is recommended as an "important first step toward deregulation."

He proposes that all new gas be subject to a ceiling of $1.75 per Mcf (thousand cubic feet). However, converted through its Btu equivalency, this is equal to oil priced at approximately $10.50 per barrel. Oil competes with No. 2 distillate currently selling for approximately $14.50 per

barrel. Thus, under the President's proposal natural gas would continue to be
a bargain and large scale shortages would
persist. In addition, the President proposes
a complex six-tier system of producer
prices for natural gas, plus a confusing
system of user taxes which would discriminate against specific user groups corresponding closely to their political power.

With respect to both oil and gas, the
President correctly observed that these
products are priced "below their marginal
replacement cost and, as a result, the
nation uses them wastefully with little
regard to their true value." This statement
is true, and one might take encouragement
from the fact that it is enunciated by the
President. However, in the next paragraph
he states that "the residential sector is
sheltered as the plan would keep natural
gas prices to residential users down and
provide tax rebates for home oil use." His
policy recommendations thus perpetuate
the very problem that he has identified.

The President also proposes an extensive new system of cash subsidies for
individuals, homeowners, schools, and
hospitals to finance weatherization and
the installation of miscellaneous "approved conservation measures." New tax
subsidies are provided for business to
encourage installation of "qualified solar
equipment," "approved conservation measures," and "co-generation equipment."
However, he also warns that in the
event voluntary programs fail to achieve
prescribed results, then mandatory measures will be undertaken relative to
weatherization and standards of efficiency
for new buildings and home appliances.
As one illustration of a force measure,
Congress is considering legislation that
would prohibit the sale or refinancing of
any home not meeting prescribed federal
insulation standards. A decision to insulate a home should be made on the basis
of the present cost of insulation and the
present value of the flow of future savings.
If costs exceed benefits, such investments
should not be made. An exception occurs
if there are net external benefits. None
are obviously present. If this calculation
is distorted by artificially low prices for
gas or other energy input, then the obvious
correction should be to eliminate the

source of the distortion—the current price
control system. The President's program
perpetuates this problem by extending gas
price controls and making both gas and
oil price controls permanent. Costs and
benefits will differ widely by geographical
area, age of the house, difficulty of retro-
fitting, temperature preferences of individuals, and the like. In the absence of
net external benefits, full insulation decisions should be made by homeowners, not
by a distant Congress.

Another proposal calls for an extension
of existing tax subsidies. For independent
oil and gas producers he proposes that the
intangible drilling cost expenditure provision of the· tax code be liberalized.
However, further liberalization of tax
subsidies will make oil production more
profitable after taxes. This is in conflict
with the President's own price control
measures, which are designed to restrain
profitability. Further, a tax subsidy, unsupported by evidence of net external
benefits, leads to overinvestment in the
subsidized industry and to resource misallocation. Instead of further liberalization,
the President and Congress should consider eliminating existing legislation which
permits expensing of intangible drilling
costs for productive wells and requires
instead the capitalization of such expenditures. In a similar vein, complete elimination of percentage depletion allowance for
all mineral production regardless of firm
size should be considered.

In addition, the President proposes
expansion of the intangible drilling cost
expensing provisions to include geothermal energy production. The reasoning
above applies here also. Further, a tax
subsidy for geothermal energy places alternative energy sources including solar,
wind, and fuel from waste, at a relative
disadvantage. Instead of extending tax
subsidies to additional energy sources, a
preferable policy would be to eliminate
such nonneutral tax provisions from all
present tax applications.

III. Summary and Conclusions

1. The record of government energy
policies over the last fifty years is poor.
From an optimum resource allocation or

a resource conservation point of view, federal policies have been counterproductive. If tax subsidies and import quotas had never been introduced, the "energy crisis" of the 1970's would be less severe or non-existent. If price controls had never been mandated, the dilemma of decontrol with its windfall profits and impact on the poor arguments would be less severe. If prices had been allowed to seek their competitive level, unaided by tax subsidies and unrestrained by price controls, resource conservation in the economic sense would be more advanced in the United States.

2. The history of energy policy reveals the nature of the political process. Congress and the Administration are responsive to the dominant organized interests which exert political pressure on them. The success of the oil industry in obtaining major tax favors, in persuading the Congress to exercise monopoly power in the form of market demand prorationing, and in obtaining restrictions on foreign competition in the form of import quotas, testifies to the historical political power of that industry. It should be noted, however, that political power rests primarily in the hands of independent producers rather than with large oil companies. (1) The recent revisions of the percentage depletion allowance which exclude large oil companies and retains this tax treatment for small companies, testifies to this point. (2) Under market demand prorationing, most small producers were exempt while the burden of output restrictions rested primarily on the more productive fields, owned by larger firms. (3) The introduction of import quotas was responsive to the needs of independent producers and was over the objections of the major firms. (4) In the administration of the import quota system, import tickets were allotted disproportionately to smaller firms. (5) Under the current entitlements system, small refiners are exempt. While the political power of the oil industry in general has declined in recent years, the power of the independents remains impressive. The loss in political power for the oil industry in general has accrued to the benefit of environmental interests groups. In an economic frame-

work, the rise of this pressure group can be viewed as nothing more than another dominant organized interest group. It does not follow that the public interest will now be served.

3. There is nothing in the history of U.S. energy policy that leads one to expect that policy currently being debated and ultimately to be passed will lead to conservation of scarce resources. Some of the problems of policies currently under governmental favor are already apparent. Other problems will become obvious with the passage of time. The conflicts of the past will be repeated in which one governmental measure requires another to correct for its problems. Congress has failed to understand a principle formulated by biologist Garret Hardin—"you can't do just one thing." Tax subsidies lead to market demand prorationing, which leads to import quotas. Price controls lead to nonprice rationing, which leads to the "administrative nightmare" of entitlements.

FOOTNOTES

[1]McDonald (1971).
[2]Energy Policy Project (1974).
[3]Sweeney (1977).
[4]Brannon (1975).
[5]Office of Defense Mobilization (1956).
[6]*Oil and Gas Journal* (1978).
[7]Tetra Tech, Inc. (1976).
[8]Mead (1977). b
[9]Mead (1977). b
[10]Jones, Mead and Sorensen (Forthcoming 1978).
[11]Erickson and Spann (1974).
[12]Mancke (1974).
[13]The White House (1977).
[14]Mead (1977). a
[15]Executive Office of the President (1977).

REFERENCES

Brannon, Gerard M. *Studies in Energy Tax Policy.* Cambridge, Mass., Ballinger Publishing Co., 1975.
Energy Policy Project, *A Time to Choose.* Cambridge, Mass., Ballinger Publishing Co., 1974.
Erickson, E. W. and Spann, R. M. "The U.S. Petroleum Industry," E. W. Erickson and L. Waverman (editors), *The Energy Question, An International Failure of Policy,* Vol. II, Toronto: University of Toronto Press, 1974.
Executive Office of the President, *The National Energy Plan.* Washington, D.C.: April 29, 1977.
Jones, R. O., Mead, W. J., and Sorensen, P. E. "Free Entry into Crude Oil and Gas Production and Competition in the U.S. Oil Industry," *Natural Resources Journal,* forthcoming July 1978.

Mancke, R. B. *The Failure of U.S. Energy Policy,* New York: Columbia University Press, 1974.

McDonald, S. L., *Petroleum Conservation in the United States: An Economic Analysis.* Baltimore: The Johns Hopkins Press, 1971.

Mead, W. J., "An Economic Appraisal of President Carter's Energy Program," *Science,* Vol. 197, July 22, 1977, 340–345. a

Mead, W. J., *Transporting Natural Gas from the Arctic, the Alternative Systems.* Washington: American Enterprise Institute, 1977. b

Oil and Gas Journal, January 9, 1978. p. 36.

Office of Defense Mobilization, *Hearings,* 1956.

Sweeney, J. L., "Economics of Depletable Resources: Market Forces and Intertemporal Bias," *Review of Economic Studies,* XLIV (1), February 1977, 125–141.

Tetra Tech, Inc., *Energy Fact Book 1976,* A report prepared for the director of the Fleet Analysis and Support Division, Office of Naval Research, 1976.

The White House, Detailed Fact Sheet, "The President's Energy Program," April 20, 1977.

11

PETROLEUM REGULATION
The False Dilemma of Decontrol

Charles E. Phelps and Rodney T. Smith

The petroleum industry in the United States remains bound by price controls originated in 1971 and recently extended until 1979 by the Energy Policy and Conservation Act (EPCA) of 1975. That extension was viewed as a way to combat higher prices for refined products, at the expense of increased U.S. dependence on foreign oil. While we concur that the extension did increase U.S. dependence, we believe that the controls have not reduced the prices of refined products. Consequently, decontrol does not pose a choice between higher product prices and less dependence. Rather, decontrol reduces dependence on foreign oil.

Existing controls regulate many aspects of petroleum production and refining in the United States. Domestic production of crude oil is subject to a three-tier price control. "Lower Tier Oil" is base-period output from properties producing in 1972. That oil can be sold at prices averaging about $5.15 per barrel. "Upper Tier Oil" is output from those properties in excess of the base-period production, as well as all output from properties beginning production since 1972. That oil can be sold for about $11.50 per barrel. Output from properties producing less than 10 barrels per day is exempt from price controls. In contrast, imported crude oil is subject to a tariff of $.21 per barrel, which, when coupled with price movements on the world market, has made the landed price of foreign crude oil approximately $14 per barrel.

The regulations also determine the price of controlled oil transferred to refiners. The "allocation program" distributes the controlled oil according to historical contracts in 1972. The

From Charles E. Phelps and Rodney T. Smith, "Petroleum Regulation: The False Dilemma of Decontrol," pp. v-viii, 1977. Rand Report R-1951-RC. Reprinted by permission of the Rand Corporation, Santa Monica, CA.

"entitlement program" offsets differences in average acquisition
costs arising from disparate access to controlled oil.

Product price ceilings administered by the Federal Energy
Administration (FEA) are intended to force refiners to pass along
to retailers the "savings" arising from the price controls on crude
oil. The product price ceilings consist of base-period prices (from
1973) plus allowable increases due to increased costs of refining
(for example, higher prices of crude oil). Controls on retail prices
are similarly intended to force retailers to pass to consumers the
alleged savings.

Existing analyses, with which we agree, conclude that the crude
oil price ceilings must certainly reduce U.S. crude oil production,
and hence increase U.S. dependence on foreign oil sources.

Prevailing analyses also conclude that decontrol would increase
the price of refined products by as much as 5¢ to 6¢ per gallon.
That conclusion has been reached by two separate arguments. First,
it has been assumed that refiners price their product on the basis
of average acquisition cost of inputs. The controls have reduced
these costs and by this logic have therefore reduced refined product
prices. Second, the entitlement program, as described below, generates a subsidy on the use of crude oil in refining, so its repeal
would increase refined product prices. Both conclusions are incorrect.

The average-cost pricing forecast is based upon an erroneous
view of the world. Product prices are based upon the cost of producing the most expensive unit, not average costs. Since foreign
oil is the most expensive, the price of refined products is based
upon imported oil prices. Refiners of controlled oil receive a
profit transfer from the producer of the oil, but those profits are
retained by the refiner. The product price ceilings attempted to
force refiners to pass on these profit transfers to consumers, but
the price ceilings are not binding. Market forces in fact impose
a greater discipline on refined product prices than do the FEA
controls.

The structure of the price controls provides evidence that the
price ceilings are indeed nonbinding. The FEA regulations allow
refiners to accumulate "banked costs"—increases in average refin-

ing costs which are not taken in product price increases--for four product categories (gasoline, fuel oil, jet fuel, and other products). Any time banked costs are positive, product prices are not controlled, since prices could legally be increased. Data from the FEA show that substantial banked costs exist, averaging 6¢ to 9¢ per gallon for the industry during 1975, drifting slightly downward during 1976. Our research has estimated that for every $1 per barrel (2.4¢ per gallon) increase in the world price of crude oil, refiners increase their product price by 28¢ per barrel (2/3¢ per gallon) less than is allowed by the FEA price controls. This attests to the rigorous discipline of the market.

While the price controls on crude oil did not influence product prices, they did transfer profits within the petroleum industry. In 1975, the crude oil price controls and allocation program transferred about $8 billion from crude oil producers to refiners. Since vertical integration is prevalent in the petroleum industry, much of this was a transfer between production and refining subsidiaries. However, at least $3 to $4 billion was transferred from crude oil producers to nonaffiliated refiners. Decontrol would eliminate these transfers.

The second forecast of a product price increase is based upon the effects of the entitlement program. This program requires that refiners have an entitlement for each barrel of controlled oil used in refining. Each firm is issued entitlements equal to their total use of crude oil multiplied by the industry average ratio of controlled oil to total oil. Some firms are issued fewer entitlements than their actual use of controlled oil would require. Such firms must purchase additional entitlements from other firms at a price determined monthly by the FEA. In 1975 the purchase and sale of entitlements transferred $1.5 billion among refiners.

Every refiner has an incentive to expand oil inputs (and hence output) to receive additional entitlements. By this logic, the expansion in domestic refining, which did occur, should have caused refined product prices to decline in the United States when the entitlement program was instituted in November 1974. Repeal of the program would reverse this hypothesized price decline.

This forecasted price increase neglects the presence of world trade in refined products. The United States has been an active participant in world markets for refined products for many years, currently as a net importer. Because of this world trade, the domestic price of refined products is established by world, rather than U.S., demand and supply, with domestic prices conforming to landed world prices of products, inclusive of the current product tariff. By subsidizing domestic crude oil use, the entitlement program expanded domestic refining and reduced U.S. demand for product imports. U.S. refiner prices would decline, only if the reduced U.S. demand for product imports lowered world product prices.

Events after the introduction of the entitlement program showed that product prices did not decline. The entitlement program decreased the volume of product imports by 16 percent, but had *no discernible effect* on refiner prices reported by the FEA. In contrast, the 1.5¢ per gallon tariff on product imports has increased U.S. prices of refined products, adding to industry profits by $2 billion per year.

The 1975 EPCA allows the Administration to decontrol any or all parts of the petroleum and refining industries, subject to consent of the Congress. Selective removal of refinery price ceilings eliminates nonbinding controls and hence would have no effect either on product prices or dependence on foreign oil. Total decontrol of oil production, allocation, refinery price ceilings, and entitlements would also have no effect on product prices, but would reduce dependence on foreign oil. However, reduction or abolition of the product tariff would reduce refiner prices. Thus the opportunities for decontrol written into the EPCA present a political challenge to the new Administration. The choice is reduced dependence on foreign oil or continuation of the current multi-billion-dollar transfers within the industry.

12

THE DECONTROL OF DOMESTIC OIL PRICES
An Overview

Congressional Budget Office

SUMMARY

On April 5, 1979, the President announced his decision to decontrol domestic crude oil prices gradually starting on June 1, 1979, so that domestic prices would reach the world price by October 1, 1981. Since the Energy Policy and Conservation Act (EPCA) of 1975 gave the President discretionary authority to decontrol prices during that period, only new legislation by the Congress could limit the exercise of that authority.

The President's decontrol plan would generate large increases in revenues to the oil producers over what they would have received under a continuation of controls. Thus, the Congress must decide how these increased producer revenues from decontrol can be put to best use. The President has proposed that the Congress enact a "windfall profits tax" to capture some of these revenues and to establish an Energy Security Fund that would channel these captured revenues to investments in energy research and development, to assistance for mass transit, and to assistance for low-income households burdened by higher energy prices. Alternative uses of these revenues that might also be considered include allowing them to remain with the private sector to finance exploration for new oil or using them to provide general tax relief.

THE DECONTROL OF DOMESTIC OIL PRICES

The Current System of Controls

Although government policy had affected the price and availability of crude oil for some time, direct federal regulation of crude oil prices was introduced by the Emergency Petroleum Allocation Act of 1973 and was modified in 1975 by

EDITORS' NOTE: The article presented here is a brief summary of a much larger analysis. The complete article, "The Decontrol of Domestic Oil Prices: An Overview," can be obtained from the U.S. Government Printing Office, Washington, DC.

From Congressional Budget Office, "The Decontrol of Domestic Oil Prices: An Overview." Washington, DC: Government Printing Office, 1979.

EPCA. Essentially, the present regulatory system divides all doemstic crude oil into the following three classifications, or tiers:

- Old oil, or lower-tier oil, which is oil from properties that began producing before 1973. Currently, about 3.0 million barrels per day of old oil are produced and it receives a price of approximately $5.86 per barrel at the wellhead.

- New oil, or upper-tier oil, which is oil from properties that began producing during or after 1973. Approximately 3.0 million barrels per day of domestic production are new oil and it receives a price of about $13.06 per barrel at the wellhead.

- Uncontrolled oil, which is oil that earns as much as refiners are willing to pay for it. Three types of oil are allowed this treatment: Alaskan North Slope oil, Naval Petroleum Reserve, and "stripper" oil—that is, oil from wells that produce 10 or fewer barrels per day. Approximately 2.6 million barrels per day of current domestic production are uncontrolled and receive a price of about $18.50 at the refinery gate.[1]

Under EPCA the average, or composite, price for these three types of domestic oil (with some special adjustments for stripper oil) can increase at a rate up to 10 percent per year.[2] Barring new legislation, all controls on domestic oil prices will end on October 1, 1981, and domestic production will receive world prices.

The President's Decontrol Decision

In order to phase out controls on domestic crude oil, the President has decided to:

- Redefine all old oil as new oil between June 1, 1979, and October 1, 1981; and simultaneously

- Raise the price of new oil to the world price by October 1, 1981, so that by that date all old oil will have become new oil and all new oil will receive the world price.

Relative to an indefinite continuation of controls, the President's plan would entail both benefits and costs. The following benefits are critical:

- Increasing domestic oil prices to the world level would encourage consumers to reduce their demand for oil through both the substitution of alternative fuels and outright conservation. The price increase for oil would also encourage investment in solar and synthetic fuels, but it would not be sufficient to make unconventional fuels such as liquefied coal or shale oil economical. By 1985, it is estimated that decontrol would decrease demand for oil by approximately 215,000 barrels per day.[3] The potential savings are expected to be substantially greater during the late 1980s and early 1990s since energy is used primarily in connection with capital goods such as industrial boilers and automobiles which take 5 to 20 years to replace.

- Decontrol would stimulate additional supply from tertiary recovery, new discoveries, and existing oil from proven reserves.[4] In total, these three major sources should provide 200,000 and 405,000 barrels per day of additional supply by 1981 and 1985, respectively.

- The demand reductions and supply increases would decrease oil imports by approximately 620,000 barrels a day by 1985, or about 5 percent of total U.S. oil imports in that year. This would represent a shift of approximately $6 billion in the 1985 U.S. balance of payments. In later years, as demand reductions continue to grow, the magnitude of the oil import relief would continue to increase.

- Adoption of the world price could improve U.S. relations with member nations of both the Organization for Economic Cooperation and Development (OECD) and the Organization of Petroleum Exporting Countries (OPEC), which view the current subsidy of domestic energy consumption created by price regulation as evidence of U.S. unwillingness to address the energy problem.

The President's plan would also impose the following costs:

- The price increases for domestic oil would increase inflation, and they might slow economic activity and increase unemployment. By the end of 1982, it is estimated that decontrol would increase the level of prices by 0.6 to 0.8 percent above that anticipated if controls were continued. If OPEC continues to increase the real price of oil over this period, the inflationary impact of decontrol could be considerably higher. The effects on real Gross National Product (GNP) and unemployment are relatively minor and generally occur after 1982.

- Low-income families would pay a disproportionate share of their income on the higher oil prices caused by decontrol. Specifically, decontrol would cost an additional $64 per family for the lowest fifth of families as ranked by income; this would represent approximately a 1.3 percent decline in their real income by 1982. In contrast, families in the highest fifth of the income distribution would suffer only a 0.5 percent decline in their real income by 1982. Any increases in real OPEC prices would worsen the impact on low-income families.

- The price increases under decontrol would transfer what has been a windfall income gain for consumers, who have been paying less than the world price for oil, to a windfall profit for producers, who will be receiving higher prices for oil that could have been produced at current prices. Relative to an indefinite continuation of controls, and assuming no increase in real

OPEC prices, this windfall profit to producers would total approximately $68.9 billion between 1979 and 1985. If OPEC prices increased by 3 percent in real terms over this period, the windfall would be an additional $25.7 billion.

The benefits and costs summarized above are all relative to an indefinite continuation of the present controls under EPCA. If EPCA were not extended—that is, if decontrol became effective abruptly on October 1, 1981, rather than phased over the 28-month period—then most of the benefits and costs would take place at that time. As compared with all-at-once decontrol, the President's program has the advantage of phasing the price increase over a longer period of time and providing for an earlier supply response. By 1985, however, the effects of a phased and a sudden decontrol would be virtually identical.

Alternatives to the President's Decontrol Plan

Two alternatives to the President's decontrol plan are analyzed in this study. The first, the middle-price option, would decontrol all truly new oil and raise old oil to the upper-tier price, but would maintain the controls indefinitely on upper-tier oil. The second, the modified EPCA option, would decontrol truly new oil and elevate all marginal wells to the upper tier, but would maintain controls on other upper- and lower-tier oil. Both alternatives are compared with an indefinite continuation of current controls.

- *The middle-price option.* This option would decrease the producer revenues substantially from the $68.9 billion attributable to the President's program to approximately $24.4 billion over the period from 1979 to 1985. It would also retain most of the supply response—that is, 335,000 of the 405,000 barrels per day estimated for the President's plan. The demand reduction would be about 100,000 barrels per day, or less than one-half of that attributable to the President's plan. This option would reduce both the burden of low-income families and the impact on inflation, which would most likely be less than one-half the impact of the President's plan.

- *The modified EPCA option.* This option would stimulate production approximately 160,000 barrels per day in new supply as a result of the provisions to decontrol new oil and to elevate marginal lower-tier oil to the upper-tier price. Very little reduction in demand would occur with this option (less than 50,000 barrels per day by 1985) because the additional producer revenues would be only about $9.3 billion over the 1979-1985 period. The benefit of this option, however, could be little additional inflation and little negative impact on low-income households.

THE TAX ISSUES

Additional profits on lower- and upper-tier oil may be considered "windfalls" if price increases were not anticipated by producers and are therefore not needed to make existing production profitable. In addition, higher prices may be deemed a windfall if they are the product of OPEC's monopoly power, which distorts world oil markets.

Whether or not windfall profit taxes are considered appropriate depends not only on these equity considerations, but also on how much new supply could be obtained under the President's plan, and on whether additional revenues are necessary to finance this supply. If the price on the new supply offers sufficient incentives for firms to borrow and invest, then the additional revenues from existing oil could be taxed away. On the other hand, if revenues are required for the investment, then they could be left with the oil producers.

The President's Tax Proposals

The President proposes to apply a 50 percent tax rate to the additional producer revenues after exempting certain types of lower-tier oil. Of the total $68.9 billion in windfall revenues that producers would receive between now and 1985, $51.4 billion is assumed to be the base for the windfall profits tax. The tax on this base would be $25.7 billion between 1979 and 1985; the residual $25.7 billion, as well as the $17.5 billion exempted from the windfall tax base, would be taxed through the normal corporate income tax. These revenues would yield a corporate tax liability of another $4 billion over the 1979-1985 period. Thus, of the $68.9 billion in windfall revenues, a total of $29.7 billion would be taxed away from the producers. If the windfall were subject only to corporate income taxes, approximately $13.3 billion would be taxed away. The windfall tax, therefore, more than doubles producers' liabilities on windfall income.

Alternative Tax Options

Three alternatives to the President's tax proposals are analyzed in this study:

- A 75 percent windfall tax rate on upper-tier oil and a 50 percent rate on lower-tier oil would, over the 1979-1985 period, collect $38 billion out of the $68.9 billion windfall; $37 billion would be collected through windfall taxes and $1 billion through corporate income taxes. As compared with the President's proposals, this option would tax an additional $8.3 billion, or 12 percent of the windfall.

- A 25 percent windfall tax rate would produce $12.8 billion in windfall tax liability between 1979-1985 and $8.6 billion in normal corporate income tax, for a total of $21.4 billion. Tax liabilities would thus be $8.3 billion less than those that would result from the President's proposals.

- A "plowback" provision would allow producers to deduct increases in drilling expenditures from the windfall profits tax base. Based on CBO assumptions about the amount of new investment in exploration and development, it is estimated that this provision would allow producers to deduct $31.9 billion from the windfall profits tax base between now and

1985, leaving a base of $19.5 billion during this period and windfall tax liabilities of $9.7 billion. Total tax liabilities, after corporate income taxes are added in, would equal $19.5 billion. This liability would be $6.2 billion more than what the total liability would have been under the normal corporate income tax.

The Marginal Tax Rate

The above tax estimates are extremely sensitive to the assumed marginal corporate income tax, which in turn depends primarily upon the amount of new investment in exploration and development. Essentially, the opportunity to treat drilling costs as expenses instead of capital outlays permits producers to shelter substantial windfall revenues and the income from new production. In recent years, with the high rate of inflation and the high level of exploration, expense deductions have been sufficient to offset nearly half of the tax that would be due if the statutory rate of 46 percent were applied to all companies. Under the CBO assumptions concerning expenditures for exploration and development, the marginal tax rate is approximately 13 percent for 1980, decreases to 6 percent in 1981 and 1982, and then increases over time to 26 percent in 1985. The marginal rate changes over time because of two factors: when producers make new expenditures on exploration and production that reduce taxable income, and when they receive revenues from new supplies that increase revenues. Over the 1979-1985 period, CBO estimates that the average marginal tax rate would be approximately 15 percent.

ENERGY SECURITY FUND

The President has proposed that the Congress establish an Energy Security Fund, which would redistribute tax revenues to low-income households, to mass transit, and to energy investments that assist in the transition to a more energy-efficient economy. Given CBO's revenue estimates and no increase in real OPEC prices, the President's program would create approximately $30 billion in revenues for the trust fund over the 1979-1985 period.

The Trust Fund Mechanism

The Congress has used trust funds in the past to finance large capital projects; the funds have been obtained by taxes on specific uses. The primary examples are the Highway Trust Fund and the Airport and Airway Trust Fund. Trust funds, however, have several important drawbacks from the standpoint of budgetary and policy coordination. First, since trust funds are only marginally affected by the budget resolutions and the appropriations process, they limit the Congress' control over the federal budget. Second, since both energy investments and mass transit already have relatively large federal programs, additional expenditures from a trust fund would create coordination problems both for the Congress in authorizing and appropriating these programs and for the Executive agencies in administering them. Finally, since revenues are extremely sensitive to future OPEC price increases, which are difficult to predict, it may be difficult to plan the expenditures from such a fund.

Energy Investments

The President recommends spending additional funds on a demonstration plant for solvent-refined coal, a development program for synthetic liquids, and additional research and development (R&D) on coal. Such technologies are feasible, and they would increase the probability that cost-effective synthetic fuel could be produced during the next 15 to 20 years. This program should, however, be viewed as providing technical information for future commercial plants rather than providing any domestic production. Alternative options for R&D funds over the longer run include fusion, solar photovoltaic, solar heating and cooling, and several fission technologies.

Mass Transit

The mass transit funding recommended by the President is primarily to purchase new buses and to rehabilitate existing rail systems. Although there are significant differences in the energy efficiencies of the various modes of urban transportation, it may nevertheless be difficult to get people to switch from automobiles to buses, which are about three times more energy-efficient than automobiles. Through 1985, it is assumed that funds would be available to purchase about 8,000 additional buses—a 15 percent expansion in the total U.S. fleet. The potential energy saving from such a proposal would, however, be less than 10,000 barrels of oil per day. The expansion would also add to current operating costs for bus companies and would thus create greater pressure for increased federal assistance.

Low-Income Assistance

CBO estimates that oil price decontrol would increase the nation's oil bill by $12.2 billion in 1982 if real OPEC prices remain constant and by $15.8 billion if there is a 3 percent per year increase in real OPEC prices. Since it is assumed that all price increases will be passed through to consumers, households will ultimately bear the burden of these additional oil expenditures. Assuming no real OPEC price increase, the increase in 1982 for families with annual incomes under $5,800 will be $64 and for families with annual incomes between $5,800 and $11,400 the increase in 1982 will be $99. (All increases are stated in 1979 constant dollars.) To offset these increases for both income classes, the federal government would have to provide assistance amounting to between $3.0 billion and $3.7 billion, depending upon whether future real increases in OPEC prices occur.

Alternatives to the Energy Security Fund

If the Congress determines that the new revenues resulting from decontrol can be put to best use through taxation, spending options other than those recommended by the President can be considered, including the following:

- *No earmarking of funds.* One major option would be to separate the tax decision from the expenditure decision. If the tax is enacted, then it would be up to the budget and appropriations committees of the Congress to decide on the use of the funds through the normal budget process. These committees could recommend spending on projects similar to those of the President or on other programs, or they could decide to decrease the size of the deficit. This option would provide the Congress with more effective budget control and with greater potential for overall planning and policy coordination than the President's proposed trust fund.

- *A fund for oil exploration.* A second option would be to use the funds to finance exploration and development of oil reserves in non-OPEC developing nations. The major advantage of such a fund is that there is probably greater likelihood of finding relatively large oil reserves outside the United States than in the United States because of the amount of exploration that has already taken place in this country. An exploratory program by the U.S. government might, however, be redundant with existing efforts.

- *Reductions in payroll taxes.* A third major option would be to allow the additional tax revenues to be used to decrease payroll taxes. If it is assumed that 50 percent of the additional revenues are applied to employee taxes and 50 percent to employer taxes, then there could be some reduction in the rate of inflation attributable to the President's decontrol plan. Although considerable uncertainty surrounds these estimates, such a proposal would improve the price level by an estimated 0.3 percentage point by 1984.

NOTES

1. Technically, Alaskan oil can only receive the upper-tier price at the wellhead, but because of high transportation costs it receives the world price at the refinery.

2. The President can authorize increases in the composite prices that are greater than 10 percent, subject to a veto by one house of the Congress.

3. This estimate, like all others presented in this paper, presumes that the full increase in the cost of crude is passed on to consumers. If refiners have to absorb a percentage of the increase, the demand response will be proportionately lower.

4. Tertiary recovery is a technology that injects either heat or chemical compounds into an oil reservoir to loosen oil so that it will flow more freely.

Pollution Control Policy

13

WHAT CAN WE GET FROM EFFLUENT CHARGES?

Clifford S. Russell

*This paper clarifies the debate over effluent charges as instruments of
environmental quality policy. The author identifies four charge schemes
that seem to have practical potential; compares them with the regulatory alternatives in terms of economic efficiency, information requirements, and susceptibility to political pressure and delaying tactics; and
discusses problems of enforcement. He concludes that effluent charges
have only one unambiguous advantage—they tend to force environment-
saving innovation—and that this advantage might be obtained by graft-
ing a charge onto discharge limitations.*

The United States may now be approaching one of those slick,
downward-sloping surfaces we so frequently create by our all-or-
nothing approach to gratifying our shifting enthusiasms. For example, a little over a decade ago we decided it was unconscionable
that elderly people with fixed incomes and poor people with virtually
no incomes should face the possibility of ruinously large medical
bills. Now we are all up to our elbows in an enormous and seemingly
uncontrollable medical care cost inflation, to which Medicare and
Medicaid have greatly contributed. Similarly disquieting examples

I am grateful for comments on earlier drafts from my colleagues Emery
Castle, A. M. Freeman III, Charles Hitch, Robert Mitchell, Henry Peskin,
Kerry Smith, Walter Spofford, William Vaughn, and William Watson. Nina
Cornell, Terry Davies, Ernst Habicht, David Kinnersley, and Allen Kneese
also saw and were kind enough to react to an early version. An anonymous
reviewer for this journal also provided useful suggestions. None, of course,
bear any responsibility for my use (or misuse) of their suggestions or for the
resulting product.

From Clifford S. Russell, "What Can We Get from Effluent Charges?" 5(2) *Policy Analysis* pp.
155-180 (Spring 1979). © Copyright 1979 by the Regents of the University of California.

might be drawn from our experience with public housing, with urban renewal, with price and income controls, and with regulation of energy prices. Now, disenchanted with our efforts at "command and control" intervention in the economy, we are beginning to remember the virtues of prices and markets and are being shown how at least some of these virtues might be obtained if we used price-like ways of public intervention. A healthy and long-overdue message—up to a point. The danger, which ought to be familiar by now, is that by speaking loudly, simply, and enthusiastically enough to get the attention of Congress and the executive branch the proponents of "the public use of private incentives" will push us over the edge, inspiring a rush of ill-considered legislation that will damage the future acceptability of markets and price-like incentives.[1]

My aim in this paper is, for the narrow but important field of environmental quality, to clarify what we can and cannot expect from publicly prescribed prices—here usually in the form of effluent charges.[2] As a proponent of greater reliance on pricing in public activities generally, I certainly do not wish to be interpreted as a debunker, a nay-sayer trying desperately to kill an idea whose time has come. But it does seem to me that the rhetoric of the major proponents of charges may have created expectations that any particular real charging scheme will never be able to fulfill. This danger is related to, but separate from, a tendency for the ongoing debate about effluent charges to confound a number of logically distinct possibilities for such a scheme. The importance of the resulting confusion lies in the fact that different possible charging systems have different characteristics in terms of some key dimensions of the debate: static economic efficiency; information requirements; scope for political bargaining and compromise; opportunity for legal challenges. Thus, until we know clearly what kind of system we are setting up, we cannot hope to know what mix of good and bad attributes we are buying—except in one dimension: all the effluent charge possibilities discussed here share a common and highly desirable dynamic incentive effect, for they lift air and water out of the zero-priced resource category and spur firms to think about

1. Charles L. Schultze, *The Public Use of Private Interest* (Washington, D.C.: Brookings Institution, 1977).

2. Other forms have been suggested, including a tax on fuels by sulfur content and a tax on automobiles that do not meet the auto emission standards. Both of these are conceptually very close to effluent charges because of the close link between the taxed "object" and pollution discharges.

short- and long-term technological changes that allow more economical use of the waste assimilating capacity of air and water.[3] One major message of this paper is that this incentive effect is probably the strongest argument for effluent charges. In obtaining it, however, we shall have to face the real shortcomings of particular systems more squarely than we have so far.

PRACTICAL EFFLUENT CHARGE ALTERNATIVES

The number of theoretically possible effluent charge schemes is, of course, quite large because such schemes may differ according to (1) the type of policy target each is designed to achieve; (2) the manner in which the charge levels are chosen; and (3) whether the charges applied are uniform for all dischargers in the relevant jurisdiction or different for differently situated sources.[4]

Within these distinctions further refinement is possible. For example, one can differentiate between policy targets that are themselves uniform and those that vary in some way. Thus we can have uniform national ambient standards (standards that apply to the environment at large as opposed to the end of a discharge pipe) or ambient standards for Philadelphia that are different from those for Yellowstone National Park. As a matter of fact, our current system includes both nonuniform ambient and nonuniform effluent standards, since for air the "uniform" national primary and secondary

3. It is possible to define ways of using charges that reduce the continuing incentive to zero once some discharge or treatment technology standard is met. These are really fines to speed compliance with regulation and are discussed only in passing in the rest of this paper. For a complete description of an actual implementation program based on such charges, see U.S., Environmental Protection Agency, *Economic Law Enforcement*, EPA–901/9–76–003a, report submitted by The Connecticut Enforcement Project (Washington, D.C., 1975), vol. 1, *Overview*. This idea appears to be attaining considerable popularity in Washington and was, in fact, included in the proposed Clean Air Act Amendments of 1976 as reported from the House-Senate Conference Committee on 30 September 1976 (U.S., House of Representatives, Report 94–1742, sec. 119). At this writing, both Senate and House versions of the 1977 Clean Air Bills have similar provisions (*Air/Water: Pollution Report*, 16 May 1977, p. 194).

4. The last difference requires a little clarification. Charges set by state governments can be uniform across each state, but nonuniform when viewed from the national perspective. More important, however, within any jurisdiction that adopts the charge, nonuniformity can mean that all dischargers along one river or in one airshed pay one charge, while all along another river or in another airshed pay another; or it can mean that each discharger along a single river is, at least in principle, subject to a different charge. It is in the last sense that nonuniformity is of central interest here.

ambient quality standards exist in combination with a nondegrada-
tion policy that has been taken to mean that currently clean areas
face tougher standards than the "uniform" levels. And on the water
side, the cornerstone of policy is the National Pollution Discharge
Elimination System (NPDES), with its individual discharge permits
that, although based on guidelines using uniform definitions, are
actually written for individual plants in light of particular circumstances and hence are really nonuniform.[5] There also exist nonuniform in-stream quality standards set by the states during the
1960s.

In addition, there are real possibilities for hybrid systems involving the imposition of a charge on top of some chosen or existing set
of regulations, such as zero discharge allowances for certain toxics
or the attainment of the 1977 BPCTCA (best practicable control
technology currently available) effluent limitations. For the most
part, in order to sharpen the issues, this paper deals with pure charge
systems. Toward the end of the paper I do discuss hybrid systems as
a possible method of capturing the most telling advantages of
charges in the existing political situation and historical context.

Even within the set of pure charge schemes, not all alternatives
are of equal interest, and for the sake of clarity and brevity I confine most of my discussion to the characteristics of what seem to be
the principal competitors for policymakers' attention. There are, I
believe, four such major alternatives, and they are summarized in
table 1. The reader may well wonder, however, what happened to
the logical possibilities left out of the table. Why, for example, am I
ignoring the option of using trial and error to determine a uniform
charge aimed at inducing compliance with a discharge standard?
I deal below with such questions and with a few other matters of
clarification. I then provide a critique of the competing systems

5. Notice that the concept of uniformity in discharge standards is not well
defined in the absence of further language. A uniform standard could be one
involving equal quantities per unit time at each plant, regardless of size, type,
and so forth. There could also be uniformity of percentage *reductions* in
discharges from some base period, or uniform discharges by plant type per
unit of input or output. The "effluent limitation guidelines" being prepared
by the U.S. Environmental Protection Agency under the 1972 amendments
to the Federal Water Pollution Control Act are basically of this last variety,
with allowance for variation not only with plant type, but with age, production technology used, and local economic factors.

TABLE 1. PRINCIPAL ALTERNATIVES FOR AN EFFLUENT CHARGE SYSTEM

Policy Target	Method of Setting	Degree of Charge Variation over Sources
Discharge Standards	Calculation[1]	Nonuniform[2]
Ambient Quality Standards	Trial and Error[1]	Uniform[2]
Ambient Quality Standards	Calculation	Uniform
Ambient Quality Standards	Calculation	Nonuniform

[1] In the terminology used here, an effluent charge is set by calculation if the "correct" level (or what is believed to be the correct level) to attain the policy target is determined in advance by the responsible public authority on the basis of available information on costs, characteristics of natural systems, and so forth. A charge is set by trial and error if a more or less arbitrary charge level is set in advance, the results of that charge (in terms of actual discharges or actual ambient quality levels) are monitored and compared to the target, a new charge level, intended to move the system closer to the target, is chosen and announced, and so on iteratively until, it is hoped, the target is met. In a real situation, where exogenous conditions are constantly changing, any attempt to set a charge will take on some of the character of both polar approaches.

[2] Here systems are taken to be uniform if all dischargers in a water or airshed face the same charges—whether or not there are differences among entire airsheds, states, or regions. Nonuniformity means that the charge is tailored to each individual source.

given in table 1, and a discussion of the characteristics of regulatory schemes, in terms of the key dimensions already identified.

Charges as Marginal Damages

For many economists, the most glaring omission from table 1 and, indeed, from my entire discussion up to this point, is probably the theoretical possibility of setting charges so that the marginal costs of discharge reduction at each source just equal the marginal social damages attributable to that source. This, however, does not seem to be a real policy option for the foreseeable future, because of the very great difficulties in the way of measuring many important benefits (such as health and aesthetic effects), because the required computations would be enormously difficult, and because such single-minded concern with efficiency is out of character with public policy generally. But even when we eliminate this theoretically appealing alternative, we are left with more possibilities for combining type of standard, method of charge calculation, and degree of charge uniformity than appear in table 1. (In fact, of course, since the table includes three dichotomous characteristics, four of the eight possibilities have been left out of the table.) Again, there are practical arguments against the omitted alternatives.

Uniform Charges and Discharge Standards

The use of uniform charge levels is almost certainly inconsistent with discharge-standard targets. In whatever way a discharge standard is expressed, its exact attainment at each source will certainly require nonuniform charges, because marginal-cost-of-reduction schedules will differ among sources. Or, said another way, only by some miraculous chance will a discharge standard, even one that does not vary over sources, be such that its attainment at each source will just be induced by a charge set uniformly over the nation or region.[6]

Of course, in principle, it would be possible to achieve, via a single, nationally-uniform set of effluent charges, *at least* any desired level of discharge reduction or *at most* any allowed remaining discharges at every source. But the charge required to bring the highest-cost sources up to snuff would, in general, be very much greater than that required to induce most dischargers to meet such a standard. Therefore, the required uniform charge would produce, as a practical matter, greater discharge reductions than the targets called for and would imply greater costs of reduction to most dischargers than would those targets if enforced administratively.[7] This

6. There is the possibility of creating a simple and internally consistent— if tautological—system of "uniform discharge standards" using charges and not requiring prior identification of a correct set of charge levels. This possibility is to define uniformity in terms of marginal removal costs. Then any uniform charge set will (if firms are really cost minimizers) lead to the achievement of a uniform standard.

7. Any charge system that stops short of inducing zero discharges will always cost dischargers more than would the equivalent discharge standard (a standard set at the levels of discharge reached via the charge). This is because the dischargers pay not only the cost of the optimal reduction in waste loads, but also the fees for their remaining discharges—and these may in fact be of roughly the same size as the costs of reduction, or even much higher. (See, for example, the examples given in C. S. Russell and W. J. Vaughan, *Steel Production* [Baltimore, Md.: Johns Hopkins Press for Resources for the Future, 1976], pp. 300–306. For the steel mill involved, the total effluent fee payments are consistently higher than the total costs of the reductions undertaken.) It is this continuing payment to which economists look for the inducement of future discharge reductions through the development of new technologies. But its existence has often been ignored when explanations for industry's opposition to charges are under discussion. See

situation does not seem politically plausible, as the supposed discharge standard will apply in fact to very few sources, while all the
others will meet stricter standards.

Nonuniform Charges and Trial and Error

If uniform charges cannot, as a practical matter, be used to
achieve discharge standards, then it also seems that the trial and
error method of arriving at the proper charges for each individual
source is inconsistent with discharge standards. Proceeding by trial
and error to find charges that must, in principle, be tailored to each
of 60,000 or so individual sources of pollution is an awe-inspiring
task. While the number of individual prices that would have to be
determined is no greater than the number of discharge standards
required under, for example, the current NPDES system in water
pollution, each price would presumably have to be set several times
(at least) by the very nature of trial and error. There are, in addition,
more fundamental difficulties. For example, a comprehensive charge
system would have to take account of air and water pollution and
solid waste disposal, and this would land the charge-setters in the
complications raised by intermedia tradeoffs. Thus increasing the
charge on biochemical oxygen demand (BOD) for a particular plant
also might require raising the charge on particulate emissions from
that plant if the air-side discharge standard is just being met, because treatment plant sludges are often incinerated and the additional removal of BOD from the waste water would imply additional
sludge generation. While such difficulties may not constitute logical
obstacles to use of the trial and error method with individualized
charges, when combined with the sheer administrative and monitoring efforts required to promulgate, investigate, and amend each

W. J. Oates and W. E. Baumol, "The Instruments of Environmental Policy,"
in *Economic Analysis of Environmental Problems,* ed. Edwin S. Mills (New
York: National Bureau of Economic Research, 1975); and A. V. Kneese and
C. L. Schultze, *Pollution, Prices, and Public Policy* (Washington, D.C.:
Brookings, 1975). But, for discussions that do explicitly include this feature,
see A. M. Freeman III and R. H. Haveman, "Residuals Charges for Pollution
Control: A Policy Evaluation," *Science* 177 (28 July 1972): 322–29; and
National Academy of Sciences, *Decision Making in the Environmental Protection Agency* (Washington, D.C., 1977), p. 158. If the comparison is between a uniform charge and a uniform discharge standard designed to meet
the same ambient quality standard, it need not be true that in the aggregate
the charge scheme will cost dischargers more.

round of the trial, I believe they justify omitting these combinations from the list of practical options.

Uniform Charges and Ambient Standards

It is natural at this point to ask why the argument above about uniform charges as instruments for achieving discharge standards cannot also be used to rule out the use of uniform charges to meet an ambient quality standard. Certainly, because, as discussed in the next section, uniform charges cannot in general achieve an ambient standard at least cost, under a uniform charge some sources will be cleaning up too much and others not enough, relative to the efficient solution. As a practical matter, however, which sources fall into which categories will not be known *unless* enough information is available to allow calculation of the efficient set of nonuniform charges. There will not, in any event, be the disparities, obvious to each plant manager, between a stated discharge standard and a least-cost response to the uniform charge. Therefore we could expect less political heat whether calculation or trial and error were used for determining the charge.[8] Note, however, that some element of uniformity will almost certainly be required if trial and error is used to find the correct charges to meet chosen ambient standards. As argued above, attempting to find tens of thousands of "correct" charges by trial and error is simply too difficult a job. It does, in addition, imply hopelessly large degrees of freedom for the agency charged with meeting the standard. Any action taken under these circumstances would almost certainly be challenged as arbitrary and capricious by those affected. How such actions could be defended is unclear, because there would, by assumption, be no information base to which the agency could point in justifying any particular decision.

The above arguments and observations lead me to believe that the practical universe of policy options, a subset of the logical possibilities, is that shown in table 1. This is the basis of my discussion below of efficiency, information, politics, and litigation.

8. It does not follow that if we had the information necessary to calculate efficient, nonuniform charges there would be no point in using uniform charges to meet ambient standards. Uniform charges, while not efficient, *may* be seen as fairer by some parties.

Charges as Policy Targets

A final matter may be mentioned in passing. When reading some of the statements of proponents of charges, one may get the impression that charges should, in fact, be the target of our policy rather than only instruments for the attainment of other targets. This interpretation is possible because these proponents are willing to advocate the introduction of charges while recognizing that in the current state of the relevant arts we cannot really predict what will result in the environment from the introduction of any specific charge set.[9] The nature of the political process also provides arguments to support the notion of charges as targets. First, of course, some would maintain that the distinction between targets and instruments is false and misleading, and meaningful, if at all, only in the rarified world of certain econometric models. Every product of the public policy process is in some way both an instrument and a target. For example, the rate of interest, while a key instrument of macro policy, carries so much historic, nearly ideological, freight, that its level is important in itself. More to the point in terms of environmental issues, since targets are usually expressed by Congress in imprecise though high-sounding terms, the making of public policy really involves simultaneous creation of targets and instruments in the administrative process.

A second line of support for the charges-as-targets argument is a more practical one. It says that what is important is establishing the principle that charges are acceptable and useful; much later we can worry about adjusting the charge levels to achieve particular levels of ambient quality.[10] To some extent, roughly analogous posi-

9. The most accessible source for this line of argument is chapter 7 in Kneese and Schultze, *Pollution, Prices, and Public Policy*. Kneese and Schultze explicitly make the point that we do not now know enough to levy charges designed to achieve particular goals, but that getting the incentive effects is worthwhile even though we cannot know exactly what we are buying in either the short or the long run. (See p. 106.)

10. See Kneese and Schultz, *Pollution, Prices, and Public Policy*, p. 95. Notice that our existing (as of September 1977) water quality legislation might be said to treat pollution discharges, or even particular discharge reduction technologies, as targets, when ultimately we must be concerned about ambient environmental quality. This confusion is behind the current debate over the desirability of proceeding to the 1981 BATEA (best available technology economically achievable) discharge standards.

tions appear to arise among the enthusiasts for any major public initiative. For example, social security was sold as an insurance system by those who were dead set on its eventually becoming a powerful instrument for income redistribution.

If one accepts the position that charges may be seen as an end in themselves, then there is only one general choice left: the degree of uniformity imposed on the system. Since the charges are themselves the target, there are no ambient or discharge standards and no "correct" charges to calculate or arrive at by other means. Indeed, if charges are an end in themselves, it is difficult to see any firm grounds on which to choose their level, though it would be reasonable to pick a uniform level high enough to produce some response, simply on the grounds that otherwise the law would be called into disrepute. The fundamental question then becomes, Are charges really so desirable that we should be willing to pick a uniform charge set arbitrarily (but subject, of course, to intense political pressures) and to live with it for quite a long time? For I suspect that a set of charges, once established by Congress, will be very difficult to change and especially difficult to increase.

THE CHARACTERISTICS OF EFFLUENT CHARGE SYSTEMS
Static Efficiency

Static efficiency is a measure of alternative policies particularly dear to the hearts of economists, for obvious reasons, and figures prominently in the debate over effluent charges, since these instruments are frequently claimed to be superior in this dimension of comparison. Not all the schemes depicted in table 1 display this characteristic to the same extent, however, and the major burden of this subsection will be to show that the attainment of static efficiency cannot be called upon as support for some of the most commonly suggested policy initiatives.

The efficiency claim may validly be made for effluent charges in the context of a system of discharge standards with calculated "correct" (and, in general, nonuniform) charges as the instruments. There, each discharger can, in principle, be induced to meet the required standard at least cost (assuming, as always, profit maximizing behavior). Notice, however, that only one definition of the discharge standard will result in the *sum* of all the discharges being achieved at least cost (efficiently). That is a discharge standard based on uniformity of marginal costs across dischargers. Any of the infinite number of other discharge standards can be efficiently achieved using effluent charges, but the possibility will remain that the standard itself is essentially arbitrary in relation to the fundamental matter of actual environmental quality.

Where ambient environmental quality targets are concerned, two important points may be made. First, the efficient attainment of any ambient standard will, in general, require individualized charges—that is, a different charge set for each source. Uniform charges equalize marginal costs of changing discharges at each source, but to meet an ambient standard efficiently what is necessary is the equalization of the marginal costs of changing each source's contribution to the ambient concentrations being constrained.[11] Or, said another way, advocating the use of uniform charges to meet standards efficiently amounts to ignoring the role of natural systems (terrestial and aquatic ecology and local meteorology) that fill the space between the dischargers and the points at which concentrations are measured and constrained.[12] In the real world, location matters.[13] It follows that a system based on uniform (national or regional) charges with trial and error attempts to meet a desired ambient standard will *not*, in general, produce efficiency. (The same

11. A simple and elegant proof of this proposition, attributable to Walter Spofford, may be found in A. V. Kneese, "Costs of Water Quality Improvement, Transfer Functions, and Public Policy," in *Cost Benefit Analysis and Water Pollution Policy*, ed. H. M. Peskin and E. P. Seskin (Washington, D.C.: Urban Institute, 1975), pp. 195–97.

12. This is a common error among economists. Even Freeman and Haveman in their otherwise excellent analysis of charges as an alternative to regulation ("Residuals Charges for Pollution Control") are confused, referring to "the exact charge at which the quality standard is attained" as the one "which equates the marginal costs of waste reduction of all dischargers [and achieves] the standard at minimum total cost" (p. 326).

13. It is worth making explicit here the implicit model behind many of the statements about ambient standards in this paper. Basically, this model involves a small set of points in the environment at which ambient conditions are measured. In general, the conditions at any such point will be affected by more than one discharger, and each of the dischargers will be located differently with respect to the monitoring stations. If, at the other extreme, the system involved one monitoring station per source, with each station located so that conditions at it were effectively influenced only by the single source, the line between ambient and discharge standards would disappear, but individualized charges would still be the efficient way to induce achievement of a given ambient standard.

comment, by the way, applies to uniform discharge standards seen as instruments for achieving desired ambient quality levels, although, as pointed out in footnote 5 above, the concept of uniformity here is ambiguous in the absence of further definition.) Correctly calculated charges could achieve the desired standard more cheaply. Thus, the second observation: static efficiency of an effluent charge in the ambient standard context depends on calculation of the correct, individualized, charges.

There are, of course, complications that must be mentioned. All these statements reckon without the stochastic, non-steady-state character both of nature and of most production operations. Consistent attainment of a given ambient quality standard using effluent charges may be essentially impossible, and efficient attainment completely beyond the pale. The very best we can probably aspire to is a seasonally varying charge system, reflecting average changes in natural assimilative capacity and in production patterns. Superimposed on this might be a set of supercharges for unusually severe natural conditions such as extreme low stream flows or meteorological inversions. Even then it might be preferable to deal with extreme events just as most writers propose to deal with extremely toxic discharges—by discharge standards, rather than by effluent charges.

Another set of problems so far ignored here (and in almost all the literature) is that associated with economic growth and decline and with technological innovation. If the desired ambient standard stays fixed over time, and if in period zero it is just being met and is being met efficiently, changes in numbers and sizes of sources and changes in production and treatment technology will all, in general, call for recalculation of the optimal charge sets.[14]

14. As a practical matter, other ways might be found to deal with these problems. For example, the planning period could be begun with slack in the system—that is, with charges high enough that the ambient standard would be, in fact, exceeded. Or something along the lines of EPA's policy of compensatory reductions—a close kin of Dale's system of pollution rights —could be instituted (see J. H. Dales, *Pollution, Property and Prices* [Toronto: University of Toronto Press, 1968]). Since location matters, of course, the appropriate compensating reductions will not generally involve simple pound-for-pound exchanges by two distinct dischargers. The problem exists for the pollution-rights schemes as well. See, for example, W. D. Montgomery, "Markets in Licenses and Efficient Pollution Control Programs," *Journal of Economic Theory* 5 (December 1972): 395–418.

A different way of approaching the static efficiency issue is to ask in what situations uniform charge systems would be efficient. The answer is that in any situation in which location does not matter (such as a lake or airshed with perfect mixing of pollution from all sources) uniform charges will achieve any particular level of ambient quality most cheaply.[15] In such a situation, the charge could be arrived at by trial and error (ignoring for the moment problems of dynamic inefficiency arising from the adjustment process).[16]

Regulatory approaches to the achievement of particular environmental management targets are not, of course, automatically inefficient any more than charges are automatically efficient. If a discharge standard is the public policy target, then the question of efficiency really involves the extent to which each source is induced to produce its mandated discharges at least cost. If the levels are simply specified, we can assume, without doing much violence to the world, that cost-minimizing firms will meet them as cheaply as possible. But with capital cost subsidies, biases toward particular end-of-pipe technologies, and the tendency to reduce allowed standards as new and cheaper discharge-reduction processes are developed, the existing system probably tends to introduce considerable inefficiency even in this simple context. As far as ambient quality standards are concerned, there does of course exist an efficient set of

15. With perfect mixing of all discharges as assumed above, no non-uniform ambient standard could be achieved at all. Clearly such situations seldom exist, and when they do they often involve especially severe conditions, such as when an atmospheric inversion creates a mixing-bowl effect over a metropolitan area. These situations may be precisely the kind in which we desire the certain and quick response of emergency prohibitions and other direct regulations.

16. Marc Roberts has pointed out another potential problem with trial and error determination of the optimal charge set. Knowing that such a process is underway, dischargers may consider themselves to be in a gaming situation and may not react "sincerely" (that is, optimally as seen in the short run) to a particular trial set of charges. (See Marc J. Roberts, "Environmental Protection: The Complexities of Real Policy Choice," in *Managing the Water Environment*, ed. N. A. Swainson [Vancouver: University of British Columbia Press, 1976], p. 188.) This would not seem likely to be a problem with discharge standards except insofar as the costs of compliance reported to government agencies and to the public might well be distorted—probably exaggerated—to stave off future tightening of standards. One can, however, view the rather naked bluff of the auto companies on the 1978-model emission standards as "sophisticated gaming"; if so, the above differentiation would tend to crumble.

discharge standards that could be mandated by a regulatory agency interested in meeting the target at least cost. These are the discharges corresponding to the efficient effluent charge-set discussed above, and their calculation may be thought of as the mirror image (technically, the dual problem) of the calculation of that charge set. Thus, there is very little choice between charge schemes and regulatory schemes, in principle, when the sole criterion is static efficiency.[17]

Finally, if effluent charges are seen as the target of public policy, static efficiency has no real meaning. A particular goal, such as the production of a given quantity of output in the economy, may be achieved efficiently or inefficiently, but with charges as target there is, as was stressed above, no such goal. True, profit-maximizing dischargers will equate their marginal costs to the charge (which, I have argued, will necessarily be uniform if the "targets" approach is used), and therefore whatever aggregate discharge is achieved cannot be achieved more cheaply. But if that aggregate discharge was not chosen as the target in advance, it is misleading to shift gears after the fact and claim that it has been achieved "efficiently."

Information Requirements

One gets the impression that claims and counterclaims about the information requirements of charge systems vis-à-vis those of other approaches have frequently been based upon the characteristics of improbable arrangements, the particular features chosen to suit the position of the claimant. For example, opponents of charges some-

17. One reason the efficiency question looms so large in the effluent charge literature is that writers do not always distinguish between the efficiency with which a discharge standard is met and the efficiency with which the resulting environmental quality is being attained. Thus, for example, a regulatory scheme that involves, as target, the uniform percentage reduction in the discharges from all sources, will produce a certain level of ambient quality. But that same result in the environment could, with the rarest of exceptions, be attained more cheaply using the correct set of effluent charges. This observation, however, involves the implicit dismissal of the percentage reduction standard as a valid social target. Or, said another way, a standard-setting approach to implementation does not produce inefficiency just because we, as critics, can think of an *alternative target* that will not be met efficiently by the chosen standards.

When we extend our analysis to include industry entry and exit over time, charges and regulatory systems will have different effects, by extension of the arguments applicable to the comparison of charges and subsidies. See, for example, William J. Baumol and Wallace E. Oates, *The Theory of Environmental Policy* (Englewood Cliffs, N.J.: Prentice-Hall, 1975), ch. 12.

times implicitly assume that any charge system must match the idealized variety found in economics textbooks, in which both marginal cost-of-reduction and marginal social damage schedules must be known at least over the range of their intersection. If all proponents of charges were, in fact, seeking such a system, their adversaries would have a telling point because the information load required in that case is immense, and even the methodologies necessary to generate parts of it (such as health damages) are currently unavailable or at least not widely agreed upon.

On the other side, some charge boosters argue as if it were possible to begin with virtually no information, even about costs of discharge reduction; to set effluent charges more or less arbitrarily and observe the effects obtained in the environment; then to compare these effects with a desired ambient standard, adjust the charges (perhaps several times), and end up with a nationally (or regionally) uniform charge set that results in the meeting of the desired standard at least cost. As has already been observed, this is simply not a possibility. In general, the achievement of static efficiency, whether in the context of discharge standards or of ambient standards, requires charges tailored to each discharger. Such nonuniform charges do not lend themselves to the trial and error approach; and so a basic choice exists between efficiency and small initial information requirements.

Granted, then, that with effluent charges we cannot have our cake and eat it too, are we better or worse off than with direct regulation? The answer depends to some extent on the target of the regulation. If the aim is to meet given ambient quality standards at least cost, then, as has just been pointed out, calculating the required discharge limitations is symmetric with calculating the required (nonuniform) charges.[18] If static efficiency is not sought in meeting an ambient standard, then the process of trial and error using effluent limitations is symmetric with that using charges. Asymmetry, however, appears to exist for discharge standard targets. If we wish to achieve uniform

18. Examples of models designed to allow such dual calculation include the Resources for the Future Delaware model (see W. O. Spofford, Jr., C. S. Russell, and R. A. Kelly, *Environmental Quality Management: An Application to the Lower Delaware Valley* [Washington, D.C.: Resources for the Future, 1976]) and the St. Louis Air Quality Control Region model of EPA (see S. E. Atkinson and D. H. Lewis, "A Cost-Effectiveness Analysis of Alternative Air Quality Control Strategies," *Journal of Environmental Economics and Management* 1 [1974]: 237–50).

percentage reductions (perhaps for reasons of perceived "fairness") or particular quantity restrictions at each source, a regulatory scheme can simply mandate them. In that case, we apparently do not need to know the cost-of-reduction schedules for the sources.[19]

There is, however, an additional problem. If society is intent on achieving a particular discharge standard and has reduced its emphasis on ambient quality in consequence, it still has to be prepared to say, If you fail to meet this standard, then you will be (1) fined, (2) thrown in jail, (3) shut down, or (4) subject to some other penalty. But many thoughtful students of the current system are disturbed by the all or nothing character of (2) and (3) because criminal sanctions or severely disruptive penalties do not differentiate between a small failure to meet a standard and a complete lack of effort. The option of a fine or a civil penalty that does allow for gradation, if it is to be really credible, requires that the amount of the fine be neither absurdly large nor laughably small relative to the costs saved by noncompliance—hence, suggestions for a schedule of charges (really fines) linked to the cost of compliance.[20] Thus, in fact, when stimulating compliance is taken into account, we are brought back to something like a charging scheme, and it is largely illusory to think that a system of discharge standards can be made truly effective without at least some prior knowledge of source-by-source cost schedules.

Before going on to consider the political and legal dimensions of charging systems, I believe I should follow up the train of thought suggested by the mention of "compliance." In particular, opponents of the effluent charge idea sometimes assert that an effluent charge system (no more finely specified) will be "harder to administer and enforce" than a scheme of, for example, technologically-based effluent standards. Again, this judgment seems to rest on a contrast between two extremely drawn approaches. On one side, those who assert this apparently assume that an effluent charge scheme will require continuous monitoring of every residual (on which there is a charge) from every source. These opponents further argue that a

19. I should emphasize that this discussion concerns alternative ways of stimulating the achievement of given social targets. In fact, of course, it is unlikely, but far from inconceivable, that a discharge standard would be set in the absence of some notion of what it would cost.

20. See footnote 3 above, on the Connecticut system of civil penalties tied to the treatment costs avoided by noncomplying sources.

technology-based standard is simple to monitor because all that is necessary is to see that the required equipment is in place—and presumably that it is operating.

In fact, it seems to me that each of these alternative approaches requires about the same kind of monitoring approach and about the same level of effort.[21] As a start, I see no logical or technical bar to having an effluent charge scheme run on a self-reporting basis, with random "audits" of actual discharges to encourage honesty. While the income tax system provides an obvious analogy, it is perhaps even more to the point to observe that the existing NPDES system is supposed to operate on these same lines. Individual sources file reports of their own sampling activity and results with state agencies and the U.S. Environmental Protection Agency (EPA).[22] (Indeed, it currently appears that the enormous bulk of resulting reports is preventing any serious effort even to discover *reported* violations of permit guidelines, while resources for audits of actual discharges are quite inadequate.)

But what of the contention that ensuring compliance is much easier with technology-based standards? This position seems to me to be either naive or disingenuous. To claim that a successful monitoring and enforcement program can consist of visits to see that certain pieces of equipment are in place ignores all we have learned about the possibilities for avoiding operating costs by installing but not operating required equipment.[23] So a check for operation is mandatory—but there are two problems with such inspections. First, some equipment may be easy to turn on and off, meaning that operation may begin when the inspector enters the plant gate and stop when he leaves. Second, and probably more important, there is

21. Indeed, Roberts suggests it might require *fewer* resources to audit and enforce a self-reporting effluent charge scheme than to ensure compliance with a regulatory standard (Roberts, "Environmental Protection," pp. 188–89).

22. See, for example, L. D. Wisniewski and W. M. Wisnor, "Environmental Control—Water Effluent Analysis and Reporting System" (Paper presented at the Eighty-third Meeting of the Steel Industry Systems Association, Pittsburgh, Pa., 17 February 1977).

23. At the simplest level, we need only recall the fate of some of the earlier auto control equipment and even of seat belts and their associated interlocks. Situations no doubt exist, however, in which bypassing a particular piece of required treatment equipment may be more expensive than using it once installed. A possible example is a holding pond at the end of an industrial plant's sewer.

usually good operation and poor operation. For example; running waste water through primary and secondary water treatment plants does not begin to guarantee that the effluent will meet standards that are based on effective operation of these complex, even ornery, units. But mere observation of complicated equipment will not be enough to tell the public authorities whether or not effective operation is being carried out. Even the appearance of the effluent will generally be a seriously inadequate guide in this matter. (This is most obviously true for any equipment designed to remove a colorless gas from a waste-gas stream, but applies with equal force to equipment for dealing with dissolved organics, salts, toxics, and other components of waste water.) If mere visual inspection is not enough, some system of effluent monitoring is necessary. Therefore I contend that the monitoring requirements of charges and regulatory systems are really very much alike.[24]

Scope for Political Pressure and Bargaining

Is there likely to be a significant difference between charges and direct regulatory approaches in the extent of opportunities for influencing the results through political pressure or political bargains? Proponents of charges seem to feel that there is, but I see no reason to believe that this will be true. Indeed, Giandomenico Majone has recently argued persuasively that not only should we expect no difference, but that in fact no differences may be observed in the experience of nations using effluent charge systems—for example, France.[25] There is no point in reproducing Majone's arguments here, but it may be valuable to add a few observations that are only implicit in his paper.

In the first place, this part of the argument for charges rests on the pejorative connotations of the words *political* and *bargain*. The vision seems to be of interference in a straightforwardly technical enterprise by organized groups of polluters. The reality behind this vision is the problems EPA has faced in promulgating effluent limi-

---

24. It is true that, with a standard, monitoring is in principle necessary only to check that effluent quality exceeds some minimum standard, and that there is no need to know exactly how much of each residual is being discharged. In practice this advantage may be illusory, because monitoring equipment is generally designed to give absolute, not merely relativistic, read-out.

25. Giandomenico Majone, "Choice Among Policy Instruments for Pollution Control," *Policy Analysis* 2 (June 1976): 589–613.

tation guidelines, new source performance standards, and similar parts of existing regulatory apparatus, in the face of determined industry opposition. In fact, of course, the existing system does *not* involve straightforward, technical actions on the part of EPA. The laws leave EPA holding such hot political potatoes as "best practicable," "currently available," "economically achievable," "protect and enhance," "the public health," and "the public welfare." Translating phrases like these into operating policy is bound to involve making intensely political decisions, and it seems both unrealistic and normatively indefensible to imply that the situation should be otherwise. If any future legislation leaves to EPA the setting of effluent charges based on no more precise guidance than this, the same kinds of activities will go on—and rightly so.

Two situations, however, could produce quite different results as far as political activity is concerned. First, if Congress accepts the charges-as-targets approach *and* sets those charges itself, then at least a very different forum for political activity will be involved—one with well-worked-out formulae for the representation of affected interests, and one in which the political counters are different from those most useful in the offices and hearing rooms of an executive agency such as EPA.[26] We may very well judge it desirable to make such a shift. A second possibility is to attempt to maximize the extent to which the charge-setting process within EPA *is* purely technical. Here, one possibility might be for Congress to choose (or ratify already chosen) ambient quality standards, and to specify with some care how EPA is to proceed in passing from those targets to the charges designed to implement them. At the extreme, EPA would be delegated an enormous data collection and modeling effort, but the "correct" charges to reach the mandated ambient standards would be implied by the models (possibly one for each major region). This would bring EPA back toward the idealized "implementation" role and should reduce, though it certainly would not eliminate, the scope of the administrator's discretion.[27]

26. Space limitations preclude following up this point here, but what is involved are such differences as those between locally elected representatives and nationally appointed officials, between threats of law suits and threats of grass roots lobbying, and between (probably vague) promises of future jobs and promises of campaign contributions.

27. This discussion is couched in terms of the national government, but it could apply with equal force to the states, even though federal actions continue to circumscribe the freedom of action of state governments in the environmental area as in most others.

Many will argue that either of the above exercises would be beyond the technical capability of the legislature. This may or may not be true. We certainly have evidence, as in the auto-emission limitation provisions of the Clean Air Act of 1970 that Congress will, under some circumstances, take on highly technical tasks. We can reasonably conclude, however, that only infrequently do our legislators perceive political advantage in such undertakings. But the point here is not to argue that the legislature must set the charges or specify the technical procedure for passing from other targets to correct charges. Rather it is to stress that if Congress does not do one of these, an effluent charge system will be subject to the same political pressures and will be fought over on the same political ground as are existing regulatory approaches. That is, so long as this charge is a key part of a rather vaguely defined public policy that implies gains for some and losses for others, we can expect its level and other terms of its application to constitute political issues. Nothing in the nature of a charge makes it immune to the political virus.

Incentives for Delay

One argument for charges begins with the assertion that our existing system of regulation contains incentives for noncompliance and that, in contrast, an effluent charge instrument would be a powerful incentive for rapid compliance. Thus, the argument runs, under an effluent charge system there would be much more rapid attainment of the desired targets—whether discharge standards or ambient standards. On examination, this argument may be seen to turn on a particular (and most often implicit) view of the cause of the observed delays. From an alternative perspective that is, to my mind, fairer and more accurate, the question of whether charges will in fact destroy incentives for delay becomes a more difficult one, the answer to which may well be no except in rather special circumstances.

The argument that charges will speed up the process of compliance with our environmental policies begins with the observation that the existing system almost never involves any cost to a pollution source until the polluter actually installs the control equipment required to meet its permit or to comply with some technological standard. In the extreme, a totally recalcitrant polluter might eventually face criminal sanctions or at least very heavy civil penalties, but, given the inadequacy of the enforcement staffs and budgets of EPA and relevant state agencies, there is every chance that such confrontations can be postponed for years. Whenever the source does actually comply, probably no penalty will be set for the years of noncompliance, and so the present value of a policy of foot-dragging is very much higher than a policy of obeying the law. During the period of noncompliance the polluter may have to spend some money on legal talent that can file the proper objections, requests for delays or exceptions, and so forth, but the cost of this protection is much lower than the cost of abatement equipment.[28]

There is, however, an alternative view of the causes of delay in achieving our goals. This view departs from the fact that any pollution control system involves government imposition of substantial costs on specific private parties and on lower political jurisdictions (that is, on taxpayers in those jurisdictions). It further recognizes that our Constitution and the administrative law that governs the behavior of agencies like EPA are admirably and intentionally set up to make such impositions difficult. The fundamental support for the relevant structure may be said to be the due process and taking clauses of the Fifth Amendment. But the complex edifice of administrative law embodies this notion that the bureaucracy must be made to move slowly and reasonably and that it must be subject to challenge for arbitrary or capricious actions affecting citizens.[29] To some extent, then, observed foot-dragging, involving legal maneuvering, is nothing but play by the rules of the game.

The presentation of these two alternative interpretations raises an empirical question, albeit a slippery one: How much of the widely deplored delay in our current system results from bad faith and recalcitrance and how much from efforts to protect legitimate interests through full use of the possibilities of the legal system? To my knowledge there has not been sufficient research to produce even

28. The marginal cost of legal challenges is especially likely to be very low for large corporations, as they pay retainers to major law firms and probably need only to pick up the direct costs of the legal steps taken at any stage of a delay sequence.

29. For a superb discussion of administrative law generally, but with many examples from environmental cases, see Richard Stewart, "The Reformation of American Administrative Law," *Harvard Law Review* 88 (June 1975): 1669–1813.

a rough answer, and looking over the widely publicized cases—such as U.S. Steel's Gary open hearth plant and Clairton coke plant, or the auto industry's response to the mandated 1978-model emission standards—must surely result in a distorted perception. But an answer to the question is central to a reliable prediction of the impact of charges on delay. If bad-faith delays predominate, and if we can identify these bad-faith delays in individual cases, we can reasonably expect an effluent charge system to create a powerful incentive for prompt compliance. Those sources that are simply sitting tight, counting on a lack of public enforcement capability to save them a few years of compliance costs with no backward reaching penalty when the day of reckoning does arrive, will find under a charge that they begin running up a bill at once. Delay in taking the actions that minimize the sum of treatment costs and remaining charges can only cost them more money. Compliance will be cheaper than delay.

On the other hand, if our inability to move the system rapidly in the desired direction results from our prior commitment to procedural safeguards for private property, we are faced with two additional questions before we can judge the competing implementation systems. First, we must consider whether a charge system would differ from the regulatory approach in terms of these protections. And, if we find no real difference in that regard, we must ask ourselves whether we are willing to introduce distinctions that would allow more rapid progress with charges.

Whether charges differ from regulations in terms of legal and administrative delay seems to boil down to whether charges can be expected to "run" during the period of procedural and substantive challenges allowed to those affected by executive agency actions. If a discharger sees that one cost of a challenge will be a continuously mounting effluent charge bill—even if that bill may be smaller if a challenge is successful—the firm or municipality may conclude that pursuing available challenges is simply not worthwhile, since more could be saved by immediate cost-minimizing action.[30] In the

30. The rational firm's calculation here will be sensitive to whether payments on a running charge have to be made into an escrow account as accrued or are truly postponable. In the latter case, present-value calculations would be somewhat more likely to indicate that a strategy of legal challenge was optimal.

absence of a definitive legal opinion on this question of temporary avoidability let me tentatively suggest the following considerations.[31]

If Congress sets uniform national charge levels as, for example, in the charges-as-targets approach, there might be room for an initial flurry of challenges on constitutional grounds, but even during the course of these it is at least possible that no payment could be avoided. In particular, if the charge is viewed by Congress, and hence by the courts, as at least in part a tax, then it might be impossible for affected sources to have its application and collection enjoined.[32]

On the other hand, were charge levels individually calculated by EPA using complex models with the aim of finding the most efficient way of meeting a target ambient standard (also chosen by the agency), it seems much more likely that real delays could be engineered. Here, the crucial numbers would not be generally applicable to all dischargers, so that arguments from certain simple notions of fairness would have more force. In addition, because the actual numbers would be produced by a complicated process, involving the application of bureaucratic judgment and even of "art" in constructing and running the necessary mathematical approximations of reality, there would seem to be ample scope for challenges to the entire process.

Somewhere between the extremes of a uniform charge passed by Congress as a tax and an individualized charge calculated by EPA under vague congressional policy guidance will fall almost any conceivable scheme. On balance I think it unlikely that most of these would be immune to injunction during challenges of procedure or

31. It should be clear that whether or not charges can be avoided during periods of legal challenge is quite separate from the question of the constitutionality of charging schemes generally. The latter has, I believe, been impressively answered in the affirmative by Frederick R. Anderson et al., "The Law of Charges," in *Environmental Improvement through Economic Incentives* (Washington, D.C.: Resources for the Future, 1977).

32. The Anti-Injunction Act (Int. Rev. Code of 1954, S 7421 [a]) prohibits any "suit for the purpose of restraining the assessment or collection of any tax in any court," although the application of this act is inappropriate where "a challenged action is intended not to produce revenue but rather 'to accomplish a broad policy objective through the medium of federal taxation'" (Jim Dragna, "Environmental Organizations and Legislative Activity Restrictions: The 'Substantial' Deterrent to Environmental Protection," *Natural Resources Lawyer* 9 [1976]: 690).

substance, and therefore I am inclined to believe that the delay-reducing advantage of the effluent charge has been overstated.[33]

CONCLUSIONS AND A POSSIBLE POLICY

The arguments above may best be summarized in the form of propositions:

1. We cannot have a statically efficient effluent charge system that can be established by trial and error or that will be free of political bargaining and immune from legal delaying tactics.

2. A statically efficient charge, whether designed to achieve an ambient standard or a discharge standard, will be information-intensive and will be most vulnerable to delay by litigation. Politics, in these cases, ideally would be involved in the choice of the targets rather than of the charge.

3. If having a charge is viewed as a *target* of policy, static efficiency is no longer a particularly meaningful concept. (*a*) If the charge levels are set by Congress, information requirements need not be very large, but political considerations will be central to the levels chosen. There may be little to be gained by legal challenges to such charges. (*b*) If Congress contents itself with a general expression of intent and leaves the choice of charge levels to EPA, the resulting system may resemble the current one in many important respects. Information will be required to "justify" technically decisions with heavy political overtones. Political pressure and bargaining will be important at every stage of the proceedings, and legal challenges to the results of agency discretion may very well involve successful delays in charge implementation.

4. Once in operation, any charge system will, over the long run, spur firms and public bodies to search for better and cheaper ways to avoid discharging pollution into air and water. This may involve the development of new products, new production processes, new ways of recycling materials and energy, or new control technologies.

33. It is worth pointing out that the Connecticut law referred to above, the closest we have come to a real charge scheme, appears to have the feature that bills for noncompliance, while they may be calculated to include periods before any enforcement actions were taken by the state agency, do not grow in proportion to the discharges occurring during any of the administrative and legal challenges provided for in the act (see *Economic Law Enforcement*, Attachments A and B).

It is almost impossible to imagine any way of calculating how high charges "ought" to be from this perspective.

In these circumstances, it has been suggested that a realistic and potentially useful policy would be to combine part of our existing regulatory apparatus with a set of nationally uniform effluent charges covering all significant pollutants.[34] For water quality management, we could continue and complete the job of specifying permissible discharges consistent with BPCTCA, the 1977 goal of the 1972 Water Quality Act Amendments. For air, we could get into operation the state implementation plans designed to achieve at least the primary national air quality standards. In addition, all discharges, even those legitimately continuing after the achievement of those regulatory goals, would be subject to the national effluent charge. This charge-on-top policy would have as its most important effect the creation of continuing incentives for the development and adoption of environment-saving (and probably, at the same time, resource-saving) innovations.

This policy would be roughly consistent with the charges-as-targets position, but would build on a reasonably firm base of previous target achievement. At the same time, it should be explicitly recognized that such a course would not produce economic efficiency in the static sense of minimum pollution expenditures for the level of ambient quality attained. Further, we should not delude ourselves into thinking that the setting of such a charge set would be anything but a political action, and therefore we should be ready for intense lobbying over the levels to be chosen and continuing pressure for reduction from the adversely affected interests. In this connection, we should not expect anything but great difficulty in adjusting the charge levels and should certainly not expect that there would be anything even remotely market-like about that adjustment process. We can hope, however, that such a system could be put into operation without the seemingly infinite delays occasioned by numberless individual challenges of discretionary executive actions. In short, we would consciously be trading the efficiency of effluent charges as policy instruments for a simpler system retaining the

34. See, for example, Oates and Baumol, "Instruments for Environmental Policy," pp. 107ff; Kneese and Schultz, *Pollution, Prices, and Public Policy,* p. 98; and National Academy of Sciences, *Decision Making,* pp. 160–61.

dynamic incentive effects that seem to be the major positive attribute of charges.[35]

35. One possibility not discussed in this paper is that an effluent charge may be viewed primarily as a source of revenue to be committed to pollution control projects, the claim being that the thrust toward efficiency comes from the selection of projects undertaken. This is apparently the main motivation for several European schemes (personal communication to the author from David Kinnersley, on the staff of the National Water Council of the United Kingdom).

14

SPATIALLY DIFFERENTIATED AIR POLLUTANT EMISSION CHARGES
An Economic and Legal Analysis

T. H. Teitenberg

I. INTRODUCTION

The basic strategy to be employed in this country for controlling air pollution has been articulated in the Clean Air Act.[1] Under this act the national government has established national ambient air quality standards for a variety of pollutants[2] and, with certain exceptions where the federal government exercises direct control over emissions,[3] the choice of policy instruments used to meet these standards is left up to the states.[4] Although emission taxes or charges are not mentioned in the Clean Air Act, they are specifically mentioned as an appropriate policy instrument in the regulations promulgated by the Environmental Protection Agency to implement the act.[5] Thus, in contrast to water pollution control policy which specifically relies on effluent standards, emission charges are compatible with the existing legislation in air pollution control.[6]

The purpose of this paper is to explore a number of economic, administrative and legal issues which impinge on the design of a system of emission charges to achieve the national ambient air quality standards at minimum cost. The question of interest is, "if an emission charge is to be levied, what should the nature of that charge be?" Two related dimensions of this issue are whether the tax rate should

be spatially differentiated or uniform and whether the charge should be implemented nationally by Congress or by some lower level of government.

The existing literature on this subject.[7]

The author is Associate Professor, Department of Economics, Colby College, Waterville, Maine. An earlier version of this paper was presented at the Eastern Economic Association meetings in Hartford, Connecticut, April 15, 1977. The author wishes to acknowledge the capable research assistance of Rick Abrams and helpful comments from A. Myrick Freeman III and Thomas Crocker. The reader is asked to absolve them from any responsibility for remaining errors. This research was supported by a grant from the Social Science Grants Committee, Colby College.

[1] The composite law designated as the Clean Air Act (42 U.S.C. 1857 et seq.) includes the Clean Air Act of 1963 (P.L. 88-206), and amendments made by the "Motor Vehicle Air Pollution Control Act"—P.L. 89-272 (October 20, 1965), the "Clean Air Act Amendments of 1966"—P.L. 89-675 (October 15, 1966), the "Air Quality Act of 1967"—P.L. 90-148 (November 21, 1967), the "Clean Air Amendments of 1970"—P.L. 91-604 (December 31, 1970), section 302 of P.L. 92-157 (November 18, 1971), P.L. 93-15 (April 9, 1973) and P.L. 95-95 (August 7, 1977).

[2] 42 U.S.C. 1857c-4. The actual standards can be found in 40 C.F.R. § 50.

[3] See, for example, 42 U.S.C. 1857c-6, 52 U.S.C. 1857c-7 and 42 U.S.C. 1857f-1 et seq.

[4] 42 U.S.C. 1857c-5.

[5] 40 C.F.R. § 51.1, note 2.

[6] Although nothing in the Federal Water Pollution Control Act Amendments of 1972 authorizes emission charges, neither does the act preclude states from adopting them independently. Thus in water pollution control they could be employed but not as a coherent part of the federal program.

[7] See, for example, Lerner [1971, 1974, 1977]; Stein [1971, 1974]; Peltzman and Tideman [1972]; Tietenberg [1973, 1974a]; Rose-Ackerman [1973]; Menz and Miller [1977].

From T. H. Teitenberg, "Spatially Differentiated Air Pollutant Emission Charges: An Economic and Legal Analysis," 54(3) 265-277 *Land Economics* (August 1978). Copyright 1978 by the University of Wisconsin Press.

including my own articles, is characterized by a high degree of abstraction. The chief limitation imposed by this abstraction has been a lack of sensitivity in the literature to the institutional context within which an emission charge would be implemented. A major contention of this paper is that this institutional context places important constraints on the design of an efficient emission charge system, and furthermore, that when these constraints are recognized and integrated into the analysis the basis for the apparent preference for uniform national charges is weaker than otherwise would appear to be the case.[8]

The paper opens with a definition of spatially differentiated emission charges and discusses the specific sense in which it is possible to think of the degree of spatial differentiation as a policy variable. This is followed by a brief summary of the theoretical and empirical evidence which has been accumulated on the relative merits of spatially differentiated charges. The paper then turns to the question of the appropriate level of government to implement these charges and concludes by examining some of the administrative problems associated with the local implementation of a spatially differentiated system which have been raised in the previous literature.

II. THE DEGREE OF
SPATIAL DIFFERENTIATION

The method of pollution control under consideration involves the use of a per unit charge on the flow of emissions of a particular pollutant from a particular source. This emission charge would have units such as $/gram and when multiplied by the number of grams emitted would yield the total tax to be paid by the emitter.[9] Spatially differentiated charge systems are those in which the tax rate paid by an emitter is functionally related to the location of that emitter.

Much of the literature on emission charges tends to dichotomize the rate structure choice — the control authority is presumed to be able to choose only uniform charges or non-uniform charges.[10] In practice, however, there are many different degrees of differentiation which could be chosen, and uniform charges represent merely the very special case of zero spatial differentiation in the rate structure.

Spatial differentiation can be built into an emission charge system in two main ways. The first is by increasing the number of geographically distinct taxing authorities, assuming that each authority has independent control over its tax rate. By delegating the control authority to lower levels of government, each independently setting tax rates to achieve its own ambient air quality standards, Congress would assure an interjurisdictional variance in charges even with nationally uniform air quality standards. The jurisdictions for which the marginal cost of control was high at the degree of control necessary to meet the standards would impose higher tax rates; conversely, jurisdictions which could meet the standards

---

[8] This preference can be found in Kneese and Schultze [1975, pp. 99–100] and Seneca and Taussig [1974, p. 242].

[9] It is worth noting that the emission charge envisioned here does not vary diurnally or seasonally, so that a charge simply on grams is equivalent to a charge on grams/hour. A case can be made for providing for temporal as well as spatial differentiation (e.g., Tietenberg [1974b, pp. 289–91]) but that issue is beyond the scope of this paper.

[10] See, for example, Ferrar and Sassone [1975, pp. 266–73] and Seneca and Taussig [1974, pp. 242–43].

with a small amount of control (e.g., if there are only a few emitters) would find that lower tax rates would suffice.[11]

The second main means of building spatial variation into an emission charge system is to allow each taxing jurisdiction to tax different emitters within its jurisdiction at different rates. The purpose such a system would serve is described in detail below.

For convenience, to keep these two types of spatial differentiation conceptually distinct, two new terms are needed. A tax zone will be defined as the geographic area within which all emitters pay the same tax rate. A taxing jurisdiction is defined as the geographic area within which the designated control authority has the legal power to tax. The taxing authority which has control over this jurisdiction is responsible for insuring that the ambient air quality standards within the jurisdiction are met and uses its power to tax to achieve this end. When a taxing jurisdiction contains more than one taxing zone, intrajurisdictional spatial differentiation results. It is possible to achieve as much spatial differentiation as desired within a taxing jurisdiction by increasing the number of taxing zones. The limiting case, perfect tax discrimination, is achieved when every emitter falls in its own unique tax zone.

Thus, emission charge systems can in general exhibit both interjurisdictional and intrajurisdictional spatial differentiation of the rates. The degree of spatial differentiation to be employed in any particular system is a function of the number and size of the taxing jurisdictions and the number and size of the taxing zones. The next sections consider some of the economic, administrative and legal factors which affect the appropriate mix of these variables.

III. SELECTING THE MIX OF TAXING JURISDICTIONS AND TAXING ZONES

Since spatially differentiated air pollutant charges are administratively more complex than uniform charges, it is appropriate to ask what is to be gained by implementing this more complicated system. The answer is that a system of spatially differentiated charges is essential if the ambient air quality standards are to be achieved at minimum cost. This point can be illustrated with the assistance of a simple partial equilibrium model of the air pollution control process.[12]

Let us assume that there are emitters of a particular pollutant across the United States. Each of these emitters can achieve a reduction in its emission rate, e_i, at some cost $C_i(e_i)$. Society's objective, as articulated in the Clean Air Act, is to achieve the air quality standard P_m, as recorded at M different receptor locations, at minimum cost.[13] Mathematically the decision problem can be represented as the minimization of control cost subject to the constraint that the ambient air quality standards cannot be exceeded at any of the M monitoring sites. Symbolically this can be stated as the selection of the e vector which minimizes the objective function given as [1]:

$$\sum_{i=1}^{I} C_i(e_i) + \sum_{m=1}^{M} \lambda_m \left[\sum_{i=1}^{I} e_i \cdot a_{im} - P_m \right] \quad [1]$$

---

[11] Because location decisions depend on many factors in addition to environmental costs, these rate differentials would be maintained even in long-run equilibrium.

[12] A rigorous general equilibrium treatment of these points can be found in Tietenberg [1974a].

[13] The law states that the ambient standards must be met everywhere. The formulation in this paper assumes that there are M locations where the standards are currently exceeded.

The coefficient a_{im} is the parameter which translates the emission rate for the ith emitter into the ambient concentration level at receptor location m. It is functionally related to average annual wind velocity and direction and the location of the emitter vis-à-vis the receptor, among other things.[14] The solution vector e will satisfy the following conditions:

$$\frac{\partial C_i(e_i)}{\partial e_i} + \sum_{m=1}^{M} \lambda_m \cdot a_{im} \geqq 0 \quad i = 1, \ldots, I \quad [2]$$

$$e_i \left[\frac{\partial C_i(e_i)}{\partial e_i} - \sum_{m=1}^{M} \lambda_m \cdot a_{im} \right] = 0 \quad i = 1, \ldots, I \quad [3]$$

$$\sum_{i=1}^{I} e_i \cdot a_{im} - \bar{P}_m \leqq 0 \quad m = 1, \ldots, M \quad [4]$$

$$\lambda_m \left[\sum_{i=1}^{I} e_i \cdot a_{im} - \bar{P}_m \right] = 0 \quad m = 1, \ldots, M \quad [5]$$

To illustrate the inefficiencies associated with uniform charges consider taking the ratio of two equations in equation system [3], assuming that the relevant e_i's are positive.

$$\frac{\dfrac{\partial C_i(e_i)}{\partial e_i}}{\dfrac{\partial C_j(e_j)}{\partial e_j}} = \frac{\displaystyle\sum_{m}^{M} \lambda_m \cdot a_{im}}{\displaystyle\sum_{m}^{M} \lambda_m \cdot a_{jm}} \quad [6]$$

In order for uniform charges to be cost effective the right-hand side of this equation has to be equal to 1.0.[15] This is clearly a very restrictive condition, as can be illustrated by a couple of realistic examples. First of all notice that for all emitters most of the a_{im} terms will be zero because the recorded concentration level at a particular monitoring site will be affected by only a few of the thousands of emitters scattered across the country. Different parameters, however, will be zero for different emitters. An emitter in New York does not affect the air quality level in Los Angeles in any measurable sense although it does affect the air quality in New York. The opposite is true for an emitter in Los Angeles. A necessary, but not sufficient, condition for a uniform charge to achieve both standards simultaneously at minimum cost is for the shadow price (λ_m) of meeting the standard to be equal in both locations. Since the value of this shadow price is functionally related both to the number and geographic concentration of emitters as well as the cost of control for each emitter, such an equivalence would be purely coincidental. Hence, aside from coincidence, uniform charges would not be cost effective because the severity of the pollution problem differs greatly among geographic areas.[16]

There are two other reasons suggested by the above model why uniform charges

---

[14] In practice this parameter is derived from air diffusion models. These models assume that the various pollutants are nonreactive with each other. The functional relationship underlying this derivation is described in Grad [1975, pp. 217–19].

[15] Cost-minimizing firms in equilibrium will equate $[\partial C_i(e_i)]/[\partial e_i]$ to T, the emission charge. Under a uniform charge system this implies:

$$\frac{\partial C_i(e_i)}{\partial e_i} = \frac{\partial C_j(e_j)}{\partial e_j}$$

[16] One would not expect full equalization of these shadow prices even in the very long run because alternative locations are never perfect substitutes and environmental costs are not the sole consideration in making location decisions.

may not be efficient. The first is that some emitters may contribute to more than one receptor location where a tax is imposed; others may not contribute to any. In a cost-effective allocation of the control responsibility the former emitter will pay a charge on each unit of emissions equal to the sum of the individual charges associated with each receptor location. The latter emitters will pay no charge at all. Clearly a uniform charge system would be unable to achieve this result.

The final reason why uniform charges can misallocate resources rests on the realization that even the non-zero meteorological parameters (the a_{im}'s) may differ in magnitude even among emitters in the same urban area. The contribution of any emitter to any particular reception location depends on the location of the emitter vis-à-vis the receptor. Thus, *ceteris paribus*, the emitters closer to and upwind from the receptor location will have larger a_{im}'s than other emitters in more remote locations of the same urban area. A cost-effective charge system will impose higher charges, *ceteris paribus*, on firms with larger a_{im}'s. A uniform charge system would be unable to make this distinction as well.

The inescapable conclusion, is, then abstracting momentarily from the costs of administration, no uniform emission charge system can be cost effective for a variety of reasons. The theory alone, however, is insufficient to suggest the magnitude of the cost increases resulting from the imposition of a uniform charge system. If they are small, then the policy maker might presume, without effective contradiction, that spatially differentiated charges are simply not worth the additional administrative costs required to implement such a system. On the other hand, if they are large, then the

additional administrative effort may yield sizable net benefits.

Unfortunately the data necessary to appraise systematically and conclusively the size of these costs are not available. It is not difficult to see why this is so. In order to compare these costs it would be necessary to collect information on the costs of control for every air pollutant emitter in the United States. The data requirements for this test are clearly prohibitive.

Fortunately some limited data are available. In a recent study Atkinson and Lewis [1974] have examined the increases in costs associated only with the last of the three sources of misallocation discussed above. Using data for Saint Louis the authors examined the costs of meeting a predetermined sulfur dioxide air quality standard using both the emission least-cost method (which would result from a uniform emission charge) and the ambient least-cost method (which would result from a spatially differentiated emissions charge). Their conclusion was that the cost saving which would result from substituting the ambient least-cost method for the emission least-cost method was on the order of 50% [Atkinson and Lewis 1974, p. 237]. Since their study deals only with one of the three reasons for costs to be higher and yet suggests such large savings, the conclusion that spatially differentiated charges could achieve the ambient air quality standards at significantly lower cost seems unambiguously supported. The additional administrative costs incurred by imposing a spatially differentiated charge would have to be very large indeed to outweigh benefits of this magnitude.

The analysis so far, however, is decidedly short run in nature; it assumes that the location of each emitter is fixed.

In fact, of course, a spatially differentiated system of emission charges creates incentives for emitters to change their locations from high-tax to low-tax regions. The argument is made by those opposed to a spatially differentiated charge that uniform national charges are necessary because any geographic variation in the rates will lead to a migration of industry from dirty regions to clean ones.[17] The flaw in this argument can be seen immediately when it is realized that there is an implicit assumption behind it. This argument implicitly assumes that the charges are being used to implement spatially uniform air quality standards. Otherwise, if there were more stringent ambient standards in clean areas, it is not at all clear the tax would be lower there. The tax rate in relatively clean areas would depend on the degree of cleanup needed to meet the standard, not merely on the actual pollutant concentrations.

Exposing the flaw conveniently suggests the solution. If the industrial migration from dirty areas to clean areas which could result from uniform ambient air quality standards is inefficient, then the solution is to control the degradation of the clean air either by controlling the rate of increase of concentrations or by placing some more stringent ambient standards in those areas. This will lead to spatially differentiated concentration levels which are not eroded by the existence of spatially differentiated charges. Such a system would internalize the externalities associated with a particular location decision. In contrast, a system of uniform emission charges will lead an emitter to be indifferent to the environmental consequences of its location decision. This is hardly consistent with the intent of the Clean Air Act.

The federal government appears to be heading toward this particular resolution of the degradation problem. Under the prod of a court suit[18] the Environmental Protection Agency has promulgated regulations to prevent the degradation of the nation's air.[19] These regulations, while not specifically setting more strict ambient standards, do have the effect of limiting the amount of increase in emissions which is permitted in various parts of the country. One of the classifications, which is generally applied to relatively clean areas, allows only a two micrograms per cubic meter increase in the concentration of sulfur oxides after January 1, 1975.[20] On August 7, 1977, President Carter signed the "Clean Air Act Amendments of 1977," which incorporated this approach into the Clean Air Act.[21] In addition the Clean Air Act specifically delegates to the states the power to set ambient standards which are more strict than those at the national level.[22] Although one would not expect local areas to invoke this provision en masse,[23] some states have established

---

[17] This argument can be found in Seneca and Taussig [1974, pp. 242–43] and Kneese and Schultze [1975, p. 110].

[18] Sierra Club v. Ruckelshaus, 344 Supp. 253 (D.D.C. 1972), which was later affirmed by the Supreme Court by a 4–4 vote, 412 U.S. 541 (1973). In this suit the Sierra Club successfully argued that uniform national ambient standards did not prevent the "significant deterioration" of the air in relatively clean areas and that significant deterioration was contrary to the intent of the act.

[19] These regulations are presented in 40 C.F.R. § 52.21.

[20] 40 C.F.R. § 52.21 (c)(i). This compares to a national primary standard of 80 micrograms per cubic meter. 40 C.F.R. § 50.5 (a).

[21] 91 Stat. 731.

[22] The power to establish ambient standards which are stricter than those set by the national government is granted to states in 42 U.S.C. 1857d-1.

[23] The unilateral invocation of this provision by a state could raise the costs for emitters in their state vis-à-vis their competitors in other states. This could lead to an

stricter standards.[24] Thus, the available evidence suggests that the degradation problem should be and will be resolved, not by imposing uniform charges, but rather by the more direct approach of stipulating different standards for air quality in different parts of the country.

The argument so far suggests that there should be multiple tax zones, but it doesn't say anything about the appropriateness of alternative tax jurisdiction choices. The fact that the Clean Air Act rules out a national taxing jurisdiction by delegating the control authority to the states increases the cost of a national taxing jurisdiction by making an amendment to the existing legislation necessary if it is to be imposed. The question, then, is whether the advantages of a national taxing jurisdiction are sufficiently strong as to recommend changing the thrust of the existing legislation.

There are some distinct advantages to using the nation as the taxing jurisdiction, but, on balance, these do not seem strong enough to argue for new legislation. The primary advantage of a national taxing jurisdiction is that it minimizes interjurisdictional spillovers. It is possible with smaller jurisdictions, for example, for one of these jurisdictions to allow or, perhaps, even coerce industries to locate near the border of the jurisdiction. In this way they can export their emissions to another jurisdiction while retaining the property tax and, to a lesser extent, employment benefits of having the emitters within the confines of their taxing boundaries. With a national juris-

diction the boundaries encompass a larger geographic area and there are fewer borders to lead to this kind of problem.

The Clean Air Act recognizes the potential for interjurisdictional spillovers and attempts to encourage cooperation among the states to prevent it. For example, the administrator is authorized to pay, for up to two years, 100 percent of the costs of planning an interstate approach to meet the ambient air quality standards.[25] The administrator is also authorized to designate any interstate area as an air quality region, which requires coordinated implementation planning.[26] In the absence of an acceptable coordinated plan, the administrator can substitute his own plan.[27] While it remains to be seen how effectively these solve the interjurisdiction problem, they do provide a concrete example of how this problem can be handled without moving entirely to a nationally uniform emission charge system.[28]

---

[24] An example is provided by the Illinois Pollution Control Board's Rule 303 which precludes any degradation of existing air quality unless the state Environmental Protection Agency finds that degradation is "justifiable as a result of necessary economic and social development" and will not interfere with human health and welfare. This rule has withstood legal challenge. Commonwealth Edison v. Pollution Control Board. 8 ERC 1531 (1976).

[25] 42 U.S.C. 1857c-1.

[26] 42 U.S.C. 1857c-2.

[27] 42 U.S.C. 1857c-5. This provision has been invoked. See, for example, the administrator's plan for transportation controls in the District of Columbia Region. The legal history of this preemption can be seen in 38 Fed. Reg. 16556-9, 16563 (June 22, 1973); 38 Fed. Reg. 20758, 20779, 20789 (August 2, 1973); 38 Fed. Reg. 30626 (November 6, 1973); 38 Fed. Reg. 31536 (November 15, 1973); 38 Fed. Reg. 33702-31 (December 6, 1973).

[28] It should be pointed out that the problem could be much more serious for some pollutants and for some regions. Sulfates, if included in the list of pollutants, will present particular problems because of the apparently long distances they travel. Also, the movement of SO_2 and TSP across state boundaries in the Northeast is common. I am indebted to A. Myrick Freeman III for calling this to my attention.

---

industrial emigration which could, in turn, create a politically unpalatable unemployment situation. Thus, while the states may collectively prefer more stringent standards, provided that other states impose them as well, in the absence of any mechanism to insure this result, they are not likely to impose them unilaterally.

A supporter of a national taxing jurisdiction might well argue that national emission charges are the only politically feasible system of charges that might be implemented, because local areas would never unilaterally impose emission charges. The chief criticism to be leveled against the political feasibility argument for national uniform emissions charges is that, even if the basic premise is correct, the institution of such a system would represent a Pyrrhic victory at best. A nationally uniform emissions charge is so grossly inefficient compared to spatially differentiated strategies that it is not clear why anyone would want one. If it were to be the sole instrument for achieving the air quality standards, the rate would have to be set high enough to insure that the ambient air quality standard would be met in the geographic area which had the highest marginal cost of pollution control at the point where the standard was achieved. Forcing every region to bear the same marginal cost of cleanup as, say, New York or Los Angeles seems to be an extremely high cost to pay to avoid what appears to be an administratively simple degree of differentiation.[29]

To summarize the argument to this point, a case has been made that nationally uniform emission charges appear inferior to spatially differentiated emission charges. These spatially differentiated emission charges, however, could be imposed either nationally by dividing the country up into taxing zones, each with its own tax rate, or by delegating the authority to lower levels of government as was done in the Clean Air Act.

There are two main reasons why the use of a national taxing jurisdiction with a number of tax zones may be inferior to local taxing jurisdictions. The first reason, discussed above, results from the fact that local taxing jurisdictions are compatible with the existing legislation while a national jurisdiction is not. Amending the existing legislation to include provision for a national spatially differentiated emission charge is difficult at best and impossible at worst; the burden of proof, therefore, falls on those arguing that such a charge is justified.

The second argument is legal. There are two possible legal bases for the Congressional control of pollution — taxing power and the commerce clause. The taxing power of congress is not unlimited. In particular, section 8 of the Constitution of the United States reads in part as follows: "The Congress shall have Power to lay and collect Taxes, Duties, Imports and Excises, to pay the Debts and provide for the common Defense and general Welfare of the United States; but all Duties, Imports and Excises shall be uniform throughout the United States...."[30] Since an emission charge would generally be considered an excise tax,[31] this clause appears to rule out spatially differentiated charges imposed at the national level. Indeed, the various judicial interpretations of this article have made it quite clear that the word "uniform" refers specifically to geographic uniformity.[32]

---

[29] One could alternatively argue that the tax rate should be set at the marginal cost of control in the areas which have the least problem meeting the standard and then augmented with local policy instruments. But since many areas are meeting the standard with no controls at all this tax rate is zero! And any tax rate greater than zero will overtax some parts of the country in the sense that the concentration in these areas will be significantly better than the standard.

[30] U.S.C.A. Const. Art. 1 § 8.

[31] The term excise tax has come to mean every form of taxation which is not a burden laid directly on persons or property. 33 C.J.S. p. 111, note 6.

[32] Patton v. Brady, Va. 1902, 22 S. Ct. 493, 184 U.S. 622, 46 L. Ed. 713. See also, Brushaber v. Union Pacific R. Co., New York 1916, 36 S. Ct. 236, 240 U.S. 1, 60 L. Ed. 493; Flint v. Stone Tracy Co., 1911, 31 S. Ct. 342, 220 U.S. 107, 55 L. Ed. 389.

Thus, while some degree of tax discrimination has been held to be consistent with the uniformity requirement, geographic tax discrimination has not. Although there have been no specific decisions on emission charges the precedent does seem sufficiently unambiguous that the constitutionality of a national taxing jurisdiction with multiple taxing zones is highly questionable. Since this provision in no way prevents local areas from imposing their own charges, interjurisdictional spatial differentiation can be achieved by delegating the control authority to state and local areas. Thus, if this precedent were to hold up when applied to emission charges, any degree of spatial differentiation at the national level would have to come from the delegation of authority and could not come from taxing different geographic regions at different rates.

It has been suggested that the uniformity requirement could be avoided at the national level if the Congressional authority to use emission charges were based on the commerce clause rather than taxing power.[33] There is sufficient precedent to argue that the control of pollution could fall under the commerce clause and that charges could be used as an acceptable pollution control policy instrument; it is much less clear that spatially differentiated charges would be allowed, however. Two pieces of evidence suggest this. First, none of the cases used to support the use of the charges under the commerce clause involved spatially differentiated charges. Thus, none of these cases provide a test of the proposition that the courts would allow Congress to use the commerce clause to escape the uniformity requirement as it applies to geographic tax discrimination. While certain types of discrimination may well

be held to be consistent with the uniformity requirement, geographic tax discrimination is not likely to be. Second, the issue of whether the commerce clause could be used as an escape will almost certainly be raised, requiring the court to make an explicit decision. It has already been raised with respect to previous attempts to impose national emission charges.[34] Thus, the only thing that can be said with some confidence is that while some emission charges could undoubtedly be rested comfortably on the commerce clause, the case for spatially differentiated charges is much weaker. Interestingly enough, as is pointed out below, this legal uncertainty is much smaller when charges are imposed at the local level.

The final issue to be dealt with is the desirability and feasibility of multiple tax zones within the local jurisdiction. Put another way, "Should we and can we have intrajurisdictional spatial differentiation of emission charges as well as interjurisdictional spatial differentiation?" The benefits to be derived from additional differentiation are clear. As mentioned above the cost reduction to be obtained from the application of intrajurisdictional spatially differentiated emission charges is on the order of 50%, even when the jurisdictions are as small as an urban area. The question then is

---

[33] See Irwin and Lirhoff [1974, pp. 40–47]. This paper does not specifically examine the constitutionality of spatially differentiated charges, but it is possible to draw an inference, as one referee did, that the commerce clause allows an out.

[34] For example, when Senator Proxmire introduced an effluent charge amendment to the Federal Water Pollution Control Act, Senator Muskie immediately raised the uniformity issue. See Irwin and Lirhoff [1974, p. 63]. Any government charge imposed for raising revenue is subject to this challenge whether it is called a tax or not. See Columbia Gaslight Co. v. Mobley, 137 S.E. 211.

whether the costs are sufficiently large as to outweigh these potentially large gains.

One might presume that the legal rules prohibiting intrajurisdictional spatial differentiation of tax rates at the national level would be equally compelling at the state and local level, but this does not appear to be the case. In *Peacock* v. *Pratt* (1903) a federal court ruled that the uniformity requirement had no application to a state or territorial legislation.[35] The governing principles, then, are those imposed by state constitutions.

Since there is no mechanism to insure that the interpretations of the various state constitutions by state courts are consistent with each other, in general they are not. While uniformity of taxation is necessary under the provisions of the constitution of many of the states,[36] and while such a constitutional provision ordinarily is applicable to'all taxes on property, it has been held in many states that it is restricted to taxes on property.[37] In other states excise taxes have been specifically excluded from being subject to the uniformity provision.[38] Since a tax on emissions would most likely be considered an excise tax rather than a property tax, in all states in which a precedent has been established the precedent seems quite consistent with the legal enforceability of spatially differentiated pollutant charges.

There is one more prevailing legal theory which seems to permit the imposition of spatially differentiated emission charges at the state and local level. It suggests that exactions imposed in the exercise of the police power rather than that of taxation have been held not to require uniformity.[39] Pollution control has generally been considered a legitimate exercise of the police power of the state, since it affects public health and welfare, and the concurrent use of the police and taxing power has been upheld by the courts.[40] In contrast to the national taxing power, however, the state uniformity requirements impose no particular constraints on geographic tax discrimination.

While uniformity is not a requirement under the police power authority the statute does have to satisfy the due process and equal protection clauses of the Constitution. The equal protection clause precludes discriminating between persons in the same classification. For spatially differentiated charges the tax zones would provide the classification system since emitters in different zones would pay different tax rates. The question of interest is whether or not this classification system, being dependent upon meteorological parameters, which are derived from analytical models, is legally defensible. The one study of which I am aware [Pierce and Gutfreund 1975] which examines this question in some depth concludes that air dispersion models are likely to be admissible provided they are used by trained professionals and are based on the best available data and methodology. In short, the prognosis is favorable.

---

[35] Peacock v. Pratt, C.C.A. Hawaii 1903, 121 F. 772. Cited in U.S.C.A. Cont. Art. 1 § 8, Cl. 1, Note 108.

[36] 84 C.J.S. § 22, Note 46.

[37] This is true, for example, in Alabama, Arizona, Arkansas, Indiana, Kansas, Louisiana, Maine, Mississippi, Oregon, South Carolina, Virginia and Wyoming. See 84 C.J.S. 24, Note 38.

[38] 84 C.J.S. § 4, Note 39.

[39] See Milwaukee Fire Dept. v. Helfenstein, 16 Wis. 145.

[40] The case histories supporting this point can be found in Grad [1973, p. III-18] and Pollock [1969, p. 139].

IV. ADMINISTRATIVE ASPECTS

The final issue to be dealt with is the administrative practicality of a spatially differentiated charge system as opposed to a nationally uniform charge system. Two recent works have suggested that this approach, while of theoretical importance, is of limited practical significance. The first, by Seneca and Taussig [1974, p. 242], suggests that the information requirements are too burdensome. The second, by Burstein and Quigley [1976, pp. 80–82], suggests that the whole concept of spatially differentiated charges is based upon an arbitrary definition of space, and since the taxes are sensitive to the definition of space, this represents the fatal flaw. Each of these criticisms will be taken up in turn.

The Seneca-Taussig arguments rest on the contention that the additional information which would be required to establish spatially differentiated charges would be sufficiently difficult to acquire that any benefits conferred by its collection would be outweighed by the costs of collecting it. This argument is diluted substantially when the exact information requirements are examined.

The establishment of an interjurisdictional differentiation in rates simply requires a repetition of the same kind of information gathering at the local level that must take place at the national level to establish a national emission charge. While there are certainly more rates to define, there is nothing qualitatively different about the information required.

Qualitatively different information is required, however, for the establishment of an intrajurisdictional differentiation of rates — the $I \times M$ matrix of meteorological parameters. At first glance one might suspect that this was a matrix of variables rather than constants since wind speeds and direction change frequently. The key, however, is that this is a matrix of annual averages and these averages tend to be very stable from year to year. Furthermore, it is possible to use these annual average parameters to meet the requirements of the Clean Air Act.[41]

It is worth calling attention to a couple of properties of this matrix which make it easier to construct than would otherwise have been the case. As pointed out above, it is a matrix of constants, which, given the locations of the receptors and the emitters, is stable over time. In addition, the collection of the information does not depend on the cooperation of the emitter in any way. Rather it is based on prevailing meteorological conditions and can, for nonreactive point source pollutants, be derived using existing meteorological models.[42] These characteristics suggest that the cost of constructing this matrix would be moderate and not likely to outweigh the large benefits to be derived from its use.

Against this background the Burstein-Quigley paper suggests that while everything said above is valid, given the location of the monitoring sites where the concentration levels are measured, the location of these sites is "inherently arbi-

---

[41] The exact procedures for this mapping can be found in Tietenberg [1974b, pp. 284–85]. The mapping holds even when the standards are expressed in averaging times shorter than one year using a transformation in Larsen [1971]. One can improve on this transformation and reduce costs still further by the imposition of temporally varying charges, but this refinement would be common to uniform and spatially differentiated charges and, hence, beyond the scope of this paper.

[42] For a discussion of one such widely used multi-pollutant, multi-source model see note 14 supra.

trary" to use their words [1976, p. 81]. And furthermore, they argue, different locations of the monitoring sites will result in different taxes.

I will not refute the second point that different sites lend to different tax rates. I do, however, emphatically reject the notion that the location of these sites is inherently arbitrary. Rather, their location is dictated by a fairly simple decision rule which is suggested by the legislation itself.

Generally, in any area, with a combination of mobile sampling facilities and computer simulation, it is possible to construct an annual average pollution surface for a region of interest.[43] These surfaces characteristically exhibit some peaks and troughs reflecting a variety of geographic and meteorological parameters. Using these surfaces one can identify locations where the concentrations exceed the legal standards and place the monitoring sites at all peaks which violate the legal ambient air quality standards. Once again this is not an arbitrary decision but one dictated by the rational enforcement of a specific policy.[44]

It is quite possible, of course, that this decision rule will be able to locate the monitoring site only approximately — say, somewhere within a city block of the true peak concentration — and that the modeling methods will be insufficient to locate it with any more precision. The point, however, is that at this level of detail it simply doesn't make much difference. The degree to which the level of the tax would be affected by this approximation would be so small as to make it a problem not worth worrying about.

If the nation is concerned about air pollutant concentrations, as our current policy suggests it is, locally administered,

spatially differentiated charges can lead to substantial reductions in the cost of meeting the Congressionally mandated ambient air quality standards. The fact that we don't actually achieve the optimum is, in a world of scarce information, neither particularly surprising nor particularly interesting. The available evidence suggests that we are much closer with spatially differentiated charges than we are with uniform charges and that is what's important.

V. CONCLUDING COMMENTS

The foregoing analysis indicates that locally administered, spatially differentiated air pollutant emission charges appear to offer a very real public policy option. Not only are they compatible with the existing legislation, but they offer potentially large savings in the costs of achieving the Congressionally mandated ambient air quality standards. While their legal basis is not totally clear because no specific legislation has been brought before the judiciary, the existing precedents appear quite favorable. And, finally, the published administrative objections to them disappear upon closer examination. Far from being merely an intellectual curiosity, spatially differentiated emission charges appear to offer the nation a realistic opportunity to achieve its air pollution goals at significantly lower cost.

[43] An example of such a pollution surface can be found in Grad [1975, p. 170].
[44] There are already in excess of 6,000 ambient air monitoring sites already located in the United States using this basic rule. See Council on Environmental Quality [1975, p. 308].

References

Atkinson, Scott E., and Lewis, Donald H. 1974. "A Cost-Effectiveness Analysis of Alternative Air Quality Control Strategies." *Journal of Environmental Economics and Management* 1 (Nov.): 237–50.

Burstein, Nancy, and Quigley, John M. 1976. "The Danger of 'Derived Decision Rules.'" *Journal of Environmental Economics and Management* 3 (June): 80–82.

Council on Environmental Quality. 1975. *The Sixth Annual Report of the Council on Environmental Quality*. Washington, D.C.: Government Printing Office.

Ferrar, Terry A., and Sassone, Peter. 1975. "The Political Economy of Effluent Charges." *Eastern Economic Journal* 11 (July): 266–73.

Grad, Frank P. 1973. "Intergovernmental Aspects of Environmental Controls." In *An Anthology of Selected Readings for the National Conference on Managing the Environment*, sponsored by the Office of Monitoring and Research. The Environmental Protection Agency (May): III/14–III/43.

Grad, Frank P., et al. 1975. *The Automobile and the Regulation of Its Impact on the Environment*. Norman: University of Oklahoma Press.

Irwin, William A., and Lirhoff, Richard A. 1974. *Economic Disincentives for Pollution Control: Legal, Political and Administrative Dimensions*. EPA 600/5-74-026 (July).

Kneese, Allen V., and Schultze, Charles L. 1975. *Pollution, Prices and Public Policy*. Washington: The Brookings Institution.

Larsen, Ralph I. 1971. "A Mathematical Model for Relating Air Quality Measurements to Air Quality Standards." Environmental Protection Agency, AP-89 (Nov.).

Lerner, Abba P. 1971. "The 1971 Report of the President's Council of Economic Advisers." *American Economic Review* 61 (Sept.): 527–30.

———. 1974. "Priorities and Pollution: Comment." *American Economic Review* 64 (Sept.): 715–17.

———. 1977. "Environment—Externalizing the Internalities?" *American Economic Review* 67 (March): 176–78.

Menz, Fredric C., and Miller, Jon R. 1977. "Local vs. National Pollution: Note." *American Economic Review* 67 (March): 173–75.

Peltzman, Sam, and Tideman, T. Nicholaus. 1972. "Local Versus National Pollution Control: Note." *American Economic Review* 62 (Dec.): 959–63.

Pierce, D. F., and Gutfreund, P. D. 1975. "Evidentiary Aspects of Air Dispersion Modeling and Air Quality Measurements in Environmental Litigation and Administrative Proceedings." *Federation of Insurance Council Quarterly* 25 (Spring): 341–53.

Pollock, L. W. 1969. "Legal Boundaries of Air Pollution Control: State and Local Legislative Purposes and Techniques." In *Air Pollution Control*, ed. Clark C. Havighurst. Dobbs Ferry, N.Y.: Oceana Publications, Inc.

Rose-Ackerman, Susan. 1973. "Effluent Charges: A Critique." *Canadian Journal of Economics* 6 (Nov.): 512–28.

Seneca, Joseph J., and Taussig, Michael K. 1974. *Environmental Economics*. Englewood Cliffs, N.J.: Prentice-Hall, Inc.

Stein, Jerome L. 1971. "The 1971 Report of the President's Council of Economic Advisers: Micro-Economic Aspects of Public Policy." *American Economic Review* 61 (Sept.): 531–37.

———. 1974. "Priorities and Pollution: Reply." *American Economic Review* 64 (Sept.): 718–23.

Tietenberg, T. H. 1973. "Controlling Pollution by Price and Standards Systems: A General Equilibrium Analysis." *Swedish Journal of Economics* 75 (June): 193–203.

———. 1974*a*. "Derived Decision Rules for Pollution Control in a General Equilibrium Space Economy." *Journal of Environmental Economics and Management* 1 (May): 3–16.

———. 1974*b*. "The Design of Property Rights for Air-Pollution Control." *Public Policy* 22 (Summer): 275–92.

15

ENVIRONMENTAL POLICY AND THE DISTRIBUTION OF BENEFITS AND COSTS

Henry M. Peskin

IT IS HARD to conceive of any federal environmental policy—or, indeed, any federal policy—that does not affect various people differently. If a policy were designed in such a way that all affected parties were made better off and none worse off, then the fact that some gained more than others would probably not be of great concern to the designers of policy. At least, this is what one might surmise from the policy designer's frequent emphasis on total benefits and costs. The fact that policies with benefit–cost ratios greater than unity have the *potential* of making everyone better off has apparently eased the conscience of many a policy maker. In the real world, however, such potential outcomes are rarely realized. Regardless of the total of benefits and costs, the usual state of affairs is that some parties gain while others lose.

Federal environmental policy is not exceptional in this respect. What may be exceptional about it is that there seems to be widespread political acceptance for the environmental policies we have adopted even though there is evidence that the number of losers may exceed the number of gainers. In this chapter we will first discuss why this disparity between gainers and losers is an expected consequence of the design of the policy. Then, using data from a study of the distributional consequences of the Clean Air Amendments of 1970, we provide evidence that substantiates these expectations. Finally, we speculate on the political implications of

From Henry M. Peskin, "Environmental Policy and the Distribution of Benefits and Costs," 144-163 in *Current Issues in U.S. Environmental Policy,* Paul R. Portney (ed.). Copyright © 1978 by the Johns Hopkins University Press.

the observed and expected distributional effects. In particular, we shall discuss those aspects of air pollution policy that have made it politically acceptable even though a minority of the population seem to enjoy benefits in excess of the costs they are forced to bear as a result of the policy. We shall also speculate on certain existing aspects of the Clean Air Amendments and certain suggested changes in them that may, in fact, make the law less politically acceptable in the future.

While one may quarrel with our methods and even more so with our quantitative estimates, we feel that such analyses are crucial to a full understanding of the political and economic implications of alternative environmental policies.

Uneven Benefits and Uneven Burdens

Our task of identifying who will benefit from and who will bear the costs of pollution control is difficult because there is no general agreement as to who are the actual beneficiaries. This lack of agreement is due to conflicting perceptions of the nature of pollution and environmental quality.

There are those who believe that environmental quality is a commodity provided equally to everyone and enjoyed by all members of society. According to this view, no individual member would be able to purchase more environmental quality than his neighbor even if he wished.[1] If this view were adopted, one might conclude that environmental quality improvements would benefit everyone equally. Yet this conclusion does not necessarily follow. For, even if the *physical* quality of the environment had improved identically for all citizens, these physical improvements might not be valued equally by all of them. As Baumol has argued, it is likely that those with more money might place a higher value on environmental quality improvements if only by virtue of the fact that they can pay more for them.[2] For this reason, if one accepted the view that environmental quality is a purely public commodity, then it could be argued that the rich would benefit the most from environmental cleanup.

On the other hand, there is another view that emphasizes the variability of pollution across geographical locations. According to this view, house-

[1] Economists call such commodities "purely public." National defense is most often used as an example of such a pure public commodity.

[2] William J. Baumol, "Environmental Protection and Income Distribution" in Harold M. Hochman and George E. Peterson, eds., *Redistribution Through Public Choice* (New York, Columbia University Press, 1974).

holds can determine the pollution to which they are exposed by choosing their residence. Households can thus, "purchase" environmental quality like any other private commodity by buying a home in an unpolluted neighborhood. However, since poorer households often have very little choice of residential location, they often end up in polluted neighborhoods where rents or property values are depressed. Therefore, under this latter view, while environmental quality is perceived to be more nearly a private commodity, adjusting the consumption of this commodity is difficult for many individuals, especially for those with low incomes.

Consequently, while the rich would appear to benefit most under the former, public-commodity view of environmental quality, the urban poor would clearly benefit most if environmental quality were viewed as "purchasable" through location. Therefore, conclusions regarding the distribution of environmental quality improvement depend critically on which view of environmental quality is adopted.

When one considers the costs of cleaning up pollution as well as the benefits, it becomes even more difficult to theorize about the distributional consequences. There are many ways to finance a pollution reduction program and each way can present its own pattern of financial burdens to members of society. A federal program financed with the federal income tax structure is likely to place a heavier burden on the rich (that is, be more progressive) than if the program were administered and financed by the states and local governments with their generally less progressive tax structures.[3]

Actually, the more prominent environmental programs—those discussed in chapters 2 and 3, for example—are characterized by a combination of control strategies, with the initial financial burdens shared by several layers of government, industrial sectors, and households. The ultimate distributional consequences of these complex programs, however, depend on the way in which their initial financial burdens are shifted to the general population. In principle, this shifting depends on the tax structures of the various levels of government, the structure of the markets within

---

[3] A tax structure is said to be progressive if the share of a taxpayer's income paid in taxes increases with his or her income. In a similar vein, we say that the cost structure of a policy is progressive if the share of income allocated to the costs rises with income, and that the benefit structure of a policy is progressive if benefits as a fraction of income *decline* with higher incomes. Finally, we say that the net benefit structure of a policy is progressive if benefits minus costs as a fraction of income decline with higher incomes. Note that if benefits minus costs are negative, this definition means that a progressive net benefit structure requires that the net-benefit-to-income ratio be less negative for poorer income classes.

which the industrial sectors operate, and the ownership of governmental debt and private capital.

One clear implication of these observations is that no realistic environmental policy is likely to have *uniform* distributional effects—that is, no policy will affect each and every person, family, or household in the same way. Moreover, the ultimate impact may be very difficult to predict. As a result, while a particular policy approach may at first appear equitable to the general public, its final distributional consequences might not be judged fair at all. For example, while it may seem fair (and it may make good economic sense) to require the steel industry to pay for its own cleanup, it is likely that these costs can easily be shifted to steel customers and ultimately to final consumers. To the extent that such a shifting is possible, the financing of the cleanup will take on the aspects of a general sales tax because steel is a major component of a large number of products destined for final consumption. What at first seemed fair ultimately may appear regressive and unfair, since the poor will bear a proportionately greater burden of the cost than the rich.

Of course, if it were also the case that the poor were the primary victims of the steel industry's pollution, they might receive proportionately larger benefits from the policy. Thus, when *net* benefits are considered, the total impact of the policy could be progressive and, again, judged fair.

To make final assessments of the distribution of benefits and costs requires a difficult type of empirical analysis. There are perhaps two unsatisfactory characteristics of such analysis. First, it will be almost impossible to draw general conclusions about all environmental policies since the analysis must be tailored to specific approaches, and the distributional effects of one pollution control strategy may easily differ from those of another. Second, the factors that determine the policy's ultimate effect on families are so complex that it is impossible to undertake the analysis without making a number of strong assumptions, many of which are disputable. Our analysis of the Clean Air Amendments, discussed in the next section, evidences both these characteristics.

Analysis of the Clean Air Amendments[4]

The Clean Air Amendments of 1970 seem typical of current environmental legislation in approach and complexity. As chapters 2 and 3 point

[4] This section is based on Leonard P. Gianessi, Henry M. Peskin, and Edward Wolff, "The Distributional Effects of the Uniform Air Pollution Policy in the United States," unpublished RFF Discussion Paper D-5, April 12, 1977.

TABLE 5-1   Annual Air Pollution Benefits and Annual Costs to Attain Benefits, 1968

(millions of 1970 dollars)

Standard industrial code	Sector	Benefits	Industry cost to meet EPA standards[a]
01	Agriculture	201	1,137[b]
07	Agricultural services	214	107
08	Forestry	864	160[b]
10	Metal mining	14	19[b]
11–12	Coal mining	72	161
13	Oil and gas drilling	27	8
14	Nonmetal mining	13	7
15–17	Construction	98	169[c]
19	Ordnance	4	3
20	Food products	138	55
21	Tobacco products	4	2
22	Textiles	49	19
23	Apparel	10	2
24	Wood products	36	63
25	Furniture	11	3
26	Pulp and paper	265	90
27	Printing, publishing	8	2
28	Chemicals	865	199
29	Petroleum products	1,316	207
30	Rubber products	97	11
31	Leather products	14	6
32	Stone, clay, glass	1,164	254
33	Primary metals	2,712	858
34	Fabricated metals	69	32
35	Machinery except electrical	63	16
36	Electrical machinery	48	10
37	Transportation equipment	117	27
38	Instruments	17	3
39	Miscellaneous manufacturing	23	3
40	Railroads	156	66[b]
41	Local and suburban transit	139	165[b]
42	Motor freight	120	133[c]
44	Water transportation	180	49[b]
45	Air transportation	46	274[b]
46	Pipelines	15	34
49	Utilities	4,760	1,634
55	Gas stations	87	540[b]
50–81	Trades and services	942	1,405[c]
82	Education	18	67[c]
88	Households	3,981	12,157[d]
91–93	Governments	153	2,303[c]
	Total	19,130	22,460

Note: Estimates revised May 15, 1976.

Source: Adapted from L. P. Gianessi, H. M. Peskin, and E. Wolff, "The Distributional Effects of the Uniform Air Pollution Policy in the United States," unpublished Discussion Paper D-5 (Washington, D.C., Resources for the Future, 1977) table 1.

ᵃ The primary data source was U.S. Environmental Protection Agency, *The Economics of Clean Air,* Annual Report of the Administrator (March 1972). Many EPA cost numbers have since been revised

out, the law attempts to attack air pollution from two sides. First, accept-able standards of ambient air quality are established. Second, there is an effort to mandate acceptable levels of emissions for particular classes of emitters—certain major stationary sources, new facilities, facilities that emit hazardous pollutants, and mobile sources. States and localities are left in the unenviable position of making both these approaches "mesh." That is, given the mandated emissions policies, states and localities are ex-pected to devise plans to achieve the mandated ambient standards.

Because of the complexities of the legislation, an analysis of likely dis-tributional consequences makes it necessary to estimate what will, in fact, be done (that is, what particular strategies will be adopted), as well as the costs and benefits of so doing. Fortunately this speculative exercise was largely accomplished by the Environmental Protection Agency (EPA) in their 1970 report to Congress.[5] This report assumes that in addition to mobile-source emissions requirements, the ambient standards in the act will be attained by certain technological responses on the part of industry. EPA has estimated the costs of these responses as well as the dollar value of the likely benefits from air pollution control at the national level.

We have made a variety of adjustments to these data, the most impor-tant being the attribution of these costs and benefits to Standard Industrial Classification (SIC) sectors, an operation that, in turn, required filling in data gaps using other published sources.[6] The results of these adjustments as well as the national totals are shown in table 5-1.

The next step in the analysis was to distribute these costs and benefits to individuals in the population. Actually, we distributed these totals to fami-lies rather than individuals since the family is more often the usual focus of

---

[5] U.S. Environmental Protection Agency, *The Economics of Clean Air,* Annual Report of the Administrator (March 1972).

[6] The biggest gap was the neglect of benefits due to automobile pollution control. This adjustment was based on the work of L. R. Babcock and M. L. Nagda, "Cost Effectiveness of Emission Control," *Journal of the Air Pollution Control Association* vol. 18 (1973) pp. 1973–1979.

---

upward. Many other sources (e.g., journal articles, contractors' reports, industry studies, and the like) were used to obtain the two-digit SIC breakdowns. Complete documentation on these sources and esti-mating methods is available from the project investigators. EPA does not provide estimates of the costs to meet standards for fuel combustion from stationary sources broken down by sector. Therefore, aggregate EPA cost estimates are distributed by estimated fuel usage. EPA cost estimates reflecting emission levels in 1977–78 were adjusted to the 1968 base year by assuming a fixed proportion between a sector's activity level and its emissions.

b EPA standards not established. Cost estimates are based on industry estimates of clean-up costs and EPA contractors' reports.

c Estimate assumes all gasoline vehicles are fitted with pollution control equipment necessary to meet 1977 standards.

d Estimate based on 1970 automobile pollution.

distributional analyses, and certain of the data needed for this step are only available by family units.[7]

Before discussing the details of our distribution techniques, we should point out the basic methodological approach. It is impossible to observe the actual impacts on millions of people of a policy that has yet to be fully implemented. Therefore, instead we "observe" the impacts on a random sample of the population of a policy that is *assumed* to be fully implemented. The random sample is the one-in-a-thousand 1970 Census Public Use File, a self-weighting sample of household and person records of the 1970 population census. Our approach is an example of a class of approaches known as microsimulation techniques.[8] These techniques have become feasible only because of the ability of the modern computer to process rapidly extremely large data sets. In our case, we have had to process over 60,000 household and 500,000 individual records.

Benefit Estimates

National benefit totals were first distributed to regions known as Census County Groups and to subportions of these groups, known as Standard Metropolitan Statistical Areas (SMSAs). Each individual within these regions was assumed to receive an even share of a region's estimated benefit total. Thus, within a region, a family's benefit was determined solely by the number of its members.

The procedure for distributing the national benefit totals to regions, the assumptions behind the procedure, and its weaknesses are fully discussed in two recent studies.[9] Here, we make only the following observations about our procedure. We basically assume that pollution damage (and, hence, the benefits from alleviating such damage) is proportional to local physical air quality or pollution concentrations.[10] Hence, we reject the pure public-commodity view of environmental quality. Two factors that

[7] Families in our analysis are defined as U.S. Census primary families and unrelated individuals over fourteen years old.

[8] See Guy Orcutt, Martin Greenberger, John Korbel, and Alice Rivlin, *Microanalysis of Socioeconomic Systems: A Simulation Study* (Harper and Row, 1961).

[9] Gianessi, Peskin, and Wolff, "Distributional Effects;" and Leonard P. Gianessi, Henry M. Peskin, and Edward Wolff, "The Distributional Implications of National Air Pollution Damage Estimates," in F. T. Juster, ed., *Distribution of Economic Well-Being* (Cambridge, Mass., Ballinger for the National Bureau of Economic Research, 1977).

[10] In turn, the relative air quality of two regions is assumed to be proportionate to the relative rate of emissions in the two regions. County groups are assumed to be large enough that spillovers can be neglected but small enough to permit an assumption of homogeneous air quality within the region.

may have nonproportional influences on damage are also neglected. The first is the income of the damaged party. As we pointed out above, Baumol and others have argued that the dollar valuation a person places on physical environmental damage can vary with the person's income; furthermore, there is reason to believe that the valuation increases as the individual becomes wealthier. Our analysis does not account for this. The second neglected factor is the possibility of "increasing returns" to bad health from pollution concentrations. There is reason to believe that when the air is rather clean, small increments in pollution concentrations will have small detrimental effects. However, increments of the same size can have very large detrimental effects when the air is very dirty.

Since we distributed a fixed national benefit total, neglect of these two factors may work in opposite directions. Ignoring income differences may imply that we underestimate the policy benefits to wealthier people relative to poor people. However, to the extent that the poor live in more highly polluted areas, and would benefit the most from improvements in very polluted air, the opposite is the case. Thus, the proportionality assumption may provide a good approximation of relative damages in spite of the neglect of the nonproportional influences of income and the potentially cumulative health–pollution concentration relationships.

Table 5-2 lists the ten areas where the average benefits per family of controlling air pollution are the highest and lowest.[11] While it is not surprising that the residents of the heavily industrialized northeastern areas have the most to gain from pollution control, it is perhaps surprising that these benefits are concentrated in so few regions. Our analysis suggests that over 30 percent of total national benefits go to the residents of the five dirtiest SMSAs, although they account for but 8 percent of the U.S. population. As we shall see, costs appear to be much more widely distributed. Therefore, the concentration of benefits in a very few areas is the major determinant of all our subsequent results concerning the ultimate distributional consequences of the 1970 Clean Air Amendments on income classes and racial groups.

Cost Estimates

The costs of air pollution abatement in table 5-1 were distributed to families in one of three ways, depending on whether the initial incidence of

---

[11] The failure of Los Angeles to appear in the list of the ten highest benefit areas is a consequence of the fact that the national damage estimates do not give a heavy weight to automotive pollutants.

TABLE 5-2   Areas with Highest and Lowest Per-Family Gross Benefits
Under the 1970 Clean Air Amendments

Rank	County group or SMSA	Dollars per family
	Ten Highest	
1	Jersey City SMSA	2,547.29
2	New York, N.Y. SMSA	1,169.94
3	Erie SMSA	1,040.37
4	Newark SMSA	864.41
5	Paterson SMSA	782.99
6	Detroit SMSA	762.77
7	Chicago SMSA	660.71
8	Cleveland SMSA	652.12
9	Providence SMSA	631.39
10	Gary SMSA	622.94
	Ten Lowest	
1	Alaska	0.32
2	Nevada, S. Utah	1.42
3	Montana	2.53
4	S. New Mexico, W. Texas	2.98
5	Wyoming, W. Nebraska	2.98
6	N. New Mexico	3.79
7	Arizona	3.85
8	S.W. Texas	4.09
9	N.W. Texas	4.15
10	C. Texas	4.63

costs fell on industries, governments, or households. Industrial costs—
which we assume to be passed on in the form of higher product prices—
were apportioned to families according to an estimate of their total consumption (which, in turn, was based on their income). The apportionment
of governmental costs—assumed to be paid for by tax increases rather
than reductions in other expenditures—was based on estimates of family
tax burden. Household costs, which for the most part, are automobile pollution control costs, were apportioned on a per-vehicle-owned basis, one
of the many household characteristics reported in the Public Use Sample.[12]

No region of the United States can claim an overwhelming preponderance of vehicle ownership or families residing in a given income class.
Therefore, average per-family costs are spread much more narrowly be-

[12] This description oversimplifies the actual task. In addition to the need for data
on consumption levels and tax rates by income class, a procedure had to be devised
for assigning cars to families. The Public Use File only reports vehicle ownership
by household, and a household may contain several families and unrelated individuals or both. Details of the procedure are reported in Gianessi, Peskin, and
Wolff, "Distributional Effects."

TABLE 5-3   Areas with Highest and Lowest Per-Family Costs Under
the 1970 Clean Air Amendments

Rank	County group or SMSA	Dollars per family
	Ten Highest	
1	Oxnard-Ventura SMSA	438.96
2	Bridgeport SMSA	422.86
3	Anaheim SMSA	416.95
4	Paterson SMSA	405.04
5	San Jose SMSA	401.18
6	S.W. Texas	400.22
7	Columbia SMSA	396.73
8	Alaska	396.11
9	Lansing SMSA	395.76
10	Dayton SMSA	395.30
	Ten Lowest	
1	S. Arkansas, W.C. Mississippi	254.56
2	Jersey City SMSA	263.18
3	M.W. Mississippi	270.16
4	N. West Virginia	274.14
5	N.W. Florida	279.63
6	Central S. Carolina	279.63
7	N.C. Missouri	282.08
8	New York, N.Y. SMSA	284.11
9	N. Mississippi, W. Tennessee, E. Arkansas	286.77
10	C. Tennessee	289.23

tween the ten highest cost areas and the ten lowest cost areas than are the
per-family benefits. These high and low cost areas are shown in table 5-3.
What differences do exist are explained by the fact that the high cost areas
have relatively fewer low income families and high per-family automobile
ownership.

Net Benefits

Net benefits are defined as the difference between per-family benefits and
costs. When one calculates average net benefits per family for all 274
county groups and SMSAs, it appears that these average net benefits are
positive for only a minority of these areas. For the air pollution policy as a
whole, there appear to be only twenty-four areas (accounting for about
28 percent of the U.S. population) where average net benefits per family
are positive. If the automobile policy is considered in isolation, only four
areas (the Jersey City, New York, Paterson, and Newark SMSAs) show
positive net benefits.

These results should not be surprising since we have seen that costs seem to be spread, geographically, far more evenly than benefits. The areas enjoying positive net benefits are those that suffer from a disproportionately large share of the nation's air pollution.

These results also imply that only a minority of the nation's population—principally those who live in the highly polluted areas—gain on net from the 1970 Clean Air Amendments. A more exact estimate of gainers and losers can be obtained by inspecting estimated benefits and costs for each family in the Public Use Sample. By this procedure, it is estimated that about 19 million families—or 29 percent of all families—enjoy positive net benefits. When the automobile policy is considered in isolation, only about 16 million families gain on net. It should be noted, however, that while net gainers appear to be in the minority, their gains on average greatly exceed the loss of net losers even though, as table 5-1 shows, total losses (costs) exceed total gains (benefits) by about $3 billion.

The rankings of net benefits shown in table 5-4 reflect both the wide dispersion in gross benefits and the relatively narrow dispersion in costs. The order of the areas with the highest net benefit is nearly the same as the order of highest gross benefits shown in table 5-2. The areas with the lowest net benefits differ insignificantly in their rankings and are representative of a large number of areas which have per-family costs in the $300–400 range, and which enjoy the very low per-family benefits common to areas with low levels of urbanization.

Income Relationships

Table 5-5 shows average benefits, costs, and net benefits by family income classes and by race. These data provide another view of the relative benefits and burdens of the air pollution control policy.

It is apparent that the industrial air pollution control policy and the household (primarily atuomobile) policy have markedly different impacts when viewed in relation to income. Nearly all income and racial groups enjoy, on average,[13] positive net benefits from the control of industrial air pollution. In contrast, no racial group or income class appears to gain from the control of automobile emissions. Except for those in the highest income class, non-whites appear to be the only net gainers from the 1970 Clean Air Amendments as a whole—a consequence of their lower average vehicle ownership (which lowers automobile control costs), their larger

[13] This qualifier is important because there are individual families that gain or lose in all income and racial classes.

TABLE 5-4   Areas with Highest and Lowest Per-Family Net Benefits
Under the 1970 Clean Air Amendments

Rank	County group or SMSA	Net benefit (dollars per family)
	Ten highest	
1	Jersey City SMSA	2,284.11
2	New York SMSA	885.83
3	Erie SMSA	700.85
4	Newark SMSA	509.59
5	Detroit SMSA	385.15
6	Paterson SMSA	377.95
7	Chicago SMSA	317.87
8	Providence SMSA	283.91
9	Cleveland SMSA	278.80
10	Gary SMSA	264.09
	Ten lowest	
1	S.W. Texas	−396.13
2	Alaska	−395.79
3	Nevada, S.W. Utah	−379.42
4	Santa Barbara SMSA	−362.08
5	Wyoming, W. Nebraska	−350.35
6	S. New Mexico, W. Texas	−349.71
7	Tucson SMSA	−347.52
8	C. Nebraska	−345.12
9	E.C. California	−343.57
10	N.E. Colorado	−342.23

average family size (which increases per-family benefits), and their tendency to reside in more urbanized locations (areas that receive the greatest pollution reductions).

Total benefits appear to increase as income rises, implying that higher income groups suffer (prior to the policy implementation) greater absolute damage than the poor. This finding, which is counter to those of Freeman and of Zupan,[14] may appear strange to those who picture the poor living in highly polluted urban slums. Although this characterization is no doubt valid, it must be kept in mind that the poorest of the poor actually live in relatively clean rural areas. Since both the Freeman and the Zupan studies dealt with specific SMSAs, and not with the entire nation, they did not observe the pollution to which the rural poor are exposed.

[14] A. Myrick Freeman III, "Distribution of Environmental Quality," in Allen V. Kneese and Blair T. Bower, eds., *Environmental Quality: Theory and Method in the Social Sciences* (Baltimore, Md., Johns Hopkins University Press for Resources for the Future, 1972); and Jeffrey M. Zupan, *The Distribution of Air Quality in the New York Region* (Washington, D.C., Resources for the Future, 1973).

TABLE 5-5 Annual U.S. Per-Family Air Pollution Control Costs and Benefits by Income Class and Race
(dollars)

Costs and benefits	Less than 3,000	3,000 to 3,999	4,000 to 5,999	6,000 to 7,999	8,000 to 9,999	10,000 to 11,999	12,000 to 14,999	15,000 to 19,999	20,000 to 24,999	25,000+
Industry and govt. costs										
Whites	59.79	81.90	102.63	130.47	155.90	177.56	210.49	248.17	299.87	457.29
Non-whites	59.79	81.90	102.63	130.47	155.90	177.56	210.49	248.17	299.87	457.29
Total	59.79	81.90	102.63	130.47	155.90	177.56	210.49	248.17	299.87	457.29
Industry and govt. benefits										
Whites	100.27	123.49	138.94	177.39	228.40	258.04	294.59	334.85	377.25	392.57
Non-whites	166.13	216.42	286.31	337.07	391.29	399.25	490.57	491.77	500.95	495.76
Total	112.57	138.76	160.33	195.48	242.19	267.16	306.99	343.27	382.75	395.22
Industry and govt. net benefits										
Whites	40.48	41.59	36.32	46.92	72.50	80.48	84.10	86.68	77.38	−64.72
Non-whites	106.34	134.52	183.68	206.60	235.39	221.69	280.08	243.60	201.08	38.47
Total	52.78	56.86	57.70	65.01	86.29	89.60	96.50	95.10	82.88	−62.07

Income class

Household costs (automobile)										
Whites	92.87	131.01	153.75	179.69	204.27	225.04	245.92	274.29	299.99	303.78
Non-whites	52.75	82.33	100.81	138.89	152.96	175.16	197.35	228.70	250.82	287.24
Total	85.25	123.01	146.03	175.04	199.91	221.82	242.83	271.83	297.81	303.35
Household benefits										
Whites	27.00	33.34	36.21	44.66	58.59	65.61	76.00	88.40	102.58	112.91
Non-whites	44.11	59.07	84.69	89.78	100.49	113.26	129.67	138.16	128.63	146.28
Total	30.25	37.56	43.28	49.79	62.14	68.69	79.41	91.08	103.74	113.77
Household net benefits										
Whites	−65.87	−97.67	−117.54	−135.03	−145.68	−159.43	−169.92	−185.89	−197.41	−190.87
Non-whites	−8.64	−23.26	−16.12	−49.11	−52.47	−61.90	−67.68	−90.54	−122.19	−140.96
Total	−55.00	−85.45	−102.75	−125.25	−137.77	−153.13	−163.42	−180.75	−194.07	−189.58
Total costs										
Whites	152.66	212.91	256.38	310.16	360.17	402.60	456.41	522.46	599.86	761.07
Non-whites	112.54	164.33	203.44	269.36	308.86	352.72	407.84	476.87	550.69	744.53
Total	145.04	204.91	248.66	305.51	355.81	399.38	453.32	520.00	597.68	760.64
Total benefits										
Whites	127.27	156.83	175.15	222.05	286.99	323.65	370.59	423.25	479.83	505.48
Non-whites	210.24	275.49	371.00	426.85	491.78	512.51	620.24	629.93	629.58	642.04
Total	142.82	176.32	203.61	245.27	304.33	335.85	386.40	434.35	486.49	508.99
Total net benefits										
Whites	−25.39	−56.08	−81.23	−88.11	−73.18	−78.95	−85.82	−99.21	−120.03	−255.59
Non-whites	97.70	111.16	167.56	157.49	182.92	159.79	212.40	153.06	78.89	−102.49
Total	−2.22	−28.59	−45.05	−60.24	−51.48	−63.53	−66.92	−85.65	−111.19	−251.65

TABLE 5-6 *Average Incidence of Air Pollution Control Costs and Benefits by Income Class and Source for the United States*

(percentage of income)

					Income class					
	Less than $3,000	$3,000 to $3,999	$4,000 to $5,999	$6,000 to $7,999	$8,000 to $9,999	$10,000 to $11,999	$12,000 to $14,999	$15,000 to $19,999	$20,000 to $24,999	$25,000+
Costs										
Industry and govt.	3.4	2.4	2.1	1.9	1.7	1.6	1.6	1.4	1.4	1.1
Household	4.8	3.6	3.0	2.5	2.2	2.0	1.8	1.6	1.3	0.7
Total	8.2	6.0	5.1	4.4	3.9	3.6	3.4	3.0	2.7	1.8
Benefits										
Industry and govt.	6.3	4.0	3.2	2.8	2.7	2.4	2.3	2.0	1.7	1.0
Household	1.7	1.1	0.9	0.7	0.7	0.6	0.6	0.5	0.5	0.3
Total	8.0	5.1	4.1	3.5	3.4	3.0	2.9	2.5	2.2	1.3
Net benefits										
Industry and govt.	2.9	1.6	1.1	0.9	1.0	0.8	0.7	0.6	0.3	-0.1
Household	-3.1	-2.5	-2.1	-1.8	-1.5	-1.4	-1.2	-1.1	-0.8	-0.4
Total	-0.2	-0.9	-1.0	-0.9	-0.5	-0.6	-0.5	-0.5	-0.5	-0.5

If a family's share of pollution control costs is viewed as a tax, while the family's benefit is viewed as a subsidy, then the "progressivity" of this tax-subsidy package can be analyzed by dividing the cost and benefit totals of table 5-5 by the average incomes of the various income classes. These results are displayed in table 5-6.

Since average per-family cost as a percentage of income declines with income, the relative burden of the air pollution control policy clearly falls more heavily on the poor. In other words, the cost structure is "regressive."[15] On the other hand, the benefits are "progressive"—the rich enjoy fewer benefits per dollar of income than the poor.

Overall, net benefits, although negative for all classes, appear neither progressive nor regressive (indeed, they are proportionally distributed for incomes above $10,000). However, there is obviously a big difference between the burdens of the policy with respect to its industrial component as opposed to its household (primarily automobile) component. The net benefits of industrial air pollution control appear not only to be positive for almost all income groups but also progressively distributed. The net benefits of the household component, on the other hand, because of its large costs relative to benefits for all income classes, are both negative and regressive.

Alternative Strategies for Air Quality Improvement

As noted earlier, final assessment of the likely distribution of benefits and costs for any specific environmental policy is quite difficult without thorough empirical analysis. Nevertheless, we can hazard a few educated guesses about the distributional effects of certain alternative air pollution control policies.

Consider, for example, the two-car strategy discussed in chapter 3. Such a policy would not only be less expensive (with little effect on benefits), but, as Harrison argues, it would also be less regressive since large SMSAs

---

[15] Although percentages differ, this regressive pattern was also observed by Freeman, "Distribution of Environmental Quality"; Nancy S. Dorfman and Arthur Snow, "Who Will Pay for Pollution Control?" *National Tax Journal* vol. 28, no. 1 (March 1975) pp. 101–115; and Robert Dorfman, *Incidence of the Benefits and Costs of Environmental Programs*, Discussion Paper No. 510 (Harvard Institute of Economic Research, October 1976). The pattern was also shown for automobile policy only by A. Myrick Freeman III, "The Incidence of the Cost of Controlling Automotive Air Pollution," in F. T. Juster, ed., *Distribution of Economic Well-Being* (Cambridge, Mass., Ballinger for the National Bureau of Economic Research, 1977); and David Harrison, Jr., *Who Pays for Clean Air?* (Cambridge, Mass., Ballinger, 1975).

tend to have wealthier car-owning populations than smaller SMSAs and rural areas.[16] These smaller SMSAs and rural areas would be relieved of the costs of controlling automobile emissions.

However, estimating the distributional consequences of changes in industrial air or water pollution control policies is more difficult. Suppose, for example, we abandon a national air pollution control policy for one that allows regions of the country freedom of choice with respect to environmental policy. Because, unlike automotive control costs, the final "location" of industrial control costs is not necessarily the location where they are initially incurred, the distributional results will depend on complex trade and market patterns.

Thus, while certain suggested policy alternatives—effluent charge systems, for example—may be attractive on grounds of economic efficiency, they may be no better or no worse in terms of their distributional equity. Much depends on how the charge system is administered, especially with respect to the purpose of the charges, their levels, and the disposition of collected revenues.

If the purpose of an effluent charge is to bring about approximately the same emission reductions that are presently the targets of current regulations, then the distributional patterns will not be very different from what they are now. However, since charges are thought to be more efficient than mandated controls,[17] total pollution control costs can be expected to be somewhat lower, thereby resulting in a larger number of net gainers. On the other hand, the distributional pattern may be greatly different if the charges are to be set in accordance with local (rather than national) preferences. It is quite possible that very clean rural areas, desirous of industrial growth, would choose to set very low charges. If so, the current high-cost, low-benefit pattern typical of these areas could change to a low-cost, low-benefit pattern, depending again on the way industrial commodities flow.

It is also difficult to predict what effect the collected revenues will have. Under many charge schemes these revenues could be substantial even if the desired level of air quality is attained.[18] If, for example, these revenues

---

[16] Harrison, *Who Pays?*

[17] See chapter 2 for a discussion of this proposition.

[18] While some schemes suggest a zero charge when a target level of water quality is attained, an ideally efficient policy requires the charge to equal the marginal social damage of a small increase in the target level and the marginal social opportunity cost of a small decrease in the target level. Generally, these marginal social damages and costs, and hence the charge, are non-zero, even when an ideally efficient pollution level obtains.

were to be used for general tax relief, the policy would tend to be more regressive, since the wealthy bear larger proportional tax burdens. An opposite result would obtain if these revenues were used for the construction of publicly owned pollution control facilities designed to substitute for private industrial facilities. Such a policy would relieve the regressive burden of the costs of the replaced industrial facilities. An even more progressive outcome would be assured if these revenues were targeted for low income populations.

However, our analysis indicates that "poor aim" is a likely feature of such policy targeting. The difficulty of determining the actual distributional pattern of the burden of policy costs makes it difficult to use the policy's revenues (or even general revenues) as a means of subsidizing or offsetting these costs. This problem is not confined to pollution control policies but to any tax or subsidy proposal such as the recent suggestions to use subsidies to offset the cost of various aspects of the president's energy policy.

Political Acceptability

Both our qualitative discussions and our empirical analysis of the 1970 Clean Air Amendments support the conclusion that the burdens and benefits of environmental policy are likely to be unevenly distributed across regions, income classes, and races. Indeed, our estimates suggest that net gainers are in the minority and are confined to a few presently highly polluted regions.

Regardless of these characteristics, Congress and the public have generally supported environmental programs, although enthusiasm may be waning. If citizens vote in their own self-interest, as many believe them to do, one might wonder why U.S. environmental policy enjoys the support it has. There are several possible explanations and we shall focus on three of them.

The Analysis Understates the Benefits

Any apparent inconsistency between public support for environmental programs and the relatively small number of net gainers may be entirely illusory. If the true benefits are greatly understated, then net gainers may, in fact, be in the majority. Indeed, a critic of EPA's benefit estimates may cite the public support of the programs as evidence that the benefits are underestimated. However, since the public might well support such a program even if the benefit estimates are accurate (as will be argued below), such "evidence" is rather weak.

Nevertheless, it is impossible to prove that all the benefits of a clean environment have been quantified or are even capable of being quantified. In particular, there may be overriding social benefits generated by cleaning up the environment that are of a public commodity nature and that are independent of any private or regional gains. Those who assert that a clean environment is a national birthright to which all are entitled are implicitly asserting the existence of such a benefit.

Lack of Knowledge of Actual Costs and Benefits

Of course, in explaining the political support, the actual existence of possibly unquantified benefits is not as important as the *perception* of their existence. It is entirely possible that our analysis has accurately pictured all the costs and benefits but that these true "facts" were not available to congressmen or the public during the mid-1960s when support for environmental legislation was most enthusiastic.

Although one may question whether there was a full understanding of the level and distribution of benefits (especially in view of the uncertainties surrounding benefit estimation), there is some evidence that policy costs and their distribution were not fully appreciated by supporters of environmental regulation. Often expressed was the view that pollution control was a problem of corporate power—that the costs of environmental quality improvements would be drawn solely from corporate profits[19] (and this was the source of corporate opposition).[20] The fact that the final cost burdens were likely to be regressive was not emphasized—at least publicly.

Certainly the early widespread support for environmental policy and the more recent and cautious attitudes could be explained by the fact that perception of the true costs and benefits is only beginning to be realized. Yet, as we shall see, there is still another plausible explanation.

Consistency with Distributive Goals

The analysis of the distributive impacts of the 1970 Clean Air Amendments indicates that those who gain when both benefits and costs are taken

---

[19] For example, see John C. Esposito, *Vanishing Air* (New York, Grossman Publishers, 1970).

[20] The inconsistency between the assumption of no shifting of control costs to consumers and the implicit assumption of corporate monopolies facing inelastic demands was not appreciated.

into account are more likely to be non-white, low income, inner-city residents. The law apparently serves to shift welfare toward a population group that is also a focus of a large body of explicit redistributive policy.[21] It is quite likely that certain pro-environment congressmen were influenced by the image of the inner-city resident living with both the burdens of poverty and dirty air. To these congressmen, the redistributive character of the environmental policy is simply another point in its favor.

If this conjecture is correct, it does not bode well for certain aspects of water quality legislation or for certain suggested amendments to the Clean Air Act. That is, it has been estimated that 70 percent of the benefits of improved water quality will be in the nature of improved recreational opportunities.[22] These benefits will be biased toward the wealthy since those in the higher income classes are the major users of water-based recreation.[23] In a similar fashion, suggested policies to limit air quality degradation in already clean areas cannot help but dampen economic growth, and, regardless of how noble the objectives may be, such growth-limiting policies, unless accompanied by substantial redistribution efforts, will almost certainly harm the poor who have yet to attain high levels of wealth far more than the rich who already have. To the extent that these and other aspects of environmental policy are perceived as primarily benefiting the wealthy, they may lose the support of welfare-oriented congressmen.

Conclusion

None or all of the above three explanations may account for congressional attitudes toward current environmental policy. It is difficult to prove or disprove any of these conjectures. What we can say with certainty is that environmental policy has potentially profound distributional implications. These policies are inherently biased with respect to their impact on different families and different geographical regions. This chapter has suggested that this lack of neutrality can have and may have had an impact on the political acceptability of the legislation. It is a possibility that should not be ignored when considering future legislation.

[21] It is obviously not the sole focus. Most welfare recipients are white and many live in rural areas.

[22] Fred H. Abel, Dennis P. Tihansky, and Richard G. Walsh, "National Benefits of Water Pollution Control" (Washington, D.C., Office of Research and Development, U.S. Environmental Protection Agency, n.d.).

[23] C. J. Cicchetti, J. J. Seneca, and P. Davidson, *The Demand and Supply for Outdoor Recreation* (New Brunswick, N.J., Bureau of Economic Research, Rutgers University, 1969).

Section
V

Income Support
and
Labor Market
Policy

16

HOW LARGE IS THE WELFARE CLASS?

Martin Rein and Lee Rainwater

Data from a ten-year survey show that a relatively small percentage of welfare recipients is committed to welfare as a "way of life."

The growing cost of this country's welfare programs —the so-called "welfare crisis"—has prompted a great deal of discussion, much of which adds up to a theory that there is a large proportion of people on welfare who have been dependent on it for such a long period of time that they can be said to constitute a welfare class.

The three main popular views about families in the welfare class are all based on the assumption that welfare has become a way of life for a great many of its recipients. The most common of these views is that members of the welfare class are victims of social, psychological, or physical pathology. They are referred to as "multi-problem" families who must remain on welfare because they are "unemployable." This kind of family, it is often felt, has become so committed to a life on welfare that it remains on welfare even when some of its problems have been ameliorated.

Another opinion is that the welfare class is an exploited group that functions in the economy like a modern reserve army, responding to cyclical changes in the demand for labor. A certain proportion of the population, therefore, is at the mercy of the ups and downs in the employment cycle, and the vagaries of the low-wage labor market.

Finally, there is the view that a substantial number of welfare clients are "cheats." People with long-term

MARTIN REIN is Professor of Urban Studies, Massachusetts Institute of Technology. LEE RAINWATER is Professor of Sociology, Harvard University.

From Martin Rein and Lee Rainwater, "How Large is the Welfare Class?" 20(4) *Challenge* 20-23 (September/October 1977). Copyright ©1979. Reprinted from *Challenge*, the magazine of Economic Affairs by permission of M. E. Sharpe, Inc. White Plains, NY 10603.

dependency on welfare are seen not as the exploited, but as the exploiters. They use the public transfer system as entrepreneurs, and make their living by manipulating the system, rather than by finding work.

Whatever one's opinion as to the reason for a family's long-term attachment to and dependence on the welfare system, it would seem important to determine just how large this welfare class really is. For what policy-makers believe about the size and characteristics of this class will significantly affect what they do in the area of welfare reform.

Our investigations suggest that the welfare class is not nearly so large as people think it is.

The Panel Study

There have been a number of attempts to estimate the size of the group with a long-term dependence on welfare, but the task has proved difficult because it has been based on routine administrative welfare statistics, which deal only with particular cases at particular times. The best way to determine the size of the welfare class is to follow a sample of families over a period of years to see how high the probability is that they will go on welfare, stay there for a considerable time, and derive a major proportion of their income from welfare. So far as we are aware, there is only one survey that provides the kinds of data which enable those probabilities to be assessed—the Panel Study of Income Dynamics, conducted by the University of Michigan Survey Research Center.

For a decade now, a national sample of over 10,000 American adults, who are members of over 5,000 families, have been interviewed to determine how their family income has been obtained. It has become clear from much previous research that the life careers of women and their children are central to the welfare experience. We therefore chose for analysis from the Panel Study women who were between the ages of 18 and 54 in 1968, the first year of the survey. We followed the patterns of their welfare experience through 1974, developed a model of that experience, and projected the model over a ten-year period. Our aim was to determine the incidence of welfare class membership. Our operational definition of such membership was attachment to the welfare system for at least nine out of ten years, and at least 50 percent dependence on the system for family income during that period. This definition is consistent with the conception of a welfare class held by researchers, policy-makers, and the general public.

We wanted to know, for a given group of women, how many were likely to become members of the welfare class. This involved three basic component questions: How many would go on welfare at all? How long would they stay on welfare? How dependent would they be on welfare for family income? (This last component is an important one. The Panel survey data reveal, for example, that a number of families on welfare for long periods derive only a small portion of their income from it, and this income consists of welfare payments on behalf of foster children being cared for by couples—hardly a situation that would qualify them for membership in the welfare class.)

The data show that from 1968 to the present, the probability that a woman between the ages of 18 and 54 would go on welfare has been about 1.5 percent. That is, of every 1,000 women who have not been on welfare during the previous year, about 15 will join the rolls. Since there are roughly 50 million women in this age range in the United States, this means that about 750,000 of them will become welfare recipients each year.

Once a woman goes on welfare, the data show, the probability of her staying on it for a second year is 60 percent; for a third year, 70 percent. The probability rises to a plateau of 80 percent for the fifth year and beyond. At any given time, about 5.5 percent of women from 18 to 54 years of age are members of families which obtain at least part of their income from welfare. The analysis suggests that the average woman who goes on welfare at all spends about four out of ten years in that position. Her four years is the sum of two consecutive years on welfare, and two years' "cycling back" to welfare, after having left it for one or more years. But this four-year period does not conform to the concept of a member of the welfare class, which requires a much longer-term dependency. If we estimate the various stages of welfare participation for 18- to 54-year-old women, we can arrive at an estimate of the size of the group which is dependent on welfare for a period of at least nine out of ten years.

Of the 50 million women in the country in that age range, 43 million, or 86 percent, will have had no welfare experience at all over the ten-year period 1968-1977. But 7 million, or 14 percent, will have had some welfare income in at least one of those years. Here is a breakdown of the welfare experience of those 7 million women:

Total women 18-54 years old in first year	50,000,000
Have been on welfare at least once in 10 years	7,000,000
On welfare for 4 or fewer years	3,500,000
On welfare more than 4 years	3,500,000
On welfare 5 to 8 years	2,730,000
On welfare 9 or 10 years	770,000
Of those on welfare 9 or 10 years, Less than 50 percent dependent on welfare	154,000
50 percent or more dependent on welfare	616,000

Thus the size of the welfare class comes to 616,000 women out of the total of 50 million. Since in any one year some 2.7 million women are likely to be on welfare, we find that only slightly over 20 percent of those on welfare at any one particular time are members of the welfare class, by our definition. The other 80 percent have short- or medium-term welfare careers. And of the 7 million women who go on welfare in any year, the welfare class represents only 10 percent. It is true, however, that although the welfare class constitutes only a fifth of those on welfare at any given time, its members consume more than a fifth of the welfare dollars. In fact, our data suggest that they consume as much as 60 percent of all welfare dollars going to the families of women between the ages of 18 and 54.

Overall, one can conclude that the welfare class is a definite minority among welfare recipients. The patterns of welfare careers, which have been studied by Susan Anderson-Khleif, who read the cases discussed here, suggest that it might be useful to think of two other categories of welfare recipients as more typical.

Common patterns among welfare clients

One of the more common groups of welfare clients is composed of those who make use of welfare in the course of some kind of family transition—usually marital breakup. These families go on welfare with every expectation of leaving it as quickly as possible; they use welfare as a resource in "digging out" of the financial hole the marital disruption puts them in. As the new female household head gets on her feet, she begins to work, sometimes after having finished her

schooling, and eventually earns enough to discontinue her welfare payments.

Another common group is made up of families in which job problems, rather than marital disruption, produce the financial crisis to which welfare is a solution. Male or female heads of households lose their jobs and have a hard time finding others, or else they have jobs in the marginal labor market and are therefore subject to recurrent unemployment. They go on welfare for a short period of time. They may, however, be "cyclers," coming back to welfare in some later period of unemployment.

Then there is a small group (perhaps as large as the welfare class) for whom welfare represents a transition to other public transfers. It consists of household heads who receive welfare while they are establishing their eligibility for workmen's compensation, or widow's or survivor's benefits. To some extent, this shifting from means-tested to social insurance benefits may lead to an underestimation of the size of the welfare class. It is quite possible that enterprising welfare departments shift cases with marginal eligibility off the welfare rolls and onto some form of social insurance program as a way of minimizing costs to the states and localities.

We have described life situations which are common among welfare recipients. Is there any pattern that might be called common among welfare class members? It is possible to discern a "locked-in" pattern in many of these families, a situation where everything is going wrong at the same time. Families like this are bereft of a social support network to which they can turn for help. They may not, as other welfare families do, have access to friends, neighbors, relatives, or their own economic resources from reported or unreported work. They may also face serious psychiatric problems. They do, in fact, conform to the image of the "multi-problem" family which many people have of the typical welfare client. But one must be cautious in attributing a hard-and-fast pattern to families in the welfare class. Their situations are actually heterogeneous, as a close reading of their case records will reveal, and some of them indicate a readiness to leave the welfare system, though, of course, they may have to come back on welfare at some future time.

Implications for welfare reform

At present, welfare seems to serve primarily as a way for society to cope with two of its problems—family disruption and labor market inadequacy. The dominant issues in welfare reform, therefore, should be those having to do with the life situations, needs, and incentives of the larger group of welfare recipients.

Since there is next to nothing that government policy can do to reduce the level of family disruption, a proper goal of family social policy would be to design income maintenance systems that smooth out the financial difficulties now accompanying marital breakup. Since as many as half of today's children will live at some time in a single-parent family, usually headed by the mother, a principal goal of welfare reform should be to provide security for that family, without at the same time discouraging mothers and other family members from pursuing work careers.

In the long run, however, a full-employment policy designed to provide more jobs and greater job security for both men and women is the key to solving welfare problems. It is likely that the effect of the so-called disincentives to work contained in present and proposed programs has been considerably exaggerated in discussions of welfare problems and welfare reform. If there were more opportunities for employment, there would be more incentive to work.

In light of these considerations, the principal goal of welfare reform should be to reduce the number of occasions when people going through the common crises of family breakup and unemployment require means-tested programs. A program of universal benefit for the working as well as the nonworking poor (for example, child allowances or tax credits), supplemented perhaps by the development of a new form of social insurance to diminish the economic risks for single heads of households, should go a long way toward reducing the number of people who use means-tested programs at all, and should also decrease the number of people who stay on welfare for even a moderate period of time.

17

CAN WELFARE REFORM ELIMINATE POVERTY?

Sheldon Danziger and Robert Plotnick

This paper describes the existing welfare system, outlines the problems with the system that have led to its being characterized as a "mess," and presents the principles on which President Carter's reform proposals were based. It then analyzes the level and trend in poverty since 1965 and the antipoverty effect of income maintenance programs in general and welfare programs in particular. The contradictions inherent in the goals of eliminating poverty and reforming welfare are discussed, and, in the final section, they are analyzed with reference to the Program for Better Jobs and Income. We conclude that if poverty is to be eliminated, there must be a greater emphasis on increasing the employment or social insurance income, rather than the welfare income, of the poor.

The elimination of income poverty has been an explicit objective of public policy since the early 1960s. In the past fifteen years numerous policies and programs designed to improve the economic welfare of our poorest citizens have been implemented. Partly as a result of this antipoverty effort, a rapid increase in the number of welfare beneficiaries and the value of available welfare benefits occurred. Although this growth in welfare led to a reduction in income poverty, a "welfare crisis" emerged. The dimensions of the crisis were perceived differently by politicians, taxpayers, and welfare recipients, but many became convinced that the existing welfare system needed reform.

In August 1977, President Carter announced the Program for Better Jobs and Income as his answer to the "welfare mess." An examination of this reform proposal illustrated a fundamental point: welfare reform is neither a necessary nor a sufficient condition for the elimination of poverty. Indeed, the elimination of poverty may require a mix of policies that violates some stated objectives of comprehensive welfare reform as generally outlined.

From Sheldon Danziger and Robert Plotnick, "Can Welfare Reform Eliminate Poverty?" 53(2) *Social Service Review* 244-260 (June 1979). Copyright 1978 by the University of Chicago.

The Welfare System and the Objectives of Welfare Reform

At present the welfare system is generally conceived as consisting principally of three income-tested programs: Aid to Families with Dependent Children (AFDC), with about 11.5 million recipients; Supplemental Security Income (SSI), with roughly 4.5 million recipients; and Food Stamps, with about 18 million recipients.[1] AFDC and SSI provide benefits in cash, while Food Stamps provides benefits in kind. These are the programs that most welfare reform plans intend to overhaul.

In addition, there exist a number of other welfare programs not directly affected by reform proposals: certain veterans' benefits and pensions, housing assistance programs, Basic Opportunity Grants for higher education, and others. Finally, there is Medicaid, the largest welfare program of all (currently about 25 million recipients), whose reform is usually addressed as part of the national health insurance debate.

These programs, plus the social insurance programs which condition benefits on previous employment and earnings experience, such as Old Age Survivors, Disability and Health Insurance, and Unemployment Compensation, provide substantial relief to the poor. In fiscal year 1977, $49 billion in public funds were spent on income-tested programs, and another $134 billion on social insurance. About two-thirds of the $49 billion of welfare expenditures were financed by the federal government. These programs have expanded rapidly since 1965, both in the number of recipients and in the average benefit per recipient. In 1965, $8.9 billion, or 1.3 percent of GNP, was spent on welfare programs; this had increased to $39.4 billion, or 2.8 percent of GNP, by 1974. These programs have successfully delivered their benefits to the poor: as of 1974, about 92 percent of AFDC benefits and about 83 percent of Food Stamp benefits were going to those who would have been poor in the absence of transfers.[2] Although the current system has been characterized as a "mess," and although President Carter stated that the welfare system is worse than he had expected, it has been successful in targeting increasing amounts of relief to an increasing number of poor beneficiaries.

Since the problems of the current welfare system have been evaluated and catalogued numerous times, this discussion will be very brief.[3] First, the existing welfare system is inequitable. It treats people who have similar needs differently. A single-parent family of four living in Mississippi was entitled to $3,071 in AFDC and food stamps in fiscal year 1978, while a similar family living in New York was eligible for $7,354.[4] In addition to the inequity itself, these geographic disparities apparently encourage migration from low-benefit to high-benefit states. Second, welfare treats differently people who have similar needs but live in different types of families. In any of the twenty-five states and Puerto Rico which do not have an AFDC program for unemployed parents (AFDC-U), a family with two parents but no earnings becomes eligible for AFDC benefits only if the father deserts the family. If the father stays with the family, it will be eligible only for food stamps and, in some jurisdictions, General Assistance.

Besides discouraging marital stability and encouraging migration, the current system discourages work. As labor income rises, benefits fall and the reward from working is diminished. Because some families participate in two or more of these programs at the same time, the total loss in benefits caused by an increase in earnings may almost completely offset that increase. In other cases, an individual's benefit is higher without work than with a job. And in some states a two-parent family of four receiving benefits from the AFDC-U program suffers a loss in income if the father goes from a part-time job to a full-time job. In taking the job and leaving the AFDC-U program, he may also lose Medicaid benefits.

Finally, each of the welfare programs has different operating rules. In a single household, one person may receive food stamps and AFDC benefits while another receives food stamps and SSI benefits. Since each program has different rules, different accounting periods, and different notions of the filing unit, administration is complex. AFDC is administered by the states, with federal sharing of payments, while SSI is a federal program with payments that the states can supplement. Because of these problems, the system is too complex for many of the poor to understand, so they may not receive benefits which they need and to which they are entitled.[5]

The administration's most recent welfare reform proposals were to be governed by a set of twelve principles set forth by President Carter in May 1977.[6] The principles emphasized the elimination of many of the problems enumerated above. They included holding welfare costs down, providing work incentives and access to employment and training, reducing incentives for family break-up by extending eligibility to all persons, and simplifying and improving welfare administration. Only one principle, the eighth, addressed the issue of poverty, and it did so indirectly: "A decent income should be provided also for those who cannot work or earn adequate income, with federal benefits consolidated into a simple cash payment." This welfare reform was to provide jobs, higher incomes, and rewards for work. As such, it did not attempt to eliminate poverty through a cash assistance (negative income tax) program.

Why was the goal of eliminating poverty absent from President Carter's statement of welfare reform principles? The answer arises from the inherent conflicts involved in providing work incentives and poverty-level income guarantees, while simultaneously holding down program costs. There are three important elements in any welfare program: the income guarantee provided to those with no income of their own, the rate at which this guarantee is reduced as earned income rises (the benefit-reduction rate), and the contemplated total costs of the program. These three elements are linked in such a way that the third results directly from the other two. For example, if the government chooses an income guarantee of $3,000 and a benefit-reduction rate of 50 percent, all households with incomes up to $6,000 will be eligible for program payments.[7] From this, we can derive the total cost of the program. If costs were higher than the amount budgeted, then to stay within budget limits the government would have to either restrict the guarantee, raise the benefit-reduction rate, or restrict eligibility. Raising the tax rate to 75 percent would lower the break-even level to $4,000 and reduce total costs. Or the government could lower the income guarantee to $2,000, retain the 50 percent benefit-reduction rate, and also reach a lower program cost with a $4,000 break-even level.

In general, the higher the income guarantee and the lower the benefit-reduction rate, the higher the program costs. Both higher guarantees and lower benefit-reduction rates alleviate poverty. Higher guarantees ensure higher incomes to those who do not work, but they increase costs and may discourage work effort. Higher benefit-reduction rates certainly discourage work. Lowering the rate promotes work effort, and the increased earnings help reduce poverty, but costs are higher than they would be with a higher benefit-reduction rate. Thus holding down costs and alleviating poverty are conflicting goals.

With this elementary background to the mechanics of welfare reform, we can anticipate why this attempt at welfare reform was not likely to eliminate poverty. Carter's first principle of May 1977 stated that the new system was to have "no higher initial cost than the present system." The next four related to access to jobs and training and the encouragement of work. These principles specified a holding down of both total program costs and benefit-reduction rates. Once those two elements had been chosen, the third, the income guarantee, was determined. In its current context, Carter's principles required an income guarantee that was below the poverty line and would not eliminate poverty for those who did not work. As will be shown below, income guarantees that are high enough to eliminate poverty would either increase program costs dramatically, or require a benefit-reduction rate so high that work would be discouraged.

The Trend in Poverty and the Antipoverty Effects of Income Maintenance Programs.

An analysis of the effect of welfare reform on poverty requires a review of the evidence on the trend in poverty and on the antipoverty effectiveness of existing welfare programs. While such a task seems straightforward, it is not. Consider two recent statements on the trend in poverty. In the first, Martin Anderson uses a definition of poverty which accepts the official government poverty lines and adds to the money income of the poor the cost of taxpayer-provided, in-kind transfers, like food stamps, Medicaid payments, and public housing. He asserts that "the 'war on poverty' that began in 1964 has been won. The growth of jobs and income in the private economy, combined with an explosive increase in government spending for welfare and income transfer programs, has virtually eliminated poverty in the United States."[8] Martin Rein, in contrast, focuses on inequality, a relative measure of poverty: "My argument is that social policies are by themselves unable adequately to offset the antiegalitarian forces in the economies of advanced industrial nations. Despite the enormous rise in public expenditures, specifically in transfer outlays . . . , a significant redistribution did not occur, as the share of income going to the bottom fifth remained stubbornly unchanged."[9]

Table 1 reveals the source of these conflicting conclusions. The incidence of poverty among persons is shown for three measures: the official measure, a relative measure, and the official measure after adjustments have been made for the receipt of in-kind transfers and for the underreporting of money income.[10] It is with reference to a measure like the adjusted official measure that Anderson concludes that there is no longer a poverty problem, that all that needs to be done has been done. Similarly, the constancy of relative poverty reinforced Rein's view that, with traditional welfare policies, nothing can be done. The official measure produces a result that lies within these two views. While poverty has declined significantly in the recent past, a serious poverty problem remains.

Table 1

THE INCIDENCE OF POSTTRANSFER POVERTY AMONG PERSONS

Year	Official Measure (%)	Relative Measure (%)	Official Measure, Adjusted (%)
1959	27.4	N.A.	N.A.
1965	15.6	15.6	N.A.
1968	12.8	14.6	10.1
1976	11.8	15.4	6.5

SOURCE. — Sheldon Danziger and Robert Plotnick, *Has the War on Income Poverty Been Won?* (New York: Academic Press, in press). The numbers in the tables are based on calculations by the authors from the 1966 Survey of Economic Opportunity and various March Current Population Surveys.
NOTE. — N.A. = not available.

Arguments about the relationship between welfare reform and poverty reduction can be made with reference to any of the series in table 1, but we have based our analysis on the official measure of poverty, for two reasons. First, data on this measure are readily available. For example, data on the effect of a suggested welfare reform plan on official poverty are published by the Department of Health, Education, and Welfare, while the effect on relative poverty is not. Second, the substance of the analysis is not changed by the use of the other series. If welfare reform cannot eliminate poverty according to the official definition, it certainly will be less successful according to a relative definition. Moreover, a major part of the analysis that follows is concerned with poverty that exists before the receipt of welfare income, so that many adjustments to the official measure become less relevant.

Even if one accepts the in-kind measure which shows the lowest aggregate incidence of poverty, one cannot ignore the disparities that exist among various groups in the population. When a disaggregated view of the incidence of poverty is taken, as in table 2, it is impossible to conclude that poverty has been eliminated for blacks or for women. The adjusted official measure, which guides Anderson's view, still shows that about one-third of persons living with black female family heads, about one in seven living with white female family heads, and one in ten living with black male heads are poor.

Table 2

INCIDENCE OF POSTTRANSFER POVERTY AMONG PERSONS BY CHARACTERISTICS OF HEAD OF HOUSEHOLD, 1974

Head of Household	Official Measure (%)	Relative Measure (%)	Official Measure, Adjusted (%)
White male	6.0	8.3	4.1
Nonwhite male	17.0	23.5	11.5
White female	27.2	34.3	13.9
Nonwhite female	54.6	64.1	30.2

SOURCE. — Danziger and Plotnick, *Has the War on Income Poverty Been Won?*

Table 3

ANTIPOVERTY EFFECTIVENESS OF GOVERNMENT TRANSFERS
(Using Official Measure of Poverty)

	% REMOVED FROM POVERTY BY			
CATEGORY	Pretransfer Income (1)	Social Insurance (2)	Welfare Programs (3)	Posttransfer Income (4)
All persons:				
1965	21.3	5.0	.7	15.6
1976	21.0	7.9	1.3	11.8
Households with head less than 65 years old:				
1965	16.6	1.9	.6	14.1
1976	15.6	3.4	.9	11.3

SOURCE. — Danziger and Plotnick, *Has the War on Income Poverty Been Won?*
NOTE. — Col. 4 = col. 1 − col. 2 − col. 3.

Because the data in tables 1 and 2 are based on posttransfer income, we cannot know whether the observed decline in poverty according to the official measure is due to greater success by the poor in the marketplace or greater reliance on government transfers. Table 3 shows poverty before all government transfers, the effect of social insurance transfers (Social Security, Unemployment Compensation, Workmen's Compensation) in column 2, and of welfare (AFDC, SSI, and General Assistance) in column 3. The table reveals that, although posttransfer poverty has declined, it has not done so because the programs of the War on Poverty provided "a hand up" so that the poor could earn their way out of poverty, but rather because government transfers increased. On the basis solely of market income, the incidence of poverty was 21 percent in both 1965 and 1976 for all persons and about 16 percent in both years for persons living in households where the head is not aged. Posttransfer poverty declined only because the size and the antipoverty effectiveness of both social insurance programs and welfare programs increased. By 1976, 9.2 percent of all persons whose pretransfer income was below the poverty line were removed from poverty by government transfers. Social insurance programs were six times as effective in eliminating poverty as were welfare programs for all persons, and four times as effective for the nonaged. The table reinforces the obvious: the volume of earnings in the economy is vastly larger than the volume of social insurance transfers, while the volume of social insurance transfers is vastly larger than the volume of welfare transfers.[11]

Changes in the level of prewelfare poverty are of particular interest in any discussion of welfare reform, since it is to the prewelfare poor that welfare programs are targeted. In addition, many people view the "real" poverty problem as centering upon the prewelfare poor. Those who are taken out of poverty by social insurance benefits, by their own market incomes, or by both are viewed as having taken themselves out of poverty. At the same time, taking those who remain poor out of poverty by welfare is judged an unsatisfactory, second-best solution to the poverty problem.

In 1965 about 16 percent of all persons were prewelfare poor (from table 3). Largely in response to a strong labor market, but also owing to increased social insurance transfers, prewelfare poverty fell to 13.6 percent by 1968 and then declined to 13.1 percent in 1976.

Posttransfer poverty remains because the poor do not receive enough market income in the first place, and not enough in transfer income in the second place, to remove them from poverty. The fact that some do not receive the transfers to which they are entitled is part of the problem, although by 1976, 80 percent of the pretransfer poor received a government cash transfer (if in-kind transfers are considered, this figure rises to about 90 percent). The income maintenance system reaches the poor, but it does not provide them with enough income to escape from poverty.

A comparison of the average size of welfare and social insurance payments emphasizes the insufficiency of welfare and reveals why so many more persons are removed from poverty by social insurance than by welfare. Table 4 shows that fewer households receive welfare than receive social security or other social insurance transfers, and that the average welfare payment is smaller than the average for these other transfers. The existing transfer system is so broad that 42 percent of all households received some form of cash transfer, which averaged $2,803 in 1974 (when the mean household income from nontransfer sources was about $11,000).

Table 4

AVERAGE SIZE OF CASH TRANSFERS, 1974

Program	% of Households Receiving Transfers	Mean Transfer ($)
Social Security and railroad retirement	25.6	2,686
Other social insurance[a]	17.3	2,024
Welfare[b]	8.1	1,701
Any transfer	42.0[c]	2,803[c]

SOURCE. — Danziger and Plotnick, *Has the War on Poverty Been Won?*
[a]Includes income from Unemployment Compensation, Workmen's Compensation, government employee pensions, veterans' pensions and compensation.
[b]Includes income from AFDC, SSI, and General Assistance.
[c]The mean transfer for all transfers is higher than the mean for any category, and the percentage of households receiving transfer income sums to more than 42% because many households receive multiple transfers.

Particularly important in any discussion of welfare reform is the situation of female family heads. They are the group at the center both of the "welfare mess" and the poverty problem. In 1974, about one-third of all females between the ages of twenty-five and fifty-four who headed families that included children received welfare income that averaged $2,379, while their own earnings averaged $1,110. Despite this aid, 69 percent remained poor.

The data in the tables explain how we could "be doing better, but feeling worse" about the poverty and welfare problems.[12] Increases in social insurance transfers and welfare transfers since the War on Poverty have produced a decline in the incidence of posttransfer poverty—we are doing better. Yet the reduction in poverty did not come about because more households earned their way out of poverty. Pretransfer poverty did not decline between 1965 and 1976. More people received higher government transfers, which increased the welfare rolls and produced the "welfare crisis" at the same time as they reduced poverty. Since our society places such a high value on self-reliance and work, the fact that so many people remain poor before transfers and that so many receive welfare makes us feel worse.

To the conflict among welfare reform goals cited above, we must add the conflict between the goals of reducing the welfare rolls and eliminating poverty. The contradiction arises because we have not reduced the pretransfer poverty count. That count cannot be reduced by welfare; it can only be reduced by programs that provide work incentives or job opportunities for the poor. Thus the neglect of poverty and the emphasis on work incentives and controlling welfare costs in Carter's statement of principles are indications that we are approaching the limits of our tolerance for the current transfer system. While a few years ago policy seemed to be moving toward a universal income guarantee that would eliminate poverty for all citizens, we are now moving toward a two-track system that distinguishes between those expected and those not expected to work. Only by a plan that eliminates poverty through work can we both "do better and feel better." It is from this viewpoint that we review the recent welfare reform proposal.

The Program for Better Jobs and Income

The Program for Better Jobs and Income (PBJI) would have consolidated three major components of the current welfare system and provided, like Nixon's Family Assistance Plan, a nationwide minimum federal cash payment for all the poor.[13] It also pledged to provide as an integral part of the welfare system a public service job for some of those able and expected to work. Earnings, welfare, manpower policy, and taxes would have been interrelated through an expanded earned-income tax credit and a new, nationally uniform system of basic income-support payments.

Compared with the current system, large gains were claimed for PBJI: (*a*) Welfare would have been integrated with earnings and both coupled with the tax system; (*b*) consolidation would have streamlined administration; (*c*) work would have always paid more than welfare; (*d*) family stability would have been enhanced by allowing married couples with children to benefit in the same manner and to the same extent as single-parent families; (*e*) the relatively high national minimum payment would have reduced incentives for migration from low- to high-benefit states; (*f*) states and localities would have received fiscal relief.

Several important attributes of the Carter plan were already present in the current system. As did the proposal, food stamp benefits have depended on the amount of earnings and other income of the family, on family size, and on willingness to work. Similarly, the SSI program, in effect since 1974, has rules of operation and a uniform national minimum payment much like those of the income-support provisions of the Carter proposal. The earned income credit, an important component of the President's proposal, is already in place.

The details of the Carter Program for Better Jobs and Income can best be understood by focusing seriatim on its four major components: job opportunities, the work-benefit and income-support provisions for those expected to work, income-support payments for those not expected to work, and tax reductions through the earned-income tax credit.

Job opportunities. — First, $8.8 billion would have been set aside to create up to 1.4 million public sevice jobs for adult workers with children who could not find a private job. Most of these jobs would have paid the minimum wage, $2.65 now, and about $3.30 in 1980 when the program was to begin. Those eligible for the jobs would have been adults—one per family—who would have been placed in the "expected to work" category if they were unable to find a regular private or public sector job.

In determining which families have an adult who is expected to work, there would obviously have been administrative discretion. But one member of all families would have been expected to work unless all the adults in the family fell into one or another of the following categories: aged, blind, disabled, or mothers without husbands (and fathers without wives) whose youngest child was less than seven years old. Mothers without husbands (or fathers without wives) whose youngest child was between seven and fourteen years would have been expected to work part-time, while such parents whose youngest child was over fourteen would have been expected to work full time. Because earnings from employment in a private job would have been accompanied by a subsidy—the earned-income tax credit (EITC)—in addition to the work benefit, a worker would always have found a private job more lucrative than a public one, and thus would have had an incentive to use the public service jobs only as a last resort.

Work benefit and income support for those expected to work. — Earnings of low-wage workers would also have been supplemented by the cash support system. Unlike the benefits from the EITC, however, the cash support system would have added to the income of those in the special public jobs as well as all other jobholders. The size of the cash supplement would have depended upon earnings, other income, and family size. Cash supplements for a four-person family would have started at $2,300 if a family had a member expected to work, and remained at that level as long as earnings were less than $3,800. The cash supplement would have declined by 50 cents for every dollar of earnings in excess of $3,800, becoming zero at $8,400. In addition, the family with regular earnings would have received benefits from the EITC to supplement both earnings and income-support benefits.

Income support for those not expected to work. — For a family of four in which no one was expected to work, a basic income-support payment of $4,200 would have been granted. Thus, the maximum support payment for a family not expected to work would have exceeded by $1,900 that for a family expected to work. For this group, benefits would have fallen by 50 cents for every additional $1 of earnings right from the first dollar earned—there would have been no $3,800 "disregard" as would have been the case for those expected to work. The not-expected-to-work group would have included most of the current AFDC recipients and all SSI recipients, and for many of them benefits would have increased under the proposed program.

Tax reduction. — The final component of the plan was tax reduction. Since 1975, we have had a tax credit for low-earnings families with children—the earned-income tax credit. The EITC supplements regular earnings by 10 cents for each additional dollar earned up to earnings of $4,000, and then reduces the credit by 10 cents for each dollar earned after $4,000 (until the credit is reduced to zero). Under the proposed program, benefits from this credit would have been increased for all families with regular earnings (that is, earnings for jobs other than the special public jobs) of more than $4,000 but less than $15,620. Indeed, all families earning between $8,000 and $15,620 would have received a benefit for which they are not now eligible. More than half of all families would have paid lower taxes because of the increased earned-income tax credit.

Under the Carter plan, the income guarantee for a family of four in which the head was not expected to work, $4,200, was about 65 percent of the poverty line for such a family. Only for the aged, blind, or disabled would the cash assistance payment have reached the poverty line when no household member was employed. Those who did not work (and were not aged, blind, or disabled), even if they were not expected to work, would have remained poor. In fact, many current welfare recipients would have suffered income losses if their states had not been required to "grandfather" their benefits for a three-year period. Under the plan, individuals who were newly enrolled in welfare and who did not work would receive PBJI benefits that were no more than half the poverty line and less than what they would have received under current policies.

Although many current recipients who do not work would not have benefited under the Carter plan, the extension of cash benefits to all persons would have increased the incomes of many who are currently ineligible for cash assistance—childless couples, unrelated individuals, and two-parent families in states without an AFDC program for unemployed parents. These persons are currently eligible only for food stamps, and possibly for unemployment insurance and general assistance. For example, a childless couple eligible for $636 in food stamps in 1978 would have been eligible, under the new plan, for $2,200 in cash assistance if neither member could find work. While this payment was only about half the relevant poverty line, it represented a tripling of available benefits. In general then, PBJI would have raised the incomes of the poor but would not have removed them from poverty unless they worked.

For those who worked, PBJI represented a significant departure from previous welfare policies. Because the program emphasized the provision of jobs and the supplementation of earnings, all those who worked at low wages, regardless of family composition or region of residence, would have had higher incomes and, in many cases, would have been taken out of income poverty. For example, the heads of families of four who work full-time, full-year at a minimum-wage job at present earn only 80 percent of the poverty line. From PBJI, however, they would have received a cash assistance payment and an earned-income tax credit, so that total family income would have exceeded the poverty line by about 15 percent. These two components of the Carter plan should have resulted in the elimination of poverty for those who worked full time as well as raised the take-home pay of many of those who were not officially in poverty but who worked at below-average wages. In fact, anyone who worked about three-fourths of the year at the minimum wage would have had his or her family income supplemented up to the poverty line.[14]

Our assertion that PBJI would have benefited mainly those who were aged, disabled, or working is validated by data presented by the Congressional Budget Office.[15] If PBJI had become law, poverty (in 1975) would have declined from 11.2 percent of all families to 9.0 percent, and the number of families in poverty would have been reduced from 8.3 million to 6.7 million. Almost half (47 percent) of the additional 1.6 million families taken out of poverty would have had aged or disabled heads; another 40 percent, a working head (28 percent full-time workers; 12 percent part-time).

PBJI would have provided a nationally uniform, minimum cash payment for all individuals. As such it would have become our first universal, cash guaranteed annual income. PBJI would have been an important change in our welfare system, but it would not have solved the poverty problem.

The constraints imposed by the presidential statement of welfare reform principles prevented poverty-line income guarantees from being proposed. PBJI could not even stay within Carter's first principle of holding costs to their current level. The Budget Office estimated that PBJI would have increased costs in 1982 by $14 billion and provided cash assistance for almost 30 million individuals. To raise the benefit structure to the poverty line would have added an additional $43 billion and an additional 20 million recipients.[16]

PBJI would have reformed welfare, but it would not have eliminated poverty. To do so, given an economy in which one-fifth of all persons live in households with pretransfer incomes below the poverty line, would have required an expansion in welfare beyond the bounds of political feasibility. If poverty-line guarantees are not politically acceptable (except for the aged, blind, and disabled), then a two-track approach, which distinguishes between those expected and those not expected to work, represents an attractive alternative. The provision of special public service jobs and the expanded supplementation of wages would refocus the approach to the poverty problem. Having the federal government accept responsibility for providing jobs and supplementing low wages would shift the onus of poverty from the unemployed and the working poor to the malfunctioning of the labor market. PBJI's emphasis differed significantly from that of the antipoverty programs of the 1960s that focused on the deficiencies of individuals and attempted to change the personal attributes of the poor. PBJI would not have changed the poor, but it would have provided jobs, cash assistance, or both.

Critics attacked the program's distinction between those expected and those not expected to work as an outdated poor-law distinction between the deserving and undeserving poor. According to this view, PBJI represented a repressive tightening of the rolls and an attempt to coerce individuals from the welfare rolls onto the work rolls. Some of these same critics, however, argued that the work motivation of the poor does not differ from that of the rest of society—that the poor want to work. These two views are inconsistent. For if the poor want to work, then a welfare program which requires work is not punitive as long as it accepts the responsibility for providing work opportunities.

PBJI would have done just that. If the poor want to work—and there is no evidence to the contrary—then the provision of jobs should improve their economic position. If unemployed family heads want to work, but cannot find a regular private- or public-sector job, they must either be offered a special public service job or paid the cash assistance benefit that would accrue to similar families in which the heads were not expected to work.[17] Although the jobs under PBJI would have paid only the minimum wage, when combined with the cash assistance payment they would have provided incomes that exceeded the poverty line.

In addition, under PBJI, a family would not have been denied aid even if the head refused to work. Consider two-parent families with two children, in which the heads are expected to work. but refuse to search or to accept a public job offer. The cash assistance payment for the families, $2,300, still exceeds the benefits that such families could expect under the existing system. If the heads of these families refuse to search for work, the families are currently excluded from all benefits—including food stamps and Unemployment Compensation.

PBJI would have raised income but would not have eliminated poverty for those who did not work, would have significantly reduced poverty for those who worked a substantial part of the year, and would have provided a work opportunity yielding an income above the poverty line to family heads who could not find a regular job.

The elimination of poverty is a goal that could be achieved only at the expense of Carter's first principle of welfare reform—holding down costs. The two most direct ways to expand PBJI from a welfare reform proposal to an antipoverty one as well would have been to raise income guarantees to the poverty line for those not expected to work and to provide a public job to all those who wanted one (i.e., to remove the cap on the number of jobs and their restriction to heads of household with children).[18] The first change might reduce work—if those not expected to work would have taken jobs under PBJI in response to their below-poverty-line guarantee. But the second would have increased work, and probably by a larger amount, so that poverty reduction and the encouragement of work would not have been in conflict.

If the program cost could not be increased, then this welfare reform could not eliminate poverty. Even if we could eliminate poverty through welfare, we would still have achieved only a second-best solution. Beneficiaries would clearly be better off, but pre-welfare poverty would have remained (although posttransfer poverty had been eliminated). Successful welfare reform could mitigate many of the defects of the current system, but could not end economic dependence on welfare.

We have argued that PBJI could not have eliminated poverty because poverty-line guarantees exceeded its cost constraint, and that even if this constraint were removed, a welfare problem would remain. This suggests that it is time to focus more carefully on two other means of reducing poverty—changes in the economy and the labor market that currently generate unacceptably high levels of pretransfer poverty, and an expansion of the social insurance system to cushion a greater variety of income losses.[19]

Notes

This research was supported by funds granted to the Institute for Research on Poverty at the University of Wisconsin—Madison by the Department of Health, Education, and Welfare pursuant to the Economic Opportunity Act of 1964. The authors wish to thank Jeannie Nakano for valuable assistance. Irwin Garfinkel, Robert Haveman, Robert Lampman, Eugene Smolensky, and Michael Taussig provided valuable comments on an earlier draft. An earlier version was presented at the 1978 meetings of the American Sociological Association.

1. This section draws heavily from Sheldon Danziger, Robert Haveman, and Eugene Smolensky, prepared for the U.S. Congress, Joint Economic Committee, *The Program for Better Jobs and Income—a Guide and a Critique* (Washington, D.C.: Government Printing Office, 1977).

2. Sheldon Danziger and Robert Plotnick, *Has the War on Income Poverty Been Won?* (New York: Academic Press, in press).

3. See, for example, Michael Barth, George Carcagno, and John Palmer, *Toward an Effective Income Support System: Problems, Prospects, Choices* (Madison: Institute for Research on Poverty, 1974); and U.S. Congress, Joint Economic Committee, *Studies in Public Welfare* (Washington, D.C.: Government Printing Office, 1974-76).

4. U.S. Congress, Congressional Budget Office, *The Administration's Welfare Reform Proposal* (Washington, D.C.: Government Printing Office, 1978), pp. 150-51.

5. Estimates of the percentage of eligible persons who do participate range from only about 50 percent for Food Stamps and SSI to about 90 percent for AFDC.

6. "Text of Carter Welfare Remarks," *New York Times* (May 3, 1977).

7. The level up to which benefits are paid, the break-even level of the program, can be found by dividing the income guarantee by the benefit reduction rate when the benefit reduction rate is constant. There are more complex plans in which the benefit reduction rate varies and in which some initial earnings are not subject to the benefit reduction rate.

8. Martin Anderson, *Welfare* (Stanford, Calif.: Hoover Institution Press, 1978), p. 15.

9. Martin Rein, "Equality and Social Policy," *Social Service Review* 51 (1977): 569.

10. The "incidence of poverty" among a specific group of persons is the percentage of persons in that group with incomes below the poverty line. For example, in 1975 there were 17.8 million poor white persons out of a total white population of 183.5 million. The incidence of poverty among whites was, therefore, 17.8/183.5 = .097, or 9.7 percent. Both the official measure and the adjusted measure use the Social Security Administration poverty lines. They differ only in what is included as income. For a complete discussion of these issues, see Danziger and Plotnick, chap. 1.

11. If in-kind transfers are counted as income, the antipoverty effectiveness of welfare programs would increase. However, it would still fall short of the effect of social insurance transfers; see Robert Plotnick, "Income Tested Transfers and Poverty Reduction," mimeographed (Madison: Institute for Research on Poverty, August 1978).

12. This phrase was coined by Aaron Wildavsky with respect to health policy; see "Doing Better and Feeling Worse: The Political Pathology of Health Policy," *Daedalus* 106, no. 1 (Winter 1977): 105-24.

13. We discuss the specifics of PBJI—which may now be considered defunct—because it is an example of the evolution toward a welfare system that emphasizes work incentives over poverty reductions. The title itself was indicative of this concern.

14. This would have been true only for families with children. Families with children would have been eligible for the earned income-tax credit and for the exemption of the first $3,800 of earnings from the benefit reduction rate. Without these two provisions, unrelated individuals or childless couples who did not work full time might still have received incomes below the poverty line.

15. Robert D. Reischauer, "Testimony to Task Force on Distributive Impacts of Budget and Economic Policy," mimeographed (Washington: U.S. Congress, Congressional Budget Office, October 13, 1977), p. 18, table 4(a). These estimates assumed that states would have chosen to supplement the PBJI benefits up to their current cash assistance and food stamp benefit levels.

16. U.S. Congress, Congressional Budget Office.

17. The program, for budgetary reasons, did not provide a job for anyone who wanted one. Rather it set a specific number of jobs and targeted them only to households with children. To make PBJI an antipoverty program, it would have to have been expanded to provide a job to anyone seeking one, but this would have increased the demand for jobs to about 6.5 million and program costs by $37 billion. See Robert Haveman and Eugene Smolensky, for U.S. Congress, Joint Economic Committee, *The Program for Better Jobs and Income: An Analysis of Costs and Distributional Effects* (Washington, D.C.: Government Printing Office, 1978).

18. Although the tone of this discussion has been optimistic, the difficulties of actually administering a two-track system or of providing special public jobs should not be minimized. Some of the difficulties are reviewed in Haveman and Smolensky and in U.S. Congress, Congressional Budget Office.

19. For example, in addition to providing for the income losses due to retirement, death and disability, social insurance could provide for income losses due to family disruption.

18

THE ANTIPOVERTY EFFECTIVENESS
OF IN-KIND TRANSFERS

Timothy M. Smeeding

ABSTRACT

In recording its poverty statistics, the U.S. Census Bureau ignores the impact of in-kind transfers on the extent of poverty. In this paper, we estimate that when in-kind food, housing, and medical care transfers are counted and measured at their cash-equivalent value, and when Census income is adjusted for underreporting, federal taxes, and intrahousehold income-sharing, the 1972 poverty count and the poverty gap are halved. In addition, we find that in-kind transfers are relatively inefficient devices for reducing income poverty, delivering only about 31 cents of antipoverty effect per dollar of program cost.

This paper estimates the effect of noncash transfer payments in the form of food, housing, and medical care on the extent of income poverty in the United States in 1972.[1] Despite their importance as a source of consumption for low-income households, in-kind transfers are not counted as income and, hence, do not contribute to poverty reduction.[2] Yet, noncash transfer payments in the form of food, housing, and medical care totaled $16.4 billion in 1972.[3] According to the Department of Health, Education, and Welfare [29], in-kind

---

The author is Assistant Professor of Economics, University of Utah.

* This investigation was supported in part by Grant No. 57811 from the Social Security Administration, U.S. Department of Health, Education, and Welfare, and has benefited from the comments of Robert Haveman, Edgar Browning, and the editor. [Manuscript received August 1976; accepted February 1977.]

1 A recent effort by Browning [4] examines the same question, though his approach and results differ from those presented here. Earlier efforts dealing with the effect of in-kind transfers on the poor in particular, and income distribution in general, include Morgan and others [15] and Reynolds and Smolensky [19].

2 See, for instance, [26].

3 See [24], pp. 13-15. We do not consider individual household benefits received in the form of educational subsidies for at least two reasons. First, the current value of an education transfer to the household is most difficult to measure. Whereas the present discounted value of the increase in expected future earnings may provide some esti-

transfers benefiting the poor exceeded cash transfers to this same group in 1972. Moreover, in-kind transfers to the poor have been growing rapidly relative to cash transfers. In 1964, in-kind benefits to the poor were less than one-quarter as large as cash-transfer benefits to poor people. During fiscal 1977, Minarik and Palmer [14] report that means-tested in-kind transfers ($21.6 billion) will be 80 percent greater than means-tested cash transfers ($12.2 billion). Hence, because of both their volume and their rapid growth,[4] the omission of in-kind transfers seriously biases existing estimates of the incidence of income poverty and how this incidence has changed in recent years.

In order to estimate the extent to which noncash transfers provide economic welfare to low-income individuals, several adjustments are necessary. The first section of this paper briefly summarizes some preliminary adjustments made to the March 1973 Current Population Survey (CPS) data tapes and their effect on the povery count and poverty gap in 1972.[5] In the second section, and more thoroughly in the Appendix, a description of the procedure employed in simulating noncash transfer benefits to survey households is given. Because the value of a noncash transfer to a recipient may differ from its market value depending on the form in which the transfer is received, each household's willingness to pay for noncash transfers must be estimated. A model for determining this cash equivalent is also presented in Section II. In the third section, the effect of noncash transfers on the income poverty gap is measured. Next, the effect of noncash transfers on the incidence and composition of income poverty is explored. Official government poverty statistics are com-

---

mate of the worth of education to the individual, there is clearly no superior way to count the current value of these benefits to the household. Second, the inclusion of this type of transfer payment would almost necessarily require some adjustment in the government poverty income threshold since educational benefits were not allowed for in determining this consumption constraint. An additional $11.3 billion in noncash benefits, primarily medical benefits extended to veterans and disabled workers, social services provided by state and local welfare agencies, and free or subsidized school lunches, are not counted here. Once these figures are adjusted to eliminate groups not counted by the CPS (e.g., the institutionalized and the military) and items not directly relevant to income poverty determination (e.g., social services), only about $5.8 billion remains, primarily concentrated among veterans and disabled workers—two groups which are not heavily represented in the poverty population. Hence, it seems that the uncounted in-kind benefits should have relatively little effect on the figures presented here.

4 One explanation of this rapid increase, suggested by Lampman [13], is that in-kind transfers may be the most politically feasible form in which to transfer income. For instance, Lampman sees food stamps as an "in-kind negative income tax," compromising the paternalistic preferences of political conservatives with the desires of political liberals for a federally administered cash income support system.

5 A detailed discussion of the data adjustments in the first two sections is beyond the scope of this paper. Interested readers are referred to Smeeding [21] for a more complete description of these procedures.

pared to estimates based on the adjusted income measure[6] which includes noncash transfers. We summarize the results and their policy implications in Section V.

I. PRELIMINARY DATA ADJUSTMENTS

From data collected in the CPS, the U.S. Bureau of the Census publishes annual estimates of the depth (poverty gap) and extent (poverty incidence and composition) of poverty. While these are official figures used by all government agencies in planning future programs and gauging the effects of current programs, they have several weaknesses.

One important shortcoming is the underreporting of money income in the CPS. In 1972, the CPS captured only about 90 percent of total cash personal income. Moreover, the extent of underreporting varies significantly among types of income. For instance, total reported cash public-assistance income, an important source of income for low-income households, was only 74 percent of aggregate disbursements of government agencies.[7] In assessing the economic welfare of low-income households, underreporting leads to an exaggerated estimate of income poverty. To correct this source of bias, reported CPS cash-income flows were adjusted for underreporting and nonreporting, employing a procedure adapted from the transfer income model of the Urban Institute.[8] These adjustments reduce the poverty gap by $2.7 billion and the number of poor households (that is, families plus unrelated individuals) by about 2.1 million.

While income underreporting produces an upward bias in the poverty count,

---

6 It should be noted that while the income measure used in this paper is a significant improvement on the Census income concept, it should not be taken as a comprehensive measure of economic well-being. Rather, we focus on basic money-income components of a poverty income threshold. For a good beginning at developing a measure of comprehensive income, including the value of leisure and other nonmarket income components, see Sirageldin [20] and Morgan and Smith [16].

7 The preceding figures on income underreporting were taken from [26], p. 149. Benchmark totals are derived by the Bureau of Economic Analysis from administrative records that have been adjusted to eliminate population groups (institutionalized persons, military personnel living on base, etc.) not covered by the CPS.

8 See Beebout and Bonina [1] for more information on the Urban Institute model. See Smeeding [21], Ch. 2 and App. 2, for a complete description of the methodology employed here. In brief, this adjustment model deals with both underreporting (i.e., an inadequate total dollar amount as compared with the adjusted bench-mark total) and nonreporting (i.e., an inadequate number of recipients as compared to recipient control counts). The key assumption is one of proportional underreporting of income, given the correct number of recipients for each income type.

the absence of information in the CPS on federal income and payroll taxes paid causes a downward bias in the poverty count—assuming that disposable income is the appropriate concept for judging income adequacy. Although the CPS income definition used to determine poverty status includes social security and other cash transfers, it makes no allowance for taxes paid. To correct for this shortcoming, a tax simulation model was developed to estimate federal personal income taxes paid by individual earners.[9] This adjustment increased the poverty income gap by $1.3 billion, and added .65 million additional households to the poverty category.

A further weakness concerns the accounting units employed by the Census in measuring poverty. While the Census Bureau treats families and unrelated individuals (one-person families) separately for purposes of poverty determination, this analysis will utilize the household unit.[10] By treating unrelated persons and families as separate economic entities even if two or more units share living arrangements, the Census disregards any intrahousehold income-sharing among these persons. While it is impossible to measure accurately the actual degree of income- and resource-sharing that occurs in such coupled units, it seems more appropriate to regard individuals sharing living arrangements as a single resource-sharing unit—a household—in estimating the minimum consumption level of individuals in the unit. The realignment of living units into households reduced the 1972 official poverty count of 9.96 million families and unrelated individuals to 8.74 million households.

The combined effects of these three adjustments are shown in Table 1. Altogether they reduce the official poverty count, and the official poverty gap, by over 25 percent.

II. ALLOCATING AND VALUING NONCASH TRANSFERS

Because of their magnitude and their rapid expansion, the omission of in-kind transfers is the most serious problem with Census estimates of the poverty population and how this population has changed in recent years. In response to this

---

9   For a complete description of the federal tax determination model, see Smeeding [21], App. 6. Tax-filing rules were selected so as to minimize federal income tax liability for each tax-filing unit. Estimated tax liability by income level corresponds closely with Internal Revenue Service estimates at adjusted gross income levels of $12,000 and below.

10 In the CPS, a family is defined as all members of a unit related by blood, marriage, or adoption, while Census households are all people sharing the same living facilities. Household and family (or household and unrelated individual for a one-person household) are equivalent terms for more than 95 percent of all Census units. For an analysis of this same accounting difference in the United Kingdom, see Fiegehen and Lansley [8]. In addition to the household figures, summary statistics will also be presented for the number of poor persons.

TABLE 1

	1972 Poverty Counts in Millions of		1972 Poverty Gap in Billions of Dollars
Basis of Estimate	Units	Persons	
Official Census figures[a]	9.96	24.455	$12.03
CPS cash income adjusted for under-reporting, taxes paid, and intra-household income-sharing[b]	7.29	18.805	8.89
Difference	2.67	5.650	3.14
Percentage difference	−26.8%	−23.1%	−26.1%

a   Figures are taken from U.S. Department of Commerce, Bureau of the Census [26], Tables 1, 5, 6. Census units are in terms of families plus unrelated individuals. See fn. 22.

b   See Smeeding [21], Table 6-6, p. 215, and Table 8-6, p. 286.

omission, in-kind transfers were allocated to households on a unit-for-unit basis according to specific eligibility rules, benefit schedules, aggregate program budget totals, and recipient counts. Computer simulations were carefully adjusted to match bench marks based on administrative agency data. While error in estimating the benefits received by any particular household may occur, a reliable estimate of the antipoverty effectiveness of health, food, and housing transfer programs will be obtained. The imputation procedures for each of these transfer programs are briefly summarized in the Appendix.

Because the monetary costs of in-kind programs fail to measure accurately the contribution of benefits to economic welfare, the value of benefits received by any given household must be adjusted.[11] This value is defined as the amount of cash income needed to induce families to forgo a particular in-kind benefit, and is referred to as the "cash equivalent" of the benefit.

It is a well-known proposition in economics that, except in special cases, an in-kind transfer is relatively less effective than a cash transfer of equivalent cost in increasing the economic welfare of recipients. While the sign of the adjustment necessary to transform the value of in-kind transfers into the increment of recipient economic welfare is known, the magnitude of the adjustment is difficult to ascertain. Because this magnitude depends upon the elasticity of substi-

---

11   It may be argued that because none of the transfers treated in this paper is of the "lump-sum" variety, even cash transfers are worth less than their market value to recipients. In addition, we take no account of donor benefits accruing to transferors (net taxpayers). For a discussion of this phenomenon, see Smolensky and others [23] and Reynolds and Smolensky [19].

tution between the subsidized commodity and nonsubsidized commodities, the shape of the recipients' indifference map determines this magnitude. In the absence of reliable estimates of these relevant elasticities,[12] an alternative procedure was followed in this study.

First, it was assumed that a hypothetical household comparable to the recipient unit in terms of cash income, age structure, and family size is awarded a cash transfer equal to the market value of the in-kind transfer. Then the budget share devoted to the in-kind commodity by this comparable household with its additional income is estimated using data on consumption patterns according to family size and money-income level as compiled by the 1960–61 Bureau of Labor Statistics *Survey of Consumer Expenditures* [32] , price adjusted to 1972. This budget share served as an estimate of the cash value of the transfer to the actual recipient household. If the amount that the comparable household receiving the cash transfer would have spent on the subsidized good exceeded the market value of the in-kind transfer, the cash equivalent and the market value were considered equal. In this case, the household receiving the noncash transfer was presumed to be indifferent between the noncash transfer and an equivalent cash grant. On the other hand, if the market value of the in-kind transfer exceeded the amount that the comparable family would have voluntarily spent on the subsidized good, the value of the subsidy is reduced by the difference between these two amounts. Since this procedure implicitly assigns zero value to subsidies that exceed the amount the hypothetical family would have spent on the subsidized good (if presented an equal cash payment), while this value is probably greater than zero, the cash equivalents estimated herein may be treated as lower-bound estimates of the true cash value of in-kind subsidies.

On the average, the estimated cash-equivalent values for food, housing, and medical care are 88, 56, and 68 percent of their market value, respectively. Table 2 shows the cash-equivalent values by income class. In addition, efficiency ratios (the ratio of the cash equivalent to the market value) for each type of transfer are shown for 1972. The table indicates that as income rises, the commodities become better substitutes for cash—that is, their average cash equivalent rises with household cash income. Hence, noncash transfers are least valuable to low-income units. In the case of food stamps, the cash-equivalent value approaches the subsidy cost at fairly low income levels. In the case of medical care, the

---

12   At least three recent studies have attempted to estimate the cash-equivalent value of in-kind benefits to the household. Smolensky and others [23] is probably the best and most comprehensive treatment of this issue. Also Kraft and Olsen [10] and Clarkson [7] deal with estimating the cash equivalents of public housing and food stamps, respectively. Smolensky and others [23] directly utilize formal utility functions and then separately select elasticities of substitution (σ) between the subsidized good and other goods. Kraft-Olsen [10] utilize a Cobb-Douglas utility function where $\sigma = 1$. As distinct from these approaches, the model used here implicitly determines the value of σ. For further information, see Smeeding [21], pp. 103–40 and App. 7.

TABLE 2
AVERAGE FOOD, MEDICAL, AND HOUSING CASH EQUIVALENTS AT VARIOUS LEVELS OF DISPOSABLE PERSONAL INCOME IN 1972

Level of Household Disposable Personal Income Per Capita[a] (000s)	Food Stamps		Medicare, SMI, Medicaid		Public Housing	
	Average Cash Equivalent	Efficiency Ratio[b]	Average Cash Equivalent	Efficiency Ratio[b]	Average Cash Equivalent	Efficiency Ratio[b]
$0-.999	$481	.73	$373	.58	$621	.68
1.0-1.999	295	.86	468	.54	683	.74
2.0-2.999	261	.88	393	.59	666	.65
3.0-3.999	316	.89	335	.64	605	.57
4.0-4.999	310	.90	326	.67	554	.56
5.0-5.999	309	.93	328	.69	395	.52
6.0-7.499	325	.95	336	.70	344	.45
7.5-9.999	323	1.00	339	.77	275	.35
10.0+	375	1.00	317	.85	214	.26
Aggregate cash equivalent value in billions, and overall average efficiency ratio[c]	$1.692	.88	$8.828	.68	$.854	.56

a Cash income as reported in the *Current Population Survey* after adjusting for federal payroll and personal income taxes and income under-reporting.

b The efficiency ratio is the average cash equivalent divided by the average market value of each type of transfer.

c The overall average efficiency ratio equals the total market value of each subsidy divided by the total cash equivalent value of that subsidy.

values rise slowly, indicating a relatively low income elasticity of medical-care consumption.[13]

III. THE ANTIPOVERTY EFFECTIVENESS OF NONCASH TRANSFER PROGRAMS: TARGET-EFFICIENCY

The antipoverty effectiveness of transfer programs can be gauged by several criteria. The target efficiency with which in-kind programs reach the poor is one such criterion. In this study, two target-efficiency ratios will be presented for each of the in-kind transfer programs. They are described in Table 3. In each case, benefits from in-kind programs are measured at their cash equivalent value to the recipient household.

The first target-efficiency measure is the income-efficiency ratio (V) defined as the value of program benefits accruing to the post-cash-transfer poor as a percentage of total benefits received. By the adjusted poverty measure described above, there are approximately 7.3 million post-cash-transfer poor households, with an aggregate poverty gap of $8.9 billion.[14] Using this measure, only 35.3 percent of all noncash benefits were target-efficient. While more than 60 percent

---

13   In the case of public-housing subsidies, the efficiency ratio first rises and then falls at higher income levels. This result is due to the peculiar form of most in-kind housing transfers which, in effect, offer a "take it or leave it" choice to prospective public-housing tenants. Recipients may either accept the transfer by living in a specific public-housing unit or they do not participate in the program. In fact, only if our comparable household with a hypothetical cash transfer were willing to consume exactly the same amount of "housing" which is provided by the public-housing unit, would the cash equivalent and the market value be equal. In estimating cash equivalents for public-housing programs, 34.1 percent of all Low Rent Public Housing and "Section 236" public-housing recipients—408,000 household units—would have consumed *more* housing than was provided by their public-housing unit if presented with an equal cash payment. The form of the subsidy discouraged the consumption of extra housing for these beneficiaries. In this case, the value of the subsidy to the household is reduced by the difference between the desired consumption share of our comparable household and the market value of the housing subsidy. One interpretation of this phenomenon (see Smolensky and Gomery [22] and Smeeding [21], p. 124) is that the average taxpayer desires not only that transfer recipients consume housing per se, but also that their residence be confined to the particular physical location of the housing unit.

14   While V could be estimated using the pre-cash-transfer poor as the target, this procedure would fail to recognize that most in-kind transfer benefits (in fact, all except Medicare) are conditioned by the receipt of cash transfers as well as earned and property income. In effect, due to this conditioning process, in-kind transfers will be considered marginal income and, hence, the benefit incidence of all other transfer programs will be first accounted for. Garfinkel and Haveman [9] follow this approach in estimating target efficiency. However, several previous poverty studies evaluated *all* transfers on the basis of the poverty count and poverty gap *before* any income transfers. For instances, see Plotnick and Skidmore [18], Lampman [11, 12], Bridges [3], Okner [17], and Browning [4].

TABLE 3
COMPARABLE TARGET EFFICIENCY RATIOS
FOR NONCASH TRANSFERS IN 1972

Type of Noncash Transfer	Income-Efficiency Ratio V	Poverty-Gap Efficiency Ratio P
Medical care[a]	27.4%	24.9%
Food stamps	61.6	56.8
Public housing[b]	65.1	44.1
All noncash transfers[c]	35.3	31.1

Note: The income-efficiency ratio (V) is the percentage of total dollar benefits received by pretransfer poor. The poverty-gap-efficiency ratio (P) is the percentage of total dollar benefits reducing the poverty-gap target. Benefits are defined as the cash-equivalent value of the program to the household. The pretransfer poor refers to households which are poor after counting revised cash income and prior to counting noncash transfer benefits (see Table 5). The poverty gap refers to the poverty gap after counting revised cash income and prior to counting noncash transfer benefits (see Table 4). A more complete description of each statistic is found in the text.

a   Medical-care transfers include Medicare, Supplemental Medical Insurance, and Medicaid.

b   Public housing includes benefits from Low Rent Public Housing, Rent Supplements, "Section 235" mortgage assistance, and "Section 236" rental assistance.

c   All noncash transfers include the combined effect of medical care, food stamps, and public housing.

of all food and housing benefits reached the target group, only about one-quarter of all medical-care benefits went to the poor. This low V ratio for medical care can be attributed to three factors: the relatively low budget shares for medical insurance in low-income families;[15] the fact that Medicare benefits are not income-conditioned and, hence, accrue to many nonpoor families receiving Social Security and Old Age Assistance benefits; and the availability of Medicaid benefits to but a subset of the poor.[16] Because medical-care benefits comprise

---

15   In another larger work, the efficiency ratio—the ratio of the cash equivalent to the subsidy value—for those units eligible for Medicaid alone, for Medicare and Supplemental Medical Insurance alone, and finally for all medical-care subsidies, are shown to be .63, .93, and .78, respectively. Hence, low-income households eligible for Medicaid benefits had a substantially lower willingness to pay for medical insurance than did other types of medical-insurance recipients. See Smeeding [21], App. 7, p. 370.

16   While most public-assistance recipients are eligible for Medicaid payments, benefits available to those households made unpoor by cash public assistance do not contribute to the V ratio. In 1972, 1.71 million households were made unpoor by cash public assistance, and less than 40 percent of all households receiving public assistance were poor after receipt of that payment. Moreover, Medicaid benefits were available only to

TABLE 4
THE EFFECTS OF REVISING CASH INCOME AND INCLUDING NONCASH TRANSFERS ON THE POVERTY GAP,[a] 1972 AND 1968

Designation	1972	1968[a]
1. Official poverty gap[b] (based on reported CPS income)	$12.032	$11.845
2. Revised poverty gap (based on revised cash income)	8.893	9.590
3. Final poverty gap (based on revised cash income plus noncash transfers)	5.353	8.330
Percentage Differences		
(Official – Revised)/Official	26.1%	19.0%
(Revised – Final)/Official	29.4	10.7
(Official – Final)/Official	55.5	29.7
(Revised – Final)/Revised	39.8	13.1
Total subsidy value of noncash transfers[a]	$16.351	$ 7.816

a   All figures in billions of dollars; 1968 figures in billions of constant 1972 dollars.
b   Official poverty gap taken from U.S. Bureau of the Census [26], Tables 5 and 6. Because the Census Bureau separately bases its poverty statistics on families and unrelated individuals (one-person families), the figures shown here are the sum of the poverty income gaps for both groups.

77 percent of all in-kind transfer benefits, the income-efficiency ratio for aggregate noncash transfers is low.

The second target-efficiency indicator is the poverty-gap-efficiency ratio (P). The P ratios, defined as percentage of total benefits which contribute to a closing of the poverty gap, are similar to the V ratios, yet are somewhat lower in every case. The P ratios are based on a more strict criterion than are the V ratios in that only those dollars received by the target poor which also diminish the poverty gap are counted as being "efficient." Except for public-housing benefits, the P ratios differ from the V ratios by less than 5 percent. For public housing, the difference is more than 20 percent and is attributable to the substantial spillover of public-housing benefits beyond the poverty-income line.[17] Because

the children of the categorically needy, i.e., poor nonpublic-assistance recipients, in about one-half of the states in 1972.
17   The reason for the large spillover of public-housing benefits is the lumpy nature of the transfer. Residence in a public-housing unit confers an average yearly benefit of nearly $600 to each recipient unit. Further, the average benefit does not fall a great deal as income rises. Food and medical-care programs have lower average benefits, $312 and $329, respectively.

public-housing benefits comprise less than 8 percent of aggregate in-kind benefits, their effect on the difference between the aggregate V and P is small.

In summary, then, the in-kind transfer programs analyzed here do not appear to be very efficient for several reasons. First of all, the inefficiency associated with in-kind transfers reduces their recipient value to about 70 percent of their market value, regardless of the target-efficiency of these benefits. Moreover, the poorest of the poor benefit least from noncash programs because they value them least. Second, target-efficiency scores are low because high-income cutoff points allow many nonpoor households, particularly many nonpoor public-assistance recipients, to benefit from noncash programs—even though many poorer households are excluded. Even the food-stamp program, which had the highest target-efficiency among the in-kind transfer programs, only reduces the poverty gap by about 50 cents for every dollar's worth of public expenditure.

Despite this relative inefficiency and because of their enormous size, these programs result in a 40 percent decline in the poverty gap in 1972. Table 4 shows that when adjustments for federal taxes paid, income underreporting, and intrahousehold income-sharing are combined with in-kind transfers evaluated at their cash equivalent, the official Census poverty gap of $12.0 billion is reduced to $5.4 billion. These statistics can be compared to the 1968 poverty gaps, where both the volume and antipoverty effect of noncash transfers is less than in 1972. If the relationship between the growth in market value of noncash transfers to the poor and the decline in the revised poverty gap has persisted, approximately $35.0 billion of food, housing, and medical-care transfers to the poor in 1976 should lead to a final poverty gap that is less than 45 percent of that indicated by the official statistics.

IV. CHANGES IN THE INCIDENCE OF POVERTY AND THE COMPOSITION OF THE POOR

In addition to reducing the number of poor households and the poverty gap, these programs alter the demographic composition of the postcash and noncash transfer poverty population. Because public tastes for income redistribution through in-kind transfers favor certain types of poor families (for example, elderly people or females with children) relative to others, it is of interest to investigate the effect of these transfers on both the composition and the incidence of poverty.[18]

---

18 Poverty incidence refers to the percentage of all households of any given demographic category which can be regarded as poor. Poverty composition, on the other hand, refers to the percentage of all poor households which are of a particular type. The results of this study may be compared with a recent study by Browning [4] which evaluates in-kind transfers (exclusive of education) at their market value. Browning allo-

In Table 5, the incidence of poverty as indicated by the official Census figures (column 1) is compared to poverty estimates based on both revised cash income (column 2) and revised cash income plus the cash-equivalent value of in-kind transfers (column 3). The final two columns indicate the percentage reduction in poverty incidence due to the combination of both the income revisions and the imputation of noncash transfers, and due to the imputation of noncash transfers alone, for several nonexclusive population subgroups.[19] By comparing percentage differences for all households (row 1) with the differences for various subgroups, the relative antipoverty impact of the program on the various demographic groups can be seen. For example, any subgroup in the final column with a percentage change greater (less) than 38.3 percent receives relatively more (less) antipoverty benefit from noncash transfers than the population as a whole.

These comparisons indicate that aged households, public-assistance recipients, people residing in the Northeast and North Central regions of the country, white female-headed households, and unrelated individuals have benefited relatively more from noncash transfers than have other population groups. Despite the fact that the in-kind transfers tend to reduce regional differences in total cash plus noncash transfer benefits in specific cases,[20] low-income residents in southern states received less assistance from these in-kind programs than did people residing in other areas. This is partially explained by the link between receipt of public assistance and Medicaid benefits and the low participation rates in public-assistance programs in the South. Those receiving public assistance also are more likely to obtain food and housing benefits, perhaps by receiving information about these programs when they apply for public assistance.[21]

---

cates a total of $43 billion of in-kind transfers, while only $16.4 billion is allocated here (see fn. 3). While he uses no microdata base, Browning (p. 22) suggests that due to the rapid growth of noncash transfers and their presumed incidence, ". . . on average poverty became virtually non-existent in the United States in 1974." The lack of microdata regarding the distribution of in-kind transfers among the poor leads Browning to conclude only that the total value of net resources distributed to the official Census poverty population was large enough to eliminate poverty in 1973. Since the official poverty gap is less than the value of in-kind transfers, this is a true statement. Yet the use of microdata in this study shows that, due to the uneven distribution of in-kind transfers among the poor, while income poverty has certainly been reduced, it has not been completely erased. See Tables 5 and 6, for instance.

19 It should be noted that several of these demographic groups overlap to a large degree. For instance, the percentage of elderly who are poor is highly correlated with the percentage of poor females and the percentage of poor unrelated individuals because many of the elderly poor are widows who live alone.

20 See Blechman and others [2], pp. 177-79.

21 Two other factors are at work here as well. First, because the southern poor are among the least well-off of the poor due to low participation rates and low benefit schedules for cash assistance, these households will have less cash equivalent per dollar of noncash transfer cost. On the other hand, due to these low cash-assistance values, the target efficiency of in-kind transfers is higher in the South for those families who do participate in these programs.

TABLE 5
POVERTY INCIDENCE IN THE UNITED STATES, 1972:
PERCENTAGE OF HOUSEHOLDS OF EACH TYPE REGARDED AS POOR

Demographic Group	Official U.S. Census Bureau Figures[a] (1)	Revised Cash Income[b] (2)	Revised Cash Income Plus Noncash Transfers[c] (3)	$\frac{(1)-(3)}{(1)} \cdot 100$	$\frac{(2)-(3)}{(2)} \cdot 100$
All households	14.6%	10.7%	6.6%	54.8%	38.3%
Age of head					
65 years and older	23.6	17.3	6.2	73.7	64.1
Under 65	12.4	9.0	6.7	45.9	25.6
Public assistance status					
Recipient	54.2	39.7	18.9	65.1	52.4
Nonrecipient	11.5	8.5	5.6	51.3	34.1
Location of residence					
Urban	13.0	10.6	6.6	49.2	37.7
Rural farm	15.9	11.5	6.9	56.6	40.0
Rural nonfarm	18.5	10.8	7.9	57.3	26.9
Place of residence					
Northeast	12.0	6.9	3.6	70.0	47.8
North Central	12.7	8.5	4.7	63.0	44.7
South	18.7	15.5	10.2	45.5	34.2
West	13.8	11.2	7.3	47.1	34.8
Race and sex of head					
White male	6.9	5.4	3.4	50.7	37.0
Nonwhite male	21.0	16.1	11.0	47.6	31.6
White female	32.3	22.5	12.7	60.7	43.6
Nonwhite female	55.3	38.7	25.8	53.3	33.3
Size of household					
Unrelated individual	38.6	24.2	11.9	69.2	50.8
Family of 2 or more	9.1	7.6	5.4	40.7	28.9
Total poor households in millions	9.958	7.293	4.517	54.7	38.1
Total poor persons in millions	24.455	18.805	12.854	47.4	31.6

a   Source: U.S. Bureau of the Census [26], Tables 1, 18, 19, 21, 23, 24, 40, 41.

b   Revised cash income is composed of original CPS-Census income which has been adjusted to take account of federal payroll and personal income taxes paid, income misreporting, and intrafamily transfers.

c   Revised cash income as described in (b) above plus the cash equivalent of noncash transfers.

TABLE 6

POVERTY COMPOSITION IN THE UNITED STATES, 1972:
PERCENTAGE DISTRIBUTION OF POOR HOUSEHOLDS AND ALL HOUSEHOLDS,
BY DEMOGRAPHIC CATEGORY

	Basis of Poverty Estimate			
Demographic Group	Official U.S. Census Bureau Figures[a]	Revised Cash Income[b]	Revised Cash Income Plus Noncash Transfers[c]	Percentage Distribution of All U.S. Households[d]
All households	100.0%	100.0%	100.0%	100.0%
Age of head				
65 years and older	31.9	32.0	18.6	19.7
Under 65	68.1	68.0	81.4	80.3
Public assistance status				
Recipient	27.2	25.9	20.9	7.3
Nonrecipient	72.8	74.1	79.1	92.7
Location of residence				
Urban	61.0	67.9	66.4	68.6
Rural farm	4.6	4.6	5.0	4.2
Rural nonfarm	34.4	27.4	28.6	27.2
Place of residence				
Northeast	19.5	15.3	12.9	23.8
North Central	23.6	21.4	19.3	27.1
South	39.7	44.3	47.8	31.0
West	17.2	19.0	20.0	18.1
Race and sex of head				
White male	33.4	35.6	36.6	70.4
Nonwhite male	10.1	10.5	11.6	7.0
White female	40.7	38.7	35.4	18.4
Nonwhite female	15.9	15.2	16.4	4.2
Size of household				
One (unrelated individual)	49.0	42.0	33.3	18.5
Two persons or more	51.0	58.0	67.7	81.5

a   Source: U.S. Bureau of the Census [26], Tables 1, 3, 4.
b   Revised cash income is composed of original CPS-Census income which has been adjusted to take account of federal payroll and personal income taxes paid, income misreporting, and intrafamily transfers.
c   Revised cash income as described in (b) above plus the cash equivalents of noncash transfers.
d   Source: U.S. Bureau of the Census [27], Tables 16, 17, 20.

In Table 6 the effect of in-kind transfer programs on the composition of poor households is described. Two sorts of comparisons are possible: first, the distribution of the poverty population as officially defined can be compared with the distribution when alternative definitions are employed, and second, the composition of the poor by alternative definitions can be compared to the composition of all households in the U.S.

One of the most significant findings is the effect of noncash transfers on the percentage of poor households that are aged. Whereas poverty counts based on official and revised income figures show a significant overrepresentation of the aged in the poverty population, the poverty count for aged households when in-kind transfers are combined with cash-income revisions indicates relatively fewer aged households among the poor than among the total population. That is, after data adjustments, aged households are *underrepresented* in the poverty population.

A second important change is in regional composition. After the full set of adjustments, it is estimated that nearly half (47.8 percent) of all poor families reside in the South. The official estimates indicate that only 39.7 percent of all poor families live in this region. Apparently the small amount of in-kind transfers received by southern households relative to in-kind benefits received by households in other regions has substantially affected the geographic distribution of the poor. Moreover, because these southern states contain about 31 percent of all households, they are decidedly overrepresented in the poverty population relative to the total population.

Finally, data revisions and receipt of noncash transfers have an important effect on the representation of unrelated individuals in the poverty population. While the Census estimates that almost half of the poor are one-person units, the revised data indicate that about one in every three poor units is an unrelated individual.[22] This latter estimate is still almost double their percentage of the total population, however.

In summary, the adjustments reported here have significantly altered both the size and the composition of the poverty population. In particular, the representation of aged households, southern households, and one-person units in the poverty population is significantly changed.

V. POLICY IMPLICATIONS

All of the data analyzed here are for 1972, at the latest. Since that time there

---

22 It will be remembered that our figures are based on household income accounting while Census figures separately count all unrelated individuals living together as single-persons units. This accounting difference explains some part of the difference between the Census estimate and our revised cash-income estimate of poor unrelated individuals. In addition, as noted above, many unrelated individuals are elderly persons receiving substantial amounts of medical benefits.

has been substantial change in the U.S. income-support system. Food-stamp benefits were almost $5.5 billion in 1976,[23] almost triple their 1972 level. While a moratorium has been placed on new public-housing projects, benefits totaling $2.3 billion continue to be paid out to existing tenants. In 1976, Medicare and Medicaid benefits totaled about $28.2 billion, more than double their 1972 value. Based on the results presented here, it seems that two major conclusions may be drawn regarding the level of income poverty in the U.S. in 1976.

First, the obsolescence of official Census Bureau poverty statistics has increased greatly since 1972.[24] Second, it is to be expected that with the rapid increase in in-kind transfers, the target-efficiency of these programs has decreased since 1972. Not only is the target—as defined by revised cash-income estimates—shrinking, but the growing size of the programs has likely led to increased spillovers.

Hence, if antipoverty effect is an important criterion in designing income-transfer programs, it appears that the budget growth of existing programs is a relatively ineffective means of poverty reduction. It may well be true that substituting a federally administered, comprehensive negative income tax or income-supplement program for the current set of cash public-assistance and in-kind programs[25] would be a more cost-effective way of reducing poverty. On the other hand, the electorate may have a preference for in-kind as opposed to cash transfers and may also be willing to give subsidies to many of the near-poor, perhaps especially to those who otherwise might be subjected to considerable medical expenses. Thus, although a relatively simple cash program such as a negative income tax has great appeal to most economists, antipoverty policies appear to be shaped by a wider variety of goals than economists often consider.

APPENDIX

Medical-care benefits from the Medicare, Supplemental Medical Insurance, and Medicaid programs are imputed on the basis of their insurance value rather than

---

23 Source of food-stamp, public-housing, and Medicaid and Medicare figures below is the *Budget of the United States Government* [5, 6].

24 It must be noted that the Census poverty lines by which we calculate the poor may be obsolete as well. If we were to raise the poverty line to one-half median income, the size of the poor population would increase substantially, and target efficiency would be considerably improved. See Smeeding [21]. Recently a poverty studies task force has recognized many of these problems and is taking steps to revise government poverty measures. See [28].

25 An Income Supplement Program (ISP) is currently being considered by both the Department of Health, Education, and Welfare and the Joint Economic Committee [25]. In addition, the author is currently undertaking a study that simulates several different income-maintenance strategies, including earnings subsidies and a negative income tax similar to the ISP plan, in order to estimate their comparative antipoverty effectiveness.

the amount of money paid a medical vendor on the recipient's behalf. Thus, all eligible persons are assigned a fair insurance value[26] from each program according to their recipient category, i.e., child, adult, disabled adult, or elderly, and their state of residence. Because of the wide variation in medical costs for equivalent levels of medical-care provision across the country, benefit levels so estimated were adjusted by Bureau of Labor Statistics regional medical-care price indices [33] to reflect geographical differences in medical-care costs. Further, since most of the rise in medical-care benefits since the advent of Medicare in 1965 is due to price increases alone, benefits are deflated by the differences between the medical price index and the consumer price index to reflect the real insurance value of program coverage. In 1972, the aggregate value of medical-care subsidies under these programs was $12.9 billion.

Public-housing benefits are imputed for four separate programs: Low Rent Public Housing, Rent Supplements, "Section 235" mortgage assistance, and "Section 236" rental assistance. Again, program-specific income and assets tests are applied in determining eligibility status. Household participation rates and benefit levels are based on Department of Housing and Urban Development estimates for specific income, age, sex, geographical location, and cash public-assistance status groups [30, 31]. Imputed benefits for participating households are adjusted by means of Bureau of Labor Statistics data [33] to take account of housing price differences due to geographical location and metropolitan-nonmetropolitan residence. The 1972 market value of housing benefits was $1.5 billion.

In much the same way, eligibility for food stamps is based on adjusted income levels and asset tests as specified by the 1972 laws. The total pool of eligibles is made consistent with actual recipient levels by means of unpublished U.S. Department of Agriculture food and nutrition studies data on participation patterns of various groups distinguished by locations, age, sex of household head, and household-income level. In 1972, $1.9 billion in food-stamp benefits were distributed.

REFERENCES

1. H. Beebout and P. Bonina. "TRIM: A Micro-simulation Model for Evaluating Transfer Income Policies." Urban Institute Working Paper. Washington: 1972.

---

26 While an actual $1,000 Medicaid payment for a poor hospitalized person may possibly prevent a $1,000 income loss, it does not follow that the recipient's welfare level has increased by $1,000. On the other hand, the availability and assurance of adequate medical care does provide a real-income increase to all actual and potential (i.e., eligible) recipients in the form of a subsidized health insurance policy. The fair insurance value of a medical subsidy is measured by: total vendor payments plus administrative costs minus premiums paid by eligibles in each eligibility category, divided by the total number of eligibles in each category.

2. B. Blechman and others. *Setting National Priorities, the 1975 Budget.* Washington: Brookings Institution, 1975.

3. Benjamin Bridges. "Redistributive Effects of Transfer Payments Among Age and Economic Status Groups." Staff Paper 10. Washington: Social Security Administration, Office of Research and Statistics, 1972.

4. Edgar K. Browning. *Redistribution and the Welfare System.* Washington: American Enterprise Institute for Public Policy Research, July 1975.

5. *The Budget of the United States Government, 1976.* Washington: U.S. Government Printing Office, 1975.

6. *The Budget of the United States Government, 1977.* Washington: U.S. Government Printing Office, 1976.

7. Kenneth Clarkson. *Food Stamps and Nutrition.* Washington: American Enterprise Institute for Public Policy Research, April 1975.

8. G. Fiegehen and P. Lansley. "Household Size and Income Unit in the Measurement of Poverty." Paper presented to the 14th General Conference of the International Association for Research in Income and Wealth, Aulanko, Finland, August 1975.

9. Irwin Garfinkel and Robert Haveman. "Earnings Capacity and the Target Efficiency of Alternative Transfer Programs." *American Economic Review* 64 (May 1974): 196–204.

10. J. Kraft and E. Olsen. "The Distribution of Benefits from Public Housing." Paper presented to the National Bureau of Economic Research Conference on Research in Income and Wealth, Ann Arbor, Mich. May 1974.

11. Robert Lampman. "How Much Does the American System of Transfers Benefit the Poor?" In *Economic Progress and Social Welfare*, ed. L. H. Goodman. New York: Columbia University Press, 1966.

12. ———. *Ends and Means of Reducing Income Poverty.* Institute for Research on Poverty Monograph Series. Chicago: Markham Publishing Co., 1971.

13. ———. "Concepts of Equity in the Design of Schemes for Income Distribution." Institute for Research on Poverty Discussion Paper 296-75. Madison: University of Wisconsin, 1975.

14. Joseph Minarik and John Palmer. "Income Security Policy." In *Setting National Priorities: The Next Ten Years*, eds. H. Owen and C. Schultze. Washington: Brookings Institution, 1976.

15. James N. Morgan and others. *Income and Welfare in the United States.* Ann Arbor: University of Michigan Press, 1962.

16. James N. Morgan and James D. Smith. "Measures of Economic Well-Offness and Their Correlates." *American Economic Review* 59 (May 1969): 450–62.

17. Benjamin Okner. "Transfer Payments: Their Distribution and Role in Reducing Poverty." In *Redistribution to the Rich and the Poor*, eds. K. Boulding and M. Pfaff, Belmont, Calif.: Wadsworth Publishing Co., 1972.

18. Robert Plotnick and Felicity Skidmore. *Progress Against Poverty.* Institute for Research on Poverty Series. New York: Academic Press, 1975.

19. M. Reynolds and Eugene Smolensky. "The 1970 Post-Fisc Income Distribution." *National Tax Journal* 27 (December 1974).

20. A. Sirageldin. *Non-Market Components of National Income.* Ann Arbor: Survey Research Center, University of Michigan, 1969.

21. Timothy M. Smeeding. "Measuring the Economic Welfare of Low Income Households, and the Anti-Poverty Effectiveness of Cash and Non-Cash Transfer Programs." Ph.D. dissertation, University of Wisconsin-Madison, 1975.

22. Eugene Smolensky and J. Gomery. "Efficiency and Equity Effects in the Benefits from the Federal Housing Program in 1965." In *Benefit Cost Analysis of Federal Programs*, Joint Economic Committee Print. Washington: U.S. Government Printing Office, 1973.

23. Eugene Smolensky and others. "Adding In-Kind Transfers to the Personal Income and Outlay Account: Implications for the Size Distribution of Income." Institute for Research on Poverty Discussion Paper 199–74. Madison: University of Wisconsin, 1974.

24. U.S. Congress, Joint Economic Committee. "How Public Welfare Benefits Are Distributed in Low Income Areas." In *Studies in Public Welfare*, Joint Economic Committee Print, Paper 6. Washington: U.S. Government Printing Office, 1973.

25. ———. "A Model Income Supplement Bill." In *Studies in Public Welfare*, Joint Economic Committee Print, Paper 16. Washington: U.S. Government Printing Office, December 1974.

26. U.S. Department of Commerce, Bureau of the Census. "Characteristics of Low Income Population 1972." *Current Population Reports*, P-60, No. 91. Washington: December 1973.

27. ———. "Household and Family Characteristics: March 1973." *Current Population Reports*, P-20, No. 258. Washington: December 1973.

28. U.S. Department of Health, Education, and Welfare. *The Measurement of Poverty*. Washington: U.S. Government Printing Office, April 1976.

29. U.S. Department of Health, Education, and Welfare, Office of the Assistant Secretary for Planning and Evaluation, Office of Program Systems. "Federal Outlays Benefitting the Poor, Summary Tables." Washington: March 1974.

30. U.S. Department of Housing and Urban Development. *Housing Yearbook, 1973*. Washington: U.S. Government Printing Office, 1973.

31. ———. *Housing in the Seventies*. Washington: U.S. Government Printing Office, November 1974.

32. U.S. Department of Labor, Bureau of Labor Statistics. *Survey of Consumer Expenditures, 1960–1961*. BLS Report 237-93. Washington: February 1965.

33. ———. "Three Budgets for an Urban Family of Four Persons." No. 75-253. Washington: June 1973.

19

THE ESTIMATION OF LABOR SUPPLY MODELS USING EXPERIMENTAL DATA

Michael C. Keeley, Philip K. Robins,
Robert G. Spiegelman, and Richard W. West

For many years there has been interest in replacing the existing complex transfer system in the United States with a nationwide negative income tax (*NIT*) program.[1] The feasibility and desirability of an *NIT*, however, depend on its effects on aggregate labor supply (and its cost). Interest in predicting these aggregate effects has motivated considerable empirical research on labor supply. The first studies used existing data, usually cross-sectional, to estimate the parameters of labor supply functions.[2] Unfortunately, the range of estimates in these studies is disturbingly large and of limited usefulness to policymakers.[3] Consequently, a new approach to labor supply research

has been followed social experimentation.[4]

Several experiments have been funded by the federal government to test the effects of alternative *NIT* programs on labor supply. The first experiment, the New Jersey Experiment, was conducted in New Jersey and Pennsylvania from 1968 to 1972.[5] Other experiments have taken place in Gary, Indiana from 1970 to 1974, and in rural areas of Iowa and North Carolina from 1969 to 1973. The largest and most comprehensive of these experiments began in 1971 in Seattle, Washington and Denver, Colorado and is still taking place.

In principle, a controlled experiment affords the opportunity to overcome most of the problems inherent in nonexperimental research, because in an experiment, the budget constraints of individuals are exogenously shifted in a measurable way. In practice, however, the experiments have been beset with their own unique set of econometric problems. These problems include the nonrandom assignment of experimental treatment, small samples, truncation of response, limited duration, participation in other welfare programs both before and during the experiment by sample members, and the selection of nonrepresentative samples.[6]

In this paper, a methodology is presented that attempts to deal with these problems. Experimental data from the Seattle and

*Economists, SRI International. The research reported in this paper was performed under contracts with the states of Washington and Colorado, prime contractors for the Department of Health, Education, and Welfare, under contract numbers SRS-70-53 and SRS-71-18, respectively. The opinions expressed in the paper are our own and should not be construed as representing the opinions or policies of the states of Washington or Colorado, or any agency of the U.S. government. An earlier version of this paper was presented at the Summer 1976 meetings of the Econometric Society and in seminars at the National Bureau of Economic Research and Mathematica Policy Research. Jodie Allen, Yoram Barzel, David Betson, Michael Boskin, Glen Cain, Joseph Corbett, Irwin Garfinkel, David Greenberg, Terry Johnson, Richard Kaluzny, Richard Kasten, Robert Lerman, Stanley Masters, Myles Maxfield, Robert Moffit, Larry Orr, Harold Watts, and Robert Willis provided valuable comments on various drafts of this paper. We are, of course, solely responsible for the views presented and for any remaining errors. Helen Cohn, Diane Hollenbeck, Paul McElherne, Gary Stieger, and Steven Spickard provided expert programming assistance.

[1] Milton Friedman is usually credited with developing the concept of a negative income tax. Robert Lampman and James Tobin (1965) among others also made early contributions to the concept.

[2] An excellent collection of such studies is presented in Glen Cain and Harold Watts.

[3] See Keeley for a survey of these studies and a discussion of some of the econometric difficulties that lead to such a wide range of estimates.

[4] Heather Ross (1966) is credited with first conceiving the idea of an *NIT* experiment. Guy Orcutt and Alice Orcutt (1968) first published a paper outlining an experimental design.

[5] The New Jersey Experiment is described in David Kershaw and Jerilyn Fair. Watts and Albert Rees (1977a, b) and Joseph Pechman and P. Michael Timpane present the results from this experiment.

[6] See Henry Aaron, Keeley, and Keeley and Robins for a critical discussion of many of these problems.

From Michael C. Keeley, Philip K. Robins, Robert G. Spiegelman, and Richard W. West, "The Estimation of Labor Supply Models Using Experimental Data," 68(5) *The American Economic Review* 873-887 (December 1978). Copyright © 1978 by the American Economic Association.

Denver Income Maintenance Experiments (*SIME/DIME*) are used to estimate the parameters of a labor supply function.[7] These parameters are then used to predict the nationwide labor supply effects of alternative *NIT* programs.

The empirical response function estimated measures the change in labor supply over a two-year period. The Tobit method is used to estimate equations for single female heads of families, husbands, and wives. Nationwide aggregate labor supply responses to six alternative *NIT* programs are predicted by applying the response function to data from the March 1975 *Current Population Survey*.

The plan of the paper is as follows: Section I describes an experimental *NIT* program; Section II presents a theoretical model of the labor supply response to an *NIT*; Section III specifies the empirical model; Section IV presents the empirical results; Section V discusses policy implications; and Section VI presents the summary and conclusions.

I. Description of an Experimental NIT Program

An *NIT* program is characterized by a support (or guarantee) level S, and a tax rate t_e. The support level is the grant provided when other income is zero, and the tax rate is the rate at which the grant declines as other income increases. In a controlled *NIT* experiment, an effort is made to ensure that the influence of other tax and transfer programs is eliminated. Public transfers, therefore, are fully taxed, and positive taxes are reimbursed. Consequently, the payment a person receives depends on gross income and both experimental and nonexperimental tax rates.

For this discussion, it is assumed that nonexperimental net nonwage income (including public transfers) is zero and that both the nonexperimental and experimental tax rates are constant. These assumptions are relaxed in the empirical analysis. The

payment P associated with a particular *NIT* program is determined as follows:

$$(1) \quad P = \begin{cases} S - t_e Y + t_n Y & \text{if } S + t_n Y \geq t_e Y \\ 0 & \text{if } S + t_n Y < t_e Y \end{cases}$$

where t_n is the nonexperimental tax rate and Y is gross income. The payment, if positive, is equal to the grant $S - t_e Y$, plus the positive tax reimbursement $t_n Y$.

Figure 1 shows a graph of the nonexperimental budget line (line ABT) and the experimental budget line (line ABE) of an individual enrolled in an *NIT* program. Point B, where the two budget lines intersect, is the point at which the payment becomes zero and is known as the tax break-even level. The tax break-even level of income, given by $S/(t_e - t_n)$, may be contrasted with the grant break-even level of income, given by S/t_e. The grant break-even level is the level of income at which the *NIT* grant ($S - t_e Y$) becomes zero.

The program support level S is designated by the line ET. Under the assumption that the nonexperimental tax rate, t_n, is less than the tax rate of the *NIT* program under consideration, t_e, the absolute value of the slope of the new budget line (ABE) to the right of B is reduced.

The Seattle and Denver Income Maintenance Experiments are testing eleven different *NIT* programs. The programs are described in Table 1. A feature of *SIME/DIME* that distinguishes it from the other *NIT* experiments is the testing of programs in which the marginal tax rate declines as income increases. Families in *SIME/DIME* are enrolled for either three or five years.[8] Different durations are being tested, because of difficulties in inferring permanent effects from experiments of finite length. According to Charles Metcalf, substitution and income effects should vary according to the length of the experiment. In our empirical analysis, we formally test for such differences. The results of these tests are presented in Section IV.

---

[7] For a description of *SIME/DIME*, see Mordecai Kurz and Spiegelman (1971, 1972).

[8] A small number of families are enrolled for twenty years but are not considered in this study.

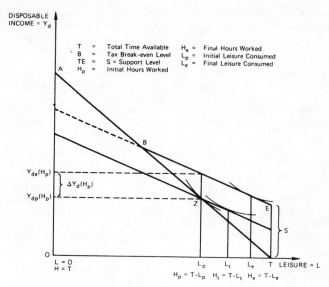

FIGURE 1. AN EXPERIMENTAL *NIT* PROGRAM

TABLE 1—PROGRAMS BEING TESTED IN THE SEATTLE AND DENVER
INCOME MAINTENANCE EXPERIMENTS
(1971 Dollars)

Support Level	Initial Tax Rate	Rate of Decline of Average Tax Rate per $1,000 of Income	Grant Break-Even Level	Tax Break-Even Level
$3,800	.5	0	$ 7,600	$10,250
3,800	.7	0	5,429	6,350
3,800	.7	.025	7,367	10,850
3,800	.8	.025	5,802	7,800
4,800	.5	0	9,600	13,150
4,800	.7	0	6,867	8,520
4,800	.7	.025	12,000	19,700
4,800	.8	.025	8,000	11,510
5,600	.5	0	11,200	15,700
5,600	.7	0	8,000	9,780
5,600	.8	.025	10,360	16,230

Note: The figures for the support level, the grant break-even level, and the tax break-even level are in 1971 dollars and are for a family of four with only one earner and no income outside of earnings. Adjustments are made to these figures for family size and for changes in the cost of living over time. Positive tax reimbursements include the federal income tax and social security taxes. The federal income tax assumes the family takes the standard deduction. State income taxes, which are relevant only for the Denver Experiment (there is no state income tax in Washington), are ignored in calculating the tax break-even level. Thus, the tax break-even level is slightly higher for the Denver Experiment.

II. Theoretical Analysis of the Labor Supply Response to an *NIT* Program

A. *The Model*

It is assumed that each individual maximizes a well-behaved utility function, $U(L, Y_d)$, where L is leisure and Y_d is consumption of market goods (or disposable income) subject to the budget constraint

$$(2) \qquad F \equiv wT + Y_n = wL + Y_d$$

where F is full income, w is the net wage rate, T is total time available, and Y_n is net nonwage income. Utility maximization implies that the individual has a labor supply function $H = H(w, Y_n)$, where $H = T - L$ is hours of work. Totally differentiating the labor supply function and substituting in the Slutsky equation[9] gives

$$(3) \qquad dH = \left. \frac{\partial H}{\partial w} \right|_U \cdot dw + \frac{\partial H}{\partial Y_n} (Hdw + dY_n)$$
$$= \alpha dw + \beta(Hdw + dY_n)$$

where U is utility, α is the substitution effect, and β is the income effect.[10] The term $Hdw + dY_n$ is the total differential of disposable income, holding constant the initial supply of labor H.

The model given by equation (3) is specified in terms of unobservable differential changes. The differential change model implies that each individual's point of compensation should be his or her initial equilibrium labor supply. If differences in initial

[9]The Slutsky equation decomposes the total effect of a wage change on labor supply into a substitution effect and an income effect:

$$\frac{\partial H}{\partial w} = \left. \frac{\partial H}{\partial w} \right|_U + H \frac{\partial H}{\partial Y_n}$$

[10]For a family with more than one potential earner, the equation can be generalized to include cross-substitution effects. In our empirical formulation of this model, it is assumed that cross-substitution effects are zero, partly because the net wage changes of both spouses are highly correlated and their effects are difficult to distinguish empirically. An attempt to apply this model to nonexperimental cross-sectional data is presented in Orley Ashenfelter and James Heckman (1973, 1974). See, however, the critique of Jonathan Dickinson (1977).

labor supply across individuals are the result of differences in equilibrium or permanent labor supply, each person should be compensated at his or her initial position. In our application of the model, we follow this compensation procedure.[11] To measure substitution and income effects empirically, finite differences are used to approximate the unobservable differential changes. In discrete form, the model described in equation (3) becomes:

$$(4) \qquad \Delta H \approx \alpha\Delta w + \beta(H_p\Delta w + \Delta Y_n) =$$
$$\alpha\Delta w + \beta\Delta Y_d(H_p)$$

where $\Delta Y_d(H_p)$ is the change in disposable income of an individual, holding constant his or her initial labor supply H_p.

B. *Analyzing the Response to an NIT Program*

Equation (4) states that the effects of shifts in the budget constraint on labor supply can be decomposed into a substitution effect, which depends on the change in the net wage rate Δw, and an income effect, which depends on the change in disposable income evaluated at initial hours of work, $\Delta Y_d(H_p)$. For a person placed on an experimental *NIT* program, Δw is equal to the gross wage rate times the difference between the pre-experimental and experimental tax rates,[12] and $\Delta Y_d(H_p)$ is equal to the payment the person would receive if initial labor supply were maintained. Referring again to Figure 1, consider a person below the break-even level who is in equilibrium at point Z before the imposition of an *NIT* program. The change in the quantity of leisure demanded is comprised of a substitution effect ($L_s - L_p$) holding disposable income constant at initial labor supply, and an income effect ($L_e - L_s$) holding relative prices (i.e., the

[11]If differences in initial labor supply are purely transitory, then such a procedure is not appropriate, because initial labor supply is not at an equilibrium position. Compensation at the initial position, however, ensures that the point of compensation is not endogenous.

[12]This assumes that the gross wage rate is unaffected by the program.

wage rate relative to the price of goods) constant.[13] Disposable income is held constant by rotating the budget line through the initial equilibrium point Z, where, at the new net wage rate and new monetary full income, the consumer could still purchase the initial consumption bundle.

The analysis thus far focuses on the response of a given individual to a particular program. Because of differences in tastes or other unmeasured variables, however, there is considerable heterogeneity of the initial equilibrium positions of individuals.[14] In fact, the best empirical labor supply equations explain only about 20–30 percent of the variance in labor supply.[15] This suggests that on a given budget line there is a distribution of initial equilibrium positions. For simplicity, it is assumed that this distribution is the result of differences in tastes.

Because separate responses resulting from compensated wage changes and income changes are not observed for each person (only total response that results from both changes is observed),[16] some a priori restriction is needed to identify the model so that income and substitution effects can be measured empirically. The restriction we impose is to assume that different individuals have equal substitution effects and equal income effects at their initial equilibrium positions.[17] If, in fact, income and substitution effects differ among individuals, the

empirical method used measures average income and substitution effects in the sample.

The assumptions underlying this model are different from those implicit in most cross-sectional studies.[18] Instead of assuming that each person has the same preference structure, it is assumed that differences in taste are reflected in differences in initial equilibrium labor supply, after controlling for differences in budget constraints. Therefore, there is no single utility function that is consistent with the model, although each person is assumed to maximize a well-behaved utility function.

C. Implications of the Model

The assumption that different individuals have equal substitution and income effects implies that response to a given *NIT* program depends on the initial equilibrium position. For example, a person with low income experiences a considerable change in disposable income and net wage rate, and a large response is expected. On the other hand, a person initially at the break-even level experiences a change only in the net wage rate. Response for this person consists only of a (Slutsky) substitution effect and is therefore smaller. Next, consider a person above the break-even level. This person experiences changes in disposable income and the net wage rate only if the elasticity of substitution in consumption is sufficiently large that the indifference curve through the initial point intersects the *NIT* segment of the new budget line. Thus, for a person initially above the break-even level, we would expect a very small probability of response. Finally, consider an individual who is not working: this person experiences a considerable change in disposable income and net wage rate, but has zero response.[19]

---

[13]This is the Slutsky, as opposed to the Hicks, decomposition.

[14]See Robert Hall (1975), and Heckman and Robert Willis for a discussion of heterogeneity.

[15]See Cain and Watts for a sampling of typical cross-section labor supply equations. These studies, however, analyze a measure of labor supply that does not correspond strictly to our concept of equilibrium labor supply. Instead, the studies use current labor supply, which is the sum of permanent or equilibrium labor supply, a transitory component, and a life cycle component.

[16]For persons at the tax break-even level initially, total response is a result of the (Slutsky) substitution effect.

[17]Although it may appear that we are assuming constant substitution and income effects for each person, this is not the case; indeed, it is impossible to have a labor supply function with constant income and substitution effects (see, for example, Dickinson, 1975, p. 31).

[18]It might be noted that the model described in this paper cannot be estimated using cross-sectional data. In a cross section, only one equilibrium position is observed, and the model is not identified.

[19]Response is subject to truncation because, at most, a person can reduce hours to zero. The estimation technique we employ accounts for this problem.

Thus, response depends on the initial equilibrium position.[20]

Differences in response to an *NIT* program arise, not because persons with different tastes for work have inherently different responses to changes in disposable income or net wage rates, but because individuals with different propensities to work (different initial equilibria on a given budget constraint) are offered different inducements to change their behavior. Those with the smallest propensities to work experience the largest changes in income.

A final implication of this model is that theory-free response models that compare the average response of persons on different programs are not meaningful. The reason for this is that persons with higher incomes (and therefore higher labor supplies) are assigned to the more generous programs in order to reduce the average cost of an observation.[21] Thus, because both response and assignment to program depend on the initial position, biased measures of program differences are obtained.[22] The response model used, however, controls for the nonrandom assignment by allowing response to be a function of preexperimental labor supply and by directly measuring the change in budget constraints caused by the *NIT*.

III. Empirical Specification

To estimate equation (4), data on heads of families in *SIME/DIME* are used. The change in labor supply ΔH, is equal to hours of work in the second year of the experiment H_e, minus hours of work in the year prior to the experiment H_p. The response variables, Δw and $\Delta Y_d(H_p)$, depend on the particular budget constraint, and on the preprogram equilibrium position. For reasons described below, several modifications are made to this equation regarding functional form, additional variables, missing data on wage rates for nonworkers, and nonlinearity of the budget constraints.

A. The Role of Control Families

Approximately 45 percent of the families in *SIME/DIME* serve as controls and are not eligible for payments. For these families, it is assumed that Δw and $\Delta Y_d(H_p)$ are zero.[23] Control families are included in the sample, however, to increase the efficiency of the estimated treatment effects.[24] Efficiency is increased because factors other than the experiment (such as changing economic conditions) cause labor supply to change over time. The inclusion of control families in the sample enables us to make a more precise distinction between experimental and nonexperimental effects. Variables used in this study to measure nonexperimental effects are called control variables. The control variables include all variables that affect assignment to experimental treatments.[25]

B. Calculating the Change in Disposable Income

The change in disposable income evaluated at the initial equilibrium hours of work

[20]Note that in a typical cross-sectional model, where it is assumed that gross wage effects and income effects are constant, response would not depend on the initial position (below break even and ignoring truncation), because the changes in nonwage income and the net wage rate do not depend on the initial position.

[21]Simple random assignment is not used in any of the *NIT* experiments. See John Conlisk and Kurz, and Keeley and Robins for a description of the *SIME/DIME* assignment model.

[22]If program dummy variables were interacted with all assignment variables, unbiased estimates of response could be obtained. Such a model would have far too many parameters, however, to be estimated with precision using our sample. See Spiegelman and West.

[23]Changes in the control budget constraints that have zero mean and are uncorrelated with the variables in the equation would not affect the consistency of the estimates.

[24]A comparison of least squares estimates for husbands, including and excluding control families, indicates that the coefficients of $\Delta Y_d(H_p)$ and Δw differ by less than 10 percent, while the standard errors are 16 percent larger when controls are excluded.

[25]The control variables include eight dummy variables for normal income categories, dummy variables for race (black/white) and site (Seattle/Denver), age, number of family members, number of children under 5 years of age, and Aid to Families with Dependent Children (*AFDC*) benefits in the year prior to enrollment.

is given by

$$(5) \quad \Delta Y_d(H_p) = Y_{de}(H_p) - Y_{dp}(H_p)$$

where $Y_{de}(H_p)$ is disposable income evaluated at H_p under the *NIT*, and $Y_{dp}(H_p)$ is disposable income evaluated at H_p before the *NIT*. For this study, $\Delta Y_d(H_p)$ is calculated on the basis of earnings and nonwage income in the year before enrollment in the experiment.[26] Thus, $\Delta Y_d(H_p)$ depends on both transitory and permanent components of labor supply. In theory, the change in disposable income should be measured at normal or permanent labor supply. Because there is likely to be a transitory component in our measure of labor supply, our estimate of the income effect will be biased because of the presence of errors in variables.[27] In a lengthier version of this paper available from the authors upon request, the bias is discussed and it is shown that the bias is not likely to be large if preexperimental labor supply is included on the right-hand side of the equation. For this reason, H_p is

---

[26] $\Delta Y_d(H_p) = S - SR100 - .5(SR50 - SA50) - [t - r(Y - E)](Y - E) + Q$, where S is the support level, t is the initial tax rate, and r is the rate of decline of the average tax rate. The term $SR100$ represents items taxed at 100 percent: bonus value of food stamps, welfare benefits other than *AFDC*, unemployment and workmen's compensation, veteran's survivors and disability benefits, training stipends net of tuition, fees and books, and social security benefits. The term $SR50$ represents items taxes at 50 percent: alimony and child support received and other support received. The term $SA50$ represents items reimbursed at 50 percent: alimony and child support paid and other support paid. The term Y represents items taxed as income: earnings, insurance benefits, pensions and annuities, payments from private disability plans, and a fraction of net worth. The term E represents items subtracted from income: child care expenses, care for the aged, and medical expenses. The term Q represents items reimbursed at 100 percent: federal and state income taxes and social security taxes. If $\Delta Y_d(H_p) > 0$, a family is defined as being below the tax break-even level; it is set equal to zero for families above the tax break-even level. Families receiving *AFDC* benefits prior to the experiment are required to give up their *AFDC* status in order to receive *NIT* payments. We subtract preexperimental *AFDC* benefits from $\Delta Y_d(H_p)$ for families below the tax break-even level.

[27] The substitution effect would also be biased to the extent that the preexperimental tax rate depends on preexperimental labor supply.

included among the explanatory variables, and H_e is used as the dependent variable.

C. *Calculating the Change in the Net Wage Rate*

The change in the net wage rate is given by

$$(6) \quad \Delta w = -W(t_e - t_p)$$

where W is the gross wage rate, t_e is the experimental tax rate, and t_p is the preexperimental tax rate. In calculating this variable from *SIME/DIME* data, two problems arise. First, the preexperimental tax function and many of the experimental tax functions are non-linear. Second, wage rates are not observed for nonworkers.

As mentioned earlier, a feature of *SIME/DIME* is the testing of declining tax rate programs. The effect of the declining tax rate programs is to make the experimental tax rate t_e an endogenous variable that depends on labor supply. To purge the tax rate of this endogeneity, we linearize the budget constraint around the preexperimental point and treat the individual as if he or she were on the tangent linear budget constraint. This procedure is deficient in that all final equilibrium points are not on the linearized budget constraint, although the rate of decline of the tax rate is small. Furthermore, because the experimental budget set is nonconvex for families on the declining tax rate programs, and because small changes in nonconvex budget sets may lead to large changes in behavior, the linearization may not be a reasonable approximation to the true budget set. To account for the linearization procedure during estimation, we include a dummy variable for persons on the declining tax rate programs.

The preexperimental budget constraint is also non-linear, because of the progressivity of the positive income tax system and the interrelations among tax rates in income-conditioned public transfer programs. Endogeneity is not a problem, however, because preexperimental labor supply is predetermined. The preexperimental tax rates are derived on the basis of preexperimental income and participation in certain income-conditioned tax and transfer programs. The income-conditioned programs we consider include federal and state income taxes, social security taxes, *AFDC*, Aid to Families with Dependent Children-Unemployed Parent (*AFDC-UP*), and Food Stamps. The tax rates are derived in accordance with the tax laws and the administrative regulations of the public transfer programs.[28]

Because wage rates are not observed for nonworkers, a wage equation is estimated for workers based on personal characteristics, and the equation is used to predict wage rates for the entire sample.[29] A variety of different wage equations can be specified; the wage equation we estimate is a simple linear formulation based on the human capital model of Jacob Mincer.[30] The change in the net wage Δw is calculated as the product of the predicted wage rate and the difference between the linearized pre-experimental and experimental tax rates. Like $\Delta Y_d(H_p)$, Δw is set equal to zero for persons above the tax break-even level.

[28] See Kurz et al. for a discussion of how the positive tax rates are derived, and Maxfield for a discussion of how the transfer program tax rates are derived. There is some evidence that legal tax rates are an over-estimate of the effective tax rates of public transfer programs. Legal tax rates are used in this paper because they are used in the computer program that extrapolates the experimental results to the national population.

[29] This approach follows Hall (1973) and Edward Kalachek and Frederick Raines. Reuben Gronau and Heckman (1974) demonstrate that the wage equation approach yields biased estimates for nonworkers, and they develop alternative estimation procedures. However, in this paper, the substitution effect is estimated as the coefficient of the change in the net wage rather than the coefficient of the gross wage rate. It is unlikely that small biases in estimating gross wages significantly affect the change variable, which depends primarily on the difference between the experimental and preexperimental tax rates. In a recent paper, Heckman (1976) finds that in a national sample of white married women (the National Longitudinal Survey) the selectivity bias in wage rates is quantitatively small.

[30] The estimated wage equations are

$$W = -.071B + .033E + .061X - .00106X^2$$
$$(.051) \quad (.012) \quad (.008) \quad (.00018)$$

$$+ 2.340 \text{ for husbands}$$
$$(.172)$$

D. *Additional Experimental Variables*

Certain families on *SIME/DIME* are enrolled in manpower programs that provide counseling and subsidize training and educational activities.[31] To capture the effects of the three manpower programs of the experiment, dummy variables for each program are included in the empirical specification.

Many of the enrolled families are initially above the tax break-even level.[32] Even though the calculated values of Δw and $\Delta Y_d(H_p)$ are zero for families with preexperimental equilibria above the tax break-even level, some of these families will respond to the experiment.[33] Response above the break-even level is measured by defining three explanatory variables that capture the location of the family relative to the break-even level: a dummy variable signifying whether or not the family is above the break-even level, the break-even level of the

$$W = .800B + .110E + .036X - .00073X^2$$
$$(.049) \quad (.014) \quad (.008) \quad (.00020)$$

$$+ .590 \text{ for wives}$$
$$(.192)$$

$$W = .010B + .102E + .045X - .00098X^2$$
$$(.045) \quad (.013) \quad (.009) \quad (.00021)$$

$$+ .816 \text{ for female heads of households}$$
$$(.183)$$

where B is a dummy variable for race (black = 1), E is years of schooling, and X is experience (defined as age minus years of schooling minus 5). Standard errors are in parentheses. The R^2s are .112, .048, and .116, respectively. Because the variance of Δw would be dominated by the change in the tax rate no matter how complicated the wage equation, the results using a more complicated wage equation are likely to be similar to the results reported in this paper.

[31] See Kurz and Spiegelman (1971, 1972) for a description of the manpower component of *SIME/DIME*.

[32] Based on preexperimental income, 10 percent of the single-parent headed families and 20 percent of the double-parent headed families in *SIME/DIME* are above the tax break-even level.

[33] Under the assumption that substitution effects are constant, it can be shown that families above the tax break-even level will respond only if income in excess of the break-even level is less than half of the absolute value of the change in income they would experience if they did respond (see Robins and West).

family earnings, and the amount of family earnings above the break-even level.[34]

E. *Estimation Procedure*

Because H_e cannot take on negative values and because there are numerous observations where $H_e = 0$, estimation of the model by ordinary least squares would yield inconsistent coefficient estimates. Furthermore, the estimates would be inefficient because the error term is heteroscedastic. To account for these statistical problems, we use a tobit model, which is designed to handle cases where the dependent variable is truncated normal.[35] The Tobit model may be written as

$$(7) \quad H_e = \max [b_0 + b_1 H_p + b_2 C$$
$$+ b_3 M + b_4 \Delta Y_d(H_p) + b_5 \Delta w$$
$$+ b_6 FABOVE + b_7 BREAK$$
$$+ b_8 EARNABV$$
$$+ b_9 DECLINE + e, 0]$$

where
H_e = experimental hours of work
H_p = preexperimental hours of work
C = vector of control variables
M = vector of manpower treatment variables
$\Delta Y_d(H_p)$ = change in disposable income evaluated at preexperimental labor supply (thousands of dollars per year)

Δw = change in the net wage rate (dollars per hour)
$FABOVE$ = dummy variable for persons above the tax break-even level
$BREAK$ = break-even level of earnings (thousands of dollars per year)
$EARNABV$ = family earnings above the break-even level (thousands of dollars per year)
$DECLINE$ = dummy variable for persons on the declining tax rate programs.
e = random error term, assumed to be distributed normally with variance σ^2.

The b_i and σ^2 are estimated by maximum likelihood using an iterative-maximization technique.

The parameters in a Tobit model cannot be interpreted in the same way as the parameters in a linear model. In a linear model, the treatment parameters are interpreted as the average response of the population to the imposition of a negative income tax. In a Tobit model, the treatment parameters give the average response only of persons who have nonzero labor supplies (interior solutions) before and after the imposition of a negative income tax. The response of all other persons is somewhat smaller in magnitude than that of persons with interior solutions because of the lower bound on the dependent variable. The coefficients of $\Delta Y_d(H_p)$ and Δw, however, can be interpreted as income and substitution effects for persons with interior solutions before and after the *NIT* program is implemented.

This empirical specification eliminates many of the problems associated with measuring the response to an *NIT* program. Nonrandom assignment by family income is taken into account because the response is allowed to vary with preexperimental income, which is the major assignment variable. Heterogeneity is partially controlled because individuals with identical budget

---

[34]Our specification of these above break-even variables is likely to suffer from errors of measurement of the same type as those present in $\Delta Y_d(H_p)$. To some extent, however, the procedure used to account for errors of measurement in $\Delta Y_d(H_p)$ should also account for this type of measurement error. The primary cause of bias in the above break-even variables is probably misclassification of persons who are near the break-even level preexperimentally; the specification would thus lead to overestimation of effects above the break-even level and underestimation of effects below the break-even level. In another paper, Robins and West present a model that unifies the response above and below the break-even level and find that the results are similar to those presented in this paper.

[35]See Takeshi Amemiya or Tobin (1958) for a discussion of the Tobit model.

TABLE 2—ESTIMATED EXPERIMENTAL EFFECTS ON LABOR SUPPLY
(Tobit Estimates)

Independent Variable	Coefficient		
	Husbands	Wives	Female Heads
Below break-even			
$\Delta Y_d(H_p)$	− 34.4	− 142.9[c]	− 101.1[b]
	(27.3)	(44.4)	(39.4)
Δw	83.2[b]	168.0[a]	125.8[a]
	(37.1)	(91.2)	(65.9)
Above break-even			
FABOVE	− 12.7	− 430.8[a]	− 344.8
	(174.6)	(255.6)	(291.3)
BREAK	− 5.5	8.3	73.2
	(21.1)	(29.5)	(64.7)
EARNABV	11.5	47.5	35.1
	(27.3)	(42.0)	(55.6)
DECLINE	− 86.3[b]	119.5	21.8
	(48.4)	(78.1)	(73.2)
χ^2	21.55[c]	26.84[c]	20.24[c]
S	720	1,086	990
	(14)	(28)	(25)
$\bar{H}_e$	1,736	659	975
	(825)	(825)	(935)
N	1,592	1,698	1,358

Notes: Standard errors in parentheses; χ^2 is the *chi*-square test for treatment effects
(6 degrees of freedom); S is the standard error of estimate; $\bar{H}_e$ is the mean of the dependent variable, hours of work per year in the second year of the experiment; N is
the sample size.
[a] Indicates significance at 10 percent level.
[b] Indicates significance at 5 percent level.
[c] Indicates significance at 1 percent level.

constraints are allowed to respond differently. Preexperimental participation in
other welfare programs is taken into account
by including welfare income and tax rates
in the definitions of the changes in disposable income and net wage rates. Finally,
the estimation of substitution and income
effects enables the prediction of labor supply
response to *NIT* programs other than the
ones being tested in *SIME/DIME*.

IV. Results

The sample consists of a subset of originally enrolled black and white family heads
who remained in *SIME/DIME* for at least
two years and for whom data were available at the time this study was undertaken.[36]

[36] About 800 Mexican-Americans are enrolled in the
Denver Experiment but are excluded from the analysis
in this paper because data were not available for them

The empirical model is estimated separately
for female heads of households and for
husbands and wives in two-parent headed
households. The subgroups for analysis are
defined as of the date of enrollment regardless of changes in marital status. This approach is used so that the estimates are not
conditional on unchanged marital status.

when this study was undertaken. It has turned out to
be a rather difficult task to build computer software
that converts data from interview form into analytical
files with reasonable flexibility and generality at low
cost. SRI International is now in the process of building such computer software and processing interview
data into a data management system. This system will
enable users to construct their own analytical files
from the basic data. When this data base system is
complete, the Department of Health, Education, and
Welfare, which is funding *SIME/DIME*, will release
a public use file. In the interim, a copy of the data tape
used for the analysis presented in this paper is available on request (at a nominal cost to cover copying
and documentation).

TABLE 3—TESTS OF SITE, RACE, AND
EXPERIMENTAL DURATION DIFFERENCES IN RESPONSE

TABLE 3—TESTS OF SITE, RACE, AND
EXPERIMENTAL DURATION DIFFERENCES IN RESPONSE

	Husbands	Wives	Female Heads
Site test	.53	.41	1.12
Race test	1.70	.52	1.34
Experimental duration test	.93	1.53	.41

Notes: Tests are based on ordinary least squares estimates. The race and site tests are performed by interacting each experimental variable with race and site dummies. The experimental duration test is performed by interacting Δw and $\Delta Y_d(H_p)$ with dummy variables for the three- and five-year programs. The coefficients of control variables are constrained to be the same in the tests. Numbers given are F-ratios with 6 and N degrees of freedom for the race and site tests, and 2 and N degrees of freedom for the experimental duration tests, where N is the sample size.

Table 2 displays the Tobit estimates for the experimental variables.[37] In Table 3, the results of tests of differences in response by race, experimental site, and experimental duration are presented. The various tests are performed using ordinary least squares to reduce computational expense.

For each group, there are statistically significant experimental effects on labor supply. The income effects are negative and statistically significant for wives and female heads, and the substitution effects are positive and statistically significant for all three groups. The F-statistics for site and race differences are not significant, implying that the hypotheses of equal experimental effects

[37] The results for the control and manpower variables are in an appendix available upon request from the authors.

in Seattle and Denver and for blacks and whites cannot be rejected. The tests of different substitution and income effects for persons on the three- and five-year experimental programs are not statistically significant; however, for all three groups, the substitution effect is larger and the income effect is smaller for persons on the three-year programs, a result consistent with the predictions of the model developed by Metcalf.[38] For families above the tax break-even level, only wives appear to be responding to the experiment. All three groups exhibit a response above the break-even level that declines in absolute value with distance from the break-even level.[39]

Table 4 presents estimated substitution and income effects evaluated at the sample means for persons below the break-even level who are working in both the pre-experimental and experimental periods (for example, persons for whom $H_e > 0$ and $H_p > 0$).

The estimated effects at the sample means

[38] *SIME/DIME* is uniquely structured to test the effects of experimental duration on behavioral response. Studies devoted to this issue are currently being undertaken.

[39] Because the functional form used for the experimental response could be considered fairly restrictive, we have estimated several less restricted versions of the model. These versions include the following sets of additional variables; 1) a dummy variable for having a financial treatment, 2) the change in the support level, 3) interactions of $\Delta Y_d(H_p)$ with preexperimental nonwelfare income, and 4) interactions of Δw and $\Delta Y_d(H_p)$ with *DECLINE*. Out of twelve tests of the null hypotheses that these additional variables have zero coefficients, only one, the test of 1) for wives, is significant at the 5 percent level; all the others are not significant at the 10 percent level.

TABLE 4—SUBSTITUTION AND INCOME EFFECTS AT THE MEAN
(Estimated Asymptotic Standard Errors in Parentheses)

	Husbands	Wives	Female Heads
Substitution effect at the mean $(\hat{b}_5 \Delta \overline{w})$	−55.7 (24.9)	−63.8 (34.7)	−59.1 (31.0)
Income effect at the mean $[\hat{b}_4 \Delta Y_d(H_p)]$	−47.1 (37.4)	−198.6 (61.7)	−117.3 (45.7)
Total effect at the mean	−102.8 (33.0)	−262.4 (55.1)	−176.4 (43.6)
Mean hours of work in preexperimental period $(\overline{H}_p)$	1,922	1,194	1,577

indicate a substantial disincentive effect, particularly for women. In percentage terms, the effects are −5.3 percent for husbands, −22.0 percent for wives, and −11.2 percent for female heads of families. It is important to note that these effects are based on mean changes in disposable income and net wage rates that result from the set of programs being tested in *SIME/DIME*, rather than from any single *NIT* program.

V. Implications of the Results for a Nationwide *NIT* Program

One of the primary reasons for undertaking the *NIT* experiments is to provide policymakers with estimates of the labor supply effects of a nationwide *NIT* program. The model developed in this paper can be used to predict the labor supply effects of a variety of nationwide *NIT* programs, including programs that are different from those being tested in the experiments. We use the March 1975 *Current Population Survey* (*CPS*) to generate nationwide predictions.[40] The *CPS* is a weighted random sample of the *U.S.* population and contains information on about 50,000 households.[41] The predictions are derived by applying the estimated response function to each individual and then summing the estimated responses over all individuals. Only the responses of heads of families between the ages of 18 and 58 are considered; nonheads of households, households with only one member, and the elderly are omitted from the analysis.

Predictions are generated for six different *NIT* programs. The six programs have constant tax rates of 50 and 70 percent and support (guarantee) levels of 50, 75, and 100 percent of the poverty level ($5,000 for a family of four in 1974). Because the poverty level increases with family size, the support level also increases with family size. The nominal support level is constant across re-

[40] For a detailed description of the methodology used to generate the predictions, see Keeley et al. and Maxfield.

[41] The income data from the March 1975 *CPS* are annual data for the year 1974.

gions, and the *NIT* program is assumed to replace the existing *AFDC*, *AFDC-UP*, and Food Stamp programs. All other nonlabor income is taxed by the program at a rate of 100 percent.

The predicted labor supply responses are presented in Table 5 and are reported in two ways: first, the average responses for all participating families; and second, the average responses for the *U.S.* population. The average responses for the *U.S.* population include the responses of certain nonparticipants, as well as the responses of participants. The nonparticipants who respond are families that previously received welfare benefits and are above the break-even level of the *NIT* program. These families increase their labor supply when the welfare programs are replaced by the *NIT* program.

In interpreting the results, it is important to keep in mind that the responses vary not only because of changing guarantee levels and tax rates, but also because of a changing pool of participants. For example, as the tax rate increases (for a given guarantee), the pool of participants decreases. On the other hand, as the guarantee increases (for a given tax rate), the pool of participants increases. The manner in which the pools change depends on the distribution of income within the relevant population subgroup.

For participating husband-wife families, the magnitudes of the average responses are positively associated with both the guarantee and the tax rate. For participating female-headed families, the responses are positively associated with the guarantee, but do not vary with the tax rate. For both groups, the results indicate fairly sizable reductions in labor supply, ranging from between 10 and 21 percent for husband-wife families and between 0 and 15 percent for female-headed families.

The average responses of the *U.S.* population are quite small relative to the average responses of participating families because most families in the United States do not choose to participate in the program. While the magnitudes of the average responses again increase with the guarantee (as they

TABLE 5—AVERAGE LABOR SUPPLY RESPONSES TO A NATIONWIDE *NIT* PROGRAM FOR
ALL PARTICIPATING FAMILIES AND FOR ALL FAMILIES IN THE UNITED STATES

NIT Support Level	Participating Families			All Families	
	Change in Hours[b]	Percent Change	Number of Families[c]	Change in Hours[b]	Percent Change
NIT Tax Rate 50 Percent					
50 Percent of Poverty Level[a]					
Husbands	−104	−7.0		−4	−0.2
Wives	−92	−23.3		−2	−0.3
Total H/W	−196	−10.3	2.4	−6	−0.2
Female Heads	0	0.0	2.3	+16	+1.6
75 Percent of Poverty Level[a]					
Husbands	−106	−5.9		−19	−1.0
Wives	−110	−22.8		−19	−2.4
Total H/W	−216	−9.5	7.6	−38	−1.4
Female Heads	−47	−6.7	3.0	−23	−2.4
100 Percent of Poverty Level[a]					
Husbands	−119	−6.2		−47	−2.4
Wives	−130	−22.7		−50	−6.3
Total H/W	−249	−10.0	15.7	−97	−3.5
Female Heads	−99	−12.0	3.6	−69	−7.1
NIT Tax Rate 70 Percent					
50 Percent of Poverty Level[a]					
Husbands	−136	−10.8		−2	−0.1
Wives	−111	−29.9		0	0.0
Total H/W	−247	−15.1	1.3	−2	−0.1
Female Heads	−10	−2.7	2.0	+20	+2.1
75 Percent of Poverty Level[a]					
Husbands	−157	−11.2		−9	−0.5
Wives	−126	−32.5		−5	−0.6
Total H/W	−283	−15.8	2.8	−14	−0.5
Female Heads	−47	−9.3	2.5	−12	−1.2
100 Percent of Poverty Level[a]					
Husbands	−164	−10.1		−23	−1.2
Wives	−144	−32.0		−18	−2.3
Total H/W	−308	−20.6	5.8	−41	−1.5
Female Heads	−95	−14.9	3.0	−52	−5.3

Notes: Average hours of work per year for all husbands in the United States before response = 1,999. Average hours of work per year for all wives in the United States before response = 793. Average hours of work per year for all female heads in the United States before response = 974. Total number of husband-wife families in the United States = 39.8 million. Total number of female-headed families in the United States = 4.9 million.

[a] Poverty level was $5,000 per year for a family of four in 1974.

[b] Average change in hours of work per year due to *NIT*.

[c] Shown in millions.

do for participants), they decrease with the tax rate for both groups. This inverse relationship between the average *U.S.* response and the tax rate is an interesting and perhaps unexpected result that is a consequence of the fact that the number of participants decreases by an amount large enough to offset the effect of a larger response among participants. Thus, we find that the total disincentive effect of a nationwide *NIT* program is smaller under higher tax rate programs.

VI. Summary and Conclusions

Social experimentation is a relatively new research tool that is being used to assess the behavioral effects and costs of alternative public transfer programs. Its success as a research tool depends on developing an empirical framework that exploits the advantages of experimental data (primarily, exogeneity of treatment) and at the same time accounts for the unique aspects of experimental design that create problems in the analysis (namely, nonrandom assignment, nonrepresentative samples, limited duration, the presence of other welfare programs, etc.).

In this paper, we present a framework for using experimental data to estimate the parameters of a labor supply response function. The nationwide aggregate labor supply effects of alternative *NIT* programs are obtained by applying these parameter estimates to a national data base. The results indicate that the labor supply responses to alternative nationwide *NIT* programs vary widely with the parameters of the program, and that for some programs, the aggregate labor supply responses are of considerable magnitude.

REFERENCES

H. J. Aaron, "Cautionary Notes on the Experiment," in Joseph Pechman and P. Michael Timpane, eds., *Work Incentives and Income Guarantees: The New Jersey Negative Income Tax Experiment*, Washington 1975, 88-114.

T. Amemiya, "Regression Analysis When the Dependent Variable is Truncated Normal," *Econometrica*, Nov. 1973, *41*, 997-1016.

O. Ashenfelter and J. Heckman, "Estimating Labor Supply Functions," in Glen G. Cain and Harold W. Watts, eds., *Income Maintenance and Labor Supply*, Chicago 1973, 265-78.

———— and ————, "The Estimation of Income and Substitution Effects in a Model of Family Labor Supply," *Econometrica*, Jan. 1974, *42*, 73-85.

Glen G. Cain and Harold W. Watts, *Income Maintenance and Labor Supply*, Chicago 1973.

J. Conlisk and M. Kurz, "The Assignment Model of the Seattle and Denver Income Maintenance Experiments," res. memo. no. 15, Center Study Welfare Policy,

SRI International, July 1972.

J. Dickinson, "Implicit and Explicit Preference Structures in Models of Labor Supply," disc. paper no. 331-75, Instit. Res. Poverty, Univ. Wisconsin, Dec. 1975.

————, "The Ashenfelter-Heckman Model and Parallel Preference Structures," disc. paper no. 411-77, Instit. Res. Poverty, Univ. Wisconsin, Dec. 1977.

Milton Friedman, *Capitalism and Freedom*, Chicago 1962.

R. Gronau, "Wage Comparisons—A Selectivity Bias," *J. Polit. Econ.*, Nov./Dec. 1974, *82*, 1119-143.

R. E. Hall, "Wages, Income, and Hours of Work in the U.S. Labor Force," in Glen G. Cain and Harold W. Watts, eds., *Income Maintenance and Labor Supply*, Chicago 1973, 102-62.

————, "Effects of the Experimental Negative Income Tax on Labor Supply," in Joseph A. Pechman and P. Michael Timpane, eds., *Work Incentives and Income Guarantees: The New Jersey Negative Income Tax Experiment*, Washington 1975, 115-47.

J. Heckman, "Shadow Prices, Market Wages, and Labor Supply," *Econometrica*, July 1974, *42*, 679-94.

————, "Sample Selection Bias as a Specification Error (with an Application to the Estimation of Labor Supply Functions)," mimeo., Univ. Chicago, Apr. 1976.

———— and Robert Willis, "A Beta Logistic Model for the Analysis of Sequential Labor Force Participation by Married Women," *J. Polit. Econ.*, Feb. 1977, *85*, 27-58.

E. D. Kalachek and F. Q. Raines, "Labor Supply of Lower Income Workers and the Negative Income Tax," in *Technical Studies*, The President's Commission on Income Maintenance Programs, Washington 1970, 159-86.

Michael C. Keeley, *The Economics of Labor Supply: A Critical Review*, forthcoming.

———— and Philip K. Robins, "The Design of Social Experiments: A Critique of the Conlisk-Watts Assignment Model," mimeo., Center Study Welfare Policy,

SRI International, Mar. 1978.

―――― et al., "The Labor Supply Effects and Costs of Alternative Negative Income Tax Programs," *J. Hum. Resources*, Winter 1978, *13*, 3–36.

David Kershaw and Jerilyn Fair, *The New Jersey Income Maintenance Experiment*, Vol. 1: *Operations, Surveys, and Administration*, New York 1976.

M. Kurz et al., "A Cross Sectional Estimation of Labor Supply for Families in Denver 1970," res. memo. no 24, Center Study Welfare Policy, SRI International, Nov. 1974.

―――― and R. G. Spiegelman, "The Seattle Experiment: The Combined Effect of Income Maintenance and Manpower Investments," *Amer. Econ. Rev. Proc.*, May 1971, *61*, 22–29.

―――― and ――――, "The Design of the Seattle and Denver Income Maintenance Experiments," res. memo. no. 18, Center Study Welfare Policy, SRI International, May 1972.

. Robert J. Lampman, *Ends and Means of Reducing Income Poverty*, Chicago 1971.

M. Maxfield, "Estimating the Impact of Labor Supply Adjustments on Transfer Program Costs: A Microsimulation Methodology," mimeo., Mathematica Policy Res., Feb. 1977.

C. E. Metcalf, "Making Inferences from Controlled Income Maintenance Experiments," *Amer. Econ. Rev.*, June 1973, *63*, 478–83.

Jacob Mincer, *Schooling, Experience, and Earnings*, New York 1974.

G. H. Orcutt and A. G. Orcutt, "Incentive and Disincentive Experimentation for Income Maintenance Policy Purposes," *Amer. Econ. Rev.*, Sept. 1968, *58*, 754–72.

Joseph A. Pechman and P. Michael Timpane, *Work Incentives and Income Guarantees: The New Jersey Negative Income Tax Experiment*, Washington 1975.

P. K. Robins and R. W. West, "Participation in the Seattle and Denver Income Maintenance Experiments, and Its Effect on Labor Supply," res. memo. no. 53, Center Study Welfare Policy, SRI International, Mar. 1978.

H. Ross, "A Proposal for a Demonstration of New Techniques in Income Maintenance," memo., Data Center Archives, Instit. Res. Poverty, Univ. Wisconsin, Dec. 1966.

R. G. Spiegelman and R. W. West, "Feasibility of a Social Experiment and Issues in Its Design," 1976 *Proc. Amer. Statist. Assn.*, *Bus. and Econ. Statist. Sec.*, Washington 1976, 168–76.

J. Tobin, "Estimation of Relationships for Limited Dependent Variables," *Econometrica*, Jan. 1958, *26*, 24–36.

――――, "Improving the Economic Status of the Negro," *J. Daedalus*, Fall 1965, *94*, 878–98.

Harold W. Watts and Albert Rees, (1977a) *The New Jersey Income Maintenance Experiment*, Vol. II: *Labor Supply Responses*, New York 1977.

―――― and ――――, (1977b) *The New Jersey Income Maintenance Experiment*, Vol. III: *Expenditures, Health, and Social Behavior, and the Quality of the Evidence*, New York 1977.

U.S. Bureau of the Census, *Current Population Survey*, Mar. 1975 (data tape).

20

UNEMPLOYMENT INSURANCE AND UNEMPLOYMENT IN THE UNITED STATES

Daniel S. Hamermesh

I. INTRODUCTION

There is no single system of unemployment insurance in the United States. Rather, there are separate systems in each of the 50 states, Puerto Rico and the District of Columbia. Accordingly, it is impossible to describe fully the institution of UI in this country; similarly, because of this heterogeneity, one cannot use a single state's system as an example that typifies the working of UI or that indicates its likely effects. Instead, we present here a discussion of those general features that characterize many of the state systems and that are essential for an understanding of how and to what extent UI affects the unemployment rate.

One way to analyze the effect of UI on unemployment is the direct approach, the standard methodology of impact evaluation. This postulates a number of variables that may produce variations in unemployment, and asks what additional effect is produced by variations in the parameters describing the UI system. If it is possible to identify this relationship satisfactorily, this method, discussed in Section III of this paper, is a simple and useful one.

An alternative, more complex approach is to recognize that the unemployment rate, $U/L \cdot$ can be written as the product of the number of spells of unemployment and their average duration, in weeks, divided by 52 times L, the labor force. Using this identity, the effect of UI on the unemployment rate can be calculated by aggregating its effects on the duration of spells of unemployment, the number of such spells, and the composition of the labor force. Sections IV, V and VI examine the available evidence on each of these effects, while Section VII synthesizes the results and summarizes the best estimates of the impact of UI on unemployment.

*This paper is partly based on the author's larger work, *Jobless Pay and the Economy*, Baltimore, Maryland: Johns Hopkins University Press, 1977.

"Unemployment Insurance and Unemployment in the United States," Hamermesh, Daniel S. in UNEMPLOYMENT INSURANCE: GLOBAL EVIDENCE OF ITS EFFECTS ON UNEMPLOYMENT, Proceedings of an International Conference, Herbert G. Grubel and Michael A. Walker eds., The Fraser Institute, Vancouver, B.C., pp. 39-58, 1978.

II. OVERVIEW OF UNEMPLOYMENT INSURANCE IN THE UNITED STATES

Since 1947 the United States has experienced six recessions in business activity. The civilian unemployment rate has varied from 2.7 per cent of the labor force (measured in the monthly household survey) in December 1952 to 8.9 per cent in May 1975. Further, there is good evidence that the measured unemployment rate consistent with a given degree of aggregate labor market tightness in the mid-1970's is higher, perhaps by as much as two percentage points, that it was in the late 1950's. This change has resulted from a shift in the demographic mix of the labor force toward groups, particularly the young, that are more prone to spells of unemployment. Presumably, with the continuing decline in birth rates since the mid-1950's, this phenomenon is reaching its extreme, and .we can expect measured unemployment rates in the 1980's to be somewhat lower than those in the mid-1970's, assuming the same degree of macroeconomic stimulus and no major changes in labor market institutions.

As a percentage of disposable income, unemployment insurance benefits have varied from .34 in 1969 to 1.55 in 1975.[1] While these numbers are small, there is evidence (Lester, 1962, and Gramlich, 1974) that UI benefits offset somewhere between 10 and 15 per cent of all earnings losses resulting from movements of the economy away from cyclical peaks. Further, weekly UI benefits per claimant have equalled between 32 and 37 per cent of average weekly earnings in covered employment since 1947. More important, Hamermesh (1977) uses both hypothetical examples and a survey of exhaustees to show that for a typical beneficiary, when the nontaxable nature of benefits is considered along with lost fringes, uncompensated parts of unemployment spells and inflation of wages as compared to benefits (based on previous year's wages), the likely replacement ratio is somewhere between 50 and 60 per cent.

Extent and diversity

To understand the diversity of UI systems in the United States, consider first a typical beneficiary, and then a typical firm.[2] The potential beneficiary is eligible for benefits if his previous employer was covered by the state UI system. Essentially all manufacturing firms are now covered, but employees in agriculture, the self-employed, domestic household workers, and some employees in state and local government activities or in certain small non-profit operations are not. (Railroad workers, ex-servicemen and Federal employees are covered by small special programs which we ignore in this discussion, and there are minor interstate differences in coverage.) Roughly 75 percent of the civilian labor force is now covered.

Eligibility and terms

Eligibility is also defined in terms of prior work attachment and the reason for separation. Regulations differ, but among the eight states that we use as examples, in Colorado the worker must have earned 30 times the weekly benefit amount and $750 in the base period. (In 35 states this is the first four of the five calendar quarters preceding his filing the claim. In most of the rest, including Massachusetts, Minnesota, Ohio and New York, the base period is the 52 weeks preceding the claim or the receipt of benefits.) California and Massachusetts require a flat amount of annual earned income for eligibility; Minnesota, New York, Ohio and Oregon place requirements both on weeks worked and earnings in the base period, and in South Carolina the claimant is required to have earned 1.5 times his *high-quarter earnings* and $300 during the base period. These examples capture the main types of provisions. The other criterion for eligibility in most states is that the worker was laid off or quit for cause. If he quit voluntarily or was fired, he will be declared ineligible, although he can appeal this decision. In some states, he will receive UI benefits after a longer waiting period (often six weeks or more).

Potential duration of benefits is uniform in a few states (New York), but in most it depends on the claimant's base period earnings and/or weeks of employment. In most states the maximum potential duration of regular benefits is 26 weeks. Practices also differ among states on weekly benefits. The weekly benefit can be some fraction of high-quarter earnings (California, Colorado, Massachusetts and South Carolina); some, possibly variable, fraction of average weekly wages during the base period (Minnesota, New York and Ohio), with the fraction equal to .5 in most cases; some fraction of entire base period earnings (Oregon), or some other method in another state. In 11 states, including Massachusetts and Ohio, the claimant can also receive extra benefits (dependents' allowances) linked to his weekly benefits, his base-period earnings and the number of dependents in his household.

In all states there is a maximum benefit beyond which the weekly benefit cannot be raised regardless of prior earnings or work history. This is defined either in dollar amounts or relative to the state average weekly wage in covered employment (in 32 states including Colorado, Massachusetts, Ohio, Oregon and South Carolina). In no state is this maximum higher than ⅔ the state average weekly wage, except where dependents' allowances are also paid. In 1972, 44 per cent of recipients received the maximum benefit.

After a one-week *waiting period* (in all but eight states), the claimant begins to receive his weekly benefit. So long as he can show he is looking for work and that he has not refused *suitable work* in a job found for him by the Employment Service, he may continue to receive his benefit check. In all states except Montana he may take part-time work and receive partial benefits up to his potential duration.

If the beneficiary has not found suitable work by the end of the period equalling his potential duration, a permanent, triggered program of Extended Benefits now allows him to receive benefits at his same weekly rate for an additional period equal to one-half his potential duration under the regular state program (or 13 weeks at most). Further, in December 1974 and March 1975 additional temporary Federal Supplemental Benefits were enacted that provide up to an extra 26 weeks of benefits at the same weekly rate. A recipient could conceivably draw UI benefits for 65 weeks under the combined regular and extended programs, Extended Benefits and (temporary) Federal Supplemental Benefits. In addition, a temporary *Special Unemployment Assistance* program was also enacted. Effective July 1975 it provided up to 39 weeks of UI benefits for otherwise eligible workers whose base-period employer was not covered. Both programs will be phased out by February 1978.

Employment taxes

In 1975 the Federal unemployment tax was 3.2 per cent of the wages of each employee up to a *tax base* of $4200 in earnings per annum. The tax is collected from employers; only in three states, Alabama, Alaska and New Jersey, is there also a contribution by the employee. States have been free to impose a higher taxable base for their own systems, as the cases of Minnesota and Oregon in Table 1 illustrate. Six states had a base above $4200 in 1975. The greater interstate variation is in the determination of the tax rate paid by the firm. Federal law has allowed states to void most (currently all but .5 percentage points) of the 3.2 per cent Federal tax. (The .5 per cent is used to finance the Employment Service, part of Extended Benefits, and Federal Supplemental Benefits.) The states can then construct sets of experience rated schedules that vary the tax rate so long as overall financial solvency is maintained.

Experience rating

As Table 1 shows, the possible degree of variation in tax rates differs substantially among states. Indeed, in 1975 the most favorable schedule in Colorado allowed firms with a good unemployment experience to pay no taxes, while on the least favorable tax schedule the maximum rate is 3.6 per cent. Colorado and Ohio are two of the 13 states in which the minimum rate on the lowest schedule is zero. Maximum rates on the highest tax schedule vary from 2.7 per cent in some states to as high as 8.5 per cent. As

TABLE 1

UNEMPLOYMENT INSURANCE PROVISIONS AS OF JANUARY 1975, SELECTED STATES

Characteristic	California	Colorado	Massachusetts	Minnesota	New York	Ohio	Oregon	South Carolina
Minimum Qualifying Employment or Wages	$750	30 x weekly benefits; $750	$1200	18 weeks with $30 each week	20 weeks; $600	20 weeks with $20 each week	18 weeks $700	1-1/2 x HQE; $300, with $180 in any quarter
Benefit Amount:								
1. Weekly Benefits	1/24-1/27 of HQE	1/22 of HQE	1/21-1/26 of HQE	50% of AWW	67-50% AWW	50% of AWW	1.25% of base period earnings	1/26 of HQE
2. Dependents' Allowances	—	—	$6 each, up to 1/2 weekly benefits	—	—	$1-$39, dep. on number & weekly benefits	—	—
Benefit Duration: (Weeks)								
1. Maximum	26	26	30	26	26	26	26	26
2. Minimum	12	7	9	13	26	20	9	10
Taxes:								
1. Base	$4200	$4200	$4200	$4800	$4200	$4200	$5000	$4200
2. Minimum Rate	.1%	0	.5	.1	.3	0	.8	.25
3. Maximum Rate	4.1%	3.6	5.1	5.0	5.2	4.3	3.2	4.1

Source: *Comparison of State Unemployment Insurance Laws*, January 1975.
NOTE: HQE is high-quarter earnings; AWW is average weekly wage.

long as the firm is already at the minimum tax rate, further layoffs, and thus further charges on its reserves, cannot lower its tax rate unless the entire tax schedule is lowered. Similarly, if its balance is so low as to place it at the highest rate, the extra charges resulting from a single layoff will not affect its rate unless the entire tax schedule is raised. Clearly, the range between minimum rate on the lowest schedule and maximum rate on the highest determines the extent to which experience rating is fully operative.

III. STUDIES OF THE TOTAL EFFECT OF UNEMPLOYMENT INSURANCE ON UNEMPLOYMENT

Four studies have been produced using the general form:

$$U/L = F(UIB/AWW; X),$$

where UIB/AWW is the ratio of average weekly benefits to average weekly earnings in covered employment; and X is a vector of variables designed to account for differences in unemployment rates not produced by UI. In time-series studies the X vector includes changes in real GNP or the relative shortfall of actual from potential GNP. In the cross-section studies variables measuring the relative industrial, occupational or demographic mix are included in this vector.

The estimates from the four studies are presented in Table 2. In order to make comparisons among them, we calculate the effect of a ten percentage point increase in the replacement rate UIB/AWW on the unemployment rate. While this clearly implies simulating outside the range of observation in the time-series studies (since the ratio only varied between .32 and .37 in the postwar period), it does allow us to analyze the likely effect of the entire system on the unemployment rate. Further, it provides a check on the reliability of the estimates, if the true structures are linear in UIB/AWW. If they are not, then it is incumbent on those who wish to use models for policy purposes to respecify them. If the simulated impact on unemployment of a replacement rate equal to zero is absurdly large, we can conclude that, at the very least, the results are of little use in analyzing the overall impact on unemployment. (They may, though, be useful for considering the effects of small changes in benefits, if the equations are otherwise well specified and the data are appropriate.)

Difficulties with the Grubel-Maki model

The implied impacts of higher benefit amounts on unemployment are truly immense in these studies. Grubel-Maki (1974) get an increase in the unemployment rate of 6.31 percentage points in response to a 10 percentage point increase in replacement, while Baily (1974) finds unemployment rates

TABLE 2
STUDIES OF THE EFFECTS OF UNEMPLOYMENT INSURANCE BENEFITS ON UNEMPLOYMENT RATES

Study	Data	Effect of a 10 Percentage Point Increase in the Replacement Rate
Baily (1974)	Annual data, 1948-69, insured unemployment rates in the United States	Average: 0 When GNP is 3 Percent above trend: - .99 When GNP is 3 Percent below trend: +.86
Grubel-Maki (1974)	Annual data, 1951-72, insured unemployment rates in the United States	+6.31
	48 states, 1971, insured unemployment rates.	+ .98
Holen-Horowitz (1974)	38 states, 1971, insured unemployment rates.	+ .47[a]
	1970 Census unemployment rates.	+ .16[a]
Komisar (1968)	45 states, changes in insured unemployment rates,	
	1953-1954	+ .06
	1957-1958	+ .15
	1960-1961	+ .20

[a]Average of effects in states with benefit formula based on annual, high-quarter or weekly earnings.

.86 percentage points higher during a recession, but .99 percentage points lower during a boom as a result of higher benefits. Both of these studies suffer from the severe defect that they use aggregate data. The lack of substantial variation in the replacement ratio since 1945 causes them to attribute any observed change in unemployment to the minute changes in replacement rates. When these effects are magnified to reflect the ten percentage point hypothetical change in replacement, the resulting estimates are huge, suggesting the studies tell us little about the likely overall impact of the system. (With an average replacement rate of .34, the Grubel-Maki results imply that abolition of benefits would reduce the unemployment rate by 21.5 percentage points. Given the postwar range of variation in unemployment, this implies that, but for UI, we would have negative unemployment.)

Even when the two time-series studies are considered on their own grounds, there is grave difficulty interpreting the results. Grubel-Maki show that replacement rates are higher cyclically when unemployment is higher. (A similar result holds in the cross-section; see Wandner, 1975.) Because of this there is a simultaneity problem that prevents us from interpreting Baily's results as reflecting induced unemployment. Grubel-Maki attempt to account for this in their unemployment equation by using two-stage least squares, but one wonders whether the equation is identified: the only variables in the equation for *UIB/AWW* are unemployment, which is the dependent variable in the other equation, and time, which is very highly correlated with the percent of workers in covered employment, another variable in the vector *X*.[3] This probable lack of sufficient identifying restrictions on the unemployment equation means that the coefficient of *UIB/AWW* cannot be interpreted in the way the authors would like.

Cross-section trials

Three studies present estimates using cross-section data on states, with either the civilian or the insured unemployment rate as the dependent variable. A different sort of simultaneity problem muddies the waters here. It is difficult to disentangle the effects of a more liberal UI system on unemployment from the effects of perpetually higher unemployment on the liberality of the state's system. None of the three studies even tries to account for this problem, and it is not an easy problem to solve, depending as it does on a political theory of differences in the institutions of UI.

The effects of this difficulty are clear when we examine the Grubel-Maki and Holen-Horowitz results. In 1971 replacement ratios (average benefits divided by average weekly earnings in covered employment) varied across states from .22 to .43. Even using this range, the Grubel-Maki parameter estimates suggest that if the replacement ratio were reduced from its mean, .35, to its minimum value, the insured unemployment rate would have been 2.8 instead of the 4.1 per cent that occurred. Abolishing the system would, according to the estimates, reduce unemployment in covered industry to essentially zero, a result that is difficult to credit. While the Holen-Horowitz estimates are somewhat lower they also must be interpreted carefully. Since the authors include a host of variables describing each state's system, while the impacts listed in Table 2 are based solely on the parameter describing the effect of variations in benefits on unemployment rates, the likely estimate of the total effect of the system is much greater.

The Komisar study circumvents some of the simultaneity problem by using the change in insured unemployment rates as the dependent variable. (Of course, there may be a similar problem on the change in unemployment; states that experience substantial fluctuations in unemployment may enact more liberal benefits. However, there is no econometric evidence on this.) Unfortunately, the independent variables include *UIB* but not *AWW*, which biases the estimated impact of *UIB* upward, given the well-known positive correlation between *AWW* and *UIB*, and the likely positive correlation between *AWW* and increases in unemployment in a recession. Thus the estimates listed for this study in Table 2 are probably too high, if anything.

Shaky foundations

The most serious difficulty with this set of studies is the lack of basis in theory. Both search theory and the consumer-theoretic analysis of the work-leisure choice suggest that the duration of unemployment will be increased by higher UI benefits, holding wages constant. They say nothing about the effect on the unemployment rate, yet they are used to justify equations that make the unemployment rate a function of the replacement rate. Further, they are theories of microeconomic behavior, yet there is no link to the more aggregated data (macroeconomic data in the time-series studies) used in the works discussed in this section. These problems may well be causing the very large estimated impacts of UI benefits. Even if not, though, they suggest that a more fruitful approach is to test specific microeconomic theories on micro data that reflect the behavior implied by those theories, then combine the results to estimate the aggregate impact of UI benefits on unemployment.

IV. UNEMPLOYMENT INSURANCE AND THE DURATION OF UNEMPLOYMENT

The first step in constructing the effects of UI on the unemployment rate is to analyze the effect on the duration of spells of unemployment. There are eleven studies of this effect for the U.S. that use micro data. Their results are shown in Table 3. Where possible I calculate the implied effect on the average duration of unemployment of a hypothetical 10 percentage point increase in the individual's replacement ratio (from 50 to 60 per cent). Where this is not possible, I list instead the impact of a 10-dollar increase in the weekly benefit amount. Since average weekly earnings in the late 1960's and early 1970's, the time when the data were collected for most of the studies, were roughly $100, the results from this second method should be fairly comparable to those from the first, other things equal.

Distinguishing features

These studies can be distinguished from each other along each of several criteria. Further, each particular choice of study design has both benefits and disadvantages:

1. The sample can consist of claimants only or include other unemployed individuals. Making the former choice (Burgess-Kingston; Classen:

TABLE 3
STUDIES OF THE EFFECTS OF UNEMPLOYMENT INSURANCE BENEFITS ON THE DURATION OF UNEMPLOYMENT

Study	Data	Effect of an Increase in Weekly Benefit on Weeks of Unemployment Per Year
Burgess and Kingston (1974, p. 106)	1719 Job-Ready Claimants; Boston, Bay Area, Phoenix, 1969-70	
	Males	.01[a]
	Females	-.04[a]
Classen (1975)	3,235 Claimants; Pennsylvania, 1967-68	1.1[b]
Crosslin (1975)	746 Job-Ready Claimants; St. Louis, 1971-73	-.09[a]
	423 Individuals; Cleveland, 1970	-.05[a]
Ehrenberg & Oaxaca (1976)	Job Changing Individuals, Nationwide:	
	39 Males, 45-59; 1966-67	1.5[a]
	156 Females, 30-44; 1968-71	.3[a]
	464 Males, 14-24; 1966-69	.2[a]
	613 Females, 14-24; 1967-70	.5[a]
Felder (1975)	Individuals; Denver; 1970	
	310 Males	1.41[b]
	148 Females	1.43[b]
Hanna, *et al.* (1975)	3,342 Claimants, Nevada; 1969-72	1.02[a]
Hills (1976)	587 Individuals Nationwide; 1969-71	1.23[a]
	67 Claimants (Job Changers); 1969-71	-.30[a]
	108 Claimants (Same Employer); 1969-71	-.18[a]
Holen (1976)	13,066 Claimants; Boston, Bay Area Phoenix, 1969-70	.60[b]
Lininger (1963)	749 Claimants; Michigan; 1955	.06[a]
Marston (1975)	Simulated Averages for Insured and Uninsured, Based on Detroit; 1969	.23-.62[a]
Schmidt (1974)	115 Job Changing Individuals, Nationwide; 1966	.31[a]
	70 Individuals, Nationwide; 1966	1.63[a]

[a] 10 percentage point increase in the ratio of benefit amount to weekly wage.

[b] $10 increase in weekly benefits.

Crosslin; Hanna, *et. al.*; Holen, and Lininger) restricts one to using compensated weeks of unemployment as the duration measure. Higher benefits may shorten filing delays among those individuals in the sample, and some persons with short spells of unemployment may be missed in sampling procedure. Both of these problems will bias upward any estimate of the effect of benefits on the average duration of all covered spells of unemployment. Making the other choice avoids this problem, but introduces possible biases insofar as the behavior of individuals not eligible for UI benefits is characterized by a different structural relation from that which describes claimants.

2. The sample can consist of individuals subject to the same state system (Classen; Crosslin; Felder; Hanna, *et al.*; Lininger) or of individuals from different systems (the other studies). The first choice prevents the sample from producing results reflecting other aspects of labor market behavior or of uncontrolled differences in the structure of UI across states.[4] On the other hand, it limits the degree of variation in the replacement ratio among individuals in the sample, since in most states the ratio is constant up to the maximum benefit and declines hyperbolically thereafter.

3. The sample can separate job-changers from other unemployed workers. It is likely that UI benefits affect duration less among workers on temporary layoff (Classen and Hills confirm this). Those studies (Classen; Ehrenberg-Oaxaca, Hills and Schmidt) that make this separation allow us to concentrate on those workers for whom the system may produce the greatest disincentive effect.

4. The sample can contain detailed demographic information on individuals that allows us to hold constant for factors that may affect the duration of unemployment spells and whose omission could bias the estimated effect of changes in replacement. These studies (Ehrenberg-Oaxaca; Felder; Hills; Lininger; Marston, and Schmidt) appear to dominate the others because of this, but the results of Ehrenberg-Oaxaca, Hills and Schmidt suggest most of these "controls" are insignificant.[5]

Effects on duration

This discussion of biases should enable us to detect patterns of differences among the results in Table 3. Unfortunately, no such patterns are apparent. Studies classified by each of the criteria that characterize choices about the underlying data produce widely varying estimates. We have learned, though, that the effect is larger for job changers. Also, except for the Burgess-Kingston and Crosslin studies, which have problems of specification, only Lininger finds no effect of benefits on duration. His result may be due to the large fraction of insured workers in Michigan who are on recall (to the auto industry) and thus whose behavior is likely to be at most only slightly affected by differences in UI benefits.

Welch (1976) concluded that the effect of a 10 percentage point increase in benefits on benefit-weeks is 1.5 additional weeks, based on his consideration of the Burgess-Kingston, Classen, Ehrenberg-Oaxaca and Holen studies. I believe the biases induced through effects on filing delays and deletion of data points with very short spells are quite large. Further, Welch appears to have overlooked some fairly careful studies—Lininger and Marston—which produce much smaller estimates of the effect. Finally, most of the studies in Table 3 use benefit-weeks per year or weeks of unemployment per year. Insofar as UI induces more spells of unemployment, the numbers in Table 3 overestimate the effect on duration per spell. My best guess is that the average duration of all spells of insured unemployment is increased .5 weeks by each 10 percentage point increase in the replacement ratio. Conversely, this means that if UI benefits were reduced to zero, the average spell of unemployment among that segment of the labor force that now receives benefits would fall by 2.5 weeks. However, this holds only if these unemployed people did not become eligible for other income transfers —Food Stamps, general assistance payments, etc.—that contain work disincentives. It is thus an upper limit of the effect of the UI system on duration.

Since most of the studies are based on data from periods of low unemployment, the estimates are not applicable to examining the impact on duration when unemployment is high. (It is likely, both because job searchers are more often hitting a capital constraint and because of the diminished marginal utility of leisure [unemployment] near the end of the long spells that occur during recessions, that the effect is smaller when labor markets are slack. Wandner [1975] provides some corroborating evidence on this.) Therefore, throughout this exercise we analyze only the effect on the unemployment rate at times of low unemployment.

This discussion deals only with the duration of unemployment spells among the roughly 50 per cent of the unemployed who are eligible for UI. It is likely that, if anything, the presence of a UI system reduces the duration of spells among new entrants and re-entrants into the labor force. A person not receiving benefits but searching for work will be more likely to accept a job if the job also entails rights to future UI benefits. As compared to a world without a UI system, the existence of UI for which new entrants are ineligible raises the costs of continued unemployment relative to taking a job, so long as the value of UI to the individual is not entirely offset by the backward shifting of taxes in the forms of lower wages. The magnitude of this effect has not been estimated, but it is not likely to be large, given the very short period of employment needed to qualify for the minimum UI benefit. (In states using the high-quarter earnings formula, a well-chosen seven weeks of work at the minimum wage qualifies the worker for benefits during his future spells of unemployment.[6]) The short duration of the qualifying period relative to the average tenure in a job makes it unlikely that a new entrant will substantially shorten his search time. Ultimately, though, this is an empirical issue, but for our purposes we assume this effect is zero, bearing in mind that this assumption introduces an upward bias into our estimate of the effect of UI on the unemployment rate.

V. EFFECTS ON LABOR FORCE PARTICIPATION AT LOW UNEMPLOYMENT

There are no empirical studies on the effect of UI benefits on labor force participation in the United States. However, Swan (1975) has estimated that the recent liberalization of the UI system in Canada raised the average labor force participation rate by 2 percentage points. The theoretical justification for such an effect is clear. In the absence of UI a person will participate if the market wage W exceeds the shadow price of his or her time spent in the household W^* net of work related expenses, (see Gronau, 1973). If there is no shifting of the costs of UI backward onto labor, and B are the expected UI benefits per period, the net returns to participation are raised by the institution of UI from $W - W^*$ to $W + uB - W^*$, where u is the fraction of time the worker expects to be unemployed (and receiving UI benefits). This increase in the net returns is an inducement to enter the labor force. Its ultimate effect depends upon the labor force participation elasticities of the groups in the working-age population.

Even if the actuarial costs of the benefits are fully reflected in lower wages (workers bear the entire cost of the system) labor force participation will rise if the average worker is risk averse. While the net money returns to participating are unchanged by the introduction of UI, the expected utility over future periods is increased by the smoothing out of the income stream. Clearly, though, the effect is stronger to the extent that people bear a greater share of the costs of UI in their roles as consumers rather than as suppliers of labor.

Calculating the effects for the U.S.

The effect on the unemployment rate of this increased labor force participation depends on the unemployment experiences of those induced to enter the labor force. If the average such person has the same experience as the average labor force participant, the unemployment rate remains unchanged. We assume that the labor force participation rate of males and females ages 25-54 is completely inelastic to changes in the net advantages of work. These groups constitute about ⅔ of the American labor force.[7] There is no evidence of *labor force participation elasticities* with respect to wages among the young and among workers 55 and over. However, the studies summarized in Cain and Watts (1973) suggest that the *elasticity of hours supplied* among these groups is somewhat above zero but less than one.

I recognize that one cannot immediately jump from hours to labor force elasticities. (See Lewis, 1971. However, I show elsewhere, Hamermesh, 1976, that the predictions are the same for weeks in the labor force, and that empirically UI benefit and eligibility variables affect labor supply in the expected ways.) However, for purposes of calculation I assume an elasticity of .25. Further, I assume that workers induced to enter the labor force experience six times as much unemployment as does the average labor force participant. (We assume that the average participant is unemployed 4 per cent of the time.) Finally, we assume that half the costs of UI are shifted backward in the form of lower wages.[8]

The expected increase in earnings plus UI benefits stemming from the introduction of a UI system is then 6 per cent (.24 times an average net replacement rate of .5 times the half of UI taxes not borne by labor in the form of lower wages). Given our assumptions about the labor force participation elasticity among secondary workers, this implies an increase of 1.5 per cent in the secondary labor force (6 times .25). The change in the aggregate unemployment rate induced by this increase is 10 percentage points (1.5 times the ⅓ of the labor force accounted for by this group times .20, the assumed difference between the fraction of time spent unemployed by the induced entrants and by the average participant).

Our assumptions are clearly arbitrary, though based on all the available empirical work. However, they probably err on the side of an upward bias, especially since 24 per cent is an unusually large fraction of time spent unemployed (when the average unemployment rate is 4.0 per cent), and more than half of the cost of UI may be shifted backward.[9] One should also note that the induced labor force entry *ipso facto* increases aggregate employment, other things equal. The induced entrants are employed much of the time they are in the labor force, so market production does rise. This can offset some of the disemployment induced by changes in the duration and number of spells of unemployment. However, this extra production in the market is at the expense of production in the home. Since in the absence of UI the economy is assumed to be efficient, if we ignore second-best arguments this shift toward market production, while raising measured GNP, lowers social welfare.

VI. EFFECT ON NUMBERS OF SPELLS OF UNEMPLOYMENT

Feldstein (1975) has shown how the firm can profit and increase workers' utility by laying off workers, in response to seasonal output changes, who would not have been laid off in the absence of UI. The argument rests on:

(1) imperfections in the experience rating of UI taxes; (2) the employer's certainty about the future path of product demand.

It is impossible to gauge exactly the extent of imperfection of experience rating. I have shown (Hamermesh, 1977) though, that in 1967 28 per cent of payrolls were at either a nonzero minimum tax rate or the maximum tax rate on that year's tax schedule. This understates the effectiveness of experience rating, since some of these employers do eventually pay for UI benefits when the tax schedules are changed in their state as the overall solvency of the state funds changes. The extent of this is unknown, as is the appropriate discount rate to apply to the future tax payments. However, Becker (1972, p. 113) shows that benefits charged to firms with negative balances in their accounts ranged from 25 to 62 per cent of all benefit payments in 1967 in the eight states listed in Table 1. While an exact figure cannot be derived, the "guesstimate" of ⅓ as the size of the wedge between the employer's cost and the worker's benefits appears the best possible.

Because Feldstein's model assumes perfect foresight about fluctuations in product demand, it is a model of seasonal layoffs only and can only be used to estimate the effects of UI in increasing the seasonality of employment. Undoubtedly layoffs in response to cyclical declines in product demand are increased somewhat by an imperfectly experience-rated UI system. (However, since most layoffs occur during the cyclical decline rather than later near the trough, it is likely that the suddenness of the decline in product demand is such that the layoffs are unexpected and that the number of additional layoffs induced by UI is small.[10]) In any case, we ignore the induced cyclical layoffs, recognizing that this neglect produces a (probably very small) downward bias in the total estimated effect of UI on the unemployment rate.

Between 1958 and 1969 seasonal variation in layoffs accounted for 31 per cent of the total variation in manufacturing.[11] (This fraction is consistent with Warden (1967), who found that for 1958-1961 in Massachusetts one-third of all recipients of UI benefits were on seasonal layoffs. The Massachusetts results may overstate the fraction nationally, since Massachusetts does not use a weeks-worked requirement that helps to render many seasonal workers ineligible for benefits.[12]) During the typical year of low unemployment, layoffs account for below half the spells of workers counted as unemployed in the Current Population Survey.[13] Using these figures of ½, and the low unemployment rate of 4.0 per cent, the best estimate is that seasonal layoffs account for .62 percentage points of the unemployment rate at low unemployment (.31 times 4.0 times .5).

We noted that the wedge between employer's UI costs and workers' benefits is one-third of total benefits. With replacement to the worker equal to 50 per cent of his wage (and .47 of total compensation), the wedge lowers the cost of the typical layoff by 16 per cent (⅓ times .47). If we assume that seasonal layoffs would fall proportionately if the wedge were removed, the current system of UI contributes .10 percentage points (.62 times .16) to the unemployment rate in the covered sector at low unemployment. Obversely, it accounts for 2.5 per cent of spells of unemployment in the covered sector at low unemployment (.10/4.0).

Undoubtedly UI benefits also induce workers to quit their jobs in those 14 states where voluntary quitters are eligible for benefits. However, in all these states there is a much longer waiting period for benefits if the worker has quit, thus blunting the incentive to take a "UI vacation." In addition, 32 states not only disqualify quitters from receiving benefits, they also require some additional wage credits on subsequent jobs before the employee becomes eligible for the minimum benefit in future spells of unemployment. This operates to lower quit rates, and the net effect of UI on quits (and through quits on the number of spells of unemployment) is unclear. We therefore use only the effect on additional layoffs (2.5 per cent) as the induced increase in spells of unemployment in the covered sector.

VII. CONCLUSIONS—PUTTING THE PIECES TOGETHER

The induced change in the unemployment rate is:

$$\Delta U/L = [(1 + \frac{\Delta DUR}{DUR})(1 + \frac{\Delta NSPELL}{NSPELL}) - 1] \cdot (U/L)_{L = \bar{L}} + \Delta (U/L)_{L\ varies}$$

where DUR is the average duration (in weeks) of insured spells of unemployment, and $NSPELL$ is the number of such spells. The induced change in the unemployment rate is essentially the product of the percentage changes in duration and number of spells of unemployment in a fixed labor force, plus the change in the rate induced by the change in the demographic mix of labor force participants.

In 1969, a recent period of low unemployment, the average spell of insured unemployment was 11.6 weeks in duration. The induced change in duration of insured spells is thus 27 per cent (2.5 divided by 9.1); since insured unemployment was 47 per cent of total unemployment in 1969, UI induces a change in the average duration of all unemployment of 13 per cent. As we saw in the previous section UI also induces a 2.5 per cent increase in the number of spells of unemployment in the covered sector. Since covered employment is 75 per cent of all civilian employment, the best guess is that UI induces a 1.9 per cent increase in spells of unemployment.

The net effect is that I estimate that UI increases the measured unemployment rate by .71 percentage points. This is the product of the 13 per cent increase in duration and the 1.9 per cent increase in number of spells, coupled with the .10 percentage point increase resulting from the induced change in the demographic mix of the labor force. Viewed differently, if a low unemployment rate in the absence of UI were 4.0 per cent, with the current UI system it is 4.7 per cent. However, this induced increase would not necessarily be removed if all UI benefits were abolished, for many UI recipients would receive other assistance that provides at least some inducement for longer spells of unemployment, and the demand for privately financed plans that also contain disincentives would rise.

Since roughly half of civilian unemployment is insured unemployment, our estimates suggest that if UI were abolished and its recipients denied other transfers linked to earnings, slightly less than one-third of the insured unemployed would be at work (.7 divided by .47 times 4.7). This may appear high, but the bulk of the effect results from the best-documented part of our evidence, namely the induced change in duration. It is not very different from Feldstein's (1973) estimate, a guess not based on a review of the now available evidence, that the induced change in 1971, when unemployment was 5½ rather than 4 per cent, was 1.25 percentage points. It is, though, far more reasonable than the estimates implied by some of the studies discussed in Section III, since at least it does not indicate that the removal of UI benefits would wipe out all unemployment in the United States.

Admittedly, the approach in this paper lacks the elegance of a simultaneous equation model. However, UI is such a complex, but small program, and its economic effects are so varied, that further work trying to develop simple aggregate models based on those discussed in Section III will not be fruitful. Instead, the inelegant approach of this paper can best be refined by replacing what are admittedly only educated guesses with sound microeconomic empirical work on the effects of UI on labor force participation and layoff and quit propensities. Just as the body of empirical work on duration has given us a reasonably narrow range of estimates on the effect of UI on duration, careful empirical work can eventually produce similarly useful results for labor force participation and employee turnover.

NOTES

1 Computed from *Economic Report of the President*, 1976, and unpublished data from the Unemployment Insurance Service, U.S. Department of Labor.
2 A detailed history and description of the institutions can be found in Haber and Murray (1966).
3 Covered employment (all programs) as a fraction of the civilian labor force rose from .59 in 1951 to .66 in 1961 to .77 in 1972.

4 One simple example of the problem with mixing data from different state systems arises from differences in potential duration. Two individuals with the same replacement ratio can look forward to a much longer duration of benefits in Pennsylvania (30 weeks) than in Georgia (where average potential duration in 1974 was 21 weeks). Insofar as differences in potential duration of benefits affect job search, as strongly suggested by the work of Hanna, *et al.* (1975), mixing state data will, at the very least, lower the explained variance, other things equal, if potential duration is not included.

5 Ehrenberg-Oaxaca include variables on schooling, local labor market conditions, assets, home ownership, health status and others. Schmidt includes a smaller set that performs equally poorly, while Hills includes age, occupation, education and industry dummies. Only the last two sets of controls produce significant coefficients.

6 In North Carolina, the most stringent state using the high-quarter earnings formula, the worker must in 1975 have earned $565 and 1½ times his high quarter earnings. At $84 per week, 5 weeks working one quarter and 2½ weeks the next, the worker can qualify for benefits.

7 In December 1975 this group accounted for 61 per cent of the civilian labor force (seasonally adjusted).

8 It is well-nigh impossible to trace the incidence of an experience-rated payroll tax that differs also among states. Suffice it to say that part of the burden can in the long run be passed'on to the consumer, since rates are similar within product groupings, and that employers, unless they are monopolists, cannot in the long run experience a cut in profits. (See Hamermesh, 1977.)

9 In October 1973, the most recent cyclical peak, the unemployment rate among workers 16-24 and 55 + was 7.3 per cent seasonally adjusted. Among youths 16-19 the rate was 14.3 per cent, and among people 20-24, it was 7.1 per cent. Only among blacks 16-19 did the rate exceed 24 per cent.

10 For example, the seasonally adjusted layoff rate in manufacturing fell sharply after reaching a peak of 3.1 per cent in January 1975, before the May 1975 trough, reaching only 1.3 per cent in January 1976. Civilian unemployment rates in January 1975 and 1976 were 7.9 and 7.8 per cent respectively.

11 This was calculated taking the average for these years of the ratios $r_i = 1_{ai}/1_{ui}$, where 1 is the layoff rate, a and u denote seasonally adjusted and unadjusted, and i is the month, $i = 1, \ldots, 12$. The fraction of variation due to seasonality is then defined as:

$$f = \frac{\sum_{1^i}^{12} (r_i - r_{min})}{12 \cdot r_{min}}$$

where r_{min} is the lowest of the 12 monthly averages.

12 For example, Haber and Murray (1966) cite some data from Oregon showing that using a weeks-worked criterion lowers the fraction of layoffs eligible for benefits from 70 to 60 per cent.

13 At the business cycle peak of October 1973, the rate was only 33 per cent. The 50 per cent figure is more typical of a recovery year, and, in any case, is another factor in assuring that our estimate of the impact of UI is not biased down.

REFERENCES

Baily, Martin N. 1974. "Unemployment and Unemployment Insurance." Unpublished Paper, Department of Economics, Yale University.

Becker, Joseph M. 1972. *Experience Rating in Unemployment Insurance.* Baltimore: Johns Hopkins University Press.

Burgess, Paul, and Kingston, Jerry. 1974. "Unemployment Insurance, the Job Search Process and Reemployment Success." Unpublished Paper, Unemployment Insurance Service, Department of Labor.

Cain, Glen G., and Watts, Harold. 1973. *Income Maintenance and Labor Supply.* Chicago: Rand McNally.

Classen, Kathleen. 1975. "The Effects of Unemployment Insurance: Evidence From Pennsylvania." Unpublished Paper, ASPER, Department of Labor.

Crosslin, Robert L. 1975. "Unemployment Insurance and Job Search." Unpublished Paper, Department of Economics, Mississippi State University.

Ehrenberg, Ronald G., and Oaxaca, Ronald L. 1976. "Unemployment Insurance, Duration of Unemployment and Subsequent Wage Gain." *American Economic Review,* 66 (December, 1976):754-766.

Felder, Henry. 1975. "Job Search: An Empirical Analysis of the Search Behavior of Low-Income Workers." Unpublished Paper, Stanford Research Institute.

Feldstein, Martin. 1973. *Lowering the Permanent Rate of Unemployment.* Washington: U.S. Congress, Joint Economic Committee.

Feldstein, Martin. 1975. "Temporary Layoffs in the Theory of Unemployment." Unpublished Paper, Harvard Institute of Economic Research.

Gramlich, Edward M. 1974. "The Distributional Effects of Higher Unemployment." *Brookings Papers on Economic Activity,* 5 (1974): 293-336.

Gronau, Reuben. 1973. "The Intra-Family Allocation of Time." *American Economic Review,* 63 (September, 1973): 634-651.

Grubel, Herbert, and Maki, Dennis. 1974. "The Effect of Unemployment Benefits on U.S. Unemployment Rates," *Weltwirtschaftliches Archiv,* 112, 2, 1976.

Haber, William, and Murray, Merrill G. 1966. *Unemployment Insurance in the American Economy.* Homewood, IL: Richard D. Irwin.

Hamermesh, Daniel S. 1976. "Uncertainty, Unemployment Insurance and Labor Supply." Unpublished Paper, Michigan State University.

Hamermesh, Daniel S. 1977. *Jobless Pay and the Economy.* Baltimore: Johns Hopkins Press.

Hanna, James S.; Butler, Robert T.; and Steinman, John P. 1975. "The Socioeconomic Impact of Extended Benefits." Unpublished Paper, Nevada Employment Security Department.

Hills, Stephen M. 1976. "Unemployment Insurance and Income Protection," Unpublished Paper, University of British Columbia.

Holen, Arlene. 1976. "Effects of Unemployment Insurance Entitlement on Duration and Job Search Outcome." Unpublished Paper, Center for Naval Analyses, Arlington, Virginia.

Holen, Arlene, and Horowitz, Stanley. 1974. "The Effect of Unemployment Insurance and Eligibility Enforcement on Unemployment." *Journal of Law and Economics,* 17 (October, 1974): 403-432.

Komisar, Jerome B. 1968. "Social Legislation Policies and Labor Force Behavior." *Journal of Economic Issues,* 2 (June, 1968):187-199.

Lester, Richard A. 1962. *The Economics of Unemployment Compensation.* Princeton: Princeton University Industrial Relations Section.

Lewis, H. Gregg. 1971. "Income and Substitution Effects in Labor Force Participation and Hours of work." Unpublished Paper, Department of Economics, University of Chicago.

Lininger, Charles A. 1963. *Unemployment Benefits and Duration.* Ann Arbor, MI: University of Michigan Institute for Social Research.

Marston, Stephen T. 1975. "The Impact of Unemployment Insurance on Aggregate Unemployment." *Brookings Papers on Economic Activity,* 6 (1975):13-49.

Schmidt, Ronald M. 1974. "The Determinants of Search Behavior and the Value of Additional Unemployment." Unpublished Paper, School of Management, University of Rochester.

Swan, Neil. 1975. "Unemployment Insurance and Labor Force Participation, With Applications to Canada and Its Maritime Provinces." *Proceedings of the Industrial Relations Research Association* (Spring, 1975):511-517.

Wandner, Stephen. 1975. "Unemployment Insurance and the Duration of Unemployment in Periods of Low and High Unemployment." Unpublished Paper, Unemployment Insurance Service, Department of Labor.

Warden, Charles. 1967. "Unemployment Compensation: The Massachusetts Experience." In *Studies in the Economics of Income Maintenance.* Edited by Otto Eckstein. Washington: Brookings Institution, pp. 73-93.

Welch, Finis. 1976. "What Have We Learned From Empirical Studies of Unemployment Insurance?" Unpublished Paper, Department of Economics, UCLA.

21

EVIDENCE OF CHANGES IN EMPLOYMENT, LABOR FORCE PARTICIPATION, AND UNEMPLOYMENT

Finis Welch

There are too many empirical studies to do justice even to those I do know. I essentially ignore earlier work, which was surveyed in a study by John Peterson and Charles Stewart and in a paper by Hyman Kaitz.[1] Many of the studies they discuss were excellent in their own time, but they have been supplanted by more recent evidence. My discussion is limited to studies of national impact and to those I feel have contributed significantly either to the measurement of the effects as we now understand them or to the current debate. Many are omitted here because I consider them too poorly specified to convey important information. Others are omitted because effects are limited to a single industry or area.

If there is a general theme to the empirical literature, it is that the simple theoretical predictions are confirmed. I believe that almost every serious scholar of minimum wages would argue on the basis of available evidence that they have reduced employment of those, particularly teenagers, who would otherwise earn low wages. Until recently, incomplete coverage was ignored in empirical work. As these effects have been incorporated, it is not surprising that estimates have sharpened. It is also true that virtually all studies of employment effects have focused on all teenagers, failing to distinguish part- and full-time workers and students, even though students represent at least 40 percent of total teenage employment and even though students who work do so for only half as many hours as nonstudents. Not surprisingly, estimates are sharpened by distinguishing between students and others.

---

[1] John Peterson and Charles Stewart, *Employment Effects of Minimum Wages* (Washington, D.C.: American Enterprise Institute, August 1969); Hyman Kaitz, "Youth Unemployment and Minimum Wages," *Bulletin 1657* of the Bureau of Labor Statistics, 1970, chap. 2.

Studies of Employment and Related Effects

Most of the available studies of the effects of minimum wages use U.S. aggregate quarterly data beginning in 1954. This "late start" simply reflects the emergence of the monthly Current Population Surveys (CPS) when information on employment, unemployment, and labor force status was first disaggregated by age, sex, and color.

Four studies have been made that explicitly allow for modification of minimum wage effects owing to expansions in coverage. Among these, the study first reported by Masanori Hashimoto and Jacob Mincer and later summarized by Mincer offers the greatest demographic detail.[2] The Hashimoto-Mincer paper contains full descriptions of the empirical work, while the one by Mincer summarizes it. The 1976 Mincer paper is a bench mark. It not only introduces an uncovered sector but also recognizes the probabilistic nature of job search, showing that whereas the implications for covered sector employment are unequivocal, effects on measured unemployment rates (that is, on job search) are conjectural.

Hashimoto and Mincer find statistically significant employment reductions associated with rising wage minimums for white and nonwhite teenagers, for white and nonwhite males aged twenty to twenty-four years, for white males aged sixty-five and more, and for white and nonwhite females aged twenty and more. With less statistical precision, their estimates also suggest employment reductions for nonwhite males aged sixty-five and more and, surprisingly, for white and nonwhite males aged twenty-five to sixty-four years.

It is not surprising that they find reduced employment for low-wage groups, but the fact that they find no corresponding increase but, rather, a probable decrease for males aged twenty-five to sixty-four years suggests that this, indeed, is not a zero-sum lottery. The evidence indicates that the minimum wage causes net losses in employment and wage income.

Hashimoto and Mincer's estimates imply that minimum wages increase measured unemployment rates for each group, but the estimates are statistically significant only for nonwhite males aged twenty to twenty-four years and for white females aged twenty and more. Here the Hashimoto-Mincer work is especially noteworthy, for it finds

[2] Masanori Hashimoto and Jacob Mincer, "Employment and Unemployment Effects of Minimum Wages" (Washington, D.C.: The National Bureau of Economic Research, April 1970), mimeographed; Jacob Mincer, "Unemployment Effects of Minimum Wages," *Journal of Political Economy*, vol. 84, no. 4, part 2 (August 1976), pp. 87–104.

that employment reductions are associated with reduced labor force participation. Estimated participation reductions are statistically significant. Evidently many potential workers are more likely to drop out than to queue for rationed jobs.

As part of a 1970 Labor Department survey, Hyman Kaitz analyzed employment and unemployment effects separately for males and females, white and nonwhite, for ages sixteen to seventeen and eighteen to nineteen. He reports significant employment reductions for white male teenagers aged sixteen to nineteen years and for white females sixteen to seventeen years old. The estimates are erratic for other groups, and show numerically large (and marginally statistically significant) employment increases for nonwhite males eighteen to nineteen years old. For unemployment, Kaitz finds significant reductions for nonwhite males and no pattern for other groups.

It is surprising that the Kaitz and Hashimoto-Mincer studies find so little agreement for nonwhites. They did partition demographic groups differently, and the Hashimoto-Mincer data extend to 1969, whereas the Kaitz data stop in 1968. Further, Hashimoto and Mincer allowed effects of changed minimums to be distributed over a two-year interval, whereas Kaitz looked only for an instantaneous effect. Some of the differences in findings may be explained by the timing flexibility Hashimoto and Mincer allow, but I doubt that it explains much. Instead, I think the explanation lies in the "fine" partitions (by age, race, and sex) used by Kaitz in contrast to the simple white and nonwhite dichotomy that Hashimoto and Mincer used for teenagers.

The CPS data come from a random sample of the U.S. population. As such, it is subject to sampling error that can be important when the data are finely partitioned. For example, the May 1973 CPS reported employment of males aged sixteen to nineteen years in the "Negro and other races" group as 339,000; a standard error for this estimate is between 17,000 and 25,000.[3] From this and the implied serial correlation the CPS reports, it follows that a quarter-to-quarter change of between 6.2 and 9.1 percent lies within two standard deviations of no change at all. If observed changes this large carry a significant chance of being only a sampling artifact, why would we expect our rudimentary techniques to be adept at distinguishing "signal" from "noise"? In contrast, for white teenage males aged sixteen to nineteen years, the proportionate two-standard-deviation band spans only 2.7 to 3.2 percent of observed employment. For these less noisy data, Hashimoto and Mincer and Kaitz agree on employment effects. In fact, when

---

[3] U.S. Department of Labor, Bureau of Labor Statistics, *Employment and Earnings*, vol. 19, no. 12 (June 1973).

Kaitz pools all teenagers into a single composite, his estimated unemployment effect is much larger than that Hashimoto and Mincer report for either whites or nonwhites.

In summarizing his results Kaitz stresses that it is difficult to disentangle effects in time-series data when so many of the relevant variables move together and tend to confound identification of their separate roles. Any economist who has analyzed aggregate time-series data can sympathize with this.

In a closely related study using the same data as Kaitz, I find statistically significant employment reductions for all teenagers aged sixteen to nineteen years, but when those aged fourteen to fifteen years (a group presumed more vulnerable) are added, the estimated effect is reduced and statistical significance is lost.[4] This is evidence of the nature of these data. If minimum wages affect anyone, it will most likely be the very young. Noisy data can conceal these effects.

James Ragan used the same sex, race, and age partition as Kaitz, but he delayed the start of the data series to 1963, when students were first distinguished.[5] As with the Hashimoto-Mincer study, Ragan infers unemployment responses from effects on employment and labor force participation estimates separately.

Unfortunately test statistics for unemployment are not reported, and since the employment and labor force data are not stochastically independent, they cannot be inferred from what is reported. Yet Ragan, who uses exactly the same minimum wage variable, finds more precise estimates than does Kaitz. For males, the estimate for each of eight groups (sixteen to seventeen or eighteen to nineteen years of age, black or white, student or nonstudent) is that higher minimums reduce employment, and five of the eight coefficients are statistically different from zero by usual standards. There is less estimation precision for both female employment and labor force participation for males and females, but the bulk of the evidence is that both employment and labor force participation fall as the minimum is increased.

By this time a fairly clear pattern has emerged. First, the Current Population Survey data cannot withstand fine partitioning for precise estimation. Yet the case for reduced employment as a consequence of minimum wage rates is much stronger than that for no effect. There is essentially no information of effects on unemployment rates.

In a recent paper Edward Gramlich, using quarterly data for the years 1948 to 1975, finds no significant effect for total teenage em-

---

[4] Welch, "Minimum Wage Legislation: Reply."
[5] James Ragan, "Minimum Wages and Youth Labor Market," *Review of Economics and Statistics*, vol. 59, no. 2 (May 1977), pp. 129–36.

ployment.[6] Yet in distinguishing full- from part-time workers (since 1963, when separate data became available) he estimates significant reductions in full-time work, with partially offsetting increments in part-time work. If the part-time work is not becoming available in uncovered sectors, should it not go the other way? After all, part-time workers earn much lower wages (see Table 5) than their full-time counterparts.

Gramlich reports significant reductions in full-time employment for adult males, but for adult females no systematic relation is identified. His finding for adult males is surprising, although there are hints of it in the Hashimoto-Mincer paper.

None of these studies took cognizance of state minimum wage laws, and only Gramlich distinguished full- from part-time work and only Ragan distinguished students. The lack of differentiation is especially troublesome in the papers of Hashimoto and Mincer and Kaitz and in my own paper (1974 and modifications reported in 1977) because 40 percent of all employed teenagers (and for that matter, unemployed teenagers) are students who work less than full time.

In a study that considers the coverage of both state and federal laws and that adjusts for the fact that students work only slightly more than half as many hours as nonstudents, James Cunningham and I find dramatic effects.[7] Our analysis relies on the "1 in 100 Public Use Sample" of the 1970 census instead of on the CPS time-series data. Observations are cross-sectional for state aggregates and take advantage of the relatively larger sample to distinguish teenage employment by age: fourteen to fifteen, sixteen to seventeen, and eighteen-

---

[6] Edward M. Gramlich, *Impact of Minimum Wages on Other Wages, Employment, and Family Incomes*, Brookings Papers on Economic Activity, no. 2 (Washington, D.C.: Brookings Institution, 1976), pp. 409–51.

The Gramlich paper (1976) is poorly specified for empirical inference of effects on employment. His theory is much in the spirit of Mincer, and he uses it to criticize—rightly—all of us who have constrained coverage effects to be proportionate to the minimum and minimum wage effects to be proportionate to coverage. His own empirical specification, however, belies his theory. In Gramlich's model the departure from proportionality (imposed by Hashimoto and Mincer, Kaitz, and me) arises from interactions between both coverage and the minimum with job search behavior, welfare, and uncovered sector alternatives. His specification at the theoretical level is even more interactive than we assume, yet at the empirical level interaction is ignored altogether. Instead, Gramlich chooses to use dummy variables for the 1961 and 1967 coverage changes. The importance of his empirical work comes subsequent to the employment analysis, in his decomposition of the low-wage work force by total family income, an idea I unabashedly confiscate here in Tables 3 and 5.

[7] Finis Welch and James Cunningham, "Effects of Minimum Wages on the Level and Age Composition of Youth Employment," *Review of Economics and Statistics*, vol. 60, no. 1 (February 1978), pp. 140–45.

to nineteen-year-olds. The minimum wage is measured in terms of its estimated effect on the costs of hiring persons eighteen to nineteen years old (these are hypothetical cost increments, and they would hold only if there were no corresponding employment reductions as in the indexed effect discussed earlier). This effect is greatest in states where wages are low, where federal coverage is high, and where state laws cover many workers at high minimums.

We estimate that for each increase of 1 percent in costs of hiring those aged eighteen to nineteen years generated by wage minimums, costs rise by 1.7 percent for persons aged sixteen to seventeen years and by 3.3 percent for those aged fourteen to fifteen years. That costs rise more for younger workers indicates only that, without minimums, they would earn lower wages. Correspondingly, for each increment of 1 percent in the costs of hiring those aged eighteen to nineteen years, the employment of eighteen- to nineteen-year-olds falls 1.3 percent, employment of those aged sixteen to seventeen years falls 2.4 percent, and for persons aged fourteen to fifteen years the drop is 4 percent. Since our estimate is that on the average (across all states) in the spring of 1970 wage minimums had increased costs of hiring persons aged eighteen to nineteen years by 11.3 percent, the inference for reduced employment is 45.6 percent for fourteen- to fifteen-year-olds, 26.9 percent for sixteen- to seventeen-year-olds, and 15.2 percent for eighteen- to nineteen-year-olds. These estimates should be viewed as conjectural because of the much smaller effects found in time series studies. Bear in mind, however, not only that procedures to obtain estimates differ but also that among available studies only this one recognizes both federal and state coverage. Further, its cross-sectional nature eliminates the necessity of estimating timing or lagged effects, which is difficult at best.

Cyclical Impacts

Aggregate U.S. employment steers an unsteady course as the currents of business activity fluctuate. Not surprisingly, the impact of fluctuating labor demand is distributed unevenly across industries and workers (classified by characteristics such as age, schooling, race, and sex). Numerous observers have noted that some workers are more marginal to the work force than others. It is as though firms divide laborers into a hard-core and a marginal group. When conditions are steady, both groups are employed and form some sort of normal composite. When demand booms, firms expand first by disproportionate reliance on marginal workers and then gradually expand the hard-core or long-term base as the boom appears to solidify and provide a firmer footing for longer term commitments. When demand busts, marginal workers are the first to go.

Since the minimum wage provides a floor below which wages cannot fall, it is not an inactive participant in distributing workers between the normal and transitory work forces. As an example, suppose a firm employs both low- and high-wage labor. In normal times the firm forms a labor mixture such that just enough low-wage workers are hired to bring their hourly wage (and value to the firm) to two dollars. In these times, high-wage workers are worth four dollars. Business conditions range between boom, bust, and normal, and labor demand is 10 percent above normal during booms and falls to 10 percent below during busts. If employment were invariant to demand, wages would be 10 percent above normal in booms and 10 percent below normal in busts. Ordinarily one would expect employment to fluctuate procyclically to dampen wage variations, but some variation would remain. Now, imagine the consequences of an hourly minimum of two dollars. What happens to low-wage workers during busts?

There are sound theoretical reasons for expecting firms to depend more than proportionately on less-skilled workers to absorb the brunt of cyclical vagaries. But, regardless of what these effects would be without minimums, the imposition of wage floors destabilizes employment of those whose productivity fluctuates about the minimum.

Marvin Kosters and I estimated minimum wage effects on the age, race, and sex composition of short-run or cyclical changes in aggregate employment based on quarterly employment data for the years 1954 to 1968.[8] We began with the idea that aggregate employment could be partitioned into two components: normal employment (that consistent with the economy's long-run trend) and transitional employment (the deviation from trend, positive in booms and negative in busts). We next adopted the tautology that, subject to measurement error, μ, the employment of a particular demographic group, i, is its "normal" share times aggregate normal employment plus its "transitional" share times aggregate transitional employment. That is, $E_i = \alpha_i E_n + \beta_i E_\tau + \mu_i$, where E_i refers to employment of group i, E_n is aggregate normal employment, E_τ is aggregate transitional employment, and α and β are the respective shares for group i. We next estimated α and β for eight demographic groups as functions of the minimum wage (adjusted for changes in average wages and with a coverage adjust-

[8] Marvin Kosters and Finis Welch, "The Effects of Minimum Wages on the Distribution of Changes in Aggregate Employment," *American Economic Review*, vol. 62, no. 3 (June 1972), pp. 323–32.

ment similar to that used in the Kaitz, Hashimoto and Mincer, and Ragan studies).

Table 8 reports our estimates of average shares for the 1954–1968 period. It shows that teenagers constitute about 6.3 percent of normal employment and 22.1 percent of transitional employment.

The coefficient of marginality, the ratio of the transitional to the normal share, is a convenient summary statistic. Quite simply, if aggregate employment falls below trend by 1 percent, the coefficient of marginality estimates the percentage reduction in employment of each of the groups. A marginality coefficient of less than one suggests less than average vulnerability to aggregate fluctuations, while a coefficient of more than one implies more than proportionate variability. Among adults, only nonwhite males experience more than average variance. White males are on the whole more immune to the cycle than any of the other groups considered. Teenagers are peculiarly vulnerable: between 1954 and 1968, in a cyclical downturn a teenager was more than four times as likely as an adult to lose his or her job (3.51 ÷ 0.83).

Table 9 reports our estimates of the way minimum wages affect employment shares and marginality coefficients. The numbers are esti-

TABLE 8

AVERAGE SHARES OF NORMAL AND TRANSITIONAL EMPLOYMENT FOR U.S. CIVILIAN EMPLOYMENT: QUARTERLY AVERAGES, 1954–1968

Group	Share of Normal Employment (percentage of U.S. total), α	Share of Transitional Employment (percentage of U.S. total), β	Coefficient of Marginality, β/α
Adults (aged 20 or more)	93.4	77.9	0.83
White males	57.0	42.5	0.75
Nonwhite males	5.8	7.9	1.34
White females	26.9	24.0	0.89
Nonwhite females	4.0	3.6	0.90
Teenagers (aged 16–19)	6.3	22.1	3.51
White males	3.2	11.7	3.66
Nonwhite males	0.4	1.8	4.56
White females	2.5	7.4	2.95
Nonwhite females	0.2	1.1	4.97

SOURCE: Marvin Kosters and Finis Welch, "The Effects of Minimum Wages on the Distribution of Changes in Aggregate Employment," *American Economic Review*, vol. 62, no. 3 (June 1972), p. 327.

TABLE 9

ESTIMATED ELASTICITIES OF EMPLOYMENT SHARES AND MARGINALITY
COEFFICIENTS WITH RESPECT TO THE COVERAGE-ADJUSTED
MINIMUM WAGE

Group	Share of Normal Employment (percentage of U.S. total), α	Share of Transitional Employment (percentage of U.S. total), β	Coefficient of Marginality, β/α
Adults (aged 20 or more)			
White males	.032	−1.44	−1.47
Nonwhite males	a	a	a
White females	.032	a	a
Nonwhite females	a	a	a
Teenagers (aged 16–19)			
White males	−.331	2.48	2.81
Nonwhite males	−.356	3.88	4.24
White females	−.241	3.30	3.54
Nonwhite females	−.301	5.31	5.61

a Not statistically different from zero.
SOURCE: Marvin Kosters and Finis Welch, "The Effects of Minimum Wages on the Distribution of Changes in Aggregate Employment," *American Economic Review*, vol. 62, no. 3 (June 1972), p. 327.

mates of percentage changes arising from an increase of 1 percent in the minimum wage. For example, we estimate that a hike of 1 percent in the minimum would reduce the marginality coefficient for white adult males by 1.5 percent—that is, such an increase would further insulate them from cyclical vagaries. Our estimates for other adults are not precise enough to be useful. For teenagers, effects are as expected.

The minimum wage heightens teenage vulnerability to the cycle. How important are these estimated effects? Because of expanded coverage the effective minimum increased greatly between 1954 and 1968. Suppose the average effective minimum that existed between 1954 and 1958 was raised in one step to the average for the 1965–1968 period. How would cyclical vulnerability be affected? We estimated that cyclical vulnerability for white adult males would fall by one-third. For each of the four teenage categories, cyclical vulnerability would more than double. We concluded that teenagers are especially vulnerable to business cycles and that no small amount of this vulnerability is owing to minimum wages.

Youth Differentials

As the preceding discussion shows, the bulk of research into minimum wage effects has focused on teenagers. Because they are an easily identifiable group for which employment data are readily available and because they earn low wages, they are likely candidates for adverse effects. Consequently there have been a variety of proposals for youth differentials, or lower minimums for teenagers.

In fact, a number of European countries have adopted such programs, as have a number of U.S. states in their supplementary legislation. The mechanics of the differential involve finding groups most adversely affected and lowering the minimum for them. This, of course, means admitting that there are adverse effects.

If there are adverse effects—and the accumulated evidence that there are is convincing—is a two-tiered minimum the solution? Unlike a uniform minimum, which raises employment costs most for those who would earn the least, a two-tiered minimum ameliorates the effects on at least one low-wage group. But what of adults—especially those just above the age break and those near or past normal retirement ages who seek income supplements through part-time work—who would earn wages close to those of teenagers? With this type of two-tiered minimum they have the worst of two worlds. First, they must convince employers that they are worth the higher of the two minimums, and, second, they must compete with youths who, under the differential, can accept lower wages. Should we not then consider differentials for young adults, the aged, the less schooled, and so forth? We have enacted temporary differentials for a limited number of students and for handicapped workers, which is an acknowledgment that lower wages are necessary to give them a competitive edge. The logic is inexorable.

Imposing a minimum on a specific group restricts that group's ability to compete for jobs and to trade nominal wages for other amenities. Others not facing the same constraint are given a competitive edge. A uniform minimum generates the greatest proportionate cost increase for those who otherwise would earn the lowest wages, and their employment is most adversely affected. A set of minimums differentiated among groups so that the same proportionate cost increase would take place for each would be more even in employment effects, but devising and administering a program of this sort is clearly impossible.

So far as I know, no attempt to account for individual wage differences has explained as much as half of observed variance. (Table 5 gives some idea of wage differences for teenagers, young adults, and the aged.) Even if we could accurately forecast wage potential, it differs so widely among geographic areas and over time that the accounting job would be simply unmanageable. I began by noting that the low-wage populace is widely distributed over demographic categories and that teenagers probably hold only one-third of all low-wage jobs. In considering questions of teenage differentials, therefore, we must consider effects on the omitted majority of other low-wage workers.

At present we have so little information about degrees of competitiveness or substitutability between teenagers and other low-wage workers that we cannot make even ballpark guesses about effects on omitted groups. In fact, in the paper by James Cunningham and me mentioned earlier, we attempted to estimate effects of youth differentials extended to some but not all teenagers. We examined employment effects on those (first fourteen- and fifteen-year-olds only, then everyone fourteen to seventeen years old) given a 20 percent differential as opposed to effects on older teenagers who were exempted from the differential. Although the statistical estimates leave too much room for error for us to be confident in the findings, there are clear hints that adverse effects on omitted groups may be smaller than many would have guessed.

Since concepts of youth differentials are fraught with unanswered questions concerning feedback effects on low-wage workers to whom the differential is not extended, advocates of youth differentials must have mixed feelings. I do think, however, that a less ambiguous case for regional differentials can be made. Wages vary among states, and some areas have much higher percentages of low-wage workers than others. In fact, in the study I did with Cunningham, we estimated that a uniform federal minimum had raised costs of employing teenagers in Arkansas by more than twice as much as it had in the least affected states.

One cruel advantage for economists of the absence of a youth differential is that teenagers have remained a clear example of adverse effects. Surely they, more than any other broadly defined group, have borne the brunt of this legislation. Consequently they have served as experimental subjects, enabling us to estimate effects. Our knowledge of these effects has increased greatly in the last few years, almost exclusively as a result of analyzing teenagers. Had Congress previously enacted a differential, the evidence for teenagers would not be available, and there is a real question whether the minimum for adults would now be higher.

One argument for youth differentials that I have not seen in published discussions stems from the notion of productivity advances associated with work experience, with learning gained on the job. If a youth differential were enacted and if the adult minimum were unaffected by it, then youth employment would expand. As a result, as teenagers approached the age at which the differential no longer applied, they would have more accumulated experience and would, therefore, be more productive than they would have been if the differential had not been legislated. Consequently, the real costs of the adult minimum to the employer would be' reduced. This suggests that adverse substitution effects against young adults would decline as experience with the youth differential lengthened. Obviously this effect would not extend to the aged.

Even if a youth differential is a good idea, there remains the question of why its logical underpinnings are not pursued to the fullest. Why not have a differential for all who would earn less than the minimum? In other words, why have a minimum wage at all?

Concluding Comment

I have avoided most of the subtle and theoretically more exacting effects of minimum wage legislation. Instead, I have concentrated on the conceptual base and the empirical evidence for obvious effects. I have concentrated more on employment than on unemployment, mainly because I see little point in distinguishing between those who, as a result of increased minimums, lose their jobs and drop out of the labor force and those who lose their jobs and report to census interviewers that they are searching for work. It is only the latter who become part of the unemployment rate statistics.

Although I have dwelt on the evidence of adverse employment effects for teenagers, I do not mean to imply that teenagers are the only ones affected by wage minimums. They may be more affected than others, but the low-wage, low-productivity population is widely dispersed, and it defies simple taxonomies. Because of this, remedial measures like youth differentials or special youth job programs, which are designed to alleviate undesirable effects but which are nonetheless targeted for selected demographic groups, may not only fail to reach most of those affected but also exacerbate their plight.

Among other welfare-related programs designed for transfers from the haves to the have-nots, minimum wages are perverse. They design transfers from some have-nots to other have-nots. Of course we have added and we will continue to add welfare programs that will partially compensate minimum wage losers, spreading the losses more broadly across the population. Perhaps this is as it should be, but bear in mind the nature of this transaction. We first impose a law that results in job losses. For those who lose their jobs and then find that they qualify for welfare, there is partial compensation. Is it not strange that at a time when a major concern of welfare programs is to increase work incentives we also push a minimum wage program, which reduces work?

The establishment of a minimum wage was one of our earliest forays into a national welfare program. It was a misguided idea even in 1938, and the world of welfare has changed since then. After forty years of evidence of adverse effects, it would seem that the time for mandated minimum wages has passed.

22

YOUTH LABOR MARKETS AND THE MILITARY

Richard V. L. Cooper

I. INTRODUCTION

Youth unemployment has become an increasingly important problem
in recent years. Youth unemployment rates have averaged nearly
20 percent since 1974, and have run as high as 40 percent in some
segments of the youth labor market (e.g., black teenagers). Developing
and implementing solutions to the youth unemployment problem has therefore become a major concern throughout the policymaking community.

Before the causes of and possible solutions to the youth unemployment problem can be identified, however, it is both important and
necessary to develop a better understanding of the youth labor market--
specifically, youth labor force participation and the youth job
market. Because the military plays such an important role in the
youth labor market, the purpose of this paper is to develop an
understanding of the effects that the military has on youth labor force
participation and the youth job market.

The next section of this paper examines briefly the military's
demand for labor--i.e., the military's effect on the youth job market.
Section III then turns to focus on the supply side effects of the

*This paper was prepared for presentation at the Policy Conference
on Employment Statistics and Youth, University of California, Los
Angeles, February 11-12, 1978. The paper was prepared with the support
of the U.S. Department of Labor (No. B-9-M-8-0653).

From Richard V. L. Cooper, "Youth Labor Markets and the Military," Rand Report P5927, 1978.
Reprinted by permission of the Rand Corporation, Santa Monica, CA.

military. That is, it examines the role of the military in youth labor supply and human capital development. Sections IV and V provide illustrative examples of the impact of the military on youth unemployment, with Section IV focusing on demographic trends over time while Section V examines the black unemployment problem. Finally, Section VI examines the implications of the military's role in the youth labor market for the development of meaningful labor statistics.

II. THE MILITARY AND THE DEMAND FOR LABOR

Because the military is such a major claimant of the nation's
resources, and of youth labor in particular, it is useful to begin by
discussing the military's demand for labor. Whether the military
enters the youth labor market through traditional market allocating
mechanisms (e.g., wages and other inducements to join) or through
nonmarket allocating mechanisms (e.g., the draft), the military demand
for labor can have important effects on the size and composition of
the youth labor force. That is, the youth labor force is shaped in
significant ways by both the military's aggregate demand for labor
and the more specific policies that govern the use of military
personnel during their service careers.

The discussion below therefore centers on the demand for military
labor. If, as is not the case, the military's demand for labor made
up, say, 0.1 percent of the labor force, then the subject might be
interesting, but of only academic interest. If, as is actually the
case, the military makes up a significant share of the youth labor
force--in the neighborhood of 10 to 20 percent--then this question of
demand becomes of supreme policy importance. To the extent that labor
statistics are not designed to measure the military's effect on either
the size or composition of the youth labor force, these statistics are
accordingly less useful for policy purposes.

Recognizing the importance of the demand side of the equation,
the discussion below focuses first on the overall size of the military,
and then turns to the impact of the military on the youth labor
market in particular.

SIZE OF THE MILITARY

With its 4 to 5 million employees, depending on who all is counted, and its approximately $400 billion worth of land and capital in fiscal 1976, the Department of Defense is the single largest employer of resources in the nation. The military's capital stock consists not only of such obviously military items as tanks, ships, and aircraft, but also the more mundane items such as forklift trucks, buildings, desks and file drawers, and so forth.

The military's labor force includes about 2.1 million active duty uniformed personnel, about 1 million reservists (i.e., the so-called "weekend warriors"), 1 million direct-hire civilian personnel (of which about 600,000 are in white-collar occupations, while the remaining 400,000 are in blue-collar jobs), about 100,000 indirect-hire civilian personnel, 500,000 contract-hire civilian personnel, and about 250,000 nonappropriated fund employees.[1] For most all of the civilian personnel, however, there is little difference between their employer and regular civilian employers.[2] What is unique about the military,

-----

[1] "Direct-hire" civilians are those civilian employees maintained directly on the defense payroll. "Indirect-hires" are those foreign nationals working on U.S. installations abroad who are formally employed by the host nation, but whose costs are actually paid by the U.S. military through a reimbursement program. "Contract hires" are those individuals who, though actually employed by civilian firms, perform contract services such as aircraft maintenance, janitorial services, and kitchen duties for the military. (Contract hires do not, however, include those civilian workers engaged in the production of equipment and construction ultimately purchased by the military.) "Nonappropriated fund" civilian personnel are individuals who are paid out of funds not budgeted out of Congressionally appropriated funds. These are largely employees of military commissaries and post exchanges who are paid out of the funds generated by the sale of goods and services.

[2] There are some "dual-hatted" civilians, primarily maintenance technicians, who though employed as civilians, are also members of the reserve forces.

though, are military personnel. For the most part, the discussion in this paper will focus on active duty personnel, but it is important to recognize that the nearly 1 million reservists represent an important type of second job holding, and need to be examined accordingly.[1]

Even when we focus only on military personnel, Fig. 1 makes it clear that military personnel comprise a significant portion of the U.S. male labor force. In the immediate post-World War II period, male military personnel made up about 3.5 percent of the total male workforce, but this jumped to nearly 7.5 percent during the Korean conflict. Between the Korean and Vietnam wars, male military personnel made up between 5 and 6 percent of the U.S. male labor force. After jumping up to more than 6.5 percent during the Vietnam War, the proportion of the U.S. male workforce in the military has declined to between 3.5 and 4 percent during the past several years. Thus, although not a dominant factor in the male workforce, the military has nonetheless maintained a significant share of the labor force in its ranks during the entire post-World War II period.

THE YOUTH LABOR MARKET

Because the military maintains a "closed" personnel system, the foregoing understates in an important way the impact of the military on the youth labor market. That is, the military maintains an "up through the ranks" personnel system, with little lateral entry. This

[1] For a discussion of moonlighting and the reserves, see Bernard D. Rostker and Robert Shishko, Air Reserve Personnel Study: Volume II. The Air Reserve Forces and the Economics of Secondary Labor Market Participation, The Rand Corporation, 1973; and Robert Shishko and Bernard D. Rostker, "The Economics of Multiple Job Holding," American Economic Review, LXVI, (June 1976).

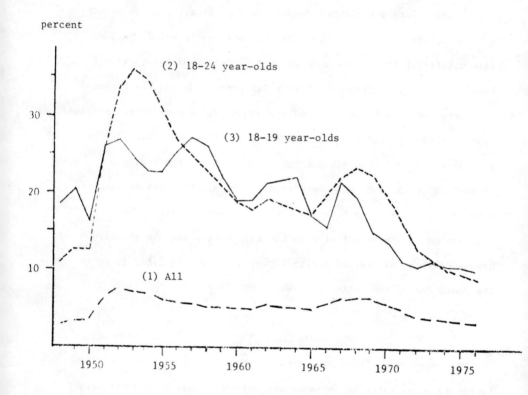

Fig. 1 -- Number of Male Military Personnel Relative to the Relevant
Male Labor Force (percent): (1) All, (2) 18-24 year-olds
and (3) 18-19 year-olds.

means, then, that the military's major influence on labor markets is
at the entry point, typically the crop of recent college graduates for
the officer corps, and the recent crop of high school graduates for
the enlisted ranks (although about 35 percent of enlisted recruits are
nonhigh school graduates). As a result, about 90 percent of all
enlisted personnel join the military between the ages of 17 and 20
years old.[1]

The implications of the closed military personnel system for
the youth labor market can be seen in Fig. 2, which shows that between
the 1950s and mid 1960s, roughly half of all young men reaching military
age served in the military. By the mid to late 1970s, however,
declining military force sizes and a substantially larger youth cohort
meant that only about 1 out of every 5 young men would serve in the
military at some time during his life.[2]

A somewhat different perspective on the effect of the military's
demand for labor on the youth labor market can be seen in Fig. 1
shown earlier. Specifically, Fig. 1 also shows the proportions of the
18 to 19 year-old youth labor force and 18 to 24 year-old labor force
employed by the military. According to either of these measures, we
see that between 20 and 35 percent of the youth labor force was
employed by the military from the time of the Korean buildup through
the Vietnam War. Only since the end of the Vietnam War, with the

---

[1] Because of the "oldest first" draft policy of the 1950s and
1960s, significant numbers of personnel then entered the military in
their mid-twenties.

[2] In fact, these demographic trends, more than anything
else, were responsible for the demise of the draft. That is, the
growing population base not only created enormous inequities (since
a small few would have to bear the "burden" of military service,
while the vast majority could escape serving), but also made it
possible to attract sufficient numbers of volunteers without the
threat of a draft.

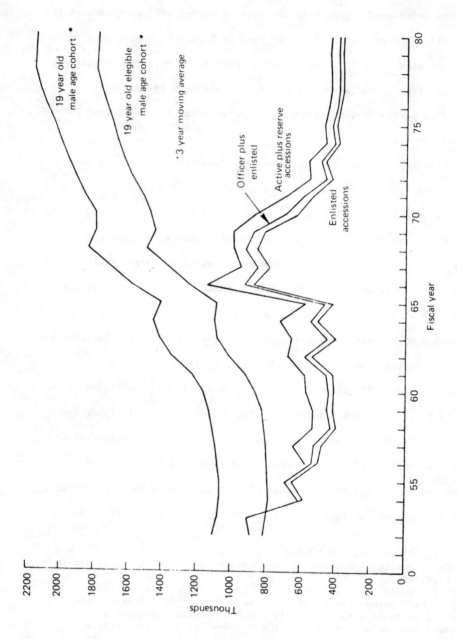

Fig. 2 — Military manpower procurement and population size

corresponding reduction in military force strengths and simultaneous
increase in the youth population cohort, has the proportion of the
youth cohort employed by the military dropped significantly--at its
current level, about 10 percent.[1]   Thus, no matter how we measure
it, the military is an important, and in some cases the dominant, player
in the youth labor market.   Accordingly, policy changes affecting the
numbers of young men entering the military--and/or the nature of their
military service--can have a significant impact on the size and
composition of the youth labor force.

In addition to the quantitative side of demand, there is an
important qualitative aspect to the military's participation in the
youth labor market.   Specifically, the military uses a variety of
criteria to screen potential applicants for enlistment.   The individual
must first take a mental aptitude test, the results of which are used
to classify the individual into one of five so-called mental categories
(with Mental Category I representing the top 7 percent of the population
and Category V representing the bottom 10 percent).   Those classified
into Mental Category V are legally ineligible to serve.   Others
ineligible include those who fail to pass the medical examination,
as well as those who fail to meet certain other criteria such as a
check of police records, talks with high school counselors, and so
forth.   Overall, about 40 out of every 100 applicants for enlistment
are rejected outright.   Moreover, of the remainder, the military
only allows some Mental Category IV (i.e., below average) and high
school dropouts to join.

---

[1] Note that these measures of the military's penetration
exclude members of the reserve forces.

The end result of supply behavior (on the part of the individual) and this demand behavior (on the part of the military) can be seen in Tables 1 and 2, which compare the mental aptitude and educational attainment, respectively, of military recruits with their civilian counterparts.[1] In general, these comparisons show that the military takes in a reasonably representative sample of the nation's youth. In terms of the nation's policy toward youth and youth unemployment, Tables 1 and 2 establish the important point that the military does not draw narrowly from any one segment of society;[2] rather the military plays a significant role in most all segments of the male youth labor force.

Finally, the discussion of the military's participation in the youth labor market would not be complete without giving consideration to two special issues: the use of women in the military and the racial composition of new recruits. Although participation of women in the armed forces was limited by law to no more than 2 percent of

----

[1] That is, theory tells us that supply behavior should lead to fewer (than a random sample of) very high mental aptitude individuals joining the enlisted ranks, since the enlisted ranks correspond more or less with blue-collar occupations and since these very high mental aptitude youth are more likely to attend college. On the demand side, the military limits (and in some cases excludes outright) the numbers of below average mental aptitude and nonhigh school graduates, so the bottom end of the mental aptitude and educational attainment spectra will also tend to be "under-represented." Thus, the enlisted ranks of the military would be expected to have proportionately fewer members from the very top and bottom ends of the mental aptitude spectrum or from those with post-secondary and no secondary education. (Commissioned officers, on the other hand, are drawn exclusively from the college graduate population.) Note, however, from Tables 1 and 2 that enlisted recruits are quite representative of the upper end of the noncollege civilian population--i.e., those individuals corresponding most closely with enlisted occupations.

[2] Other work by the author shows that the military draws a reasonably representative sample of American youth in other dimensions as well, such as region of origin and socioeconomic background. See Richard V.L. Cooper, Military Manpower and the All-Volunteer Force, The Rand Corporation, September 1977.

Table 1

Distribution of Enlisted Accessions and the General
18 to 21 Year-Old Male Population by Mental Category
(percent)

| Mental Category | Draft | AVF | US Population: Male 18–21 Year-Olds | | | |
| | | | All | | Non-College | |
			All	Non-V	All	Non-V
I	6	3	7	8	2	2
II	31	32	28	31	22	25
III	43	57	34	38	39	45
IV	19	8	21	23	24	28
V	--	--	10	--	13	--
TOTAL	100	100	100	100	100	100

Source: Office, Assistant Secretary of Defense (Manpower and
Reserve Affairs)

Table 2

Educational Attainment of Enlisted Accessions
and the U.S. Male Population
(percent)

Maximum Educational Attainment	Enlisted Accessions[a]		U.S. Male Population[b]			
	Draft	AVF	All 18-22	Not in School 18-24	18-21	Blue Collar 25-44
College Grad.	3	1	8	7	1	3
Some College	13	5	26	13	12	12
High School Grad.	54	59	41	46	49	48
Some High School	26	35	19	22	27	21
Elementary	4	1	6	11	12	16

[a]Source: Office, Assistant Secretary of Defense (Manpower and Reserve Affairs)

[b]Source: U.S. Bureau of the Census and U.S. Bureau of Labor Statistics.

[c]Includes GEDs--i.e., those who have passed a general high school equivalency test, but who do not possess a high school diploma.

military personnel strengths prior to 1972, these restrictions are now largely gone (the only major remaining restriction being that women are not to be employed in "combat," though the definition of combat is less than clear cut). As a result, participation of women in the armed forces has increased significantly over the past five years, up to more than 5 percent of total military personnel today--i.e., currently there are about 110,000 women in the military. Further increases are planned, such that women in the military should number between 150,000 and 200,000 by the 1980s. Moreover, women are being used in a variety of "nontraditional" jobs. That is, whereas women were once limited mostly to certain medical and administrative occupations, today they are entering a variety of occupational areas such as truck driver, aircraft mechanic, and in some cases combat support, among other areas. Thus, the military, which once only had a minor role in the female labor market, is now taking a much more active role and will continue to do so in the future.

For a variety of reasons, mostly economic in nature, the military enjoys an even more substantial participation in the black youth labor market than it does for the youth labor market as a whole. Unlike some areas of the civilian labor market, where blacks often face inferior economic opportunities, the military does not discriminate according to race (and this has been perceived by large numbers of black youth). As a result, blacks have historically served in larger numbers relative to their population than have nonblacks. Indeed, whereas the military employs about 10 percent of today's total 18 to 24 year-old male labor force, it employs nearly 20 percent of the black male 18 to 24 year-old labor force.[1]   Increasing

participation of black college graduates in the officer corps is

perhaps even more impressive. Whereas blacks made up only 1 percent

of all new officers in 1960, today they make up about 7 percent of the

total.

Thus, not only is the military an important factor in the youth

labor market in total, it is of increasing importance for certain

segments of that market, especially minorities and women. Stated more

simply, the above discussion has shown that the military is an

important factor in the demand side of the youth labor force.

SECULAR, CYCLICAL, AND SEASONAL VARIATIONS IN THE
MILITARY'S DEMAND FOR LABOR

Because the military plays such an important role in the youth labor

market, variations in the military's demand for labor can have an

important effect on both the size of the civilian youth labor force

and on the employment and unemployment prospects for these youths.

Three kinds of variations in the military's demand deserve attention:

secular, cyclical, and seasonal.

---

[1] The proportion of new recruits that are black has in fact
increased significantly over the past 10 to 15 years, from about
8 percent in 1960 to some 16-18 percent today. The primary reason
for this increase is the increasing proportion of black youth found
eligible for military service. During the mid 1950s, only about
12 percent of black youth were classified into Mental Categories I-III
(i.e., the upper 70 percent of the mental aptitude spectrum)--that
is, the so-called "prime" manpower pool. Today, between 45 and
50 percent are so classified. As a result, blacks have increased
their share of this prime manpower group from 2.9 percent in the mid
1950s to more than 7 percent today.

As can be seen in Figs. 1 and 2 shown earlier (and as will be shown later in Fig. 4), there has been a secular trend toward smaller military forces since the mid-1950s (excepting of course for the Vietnam War). Looking ahead, however, we expect military forces to stay at approximately their current levels--about 2.1 million members in the active duty forces. In other words, barring major unforeseen circumstances, such as another war, we should not expect to see major secular trends in the size of military forces, and hence in the numbers of youth employed by the military.

In the case of cyclical variations, the individual military services seem to exhibit some cyclical recruiting patterns (e.g., the Navy seems to still have a four-year recruiting cycle, which is a result of the Vietnam buildup and drawdown). For the Department of Defense as a whole, however, there is not much cyclical variation in the demand for labor, simply because the cycles of the individual Services have tended to be offset one another. Thus, cyclical variations in the demand for labor on the part of the military would not seem to pose significant problems for the youth labor force.

Finally, there are significant seasonal variations in the military's demand for labor, but this seasonal variation is a supply-side not a demand-side phenomenon. That is, the military has adapted itself to the seasonal variations in recruits seeking to join the military. Specifically, the military recruits particularly large numbers in the summer and fall months--i.e., following June high school graduation.

Again, seasonal variations in the military's demand for labor would not appear to pose significant problems for the youth labor force.[1]

In conclusion, there have been secular and cyclical fluctuations historically in the military's demand for labor, but these have been a result of declining force sizes and the Korean and Vietnam Wars. Barring another major buildup in force sizes, we would not expect much further secular or cyclical variation in the size of military forces, or in the military's demand for youth labor. Although there is in fact considerable seasonal variation in the military's demand for labor, this works with, rather than against, youth labor force participation, since the military is merely responding to the supply of new recruits entering the job market.

-----

[1] During the draft, there was far less seasonal variation in the demand for labor, since the military could simply draft to make up for recruiting shortfalls in the "off" recruiting months. This probably caused greater disruption to the youth labor force than the current seasonal variations which are in response to the supply of individuals entering the youth job market.

III. MILITARY SERVICE AND THE SUPPLY OF LABOR

Examination of the supply side of youth participation in the military is important for two main reasons. First, the continuity between military and civilian work experience is much greater than is sometimes perceived. That is, there are sufficient similarities between military and civilian employment that movement between the two sectors is frequently quite easy. Every year, hundreds of thousands of young men leave the civilian youth labor force to join the military, just as hundreds of thousands of young men leave the military to rejoin the civilian youth labor market. This means that modest variations in the variables affecting the desirability of military and civilian employment can have a significant effect on the flow between military and civil youth labor markets.

Second, military employment provides the individual with the opportunity to accumulate significant amounts of human capital. This human capital, in turn, can frequently be used to obtain subsequent civilian employment. As a result, the military can affect not only the size of the civilian youth labor force, but also qualitative aspects of that manpower pool, such as the skill and education mix of members of the youth labor force.

The following discussion examines these supply side aspects of military employment, focusing first on the decision to join the military, then the military work experience, and, finally, the decision to stay or leave the military.

THE DECISION TO JOIN THE MILITARY

When an individual joins the military, he or she leaves the civilian work force. Because of this, it is important to examine various aspects of the decision to join, as discussed below.

Factors Affecting the Enlistment Decision

Models of enlistment supply have been the subject of a considerable amount of reseach for at least 10 years. Among those studying the enlistment decision are economists, sociologists, and psychologists. The economists tend to formulate the enlistment decision as a model of occupational choice, where the individual presumably weighs the various advantages and disadvantages of alternative employment options and chooses the one that maximizes his or her utility. Although these are certainly not the only models used to explore the enlistment decision process, they are probably better developed than those of the other disciplines.[1]

Generally speaking, models of the enlistment decision, irrespective of their disciplinary origin, have highlighted a number of factors as critical in the individual's decision about whether or not to enlist in the military. Important among these factors are certain economic variables, including the wage rate offered by the military, the potential earnings from civilian employment, and the chances for obtaining civilian employment (as reflected by the unemployment rate). Economic factors are certainly not the only variables to affect the individual's decision to enlist, as surveys consistently show a number

---

[1] As various data collection techniques such as surveys have improved in recent years, so have the enlistment decision models of the other academic disciplines, especially sociology and psychology.

of other factors to be likewise as important, such as the training and job experience offered by the military, the chance to travel and "see the world," patriotism, and a host of other factors too numerous to mention.

The point is simply that the enlistment decision is shaped by many different things, so that modest changes in one or more of these can significantly affect both the number and types of individuals who join the military. To illustrate, a variety of economic supply studies conducted over the past 10 to 12 years show that if the military pays a wage approximating that earned by comparably aged and educated civilian workers, the military can attract between 15 and 20 percent of a given youth cohort into military service.[1] Moreover, most of these studies show that the elasticity of supply with respect to pay is somewhere in the neighborhood of 1.0. (Actually, estimates of the enlistment supply elasticity range from about 0.5 to 2.0, with 1.0 representing probably the best guess.) That is, a 10 percent increase in the military wage rate will yield approximately a 10 percent increase in the supply of labor to the military. Conversely, as the chances for obtaining civilian employment decrease, the supply of labor to the military also increases. Again, most studies done over the past several years show unemployment elasticities of between 0.1 and 0.4. In other words, a

---

[1] See, for example, Dorothy Amey, et.al., Supply Estimation of Enlistees to the Military, General Research Corporation, McLean, Virginia, June 1976; Alan E. Fechter, "The Supply of Enlisted Volunteers: Comparisons of Pre-AVF Studies with Volunteer Enlistments," in Richard V.L. Cooper (ed.), Defense Manpower Policy, The Rand Corporation, forthcoming; Stuart H. Altman and Alan E. Fechter, "The Supply of Military Personnel in the Absence of a Draft," American Economic Review, LVII (May 1967); and Harry J. Gilman, "The Supply of Volunteers to the Military Services," in Studies Prepared for the President's Commission on an All-Volunteer Armed Force, U.S. Government Printing Office, Washington, D.C., November 1970.

10 percent increase in the unemployment rate will lead to a 2 to 4
percent increase in enlistment supply.

The implication of these results is clear. Specifically, as the
military makes its employment offer more (less) attractive relative
to civilian employment opportunities, the military can expect to get
more (fewer) individuals to join. In other words, there is not a
well defined line separating military and civilian employment. This
means that in studying the factors affecting the youth labor force
and youth unemployment, it is important to recognize the role the
military plays in trying to attract young men and women.

Military Earnings

As indicated above, previous studies have shown the importance
of military pay for enlistment supply. In this regard, Fig. 3 shows
that military pay for new recruits has changed significantly during
the course of the past 10 years. Specifically, with the pressure
of the draft, there was no "need" to pay military recruits a market
wage. Indeed, as shown in Fig. 3, the wages earned by military
recruits remained virtually unchanged from 1952 through 1965, and
from 1965 to 1971 they received only cost-of-living pay increases.
Although these wages were sufficient to attract some "true volunteers,"
the draft or threat of the draft provided the vast majority of new
recruits.[1]

Given the demographic trends shown earlier in Fig. 2, it is
clear how inequitable the selective service draft had become by the

---

[1] During the 1950s and 1960s, about one-third of new recruits
were "true volunteers"; about one-third were "draft-motivated"
volunteers (i.e., individuals who volunteered in order to avoid being
drafted, but who would not have enlisted in the absence of a draft);
and about one-third were drafted outright.

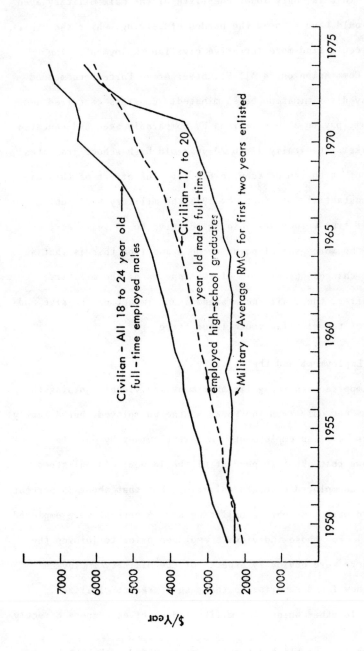

Fig. 3 — Annual Military and Civilian Wages

Source: See text.

late 1960s. That is, only about one-fifth of the male military aged
population would have to bear the burden of serving, while the other
four-fifths could find more lucrative civilian employment. The
President's Commission on an All-Volunteer Armed Force recommended
that this pay discrimination be eliminated. Congress concurred and
raised recruit pay to a level earned by comparably aged and educated
civilian workers (basically 17 to 20 year-old high school graduates),
the results of which can be seen in Fig. 3. The effect of this pay
raise was substantial. In fact, by 1975 the military had doubled
the number of true volunteers joining relative to 10 years earlier.

Again, the more general point to be drawn from this is that as
the military changes one or more of the aspects of the military
employment offer, there will be a significant impact on the size and
composition of the civilian youth labor force.

Pre-Service Employment and the Military

It is important to recognize that many individuals joining the
military come not only from the ranks of the unemployed, but directly
from previous civilian employment. A recent survey by Gay, for
example, shows that about 20 percent of the 18 year-old enlistees
in 1974 were unemployed prior to enlisting, but that about 35 percent
were employed part time before enlisting and 45 percent were employed
full time.[1] For those individuals employed prior to joining the
military, there were obviously aspects of the military employment
offer that they found superior to their then present civilian
employment. In other words, the military does often compete directly

---

[1] Source: unpublished tabulations provided by Robert M. Gay,
The Rand Corporation, 1976.

with civilian employers for young recruits. This is not altogether surprising, though, given the kinds of work that young members of the labor force often find available. That is, not only is it harder for these young members of the labor force to find work, as reflected by high youth unemployment rates, but the kinds of jobs they can obtain frequently offer less in the way of wages, challenging work, chance to accumulate human capital, and so forth, than the military can offer. Yet, it is precisely for these reasons that many young men and women seek military employment as their first or second job after leaving school.

The implication of this is clear. Although there are many young men and women who would enter the military under no circumstance, there is a sufficiently large portion of the youth labor force that, given the proper set of inducements, would (and in fact do) join the military. Thus, analysis of the youth labor market--both supply and demand--must take the military into account.

THE MILITARY WORK EXPERIENCE

Once in the military, the individual is obligated for a period of service, generally running three to six years. That is, unlike civilian employers, the military can obligate for a period of service.[1] The discussion here looks briefly at the nature of this military work experience, including the occupations that new recruits are likely to get, as well as the accumulation of human capital by military personnel.

---

[1] There are ways, however, for the individual to get out of his or her contractual obligation.

Occupational Mix of the Military

Although it is frequent to view the military in terms of the
combat arms, it is important to recognize that the military consists
of a wide range of occupations, not at all unlike what one finds in
the civilian sector. In fact, Table 3 shows that the combat arms
occupations make up only about 10 percent of the entire enlisted
work force. The other 90 percent is made up by such diverse occupations
as aircraft mechanics, medical and dental specialists, radar repairmen,
radio operators, carpenters and plumbers, military police, intelligence
experts, vehicle mechanics, and a host of other specific occupations.
In other words, young men and women joining the military find virtually
as many different types and kinds of jobs in the service as they could
in the outside civilian world.

Moreover, as part of the move to the all-volunteer force, it is
frequent to find young men and women joining the military to work
specifically in a particular job or at a particular military
installation, or with a particular military unit. Once frequent
stories about the individual who was an engineer but forced to be an
Army cook, or the cook who was forced to become a vehicle mechanic,
and so forth, are not only not common, they are rare. The military
services have made significant strides in better matching individuals'
tastes and aptitudes with actual job assignments.[1]

The foregoing is not meant as an advertisement for military
service, but rather as an indication of the very wide range of
occupational specialties that young men and women joining the service

[1] The major problem here, however, is that young recruits
are frequently unaware of what they do and do not want to do. In
fact, for many it is this indecision that led to their joining the
military.

Table 3

Distribution of the Force by
Occupational Area: FY74[a]

Officer		Enlisted	
Occupation	Percent	Occupation	Percent
Executives	1.6	Combat Arms	12.3
Tactical Operations	40.8	Electronics	10.4
Intelligence	3.2	Comm/Intelligence	6.7
Engineer/Maintenance	15.6	Other Specialists	1.9
Scientists/Professionals	6.6	Elec/Mechanics	21.6
Medical/Dental	9.4	Medical/Dental	4.6
Administrators	12.8	Admin/Clerks	18.4
Supply	6.1	Service Supply	11.0
Other[b]	3.8	Craftsmen	4.6
		Other[b]	8.6

[a]Based on "primary" occupation designators.

[b]Training, Miscellaneous, and Other.

Source: Data were furnished by the Office, Assistant Secretary
of Defense (Manpower and Reserve Affairs)

can and do engage in, and that many of these young men and women are in these occupations as a result of their own choice. The implications for the civilian youth labor force are obvious, in that individuals leaving the military bring with them a set of skills acquired during their military service. To the extent that young men and women are engaged in jobs that are found in the civil sector and that are the types of jobs in which these individuals would like to continue working, then there is the important issue of the accumulation of human capital, as discussed below.

The Accumulation of Human Capital

As indicated above, military work experience can be characterized in economic terms as the accumulation of human capital. Some of this human capital will be of a very general variety, such as the maturity that goes along with the individual's early job choices. Parts of this human capital are also very specific--in fact, they are specific entirely to the military. Examples of this would be the use of mortars, marching, drill formation, and so forth. But a substantial amount of this human capital may be of the general occupational type that is transferable to similar jobs in the civil sector.

This human capital formation takes place in several ways: through formal school training, through on-the-job training (OJT), and through actual job experience. The military maintains one of the largest educational establishments in the nation. All military recruits attend basic military training--i.e., the so-called "boot camp." In addition, about 95 percent of all new recruits attend formal technical schools. In these schools, which last from a few weeks to as much as two years (and average three to four months in length), the individual

is taught about his or her new job. These classes consist of formal
lectures and training, demonstration, and actual hands-on experience.

The on-the-job training and actual job experience in the military
constitute another form of human capital accumulation. In fact, given
the often theoretical nature of formal technical school training, the
OJT and job experience may constitute the more significant form of
human capital accumulation.

In sum, the military work experience is likely to represent a
significant amount of human capital formation by the individual.
And this fact has not gone unrecognized by potential recruits, as
military training and job experience are two of the most frequently
cited reasons for joining in the first place.

THE DECISION TO STAY/LEAVE

Upon completing the enlistment tour, the individual must decide
whether to remain in the military (if he is declared "eligible") or to
return to the civilian labor force. The discussion focuses on this
decision to stay or leave by outlining, first, the factors affecting
the reenlistment decision: second, what individuals do in their
post-service employment; and third, the migratory effects brought
about by military service.

Factors Affecting the Reenlistment Decision

As has been the case with enlistment supply, reenlistment supply
has been studied extensively during the past 10 years or so. Again,
a number of different academic disciplines have been brought to bear
on the issue, including economics, sociology, and psychology, among

others. The economic studies tend to show that reenlistment supply is
quite sensitive to military and civilian pay opportunities.
Specifically, the elasticity of supply with respect to pay has been
shown to be in the neighborhood of 1.0 to 4.0, with 2.0 probably
representing the best guess.[1] This means, then, that reenlistment
supply is quite sensitive to military pay. That reenlistment supply
should be more sensitive to pay than enlistment supply is not
surprising, though, since individuals facing the reenlistment point
are those who have already entered the military. That is, the initial
enlistment decision screens out those individuals most opposed to
military service on "taste" grounds, so that reenlistment supply is
likely to be drawing from a more homogeneous manpower pool.

For a variety of technical reasons, studies have been less
successful in pinpointing the responsiveness of reenlistment to unemployment rates. Nevertheless, the conventional wisdom is that
reenlistment supply is in fact quite sensitive to unemployment, and
a casual review of the evidence bears this point out. Clearly,
however, more thorough study of this issue is warranted before
definitive conclusions can be drawn.

Noneconomic factors have also been shown to play an important
role in the individual's decision about whether to reenlist. A
variety of studies, mainly using survey techniques, find that certain
attributes of military service will either persuade or dissuade an
individual from reenlisting. For example, job security is one of
the most frequently cited reasons for individuals deciding to reenlist,

---

[1] See, for example, John H. Enns, <u>Reenlistment Bonuses and
First-Term Retention</u>, The Rand Corporation, September 1977; and
Gary R. Nelson, "Economic Analysis of First-Term Reenlistments in
the Army," in <u>Studies Prepared for the President's Commission</u> . . .,
op. cit.

while the loss of personal freedom is perhaps the dominant noneconomic
reason why individuals choose to leave military service after the end
of their first term. Since these are clearly not the only factors
that affect the individual's reenlistment decision, the larger point
is simply that reenlistment is a function of many variables, such that
changes in one or more of these variables can in the long run
significantly affect the numbers and types of individuals reentering
the civilian youth labor force.

Post-Service Employment

As indicated earlier, military service may provide the
opportunity to accumulate human capital--human capital that can be
applied to subsequent civilian employment. The extent to which the
military does lead to the accumulation of human capital has in fact
been the subject of considerable study during the past 5 to 10
years.[1]

These studies of veterans' post-service activities have tended
to focus on one or more of the following three issues: general
employability of military veterans, the extent to which veterans

[1] See, for example, Eva Norrblom, An Assessment of the
Available Evidence on the Returns to Military Training, The Rand
Corporation, July 1977; Eva Norrblom, The Returns to Military and
Civilian Training, The Rand Corporation, July 1976; Robert B. Richard-
son, "An Examination of the Transferability of Certain Military Skills
and Experience to Civilian Occupations," unpublished Ph.D. dissertation,
Cornell University, 1966; William Mason, "On the Socioeconomic Effects
of Military Service," unpublished Ph.D. dissertation, University of
Chicago, 1970; Adele P. Massell and Gary R. Nelson, The Estimation of
Training Premiums for U.S. Military Personnel, The Rand Corporation,
June 1974; and Zvi Griliches and William Mason, "Education, Income,
and Ability," Journal of Political Economy, LXXX (May/June 1972).

use some of the knowledge and experience gained during military employment for their post-service civilian employment, and the earnings of veterans as compared with nonveterans. Although these studies differ substantially in their specific findings, one general theme does emerge. Specifically, military service in general does lead to the formation of human capital that can be applied to post-service civilian employment. As would be expected, though, the degree to which human capital accumulated during military service can be transfered to the civilian sector is obviously greater for individuals serving in military occupations with more direct civilian counterparts.

In general, these analyses of veterans' post-service employment activities show, first, that veterans trained in skill x during the military tend to be employed in larger numbers in skill x in the civil sector than would be implied by a mere random sampling. In other words, veterans tend to gravitate towards the kinds of occupations they had in the military. Thus, military service appears to have a potentially important effect on shaping the kinds of occupations that members of the youth labor force will enter in their post-service careers.[1] Second, individuals employed in a post-service occupation similar to their military occupation tend to show higher earnings than their veteran counterparts whose civilian occupations are not so directly related. In other words, veterans' post-service

_____

[1] Some of the correlation between individuals' military and post-service activities is explained by the fact that individuals' pre-service and military occupations are also correlated, so to the extent that individuals' pre- and post-service occupations are correlated, so will their military and post-service occupations be.

earnings in a given occupation are higher if the veteran's military
service was in a related occupational area.[1]

˙Part of the above-cited earnings differential may be due to a
so-called "certification" effect. That is, for individuals such as
minorities and high school dropouts whose economic and employment
opportunities are otherwise more limited, satisfactory completion of
military service may be viewed by potential employers as an indicator
of greater employability. Casual examination of the evidence bears
this point out, as black and high school dropout veterans both tend
to see greater gains from their military service in subsequent
civilian employment than do white high school graduate veterans.
In general, however, the evidence is sketchy, so further study of the
effects of military service on post-service earnings and employment
opportunities clearly deserves more careful attention.

Finally, military service has a significant effect on post-
service employment activities through the educational and training
benefits offered by the Veterans Administration. The post-World War II
G.I. Bill educated literally hundreds of thousands of former servicemen.
Although the nature of the G.I. Bill has recently changed,[2] the
military will continue to represent a potentially important source
of educational benefits for America's youth population. Only recently

---

[1] It is important to note that the studies are far from
unanimous on this point. However, the studies that fail to find
much of a relation have generally been hampered by data problems.
In cases where there are sufficient data, they tend to show their
positive earnings effect. See, Eva Norblomm, An Assessment of the
Available Evidence . . . ., op. cit.

[2] The present day GI Bill is contributory. That is, for
every dollar that the service member contributes to his or her
post-service education "fund," the Government contributes two dollars.

have the effects of military service on military education and

training begun to be studied,[1] so all the effects are far from

understood. The general conclusion to emerge from this review

of post-service activities is that military service has important

effects not only on the size of the youth labor force, but perhaps

more important, on the composition of that labor force--especially

the education and skills possessed by former servicemen reentering

civilian life.

Migration

Another possible effect of military service is on migration

patterns of America's youth. These effects have been relatively

unstudied thus far, but we do know that military retirees, for

example, tend to locate in disproportionately large numbers near

military installations. This is because of the benefits provided near

military installations (e.g., commissaries, free medical care, etc.).

Military service may have a similar effect on one-term veterans in

terms of geographic migration and location, and these effects clearly

need to be studied further.

_____

[1] See, for example, Dave M. O'Neill, Sue Goetz Ross, and
John T. Warner, "The Effect of Military Training and GI Bill Training
on Civilian Earnings," in Richard V.L. Cooper (ed.), Defense Manpower
Policy, op. cit.

IV. THE MILITARY AND YOUTH UNEMPLOYMENT

The preceding two sections have focused on the military, work, and the youth labor market in very general terms. This section provides an illustrative example of these principles, and briefly examines the relationship between military labor demands and youth unemployment.

The basic hypothesis to be presented is that high youth unemployment is due in part to the large growth in the size of the youth labor force relative to the labor force in total. Because youth carry a limited amount of human capital (i.e., job experience) with them into the job market, the economy may have difficulty absorbing young workers into the work force. Thus, the rapidly growing size of the youth labor force relative to the labor force as a whole--a trend which has been exacerbated by declining military demands on the youth labor force--has meant higher unemployment rates for American youth, simply because the economy could not absorb all of these young workers, especially given institutional rigidities such as the minimum wage.

The discussion below first reviews the trends in the youth labor force. It then turns to develop a simple model of youth unemployment, as outlined briefly above.

SIZE OF THE YOUTH LABOR FORCE: TRENDS OVER TIME

There have been two significant trends affecting the youth labor force over time. First, because of the post-World War II baby boom, the size of the youth labor force has increased substantially relative to the size of the total labor force over the past 20 years.

Second, because today's military forces are smaller than those of the
1950s, the military is placing smaller demands on the youth labor
force, not only in a relative sense, but in absolute terms as well.
As a result, the civilian youth labor force has grown even more
dramatically percentage wise than has the total youth labor force, as
can be seen in Table 4. Thus, the combination of a growing youth
population and fewer numbers of youth serving in the military has
served to increase the youth share of the civilian labor force by some
70 to 80 percent over the last 20 years. For example, 18 to 19 year-
olds made up 2.9 percent of the total civilian labor force in 1959, as
compared with 5.0 percent in 1976. Similarly, 18 to 24 year-olds made
up 10.2 percent of the total civilian work force in 1959, versus 18.6
percent in 1976.[1] Clearly, then, there have been substantial
changes in the composition of the labor force, such that youth are
making up an ever larger proportion.

A SIMPLE MODEL OF YOUTH UNEMPLOYMENT

For the sake of illustration, this section develops a simple
single equation model of youth unemployment. Although this model is
meant to be illustrative only, as a simultaneous equations system is
probably more appropriate, this simple model serves to demonstrate the
importance of taking into account such factors as the supply and
demand of military labor when addressing questions related to the
youth labor force and youth unemployment.

---

[1] Ideally, we would focus on the 18 to 21 year-old male
population, as this is where the military reaches its maximum
penetration rate. However, data limitations precluded using this
definition of "youth."

Table 4

Size of Male Youth Labor Force Relative to Total Male Labor Force

| | Index | | | | | |
	1954	1960	1964	1968	1972	1976
18-19 Year-Olds						
Total Labor Force	100	108	115	134	141	152
Civilian Labor Force	100	111	114	139	163	171
18-24 Year-Olds						
Total Labor Force	100	101	109	125	136	141
Civilian Labor Force	100	123	136	146	177	190

To begin with, assume that the youth unemployment rate is a function of the general level of economic activity--in particular, assume that the youth unemployment rate is a function of the overall unemployment rate.

Second, we will assume that an aggregate production function for the economy as a whole can be stated in terms of various categories of inputs used in the production process. Specifically, we will assume that in addition to such factors of production as capital, consumables, and land, that the production function can be stated in terms of different categories of labor. For simplicity, we can define two categories of labor: inexperienced (i.e., young) workers, and experienced (i.e., older) workers. In general, we would expect these various inputs to the production process to be substitutable for one another, but they would also be expected to be less than perfectly substitutable. Therefore, as the stock of inexperienced workers increases relative to the stock of experienced workers, we would expect inexperienced or young workers to find it relatively more difficult to secure civilian employment.

In a perfectly competitive economy, this would lead to a fall in the wage rate of inexperienced workers. But, institutional rigidities such as the minimum wage may preclude this lowering of youth wage rates. As a result, the economy will find it difficult to employ all the youth who have entered the labor force.

This leads us to the simple model of youth unemployment described earlier. Specifically, we can express youth unemployment as a function of (1) the overall unemployment rate, (2) the proportion of the total civilian labor force that would be classified as inexperienced or young workers, and (3) a measure of the institutional rigidities that work against the employment of youth. For the sake of this model, these institutional rigidities will be measured as the ratio of the minimum wage to the average hourly wage for nonsupervisory production workers in nonagricultural employment.

Defining "youth" as 18 to 19 year-old males, we obtain the following regression results (standard errors are given in parentheses):

$$(1) \quad y(t) = -7.782 + 1.864 \, u(t) + 1.021 \, c(t) + 0.156 \, w(t), \quad R^2 = 0.89$$
$$\qquad\qquad\quad (3.870) \ (0.170) \qquad (0.315) \qquad\;\; (0.070)$$

where $y(t)$ = unemployment rate (percent) for 18-19 year-old males in the civilian labor force in year t,

$u(t)$ = overall unemployment rate (percent) for the civilian labor force in year t,

$c(t)$ = 18-19 year-old male civilian work force in year t expressed as a percentage of the total male civilian work force,

$w(t)$ = Federal minimum wage as a percent of the average hourly wage in nonagricultural employment for nonsupervisory production workers, and

t = 1951, ..., 1976.

If, on the other hand, we define "youth" as 18 to 24 year-old males, we get the following results:

$$(2) \quad z(t) = -1.323 + 1.684 \, u(t) + 0.077 \, d(t) + 0.023 \, w(t), \quad R^2 = 0.97,$$
$$\qquad\qquad\quad (1.520) \ (0.071) \qquad (0.036) \qquad\;\; (0.028)$$

where $z(t)$ = unemployment rate (percent) for 18-24 year-old males in the civilian labor force in year t,

$d(t)$ = 18-24 year-old male civilian work force in year t expressed as a percentage of the total male civilian work force,

and the other variables are as described in equation (1) above.

The regression results shown in eqs. (1) and (2) provide some interesting insights into the determinants of youth unemployment. As expected, youth unemployment rates are highly correlated with the unemployment rate for the economy as a whole. Moreover, and again as expected, this relationship is stronger (as reflected by the smaller standard error) for the 18-24 year-old "youth" population than for the 18-19 year-old "youth" population. The reason for this is simply that 20-24 year-olds are more experienced than 18-19 year-olds, and are thus more substitutable for experienced workers. Because they are more substitutable, the employment (and unemployment) experience of 20-24 year-olds can be expected to mirror more closely the employment experience of the civilian labor force as a whole.

Second, both equations show that youth's share of the total civilian labor force is an important determinant of youth unemployment rates in the civilian sector. Specifically, these equations show that the rapidly increasing size of the civilian youth labor force (which, in turn, is due to both the increasing size of the total youth labor force and the constant or decreasing number of youth employed by the military) has been responsible for at least some of the secular increase over time in civilian youth unemployment rates. Again, the relationship is stronger for the 18-19 year-old "youth" population than for the 18-24 year-old "youth" population (for the same reasons as described above).

Finally, the increase in the minimum wage over time relative to wages for more experienced workers has likewise served to drive up youth unemployment rates. That is, the minimum wage has helped keep

the market from adjusting to the "excess supply" of youth labor.
Given that a smaller proportion of the 20-24 year-old population would
be expected to have a "market clearing" wage below the minimum wage,
the minimum wage variable behaves as expected, since it does less well
in equation (2) than in equation (1)--i.e., it does less well for
18-24 year-olds than for 18-19 year-olds.

Together, then, these three factors--i.e., the inceasing size of
the youth population, the constant or decreasing numbers of youth
employed in the military, and institutional barriers such as the
minimum wage--help to explain why youth unemployment rates have
increased over time relative to unemployment rates for the general
economy.

Moreover, to the extent that this simple model is reasonably
accurate, the decline in the youth population that takes place in the
1980s (and the corresponding increase in the older population) means
that youth unemployment rates would be expected to decrease somewhat
in the 1980s, other things equal. This is not to say that youth
unemployment will cease to be a problem, but rather that demographic
trends will finally begin to work in favor of reducing youth
unemployment rates in the future, especially if military force sizes
remain at or near their present levels. Indeed, equation (1)
indicates that civilan youth unemployment rates ought to fall by 10
percent or so by the mid 1980s.

Although this model was developed only for the sake of
illustration, it demonstrates how important demographic trends can be,
and specifically how important the military's demand for labor is on
the size and employability of the youth labor force.

V. BLACK UNEMPLOYMENT: A SPECIAL CASE

One of the most troublesome aspects of the recent economic
recession has been the particularly high unemployment rates experienced by black youth. Whereas black youths in the civilian labor
force had historically (1950-1970) experienced unemployment rates
about 8 percentage points higher than their nonblack counterparts
(about 20 percent for blacks as opposed to about 12 percent for nonblacks), unemployment rates for blacks jumped to about twice those
of nonblacks during the height of the economic recession--35 percent
for black 16 to 19 year-old males, versus about 18 percent for nonblacks. Unemployment problems among black youth have accordingly
become a very serious and well-recognized problem.

Some insight into this black youth unemployment problem can be
gained by examining the role of the military in the youth labor
market. To begin with, recall that the military classifies prospective
recruits into one of five so-called mental categories, with Categories
I-III representing the upper 70 percent of the mental aptitude spectrum
(i.e., the "prime" manpower pool). Using results developed elsewhere
by the author [1], columns (1) and (3) of Table 5 show the distributions of the black and nonblack 18 year-old populations, respectively,
according to Mental Category. Consistent with past studies, these
distributions show that blacks as a whole do not score as well on
the mental aptitude tests administered by the military as do nonblacks.

---

[1] See Richard V.L. Cooper, Military Manpower and the All-
Volunteer Force, op. cit.

Table 5

Distribution of the Black and Nonblack
18 Year-Old Manpower Pools According
to Mental Category: 1974
(percent)

Mental Category	Percentile	Black Population		Nonblack Population	
		Total	Civilian	Total	Civilian
		(1)	(2)	(3)	(4)
I-III	31-100	45	39	84	83
IV	11-30	32	34	12	12
V	0-10	23	27	4	5

Table 6

Distribution of the Black and Nonblack
18 Year-Old Manpower Pools According
to Mental Category: 1974
(000s)

Mental Category	Percentile	Black Population			Nonblack Population		
		Total	Military	Civilian	Total	Military	Civilian
		(1)	(2)	(3)	(4)	(5)	(6)
I-III	31-100	115	31	84	1267	139	1128
IV	11-30	81	6	75	186	11	175
V	0-10	59	0	59	62	0	62

For example, column (1) shows that about 45 percent of blacks are classified into Mental Categories I-III, while about 84 percent of nonblacks are so classified. Conversely, 23 percent of blacks are classified as Mental Category V (and, hence, legally ineligible for military service), as opposed to only 4 percent of nonblacks.

Taking the 18 year-old male population in 1974, columns (1) and (4) of Table 6 show the numerical distributions of black and nonblack males, respectively, according to Mental Category. For example, there were about 115,000 black male Category I-III 18 year-olds in 1974, versus about 1,267,000 nonblack male Category I-III 18 year-olds in the overall population. But, about 31,000 black and 189,000 nonblack Category I-III 18 year-olds were in the military in 1974, as shown in columns (2) and (5) of Table 6. The numerical distribution of the civilian 18 year-old black and nonblack populations according to Mental Category can then be found by subtracting column (2) from (1) and column (5) from (4), respectively. The results are shown in columns (3) and (6). The conversion of the numerical distributions of civilian 18 year-olds according to Mental Category to percentage distributions are shown in columns (2) and (4) of Table 5.

Three important findings emerge from Tables 5 and 6. First, and as is generally well recognized, blacks do not score as well on mental aptitude tests as nonblacks. Second, though perhaps less well recognized, Table 6 shows that the military has been very successful in attracting the most able black youth, insofar as the participation rate in the military for Category I-III blacks is high by most any standard. This is not very surprising, of course, given that black youth often face inferior employment opportunities in the civil sector, whereas the military does not discriminate according to race.

The combination of the above two findings gives rise to the third: namely, that black youth in the civilian labor pool fall disproportionately in Mental Categories IV and V. To the extent that employment opportunities are correlated with measured mental aptitude, columns (2) and (4) of Table 5 help to explain why black unemployment rates are so much larger than those for whites. Moreover, because the military is able to draw such a large fraction of the Mental Category I-III black population into service, the youth unemployment rates for black civilians are accordingly larger.

VI. CONCLUSIONS

Two important conclusions emerge from the preceding discussion.
First, the military's demand for labor is an important determinant
of both the size and composition of the youth labor force. This
means that changes in the military's demand for labor can have
significant effects on the youth labor market, including employment
prospects, the size of the youth labor force, and a host of other
variables affecting American youth. Second, the military also
exerts a major influence on the supply-side behavior of the youth
labor force. Specifically, American youth have demonstrated a
considerable degree of mobility between the military and civil
sectors. This includes both the initial decision about joining the
military and later decisions about whether to remain in or leave the
military. Perhaps the most significant from the point of view of the
civilian labor market is the human capital that former Service members
bring back with them when they rejoin the civilian work force.

The implications of these findings for the measurement and collection of youth labor market information are several fold. Specifically,
these implications concern (1) the measurement of youth unemployment
rates, (2) the collection of aggregate labor force statistics, and
(3) the collection of special labor force data.

For both theoretical and empirical reasons, the results from the
preceding discussion imply that youth unemployment rates ought to be
defined in terms of the total labor force, not just in terms of the
civilian labor force. On theoretical grounds, since military service

is entirely voluntary, [1] the military competes as only one among
many potential employers for the nation's youth. To be sure, there
are unique aspects of military service, just as there are unique
aspects of some types of civilian employment. But from the viewpoint
of measuring youth labor force participation and employment, the
foregoing means that the military is theoretically little different
from other employers of youth. This is borne out empirically as well.
Not only is military service apparently seen as an attractive employment
option by a significant portion of the youth labor force--between
10 and 20 percent of young men enter the military--but members of the
youth labor force have in fact demonstrated considerable mobility
between the military and civil labor markets.[2] In other words,
military service is an integral part of the employment pattern for a
sizeable portion of the youth labor force.

In terms of measuring unemployment rates, the above discussion
suggests that those employed in the military ought to be counted as
part of the labor force. Because those serving in the military are
employed, historical measurements based on the civilian labor force
alone have therefore overestimated "true" unemployment rates, and in

---

[1] On theoretical grounds, a case can be made (though perhaps
not too persuasively) for excluding the military during periods of
the draft. That is, since not all military participation is voluntary
during a draft, military may be a more separate and distinct entity
from civilian employment when a draft is present.

[2] If, on the other hand, the military was empirically a
distinct entity from the civilian sector, as in fact has been the case
in some countries, then a case could be made for excluding the military
from labor force measures on empirical grounds. That is, if there is
little flow between the military and civil employment markets, then
the inclusion or exclusion of the military from labor force measures
is both less interesting and less important.

some cases substantially.[1] For example, the current procedure
overestimates overall unemployment rates among black youth by
some 20 to 25 percent--as opposed to a 10 percent or so
overestimation of white youth unemployment rates--simply because
such a large fraction of the black youth labor force is employed
in the military.[2] Although this does not dismiss the problem
of black unemployment, it does suggest that the problem is not
quite as severe as a casual review of unemployment rates for
black youth in the civilian labor force would seem to imply. In
general, developing more appropriate measures of youth unemployment--
i.e., measuring youth unemployment in terms of the total labor
force--can lead to more informed policy decisions.

With respect to aggregate labor statistics, the foregoing should
not be viewed to mean much change in the ways that data are collected
or maintained. That is, although it seems desirable to define
unemployment rates relative to the total labor force, it is useful
to maintain separate statistics on the civilian labor force and on the
total labor force, as is now the case. This is simply an example of
a more general principle. Specifically, labor force statistics ought
to be maintained for major segments of the youth labor market--e.g.,
according to age, race, geographic location, and so forth. That is,
collecting and maintaining labor statistics according to these major
segments of the youth labor force helps to pinpoint and spot certain
problem areas. Because the military is in fact an important segment

_____

[1] That is, the current procedure omits those employed in the
military from the denominator of the ratio used to calculate the
unemployment rate.

[2] Moreover, because the military tends to select the "cream
of the crop" from among black youth, those not serving in the military
would be expected to be the ones that would have the most difficulty
securing employment, from either military or civilian employers.

of the youth labor force, this suggests that the current procedure of maintaining separate labor force statistics for military and civilian youth employment is a valid one.

Finally, although the preceding discussion does not suggest much change in the way aggregate statistics are collected or maintained, it does suggest that special data collection methods need to take greater recognition of military service. For example, data collection methods such as the National Longitudinal Survey, the Current Population Survey, the Census, and so forth, should place greater emphasis on collecting relevant information about the individual's military participation. This would include age of entry into the military, length of service, rank, occupational specialty, training received (both formal and on-the-job), etc. That is, it is clear from the limited knowledge available that military experience and training can have an important effect on individuals' subsequent employment and earnings prospects. To the extent that current data sources do not properly measure this training and experience, then we are failing to recognize the full effects of alternative policy options. Therefore, greater attention needs to be directed toward collecting relevant information about the individual's military experience, in conjunction with his or her civilian experience.

In general, this calls for greater coordination of data collection efforts between military and civilian authorities. Such efforts are warranted, not only because youth labor markets are affected by both military and civilian work experience, but also because the controlled nature of the military environment affords the opportunity to examine certain youth productivity and behavioral parameters that can be observed only with great difficulty in the civilian sector. For example, recent surveys of military personnel have provided valuable

information about the relationships among individuals' attitudes,

their earnings prospects, and their actual employment decisions.[1]

This was made possible largely by the fact that the military was able to

first survey these individuals, then track and compare these individuals'

actual decisions with what they said they had intended. Combined with

the vast amounts of information available on the military personnel

files, these types of surveys can be used to provide valuable infor-

mation about individuals' attitudes, supply behavior, and productivity--

not only in the military, but in the civilian labor market as well.

Areas where such cooperation and coordination between military

and civilian data collection efforts could prove to be particularly

profitable include certain ongoing and special civilian collection

efforts, including future National Longitudinal Surveys, the Current

Population Survey, and the Census. Alternatively, certain regular

and special data collection efforts in the military could provide

valuable information to civilian researchers and policy makers.

Examples include the annual survey of new recruits at armed forces

entrance and examination stations, post-service surveys conducted by

---

[1]   A number of recent data collection efforts illustrate the
point. For example, to estimate the response to the military's
health professionals scholarship program, a survey was administered
to a stratified random sample of medical students across the country.
The survey essentially asked these students to trace out their supply
curve, not only with respect to values of the stipend, but also to
such other variables as tour commitment, residency policy, and so
forth. The results have been impressive, as prediction errors over
the past three years have been in the neighborhood of 5 percent.
In another effort, individuals' productivity on the job was measured.
Combined with the attitudinal information also collected and the
information available from personnel files, valuable insights have
been gained about the determinants of productivity, attitudes, and
supply behavior.

the military, attitudes of young women toward military service, and
so forth.

In sum, this paper has argued that the military is a most important
factor in youth labor markets. On the one hand, the military is a
major source of jobs for American youth, while on the other, it is
clear that military experience and training can play a signifiant
role in the issues and problems of civilian labor market behavior.

23

SELECTIVE EMPLOYMENT SUBSIDIES:
Can Okun's Law Be Repealed?

*John Bishop and Robert H. Haveman**

Concern that structural factors impede efficient labor market performance is evidenced in both statistical analyses of economic potential and policy proposals for selective employment subsidies. Estimates of the level and expected growth of full-employment *GNP* have recently been revised downward, as has the 3.2 unemployment multiplier implicit in Okun's Law (see U.S. Council of Economic Advisers and George Perry). These indications of structural changes labor markets reinforce statistics showing excessively high unemployment rates for youths and blacks, and labor force participation rates that are increasing for women and decreasing for men.

The simultaneous concern with high inflation and high measured unemployment, in the context of major changes in labor force composition and increased variance in sectoral unemployment rates (see Perry), has brought forth numerous and sizable selective employment subsidy policies (*SESP*) in both the United States and Western Europe. The *SESP*, changes in potential *GNP*, and Okun's Law are not unrelated phenomena. This paper explores that relationship. Section I presents a brief taxonomy of the primary *SESP*s which are currently being discussed in Western industrialized countries. Section II provides the economic rationale underlying these measures. Section III explores the relationship of *SESP* to the prospective growth of aggregate output, in the context of Okun's Law. Evidence on the existence and magnitude of changes in employment decisions in response to the New Jobs Tax Credit (*NJTC*) is presented in Section IV.

*Project associate, Institute for Research on Poverty, and professor of economics and fellow, Institute for Research on Poverty, University of Wisconsin-Madison, respectively. The helpful comments of John Palmer are acknowledged.

From John Bishop and Robert H. Haveman, "Selective Employment Subsidies: Can Okun's Law Be Repealed?" 69(2) *American Economic Review* 124-130 (May 1979). Copyright © 1979 by the American Economic Association.

I

Wage (or employment) subsidies have been the primary measure designed to target employment demands on those sectors with substantial excess supply. They have appeared in various guises. A *SESP* can be a function of recruitment (additional hires), the existing employment stock, or changes in the employment stock. Each of these subsidies can be targeted on particular types of labor (say, by age, sex, region, unemployment duration, or education), or they can be general in nature. Moreover, the subsidy can be a flat amount or it can vary with the level of earnings, the wage rate, or the duration of coverage. It can be paid to the employer or to the worker, either directly or via a tax credit.

Examples of several of these variants have been recently implemented (see Haveman and G. B. Christainsen). The United States' *NJTC* is a constrained marginal stock subsidy with no targeting. In calendar years 1977 and 1978 firms expanding employment above 102 percent of the previous year's employment level receive a tax credit equal to 50 percent of the first $4,200 of wages paid each additional employee up to a maximum of 47 employees or $100,000 of credit. On the other hand, the 1975 British Temporary Employment Subsidy is a reverse recruitment rather than a stock subsidy, and like the *NJTC* it is temporary and nontargeted. This program subsidizes about 30 percent of the wage costs for up to one year of workers who would otherwise be laid off. In 1974, the West German government introduced a temporary targeted recruitment subsidy with a marginal stock constraint. For six months, a wage subsidy of 60 percent was paid to firms in specified regions for employing registered unemployed workers, if the firm's employment increased from that of a stipulated date prior to the passage of the act.

The Netherlands, France, and Sweden have also recently adopted targeted employment subsidies. The percentage of the labor force on which *SESP*-type subsidies are paid varies from about .3 percent of the labor force in West Germany to 3-4 percent in Sweden. In 1978, the *NJTC* will be paid on the employment of nearly 1 percent of the United States labor force at a total budget cost of at least $2 billion.

While few reliable evaluations have been made of these *SESP*s, the numerous extensions of what were to be temporary programs suggest that they have not been viewed as failures in achieving the primary objective—employment increases—set for them. In the United States, the Carter Administration has proposed replacing the lapsing *NJTC* with a Targeted Employment Tax Credit that would subsidize firms for 33 percent of the first $6,000 of first-year wages paid to low-income workers who are either 18-24 years of age or handicapped, and for 25 percent in the second year. As revised in Congress, the proposal will likely become a hiring subsidy rather than a stock subsidy, and the target group will be expanded to include welfare recipients.

II

The economic rationale for *SESP* is straightforward: By reducing the price of labor at the margin, employment will be encouraged, unemployment reduced, price pressure will be reduced in competitive markets through a reduction in the marginal cost function for incremental output and, in the case of marginal stock subsidies, entry will be encouraged. Further, for firms engaged in external trade, *SESP* operates as an export subsidy (see Layard and Nickell). Indeed, for a number of Western European nations, this characteristic is viewed as a primary rationale for *SESP*. A temporary *SESP* encourages firms to incur labor costs earlier than otherwise. As a result, inventory accumulation or accelerated maintenance and investment spending will tend to increase. Finally, *SESP* (particularly nontemporary programs) will tend to induce the substitution of targeted labor for nontargeted labor. For example, it may induce adding a second shift rather than increasing overtime (see Jonathan Kesselman, Samuel Williamson, and Ernst Berndt).

Inevitably, however, the net job creation impact of a *SESP*—defined as the employment level in the economy with the policy less that without it—will, because of financial, output, and labor market displacements, be smaller than the gross number of jobs subsidized. A fully specified general equilibrium model is necessary to accurately estimate the net effects of a *SESP*.

If *SESP* is targeted on a resource in excess supply or with a positive and nontrivial supply elasticity (such as handicapped workers, transfer program recipients, and low-income youth (see Stanley Masters and Irwin Garfinkel)), potential *GNP*—defined as the level of *GNP* when *NAIRU* (the rate of unemployment that does not accelerate inflation) is attained—will rise. Even if the labor markets for these workers were free from distortions associated with minimum wage and tax and transfer programs, a wage subsidy of their employment paid for by a tax on other workers would raise potential *GNP* (see Bishop, 1977). Indeed, *SESP* can also increase potential *GNP* even if the labor force participation rate of each demographic group is fixed by reducing a wage-weighted *NAIRU* through concentrating employment increases on sectors with elastic sectoral Phillips curves (see Martin Baily and James Tobin).

The benefits of expanding the potential *GNP* in this manner are increased by the fact that the labor supply decisions of targeted groups are distorted by high employer- and employee-paid taxes, and even higher marginal reduction rates of transfer benefits. Consequently, any resulting increase in actual and potential *GNP* through such employment increases will be positively correlated with the change in economic welfare. Moreover, pecuniary externalities for taxpayers are created by the increase in tax revenues and the decrease in transfer costs associated with *SESP*, both of which reduce the net budgetary cost of the program.

Further a subsidy of one of the major costs of doing business will exercise downward pressure on prices during the transition to a new price level. This temporary reduction in inflationary pressure may feed back into inflationary expectations, and have a longer-run impact on price inflation.

In addition to its effects on actual and potential *GNP* and prices, *SESP* will tend to shift the composition of employment and earnings toward low-skill, target-group workers. If less inequality in the distribution of the adverse effects of poor economic performance is desired, this is a major benefit of *SESP*. One consequence of this redistribution is that, even with a constant *GNP*, the number of employed persons will increase as low-productivity workers are substituted for those with higher skills.

III

Because of these likely effects of *SESP*, the macro-economic relationships between changes in *GNP*, the *GNP* gap, and the unemployment rate will be altered. In standard policy models, increases in aggregate demand are viewed as closing the gap by increasing actual *GNP* toward some exogenously determined full-employment *GNP*. However, as indicated above, *SESP* is likely to increase simultaneously both the actual and a *NAIRU*-based potential *GNP*. Hence, a *SESP*-induced increase in *GNP* will reduce the conventionally measured *GNP* gap by more than it reduces the true gap. The *SESP* will also alter the relationship between the measured *GNP* gap and the unemployment rate. A *SESP*-induced increase in *GNP* will tend to be associated with a larger increase (decrease) in employment (unemployment) than is typically associated with general aggregate demand-induced changes in *GNP*.

Consider the following accounting relationship between *GNP*, productivity (*A*), employed capital (*K*), hours worked per week (*H*), and labor force participation rate (*L*):

$$dGNP = dA + (1 - B_L) \, dK + B_L \, (dH + S_n dL - S_n dU) \qquad [1]$$

where dx indicates the percentage rate of change of x, $U = -100 \cdot log$(employment/labor force) $\approx$ the unemployment rate, B_L is the share of labor, and S_n is the ratio of the skill level of newly employed workers to the economy-wide average. Okun's Law is a reduced form of (1) which states that a 1 percentage point cyclical change in U is associated with a 3.2 percent change in *GNP*. While a percentage point decrease in U is directly associated in (1) with an increase in *GNP* equal to $B_L S_n$ (approximately .7 of a percentage point), cyclical changes in other determinants of *GNP*—namely, *L*, *H*, *K*, and *A*—are negatively associated with *U*. It is the sum of these effects that makes up the difference between .7 and 3.2.

There are at least three reasons why a 1 percentage point change in *U* induced by a *SESP* is not likely to increase *GNP* by 3.2 percentage points. First, a *SESP*-induced reduction in *U* will shift the composition of employment toward workers with $S_n < 1$ and increase the training costs of the firm. The inevitable result of such substitution is to reduce measured productivity, at least in the short run, and S_n and $|dA|dU|$ will fall as these costs are recorded in firm accounts.

Second, *SESP* encourages the hiring of part-time workers (especially if the per worker subsidized earnings level is capped) or the substitution of additional workers for increased overtime of existing workers. As a result, the response of H to changes in U will be smaller than otherwise—$|dH|dU|$ will fall.

Third, to the extent that target group labor is not complementary with capital services, as is likely, the utilization of capital will not increase as much as in the case of an equivalent general demand stimulus—$|dK|dU|$ will fall.

Finally, because of the limited knowledge on behavioral responses, the effect of *SESP* on $|dL|dU|$ is unknown. On the one hand, target group workers form a high proportion of the discouraged worker, nonlabor force participant category. On the other hand, *SESP* may not generate as large an increase in labor force participation as an equivalent reduction in U stimulated by a general expansion in demand.

Thus, at least during the period of adjustment following enactment of a nontrivial *SESP*, Okun's Law is likely to be repealed. The reduction in the Okun unemployment multiplier associated with *SESP* is evidence that the policy is having the effects for which it is designed—increasing potential *GNP* and redistributing the costs of unemployment.

However, these effects do not come at zero cost. The *SESP* is not easy to administer. A marginal stock variety of *SESP* tends to favor new and fast-growing firms and regions. In addition, *SESP* may increase labor turnover, especially if it is temporary or of the recruitment variety. Finally, *SESP* with narrowly defined target groups (for example, low-income youth or welfare recipients) may result in the displacement of equally disadvantaged workers who have more central positions in family units.

IV

None of these impacts of *SESP* will materialize if firms fail to change their behavior in response to the subsidy. In some past programs (for example, *WIN* and *JOBS*), that response was not substantial (see Daniel Hamermesh). Administrative costs or the low-productivity signaling effect of the subsidy apparently weakened the employment incentive for which the programs were designed.

The *NJTC* has been in operation for more than a year. While a definitive assessment of its effect on employment and prices is not yet possible, a preliminary evaluation can be made. In theory, the *NJTC* should provide a major stimulus to employment, as firms which typically hire part-time or part-year workers will find that the labor costs of an expansion are cut nearly in half. The

$100,000 per firm limit on the subsidy suggests that small and medium sized firms will experience the largest employment incentive.

Nonseasonally adjusted monthly data on employment and man-hours in construction and retailing were regressed on seasonal dummies, trends on the seasonal dummies, and three-year distributed lags of input prices (gross employer wages, W; wholesale price of construction materials, M, or consumer finished goods, P; materials, services, and energy prices, Q; gasoline and electricity prices, G; and a rental price of capital, R). The lag structures were freely estimated, with each input price or price ratio being represented by its contemporaneous value, and that of each of the previous four quarters and four half-years. Exogeneity tests which entered future values of the wage rate into the equation tended to confirm the hypothesis that wage and man-hours are simultaneously determined. Consequently, all models were estimated using two-stage least squares.

The *NJTC* variable is an average over the past six months of the proportion of firms (weighted by employees) that had knowledge of the credit. It has a value of .057 in June 1977 and rises at an average rate of .0424 per month, reaching .343 in January 1978 and .572 in June 1978.

All of the *NJTC* coefficients are positive and significant in Models I and II, where input prices enter as ratios (see Table 1). When input prices enter nominally (Models III and IV), the coefficients are smaller and insignificant. Across all of the regressions the (point) average *NJTC* employment stimulus over the mid-1977 to mid-1978 period ranges from 150,000-670,000. For these industries, actual total employment growth over the period was 1.3 million. The Model III and IV estimates attribute at least 20-30 percent of the observed employment increase in these industries to *NJTC*. These results are consistent with the observation that between 1977II and 1978II rates of employment growth have substantially exceeded rates of output growth in both construction and retailing. In construction, employment grew at an 8.2-9.9 percent rate— double the 4.5 percent growth rate of real construction output. Even in retailing, where cyclical changes in employment are small, the 3.0 percent growth of real sales lagged behind the 3.4-4.0 percent growth of employment. The contrast between construction man-hours and employment regressions also suggests that the *NJTC* has, as predicted, caused a reduction in average hours per week (see Bishop, 1978).

To test the relationship between prices and subsidy-induced marginal cost reductions, the monthly change in retail price was regressed on current and lagged changes in a number of industry cost variables (wages, wholesale product prices, materials, services, and energy prices, a rental price of capital, and excise taxes), the unemployment rate, and the level and trends in seasonal dummies. For nonfood commodities and restaurant meals the retail trade margin is negatively and significantly related to the *NJTC* variable (see Table 2). Between May 1977 and June 1978, retail nonfood commodity prices rose 4.73 percent, while the counterpart wholesale prices rose 6.56 percent. This

TABLE 1

Impact of the *NJTC* on Employment in Construction and Distribution

Sample—1952-78:06	Coefficient on NJTC under Alternative Specifications[a]			
	I	*II*	*III*	*IV*
Employment				
Wholesale and retail	.076[b]	.101[c]	.064	.061
Household data	(.048)	(.050)	(.059)	(.044)
	.0121	*.0119*	*.0121*	*.0122*
Retail	.045[c]	.047[c]	.030	.031
Establishment data	(.019)	(.020)	(.023)	(.020)
	.0044	*.0045*	*.0044*	*.0050*
Construction	.196[c]		.166	.052
Household data	(.079)		(.108)	(.102)
	.0336		*.0297*	*.0353*
Construction	.180[c]		.020	.052
Establishment data	(.053)		(.108)	(.102)
	.0175		*.0155*	*.0173*
Man-Hours				
Construction	.110		.025	.007
Establishment data	(.078)		(.108)	(.091)
	.0340		*.0302*	*.032*
Average *NJTC*-Induced Employment Δ in 12-month period preceding June 1978 (in thousands)				
Household data	669	575	565	410
Establishment data	412	203	154	255

SOURCE: See Bishop (1978).

a. Estimated with two-stage least squares. The standard error of the coefficient is shown in parentheses, and the standard error of the estimate in italics beneath the coefficient. Model I: $E = \beta_0 \cdot NJTC + \beta_1 X + \beta_2 (W/P) + \beta_3 (R/P) + \beta_4 (Q/P)$ for retailing and $E = \beta_0 \cdot NJTC + \beta_1 X + \beta_2 (W/M) + \beta_3 (R/M)$ for construction where X is the vector of output lags, seasonal dummies and trends. Model II: Adds $\beta_5 (G/P)$ to Model I. Model III: Enters W, R, Q, M, and P nominally, rather than as ratios. Model IV: Same as III, but with distributed lags limited to 1.5 rather than three years.

b. Significant at .05 level on a one-tail test.

c. Significant at .025 level on a one-tail test.

discrepancy of 1.83 percentage points approximates the preferred *NJTC* estimated effect of 2.2 percent ($.038 \cdot .572 \cdot 100$) (col. 1). The observed decline in the margin is particularly surprising given recent increases in the relative price of imported consumer goods. (Imported products, it should be noted, are included in retail but not wholesale price indexes.)

Among the subsectors, the pattern of coefficients is consistent with expectations. The large negative coefficients for the low-skill-intensive restaurant industry suggest that the 8-12 percent induced reduction in marginal costs caused a 1.1 percent decline in output price. On the other hand, the small margin, nonwage-intensive retail food industry has a nonsignificant positive coefficient,

TABLE 2

Impact of the *NJTC* on the Margin between Retail and Wholesale Prices

	Coefficient on NJTC under Alternative Specifications[a]			
	One-Year Distributed Lag			Six-Month Lag
	Trends on Seasonals		No Trends	Trends
CPI Component	with Q	without Q	with Q	with Q
Food away from home	−.036[c]	−.037[c]	−.032[c]	−.033[c]
	(.013)	(.012)	(.013)	(.013)
	.0017	*.0017*	*.0017*	*.0018*
Nonfood commodities	−.038[c]	−.038[c]	−.031[b]	−.038[c]
	(.015)	(.015)	(.016)	(.015)
	.0020	*.0021*	*.0022*	*.0020*
Food at home	.051	.041	.051	.051
	(.039)	(.038)	(.040)	(.038)
	.0053	*.0053*	*.0052*	*.0052*
All commodities	−.018	−.019	−.013	−.018
	(.016)	(.016)	(.017)	(.016)
	.0022	*.0022*	*.0023*	*.0022*
Reduction in consumer costs between June 1977 and June 1978 (in billions)				
All commodity regression	3.4	3.6	2.4	3.4
Disaggregated regressions	2.8	3.3	1.9	2.8

SOURCE: See Bishop (1978).

a. The standard error of the coefficient is shown in parentheses and the regression is shown in italics beneath the coefficient. Models estimated on monthly data 1953:03 to 1978:06. Weights for *Q* are based on the 1967 input-output table, which includes gasoline, electricity, telephones, containers, cellophane packaging, supplies, insurance, auto repair, and legal fees.

b. Significant at .05 level on a one-tail test.

c. Significant at .025 level on a one-tail test.

reflecting the greater contribution of incremental employment in this sector to quality than to the volume of output.

The final rows of the table indicate that the reduction of consumer costs attributable to the *NJTC* ranges from $1.9-3.6 billion. By comparison, it is predicted that over its two-year life, *NJTC* credit claims will be $3-6 billion.

These estimates of the impact of *NJTC* are for those sectors with the largest expected response. While across-industry displacements might offset these impacts, there is no clear reason why this would occur. While limited awareness of *NJTC* may have reduced its measured effectiveness, its temporary character may have led to inventory accumulation which a more permanent program would not induce.

No impact estimates based on only the first year of program experience can be conclusive. Perhaps the *NJTC* variable is capturing other exogenous forces inducing contemporaneous employment increases and price decreases, in which case improved specifications may reduce the estimated *NJTC* impacts.

While a number of possibilities have been tried (for example, varying lags, trend shifts in 1974, and the addition of an energy price variable) without significant effects on the *NJTC* variable, other factors may be at work. Hence, the finding that *NJTC* has had sizable employment and price effects must remain tentative. It should be noted, however, that the procedure employed is more robust with respect to assumptions on the impact of taxation changes than those used to estimate the response of investment spending to taxation changes.

V

In sum, the case for *SESP* is a strong one. The level of employment is likely to be increased, its composition improved, *NAIRU* reduced, and the associated price increase lower with *SESP* than with an equivalent general stimulus to aggregate demand. And the (at least temporary) reduction in the Okun multiplier is evidence that *SESP* is inducing the behavior for which it was designed. The results from the *NJTC* regressions suggest that such employer hiring and price responses do occur. However, these responses are for a nontargeted program; extrapolation of them to a targeted *SESP* would be inconsistent with evaluations of previous such programs.

REFERENCES

M. BAILY and J. TOBIN, "Inflation-Unemployment Consequences of Job Creation Policies," in John Palmer, ed., *Creating Jobs: Public Employment Programs and Wage Subsidies*, Washington 1978.

J. BISHOP, "The General Equilibrium Impact of Alternative Anti-Poverty Strategies: Income Maintenance, Training, and Job Creation," *Ind. Labor Relat. Rev.*, forthcoming.

———— "Pricing and Employment in Construction and Distribution: The Impacts of Tax Policy," paper presented at Universities-Nat. Bur. Econ. Res., Conference on Low Income Labor Markets, June 9-10, 1978.

D. HAMERMESH, "Subsidies for Jobs in the Private Sector," in John Palmer, ed., *Creating Jobs: Public Employment Programs and Wage Subsidies*, Washington 1978.

R. H. HAVEMAN and G. B. CHRISTAINSEN, "Public Employment and Wage Subsidies in Western Europe and the U.S.: What We're Doing and What We Know," National Commission on Manpower Policy, forthcoming.

J. KESSELMAN, S. WILLIAMSON, and E. BERNDT, "Tax Credits for Employment Rather Than Investment," *Amer. Econ. Rev.*, June 1977, 67, 339-49.

STANLEY MASTERS and IRWIN GARFINKEL, *Estimating the Labor Supply Effects of Income Maintenance Alternatives*, New York 1978.

G. L. PERRY, "Potential Output and Productivity," *Brookings Papers*, Washington 1977, *I*, 11-47.

U.S. Council of Economic Advisers, *Economic Report of the President*, Washington, Jan. 1977, 52-56.

24

HEALTH, USE OF MEDICAL CARE, AND INCOME

Karen Davis and Cathy Schoen

Since improved access to medical care services for the poor is a common objective of many federal health care programs, it is useful to examine overall trends in medical care utilization and health status before analyzing individual programs. This chapter sets forth the best available evidence on the health problems of the poor, on how these problems differ in severity and type from those of other Americans, and on whether the poor receive adequate medical services. The care received by the poor is compared with that of others to determine whether the amount, type, convenience, quality, or setting of medical care differs by the patient's income. But more important, the *changes* in these differences between income classes from the early 1960s to the 1970s—the years during which so many new programs were introduced—are examined.

It is evident that the poor's access to medical services greatly improved between 1965 and 1975. At the same time, considerable progress was made in selected areas of health that have traditionally been poor for low-income people and that are amenable to medical care—infant mortality rates (particularly postneonatal mortality rates) and deaths from pneumonia and influenza, cervical cancer, cerebrovascular disease, diabetes mellitus, and accidents. It seems plausible, therefore, that in addition to providing the usual benefits of medical care—relief from acute conditions, management and amelioration of chronic conditions, preventive care, prenatal and well-baby care—improved access has contributed to a reduction in mortality from causes sensitive to medical intervention.

Caveats

An effort to document the effects over ten years of federal health care programs cannot be expected to complete the history of these programs. In many ways, an appraisal after only ten years is premature because both

From Karen Davis and Cathy Schoen, "Health, Use of Medical Care, and Income," in *Health and the War on Poverty: A Ten-Year Appraisal* (Brookings Institution, 1978). Copyright © 1978 by the Brookings Institution.

the occurrence of changes in health and the reporting of these changes frequently take place after considerable time has elapsed. For example, some studies have stated that the health of babies is dependent on how healthy their mothers were as young children.[1] Thus it takes more than a generation to detect the full effects of improved health. Shorter periods will do for other types of intervention, but still a considerable amount of time must pass before changes appear. Uncorrected ear infections are likely to produce hearing loss only after scar tissue has built up for five to seven years. Uncorrected urinary tract infections may take even longer to show up in permanent kidney damage. The long-term effects of untreated venereal disease, including sterility, blindness, and senility, do not become fully apparent for decades. Many of the untreated acute conditions of childhood and adolescence show up as debilitating and crippling chronic conditions only in middle and old age. The ability of the aged to move about with ease, retain their auditory, visual, and mental faculties, and care for themselves is related, in part, to the adequacy of health care in earlier years.

Systemic changes in the provision of health care also take place only after a considerable time. Programs to help the poor purchase medical services may have limited effects for residents of geographical areas with few physicians or other health professionals. Changes in the distribution of health professionals—brought about by increased emphasis on family practice in medical schools, admission of students from underserved areas, changed attitudes and value orientation, and the guarantee of adequate professional income provided by a medical care financing program—take time.

Another difficulty is that all new programs make jagged steps toward progress. Some efforts inevitably fail, and the experimental approach has to be altered and then tried again. Failures do not imply that the effort is impossible or unworkable but only that rethinking and improvements in design are required. Too precipitate a judgment about success or failure may preclude the growth of an effort that might be successful in the long run.

The Difficulty of Detecting and Measuring Changes

The science of detecting changes in health is inexact and imperfect. Evaluations of public programs are impeded by such obstacles as multiple

1. See, for example, Herbert G. Birch and Joan D. Gussow, *Disadvantaged Children: Health, Nutrition, and School Failure* (Grune and Stratton, 1970).

objectives, not all of which are quantifiable or measurable; crude measurements of even quantifiable effects; inadequate baseline and follow-up data; and the presence of countervening factors that make it difficult to isolate the effects attributable to specific programs.

Most of the literature on operational measurements of health employs a single or composite health index, such as life expectancy or expected disability-free days over the remaining life span.[2] These fail, however, to detect changes in health resulting from government medical care programs. To detect changes, it is important to look not only at overall measurements but also at disaggregated measurements that are expected to be particularly sensitive to improved access to medical care.

Disaggregated measurements of health would include infant and general mortality by cause of death; incidence and severity of acute conditions by type (infective and parasitic, ear, nose, and throat infections, respiratory, digestive, and urinary conditions, dietary deficiencies, skin infections, and so on); incidence of and degree of deterioration from chronic conditions (hypertension, diabetes, kidney disease, heart conditions, arthritis, asthma, and obesity, among others); pregnancy outcomes (prematurity, low birth weight, stillbirth, and miscarriage); functional capacity (disability, handicap, limitation of activity or mobility, inability to work, go to school, or care for oneself, loss of teeth, of hearing, or of vision, for example); accidental death and injuries; deviations from individually

2. See, for example, Warren Balinsky and Renee Berger, "A Review of the Research on General Health Status Indexes," *Medical Care,* vol. 13 (April 1975), pp. 283–93; Robert L. Berg, ed., *Health Status Indexes* (Chicago: Hospital Research and Educational Trust, 1973); J. W. Bush, W. R. Blischke, and C. C. Berry, "Health Indices, Outcomes, and the Quality of Medical Care," in Richard Yaffee and David Zalkind, eds., *Evaluation in Health Services Delivery, Proceedings of an Engineering Foundation Conference, South Berwick, Maine, August 19–24, 1973* (Engineering Foundation, n.d.), pp. 313–39; C. L. Chiang, *An Index of Health: Mathematical Models,* Vital and Health Statistics, series 2, no. 5 (GPO, 1965); S. Franshel and J. W. Bush, "A Health-Status Index and Its Application to Health Services Outcomes," *Operations Research,* vol. 18 (November–December 1970), pp. 1021–66; Seth B. Goldsmith, "A Reevaluation of Health Status Indicators," *Health Services Reports,* vol. 88 (December 1973; published by GPO), pp. 937–41; Donald L. Patrick, J. W. Bush, and Milton M. Chen, "Methods for Measuring Levels of Wellbeing for a Health Status Index," *Health Services Research,* vol. 8 (Fall 1973), pp. 228–45; Richard M. Scheffler and Joseph Lipscomb, "Alternative Estimations of Population Health Status: An Empirical Example," *Inquiry,* vol. 11 (September 1974), pp. 220–28; Daniel F. Sullivan, "A Single Index of Mortality and Morbidity," *HSMHA Health Reports,* vol. 86 (GPO, 1971), pp. 347–54; Daniel F. Sullivan, *Conceptual Problems in Developing an Index of Health,* Vital and Health Statistics, series 2, no. 17 (GPO, 1966); James E. Veney, "Health Status Indicators," *Inquiry,* vol. 10 (December 1973), pp. 3–4.

desired family sizes and spacing of children; unremedied health defects in children (hearing, visual, dental, growth and development); and level of preventive services (as indicators of the probability of future impairment or death).

Even if sensitive indicators of health could be isolated, gaps and deficiencies in the available data impede extensive analyses. Few data correlating health statistics with socioeconomic characteristics are available. Mortality data, for example, though based on one of the most clear-cut and measurable dimensions of health, are drawn from death certificate records, which do not indicate family income or socioeconomic status.

Nor are data often disaggregated by important subpopulations. Migrant workers, sharecroppers in the Mississippi delta, or mountaineers may have severe health problems or marked improvements in health, but these are not adequately captured by averages for the poor as a whole.

Measurements of health for those covered by public programs are particularly rare. For example, the infant mortality rate for mothers covered by Medicaid or by other health programs for the poor is not currently known and cannot be compared with the rate for low-income mothers not covered by a health program.

Clearly, the methodological difficulties of isolating the contribution of medical care to health are great. Interactions between indexes of health and medical care utilization make it difficult to disentangle the causes of change. Increases in life expectancy may lead to increases in chronic conditions and disability. Infant mortality may have been reduced because more premature or low-birth-weight babies survive, but their average health may be poorer than that of the babies who survived when many died at birth. As more people receive regular physical examinations, they may learn of health conditions of which they were previously unaware. Responses to household interview surveys are therefore likely to show increases in health problems for groups that are making increased use of medical care services.

The many factors that affect health make it difficult to isolate the contribution of any one, whether it is medical care, adequate income, diet and nutrition, housing, education, personal habits, sanitation, environmental conditions, or genetic factors. At a given time, the poor may be less healthy than others for several reasons: they are less able to pay for necessary medical care; medical care is less available in their communities; with limited education they are unaware of good health practices or unable to use the medical care system effectively; cultural barriers keep them from recognizing health problems and seeking care for them; they may work in jobs or live in communities that are deleterious to health because of occupational health and safety hazards or environmental conditions; conditions in the home related to family size, marital stability, and age and spacing of children may not be conducive to good health; and so forth.[3] The relation between poverty and health may also exhibit two-way causality, with poor health leading to a reduction in productivity and consequent diminished earning power and income.[4]

Detecting the contribution of changes in any of these elements to changes in health is also difficult, because past patterns of poor health or lack of medical care may have adverse effects that persist for a long time. For example, a chronic condition, once incurred, may not be reversible and may continue to deteriorate even with the best of ameliorative medical care.

There are many factors that may explain different changes in health among income classes: improved medical care received by the poor; reduction in poverty and higher real incomes among lower-income families; general economic conditions of unemployment and inflation; food stamp, nutrition, and other governmental programs to improve the economic and social well-being of the poor; better birth control methods; worsening environmental conditions such as air and water pollution, noise pollution, and the use of chemicals and food additives; and changes in personal

3. For annotated bibliographies of the extensive literature on health and poverty, see Robert L. Kane, Josephine M. Kasteler, and Robert M. Gray, eds., *The Health Gap: Medical Services and the Poor* (Springer, 1976); Lu Ann Aday and Ronald Andersen, *Development of Indices of Access to Medical Care* (University of Michigan, Health Administration Press, 1975); and James C. Stewart and Lottie Lee Crafton, *Delivery of Health Care Services to the Poor: Findings from a Review of the Current Periodical Literature, With a Key to 47 Reports of Innovative Projects* (University of Texas at Austin, Center for Social Work Research, School of Social Work, 1975), and Crafton and Stewart, *Delivery of Health Care Services to the Poor: Abstracts from Health Care Journals, 1967–1974* (University of Texas at Austin, Center for Social Work Research, Graduate School of Social Work, n.d.), boxed cards. Other general references on the subject include Ronald Andersen, Joanna Kravits, and Odin W. Anderson, eds., *Equity in Health Services: Empirical Analyses in Social Policy* (Ballinger, 1975); E. Gartly Jaco, ed., *Patients, Physicians, and Illness: A Sourcebook in Behavioral Science and Health* (Free Press, 1972); John Kosa and Irving K. Zola, eds., *Poverty and Health: A Sociological Analysis,* rev. ed. (Harvard University Press, 1975); Judith R. Lave and Samuel Leinhardt, "The Delivery of Ambulatory Care to the Poor: A Literature Review," *Management Science,* vol. 19 (December 1972), pt. 2, pp. P-78–P-99.

4. For an exploration of the effect of poor health on earnings, see Harold Stephen Luft, "Poverty and Health: An Empirical Investigation of the Economic Interactions" (Ph.D. dissertation, Harvard University, 1972).

habits such as diet, exercise, smoking, alcohol consumption, and drug usage.[5] Although some of them may affect all income groups, they are unlikely to do so equally. Not all of them can be expected to work in the same direction; some may improve health but others may undercut such improvements.

Does Medical Care Improve Health?

The combination of conceptual difficulties and inadequate data have led some investigators to conclude that medical care can do little to improve health.[6] Views range from the proposition that Americans now receive so much medical care that more would have little effect on health to the stronger assertion that medical care as a whole does little for health. The most extreme critics suggest that medical care does more harm than good—through excessive surgery, overmedication, adverse drug reactions,

5. Literature stressing one or another of these factors includes Leon Gordis, "Effectiveness of Comprehensive-Care Programs in Preventing Rheumatic Fever," *New England Journal of Medicine,* vol. 289 (August 16, 1973), pp. 331–35; Nedra B. Belloc and Lester Breslow, "Relationship of Physical Health Status and Health Practices," *Preventive Medicine,* vol. 1 (August 1972), pp. 409–21; David M. Kessner, project director, *Infant Death: An Analysis by Maternal Risk and Health Care* (National Academy of Sciences, 1973); M. Harvey Brenner, *Mental Illness and the Economy* (Harvard University Press, 1973); U.S. Environmental Protection Agency, *Pollution and Your Health* and *Health Effects of Air Pollution* (both EPA, Office of Public Affairs, 1976); World Bank, *The Assault on World Poverty: Problems of Rural Development, Education, and Health* (Johns Hopkins University Press, 1975).

6. See, for example, Victor R. Fuchs, *Who Shall Live? Health, Economics, and Social Choice* (Basic Books, 1974); Nathan Glazer, "Paradoxes of Health Care," *Public Interest,* no. 22 (Winter 1971), pp. 62–77; Leon R. Kass, "Regarding the End of Medicine and the Pursuit of Health," *Public Interest,* no. 40 (Summer 1975), pp. 11–42; *Economic Report of the President, January 1976,* chap. 3; and Lee Benham and Alexandra Benham, "The Impact of Incremental Medical Services on Health Status, 1963–1970," in Andersen and others, *Equity in Health Services,* pp. 217–28. A similar argument for Canada is presented in Marc Lalonde, *A New Perspective on the Health of Canadians* (Ottawa: Information Canada, 1975). Ivan Illich, *Medical Nemesis: The Expropriation of Health* (Random House, 1976), and Rick J. Carlson, *The End of Medicine* (Wiley, 1975), are among the most outspoken critics. Excesses of medicine and overuse are documented in John P. Bunker, "Surgical Manpower: A Comparison of Operations and Surgeons in the United States and in England and Wales," *New England Journal of Medicine,* vol. 282 (January 15, 1970), pp. 135–44; and *New York Times,* January 26–30, 1976: Boyce Rensberger, "Few Doctors Ever Report Colleagues' Incompetence"; Boyce Rensberger, "Unfit Doctors Create Worry in Profession"; Jane E. Brody, "Incompetent Surgery Is Found Not Isolated"; Boyce Rensberger, "Thousands a Year Killed by Faulty Prescriptions"; and Jane E. Brody, "How Educated Patients Get Proper Health Care."

and other such iatrogenic illnesses. Illich, for example, begins *Medical Nemesis* with the statement: "The medical establishment has become a major threat to health."[7]

In the abuse directed at the medical profession, fact, fiction, and fantasy are indiscriminately intertwined. Some claims are based on spotty or inaccurate evidence; contraindicative evidence is frequently ignored.[8]

The indisputable claims that have been made include: (1) historically, most of the reduction in death rates has resulted from public health and nonmedical improvements, such as immunizations, sanitation, and standard of living; (2) many of the leading causes of death today (suicide, homicide, accidents, cirrhosis of the liver, heart attacks, and some forms of cancer) are closely linked to environmental health hazards, life style, and personal habits, and thus for those currently receiving adequate medical care, the greatest contributions to better health are likely to be found in altered life styles and elimination of personal and occupational or environmental hazards; and (3) excessive confidence in the all-healing power of medicine has led in some instances to the provision of medical services of negligible benefit or demonstrable harm.

It is an overstatement, however, to assert that medical care does no good or that there are no groups in the United States that could benefit from improved access to it. There can be little doubt that for a wide range of conditions such care is essential to the preservation or restoration of health, as anyone who has ever suffered a broken bone, acute appendicitis, venereal disease, pneumonia, hypertension, or a ruptured spleen can attest. Nor is there much doubt that additional medical care would be of value to those who find it difficult to obtain even basic services—many poor people, members of minority groups, and residents of inner cities or rural areas. Even for these people, however, the most effective strategies for improving health may well be approaches that combine both medical care and attacks on the nonmedical causes of poor health.

A balanced assessment of the claims made about the relation of medical care to health requires evidence on the composition of medical care expenditures by kinds of care and on the kinds of improvements in health that can be reasonably expected. Much of the distortion of the discussion

7. Illich, *Medical Nemesis*, p. 3.
8. An evaluation of some of the econometric evidence—most of which is seriously flawed methodologically—is presented in the appendix. The rest of this chapter discusses the evidence on health trends by income class. Chapters 5 and 6 survey a number of case studies documenting the relation between the care provided by the comprehensive health centers and the health of the patients they served.

of health and medical care derives from a preoccupation with mortality. While medical care is essential to avert death in some emergencies, most medical expenditures are incurred in the diagnosis, treatment, and rehabilitation of acute and chronic conditions that are not immediately life-threatening (although without adequate care these conditions may result in avoidable pain and discomfort, gradual deterioration into more serious conditions, loss of functional capability, and shortened life span). Care that is largely informational (family planning, counseling, assessment of physical state and risks of future conditions) is also of considerable value and might appropriately be classified as a health benefit.

In short, the potential benefits of medical care vary from case to case. The effect of improved medical care on health can best be detected by looking at disaggregated measures of health status and the content of medical care.

The Human Side of Health

No examination of statistics depicting overall trends in health can reveal the human suffering and agony that lie behind them. One of the most poignant accounts of what it means to live in poverty and not receive adequate health care is contained in a report by Raymond Wheeler, M.D., who examined children in the South and in the ghettos of northern cities as a member of the Citizens Board of Inquiry into Hunger in the United States in the spring of 1970. He recounts:

Wherever we went, in the South, the Southwest, Florida or Appalachia, the impact was the same, varying only in degree or in appalling detail. . . .

We saw housing and living conditions horrible and dehumanizing to the point of our disbelief. In Florida and in Texas, we visited living quarters constructed as long cinder-block or wooden sheds, divided into single rooms by walls which do not reach the ceilings. Without heat, adequate light or ventilation, and containing no plumbing or refrigeration, each room (no larger than 8 x 14 feet) is the living space of an entire family, appropriately suggesting slave quarters of earlier days. . . .

In all of the areas we visited, the nearly total lack of even minimally adequate medical care and health services was an early and easily documented observation. Again, that which most Americans now agree to be a right of citizenship, was unavailable to most of the people whom we saw. . . .

We saw hundreds of people whose only hope of obtaining medical care was to become an emergency which could not be turned away. . . .

Most of these people live constantly at the brink of medical disaster, hoping that the symptoms they have or the pain they feel will prove transient or can somehow be survived, for they know that no help is available to them. . . .

For the majority of the hundreds of people we examined, it was a different, frustrating, and heartbreaking story. We saw people with most of the dreadful disorders that weaken, disable, and torture, particularly the poor.

High blood pressure, diabetes, urinary tract infections, anemia, tuberculosis, gall bladder and intestinal disorders, eye and skin diseases were frequent findings among the adults.

Almost without exception, intestinal parasites were found in the stool specimens examined. Most of the children had chronic skin infections. Chronically infected, draining ears with resulting partial deafness occurred in an amazing number of the smaller children. We saw rickets, a disorder thought to be nearly abolished in this country. Every form of vitamin deficiency known to us that could be identified by clinical examination was reported.[9]

Nor have these conditions been eradicated since 1970. A report on the Rio Grande valley in Texas in the fall of 1975 echoed many of the same problems:

Almost a decade later, conditions are still the same. The floor in de Hoyas's one-bedroom shack sags dangerously. A single 40-watt bulb burns in the tiny living room, which serves as the bedroom for the four de Hoyas children. A mosquito-infested drainage canal runs alongside the house. . . . Ninety-five percent of the homes have outdoor toilets. Most have been hand-built and are badly in need of repairs.

Balboans have to haul in household and drinking water in broken-down pickups and trailers from a faucet nearly a mile away. The water comes from an irrigation ditch with an abnormally high concentration of fecal organisms. . . . Farmworker Pablo Castañeda says that his children are sick much of the time from the *agua peligrosa*. "I feel anger and I feel pain," he says. "People want to shut their eyes and not think about us. But we have suffered for quite a while now." . . . There are diseases in the magic valley that were virtually wiped out years ago in other parts of the country—whooping cough, tuberculosis, typhus and amoebiasis. Infant mortality is also very high, and Dr. Paul Musgrave, medical director for twenty of Texas's southernmost counties, says, "We don't exactly advertise it, but it's not uncommon for us to have leprosy down here."[10]

Health Status: Trends in the Differences between Socioeconomic Groups

Although the gap between the health of the poor and that of others narrowed in the decade 1965–75, it has not disappeared. Of the health trends for which data are available, reduction in mortality rates was the most dramatic. Mortality data by income are available for the earlier period,

9. Raymond Wheeler, "Health and Human Resources," *New South*, vol. 26 (Fall 1971), pp. 3–4.

10. "Mañana," *Newsweek* (November 24, 1975), pp. 16, 21, 22.

but have not yet been reported for the mid-1970s. Strong evidence suggests, however, that reductions in mortality have been concentrated disproportionately in the lower income classes. Rates for blacks and Indians have declined at a faster rate than for whites. The rates for the causes of death that have traditionally been highest among the poor are the ones that have fallen the most rapidly.

By contrast, little progress in reducing the prevalence of chronic conditions was made from 1965 to 1975. Restriction of activity from acute and chronic conditions increased slightly, and the poor made no gains relative to others. Perhaps this is not surprising. Better medical care for the poor cannot be expected to show up in reduced prevalence of chronic conditions for decades yet. Most of the immediate benefit would take the form of amelioration or a more gradual deterioration of functional capability. Better medical care would also affect the incidence of only a small portion of acute conditions, those such as contagious diseases, which can be prevented by immunization. For most acute conditions, better medical care provides relief of pain and discomfort and lessens the probability that serious, chronic conditions will develop.

General Mortality by Cause of Death

One of the oldest and most common ways to measure health is mortality. Its popularity can be traced in part to the fact that counting deaths provides a readily quantifiable measure and one that is reported with reasonable accuracy over a long period of time. But it is also undeniable that extending life or averting death is one of the most socially valued "improvements" in health.

Several measures of mortality are available: the crude death rate, or simply the number of deaths divided by the population; age-adjusted death rates, which are based on a standard age composition of the population; and life expectancy rates, which indicate the average number of years remaining for an age group at different points in the life cycle.[11]

11. In recent years, there have been divergences between the crude death rate and the age-adjusted death rates. As birth rates decline, the average age of the population rises. With old people accounting for a larger share of the population, the proportion of deaths automatically rises. Therefore, in making comparisons over time or in comparing current populations with markedly different age distributions, it is important to look at age-adjusted death rates or life expectancy rates.

See, for example, U.S. Department of Health, Education, and Welfare, National Center for Health Statistics, *Mortality Trends: Age, Color, and Sex, United States— 1950–69*, Vital and Health Statistics, series 20, no. 15, DHEW (HRA) 74-1852 (GPO, 1973), pp. 11–13.

Table 2-1. Age-adjusted Death Rates per 100,000 Population, All Causes of Death and Fifteen Causes, Selected Years, 1950-74

Cause of death	1950	1960	1965	1969	1974	Percentage change 1950-74	Percentage change 1965-74
All causes[a]	841.5	760.9	741.8	730.9	666.2	-20.8	-10.2
Leading causes with a downturn in mortality							
Diseases of the heart	307.6	286.2	275.6	262.3	232.7	-24.3	-15.6
Cerebrovascular diseases	88.8	79.7	73.1	68.5	59.9	-32.5	-18.1
Accidents	57.5	49.9	53.4	55.3	46.0	-20.0	-13.9
Influenza and pneumonia	26.2	28.0	23.4	24.6	16.9	-35.5	-27.8
Certain causes of mortality in early infancy[b]	40.5	37.4	28.6	21.4	13.6	-66.4	-52.4
Diabetes mellitus	14.3	13.6	13.5	14.5	12.5	-12.6	-7.4
Arteriosclerosis	16.2	13.2	12.0	9.2	7.6	-53.1	-36.7
Congenital anomalies[b]	12.2	12.2	10.1	8.4	6.4	-47.5	-36.6
Nephritis and nephrosis	16.6	6.5	5.2	3.9	n.a.	...	...
Peptic ulcer	5.0	5.2	4.3	3.6	n.a.	...	...
Leading causes with an upturn in mortality							
Malignant neoplasms	125.4	125.8	127.9	129.7	131.8	5.1	3.0
Bronchitis, emphysema, and asthma	3.7	8.2	11.6	12.0	9.2	148.6	-20.7
Cirrhosis of the liver	8.5	10.5	12.1	14.2	14.8	74.1	22.3
Suicide	11.0	10.6	11.4	11.3	12.2	10.9	7.0
Homicide	5.4	5.2	6.2	8.6	10.8	100.0	74.2

Source: U.S. Department of Health, Education, and Welfare, Division of Vital Statistics.
n.a. Not available.
a. Includes causes not shown separately.
b. Crude death rates.

The twenty-five years from 1950 to 1974 were characterized by steady reductions in the age-adjusted death rate, which fell from 842 per 100,000 in 1950 to 666 per 100,000 in 1974, a decline of 21 percent (see table 2-1). From 1965 to 1974 the age-adjusted death rate declined by 10 percent, and deaths from ten of fifteen leading causes dropped. Between 1965 and 1974 deaths from diseases of the heart declined 16 percent; cerebrovascular diseases, 18 percent; accidents, 14 percent; influenza and pneumonia, 28 percent; diabetes mellitus, 7 percent; and arteriosclerosis, 37 percent. Since these causes of death are potentially amenable to medical intervention, it is plausible that increased use of medical care played a part in achieving the reduction.

Over this period the only increases in major causes of death were for cancer (up 3 percent), cirrhosis of the liver (up 22 percent), suicide (up 7 percent), and homicide (up 74 percent). Deaths from these causes are believed to be linked to personal habits or adverse environmental conditions—alcohol consumption, cigarette smoking, violence, stresses of urban living, pollution, use of hazardous chemicals and substances. Improved medical care could not be expected to reduce deaths from these causes substantially.

One important exception is cervical cancer. With early detection through Pap smears, a reduction in cancer of this type might be expected to follow greater use of medical services by women. The age-adjusted rate for deaths from malignant neoplasms of female genital organs did in fact decline steadily, down 10 percent for white women and 12 percent for women of other races from 1965 to 1969.

Data on trends in mortality rates by income classes are not yet available, but a common proxy for income differences is comparing mortality rates by race. Although a higher proportion of blacks than of whites are poor,[12] a minority of both races are poor, so differences by income may not be detected by racial comparisons.

Mortality rates for blacks and other nonwhites declined more than those for whites from 1965 to 1974. Age-adjusted death rates fell 10 percent for whites and 13 percent for blacks and others, but blacks continued to have substantially higher death rates than whites—more than 40 percent higher. Relative improvements for blacks and other nonwhites were

12. In 1973, 9 percent of the white population fell below the poverty level as against 32 percent of blacks and persons of other races. Bureau of the Census, *Current Population Reports,* series P-23, no. 46, "The Social and Economic Status of the Black Population in the United States, 1972" (GPO, 1973), p. 28.

particularly notable for cerebrovascular diseases and influenza and pneumonia. Rates for deaths from malignant neoplasms and cirrhosis of the liver increased more rapidly for nonwhites than for whites, however, widening the differences by race for these causes of death.

Statistics on American Indians suggest that, during a period of greatly increased expenditures for Indian health care, there have been quite astonishing drops in mortality rates from a number of causes amenable to better medical care. Between 1960 and 1974 crude death rates of Indians from influenza and pneumonia fell 68 percent and death rates from certain diseases of early infancy fell 81 percent. Infant mortality rates plummeted from 50 deaths per 1,000 live births in 1960 to 19 in 1974.[13] Between 1955 and 1971 death rates from tuberculosis fell 86 percent, and death rates from enteritis and other diarrheal diseases 89 percent. In 1971, however, both rates were still four times as high as those for the U.S. population.[14] Offsetting these declines somewhat was a tripling of the death rate from cirrhosis of the liver.

It is a well-documented fact that the poor and less educated have higher death rates than others.[15] A 1962–63 study of death rates by age, sex, and family income in the year before death showed that death rates of males and females under fifty-five were about six to ten times higher for those with family incomes below $2,000 than for those with family incomes above $8,000.[16] Some of the difference might be because people with long illnesses may have had abnormally low incomes in the year before death.

13. *Special Analyses, Budget of the United States Government, Fiscal Year 1978,* p. 222.

14. *Federal Health Policies in Rural Areas,* Appendix to Hearings before the Subcommittee on Family Farms and Rural Development of the House Committee on Agriculture, 93:2 (GPO, 1974), pt. 2, p. 88.

15. See, for example, Evelyn M. Kitagawa and Philip M. Hauser, *Differential Mortality in the United States: A Study in Socioeconomic Epidemiology* (Harvard University Press, 1973); HEW, National Center for Health Statistics, *Socioeconomic Characteristics of Deceased Persons, United States—1962–1963 Deaths,* series 22, no. 9 (GPO, 1969); NCHS, *Selected Vital and Health Statistics in Poverty and Nonpoverty Areas of 19 Large Cities, United States, 1969–71,* Vital and Health Statistics, series 21, no. 26, DHEW (HRA) 76-1904 (GPO, 1975); HEW, Office of the Assistant Secretary (Planning and Evaluation), *Delivery of Health Services for the Poor* (GPO, 1967); Lawrence Bergner and Alonzo S. Yerby, "Low Income and Barriers to Use of Health Services," *New England Journal of Medicine,* vol. 278 (March 7, 1968), pp. 541–46, reprinted in Kane and others, *The Health Gap,* pp. 27–39; Aaron Antonovsky, "Social Class, Life Expectancy and Overall Mortality," *Milbank Memorial Fund Quarterly,* vol. 45 (April 1967), pt. 1, reprinted in Jaco, *Patients, Physicians and Illness;* and NCHS, *Health, United States, 1976–1977,* DHEW (HRA) 77-1232 (GPO, 1977).

16. National Center for Health Statistics, *Socioeconomic Characteristics of Deceased Persons, United States—1962–1963 Deaths,* p. 21.

However, this seems less likely to explain high death rates among low-income younger women, since family income is not usually as dependent on the employability and health of female family members.

Kitagawa and Hauser matched death certificates with 1960 census records for deaths in the United States from May to August 1960. They found that age-adjusted mortality rates were 80 percent higher for white male family members twenty-five to sixty-four years old with family incomes under $2,000 than for similar males with family incomes of $10,000 or more. For white female family members, the mortality rate was 40 percent higher in the lowest family income class than in the highest.[17]

Kitagawa and Hauser also compared death rates by cause with educational levels (without holding income constant). They found that in 1960 for white males twenty-five years old and over those with less than eight years of education had higher death rates than those with a year or more of college from the following causes: tuberculosis (four times as high), malignant neoplasms (13 percent higher), diabetes mellitus (25 percent), cerebrovascular diseases (24 percent), hypertensive disease (23 percent), influenza and pneumonia (60 percent), accidents (71 percent), and suicide (87 percent). But college-educated white males had higher age-adjusted death rates than white males with less than eight years of education for malignant neoplasm of the prostate (95 percent) and cirrhosis of the liver (6 percent). Deaths were not appreciably different for many types of cardiovascular and renal diseases. Among white women, those with a college education tended to have similarly lower death rates with the exception of malignant neoplasms of the breast, where death rates were 42 percent higher for college-educated women than for women with less than eight years of education, and cirrhosis of the liver, where death rates were about the same for both groups.[18]

Conclusive evidence on trends in mortality rates by income and educational class from the mid-1960s to the mid-1970s will have to await follow-up studies linking death certificate information with other sources of data on socioeconomic characteristics. It is interesting to note, however, that the death rates that have declined most rapidly over this period are those for the same causes that have traditionally had the highest incidence among the poor and less educated. This strongly suggests that when follow-up data do become available a narrowing of the differences in death rates by income and education will be found.

17. *Differential Mortality in the United States,* pp. 8–10, 18.
18. Ibid., pp. 76–77.

Infant Mortality, Maternal Mortality, and the Deaths of Young Children

A second, widely used way of measuring health status is infant mortality. This way of measuring is popular because it has been recorded over long periods of time for many subpopulations of the United States. Beyond these advantages, however, the infant mortality rate is believed to be especially sensitive to the adequacy of medical care and thus a good indicator of the influence of improved medical care on health.[19]

Table 2-2. Infant and Maternal Mortality Rates in the United States, by Race, Selected Years, 1950–74

Rate per 1,000 live births

Age and race	1950	1955	1960	1965	1970	1974	Percentage change 1965–74	Percentage change 1950–74
				Infant mortality				
Under 28 days								
White	19.4	17.7	17.2	16.1	13.8	11.1	−31.1	−42.8
Nonwhite	27.5	27.2	26.9	25.4	21.4	17.2	−32.3	−37.5
All races	20.5	19.1	18.7	17.7	15.1	12.3	−30.5	−40.0
28 days to 1 year								
White	7.4	5.9	5.7	5.4	4.0	3.7	−31.5	−50.0
Nonwhite	16.9	15.6	16.4	14.9	9.5	7.7	−48.3	−54.4
All races	8.7	7.3	7.3	7.0	4.9	4.4	−37.1	−49.4
Total, under 1 year								
White	26.8	23.6	22.9	21.5	17.8	14.8	−31.2	−44.8
Nonwhite	44.5	42.8	43.2	40.3	30.9	24.9	−38.2	−44.0
All races	29.2	26.4	26.0	24.7	20.0	16.7	−32.4	−42.8
				Maternal mortality				
White	0.6	0.3	0.3	0.2	0.1	0.1	−50.0	−83.3
Nonwhite	2.2	1.3	1.0	0.8	0.6	0.4	−50.0	−81.8
All races	0.8	0.5	0.4	0.3	0.2	0.1	−66.7	−87.5

Source: HEW, Division of Vital Statistics.

Infant mortality rates are defined as the number of babies alive at birth who die within the first year. Neonatal death rates measure deaths under the age of twenty-eight days per 1,000 live births; postneonatal death rates measure deaths between the ages of twenty-eight days and one year.

Infant mortality rates dropped markedly from 1965 to 1974, from 24.7 deaths per 1,000 live births in 1965 to 16.7 in 1974 (see table 2-2). This

19. See, for example, Kessner, *Infant Death*.

followed a period of relative stability from 1950 to 1965. From 1965 to 1974 postneonatal death rates fell slightly more rapidly than neonatal rates—37 percent and 30 percent, respectively. Infant mortality rates for several gastrointestinal diseases declined markedly, as did those for influenza and pneumonia and for prematurity. Maternal deaths resulting from complications of childbirth—much rarer than infant deaths—declined by two-thirds between 1965 and 1974 and by almost 90 percent between 1950 and 1974.

These improvements were also shared by young children. Death rates for children one to four years old fell by 14 percent from 1965 to 1973 (table 2-3). An increasing number of small children as well as of children aged five to fourteen died in motor vehicle accidents. Deaths from influenza and pneumonia, however, declined dramatically for both age groups from 1965 to 1973. In contrast to trends for older people, malignant neoplasms took a smaller toll among children during this period, perhaps because of the breakthroughs made ten years ago in the treatment of acute leukemia.

Table 2-3. Death Rates of Children per 100,000, All Causes of Death and Five Leading Causes, Selected Years, 1950–73

Age and cause of death	*1950*	*1960*	*1965*	*1970*	*1973*	*Percentage change*	
						1950–73	*1965–73*
One to four, all causes	139.4	109.1	92.9	84.5	79.5	−43.0	−14.4
Motor vehicle accidents	11.5	10.0	10.5	11.5	12.3	7.0	17.1
Accidents other than motor vehicle	25.3	21.6	21.3	20.0	19.6	−22.5	−8.0
Congenital anomalies	11.1	12.9	10.2	9.7	9.6	−13.5	−5.9
Malignant neoplasms	11.7	10.9	8.6	7.5	6.4	−45.3	−25.6
Influenza and pneumonia	18.9	16.2	11.4	7.6	5.9	−68.8	−48.2
Five to fourteen, all causes	60.1	46.6	42.2	41.3	41.0	−31.8	−2.8
Motor vehicle accidents	8.8	7.9	8.9	10.2	10.6	20.5	19.1
Accidents other than motor vehicle	13.8	11.3	9.8	9.9	10.2	−26.1	4.1
Congenital anomalies	2.4	3.6	2.8	2.2	2.2	−8.3	−21.4
Malignant neoplasms	6.7	6.8	6.5	6.0	5.4	−19.4	−16.9
Influenza and pneumonia	3.2	2.6	2.1	1.6	1.4	−56.2	−33.3

Source: Department of Health, Education, and Welfare, National Center for Health Statistics, *Health, United States, 1975*, DHEW (HRA) 76-1232 (NCHS, 1976), pp. 359, 361.

As is the case for general mortality rates, data on trends in mortality rates for infants and young children by income group are not yet available. Indirect evidence, however, suggests that the poor may have experienced relatively more improvement than others. Infant mortality declined for both whites and nonwhites, but declined somewhat more rapidly for nonwhites between 1965 and 1974 (see table 2-2). In 1965 the infant mortality rate for blacks and other nonwhites was 87 percent higher than for whites; by 1974 it was 68 percent higher. Nearly all of the improvement in the infant mortality rate of nonwhites relative to whites occurred in the postneonatal period.

Other indirect evidence on trends in infant mortality rates by socioeconomic class is discovered when trends in infant mortality rates are broken down by states. Table 2-4 shows total, neonatal, and postneonatal infant mortality rates by states arranged in groups of ten according to the incidence of poverty. In 1965 the infant mortality rate in the ten states with the highest rates of poverty was 29.5 deaths per 1,000 live births, 1.3 times that of the ten states with the lowest rates of poverty. Between 1965 and 1974 infant mortality declined more rapidly in the ten highest-poverty states than in most of the other states, reducing this ratio to 1.19 by 1974. The neonatal and postneonatal components of the total infant mortality rate make it apparent that the major gains in the high-poverty states relative to the low-poverty states came in postneonatal death rates.

Several studies have documented the wide variation in infant mortality rates by the socioeconomic characteristics of families.[20] One study for the period 1964–66 found that infant mortality rates were 61 percent higher for families with incomes below $3,000 than for families with incomes of $10,000 and above. Furthermore, the date of death and cause of death differed greatly among families. The death rate for infants seven to twenty-seven days old in low-income families was 2.7 times higher than for those in high-income families, and the death rate for infants of one to five months in low-income families was four times as high as for those in high-income families.[21] Babies of low birth weight are also more common in

20. National Center for Health Statistics, *Infant Mortality Rates: Socioeconomic Factors, United States,* Vital and Health Statistics, series 22, no. 14, DHEW (HSM) 72-1045 (GPO, 1972); NCHS, *Health, United States, 1975;* NCHS, *Trends in "Prematurity," United States, 1950–67,* Vital and Health Statistics, series 3, no. 15, DHEW (HSM) 72-1030 (GPO, 1972); NCHS, *Selected Vital and Health Statistics in Poverty and Nonpoverty Areas of 19 Large Cities, 1969–71;* and Kessner, *Infant Death.*

21. National Center for Health Statistics, *Infant Mortality Rates.*

low-income families, with a concomitantly higher risk of death, mental retardation, and other crippling defects.[22]

Causes of infant deaths that are more prevalent in low-income families are infective and parasitic diseases, influenza, pneumonia and other respiratory diseases, accidents, and gastritis, duodenitis, and other diseases of the digestive system. These types of conditions are the most dangerous for babies who have been discharged from the hospital and taken home. Improper sterilization of bottles, impure water, or unsafe sanitation may cause diarrhea, which can quickly lead to severe dehydration, hospitalization, and death. Crowding, inadequate heating and ventilation, and the presence of siblings increase the incidence of respiratory illness. These illnesses, which strike babies during vulnerable, formative stages, can in many cases be effectively combated by prompt medical attention. Delay in seeking medical care is probably more common among low-income families.

Chronic Conditions and Limitation of Activity

There is little evidence that the poor experienced any reduction in the incidence of long-term chronic health problems in the ten-year period. For people between forty-five and sixty-four, the prevalence of chronic conditions such as arthritis, diabetes, hearing and visual impairments, heart conditions, and hypertension remains two to three times higher for those with low incomes than for others.[23]

It would be incorrect to conclude, however, that medical care programs for the poor have had no effect. As the death rate falls, the incidence of chronic conditions can be expected to increase.[24] Thus the relative stability of the prevalence of chronic conditions during a period when the death rate declined may be a significant achievement.

Improved medical care, moreover, can be expected to reduce the prev-

22. National Center for Health Statistics, *Health, United States, 1975,* p. 371.

23. National Center for Health Statistics, *Current Estimates from the Health Interview Survey, United States,* Vital and Health Statistics, series 10, various issues; NCHS, *Health, United States, 1975,* pp. 247, 487, 557. For those sixty-five and over, the gap narrows. The National Center for Health Statistics considers a condition chronic if it has existed for three months or more or if it falls within a list of defined chronic conditions ranging from allergies to strokes.

24. For example, as the number of deaths from heart attacks is reduced, the incidence of heart conditions among the living may increase. As more people receive regular medical care, they may also become more aware of the existence of chronic conditions such as hypertension, which is probably underreported by those not seeing a physician regularly.

Table 2-4. Average Infant Mortality Rates by States in Groups of Ten, in Descending Order of the Poverty Rate, 1965 and 1974
Mortality rates = deaths per 1,000 live births

States grouped from highest to lowest poverty rates	Poverty rate, 1969ᵃ (percent)	Mortality, all infantsᵇ			Neonatal mortalityᵇ			Postneonatal mortalityᵇ		
		Rate		Percentage change, 1965-74	Rate		Percentage change, 1965-74	Rate		Percentage change, 1965-74
		1965	1974		1965	1974		1965	1974	
Group 1										
Mississippi, Arkansas, Louisiana, Alabama, South Carolina, Kentucky, New Mexico, West Virginia, Tennessee, Georgia	24.9	29.5	19.0	−35.6	19.3	13.7	−29.0	10.2	5.3	−48.0
Group 2ᶜ										
North Carolina, Oklahoma, Texas, South Dakota, District of Columbia, Florida, North Dakota, Virginia, Arizona, Missouri, Maine	16.8	25.8	18.2	−29.5	17.9	13.5	−24.6	7.9	4.7	−40.5

Group 3 Montana, Idaho, Nebraska, Kansas, Alaska, Colorado, Vermont, Wyoming, Iowa, Oregon	12.4	24.1	15.6	−35.3	16.8	11.5	−31.5	7.3	4.1	−43.8
Group 4 Utah, California, New York, Rhode Island, Delaware, Minnesota, Pennsylvania, Illinois, Washington, Maryland	10.7	22.6	15.6	−31.0	16.6	11.6	−30.1	6.0	4.0	−33.3
Group 5 Ohio, Wisconsin, Indiana, Michigan, Hawaii, Nevada, New Hampshire, Massachusetts, New Jersey, Connecticut	9.0	22.6	15.9	−29.6	17.0	11.7	−31.2	5.6	4.2	−25.0
United States	13.7	24.7	16.7	−32.4	17.7	12.3	−30.5	7.0	4.4	−37.1
Ratio, group 1 to group 5	2.77	1.30	1.19	...	1.14	1.17	...	1.82	1.26	...

Sources: U.S. Bureau of the Census, *Statistical Abstract of the United States, 1974* (GPO, 1974), p. 391, and HEW, Division of Vital Statistics.

a. Percentage of people below the official poverty level for 1969.

b. All infants, under one year; neonatal, under twenty-eight days; postneonatal, twenty-eight days to one year.

c. The District of Columbia is included as the eleventh unit.

alence of chronic conditions only after considerable time has elapsed. No amount of medical care will eliminate chronic conditions for those who already have visual and hearing impairments, arthritis, diabetes, or heart conditions. Improved medical care or other types of intervention may affect the future incidence of these conditions, but such changes cannot be expected to become evident for decades. For many of those with chronic conditions, greater access to medical care can mean the relief of pain or discomfort and the ability to function more capably (through corrective visual and hearing assistance, regulation of blood pressure and diabetes, control of hernias and ulcers, relief of asthmatic symptoms, and the like).

Table 2-5. Prevalence of Selected Chronic Conditions, by Family Income Class, Fiscal Years 1964 and 1965 and Calendar Year 1971[a]
Rates per 1,000 population

Chronic condition and income class[b]	All ages		65 and over	
	1964 and 1965	1971	1964 and 1965	1971
Visual impairment				
All incomes	28.8	47.4	145.6	204.6
Lowest	71.2	96.3	177.5	232.1
Lower middle	21.7	37.7	115.4	163.2
Upper middle	14.3	28.9	110.1	181.3
Highest	15.2	34.5	105.7	169.2
Hearing impairment				
All incomes	45.7	71.6	216.3	294.3
Lowest	90.0	132.9	242.5	323.0
Lower middle	38.2	63.3	199.4	271.4
Upper middle	30.4	49.4	173.3	247.3
Highest	32.4	48.6	190.4	259.2
Impairment of back or spine[c]				
All incomes	34.7	39.6	55.4	67.1
Lowest	45.0	57.6	67.1	78.6
Lower middle	33.1	37.7	52.2	51.2
Upper middle	32.5	34.0	34.3	30.0
Highest	31.4	32.1	25.6	27.7

Sources: HEW, National Center for Health Statistics, *Prevalence of Selected Impairments, United States, July 1963–June 1965*, Vital and Health Statistics, series 10, no. 48 (GPO, 1968), pp. 28, 34, 55; and NCHS, *Prevalence of Selected Impairments, United States, 1971*, Vital and Health Statistics, series 10, no. 99, DHEW (HRA) 75-1526 (GPO, 1975), pp. 24, 27, 32, 36.
   a. Data in the first and third columns based on interviews conducted from July 1963 through June 1965; data in the second and fourth columns based on interviews conducted during 1971.
   b. Income classes (in dollars) are as follows:

	1964 and 1965	1971
Lowest	Under 3,000	Under 5,000
Lower middle	3,000–6,999	5,000–9,999
Upper middle	7,000–9,999	10,000–14,999
Highest	10,000 and over	15,000 and over

   c. Excludes paralysis.

While the limited data on trends in chronic conditions convey an overall picture of little change, there are isolated, modest improvements. The aged, poor or not, experienced a reduction in limitation of activity caused by chronic conditions.[25] And although children as a group experienced slightly increased limitation of activity, poor children were less affected than other children.

For the most part, data on selected chronic conditions are not comparable over time because of a change in reporting methods in 1968.[26] Roughly comparable data by family income are available only for visual, hearing, and back or spine impairments. Table 2-5 shows that the prevalence of selected chronic impairments increased between 1964–65 and 1971. In both periods low-income persons experienced higher rates of impairment of vision, hearing, and the back or spine than high-income persons.

Incidence of Acute Conditions and Restricted Activity

There has also been little change in the incidence of acute conditions (such as respiratory or gastrointestinal diseases) in the last ten years. These conditions are more prevalent among the poor, who reported slightly more acute illness and injury in 1973 than they did in 1964.[27]

Suffering an acute illness or injury, with the exception of certain types of contagious diseases, has little to do with the receipt of medical care. Most medical care for acute conditions provides relief of pain or discomfort, lessens the severity (though not usually the duration) of illness, and

25. These statistics are based on the noninstitutionalized population. For example, more elderly people were cared for in nursing homes in 1973 than in 1964. Since nursing home patients may be expected to have more chronic conditions and more limitation of activity, it is possible that the rates for all elderly people did not change markedly over the period.

26. The major information on chronic conditions by income comes from the household health interview surveys conducted annually by the National Center for Health Statistics. Unfortunately, the center changed its reporting procedures in 1968; before the change it collected information on all chronic conditions, but afterward it reported them only if they resulted in a limitation of activity or caused the patient to seek medical attention. The center also selected one major type of chronic condition for more detailed reporting each year after 1968. The impairment data in table 2-5 are based on detailed reporting in 1971 but on the more general approach for fiscal years 1964 and 1965.

27. Some studies have shown, however, that people are more likely to report an acute condition if they have seen a physician. With the greater use of physicians' services by the poor over this period, some of the increase in acute conditions may reflect higher reporting rates rather than a change in incidence.

in some cases halts the development of long-term chronic conditions. Unfortunately, there are few statistics that capture these benefits of medical care. Instead, the duration of restriction of activity (that is, confinement to bed or home, inability to work or go to school) is the major fact routinely reported.

The number of days of restricted activity resulting from acute and chronic conditions increased among the poor between 1964 and 1973. Only for the aged did significant declines occur. Fewer days of restricted activity were reported for poor children than for nonpoor children in 1964, but by 1973 more restricted activity days were reported for poor than for nonpoor children. Among the communicable diseases, there were declines in the incidence of measles, German measles, and whooping cough.[28]

Use of Medical Care

One of the most striking changes to occur between 1964 and 1974 was the increased use of medical care services by low-income people. Historically, the poor have been much sicker than other Americans but have had less care from physicians. The period 1964–74 brought a major reversal in this pattern of abnormally low use, and for the first time the poor began to visit physicians as frequently as the nonpoor. To a lesser extent the poor also made greater use of dental services. Their hospitalization rate increased by 40 percent, far surpassing that of other income classes.

Since increasing the access of the poor to health care services was a common objective of many of the federal health care programs instituted in the mid-1960s, this change suggests that progress has been substantial and that the health programs of the Great Society and the War on Poverty have been largely successful in this respect.

It does not detract from this achievement to probe for possible shortcomings. Various questions should be raised. Has the increased use of services been shared equally by all the poor? Is the job of improving their access to medical services completed? Has their receipt of health care services brought tangible or intangible benefits? Do some of them now receive too much medical care, and are economic incentives to treat them so strong that they have become vulnerable to excessive testing, hospitalization, and surgery? Is the care they receive of the same quality and convenience, and in the same type of setting, as that of others? Although

28. National Center for Health Statistics, *Health, United States, 1976–1977*, pp. 248–49.

not all of these questions can be answered adequately because of incomplete data and information, the evidence currently available is summarized below.

Physicians' Services

In 1964 the nonpoor saw physicians about 20 percent more frequently than the poor. In the 1970s the poor overtook those with higher incomes—by 1975 they saw physicians 18 percent more frequently than the nonpoor (see table 2-6). These gains by the poor were true of every age group from 1964 to 1975.

The average annual number of visits to physicians by poor children increased from 2.7 in 1964 to 4.7 in 1975. Higher-income children's use of physicians' services dropped during this period, eliminating the difference by income of 89 percent in 1964: by 1975 lower-income children visited physicians as frequently as children in high-income families.

Increases in visits to physicians may occur either because more people go to see physicians or because those who go do so more frequently, or both. The proportion of the poor seeing a physician over a two-year interval rose: in 1964, 28 percent had not seen a physician for two years or more; by 1973 this percentage was only 17. Progress was especially evident for poor children, one-third of whom had not seen a physician for two years or more in 1964. By 1973 this figure was reduced to one-fifth. Despite this gain, poor children were still 57 percent less likely to have seen a physician in the two years before 1973 than nonpoor children.[29]

Since periodic examinations by physicians are considered good medical practice, the reduction in the number of those who have not had recent contact with the medical care system is a particularly good indicator of progress. Unlike the annual number of visits, however, this way of measuring utilization indicates that the poor still lag somewhat behind the nonpoor in access to physicians' services for all age groups except young adults.

While data on the trend in preventive examinations are not available, recent statistics indicate that the poor are still considerably behind others. Fifty-seven percent of low-income women but only 34 percent of high-income women did not have a Pap smear between 1971 and 1973; similar differences occur for breast examinations. Forty-five percent of the low-

29. National Center for Health Statistics, *Health, United States, 1975*, pp. 289, 409, 507, 509, 569.

Table 2-6. Physicians' Visits per Person per Year, by Age Group and Family Income, Fiscal Year 1964 and Calender Year 1975

Income in dollars

	1964		1975	
Age group	*Income*	*Number of visits*	*Income*	*Number of visits*
All ages	All incomes	4.5	All incomes	5.1
	Under 4,000	4.3	Under 5,000	6.0
	4,000–6,999	4.5	5,000–9,999	5.2
	7,000–9,999	4.7	10,000–14,999	4.8
	10,000 and over	5.1	15,000 and over	4.9
	Ratio, highest to lowest	1.19	Ratio, highest to lowest	0.82
Under 15	All incomes	3.8	All incomes	4.4
	Under 4,000	2.7	Under 5,000	4.7
	4,000–6,999	3.8	5,000–9,999	4.0
	7,000–9,999	4.1	10,000–14,999	4.4
	10,000 and over	5.1	15,000 and over	4.7
	Ratio, highest to lowest	1.89	Ratio, highest to lowest	1.00
15–44	All incomes	4.5	All incomes	4.8
	Under 4,000	4.1	Under 5,000	5.7
	4,000–6,999	4.5	5,000–9,999	5.0
	7,000–9,999	4.7	10,000–14,999	4.5
	10,000 and over	4.9	15,000 and over	4.7
	Ratio, highest to lowest	1.20	Ratio, highest to lowest	0.82
45–64	All incomes	5.0	All incomes	5.6
	Under 4,000	5.1	Under 5,000	7.4
	4,000–6,999	5.0	5,000–9,999	5.8
	7,000–9,999	5.3	10,000–14,999	5.5
	10,000 and over	5.1	15,000 and over	5.3
	Ratio, highest to lowest	1.00	Ratio, highest to lowest	0.72
65 and over	All incomes	6.7	All incomes	6.6
	Under 4,000	6.3	Under 5,000	6.5
	4,000–6,999	7.0	5,000–9,999	7.2
	7,000–9,999	7.0	10,000–14,999	6.9
	10,000 and over	7.7	15,000 and over	6.4
	Ratio, highest to lowest	1.22	Ratio, highest to lowest	0.98

Sources: Department of Health, Education, and Welfare, National Center for Health Statistics, *Volume of Physician Visits by Place of Visit and Type of Service, United States, July 1963–June 1964*, Vital and Health Statistics, series 10, no. 18 (GPO, 1965), pp. 18, 19, 29; and National Center for Health Statistics, *Health, United States, 1976–1977*, DHEW (HRA) 77-1232 (GPO, 1977), p. 265.

income adult population had not had a physical examination in the previous two years as against 31 percent of high-income adults.[30]

Another indicator of the increased use of medical care is the percentage of pregnant women receiving early prenatal care. Low-income women who saw a physician early in pregnancy increased from 58 percent in 1963 to 71 percent in 1970, although high-income women were still 20 percent more likely to have sought early care.[31]

Dental Services

Most of the federal health programs of the last decade have been primarily concerned with medical care, but some programs also include dental care. Most of the comprehensive health centers provide routine dental care. The federal Medicaid program covers dental care as an optional service, and most states have elected to extend at least some dental services to Medicaid recipients.

The dental health of the poor has long been shockingly bad. In 1971 low-income adults between the ages of forty-five and sixty-four were almost three times as likely to have lost all their own teeth as were adults of the same age with incomes above $15,000. Among the aged, almost 60 percent of those with incomes below $3,000 had lost their teeth but only 35 percent of those with incomes above $15,000 had lost them.[32]

Poor dental health begins in childhood. In the mid-sixties among children between six and eleven, those whose family's income was less than $3,000 had an average of 3.4 decayed, unfilled teeth, but children in families with incomes of $15,000 or more had an average of only 0.7. Nearly four times as many low-income children as high-income children between twelve and seventeen had decayed or missing permanent teeth.[33]

30. Ibid., p. 273.

31. Ronald Andersen and others, *Health Service Use: National Trends and Variations, 1953–1971,* DHEW (HSM) 73-3004 (HEW, Health Services and Mental Health Administration, 1972), p. 22.

32. National Center for Health Statistics, *Edentulous Persons, United States—1971,* Vital and Health Statistics, series 10, no. 89, DHEW (HRA) 74-1516 (GPO, 1974), pp. 9, 11.

33. HEW, Health Resources Administration, *Decayed, Missing, and Filled Teeth Among Children, United States,* Vital and Health Statistics, series 11, no. 106, DHEW (HRA) 74-1003 (HRA, 1974); National Center for Health Statistics, *Decayed, Missing, and Filled Teeth Among Youths 12–17 Years, United States,* Vital and Health Statistics, series 11, no. 144, DHEW (HRA) 75-1626 (GPO, 1974), pp. 19, 20.

Although the dental health of the poor remains at substandard levels, they made steady progress in availing themselves of dental services from 1964 to 1975. In 1964 those with high incomes visited the dentist 3.5 times as often as those with low incomes. By 1974 this had been reduced to 2.0 times as often.

For poor children the average annual number of dental visits increased from 0.5 to almost one visit per child. Despite this, about 58 percent of poor children had not seen a dentist in the two years before 1973.[34]

Hospital Services

Because the poor are afflicted with more chronic conditions than others and because their health problems are generally more severe, it is not surprising that low-income people are hospitalized more than others. The period 1964–73 brought a fairly sharp increase in low-income people receiving hospital care; in 1964 discharges from short-stay hospitals averaged fourteen for every hundred low-income people; by 1973 this had risen to twenty-four per hundred people, a 70 percent increase over the period.[35] At the same time there was only a moderate increase in the hospitalization rates of higher-income people.

A major shift in the hospitalization rate also occurred for older people. In 1964 there were nineteen hospital discharges for every hundred people sixty-five or over; this had increased to thirty-five discharges in 1973.

An Assessment of Trends

These trends in the use of medical care by the poor make it clear that there has been a significant narrowing of the gap in opportunity to receive medical care. Some observers conclude that medical programs for the poor have been so successful that the job is complete and there is no longer cause for special concern about the health care of the poor. Others cite

34. Ronald W. Wilson and Elijah L. White, "Changes in Morbidity, Disability, and Utilization Differentials between the Poor and the Nonpoor: Data from the Health Interview Survey, 1964 and 1973," *Medical Care*, vol. 15 (August 1977), table 5.

35. National Center for Health Statistics, *Health, United States, 1975*, p. 309; and NCHS, *Hospital Discharges and Length of Stay: Short-Stay Hospitals, United States—July 1963–June 1964*, Vital and Health Statistics, series 10, no. 30 (GPO, 1966), p. 36.

Table 2-7. Number of Physicians' Visits per Capita Adjusted for Health Status of
Patient, by Family Income, Public Assistance Status, and Age Group, 1969

Family income (dollars)	All ages	Under 17	17–44	45–64	65 and over
All incomes	4.6	3.8	4.4	4.9	6.6
Under 5,000	3.7	3.0	4.2	4.0	6.1
Aid	4.5	3.5	5.9	5.2	6.4
No aid	3.6	3.0	4.1	3.9	6.1
5,000–9,999	4.6	3.9	4.5	5.2	6.8
10,000–14,999	4.9	4.2	4.6	5.1	7.5
15,000 and over	5.2	4.5	4.8	5.5	10.4
Ratio, aid to no aid, income under 5,000	1.25	1.19	1.42	1.32	1.05
Ratio, income of 15,000 and over to income of under 5,000, no aid	1.44	1.53	1.17	1.40	1.72

Source: Estimated from National Center for Health Statistics, 1969 Health Interview Survey. For a discussion of the method of adjustment for health status, see Karen Davis and Roger Reynolds, "The Impact of Medicare and Medicaid on Access to Medical Care," in Richard N. Rosett, ed., *The Role of Health Insurance in the Health Services Sector* (Neale Watson Academic Publications for National Bureau of Economic Research, 1976), pp. 391–425 (Brookings Reprint T-013). Figures are rounded.

instances in which the poor now surpass others in the use of health care services and suggest that perhaps the poor use them excessively.[36]

Neither of these conclusions is warranted by the evidence gathered so far. When the poor make greater use of services than others, it can be attributed to the greater incidence of illness and injury among them.[37]

The claims that access to health services for the poor is now adequate are also premature. Significant groups of the poor have not shared equally in the advances that have been achieved. About one-third of the poor are excluded from the Medicaid program. Low-income people not covered by public assistance use physicians' services much less frequently than other people (table 2-7).

Minority groups and residents of rural areas, where poor people are heavily concentrated, continue to lag well behind others in using physi-

36. Thomas W. Bice, Robert L. Eichhorn, and Peter D. Fox, "Socioeconomic Status and Use of Physician Services: A Reconsideration," *Medical Care,* vol. 10 (May–June 1972), pp. 261–71; Myron J. Lefcowitz, "Poverty and Health: A Reexamination," *Inquiry,* vol. 10 (March 1973), pp. 3–13; Martin S. Feldstein, "The Medical Economy," *Scientific American,* vol. 229 (September 1973), pp. 151 ff.; and *Economic Report of the President, January 1976,* pp. 121–22.

37. When adjustment is made for this greater incidence, the poor visit physicians slightly less frequently than others with comparable health problems (see table 2-7).

cians' services. By 1973 whites averaged 5.1 visits to physicians a year; blacks and other races averaged 4.5 visits. Differences by race are particularly marked for children.[38] Since blacks and other minority groups tend to have more severe health problems than whites, disparities in the use of physicians' services relative to health needs are even greater than these figures suggest. There were substantial improvements for blacks and other races relative to whites, however, between 1964 and 1973. In 1964 whites averaged 42 percent more visits to physicians than blacks and others; by 1973 the gap had been narrowed to 13 percent.[39]

Rural residents, representing 55 million people, continued to lag behind urban residents in using physicians' services, and the differences remained remarkably stable for a fairly long time. Some increases occurred for non-metropolitan children between 1964 and 1973, but elderly people in non-metropolitan areas fell even further behind the aged in metropolitan areas.

Although data indicating trends in the frequency of visits to physicians by race and income or by residence and income are not currently available, the overall trends suggest that not all poor people have made equal progress in gaining access to physicians' services. Instead, some groups that face special barriers—whether of distance, physical availability, cultural attitudes, or discrimination—continue to lag well behind in the use of medical services.

And even though the poor as a whole receive more care from physicians than formerly, major differences do remain in the setting, continuity, and type of health care available to them. In 1974 almost 27 percent of families earning less than $5,000, but 15 percent of families earning over $15,000, had no "usual" place for obtaining care. Eight percent of the low-income families used hospital emergency rooms as usual sources of care; only 2 percent of those earning over $15,000 used hospitals regularly.[40] Care is usually less convenient for the poor. They spend 58 percent more time than those with higher incomes traveling and waiting to see a physician.

It is not possible to conclude from the evidence currently available whether the care the poor receive is as good as, the same as, or inferior to

38. National Center for Health Statistics, *Health, United States, 1975,* pp. 291, 295, 405.

39. Ibid.; NCHS, *Volume of Physician Visits,* p. 17.

40. National Center for Health Statistics, *Health, United States, 1976–1977,* p. 213.

that received by others.[41] Apparently the poor go to physicians and hospitals for much the same reasons as other people. The Georgia Medicaid program, for example, found that the ten most frequently reported conditions of patients visiting physicians were acute upper respiratory infection, high blood pressure, acute tonsillitis, bronchitis, diabetes mellitus, kidney infection, otitis media, acute pharyngitis, heart disease, and abdominal pain.[42] The ten most common final diagnoses of Kentucky Medicaid hospital patients in fiscal 1972–73, in order of declining frequency, were childbirth, pneumonia, gastroenteritis and colitis, hypertrophy of the tonsils and adenoids, chronic ischemic heart disease, diabetes mellitus, bronchitis, false labor, acute bronchitis and bronchiolitis, and asthma.[43] In the absence of any definitive evidence to the contrary, it must be assumed that physicians and other health care providers treat these conditions when encountered in the poor as professionally as they do when encountered in other patients. The poor presumably benefit from the relief of pain or discomfort, cure of acute conditions, control of chronic conditions, and return to normal functioning as much as any other patients who receive medical treatment for similar conditions.

More information on the content and style of care the poor receive would be desirable, however. Economic incentives in public medical programs, as well as in private health insurance plans, frequently reward unprofessional practice. There is some danger that when there are alternative methods of treating a condition a physician or other health provider might be influenced to select the method of diagnosis or treatment that is most remunerative. Some conditions, for instance, can either be treated surgically or be monitored over longer periods of time and treated with nonsurgical techniques. One report on surgical procedures among Medicaid patients found high rates of tonsillectomies, hysterectomies, and

41. For a survey of the available evidence, see Avedis Donabedian, "Effects of Medicare and Medicaid on Access to and Quality of Health Care," *Public Health Reports*, vol. 91 (July–August 1976), pp. 322–31; and Robert H. Brook and Kathleen N. Williams, *Evaluating Quality of Health Care for the Disadvantaged: A Literature Review*, R-1658-HEW (Rand Corp., 1975).

42. Letter from Sam T. Thurmond, Director, Georgia Medicaid Program, to William C. Pembleton, Social and Rehabilitation Service, Department of Health, Education, and Welfare, January 23, 1976.

43. Kentucky Bureau for Social Insurance, *The Kentucky Medical Assistance Program: Report of Services Rendered, Fiscal Year 1972–73* (Frankfort: Department for Human Resources, 1973), p. 70.

Table 2-8. In-Hospital Surgical Procedures per 100 People a Year, by Family Income, United States, 1963 and 1970

Family income (dollars)	1963	1970
Under 2,000	3	7
2,000–3,499	4	6
3,500–4,999	4	7
5,000–7,499	6	7
7,500 and over	6	5
All incomes	5	6
Ratio, under 2,000 to 7,500 and over	0.5	1.4

Source: Ronald Andersen and others, *Health Service Use: National Trends and Variations, 1953–1971*, DHEW (HSM) 73-3004 (HEW, Health Services and Mental Health Administration, 1972), p. 21.

cholecystectomies.[44] Other data bear out the claim that Medicaid may have caused physicians to select surgical methods of treatment more frequently than they did in the past. Table 2-8 shows that in 1963 the number of surgical procedures per capita performed on low-income people was half that performed on high-income people, but by 1970 surgical procedures performed on the poor had doubled. The number performed on the elderly also rose after the introduction of Medicare. One study found that hospital admissions for surgery rose 30 percent in the first year; admissions for gall bladder operations tripled.[45]

A higher rate of surgery does not, in itself, suggest poor care. Survival rates, relief of pain or discomfort, and recovery times may be favorably affected by better surgical care. This is an area, however, where further exploration would clearly be of value.

44. *Getting Ready for National Health Insurance: Unnecessary Surgery*, Hearings before the Subcommittee on Oversight and Investigations of the House Committee on Interstate and Foreign Commerce, 94:1 (GPO, 1975), pp. 263–67. Data in this report for some states are questionable because of a misunderstanding of the term "surgical procedures." Some states reported every bill for a surgical procedure separately (including those of anesthesiologists, hospitals, surgeons, attending physicians, and others), which led to overcounting of surgical procedures.

45. Regina Loewenstein, "Early Effects of Medicare on the Health Care of the Aged," *Social Security Bulletin*, vol. 34 (April 1971), pp. 8–9. See also Donabedian, "Effects of Medicare and Medicaid on Access to and Quality of Health Care," p. 327.

25

A STRATEGY FOR NATIONAL HEALTH INSURANCE

Lawrence S. Seidman

It is often assumed that national health insurance (NHI) should increase health insurance coverage. Many (though not all) health economists, however, hold a very different view.[1,2,3] They agree that NHI should increase insurance against "major risks," so that each household is fully protected against financial catastrophe. On the other hand, they also believe NHI should sharply *reduce* health insurance for medical expenses that are moderate relative to a household's income. From this perspective, our society currently has too little "major risk" insurance, but far too much "minor risk" insurance. To advance the goals of equity and efficiency, the strategy for NHI should be to remedy both of these defects.

This paper will attempt to explain this approach to national health insurance through an analogy. Any analogy is imperfect. Given the complexity and special features of the health sector, an analogy is bound to differ in many respects. Nevertheless, it is the very complexity of the health sector that makes a good analogy useful. Only by simplifying can the source of the problem, and a strategy to combat it, be clearly illuminated.

The Restaurant Bill-Splitting Analogy

Our current situation, prior to NHI, can be understood by a familiar experience: restaurant bill-splitting. Suppose a group of individuals goes out to lunch together every day.

Laurence S. Seidman, Ph.D., is Assistant Professor of Economics and Assistant Professor of Health Care Systems (Leonard Davis Institute of Health Economics), University of Pennsylvania, Philadelphia, PA 19174.

This research was supported by funds from the Leonard Davis Institute of Health Economics, University of Pennsylvania, Philadelphia, PA 19174.

To ease the burden on the waiter—and in the spirit of comradeship—they decide that from now on they will split the bill evenly, regardless of what each has ordered. What will happen?

Each person will now discover, to his delight, that high-priced items on the menu are no longer unthinkable. If the group is small, of course, conscience may restrain indulgence. But the larger the group, and the less intimate the friendship, the weaker will be this source of restraint. Indeed, in a large impersonal group, it may be expected to vanish. Moreover, the larger the group, the smaller will be the impact of a person's own order on his own payment. For each additional $1's worth a person orders, his own payment will go up $1/n (where n is the number in the group), so that p/n is the "effective price" to the individual of an item with a price p. In a group of 20, lobster may be priced $4 above an individual's customary order; but under bill-splitting, his share of the total bill will rise only 20¢ if he indulges.

The result, obviously, is that bill-splitting will cause the total bill to be much greater than it would have been under individual checks. Each person's daily lunch expense will be much more. Before too long, it is likely that the group will decide that, while bill-splitting is fine for special occasions, they had better go back to individual checks.

It should be emphasized that the inflationary effect of bill-splitting does not depend on whether the bill is split evenly. The individual will have an incentive to inflate his order as long as his share of the total bill is largely independent of his own order. For example, in a group of 20, instead of each person paying 5% of the bill, suppose that half of the group with higher salaries were each assigned 6%; the half with lower salaries, 4%. The inflationary incentive would remain, since each individual's payment is hardly affected by his own order.

The main reason for the inflation of the total bill is likely to be the increase in the quality of food and style of service, rather than the quantity consumed. The quantity an individual can consume is constrained by his physical capacity. Even if he regards his own order as virtually "free" to him, the quantity he orders will respond "inelastically." Nevertheless, the cost of his order can easily be multiplied several times by raising quality and style.

The hospital sector today is characterized by widespread bill-splitting. Nearly 95% of the nation's hospital bill is paid by third parties—private insurance companies and the government.[4] These insurers, in turn, bill us for a share of their expense. Each household's share of the nation's hospital bill is its private health insurance premium and its tax payment that helps finance public insurance, such as Medicare and Medicaid. Many households may be unaware of the premium they pay, since it is often contributed on their behalf by their employer. The more an employer contributes to an employee's health insurance premium, however, the smaller the cash wage (salary) he can afford to pay the employee. Thus it is likely that most, if not all, of these employer contributions are in reality being borne by employees.

The nation's hospital bill is not split evenly, because premiums and taxes vary across households. The key point, however, is that each household's share of the total bill is largely independent of its own use of hospital service. The "effective price" to the patient of his own hospital care is therefore close to zero.

Complete bill-splitting is as wasteful and inflationary in the hospital sector as it is in our restaurant analogy. This is sometimes denied, on the grounds that doctors make all decisions uninfluenced by the degree of patient cost-sharing—or that patients themselves are completely insensitive to effective price. Usually a life-and-death situation is cited to show the irrelevance of financial incentives on the patient.

Nevertheless, a substantial body of econometric evidence has now accumulated supporting the response of hospital utilization to the effective price faced by patients.[4,5,6] This should not be surprising. First, many utilization decisions are not matters of life-and-death. Second, physicians do not always make decisions unilaterally, but sometimes present options so that the patient participates in the decision. Third, even when the physician makes the decision on his own, he may consider the financial consequences for the patient. For example, if a patient's insurance covers hospitalization, but not nursing care at home, the physician may extend the length of hospital stay.[4]

The fourth reason is perhaps most important. Some skeptics of the inflationary impact of bill-splitting have in mind the quantity of hospital care—i.e. the number of days—rather than its quality or style. As in the restaurant analogy, they believe the quantity of hospital days that patients (and their physicians) seek is largely insensitive to the effective price. They argue that certain medical conditions require hospitalization and a specific length of stay. Even if this were true, the key question is: How expensive is a hospital day? The cost per day is determined by the quality and style (amenities) of service, as well as the inefficiency of hospital production. Suppose medical condition A requires eight days of hospitalization. Should the patient stay in hospital X, with a cost of $150 per day or hospital Y, with a cost of $300 per day?

Currently, since most patients are under complete bill-splitting, they naturally prefer the most costly hospital. Physicians have no reason to seek admission privileges at less expensive hospitals, since patients are not interested in this option. Hospitals compete for patients and physicians by raising their style of service, regardless of cost. There is no incentive to avoid wasteful duplication of costly technology, since these costs can be passed on to third parties without deterring patients and physicians.

In contrast to today's situation, suppose most patients were required to pay a fraction of the cost of their *own* hospital care. Then the physician for the patient with medical condition A might place him in hospital X (cost per day, $150) instead of Y (cost per day, $300) if the difference in quality and style were not worth the cost to the patient, given his particular medical condition and preferences. Physicians would have an incentive to admit patients to efficient hospitals that avoided wasteful duplication of technology, since patients would appreciate a physician's concern for their financial burden. Hospitals, in turn, would have an incentive to provide only the quality and style of service that patients felt were worth its cost, and to provide that quality and style at minimum possible cost.

The hospital sector is not unique in its potential to utilize expensive technology and provide an expensive quality and style of product. It is unique in that complete bill-splitting removes the incentive to avoid quality, style, and technology that individual consumers do not believe is worth the cost. A cost crisis could be created in almost any sector of our economy by instituting complete bill-splitting for consumers for that sector's output.[7]

Bill-Splitting and Individual Checks: A Compromise

Why, then, is bill-splitting so prevalent in health care? In our restaurant analogy, the group quickly abandoned the bill-splitting experiment. In order to explain the persistence of bill-splitting, our analogy requires a crucial modification.

The weakness of our analogy, thus far, is that it ignores the key motivation for bill-splitting, or insurance, in the health sector—namely—risk-reduction. The most important reason why people want health insurance is to protect them against medical bills that are large relative to their income. Although only a minority of households incur such bills, the fear of financial catastrophe makes many households prefer bill-splitting to individual checks.

This key feature can be incorporated into our analogy as follows. Suppose that, in any group, a minority develops a dangerous nutritional deficiency at lunchtime, causing an overwhelming craving that can only be satisfied by an enormously expensive lunch. This craving appears to strike at random, although some unlucky persons are overcome by it repeatedly. Their burden is catastrophic under the individual check management.

Given this "major risk," it is no longer likely that the group will abandon bill-splitting, even though they realize that it causes each person to inflate his order, and therefore will result in a higher average lunch payment per person. The larger the "craving" bill, and the more risk-averse the individuals, the more likely they will prefer complete bill-splitting to individual checks, if these are the only two options.

It is bound to occur to some imaginative members of the group, however, that a third option is available. Why not use individual checks for routine lunches, but bill-splitting when the craving strikes? Most persons on most days will pay according to what they or-

der, thereby retaining the incentive to economize. At the same time, the unlucky minority will be protected against financial catastrophe by bill-splitting. It seems plausible that most will prefer this hybrid option to the other two.

It will be useful to illustrate this new option with a numerical example. Under individual checks, suppose each person in the group would ordinarily spend $2 for lunch. If the craving overcomes an individual, however, he is forced to spend $43 to satisfy it; 5% of the group is struck with the deficiency each day. While the median daily expense is $2, the mean is $4.05:

$$(.95) \times (\$2) + (.05) \times (\$43) = \$4.05$$

Under complete bill-splitting, assume each person (including the person with the craving) orders $4 more than he would under individual checks, so that the median order is $6, and the mean bill is $8.05:

$$(.95) \times (\$6) + (.05) \times (\$47) = \$8.05$$

Then under complete bill-splitting, each person's daily expense would be $8.05, $4 more than the mean expense under individual checks. It is quite possible, however, that the fear of a $43 burden would cause the group to choose complete bill-splitting, faced with only these two options.

The hybrid option would work as follows. Craving insurance would be provided, guaranteeing each person a limited burden should the craving strike. Each day, prior to lunch, each person would pay a premium into a craving insurance fund. This fund would then pay 100% of a person's bill in excess of $7. Thus, craving insurance would limit a person's burden to $7 (excluding the premium).

What premium must each person contribute, if the fund is to meet its obligation? Since the craving strikes 5%, the fund will pay no benefits to 95% of its members on a given day. For the 5% who are overcome—and order $47's worth (under craving insurance, a person will expand his order from $43 to $47, since food is "free" above $7, just as under complete bill-splitting), the fund pays $40 ($47–$7) in benefits. The mean benefit per insured member is $2:

$$(.95) \times (\$0) + (.05) \times (\$40) = \$2$$

The craving insurance premium must therefore be set at $2. It is likely that most persons would prefer individual checks, plus craving insurance, to the other two options. Table 1 compares the three options.

Table 1. Burdens under three options

	Median burden (95%)	Maximum burden (5%)	Mean burden
I Individual checks	$2.00	$43.00	$4.05
II Complete bill-splitting	$8.05	$ 8.05	$8.05
III Individual checks plus craving insurance	$4.00	$ 9.00	$4.25

If $43 is a catastrophic burden, then most would not risk category I (individual checks), despite the fact that its mean burden is lowest. It is likely that most will prefer category III (individual checks plus craving insurance) to category II (complete bill-splitting). If a person is struck with the craving (5% chance), he will spend only $7 out-of-pocket under III; together with his $2 premium, his burden will be $9, somewhat greater than the burden of $8.05 under II. But if he is not struck with the craving (95% chance), his burden under III will be only $4 (a $2 individual check plus the $2 premium), compared to $8.05 under II. On average, the burden under III will be $3.80 ($8.05–$4.25) less per day than under II. The reason: The 95% will economize under III, but not under II.

Thus far we have ignored differences in income. If incomes differ, the arrangement can be made more equitable by two modifications. First, the ceiling can be varied with income, instead of being $7 for all persons. Second, the insurance premium can be varied with income, instead of being $2 for all persons.

To simplify, suppose that half the members have income $H, and half have income $L; and that the ratio of $H to $L is 3:2. Suppose the ceiling and insurance premium are also set in the same 3:2 ratio. Thus, the ceiling for H would be $8.40, and for L would be $5.60 (the mean would remain $7); the premium for H would be $2.40, and for L $1.60 (the mean would remain $2). To allow a meaningful comparison, it is assumed that under II, the shares of the bill would also be in the 3:2 ratio; H's share would be $9.66, and L's would be $6.44 (the mean share would remain $8.05). Table 2 shows the burdens for H and L under the three options.

Persons in both group H and group L are still likely to prefer III over I or II. Under III, the burdens of a person in L have been reduced below those given in Table 1, at the expense of raising the burdens of a person in H above those given in Table 1. Since this shift in burdens better matches the person's ability-

Table 2. Burdens under income-related options

	Median burden (95%)	Maximum burden (5%)	Mean burden
Group H			
I Individual checks	$2.00	$43.00	$4.05
II Complete bill-splitting	$9.66	$ 9.66	$9.66
III Individual checks plus craving insurance	$4.40	$10.80	$4.72
Group L			
I Individual checks	$2.00	$43.00	$4.05
II Complete bill-splitting	$6.44	$ 6.44	$6.44
III Individual checks plus craving insurance	$3.60	$ 7.20	$3.78

to-pay, most would regard it as an improvement in equity.

Thus, a compromise arrangement, where both the ceiling and insurance premium are *income-related*, should promote both equity and efficiency and prove attractive to individuals at all income levels. Why, then, does complete bill-splitting prevail for hospital care, rather than "major risk" insurance which excludes coverage for moderate bills? It is theoretically possible, of course, that most people are so risk-averse, or value so highly the convenience of bill-splitting, that they simply prefer II to III. While a minority may feel this way, it seems unlikely that a majority does. An alternative explanation seems more plausible. There are at least two other causes of the prevalence of II over III. First, substantial tax subsidies encourage bill-splitting for all medical bills—routine as well as exceptional. Second, employers and unions may receive a special return from providing "shallow" insurance. Each will be considered in turn.

Given the illustration in Table 1, suppose that persons were subsidized for bill-splitting. For example, a 20% subsidy for bill-splitting would reduce the burden under II from $8.05 to $6.44, clearly increasing the relative attractiveness of II.

The federal tax system provides a substantial subsidy to bill-splitting in medical care. If an employer pays an employee a cash wage of $100, it is subject to payroll and personal income tax, hence the employee actually receives only a fraction of the gross—say, $70. If the employer instead uses the $100 to buy health insurance for the employee, no tax must be paid. Thus, given that the employer is willing to spend the $100 either way, the employee's choice is between $100's worth of health insurance, or $70 in cash. Also, an individual can deduct one-half the cost of any health insurance premium he buys up to $150 (rather than his employer deducting it). This artificial encouragement of bill-splitting has been estimated to be substantial in its impact.[2,4]

Employers and union leaders may receive a special return from providing extensive insurance, even if there were no tax distortion. Suppose the average employee would choose $100 cash rather than $100 of "shallow" insurance if the choice were his. Paradoxically, it is possible he will rate his employer, or his union leaders, more highly if they provide $100's worth of insurance. Employees consider both cash wages and fringe benefits (such as insurance) in judging their employer or union. Because medical care is so important to the employee's family, however, employees may attribute special weight to the degree of health insurance when they rate the fairness of their employer or the competence of their union. If the coverage of the health insurance plan has symbolic value, the employer and/or union may provide more insurance than the average employee would choose for himself.

A Strategy for National Health Insurance

To foster both efficiency and equity, the strategy for national health insurance should be twofold: to return to individual checks for bills that are moderate relative to a household's income, in order to reduce waste and cost inflation; to extend bill-splitting to every member of society for bills that are large relative to a household's income, so that no one is vulnerable to financial disaster because of a medical problem.

It will be convenient to label this kind of NHI as *income-related* major-risk (catastrophic) national health insurance (MRNHI). Under MRNHI, each household would be assigned a deductible, a coinsurance range and rate, and an out-of-pocket ceiling. For example, a family with an income of $16,000 might be responsible for its first $800 (its deductible), and 20% of its additional medical bill (its coinsurance rate) until it has spent $1,600 (10% of its income) out-of-pocket (when its annual medical bill reaches $4,800). Beyond this, MRNHI would pay 100%.[1]

To be equitable, the deductible, coinsurance rate and out-of-pocket ceiling must vary with a household's income, so that the subjective burden of out-of-pocket expense is comparable for all households. Without such variation, NHI will either be unfair or highly inefficient. If the deductible, coinsurance rate, and out-

of-pocket ceiling are small enough to avoid inequity to low-income families, they will be trivial for middle and upper-income families. Hospital care will continue to be nearly free for such households, weakening their incentive to economize. Furthermore, the federal budget cost of NHI will be unnecessarily large, because NHI will pay a large fraction of the medical bills that these households could afford to pay on their own. The high federal budget cost will in turn squeeze other federal programs which are often aimed at assisting the poor and the elderly. Unintentionally, the result will be to shift federal dollars away from the poor and elderly to middle and upper-income households. Few would find this desirable.

Income-related MRNHI can be implemented most easily through the federal personal income tax. Our family with an income of $16,000 would file, on its annual tax return, for a tax credit of 80% of its medical expense from $800 to $4,800, and for a tax credit of 100% of its medical expense in excess of $4,800. If the tax credit exceeds the family's tax liability, it would receive a net cash payment from the Internal Revenue Service, so that full payment would be made to all households whatever their tax liability. The MRNHI tax credit would replace the current medical deduction under the personal income tax.[2,8]

Under MRNHI, implemented through tax credits, many households would face a severe cash flow problem since they would not receive their tax credit from IRS until their tax returns were filed and processed. Even if it were feasible for IRS to process medical tax credit applications throughout the year, the household's cost-sharing (deductible and coinsurance) could still create a cash flow problem. The federal government should therefore guarantee the availability of medical loans to households unable to afford immediate payment.[1,9] Elsewhere in the literature, principles have been set out that should guide the design of the medical loan program under MRNHI.[10]

The Treatment of Private Health Insurance

In our restaurant analogy, it seemed likely that most persons would choose III and reject complete bill-splitting (II). Nevertheless, it is possible that some will be so "insurance-minded" that they prefer to pay the much higher mean cost of complete bill-splitting. As long as they bear the full cost of complete bill-splitting, choosing it freely, they should be able to obtain arrangement II. Indeed, their well-being would be reduced if they were denied this opportunity.

The same principle should guide the treatment of private health insurance under MRNHI. A household that buys private insurance (PI) should have to pay its full social cost and should have the option of saving its money for other uses, if it prefers.

To implement this principle, three policies are required. First, the current tax subsidy to workplace health insurance should be eliminated. Second, if workplace health insurance is offered, the employer should be legally required to give each employee the option of taking cash, instead of the insurance. Third, a household's expense on a PI premium should be counted toward the MRNHI tax credit only to the degree required to make it bear the full social cost of such insurance. Each policy will be considered in turn.

The current tax subsidy to workplace health insurance has been criticized by several prominent health economists, who have urged its elimination.[1,2,4] Prior to the enactment of MRNHI, a paternal argument may have justified this subsidy. Under income-related MRNHI, however, every household would be fully protected against financial catastrophe. There is no reason why "shallow" health insurance should be artificially encouraged. The subsidy can be eliminated simply by including the employer's contribution toward health insurance in the employee's adjusted gross income on his tax return.

Today, most households do not freely weigh the cost of PI against its benefit. Instead, PI is provided for them at their workplace. It is compulsory, in the sense that an employee who rejects the insurance cannot obtain cash instead.

Even if the workplace health insurance is exactly what the average employee would freely purchase (at group rates), this cannot be true of all employees, who vary in their attitude toward insurance. Earlier, moreover, it was argued that it is possible that employers and unions tend to provide more insurance than the average employee would freely purchase, because the extensiveness of the health insurance policy may have symbolic value.

To guarantee that a household's PI truly reflects its own preference, a cash-equivalent option should be enacted. Under the option, if an employer offers PI to his employees, he would be legally required to give each employee the option of taking an equivalent amount of cash instead. For example, if the insurer charges a premium of $600 for employee X and his family, employee X would have the option of taking the $600 in cash instead of the insurance. Elsewhere in the literature, the cash-equivalent option proposal is explained in greater detail.[11]

The tax credit to which a household is entitled under MRNHI depends on its out-of-pocket expense for medical care. This expense will equal its medical bill, if it has no PI. If the household has complete PI, then its out-of-pocket expense would equal its PI premium, not its medical bill. At first glance, it might seem proper to count expense on a PI premium toward MRNHI tax credit, exactly as payment to a provider (hospital or physician) is counted. For example, if our family with an income of $16,000—and an MRNHI deductible of $800 and a coinsurance rate of 20%—bought PI for $1,000, then it would be entitled to a tax credit of $160 (80% of the $200 above its deductible). This approach might appear to achieve "neutrality," biasing the household neither for nor against PI.

It turns out, however, that full counting of expense on a PI premium may not achieve neutrality. Proper treatment requires that if a household buys PI, the increase in its expected financial burden should equal the increase in the expected medical cost induced by PI. Such treatment would make a household bear the full expected social cost of any insurance it buys. It is not obvious whether fully, partly, or not counting expense on a PI premium will achieve this.

Elsewhere, this problem has been examined in depth.[12] In this study, the tentative conclusion emerged that neutrality requires only partial counting of such an expense toward tax credit for the average household.

Why is neutrality likely to require partial counting, instead of the more natural approach of fully counting such expense toward MRNHI tax-credit? The answer is that the purchase of PI by a household may generate a significant "externality." When a household buys PI, not only will its own medical bill tend to be inflated, but so will the medical bill of others, owing to the special behavior of physicians and non-profit hospitals. The inflation of its own medical bill will be fully reflected in the premium it must pay. But the inflation of others' medical bills will not. Thus, if the prospective buyer of PI is to confront its full social cost, including the external cost imposed on others, somewhat "tougher" tax-credit treatment will be required.

Why does the purchase of health insurance by one set of households tend to inflate the medical bills of non-insured households? This assertion is contrary to our restaurant analogy. If one set of customers opt for complete bill-splitting, and therefore inflate their own orders, this does not cause persons with individual checks to do the same. The difference lies in the special role of physicians and non-profit hospitals in transmitting bill inflation from the insured to the uninsured.

If a physician were a "perfect agent" for each of his patients, he would vary his recommendations according to the insurance status of each at a point when the patient would do so—if he possessed the MD's knowledge.[5] Sometimes physicians do this. For example, an MD may advise an insured patient to stay an extra day in the hospital, yet advise an uninsured patient to go home a day earlier.

For many decisions, however, MDs probably do not take account of each patient's insurance status. Instead, it is plausible that the *average* insurance of all patients will influence MDs as they adopt procedures and practices, which are then applied to most patients. For example, if most patients are completely insured for hospital care, physicians may seek admission privileges only at the most expensive hospitals, sending most patients there regardless of the insurance status of each.

This averaging process probably will be reinforced by the behavior of non-profit hospitals. As an important fraction of households obtain complete insurance, hospitals—like physicians—will sense less resistance, on average, to more expensive services and amenities. Although for-profit hospitals may still find it profitable to offer moderate-cost services and amenities to attract uninsured patients, non-profit hospitals are likely to regard such behavior as "unethical" and remain satisfied with revenues from high-cost services and amenities.

If this argument is correct, then households that buy PI will cause doctors and hospitals to inflate the bills of uninsured households, as well as their own. The transmission process can be incorporated into our restaurant analogy as follows: First, suppose customers depend heavily on waiters to advise them because they cannot judge their own nutritional needs. Each waiter does not know which customers are bill-splitters and which are on indi-

vidual checks. Also, each waiter seeks to please his customers, to earn the highest tip. If all his customers were on individual checks, the waiter should advise items with a moderate price; if all were bill-splitters, he should advise the most expensive items. Suppose restaurant customers have been solely on individual checks in the past, but now half have become bill-splitters. Waiters will react by advising more costly items for all customers, including those still on individual checks.

Second, suppose most restaurants are non-profit and do not pursue every available profit opportunity. If the majority of customers become bill-splitters, these restaurants might offer only very expensive food, because they are satisfied to cater to the preferences of bill-splitters and willing to forego a special effort to attract individual check customers with moderate-priced items. The result would be that individual check customers would have no choice but to attend high-priced restaurants.

If bill-splitting imposes costs on those with individual checks, then it is appropriate that bill-splitting be discouraged to the degree that reflects this external cost. This is why less than full counting of expense on PI toward MRNHI tax credit is likely to be proper.

Conclusion

To promote the goals of equity and efficiency, the strategy for NHI should be to: 1) provide complete protection for every household against medical expenses that are large relative to the household's income; 2) sharply reduce health insurance coverage for expenses that are moderate relative to a household's income, in order to increase the household's incentive to economize.

Using a restaurant analogy, we currently have too much bill-splitting for moderate medical bills, while still allowing an unlucky minority to get caught with individual checks for enormous bills. The solution is a compromise. We should design NHI so that there is bill-splitting for medical expenses that are large relative to a household's income, while retaining individual checks for expenses that are moderate relative to a household's income.

Income-related, major-risk (catastrophic) national health insurance (MRNHI) can be most easily implemented through the federal personal income tax. Each household would be eligible for a tax credit when its annual medical expense rises above its MRNHI deductible (which varies directly with its income). The tax credit would be a fraction of the additional medical expense until the household's out-of-pocket burden reaches its MRNHI ceiling (which also varies directly with its income). At this point, the tax-credit would equal 100% of all additional expense, thus the household's burden cannot exceed its ceiling. A household with a tax liability less than its MRNHI tax credit would receive a net cash payment from the Internal Revenue Service. The MRNHI tax-credit would replace the current medical deduction under the personal income tax.

Several complementary policies should be implemented. The federal government should guarantee the availability of medical loans to households unable to afford immediate payment of their medical bills. The current tax subsidy for workplace health insurance should

be ended, by including an employer's contribution to health insurance in the employee's adjusted gross income (on the employee's annual tax return). If an employer offers health insurance, he should be legally required to offer each employee the option of taking cash instead of the insurance. Finally, a household's expense on a private health insurance premium should be counted only partly toward MRNHI tax credit, assuming this is required to make the household bear the full expected social cost of such insurance. Probably this will be the case, since the purchase of insurance by one set of households may cause physicians and non-profit hospitals to inflate the bills of uninsured households. Because of the external cost imposed on others, special discouragement of private health insurance is appropriate under MRNHI.

References and Notes

1 Feldstein, M.: "A New Approach to National Health Insurance," *The Public Interest*, (Spring 1971).
2 Mitchell, B. and Vogel, R.: "Health and Taxes: An Assessment of the Medical Deduction," (Rand 1973).
3 Pauly, M.: "The Economics of Moral Hazard," *The American Economic Review*, (June 1968).
4 Davis, K.: *National Health Insurance* (Brookings 1975).
5 Feldstein, M.: "Econometric Studies of Health Economics," in Intriligator and Kendrick (eds.), *Frontiers of Quantitative Economics II* (1974).
6 Newhouse, J. and Phelps, C.: "Coinsurance and the Demand for Medical Services," (Rand 1973).
7 Seidman, L.: "The Aroman Food Crisis: A Fable with a Lesson for National Health Insurance," *Medical Care*, (forthcoming).

8 Marmor, T.: "Rethinking National Health Insurance," *The Public Interest*, (Winter 1977).
9 Eilers, R.: "Postpayment Medical Expense Coverage: A Proposed Salvation for Insured and Insurer," *Medical Care*, (May–June 1969).
10 Seidman, L.: "Medical Loans Under Major-Risk National Health Insurance," *Health Services Research*, (Summer 1977).
11 Seidman, L.: "A Cash-Equivalent Option for Supplementary Insurance Under Major-Risk National Health Insurance," *Policy Analysis*, (forthcoming).
12 Seidman, L.: "Supplementary Health Insurance and the Cost-Consciousness Strategy," Economics Department Discussion Paper, (April 1977).

26

CONTEMPORARY HEALTH POLICY
Dealing with the Cost of Care

Robert B. Helms

Summary

Justifications for National Health Insurance (NHI) have undergone a gradual but noticeable change in recent years. In the early 1970s the most common arguments for NHI were based on the need for improving access to medical care among people who did not have adequate insurance coverage or who could not otherwise afford adequate care. Since that time an argument has evolved that NHI is needed to control rapidly expanding costs for medical care.

The medical sector has not been spared the effects of the relatively high rates of inflation this country has experienced since 1968. But most indexes of medical prices have increased at a faster rate than indexes for the economy as a whole. These recent price increases have strengthened the political arguments in support of NHI and caused many to question traditional explanations of economic behavior in medical markets. It is not an exaggeration to say that in the popular view medical markets are somehow considered a special case among economic markets. Competitive forces and economizing decisions by consumers have seemed inadequate to the task of controlling medical costs. When medical markets are viewed in this way, it is not difficult to understand why a system of government finance under NHI is seen as an easy way to control an otherwise uncontrollable market.

But is this popular perception correct? It should be obvious that a clear understanding of how medical markets work is essential if we are to develop a national health policy that provides the kind of health care we want at reasonable cost. This paper looks at what we know about economic behavior in medical markets in an attempt to identify ways in which they differ from other markets. Specifically, the discussion deals

From Robert B. Helms, "Contemporary Health Policy: Dealing with the Cost of Care," pp. 327-353 in William Felkner (ed.) *Contemporary Economic Problems.* Copyright 1978 by the American Enterprise Institute for Public Policy Research.

*with three broad aspects of medical markets that economists have iden-
tified to explain perverse economic behavior in those markets. These
are the role of tax subsidies for the purchase of medical insurance, lack
of consumer control of demand, and lack of market competition.*

*A central conclusion of this paper is that there is no inherent dif-
ference in medical markets that cannot be explained by standard economic analysis. The perverse effects of rapidly increasing expenditures
and prices are seen as consequences of rational behavior on the part of
consumers and providers of medical care in response to the distorting
effects of government subsidies. These subsidies (both tax subsidies
for the purchase of medical insurance and direct, government payments
through Medicare and Medicaid) have promoted a system in which consumers and physicians make decisions about the use of medical facilities and services with very little consideration of the costs of these decisions. It is argued in this paper that this situation of minimal cost-
sharing at time of treatment has pervasive effects on the performance
and structure of medical markets. It is also argued that our public policies to subsidize medical care are largely responsible for the development of other problems in medical markets, such as physicians' influence over consumers' medical decisions and the apparent lack of
competition in some medical markets. In other words, there are logical
economic explanations for what many perceive to be a "market failure"
in medicine.*

*The policy implication of this analysis is that the predominant
argument now being given for national health insurance is based on a
fundamental misunderstanding of how medical markets function—
why they have developed in the way they have and how they could be
expected to perform either under more extensive regulation or, alternatively, under a policy designed to increase consumer cost-sharing. If
we are interested in formulating a national health policy that avoids the
detrimental effect of regulation experienced in other industries, while
maintaining such strong features of our medical system as high quality,
rapid innovation, and freedom of individual choice, we should not so
readily abandon the principles of a market economy.*

Introduction

Given the public concern about the rising cost of medical care, it is not
surprising that health policy is now considered a principal policy issue.
President Carter ran on a platform promising the passage of national
health insurance and has stated that an administration bill will be in-

Table 1

PRIVATE AND PUBLIC HEALTH EXPENDITURES, 1929–1976

(billions of dollars)

Fiscal Year	Total Expenditures	Percent of GNP	Out-of-Pocket Private Expenditures			Public Expenditures		
			Total	Percent of total	Average annual percent change[c]	Total	Percent of total	Average annual percent change[c]
1929	3.6	3.5	3.1	86.7	—	0.5	13.3	—
1935	2.8	4.1	2.3	80.9	−4.9	0.5	19.1	2.2
1940	3.9	4.1	3.1	79.9	6.1	0.8	20.1	7.6
1950	12.0	4.5	9.0	74.5	11.2	3.1	25.5	14.6
1955	17.3	4.5	12.9	74.5	7.6	4.4	25.5	7.6
1960	25.9	5.2	19.5	75.3	8.6	6.4	24.7	7.7
1965	38.9	5.9	29.4	75.5	8.6	9.5	24.5	8.3
1970	69.2	7.2	43.8	63.3	8.3	25.4	36.7	21.6
1975[a]	122.2	8.4	71.4	58.4	10.2	50.9	41.6	14.9
1976[b]	139.3	8.6	80.5	57.8	12.8	58.8	42.2	15.6

[a] Revised estimates.

[b] Preliminary estimates.

[c] Average annual percent change in expenditures during period from previous entry.

Source: Robert M. Gibson and Marjorie S. Mueller, "National Health Expenditures, Fiscal Year 1976," *Social Security Bulletin*, vol. 40, no. 4 (April 1977), Table 1, p. 4; U.S. Department of Health, Education, and Welfare, *Health, United States, 1976–1977* (Washington, D.C., 1977), Table 140, p. 345.

troduced in 1978.[1] There also seems to be substantial congressional and popular support for some kind of national program to provide more extensive health coverage and to control costs. However, given what is currently known about the working of medical markets and the anticipated costs of more extensive medical coverage, a government program to control the rapid rise in medical costs is popularly perceived to be a prior condition for passage of national health insurance.

Thus policy makers are faced with the dilemma of wanting to pass politically popular programs to extend subsidies for medical care but not wanting to interfere with a responsible budgetary policy. Table 1 presents some summary data illustrating the relative growth in public

[1] Executive Office of the President, *The United States Budget in Brief, Fiscal Year 1978* (Washington, D.C., 1978), p. 53.

and private health expenditures. When Congress is faced with containing these increasing public expenditures, it has two broad choices: it can reduce the coverage provided by the policy or it can attempt to persuade (or require) the providers of that service to supply the given quantity and quality at controlled prices. The policies that might be adopted to carry out either of these choices involve important questions of "efficiency," a term which refers to the general concept of using scarce resources in such a way that the benefits of health services are kept in line with the benefits of alternative uses of those resources, such as for education, housing, or food.

This essay will look at the economics of this fundamental public policy choice now being debated by Congress, the medical profession, and the general public. What are the causes of medical cost increases and what are the likely consequences of increasing our reliance on planning and regulation as opposed to a greater reliance on market incentives?

This country is already well on the way to establishing an extensive system of economic regulation in health. What we are witnessing is a classic case of the political process overlooking the fundamental economics of the marketplace and ignoring the long-term consequences of an expedient policy. As we have seen with other cases of economic regulation such as natural gas, airlines, railroads, and trucking, the potential economic loss from such a regulatory approach is not insignificant.[2] Contemporary health policy, it is argued here, should not so readily abandon the principles of a market economy.

Regulation versus the Market: A Choice of Policies

The future of health policy is being debated in an atmosphere of increasing concern about government expenditures, deficits, and inflation, and growing skepticism about the efficacy of government regulation. While we are already in the process of establishing a system of health regulation with emphasis on planning, certification of additional capacity, and revenue controls, the ongoing debate about cost control and national health insurance still leaves room for some basic choices about the part market principles should play in health policy.

A theme often heard in the debate about medical care costs is that medical markets "do not work" and therefore that the government must control costs. Several important interim questions should be

[2] Roger Noll, "The Consequences of Public Utility Regulation of Hospitals," in *Controls on Health Care* (Washington, D.C.: Institute of Medicine, National Academy of Sciences, 1975), pp. 25–48.

asked about medical markets before a policy of government regulation is adopted by default: In what sense do medical markets perform differently from other markets? In what sense do they perform similarly? What forces can be identified that make people less cost-conscious in medical markets? This paper will discuss some of the economic forces at work in medical markets in an attempt to identify the causes of medical cost increases. The presumption is that if we can determine what is different about economic behavior in medicine, we can then propose policies that promote economic efficiency and individual freedom of choice while avoiding the costs of government regulation.

A premise of this paper is that the regulatory approach to controlling medical expenses is not likely to be successful in the long run. Controlling hospital capacity, some medical prices, or even the total revenue of hospitals may have some measurable success in reducing expenditures for medical care for a few years. But if we are to learn from predictions of economic theory and our experience with regulation in other industries, we can anticipate that a system of health regulation will be subject to strong political pressures that will dissipate the short-run effects of such regulation. The result will be a health care system that retains the inefficiency of the present one while protecting existing interests from competition and technological change. As has been shown with other regulatory programs, consumers (patients) will very likely to be worse off.[3] We do know from the history of regulation, however, that the elimination, or even reform, of an established regulatory system is extremely difficult to achieve. For that reason alone we should be extremely careful about abandoning market principles in favor of a regulatory approach to health care.

Do Medical Markets Work?

A widely held perception about medical markets is that they are so inherently different from other markets that they cannot be relied on to maximize consumer well-being in the absence of direct government interference. This perception is continually reenforced by statements of both economists and noneconomists that the laws of supply and de-

---

[3] Research into the effects of various types of health regulation is in an elementary stage. For some discussion of the probable effects, see Noll, "The Consequences of Public Utility Regulation of Hospitals"; Penny H. Feldman and Richard J. Zeckhauser, "Some Sober Thoughts on Health Care Regulation," in *Regulating Business: The Search for an Optimum* (San Francisco: Institute for Contemporary Studies, 1978), pp. 93–120; David Salkever and Thomas Bice, "The Impact of Certificate-of-Need Controls on Hospital Investment," *Milbank Memorial Fund Quarterly: Health and Society*, vol. 54, no. 2 (Spring 1976), pp. 185–214.

mand do not apply to medical markets.[4] Medical markets—like markets for everything from automobiles to zucchini—have certain distinctive characteristics. They are different in some respects from other markets. But this does not mean that the concepts of supply and demand are not useful tools of analysis. Attacks on these concepts are based on misconceptions about the use of abstract models and the role of prices as an equilibrating mechanism.

The economist's attention to price (and economic incentives) may seem inconsistent with casual observations about the apparent unimportance of prices to participants in medical markets. Prices refer to the cost of foregone alternatives, that is, what consumers must give up in other consumptive opportunities and what resources are required to produce that good or service. For example, the price of an operation may represent both the sacrifice of a vacation trip to a consumer and the necessary inducement to physicians and hospitals to "produce" the operation. Other factors that may affect the consumer's choices (such as taste, income, and prices of other goods), or the producer's willingness to supply what the consumer wants (such as the costs of inputs and technological knowledge), can be considered in an orderly fashion using the concepts of supply and demand. Even when certain market conditions relating to structure and the availability of information are not strictly met, the supply and demand model can be useful because, even as an abstract model, it allows for an analysis of a multitude of forces affecting the behavior of individuals in markets.

Before discussing those aspects of medical markets that may differ from other markets, consider for a moment the many changes in medical markets that are obviously consistent with the standard analysis. In an industry sometimes described as the third largest in the country (behind agriculture and construction), there are obviously many examples of medical markets responding to outside forces (such as changes in income or shifting population patterns), which are predictable from standard economic theory. Economists have provided some empirical backup for a few examples.

First, there is substantial evidence that physician supply is affected by population shifts.[5] For example, in such areas as the Sun Belt where

---

[4] "Health care is not and should not be considered a commodity, perceived to be the same kind as other goods and services. Health care is not governed by marketplace economics. People consider health services to be qualitatively different from other goods and services." Statement by Philip Caper, M.D., in W. S. Moore, ed., *Regulatory Reform: Highlights of a Conference on Government Regulation* (Washington, D.C.: American Enterprise Institute, 1976), p. 26.

[5] For example, see Lee Benham, Alex Maurizi, and Melvin Reder, "Migration, Location, and Remuneration of Medical Personnel: Physicians and Dentists," *Review of Economics and Statistics*, vol. 50, no. 3 (August 1968), pp. 332–347; and Henry B.

there has been a net migration of the population, physicians, dentists, nurses, and others serving medical markets are responding to the demand by moving there.

There is also evidence that the traditional fee-for-service medical profession responds to increased competition from an alternative form of delivery, just as would be predicted by the standard economic theory of the firm.[6] Goldberg and Greenberg have found that in response to the success of Kaiser Permanente (a health maintenance organization—HMO) in northern California, Blue Cross broadened its hospital and physician benefit packages (including maternity coverage) and established competing HMOs. Private physicians have also responded to the success of Kaiser by forming foundations for medical care (FMCS), which provide consumers with another form of prepaid coverage.[7]

Evidence also exists that physicians, even when acting as agents for their patients rather than for their own direct pecuniary gain, prescribe relatively more drugs in certain therapeutic markets where prices have declined.[8]

While few economists would dispute that there are many aspects of medical markets that work, these examples serve to remind us that, contrary to popular belief, strong economic forces do operate in medical markets. If the market seems to produce perverse effects, such as excessive price increases or a misallocation of certain resources, then what is required is not an abandonment of economic reasoning but a deeper

---

Steele and Gaston V. Rimlinger, "Income Opportunities and Physician Location in the United States," *Western Economic Journal*, vol. 3 (Spring 1965), p. 191.

[6] See Lawrence C. Goldberg and Warren Greenberg, *The Health Maintenance Organization and Its Effects of Competition* (Washington, D.C.: Federal Trade Commission, July 1977). Health maintenance organizations (HMOs) provide medical care in exchange for a fixed annual capitation payment. In contrast to the more traditional fee-for-service providers, HMOs bear the risk of providing complete medical care for their enrolled population. Foundations for medical care (FMCS) refer to a wide variety of organizations that in general provide a form of prepaid coverage to patients but retain the fee-for-service aspect of payment to private physicians. Financial discipline is imposed through a system of peer review.

[7] Goldberg and Greenberg, *The Health Maintenance Organization*, pp. 72–84. They have also found that similar but less dramatic competitive effects have been found in other areas of the country where HMOs have become established. See also Jon B. Christianson, *Do HMOs Stimulate Beneficial Competition?* (Excelsior, Minn.: InterStudy, 1978).

[8] See Douglas L. Cocks, "Product Innovation and the Dynamic Elements of Competition in the Ethical Pharmaceutical Industry," in Robert Helms, ed., *Drug Development and Marketing* (Washington, D.C.: American Enterprise Institute, 1975), pp. 225–254, and the discussion by Yale Brozen et al., pp. 281, 289–290. Similar evidence for the United Kingdom is presented by W. Duncan Reekie in *Pricing New Pharmaceutical Products* (London: Croom Helm, 1977) and, for the United States, in "Price and Quality Competition in the United States Drug Industry," *Journal of Industrial Economics*, vol. 26, no. 3 (March 1978), pp. 223–237.

look at what may be causing the perverse market behavior. Discussed below are three broad arguments considered by economists as more serious explanations of why medical markets are "different."[9]

Tax Subsidies and Insurance. The principal reason for what appears to be different modes of economic behavior by individuals in medical markets is the effect of tax subsidies for the purchase of health insurance. Tax exemptions for medical insurance have prompted the growth of insurance coverage, which in turn has had the effect of removing some financial constraints on decisions made by both medical providers and patients.[10] While these general effects are quite well known to economists and health policy analysts, the more pervasive effects on the behavior of individuals and the structure of the medical industry are generally unappreciated.

First, consider the role of tax exemptions in promoting the growth of medical insurance coverage. In an unsubsidized market, some rational consumers would choose to purchase insurance to protect themselves from the risk of large medical payments. But tax exemptions induce the purchase of more complete insurance than consumers would otherwise buy—that is, more complete in terms of the medical problems covered and the financial cost of treatment. These effects occur not only because individuals can deduct part of their expenditure for medical insurance from taxable income, but because the tax system promotes the purchase of medical insurance through employment-related

---

[9] For other discussions of how medical markets differ, see Mark V. Pauly, "Is Medical Care Different?" in Warren Greenberg, ed., *Competition in the Health Care Sector: Past, Present, and Future* (Washington, D.C.: Bureau of Economics, Federal Trade Commission, March 1978), pp. 19–48; Cotton M. Lindsay and Keith B. Leffler, "The Market for Medical Care," in Cotton M. Lindsay, ed., *New Directions in Public Health Care* (San Francisco: Institute for Contemporary Studies, 1976), pp. 66–82. It is sometimes argued that because medicine involves questions of life and death, it is in no sense a "market" with emphasis on price and therefore is not subject to the laws of supply and demand. But economic theory is an abstract model that can be applied as a tool of analysis to any situation where consumers and producers make choices and where scarce resources are used. The concept of elasticity of demand is capable of incorporating those few medical decisions (such as emergencies) where price is given little apparent consideration.

[10] The literature on health finance and insurance is now rather extensive. For a recent popular treatment, see Martin S. Feldstein, "The High Cost of Hospitals—and What To Do About It," *Public Interest* (Summer 1977), pp. 40–54; for a more technical treatment, see Martin S. Feldstein, "The Welfare Loss of Excess Health Insurance," *Journal of Political Economy*, vol. 81 (March/April 1973), pp. 252–280. See also Joseph P. Newhouse, Charles E. Phelps, and William B. Schwartz, "Policy Options and the Impact of National Health Insurance," *New England Journal of Medicine*, vol. 290 (June 13, 1974), pp. 1345–1359; Mark V. Pauly, "Health Insurance and Hospital Behavior," in Lindsay, ed., *New Directions in Public Health Care*, pp. 103–129.

group policies. Since the employer's cost of providing medical insurance is not considered part of the employee's taxable income, employees have an incentive to bargain for more insurance coverage rather than for more wages which can be taxed. Feldstein has calculated that the employee can gain about 50 percent more in benefits from nontaxable income spent for medical insurance than he can from an increase in wages. That is, instead of a $1.00 increase in wages which are subject to taxes, he can obtain $1.50 worth of medical insurance.[11] And the employer has an incentive to provide more insurance coverage rather than to increase wages because his expenditures for social security and state taxes would be higher if he increased wages. Enthoven has estimated the federal tax subsidy for fiscal year 1978 to be $10.1 billion, which consists of $5.84 billion for the exclusion of employee contributions to insurance premiums, $2.87 billion for medical expense deductions, and $1.43 billion from foregone social security taxes.[12]

To summarize developments since World War II: (1) there has been a great increase in the percentage of the population having some medical insurance; (2) the coverage has become more complete both in terms of medical events insured and in the proportion of medical costs covered—that is, there has been more "first dollar" or "shallow" coverage; and (3) the proportion of coverage provided through employment-based group policies has increased. Recent government surveys show that in 1974, 81.3 percent of the population had some hospital insurance and 63.3 percent of the population had some group coverage.[13] As would be expected from an income effect and from a subsidy system related to income, the amount of insurance coverage

---

[11] Feldstein, "The High Cost of Hospitals," p. 45.

[12] Alain C. Enthoven, "Consumer Choice Health Plan (CCHP): An Approach to National Health Insurance (NHI) Based on Regulated Competition in the Private Sector," unpublished memorandum to Joseph A. Califano, secretary of health, education, and welfare, dated September 22, 1977, p. 3 and Appendix 21, pp. 3–4. It is interesting to note that Mitchell and Vogel estimated the tax subsidy to be $2.5 billion for 1970, though they apparently did not allow for social security taxes as Enthoven has. Still this illustrates how inflation has pushed people into higher tax brackets, causing a rapid increase in tax subsidies to health insurance. See Bridger M. Mitchell and Robert J. Vogel, *Health and Taxes: An Assessment of the Medical Deduction* (Santa Monica: Rand Corporation, August 1973), Table 5, p. 16.

[13] Charles S. Wilder, *Hospital and Surgical Insurance Coverage, United States— 1974* (Washington, D.C.: National Center for Health Statistics, August 1977), p. 5, Table A and Table 16. It should be noted that there are difficult problems of double counting when individuals are covered by more than one source of insurance or government program. Using a different procedure to count that part of the population covered under Medicare, Medicaid, and other government programs (VA and military hospitals), Sudovar and Sullivan estimate that 94.2 percent of the population now has some protection for health expenses. See Stephen G. Sudovar, Jr., and Kathleen Sullivan, *National Health Insurance Issues: The Unprotected Population* (Nutley, N.J.: Roche Laboratories, 1977), p. 3.

increased with the level of income.[14] For persons under the age of sixty-five with private insurance, only 37.2 percent of those with incomes less than $3,000 were covered while 91.8 percent of those with incomes more than $15,000 were covered.[15] Given the preponderance of work-related group policies, it is not surprising that the under-sixty-five age group also shows 85.3 percent coverage for those currently employed but only 64.0 percent coverage for those currently unemployed.[16]

Data illustrating the growth of shallow coverage are less precise because of the diversity in insurance policies. The Health Insurance Institute does show, however, that the percentage of insurance policies covering 80 percent or more of medical expenses has been above 85 percent since 1966 and above 90 percent since 1970.[17] Perhaps the best evidence of the growth of shallow coverage is found in Martin Feldstein's study of what has happened to out-of-pocket medical expenditures as hospital coverage has been extended.

> In 1950, when average cost per patient-day was a little less than $16, private insurance and government programs paid 49 percent of hospital bills. This meant that, on the average, the net cost to a patient of a day of care was just under $8. By 1975, average cost per patient-day had jumped to about $152—but private and public insurance were paying 88 percent of the hospital bill, leaving a net cost to the patient of only $18. Thus, although the cost of providing a day of hospital care had increased more than ninefold (from $16 to $152), the net cost to patients had only just about doubled (from $8 to $18). Moreover, the general increase in the prices of all goods and services meant that $18 in 1975 could only buy as much as $8 in 1950! So in real terms, the net cost to the patient at the time of illness has not changed at all during the past 25 years.[18]

While insurance companies pay about 27 percent of total expenditures for personal health care, the other large third-party payer (about 40

---

[14] For a discussion of this effect and evidence that the tax subsidy is strongly related to income, see Mitchell and Vogel, *Health and Taxes*, pp. 4–13.

[15] Wilder, *Insurance Coverage*, Table D, p. 6.

[16] Ibid., Table 9, p. 20. For those not in the labor force, 70.1 percent had hospital coverage in 1974.

[17] *Source Book of Health Insurance Data 1976–77* (New York: Health Insurance Institute, 1977), p. 38. See also the discussion of the completeness of coverage by Frech and Ginsburg, "Competition among Health Insurers," in Greenberg, ed., *Competition in the Health Care Sector*, pp. 216–219. They show some evidence that coverage by Blue Cross and Blue Shield is more complete than that provided by non-Blue companies.

[18] Feldstein, "The High Cost of Hospitals," pp. 41–42.

percent) is the government.[19] Medicare and Medicaid were passed in 1965 to provide coverage for the aged and poor. In 1975 Medicare covered approximately 24.2 million people and disbursed $15.6 billion. Medicaid provided $12.7 billion in fiscal year 1975 to an estimated 22.9 million people.[20] The latest federal budget includes $29.4 billion for Medicare and $12.1 billion for Medicaid.[21] Total federal expenditures for hospital and medical services have been growing at an average annual rate of roughly 16 percent since 1968 and roughly 18 percent since 1973.[22]

Table 2 shows some trends in medical prices and out-of-pocket private expenditures for three broad segments of medical markets. As can be seen in the table, prices have increased at a faster rate in those segments of medical markets (hospital and physicians' services) where insurance coverage has become more extensive than they have in less insured markets (other services). An explanation is that tax exemptions and government programs that have promoted the growth of third-party payments for medical care have removed most financial considerations from decisions about the use of medical facilities and services. This has led to a system that increases expenditures for medical care, increases both medical and insurance prices, and fosters a demand for alternative ways of controlling usage that do not rely on personal consumer choice. The individual behaves differently because the insurance coverage has changed what he perceives as the marginal cost of treatment. When a person becomes ill and seeks care, the tendency is to "get what's coming to me," that is, to seek the highest quality care, and larger quantities of care, up to the point where the marginal benefits are thought to be equal to the individual's marginal cost (including his time). Shallow insurance coverage, which lowers the individual's marginal cost, increases the amount of care demanded even though the additional cost may be much greater than its value to the individual. Thus, the individual not only seeks more care but he also has less incentive to be cost-conscious about the care sought.[23] The resulting higher prices for medical care in turn increase the demand for insurance because of the increase in the individual's financial risk.[24]

---

[19] Sudovar and Sullivan, *National Health Insurance Issues*, p. 4.

[20] *Source Book of Health Insurance Data 1976–77*, pp. 41–42.

[21] *United States Budget in Brief, Fiscal Year 1978*, p. 54.

[22] Calculated from the Office of Management and Budget's *Special Analyses of the Budget for Fiscal Years 1970–79*.

[23] Clark C. Havighurst and James F. Blumstein, "Coping with Quality/Cost Trade-Offs in Medical Care: The Role of PSROs," *Northwestern University Law Review*, vol. 70, no. 1 (March/April 1975), pp. 15–20.

[24] Feldstein, "The High Cost of Hospitals," p. 44.

Table 2

TRENDS IN MEDICAL COST-SHARING AND PRICES, 1955–1976

	Fiscal Year					
	1955	1960	1965	1970	1975	1976
Hospital Care						
Percent private direct payments[a]	23.6	18.6	18.5	12.3	9.8	8.9
Hospital service charges[c]						
Semiprivate room charges	6.9	6.3	5.8	13.9	10.2	13.8
Operating room charges	—	—	—	11.4	10.9	14.8
X-ray services	—	—	—	5.1	7.2	11.8
Physicians' Services						
Percent private direct payments[a]	71.2	66.0	63.2	44.9	39.0	38.7
Physician fees[c]						
Office visits	3.6	3.0	2.9	7.0	7.2	11.4
Tonsillectomy and adenoidectomy	2.6	3.1	2.5	5.2	6.9	9.7
All Other Services[b]						
Percent private direct payments	85.7	84.5	82.3	71.7	63.2	62.0
Selected indexes[c]						
Dentist fees	2.7	2.4	2.4	5.3	6.3	6.4
Eyeglasses	1.0	2.0	1.7	4.1	5.7	6.2
Drugs	1.4	2.0	0.8	0.7	2.8	6.1
Consumer Price Index[c]	2.2	2.0	1.3	4.2	6.8	5.3

[a] In addition to private direct payments, other sources of health care payments are private insurance benefits, private other, and public expenditures.

[b] All other services consist of dentist services, other professional services, drugs and drug sundries, eyeglasses and appliances, nursing-home care, and other health services.

[c] Figures refer to the average annual percent change in each index during the previous five years, except for 1976 where the period is 1975–1976.

Source: Robert M. Gibson and Marjorie S. Mueller, "National Health Expenditures, Fiscal Year 1976," *Social Security Bulletin*, vol. 40, no. 4 (April 1977), Table 7, pp. 19–20; U.S. Department of Health, Education, and Welfare, *Health, United States, 1976–1977* (Washington, D.C., 1977), Table 163, p. 377.

A system dominated by third-party payers also weakens the physician's incentive to resist the patient's demand for more extensive care. The physician does not bear the additional cost of the decision to provide more extensive care and may receive both financial and professional benefit from prescribing additional and higher quality care. In addition to the increased monetary reimbursement, additional tests or a longer hospital stay may increase the probability that a correct diagnosis has been made and thus lower the physician's risk of a malpractice suit.[25] Some of the effects of more complete insurance are translated into physician and hospital demand for more elaborate and expensive equipment whose use increases the cost of care.[26] The Congressional Budget Office estimates that almost half the 14.7 percent increase in the 1976 hospital cost per patient-day was attributable to increased services rather than to higher wages and prices paid by hospitals.[27]

Medical market behavior is also affected by a tax policy that induces people to obtain insurance coverage through employment-related group policies. There do seem to be some economies of scale in the purchase of group policies when compared with individually purchased policies.[28] But the preponderance of purchases of group policies has the effect of adversely selecting out those who do not work because they are less healthy, thus raising the price of individually purchased policies. The higher cost of individual policies and the tax subsidies on group policies lessen the chance for individuals to express their own preferences about the amount and kind of insurance they desire, a situation quite different from other insurance markets such as automobile, life, and fire insurance.[29] The effective demand on the part of those

---

[25] Michael D. Intriligator and Barbar H. Kehrer, "An Economic Model of Medical Malpractice," in Simon Rottenberg, ed., *The Economics of Medical Malpractice* (Washington, D.C.: American Enterprise Institute, 1978), pp. 89–98.

[26] See Martin Feldstein and Amy Taylor, *The Rapid Rise of Hospital Costs* (Washington, D.C.: Council on Wage and Price Stability, January 1977), pp. 20–28. For evidence that the level of insurance increases the rate of product innovation, which will in turn cause a higher rate of increase in expenditures, see Joseph P. Newhouse, "The Structure of Health Insurance and the Erosion of Competition in the Medical Marketplace," in Greenberg, ed., *Competition in the Health Care Sector*, pp. 270–287.

[27] Congressional Budget Office, *Expenditures for Health Care: Federal Programs and Their Effects* (Washington, D.C., 1977), p. 29.

[28] Mitchell and Vogel report that loading costs (premiums minus benefits) for group policies of even moderate-sized firms are only 8 to 10 percent while individual policies have loading costs of 50 to 100 percent. Mitchell and Vogel, *Health and Taxes*, p. 14.

[29] H. E. Frech III and Paul B. Ginsburg, *Public Insurance in Private Medical Markets: Some Problems with National Health Insurance* (Washington, D.C.: American Enterprise Institute, 1978).

who would prefer to have policies with higher deductibles and copayments (and lower premiums) is reduced. With less diversity in the type of policies offered, there is less pressure on the providers of care to be concerned about the cost-effectiveness of their care.

Another consequence of tying health insurance to employment is that some people lose their coverage when they become unemployed. While it is quite common for group policies to continue to cover an individual and his family for a limited period after the termination of employment, unless the unemployed worker takes definite action to purchase an individual policy, he and his family will be uncovered for some period of time. With the uncertainty of finding a new job and the financial strain of being unemployed, it is not difficult to understand why surveys show 34.3 percent of the unemployed do not have hospital insurance coverage.[30] The greater the number of uninsured people, the larger will be the financial strain placed on personal savings, relatives, Medicaid, or charitable institutions that attempt to pay for uninsured and unpaid medical care.

Several empirical studies show that a change in the consumer's copayment does affect the consumer's demand for care. Rosett and Huang use a 1960 Bureau of Labor Statistics survey of consumer expenditures to estimate a model that tests the effects of several variables on household medical expenditures. In a numerical illustration based on their findings, they show that for a family with an income of $7,000, 80 percent of all standard households would spend less than $834 per year when the coinsurance rate is 20 percent but that 80 percent of the households would spend less than $709 when the coinsurance rate is 30 percent. If the coinsurance rate were 40 percent, the figure would decline to $597. Furthermore, they estimate empirically that when the coinsurance rate is 20 percent, the $834 for medical expenses includes an additional amount of care that the family values at $325 but that costs an additional $634 to produce.[31]

Feldstein has estimated the effects of increasing the coinsurance rate from 33 percent to 50 and 67 percent. After allowing for the costs imposed by bearing increased risk, he finds that there would be a net gain to society in excess of $4 billion per year (based on 1969 private

---

[30] Wilder, *Insurance Coverage*, Table 9, p. 20. This compares with 12.7 percent not insured among the currently employed. The percentage of those not having surgical insurance was 14.5 percent for the currently employed and 36.0 percent for the currently unemployed.

[31] Richard N. Rosett and Lien-fu Huang, "The Effect of Health Insurance on the Demand for Medical Care," *Journal of Political Economy*, vol. 81, no. 2, part 1 (March/April 1973), pp. 296–297.

hospital expenditures of $12.6 billion) when reasonable assumptions are made about supply and demand elasticities.[32]

In a 1973 study of the effects of coinsurance, Phelps and Newhouse obtain evidence using insurance company data that when coinsurance rates are reduced from 25 percent to zero, total medical expenditures increase by 12 percent (an arc elasticity of 0.043). But when they measure separate responses to coinsurance in several different medical markets (hospital services, physician office visits, ambulatory ancillary services, physician house calls, and prescription drugs) and aggregate these (using expenditure weights), they find an arc elasticity of 0.10, which implies a 28 percent increase in expenditures from a decrease in coinsurance rates from 25 percent to zero. They conclude from these results that

> some persons feel coinsurance is irrelevant to decisions about consumption of medical services, because physicians make all the relevant choices. The results presented here are strong evidence against that hypothesis. Consistently, across a number of studies based upon diverse data, coinsurance has been found to exert an impact on utilization of various services.[33]

In a recent study of the effects of imposing a $1.00 per visit charge (strictly a deductible rather than a percentage copayment) on physician office visits among welfare patients in California, Helms, Newhouse, and Phelps found the charge reduced office visits by 8 percent. While the $1.00 charge reduced the program's cost for physician service by $1.04 per person per quarter, the experiment was not judged a success because it induced the patients who were eligible for hospital coverage to increase their hospital care by 17 percent. The switch to the more expensive hospital services cost the program an additional $2.64 per person per quarter.[34] While the authors conclude that the imposition of out-of-pocket payments for ambulatory care may not be effective in controlling costs in a welfare population, it should be noted that the experiment did not consider consumer behavior when cost-sharing was applied to both hospital and physician care.

---

[32] Feldstein, "The Welfare Loss of Excess Health Insurance," pp. 251–280, especially p. 277.

[33] Charles E. Phelps and Joseph P. Newhouse, "Coinsurance, the Price of Time, and the Demand for Medical Services," *Review of Economics and Statistics*, vol. 56, no. 3 (August 1974), pp. 337–341.

[34] Jay Helms, Joseph P. Newhouse, and Charles E. Phelps, "Copayments and Demand for Medical Care: The California Medicaid Experience," *Bell Journal of Economics*, vol. 9, no. 1 (Spring 1978), pp. 200–201.

In summary, it appears that there is nothing inherently different about the behavior of medical markets that cannot be explained by the effects of tax subsidies and direct government subsidies for care. Individuals are responding in predictable ways both to the tax subsidies that increase insurance coverage and to the direct governmental subsidy through Medicare and Medicaid. It is not a matter of "market failure" resulting from some fundamental difference in the pursuit of health, but only of efficient responses on the part of individuals to deliberate government policy to subsidize health. It is obvious that the intent of our public policies was to increase access to medical care among the aged and the poor and to reduce the financial burden of medical expenditures among all taxpayers. It is not so obvious that we intended these subsidizing policies to have such perverse and cost-increasing effects on individual incentives. But the fact remains that if we now want to revise public policies to control health cost increases in a way that maintains efficiency in medical markets, we must first take into consideration the effects of tax subsidies.

Even if we had fewer tax subsidies for the purchase of health insurance so that individuals would choose more cost-effective policies, there are other popular arguments about why medical markets will not work. The following two sections consider two of these arguments.

Lack of Consumer Control of Demand. If we assume for the moment that we can ignore the effect of overinsurance caused by tax subsidies, there are two varieties of criticisms of medical markets that are based on demand considerations: the apparent unresponsiveness to price of demand for medical services and physicians' influence over patients' demand for care.

Inelasticity of demand. The unresponsiveness (inelasticity) of medical demand refers to those situations where substitutes are not readily available or there is little time to make alternative arrangements. Consumers, under such circumstances, apparently give relatively little consideration to price. This is often illustrated by the case of the unconscious accident victim about to undergo emergency surgery.

If unresponsiveness to price is common across medical markets, the policy implications are that changes in supply will have little effect on the amount of medical services demanded but large effects on the revenue (income) of those being paid to deliver the services. It also follows that medical markets will be relatively immune from ordinary price competition because new entrants will have little chance to gain a larger share of the market by offering the consumer a lower price.

While there may be individual markets relatively unresponsive to price, it is highly simplistic to take this view of medical markets in general.[35] It would be expected from standard demand analysis that the elasticity of demand would vary among individual medical markets depending on consumer tastes, the availability of substitutes, and consumer knowledge about these alternatives. While emergency treatment may be an example of a market with a relatively inelastic demand, it is not characteristic of most medical situations where consumers have considerable time to decide among several available choices. These more ordinary medical choices involve such things as the choice of a family physician, whether or not to have minor surgery or a certain symptom investigated, or even an advance decision about which hospital one would prefer for emergency care should the need arise. Under such situations of deliberate choice, not only price but other aspects of the service, such as travel and waiting time, the quality of the care, and the "bedside manner" of the physician, all become more important.

In addition, there are numerous ways in which consumers may make substitutions in medical markets. For example, a consumer may follow a pharmacist's advice about an over-the-counter drug for a rash rather than consult a dermatologist, or a consumer may choose between living with a certain amount of pain as opposed to having a heart bypass operation. The greater the conceivable choices, the more elastic the demand.

Consumers can also make advance decisions to protect themselves from the risk of medical events requiring treatment when they can predict they would not want to be concerned at time of treatment with price or cost (that is, treatment having an inelastic demand). The market for insurance is a response to such situations. Even if there were no tax subsidies inducing people to purchase insurance, consumers could be expected to insure against the uncertainty of large medical expenditures in the event of an accident or a catastrophic disease.[36] It is not obvious, however, that consumers will purchase enough accident or catastrophic (deep) insurance to cover the total cost to society of such treatment if some individuals anticipate they will be taken care of once their own resources are depleted.

While obtaining empirical estimates of demand elasticities is a

---

[35] R. D. Fraser, *A Research Agenda in Health Care Economics* (Toronto: Ontario Economic Council, 1975), chapter 4, p. 2. See also Mark V. Pauly, "Is Medical Care Different?" pp. 20–27.

[36] The more inelastic the patient's demand for a particular medical service, the greater is the insurance company's role in controlling the cost of that service. See below for a discussion of limitations on insurance companies' ability to control costs.

complex task,[37] there is some evidence against the popular perception that prices for medical care are unimportant to patients. In the previously mentioned study, Rosett and Huang found consumers were more responsive to price changes for hospital and physicians' services when the coinsurance rate was increased. Specifically, they found the price elasticity of demand to be -0.35 when the coinsurance rate was 20 percent but -1.5 when consumers had to pay 80 percent of their bill.[38] Feldstein has found the elasticity of demand for hospital services to be -1.12.[39]

The previously mentioned study of the effects of coinsurance and time on medical demand by Phelps and Newhouse also contains findings of different elasticities among different kinds of medical markets. By converting a number of previous elasticity measures, they estimate elasticities which imply that for a decrease (increase) in the coinsurance rate from 25 percent to zero, the following approximate percentage increases (decreases) in expenditures could be expected:

physician house calls	108 percent
dental services	38 percent
physician office visits	33 percent
hospital expenses	17 percent
ambulatory ancillary services	15 percent
prescription drugs	15 percent
hospital admissions	8 percent[40]

These estimates are consistent with the argument that if consumers

---

[37] In addition to having adequate data, the principal problems are those associated with separating the effects of changes in prices from all other supply and demand factors affecting real world medical markets. In particular, there is the problem of separating price effects from changes in incomes and coinsurance rates. For a discussion of these complexities, see Joseph P. Newhouse and Charles E. Phelps, *On Having Your Cake and Eating It Too: Econometric Problems in Estimating the Demand for Health Services* (Santa Monica: Rand Corporation, R-1149-NC, April 1974).

[38] Rosett and Huang, "The Effect of Health Insurance," p. 301. The minus sign indicates the negative relationship between an increase (decrease) in price and a decrease (increase) in quantity demanded. A higher absolute value (1.5) indicates a greater quantity response (15 percent) for a given change in price (10 percent) than a lower absolute value (0.35).

[39] As reported by Rosett and Huang, "The Effect of Health Insurance," p. 301. For additional evidence, see Joseph P. Newhouse and Charles E. Phelps, "New Estimates of Price and Income Elasticities of Medical Care Services," in Richard N. Rosett, ed., *The Role of Health Insurance in the Health Services Sector* (New York: National Bureau of Economic Research, 1976), pp. 261–313.

[40] Charles E. Phelps and Joseph P. Newhouse, *Coinsurance and the Demand for Medical Services* (Santa Monica, Calif.: Rand Corporation, October 1974), table 12, p. 44.

paid a larger proportion of their medical bills directly rather than having them paid through third parties, they could be expected to reduce expenditures for such things as home visits, office visits, and dental care relatively more than for hospital services where more serious medical problems are treated.

Physician control of demand. The second argument about the consumer's "peculiar" behavior in medical markets concerns physician control over the demand for care.[41] In the medical context, the physician is seen to have such extensive influence over the individual that he determines the demand and hence the level of his own income. This perception of medical markets gains strength from observations that consumers have little technical information about medical choices and so put great (some would say, too much) faith in the physician's opinion. Medical training, peer pressure, and concern about malpractice liability encourage physicians to prescribe more care and a higher style of care. The policy implications are that medical markets may be less competitive and therefore less resistant to increases in prices and total expenditures.[42]

This reasoning explains much of the popular perception that medical markets "don't work." It is argued here, however, that this behavior is largely a function of the method of paying physicians through third parties. To the extent that it can logically be separated from the third-party payment effect, the propriety of physician control of demand becomes a question of the medical correctness of information supplied by physicians to patients. To what extent do physicians induce patients to consume more medical goods and services than they would buy with full and accurate information? Given the diversity of professional opinion that exists for almost any medical problem and the difference in the ways individual patients respond to treatments, not even a system of peer review could be expected to have much effect on whatever amount of inappropriate demand may have been created. To state the problem this way is to illustrate what a hopeless morass it would be to distinguish between appropriate demand and actual use.[43]

---

[41] This is conceptually a different point from the inelasticity argument because in this case the physician's influence is to increase a demand curve of a given elasticity. For an extended treatment of this topic, see Frank A. Sloan and Roger Feldman, "Competition among Physicians," in Greenberg, ed., *Competition in the Health Care Sector*, pp. 57–131.

[42] For a recent government report arguing this point, see Zachary Dyckman, *A Study of Physicians' Fees* (Washington, D.C.: Council on Wage and Price Stability, March 1978).

[43] For an analysis of the government's Professional and Standards Review Organizations (PSRO) program designed to control cost and quality of medical care, see Havighurst and Blumstein, "Coping with Quality/Cost Trade-Offs," pp. 6–68.

While an empirical attempt to measure inappropriate demand is not likely to be successful, economic analysis can be used to predict that physician control of demand (in the absence of the third-party payment effect) is not likely to be different from the system in other markets where agents are paid by consumers for information.

First, consider a medical market where there is a well-defined product or procedure such as the treatment of a skin disease, a pap smear, a hysterectomy, a heart bypass operation, or even the removal of a known tumor. The extent to which the physician can increase demand for these services will be a function of the information consumers have about the probable effectiveness of each procedure, the cost of the procedure (both in terms of time and money), and the availability of alternative sources of supply. As Pauly has pointed out, the consumer can be expected to be more informed about those procedures that are repeatedly purchased, either by the individual or his friends and relatives.[44] Thus, to the extent that the physician's control of demand can be logically separated from the third-party payment effect, such control should not be a problem for the great majority of medical procedures in which repeat purchases by the same person are common. The problem of physician control of demand can then be largely confined to those procedures that are rarely purchased, such as emergency operations and procedures of a more experimental nature.

Even in these cases, however, there are several constraints on physician behavior that may mitigate against the temptation to abuse patient trust. The first is the physician's role in supplying medical information. Consumer purchases of goods or services that are difficult to evaluate are not restricted to medicine. If there is a real demand for information, in the absence of restrictions or prohibitive costs, institutions can be expected to evolve to supply it. Middlemen traditionally perform this service in most markets (real estate, insurance, stocks) but other examples include the Consumers' Union, Good Housekeeping seal, technical magazines, and computer consulting firms. It is quite likely that there would be more of these if physicians were not so efficient in supplying information to consumers. Personal communication between physician and patient is obviously quite important.

Note that such a view amounts to dropping the assumption of a well-defined medical product. This suggests that medical markets should be more broadly defined in terms of what consumers are demanding and physicians are supplying.[45] It can be argued that one of

44 Pauly, "Is Medical Care Different?" pp. 20–27.
45 As Armen Alchian used to say in economic theory classes at UCLA, some of the biggest disputes in economics are over what is on the horizontal axis (of a supply and demand diagram).

the largest components of medical "output" is the information provided to consumers. For example, from the consumer's point of view, information that a disease is not present will obviously be productive in reducing anxiety. Because the value of medical information depends largely on personal perceptions of its worth, it is nearly impossible to measure objectively. This has led to considerable debate about the extent to which physicians overtreat patients and thus distort the ordinary workings of the market. There is no reason to believe that the demand for medical information is any less elastic than the demand for other information or that physicians have unusual powers to increase consumers' demand for information.

In addition, as Lindsay and Leffler point out, if consumers learn that a particular physician has a bias toward too much service, they may discount the physician's advice. The possibility arises that more skeptical consumers may then purchase too little medical care compared with some standard of optimal care. Other factors constraining the physician in his relations with his patients are his concern for his professional reputation among his peers, the importance consumer trust plays in building and maintaining a practice, and the availability of prepaid forms of care such as HMOs where physicians have stronger incentives to prescribe a cost-effective amount and quality of care.[46] Thus, it is argued, there are reasons to doubt the seriousness of concern over physician control of demand.

Lack of Competition. Because all markets deviate in some respects from an abstract model of perfect competition, it is not surprising that medical markets have been accused of a lack of competition. From a policy perspective, the important point is that this so-called lack of competition in medical markets is used as a justification for regulation. It is therefore important to determine in what respect competition may be lacking and why. If competition is lacking, economic theory predicts that some monopoly returns will be earned, prices will be higher than under more competitive conditions, and fewer services will be provided to consumers than they desire.

The issue of the competitiveness of medical markets cannot be separated from the effects of tax policies and insurance because the existence of third-party payments increases the demand for care and also decreases the elasticity of demand.[47] The more complete the insurance coverage, the less the incentive to search for a lower-cost pro-

[46] Lindsay and Leffler, "The Market for Medical Care," pp. 67–68.

[47] Mark V. Pauly, "The Economics of Moral Hazard," *American Economic Review*, vol. 53, no. 3 (June 1968), pp. 531–537.

vider of care. As stated earlier, a tax policy that promotes the purchase of complete medical insurance has pervasive effects on medical markets. Policies to reduce the effect could be expected to put more competitive pressure on medical markets because of the savings to consumers from lower prices and less waste of resources.

Still other considerations about competition are relevant to the discussion of how well medical markets perform or can be made to perform. These will be discussed under two broad headings, barriers to entry and competition among insurance companies.[48]

Barriers to entry. A "barrier to entry" is the term used to describe any factor tending artifically to raise the cost of entering a market. While there are many markets such as for hospitals, nurses, or blood where some barriers may be effective, we will start with the market for physicians. It has important effects on competition in other medical markets and is most commonly considered to be affected by barriers to entry.

The late Reuben Kessel in his 1958 article, "Price Discrimination in Medicine," reviewed the history of the American Medical Association's (AMA) attempts to strengthen its control over medical markets by controlling entry into medical schools, supporting more restrictive state licensing, and discouraging price competition among physicians and various modes of prepaid health care.[49] Dyckman reports that the number of physicians per 100,000 population declined from 146 in 1910 to 133 in 1959. Dyckman also points out that because of a change in both government and AMA policies, physician supply increased from 149 per 100,000 population in 1965 to 177 per 100,000 in 1975. He concludes that while earlier restrictions on physician supply may have been responsible for rapid fee increases, the dominant force affecting these fee increases in the 1960s and 1970s was the growth of insurance.[50]

In discussing physicians' incomes, Dyckman concludes from the evidence that physicians' incomes, which averaged $68,800 in 1976, are now higher than necessary to attract a sufficient supply of physicians. To support the finding he uses AMA figures showing that between

[48] For recent literature on competition in medical markets, see Warren Greenberg, ed., *Competition in the Health Care Sector.* A topic not considered here is the lack of the profit-maximizing motive in medicine. For discussion of this difference in medical market behavior, see Kenneth W. Clarkson, "Some Implications of Property Rights in Hospital Management," *Journal of Law and Economics,* vol. 15, no. 2 (October 1972), pp. 263–284; and Mark Pauly and Michael Redisch, "The Not-for-Profit Hospital as a Physician's Cooperative," *American Economic Review,* vol. 63, no. 1 (March 1973), pp. 87–89.

[49] Reuben A. Kessel, "Price Discrimination in Medicine," *Journal of Law and Economics,* vol. 1 (October 1958), pp. 20–53.

[50] Dyckman, *A Study of Physicians' Fees,* pp. 9–11, 43.

1965 and 1975 the ratio of medical school applicants to acceptances increased from 2.1 to 2.8 per person accepted even though actual first-year enrollments almost doubled. In addition, the quality of those accepted in medical schools is apparently increasing (as measured by grades), and a growing (but undocumented) number of Americans are now enrolled in foreign medical schools.[51]

It is·obvious that higher incomes and other prestigious factors related to a medical career are still attracting medical students and foreign-trained physicians. It may be that while entry into medicine is now easier than before 1965, increasing insurance coverage and income (and perhaps the efficacy of care) is causing demand to grow faster than the increasing supply of physicians can accommodate. Even though organized medicine's control over entry may have declined, there is reason to suspect that state and federal policies may now be increasing barriers to entry. Among health policy analysts, there is a general acceptance that federal subsidies to medical education have now produced a surplus of physicians. The administration is proposing a reduction in these subsidies to medical schools with aid directed more to individuals as an inducement to practice in rural and urban areas now considered to be underserved.[52] Demand is growing for government policies to increase barriers to entry as a way of controlling costs. A more direct approach would be to deal with incentive-changing effects of tax subsidies, which would help restore more price competition among physicians.

Should government policy succeed in controlling the supply of physicians without reducing the inflated demand and price insensitivity that have resulted from insurance programs, physicians' incomes will increase even more, thus increasing political pressure for their direct control. Some parties are already calling for the replacement of the traditional fee-for-service system with a budget approach to control physicians' revenues under National Health Insurance.[53] This situation suggests that common phenomenon of one regulation begetting another, which McKie so aptly refers to as "the tar baby effect."[54]

---

[51] Ibid., pp. 73–93, especially pp. 78, 84–85.

[52] United States Budget in Brief, Fiscal Year 1979, p. 55.

[53] The Health Security Act (the Kennedy-Corman bill) would establish a national health budget in which, "Medical societies would be obligated to negotiate realistic fee schedules so that the budget for physician services could not be exceeded" (Statement of Bert Seidman, director, Department of Social Security, AFL-CIO in Government Research Corporation, Controlling Health Care Costs: A National Leadership Conference, Washington, D.C., June 27–28, 1977, p. 70).

[54] James W. McKie, "Regulation and Free Markets: The Problem of Boundaries," Bell Journal of Economics and Management Science, vol. 1, no. 1 (Spring 1970), p. 9.

Of the several other factors known to be increasing the cost of entry, professional restrictions on advertising deserve some mention. Kessel has analyzed the effects of these in medicine.[55] The usual justification for these restrictions is that they prevent such unethical behavior as making claims about the effectiveness of one's treatment or attracting patients by lowering prices. Regardless of the stated purposes of restrictions on advertising, they are seen by economists as reducing price competition and protecting those already established in a medical practice. A young physician wishing to enter a market has the option of establishing a new practice or purchasing an existing one. If professional restrictions prevent him from advertising, he will be at a disadvantage in attracting patients and will have to go through the slower process of building a practice through word-of-mouth. The result, whether intended or not, is that the cost of entry is increased and the market value of existing practices is protected.[56] Recent Supreme Court decisions regarding professional advertising as well as continuing pressure by the Federal Trade Commission and various consumer groups may have the effect of providing more information about prices and comparative performance to consumers. This should result in a lower cost of entry for new physicians, more direct price competition, and more alternative forms of care such as prepaid plans, nurse practitioners, or "surgicenters," which provide out-patient minor surgery.

Again the policy debate returns to the effects of tax exemptions on insurance. In a system of medical finance with less complete insurance and more direct consumer payment for medical care, a reduction in barriers to entry could be expected to bring about increased market competition and lower prices.

Competition among insurance companies. For policy purposes, the question must be raised of why insurance companies have not exerted more pressure on hospitals and physicians to restrain medical expenditures. These companies obviously have some incentives to keep the cost of reimbursements under control as they do in other insurance markets such as automobile and fire insurance. Why then has the market behavior of medical insurance been so different and why has the growth of insurance resulted in such large increases in medical expenditures and prices?[57]

---

[55] Kessel, "Price Discrimination in Medicine," pp. 43–44.

[56] Casual discussions with physicians indicate that a new physician can expect to retain a very large percentage (some say 90 percent) of the clientele of an ongoing practice.

[57] This discussion relies heavily on Frech and Ginsburg, "Competition among Health Insurers." For additional discussion of medical insurance, see Lawrence E. Goldberg and Warren Greenberg, "The Effects of Physician-Controlled Health In-

The health insurance industry has been described as consisting of two segments: (1) the commercial (for-profit and mutual) firms where entry is easy and the structure is unconcentrated, and (2) the Blue Cross and Blue Shield plans (referred to as "the Blues"), which are organized and controlled by hospitals and physicians. State laws sometimes give the Blues protection from new entrants and special tax treatments. Collusion among the plans to divide markets on a geographical and functional basis is common. Commercial firms offer a wider range of types of coverage while the Blues prefer more standardized policies with lower deductible and copayment (more complete) provisions.[58] Given the close ties between hospitals, physicians, and the Blues, it is not surprising that a system of reimbursement based on "usual, customary, and reasonable" (UCR) fees for physicians and cost reimbursement for hospitals has led to higher payments than under indemnity policies, which pay only a set amount for a given procedure.[59] Because the Blues provide about half the medical insurance, this deliberate policy of providing full reimbursement makes it more difficult for the non-Blue insurers to control cost. An individual insurer, such as Aetna, can be expected to have little success in negotiating lower fees with physicians and hospitals when it does not have a large share of the market. In addition, even though one company may succeed in reducing fees, it will not capture all of the gain because the reduced fee will benefit all insurers.[60]

Various proposals have been made to strengthen market competition among medical insurers. Some of these have been reform of state regulations of insurance, a change from retrospective cost reimbursement to prospective reimbursement, and application of antitrust laws to the Blues to diminish the influence of providers on the insurance companies.[61] The effectiveness of any of these policies would be increased if there were a change in tax policy that induced consumers to demand less complete coverage and gave them a greater incentive to search for

---

surance: U.S. vs. Oregon State Medical Society," *Journal of Health Politics, Policy and Law*, vol. 2, no. 1 (Spring 1977), pp. 48–78; Dyckman, *A Study of Physicians' Fees*, pp. 21–33; Pauly, "Health Insurance and Hospital Behavior"; and Clark C. Havighurst, "Improving the Climate for Innovation in Health Care Financing and Delivery" (paper presented at the American Enterprise Institute conference on "The Antitrust Laws and the Health Service Industry," Washington, D.C., December 19–20, 1977).

[58] Frech and Ginsburg, "Competition among Health Insurers," pp. 216–219.

[59] Dyckman, *A Study of Physicians' Fees*, pp. 25–27.

[60] Ibid., p. 31; and Pauly, "Health Insurance and Hospital Behavior," p. 116.

[61] Clark C. Havighurst, "Controlling Health Care Costs: Strengthening the Private Sector's Hand," *Journal of Health Politics, Policy and Law*, vol. 1, no. 4 (Winter 1977), pp. 471–498.

an insurance company that provided a plan more suitable to their desires. Insurance companies, including the Blues, could still sell insurance, but they would have to compete more vigorously by offering more cost-effective policies at lower premium costs. Under an insurance system with greater consumer cost-sharing, both consumers and insurance companies could be expected to put more pressure on providers to control costs.

To summarize, standard economic analysis is useful to identify those aspects of medical markets that are different and in this way help correct the popular perception that medical markets cannot be relied upon to maintain an efficient use of resources.

Conclusion

This paper has discussed the arguments behind the popular perception that economic behavior in medical markets is inherently different from behavior in more traditional markets. It has pointed to medical tax exemptions as the primary factor behind the increasing cost of medical care. The analysis indicates that if we want to establish a health policy that benefits consumers through greater efficiency and freedom of individual choice, we must face up to the role played by tax subsidies in promoting the spread of shallow insurance coverage. It is contended that if the individual consumer is given a greater role in sharing the cost of care, his economic behavior in the medical market will be more cost effective. Efficiency will be improved because reductions in expenditures will tend to be those which the consumer and his physician agree will be less productive.[62]

It should be noted that increasing the consumer's participation in the direct payment for medical care does not mean denying care to the poor or to those who experience catastrophic health expenses. We already have Medicare and Medicaid to provide care for the aged and the poor. These programs could be improved so that the lower the income of the individual or family, the smaller the proportion of direct payment. If we choose, at some cost we could even eliminate cost-sharing for the extremely poor by completely subsidizing their care. It would also be relatively inexpensive to eliminate cost-sharing for the

---

[62] For literature on proposals aimed at restoring consumer cost-sharing to medical markets, see Havighurst, "Controlling Health Care Costs"; Joseph P. Newhouse and Vincent Taylor, "How Shall We Pay for Hospital Care?" *Public Interest*, no. 23 (Spring 1971), pp. 78–92; Mark V. Pauly, *National Health Insurance: An Analysis* (Washington, D.C.: American Enterprise Institute, 1971), pp. 33–40; Feldstein, "The High Cost of Hospitals—and What To Do About It," pp. 40–54; Enthoven, "Consumer Choice Health Plan (CCHP)."

small number of cases experiencing a catastrophic health situation. (Approximately 1 percent of the population under age sixty-five have medical expenses over $5,000 annually.)[63] Because the relatively rare occurrences of catastrophic diseases are readily insurable, such insurance could be provided directly by the government or through private insurance if mandated in some way by the government. The obvious social concern for the well-being of the aged, the poor, or those facing catastrophic medical expenses should not be used as an excuse for not establishing policies that restore cost-conscious behavior among the much larger segment of the population that has both the income to pay for normal amounts of care and the willingness to make decisions.

The pessimistic view is that it will take a deliberate change in policy together with strong political leadership to make the case for a return to market principles in health. But perhaps it would be best to end on at least this grace note of optimism. It took the economics profession approximately thirty years to begin to develop the methodology to measure the costs and benefits of regulation established during the 1930s and before. It has taken approximately another ten years of hard work to begin to invoke a public awareness of the cost of regulation. Possibly health economists and others analyzing health markets have now enough of a headstart so that it will be somewhat less than forty years until this country begins to realize the economic and personal costs of health regulation and attempts to deal with the real factors affecting health costs.

---

[63] The aggregate expenses over $5,000 of that 1 percent of the population are about $13.1 billion. Congressional Budget Office, *Catastrophic Health Insurance* (Washington, D.C., 1977), p. xiv.

27

DOCTORS, DAMAGES, AND DETERRENCE
An Economic View of Medical Malpractice

William B. Schwartz and Neil K. Komesar

The growth during the 1970s in the number of malpractice suits and in the size of the damage awards has led to widespread attacks on the medical malpractice system. It is the thesis of the present study—being published simultaneously as a report by The Rand Corporation and as an article in the June 8, 1978, issue of *The New England Journal of Medicine*—that damages awarded in a malpractice suit should be viewed not only as compensation for victims but also as a means of deterring health-care providers from negligent behavior. Economic analysis of the malpractice system indicates that such awards can send a "signal" to providers which informs them how much to invest in avoiding mishaps.

The work reported here was sponsored in part by a grant to Dr. Schwartz from the Robert Wood Johnson Foundation, in part by a general research support grant (5-S07-RR05710-07) from the National Institute of Health to The Rand Corporation, and in part by Rand from its own research funds.

Dr. Schwartz is Vannevar Bush University Professor and Professor of Medicine, Tufts University, and Principal Program Adviser to the Rand Health Sciences Program. Dr. Komesar is Professor of Law, University of Wisconsin Law School.

Attacks on the malpractice system are widespread and intense. According to some critics, too many claims are brought, and excessive damages are awarded. Others decry the lawyers' contingency fee as an inducement to unwarranted suits, or assert that the system penalizes physicians randomly. These, and other criticisms, have led to demands for major reform—even to proposals that the tort system be replaced wholly or in part by other methods for dealing with

The authors wish to acknowledge the valuable criticisms and comments of Drs. Patricia Munch, Joseph P. Newhouse, Charles E. Phelps, Rodney T. Smith, and Albert P. Williams of the Rand Corporation, Dr. William Bennett of Harvard University, Professor Paul I. Joskow of the Massachusetts Institute of Technology, Professor Robert C. Ellickson of Stanford Law School, and Professor Richard A. Posner, The University of Chicago Law School.

medical injury. Curiously enough, the perceived failings and proposed correctives are rarely subjected to critical scrutiny; rather, they are taken as self-evident.

These critiques of the existing system rest largely on an assumption that the primary or sole purpose of malpractice law is to compensate injured patients.[1,2,3] But it can be argued, on the basis of modern economic analysis, that this rationale is unduly narrow:[4,5,6] findings of negligence are seen not only as redressing past wrongs but also as giving providers an incentive to avoid future careless injuries.[5,6] Viewed in this way, the malpractice system and its problems dramatically change character.

ECONOMIC ANALYSIS OF NEGLIGENCE

As early as 1881, Oliver Wendell Holmes, Jr., in a classic treatise on the subject, observed that compensation should not be viewed as the rationale of negligence law.[7] Because individuals could, if they wished, insure themselves against accidents, he could see little reason for a government-operated system of compensation. More recently, critics of the compensation rationale have pointed out that patients could be indemnified against medical accidents through insurance programs, private or social, at a much lower administrative cost than that exacted by tort proceedings.[8,9,10,11] Indeed, the legal apparatus required to determine negligence and place blame is so expensive that only about 35 cents of every dollar in malpractice premiums is paid to successful claimants;[12] by contrast, 80 cents of every premium dollar reaches patients with health insurance.[13]

Even if negligence litigation were not expensive, as a means primarily to compensate the innocent injured, it would have puzzling features: two different individuals may sustain an identical injury and be equally innocent of its cause, and yet their prospects for receiving damages may be entirely different. Eligibility for compensation is determined by the behavior of the person responsible for the injury; so if negligence is present in one case and not in the other, one person will be compensated and the other will not.

The negligence system makes a great deal more sense if it is understood primarily as a means to deter careless behavior rather than to compensate its victims. By finding fault and assessing damages against the negligent provider, the system sends all providers a signal that discourages future carelessness and reduces future damages.

The concept of negligence is fundamental to malpractice law, but the usual definitions of negligence, even in law books, suffer from vagueness. Legal formulations, such as "conduct which involves an unreasonably great risk of causing damage" or "conduct which falls below the standard established by law for the protection of others against unreasonably great risk of harm"[14] are intuitively appealing. But such definitions only substitute, by implication, a term like "unreasonable conduct" for "negligence"; they do not specify what "unreasonable" means.

Some 30 years ago, the distinguished jurist Learned Hand formulated an explicit definition of negligence,[15] which has now become a textbook definition.[14] Negligence occurs, he stated, whenever it would cost less to prevent a mishap than to pay for the damages predicted to result from it. More explicitly, the cost of preventing a mishap (C) must be less than the probability it will occur (P) multiplied by the loss suffered when it does occur (L). Restating the rule in symbols: negligence occurs whenever $C < P \times L$. The product $(P \times L)$ is usually called "expected loss" or "expected damages."

In many situations it is impossible to prevent all injuries, and the Learned Hand Rule must, therefore, be modified as follows: negligent behavior is the failure to invest resources up to a level that equals the anticipated saving in damages.

There is an intuitive appeal to the notion that "unreasonable" or "careless" behavior can be equated with underinvesting in accident avoidance. The harmony between common sense and this interpretation of the law is best illustrated by an example. A customer walking down the aisle of a supermarket knocks a jar of baby food to the floor, where it shatters. A few seconds later, another customer turns into the aisle, fails to see the puddle on the floor, slips, and breaks a leg. It would not have been "reasonable" to expect that the owner of the market would station personnel in each aisle to offer continuous warnings about wet spots and to provide for instant cleanup. In this case, the cost of preventing the injury would far exceed the expected loss $(P \times L)$. Common sense would almost certainly lead a jury to conclude that negligence had not occurred. But if the wet spot had been left for thirty to forty minutes, the verdict would be likely to go the other way, because the cost of policing the aisles at such an interval is relatively low, and the likelihood of injury occurring during the longer interval is considerably greater. As the cost of preventing a mishap rises and the likelihood becomes more remote, failing to avoid it becomes increasingly reasonable.

More than just an explicit formulation of what is "fair" and "reasonable," the Learned Hand Rule serves to assure that resources are being efficiently allocated. It does so by establishing procedures that minimize the total cost incurred by accidents and accident prevention.

As the supermarket cases illustrate, someone who is injured is not automatically entitled to compensation, even though everything about his injury is identical to that of another person who is compensated. What matters is identical to that of another person who is compensated. What matters is that someone was negligent. Thus, litigation, beyond providing a means to redress the loss and suffering caused by carelessness, signals potentially negligent individuals that it will cost them more to be careless than to invest in an appropriate level of prevention. Damages awarded to a victim induce potentially negligent individuals to compare the cost of avoiding an injury with the cost of paying for it.[36] The importance of compensation in this view of the system is that it provides the victim with an incentive to bring suit; only thus can the signal be initiated. Compensation, in this sense, is an indispensable *ingredient* of the deterrence mechanisms, even though compensating the victim is not its main *purpose*.

The Learned Hand Rule has a rather obvious corollary, which some people find difficult to accept: there are accidents which, from society's point of view, are not worth avoiding. The cost of prevention far exceeds the expected loss; so the accident should be allowed to occur.

MEDICAL MALPRACTICE AND PROFESSIONAL CUSTOM

Because judges and juries may find it exceedingly difficult to evaluate a medical dispute, the courts have largely accepted "customary standards of medical practice" as a measure of reasonable investment in mishap avoidance.[14] The physician can plead that he has followed customary practice in his care of the patient, and the courts will usually substitute expert testimony about professional custom for a more specific accounting by the negligence standard.

This substitution reflects the faith of the legal system that physicians as a group, or at least those who set standards, are correctly investing in mishap avoidance and that medical custom can be used as the bench mark of adequate performance. And it conforms to the view, held both by providers of health care and by observes of the system, that most physicians tend to guard the welfare care and by observers of the system, that most physicians tend to guard the welfare of their patients without need for external regulation. The malpractice system exists to discipline the occasional physician who does not (or cannot) protect his patients.

In the face of conflicting testimony as to what constitutes customary and acceptable practice, the courts may undertake more explicit (if informal) application of the Learned Hand Rule.[16] Even if a defendant can show that his performance has met the accepted standard of medical practice, the courts retain ultimate responsibility for determining whether that standard also constitutes "reasonable care." And they may find that it does not.

For example, custom has been rejected as the defense in a suit brought by a 32-year-old woman who became blind from glaucoma because tonometry was not performed.[17] The appellate court weighed the cost of the test ("inexpensive and harmless") against the probability that a young person would develop glaucoma ("one in 25,000") and the magnitude of the loss (blindness). The court concluded that "reasonable prudence" required the test and faulted the profession for not routinely carrying out tonometry in patients under the age of 40. Here, custom did not meet the standard of efficiently allocating resources; the court measured custom against the Hand standard and set custom aside.

This decision, when expressed quantitatively, yields a result consistent with the Learned Hand Rule. If we take cost of tonometry as not exceeding $5 and the average jury verdict for total or legal blindness at $678,000 (for period 1973-1977),[18] we arrive at the following formulation:

$$\$5 < 1/25,000 \times \$678,000,$$
$$\$5 < \$27.$$

No reasonable adjustment of the figure for the cost of avoidance would alter this conclusion. Cases like this one indicate that professional custom serves only as a provincial substitute for the negligence rule.

RECEIVING THE SIGNAL:
THE PHYSICIAN'S RESPONSE

As with negligence law in general, the malpractice system may be understood as a mechanism for signaling the potentially negligent—in this case, a subpopulation of physicians. The signal, when properly received, informs the doctor how much to invest in avoiding mishaps; the "correct" response, then, is for him to invest his resources up to the level of expected damages.

To the extent that the usual fee for a service accurately reflects the training and the investment of time needed to meet customary standards of care, nonnegligent physicians are appropriately remunerated. By contrast, the negligent physician, who fails to provide the full service but accepts the full price, is short-changing his patient. With an effective malpractice signal, the potentially negligent physician would be stimulated to invest more time for no increase in pay because he probably could not set his fees higher than those of his more competent colleagues.

In practice, the negligent physician may modify his behavior in one of several ways. The doctor who tends to skimp on history or physican examination or to rush through procedures must take the time needed for more careful work. But increasing his investment of time on each case may be insufficient. An inadequately trained physician is notified by the damages award that he should invest in further training. The cost of training must then be amortized over future cases. Alternatively, a physician may abandon procedures that he is not competent to perform, even though these procedures are relatively more remunerative than others in his practice.

THE IDEAL SIGNAL

The ideal negligence signal is achieved when every significant incident of malpractice leads to a claim and every valid claim to a full award. Then (in an ideal or, so to speak, "frictionless," system) the physician is stimulated to invest appropriately in mishap reduction.

Let us consider a theoretical world in which there is a doctor with 100 patients in his practice. He works only to maximize his income and is completely aware of these facts: the incidence of a given mishap, the cost to him of reducing that incidence, the loss to him if the mishap occurs, and the proportion of such mishaps that lead to a suit and award.

To reduce the occurrence of mishaps he must invest his own resources, specifically his time, to prevent each occurrence. As with any attempt to approach a zero incidence of accidents, each further reduction in probability is more expensive than the previous one. So, as shown in Figure 1, reducing the frequency of a mishap from .05 to .04 costs more than reducing it from .06 to .05.

If we look at it the other way around, this is the familiar phenomenon of diminishing returns: every additional $5 spent to reduce the frequency of a mishap buys a smaller reduction than the previous $5 did. In real life, for example, repeatedly checking a cross-match of bloods or rereading a label before administering a drug would cost the same each time it was done, but would yield progressively smaller increases in accuracy as perfection was approached.

Against this background, let us examine the hypothetical situation illustrated in Figure 1. In the example, the physician knows that a particular injury will result in damages of $5000. Thus, every time he reduces the probability of mishap by one percentage point (an average of one patient per 100) he saves $50 in expected loss per patient (.01 × $5000). He also knows that reducing the frequency of a $5000 mishap from .10 to .09 costs $5, as shown by the vertical bar, but it yields an expected saving of $50, as indicated by the dashed horizontal line. For each successive decrement of .01, the costs are higher, but the saving remains constant at $50 for each .01 reduction. When the probability is reduced from .06 to .05 the cost is $50, but this expense exactly equals the saving in damages. At this point of indifference, further investment will yield no further saving. To stop here and invest no more in protection would not, therefore, be negligent. The purpose of the malpractice system is to bring the physician to this point; further investment would actually increase the net costs to society.

If only some mishaps result in suits, the physician can be expected to invest less than the optimum. Suppose, for example, that only one-fifth of his incidents lead to a negligence suit. As shown in Figure 1, the savings to the physician would then amount to only $5 when he reduces the frequency of a mishap from .10 to .09. That is, he is now saving only the difference between a $10 reduction in expected damages per patient (.20 × $50) and $5 spent to achieve the reduction. Thereafter the cost of averting a mishap exceeds the savings. Should the rate of suits be increased to 60 percent, it would become worthwile to reduce the frequency of mishaps to .07, but not lower. Pushing it down to .06 would cost $30 but save only $30. Thus, in this "ideal" system, the optimum response is achieved only when the maximum number of valid suits is brought. Below 100 percent, the signal is too weak.

Although the signal itself is suboptimal at a low frequency of suits, the gains are greatest when physicians are stimulated to move from the lowest levels of investment to a somewhat higher level, as shown by Figure 2, which diagrams the cumulative rather than the incremental gains achieved. Becauses costs

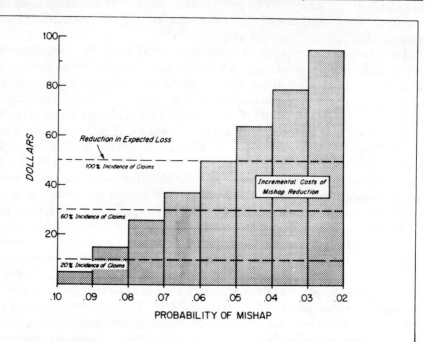

Each vertical column represents the cost to produce a reduction of one percentage point in the probability of a mishap; the top dashed line represents the corresponding reduction in expected loss. For each reduction, the cost is higher than the previous one. At a mishap probability of .06, the cost of another .01 reduction exactly equals $50, the amount by which the expected loss would be diminished if all valid claims were brought. At this so-called point of indifference, savings are balanced by the costs, and the ideal negligence standard has, in theory, been reached.

If the incidence of suits is less than 100 percent, the incentive to invest in mishaps avoidance is reduced. For example, at a 20 percent incidence (represented by the lowest of the dashed lines), the expected loss is only one-fifth of the actual. The physician who maximizes income now has no financial incentive to invest more than $10 in mishap reduction, and thus will be satisfied with a rate of .09.

Figure 1: Costs of Progressively Reducing the Probability of a Mishap and the Effect of Reduced Rates of Claims

of avoidance at low levels of protection are small relative to the reduction in damages, the benefits are large. But as the negligence standard—the point of indifference—is approached, additional savings become small and then vanish.

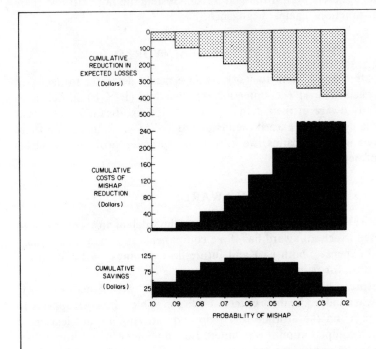

The costs of mishap reduction accumulate more rapidly than the reduction in expected losses. As a result, the cumulative savings are greatest when the negligent physician is stimulated to move from the lowest level of investment to a somewhat higher level. As the negligence standard is approached--in this instance a probability of mishap of .06--additional savings become small and then vanish. Further reduction of mishaps eventually depletes the initial savings. (Note that last two cost bars are not drawn to full height.)

Figure 2: Effect on Cumulative Savings of Expenditures on Mishap Reduction

The doctor in our example is far more explicit in his quantitative analysis than we would expect him to be in real life, even if a real-life physician did seek only to maximize his income. The example does, however, correspond to the intuitive analysis that an income-maximizing doctor would have to carry out.

It is unlikely that more than a handful of physicians, if any, are concerned solely with financial return. A substantial number, it can fairly be assumed, incorporate the welfare of their patients into their calculations and, therefore, invest appropriately in avoiding mishaps. Such physicians would continue to behave appropriately even if the malpractice system did not exist and there were no other sanctions against negligence.

THE SIGNAL IN THE REAL WORLD

For the malpractice system to work as an efficient deterrent to negligent behavior, physicians must encounter an expected loss ($P \times L$) sufficient to make them fully aware of their deficiencies, but not significantly above that level. If awards do, in fact, exceed the losses suffered by claimants and if there are too many successful claims, we have a "malpractice problem" much as the critics represent it.

SIZE OF AWARDS

The theoretical aim of the tort system is to set the value of an award equal to the loss suffered. Such an award has three components in a malpractice judgment: medical expenses, both past and future; lost earnings, past and future; and compensation for pain and suffering.

It is a widespread belief that damages being awarded by the American courts are excessive when judged by these criteria. Criticism of high damages appears to be based, in part, on the attitude that pain and suffering are not legitimate losses for which compensation is warranted. But someone whose injury affects his life style—say the ability to participate in recreation or the ability to have children—is paying a price that is properly included in a damages award.[19]

The highest, and therefore the most conspicuous, awards—those in excess of $50,000—have the largest element of compensation for pain and suffering.[20] Such awards occur almost exclusively when a catastrophic injury, such as paralysis or brain damage, has resulted from negligence. In such circumstances, the effect on life style is enormous, and a jury properly assesses the loss as a real injury that can only be compensated monetarily.[19] In these terms, even the largest awards do not seem excessive.

The average payment in the award range of less than $50,000 was substantially below medical expenses and lost earnings—typically in the range of one-third to two-thirds of such losses. Indeed, in the aggregate, awards in 1974 were slightly below medical expenses and lost earnings.[20]

NUMBER OF CLAIMS

Many more incidents of malpractice occur, it appears, than result in a claim for damages. Records of patients discharged from two hospitals during 1972 revealed a large number of significant injuries resulting from malpractice; of these, only one in every 15 led to malpractice claims.[21] The same study also suggested that many more incidents of malpractice had actually occurred than could be established from the records (this finding will hardly surprise physicians familiar with hospitals' record-keeping practices).

The conclusion that many incidents never lead to a claim is bolstered by the observation that 40 percent of the file entires held by insurance companies consist of mishaps reported by a physician but never pursued by the patient.[22] There is, moreover, a large pool of malpractice incidents in which the decision to carry out a procedure, rather than a bad outcome, is a form of negligence. Unnecessary surgery, most often hysterectomies and tonsillectomies, probably comprise the bulk of these instances. Numerous as they are, unnecessary operations rarely lead to malpractice claims and have not been included in the analysis of incidents versus claims.[21,23]

Since 1972, the number of malpractice claims has risen by nearly 50 percent.[24] Even after estimates are adjusted to account for this change, at most only one out of every 6 or 7 incidents can be expected to result in a claim. A recent study in California supports this estimate: Of malpractice incidents detected in hospital records, no more than one-sixth eventuated in a claim. This conclusion is based on the calculation that there were approximately 24,000 instances of malpractice in California hospitals during 1974[23] but that not more than 400 of the injured filed claims.[25]

The fraction (detected from the record) of malpractice incidents manifested in claims against the provider is thus quite small, probably below 20 percent. Given the degree of uncertainty in the data, we calculate, however, that the ratio of claims to incidents could be as high as .3 or less than .1. In any case, the number of suits, even though it is burgeoning, remains far below the theoretical level required to fully signal the expected loss ($P \times L$) resulting from negligence. On the other hand, from society's point of view, some of the suits required to convey the full message may actually not be "worth" bringing. This seeming paradox results from the effect of administrative costs.

ADMINISTRATIVE COSTS

The balance sheet laid out earlier in Figure 2 is incomplete because it has ignored a significant component of costs. The time spent by lawyers, physicians, patients, witnesses, judges, and juries are all resources that society must expend to maintain the malpractice system, as are the costs of maintaining the courts and the administrative outlays of such tangential institutions as the insurance industry. These costs reduce whatever level of savings may be achieved by the system. As illustrated in Figure 2, when the cumulative costs of preventing mishaps are subtracted from the savings in expected damages, a curve of net savings is obtained. When administrative costs are also subtracted, the net savings at each level of mishap prevention are reduced and the point of maximum savings is thus shifted to the left. This reduction in savings means that some number of mishaps is not worth preventing through the malpractice system, and it implies that some fraction of otherwise justifiable suits is not worth bringing.

ERRONEOUS FINDINGS

The net saving to society that can theoretically be achieved by a system of malpractice litigation is reduced when the courts make errors. These mistakes can be of two kinds—failure to detect real negligence or penalizing non-negligent behavior—and both are costly.

A court's failure to recognize negligent behavior has the effect of reducing the expected loss and thus permits physicians to set their investment in mishap avoidance below the ideal level. At the same time, the malpractice system as a whole is made more expensive because the proceeding raises administrative costs but yields no benefits.

When non-negligent physicians are penalized, the result is also costly. Physicians, realizing that such errors occur, are induced to practice inappropriately "defensive medicine," i.e., to provide medically unjustified care to reduce the probability of a malpractice suit.[26] The availability of third-party payment permits the physician to use diagnostic tests and hospitalization without restraint from the patient or cost to himself, and thus to demonstrate a level of care so painstaking that neither a patient nor a jury would be likely to make the error of calling him negligent. But this immunity is bought at a cost to society far in excess of anticipated benefits.[37] The excesses of medicine will be discouraged only if providers of health care can be encouraged to compete with each other. When a provider, such as a prepaid health plan, lowers its expenditures on defensive medicine and then passes the savings on to its members, it can attract patients away from the more wasteful, and thus more expensive, providers.

Any system is liable to error, the costs of which must be subtracted from the profits of the system as a whole. In the case of negligence procedures, there are two incentives to avoid mistaken judgments: the economic loss sustained by society and the personal injuries suffered by a plaintiff or defendant.

MALPRACTICE INSURANCE AND ATTENUATION OF THE SIGNAL

Even if the signal were perfect—every incident of malpractice leading to a proper claim, and every award equal to the loss suffered by a patient—under existing conditions it would fail to elicit the appropriate response from physicians. Malpractice insurance, as it is currently adminstered, virtually insulates the negligent physician from the damages award and, thus, from the malpractice signal.

The reason is simple: the malpractice premiums of individual physicians are rarely influenced by their record of claims, settlements, and verdicts. (Haldi,

J.: personal communication, April 1, 1977.)[27,28,29] Rather, premiums are usually set for an entire specialty group in a given region. Thus the physician with a record of frequent negligence bears no larger a share of the burden than his colleages with excellent records. No individual physician has more than a slight pecuniary incentive to reduce the expected losses resulting from his own behavior.

Under the prevailing system of group rating, we can imagine a physician who could avoid an expected loss of $1000 by spending $100. And yet, if his malpractice premiums are set for a group of 100 physicians, his own premium will rise, as a result of the mishap, by only $10 (and so will that of 99 other physicians). The individual is thus assessed only one-tenth of what it would have cost him to prevent the injury. In reality, the physician may not lose even the $10; for in most instances all physicians in a given group can pass on nearly all of the cost of their rising premiums, as increased fees, to third-party payers. Thus, the burden of higher malpractice premiums falls largely on the patient in the form of a higher health insurance premium.

As a rule, the system of group rating successfully interferes with transmission of the signal, but there is one partial exceptions. Part-time practitioners of a specialty must pay the full premium, even though only a fraction of their income derives from it. To the extent that a part-time practitioner—say, the otolaryngologist doing some plastic surgery—is incompetent, he is successfully weeded out by the group rating. In this situation, the malpractice system still has a deterrent effect, as was demonstrated by a recent study of California physicians who have been relinquishing part-time activity and reclassifying themselves exclusively into their primary area of competence.[30] Of course, the effect is clumsy, in that it also eliminates part-time specialists who are competent but cannot or will not pay the full specialty premium. Group rating is, then, an exceedingly insensitive method of identifying the negligent physician.

Malpractice insurance, on the other hand, has important social value and our comments should not be taken as argument for abolishing insurance protection. Because insurance spreads risks, it protects the physician against the financial catastrophe that could result from even a single large finding against him, and also against erroneous findings of negligence. A balance must therefore be struck between the risk-spreading value of insurance and the need for experience rating as a means of sending the deterrent signal to the physician.

The lack of individual experience rating in malpractice premiums has, in the past, been economically acceptable to both the insurance industry and the medical profession. For the industry, the cost of identifying individual bad risks has probably not been worth the potential savings. Now, as malpractice litigation comes to involve ever larger amounts of money, the interests of both the industry and the profession may shift toward a system of experience rating.

If a physician were rated by his individual experience, his premium would reflect, to at least some degree, the risk that he poses to the insurer. Moreover, given the procedures employed by health insurance companies, such physicians would probably not be able to raise fees much above those prevailing in the community. Thus, physicians who pose substantially more risk than others would themselves have to absorb much of the extra burden of premium costs.

Experience rating of physicians is, of course, justifiable only if suits are not brought randomly or capriciously. It has been argued that "good" physicians are sued as often as the "bad." In support of this contention, the belief is expressed that doctors with board certification are sued as often as those who are less well trained. Even if this statement should prove correct, it is not evidence that negligence is inaccurately found. Many factors could lead well-trained specialists to perform below their presumtive level of competence. Some well-trained physicians may take on too many patients and invest less time per case than is appropriate. Others may assume responsibilities in areas for which they are not trained or experienced. Moreover, the thesis that suits are brought randomly is not supported by a recent study of 8000 physicians in the Los Angeles area. In a four-year period, 46 physicians (0.6 percent of the 8000) accounted for 10 percent of all claims and 30 percent of all payments made by the insurance plan.[3] The average number of suits against the 46 doctors was 1¼ per year. Analysis indicates that doctors against whom multiple suits are brought do, indeed, represent a higher-risk population than their colleagues.[32]

Virtually the only penalty currently paid by the negligent physician is the value of his time spent in defending a suit and the costs of his embarrassment. In the absence of experience-rated premiums, these factors may be the only effective component of the signal and may serve some useful purpose. But because the costs cannot be purposely set, they are not likely to equal the damage assessment that the physician should experience if resources are to be efficiently allocated. "Time and embarrassment" costs may be either larger or smaller than the optimum.

CONTINGENCY FEES AND SIGNAL QUALITY

According to a popular line of reasoning, lawyers are encouraged to bring malpractice suits that lack merit because they are paid of percentage, usually one-third, of the damages awarded; if they were paid a flat fee for service they would not be so indiscriminate. Even if its true that too many frivolous suits are brought, this analysis of the contingency-fee system would be incorrect.

The lawyer who is paid a contingency fee is compensated only if he succeeds in obtaining either a settlement out of court or an award from a jury. He is not likely to invest time and several thousand dollars in out-of-pocket expenses on a case with little prospect of success. Under the system of contingency fees, lawyers thus have the incentive to filter out capricious suits, which otherwise would overload the courts, harass physicians, and produce no social benefits.

Payment by contingency fee not only encourages the lawyer to turn away baseless claims but permits him to accept clients lacking the funds to pay a fee for service. The contingency fee offers "a key to the courthouse door" to some individuals with valid claims that would otherwise be lost to the system. Without contingency fees, the deterrent signal to the physician would be reduced.

Why then, if contingency fees are such an incentive to careful selection of cases, are 80 percent of claims that reach trial ultimately resolved in the physician's favor?[25] During periods of rapidly changing technology, like the present one, we must expect that individual doctors and lawyers cannot always be certain of correct medical practice. Litigation can serve to establish proper standards and thus to provide important information about the changing limits of malpractice. The suits providing this information may well be appropriately brought, even if the accused physician is exonerated.

Fee-for-service payments to lawyers would be likely to have perverse effects on the malpractice system because lawyers would actually have an incentive to encourage suits, regardless of their merits. Responsibility for screening suits would then devolve on the client himself, who is unlikely to be adequately informed about prospects for success. The number of suits might be reduced, but not because the frivolous ones had been eliminated. Rather, those who simply could not afford to pay for litigation would be discouraged.

ALTERNATIVES TO MALPRACTICE

Dissatisfaction with malpractice proceedings has produced various suggestions for changing the system, such as ceilings on the size of awards and a shift to fee-for-service payment of lawyers, changes that might well have undesirable effects. Also advocated is a system of arbitration whereby a panel of experts would reach a finding through less formal means than a full-fledged jury trial. With this system, the gains in efficiency might be offset by significant losses: the protection against bias and influence that a broadly based, rotating jury provides and the accuracy attained by complete and careful presentations in court.

The negligence standard might be abandoned altogether and another form of liability substituted for it. One approach, for example, would establish a system of negotiations between patient and physician who would agree, in advance, to a given investment in mishap avoidance.[33,34] This "contractarian" approach, as it is called, neglects the basic problem that necessitated regulation of medical care, in the form of malpractice law, to begin with: the consumer of medical services, more than the consumer of most goods and services, lacks the information and sophistication needed for bargaining. It is precisely this market failure that created the need for regulation of health services, whether in the form of licensing or litigation.

At another extreme and currently receiving the widest attention, is a proposal to make the physician automatically responsible for many types of mishap, regardless of fault.[8,9,10,11] The no-fault alternative deserves some scrutiny because it may prove to be a problematic "solution" to existing problems.

Under most of the proposed no-fault programs, the physician would be held liable for any bad outcome associated with a particular "compensable event"— any complication of a blood transfusion, for example—and would be insured accordingly. Such no-fault liability would remove from litigation a number of events in which bad outcomes are usually, but by no means exclusively, the results of negligence. In such instances, the costs and unpleasantness of malpractice proceedings could be avoided and, proponents argue, a net saving relative to current expenditures would be achieved.

It is not clear how great the real savings under a no-fault system would be, because a no-fault system could hardly eliminate disputes and litigation. As with workmen's compensation (another form of no-fault insurance), disagreements might arise as to whether a particular outcome, say hepatitis, was in fact the result of a compensable event, such as a blood transfusion, or was the untoward effect of a drug concomitantly administered and known occasionally to cause liver damage. Litigation would be inevitable. The combined cost of such litigation, and of payments to patients who were injured but not as a result of negligence, could well offset the overall saving that a no-fault system might otherwise achieve.

In the design of a no-fault system, the most serious question must be: Who will pay the damages? If the individual physician's premiums do not reflect the costs of compensable events attributed to him, he will not be deterred from negligence. To achieve deterrence, the individual physician must be rated by his experience. But the use of individual experience ratings for no-fault insurance premiums could be expected to have some distinctly perverse effects. The practice of "defensive medicine" based on third-party resources would be encouraged because the physician would be liable for any bad outcome and would thus gain maximum protection from highly redundant safeguards. The savings would go directly to the physician; the costs would be borne by the patients.

Perhaps more seriously, physicians would be deterred from undertaking risky procedures, even when such procedures were, on medical grounds, most appropriate and should, for the patient's sake, be ventured. The cost of a bad outcome from the procedure would be borne solely by the physician, and in this case, the patient would likely be deprived of an opportunity for proper care. Skilled physicians, to whom difficult and high-risk patients are referred, would be especially penalized. In principle, a complex schedule of premiums could offset this tendency by comparing liability payments with the risk profile of a given doctor's practice. In reality, such a scheme would be difficult to implement and open to abuse.

If, on the other hand, experience ratings were abandoned, the physician would have little or no economic incentive to prevent mishaps, and a rise in the number of bad outcomes—compensable events—could be reasonably predicted. (not only would premiums fail to reflect negligence, but time and embarrassment costs would have disappeared.) An increased frequency of bad outcomes would also raise the costs of a no-fault system above currently predicted levels.

The no-fault alternative does not a priori appear to offer significant advantages over the present system. And even if it could be implemented for some selected group of events, the malpractice system would still be needed to deal with the very large number of cases that could not feasibly be dealt with under a no-fault system. The prospect of two systems, both of them complex and fraught with problems, is not an attractive one.

Our purpose has not been either to defend the system of malpractice litigation or to gloss over its shortcomings. Rather, we have demonstrated an analytic approach that helps to clarify the role of malpractice proceedings in maintaining the quality of medical care. The same kind of analysis should be applied to proposals for change before policy decisions affecting the system are made.

REFERENCES

1. American Surgical Association Statement on Professional Liability, September 1976. N Engl J Med 295:1292-1296, 1976.
2. Welch CE: Medical malpractice. N Engl J Med 292:1372-1376, 1975
3. American Bar Association Fund for Public Education: Legal Topics Relating to Medical Malpractice. Washington, DC, Government Printing Office, 1977
4. Calabresi G: The Costs of Accidents: A legal and economic analysis. New Haven, Connecticut, Yale University Press, 1970
5. Posner RA: A theory of negligence. J Legal Stud 1:29-96, 1972
6. *Idem:* Economic Analysis of Law. Boston, Little, Brown, 1972
7. Holmes OW Jr: The Common Law. Boston, Little, Brown, 1881
8. O'Connell J: Elective no-fault liability by contract—with or without an enabling statute. University of Illinois Law Forum 1975, pp. 59-72
9. O'Connell J: Ending Insult to Injury: No-Fault Insurance for Products and Services. Urbana, Illinois, University of Illinois Press, 1975
10. Havighurst CC, Tancredi LR: "Medical adversity insurance"—a no-fault approach to medical malpractice and quality assurance. Milbank Mem Fund Q 51:125-168, 1973
11. Havighurst CC: Medical adversity insurance: has its time come?, Medical Malpractice: The Duke Law Journal Symposium. Cambridge, Massachusetts, Ballinger Publishing, 1977, pp. 55-105
12. Munch P: Costs and Benefits of the Tort System if Viewed as a Compensation System. Santa Monica, California, Rand Corporation, 1977
13. A. M. Best Company: Best's Review. Property/Casualty. Oldwick, New Jersey, Insurance Editions, July 1977
14. Prosser WL: Handbook of the Law of Torts. Fourth Edition. St. Paul, Minnesota, West Publishing, 1971
15. United States v. Carroll Towing Co., 159 Federal Reporter 2d 169 (1947)
16. The T. J. Hooper, 60 Federal Reporter 2d 737 (1932)
17. Helling v. Carey, 519 Pacific Reporter 2d 981 (1974)
18. Injury Valuation Reports, Tables of Verdict Exptancy Values for Eye Injuries, Personal Injury Valuation Handbooks. Cleveland, Ohio, Jury Verdict Research, in press
19. Komesar NK: Toward a general theory of personal injury loss. J Legal Stud 3:457-486, 1974
20. Miller PD: Report of the All-Industry Committee Special Malpractice Review: 1974 closed claim survey. Technical analysis of survey results. New York, Insurance Services Office, 1976
21. Pocincki LS, Dogger SJ, Schwartz BP: The incidence of iatrogenic injuries. Appendix, Report of the Secretary's Commission on Medical Malpractice (DHEW Publication No. [OS] 73-89). Washington, DC, Government Printing Office, 1973, pp. 50-70

22. United States Department of Health, Education, and Welfare. Study of Medical Malpractice Claims Closed in 1970: Prepared for the Secretary's Commission on Medical Malpractice, Office of the Secretary, Rockville, Maryland, Westat, 1973

23. California Medical Association, California Hospital Association: Report on the Medical Insurance Feasibility Study. San Francisco, California, Sutter Publications, 1977

24. Malpractice Digest. St. Paul, Minnesota, St. Paul Fire and Marine Insurance Co., April/May 1977

25. Malpractice Claims. Vol. 1. Milwaukee, Wisconsin, National Association of Insurance Commissioners, May 1977

26. The medical malpractic threat: a study of defensive medicine. Duke Law J 1971, pp. 939-993

27. Kendall M, Haldi J: The medical malpractice insurance market. Appendix, Report of the Secretary's Commission on Medical Malpractice (DHEW Publication No. [OS] 73-89). Washington, DC, Government Printing Office, 1973, pp. 494-608

28. Malpractice Digest. St. Paul, Minnesota, St. Paul Fire and Marine Insurance Co., October/November 1977

29. Steves MF Jr: A proposal to improve the cost to benefit relationships in the medical professional liability insurance system, Medical Malpractice: The Duke Law Journal Symposium. Cambridge, Massachusetts, Ballinger Publishing, 1977, pp. 131-159

30. Lipson AJ: Medical Malpractice: The response of physicians to premium increases in California. Santa Monica, California, Rand Corporation, 1976

31. Ferber S, Sheridan B: Six cherished malpractice myths put to rest. Med Econ 52:150-156, 1975

32. Phelps CE: Experience Rating in Medical Malpractice Insurance. Santa Monica, California, Rand Corporation, 1977

33. Epstein RA: Medical malpractice: the case for contract. Am Bar Found Res J 1:87-149, 1976

34. Epstein RA: Contracting out of the medical malpractice crisis. Perspect Biol Med 20:228-245, 1977

35. The two pieces are identical except for a few minor editorial changes and the addition to the report of a preface and two footnotes.

36. A simple example will illustrate this point: a power lawnmower causes a severe injury to the leg of an operator. This particular type of accident could be eliminated if a footguard were added to each lawnmower at an ultimate cost to the manufacturer of $10 per machine. Without the protective device, the probability of the injury is one for every 100 lawnmowers sold, and the damages entailed by each injury are assumed to be $2000. The expected loss (P × L) is .01 × $2000, or $20 per lawnmower. Therefore, the cost of prevention, $10, is less than the expected loss, and the manufacturer is found to be negligent. If, on the other hand, the ultimate cost of adding the footguard were $30 per lawnmower, negligence could not be established.

37. the availability of health insurance may have another perverse effect on the malpractice signal. Physicians may respond even to a valid finding of negligence by substituting resources that are "free" to them (such as X-rays or consultations) for increased expenditure of their own time. Although the result seems desirable—an appropriate reduction in the incidence of mishaps—it may be purchased at too high a social cost.

Section
VII

Taxation Policy
and
Public Sector
Limits

28

PROPOSITION 13—GENESIS AND CONSEQUENCES

William H. Oakland

California's voters recently enacted a revolutionary measure for reducing the level and growth of state-and-local government expenditure, and for sharply restricting the use of the property tax as a source of government revenue. The Jarvis-Gann Amendment (Proposition 13): (1) restricts the property tax rate to no more than one percent of assessed value;[1] (2) sets assessed value for a property which has not been transferred since 1975-76 equal to its 1975-76 fair-market value plus two percent per year (compounded)—or in the case of subsequent transfer, sets assessed value equal to market value at time of sale plus the two-percent growth factor; and (3) requires that new taxes or increases in existing taxes (except property taxes) receive a two-thirds approval of the legislature in the case of state taxes, or of the electorate in the case of local taxes.[2]

These provisions have had an enormous fiscal impact. First, the rate limitation alone cut property-tax collections by half,[3] since the effective rate of property tax previously had averaged about 2.5 percent statewide. Moreover, the reduction was accentuated by the fact that the rollback of assessments applied to a period when property values had escalated rapidly. Hence, the overall impact amounted to a 57-percent ($7 billion) reduction in property-tax receipts. This constituted nearly 20 percent of the total revenues raised by all levels of California governments, and 37 percent of the revenues raised by local governments alone.

Before the fact, Proposition 13's critics had predicted disastrous fiscal consequences from such a massive reduction in local-government revenues. They predicted a loss of more than 200,000 public-sector jobs, on the assumption

* Professor of Economics and Public Administration, Ohio State University, and Visiting Scholar, Federal Reserve Bank of San Francisco, Summer 1978.

that slightly more than half of the lost $7 billion would have been spent on payroll (the national average is 57 percent). The total employment loss was estimated at 400,000 public and private jobs, allowing for such indirect effects as the money public employees would no longer spend. Equally important, the critics predicted that a massive disruption of public services would accompany the revenue shortfall. San Francisco officials, for example, estimated that outlays on police and fire services would be cut by one-third, the budget for libraries cut by 80 percent, the city zoo entirely eliminated, and funds for other recreation and cultural activities reduced by two-thirds.[4] These dire forecasts have not yet materialized, because of substantial State relief—and because of a number of other factors discussed in this paper. However, the critics argue that severe consequences can still be expected, since the State program was only enacted for one year and the surplus from which it was financed may not recur.

While Proposition 13's employment and public-expenditure effects have received the most attention, numerous other ramifications also demand attention. The amendment, for example, has major implications for financial markets, for individual taxpayers, for the housing market, for state and local governments, and perhaps, most dramatically, for the Federal Government. Because of this complexity, it would be foolish to attempt a comprehensive evaluation in the space available here. Instead, the paper will focus upon three broad questions or issues:

1. What was the general fiscal climate during the period in which the amendment was formulated and debated?

2. To what extent will Proposition 13 succeed in reducing the size and growth of California's public expenditures?

From William H. Oakland, "Proposition 13—Genesis and Consequences," *Economic Review* 7-24 (Winter 1979). Copyright 1979 Federal Reserve Bank of San Francisco. Reprinted by permission.

3. What does the amendment imply for California's future revenue structure?

The answer to the first question should help to resolve a basic controversy--was Proposition 13's success due to fiscal conditions characteristic of state-and-local governments in general, or was it simply a response to fiscal tensions unique to California? The evidence presented below supports the latter position. More specifically, we argue that California's fiscal climate in the pre-Proposition 13 period was characterized by: a) a heavy and growing state-and-local tax burden during a period when such burdens had levelled off in most other states; b) a massive shift of property taxes towards homeowners; and c) a rapidly expanding State budget surplus.

Although difficult to quantify, each factor undoubtedly contributed to Proposition 13's emergence and eventual adoption. More importantly, however, the second and third factors were almost unique to California. The fact that other states considered similar measures, therefore, is more a reflection of their attempt to replicate California's "success" with voter-induced tax reduction than a response to similar fiscal pressures. Largely for this reason, California's experience provides little guidance for other communities. For example, unless they amass a substantial budget surplus somewhere in the state-local fiscal system, as California has done, they cannot avoid painful disruptions in public services.

This leads us to the second question—the impact on the size and growth of public expenditure. Some Proposition 13 advocates have argued that one of its major effects will be a curb on the growth of the public sector. Our evidence suggests that such effects are and will continue to be relatively minor. Specifically, in its first year, Proposition 13 reduced the level of public services by roughly 3 percent, and in subsequent years, it may reduce the growth rate of public services by less than 1 percentage point. Such results primarily reflect the significant earlier build-up in the State government's budget surplus, the highly responsive character of the State revenue system, and the substantial growth expected in future property-tax revenues.

Despite this small expenditure impact, Proposition 13 has affected the revenue structure of California governments in a major way. Because it largely substitutes State revenues for local revenues, the share of local-government expenditures financed by local sources has dropped precipitously. This has obvious consequences for home rule. In addition, the progressivity of the state-local revenue system has increased, because State revenue sources tend to be more progressive than the local property tax. Finally, property-tax proceeds have come to be shared, on a defacto basis, by local-government units within a county area. In effect, Proposition 13 has introduced tax-base sharing at the county level. This important (although unintended) effect has tended to strengthen fiscally weak jurisdictions (e.g., central-city governments) at the expense of the more affluent (e.g., suburbs).

I. California Tax Climate

In this section we focus upon three major facets of California's fiscal climate: (1) the behavior of the total state-local tax burden over the past two decades; (2) the behavior of the relative property-tax burden of owner-occupied residential property; (3) the recent growth of the State surplus and fiscal prospects for the near-term future.

Total state-local tax burden

California governments collected $20.8 billion in taxes in fiscal year 1975-76, more than their counterparts in any other state.[5] California's per capita tax collection of $965 placed it behind only Alaska ($1,896) and New York ($1,139). Accordingly, per capita taxes in California stood 32 percent above the national average and 44 percent above the state median. In relation to personal income, a similar picture emerges. Californians paid 14.9 percent of their personal income in 1975-76, ranking behind only New York and Vermont residents—and standing 19 percent above the national average. Thus, regardless of the measure, California emerges as a high-tax state.

Additionally, the tax burden has increased sharply in recent years. Without Proposition 13, California governments would have absorbed nearly 16 percent of the state's personal income in fiscal year 1978-79, as compared to 9.3 percent in 1957—an increase of more than 6.5 percentage points. (Table A.1 and Chart 1). For the U.S. as a whole, this measure also increased during the period, but at a much less rapid pace. Thus, the differential between California and the rest of the nation widened from 1 percentage point to more than 4 percentage points over the past two decades, with much of that widening occurring just within the past five years. While the effective tax rate elsewhere actually decreased slightly during the seventies, California's effective rate continued to grow as rapidly as before. This suggests that California has gotten out of step with the rest of the country in recent years. Proposition 13 may thus reflect taxpayers' attempts to bring their government back into line with historic relationships.[6] But even after the adoption of the amendment, as Table A.1 indicates, California's tax rate remains above the average for the rest of the nation.

Property tax burdens

Consequently, significant pressures for tax relief have developed in California during recent years. But where would we expect those pressures to erupt? The sharpest increase in recent years has occurred in property taxes, especially those affecting homeowners. Thus, it is not surprising that the taxpayer chose this particular avenue for tax reduction.

The property tax plays a major role in the California tax structure, comprising approximately 41 percent of total state-local tax revenue in 1975-76.[7] The corresponding figure for the U.S. as a whole is 36 percent.[8] And since California is a high tax state, its property-tax burden is relatively high. In per capita terms, California's 1975-76 property tax receipts of $415 stood 47 percent above the national norm, and were surpassed only by New Jersey ($446) and Alaska ($1,048).[9] As a share of personal income, the relevant figures are 6.4 percent for California and 4.5 percent for the nation as a whole (see Appendix Table A.2 and Chart 1). The introduction of General Revenue Sharing narrowed this gap in the early seventies, but it widened again after 1973.

The growing burden was especially heavy for homeowners. In the absence of Proposition 13,

Chart 1

Property Taxes, and Total State-Local Taxes, as Percent of Personal Income

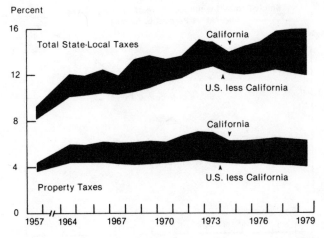

Source: U.S. Bureau of Census; 1977-79 data estimated by author (see Tables A.1 and A.2). Effect of Proposition 13 not shown on chart.

the share of property taxes accounted for by single-family dwellings would have risen from 32 percent in 1973-74 to 44 percent in 1978-79 (Table A.3 and Chart 2). Thus, relative to *total* state personal income, homeowner property taxes increased 38 percent over the same period.[10] The single-family share of total assessments had been relatively constant during the sixties and early seventies, despite substantial adjustments in the shares of other types of property. Indeed, an increase in the homeowner's exemption caused the share to dip momentarily in 1973-74, but then it began a rapid rise because of an unparalleled boom in the single-family housing market. Prices for existing homes in the San Francisco area, for example, jumped 120 percent between April 1973 and April 1978—roughly 18 percent a year[11]—and the Los Angeles area experienced even faster growth. The price upsurge could not be attributed to inflation alone, since the GNP price deflator increased only 55 percent over the same five-year period. The boom was confined primarily to single-family housing, and did not spill over into nonresidential building.

Because reassessment in California is conducted on a three-year cycle, the full effects of the housing price upsurge had not yet been felt by the fiscal year 1978-79. Given a 9-percent annual rate of property appreciation—a conservative estimate—and given a continuation of the recent pace of construction activity, the single-family share of assessments (without Proposition 13) would have risen to about 48.6 percent in the year 1981-82. (In contrast, the combined share of assessments, for homeowners and renters alike, amounted to only 47 percent for the nation as a whole in 1975.)[12] In the space of only seven years, then, the homeowner's share of the property tax would have risen 54 percent.

Therefore, it is not surprising that California's taxpayer revolt focussed upon property-tax reduction. The property-tax burden generally was heavier than elsewhere, and in addition, the rapid escalation of real-estate prices had created a massive shift of the property-tax burden toward homeowners. As a class, homeowners were made better off by the capital gains on their homes, but most were not in a position to realize them. Consequently, a large number of homeowners found themselves with property-tax bills doubling and even tripling without a corresponding increase in their income flow. Thus considerable pressures arose for some form of property-tax relief.

Chart 2

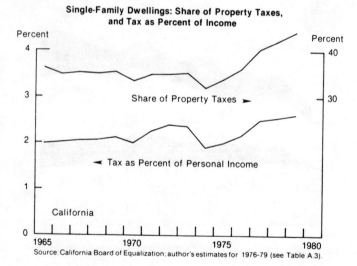

Single-Family Dwellings: Share of Property Taxes, and Tax as Percent of Income

Source: California Board of Equalization; author's estimates for 1976-79 (see Table A.3).

State budget surplus

No story about California's fiscal climate would be complete without a discussion of the budget surplus accumulated by the State government in the past several years. Without the passage of Proposition 13 and its impact on the 1978-79 budget, the cumulative surplus would have grown to at least $10.1 billion by 1979-80 (Table 1)[13]. That amount would have been almost as great as the combined yield ($11 billion in 1979) of the State's two major revenue sources, the personal income tax and the general sales tax.[14]

The growth in the State surplus reflects a virtual explosion of California tax revenues (Table 2). Between 1975-76 and 1977-78, three of the State's major revenue sources showed growth rates of 43 percent or more, and a fourth grew by about one-third. Overall, growth of revenues amounted to a staggering 40 percent. More impressively, this growth was accomplished without any rate increases and was accompanied by an increase of only 23 percent in state personal income. In the aggregate, the latter implies a revenue elasticity of 1.75. Although State expenditures also grew rapidly over the same period (27 percent), this growth was not sufficient to prevent the accumulation of a considerable surplus.

The rapid growth of State-tax revenues can be explained in part by the rapid recovery of the national and regional economies from the severe 1974-75 recession. Corporate profits and per-

Table 1
Budget Surplus of the State of California, Prior to Adoption of Proposition 13, 1975-76 to 1979-80
($ millions)

Fiscal Year	Cumulative Surplus At Beginning of Fiscal Year	Change in Cumulative Surplus from Preceding Year
1975-76	570	
1976-77	1,211	641
1977-78	3,800	2,589
1978-79a	7,100	3,300
1979-80a	10,100	3,000

a Does not allow for $4,100 million Proposition 13 relief and temporary income-tax cut of $1,000 million, both for fiscal year 1978-79.

Source: (1975-76) and (1976-77), California Legislature, *Analysis of the Budget Bill, July 1, 1978 to June 30, 1978;* (1977-78) to (1979-80) *San Francisco Chronicle,* August 25, 1978.

sonal income, of course, are highly sensitive to aggregate economic conditions. But as the economy approaches full-employment, revenue increases from these sources should slow down. However, one other factor tends to keep state revenue growth above that of personal income—inflation. Since the State's personal income tax is steeply progressive over a wide range, increases in income due to inflation generate disproportionately large increases in tax receipts. Specifically, the elasticity of the State income tax with

Table 2
Growth of Major State Taxes in California
1975-76 to 1977-78

Tax Source	Receipts 1977-78 ($ millions)	Change Since 1975-76 ($ millions)	Percent Growth 1975-76 to 1977-78 (percent)
Personal Income Tax	$ 4,391	$ 1,432	48
General Sales Tax	5,020	1,278	34
Selective Sales Taxes	2,234	672	43
Corporation Income Tax	1,900	616	48
Death and Gift Taxes	369	48	17
Property (auto excise) Tax	445	70	19
TOTAL	14,359	4,116	40

Item: California Personal Income   23

Sources: U. S. Bureau of the Census, *Governmental Finances; Economic Report of the Governor,* 1978.

respect to personal income has averaged about
1.7 over the last decade. This means that for
every one-percent inflation-induced growth in
personal income. income taxes have increased by
1.7 percent   a 0.7-percent bonus for the State.
At inflation rates of 7 to 8 percent. this translates
into an additional 5-percent real increase in the
State government's revenue.

Inflation makes the short-term outlook for
State revenue growth particularly bright. Continued inflation should enable the State to sustain personal-income growth of 11 percent. its
average for the past five years. If the growth of
other tax revenue matches the growth of personal income. total tax revenue could expand
13.5 percent per year   nearly doubling within
five years.[15] More importantly. if State Government expenditures grow in proportion to State
personal income. the budget surplus would continue to expand. By the year 1983-84. the annual
surplus would rise to $6.3 billion. and the cumu-
lative surplus to more than $30 billion (Table 3).
In other words. the budget surplus would grow
to untenable levels without some action to reduce taxes. Of course the State government
could increase expenditures more rapidly than
the 11 percent assumed in our projections. But
this would run counter to the national trend   a
falling share of income absorbed by state and
local taxes (see Table A.1). The State.
alternatively. could provide greater financial
relief to local governments. but this would only
shift the locus of the surplus. Tax reduction of
some form appears inevitable. Indeed. this helps
explain the recent one-time-only State income
tax cut of $1 billion. at a time when government
finances were supposedly in a state of crisis. A
glance at Table 3 suggests that this action was no
more than a "drop in the bucket."

Three major factors

We can now weave together the three major
strands of our fiscal-climate story. Not only were
taxes considerably higher in California than
elsewhere. but they were also diverging from the
national norm. Pressures therefore were developing to bring the state back into line. In effect.

Table 3
Projected Budget Surplus of
the State of California
1978-79 to 1983-84
($ millions)

Fiscal Year	Cumulative End-of-Year Surplus a	Yearly Surplus a
1978-79	$ 7.100	$3.300
1979-80	11.202	4.102
1980-81	15.767	4.565
1981-82	20.846	5.079
1982-83	26.489	5.653
1983-84	32.780	6.291

a For derivation see text. No allowance is made for State
    relief or tax-cut programs enacted for fiscal year 1978-79.

this amounted to resistance to abnormally high
levels of government expenditure.[16] At the same
time. the combination of economic recovery and
inflation had produced a substantial budgetary
surplus which. if left unchecked. would have
soon grown to unreasonable proportions.
Hence. pressures were building to bring taxes
back into line with expenditure. Finally. a boom
in the single-family housing market produced a
sharp jump in the homeowner's share of the
property-tax burden. Thus. there was considerable pressure to provide tax relief to this subset
of taxpayers.[17]

Proposition 13. then. was California's method
of dealing with these diverse pressures. It accomplished the necessary tax reduction. and at the
same time provided a change in tax structure
designed to promote equity. This is not to say.
however. that the amendment was the optimal
way of achieving these goals. The fact that no
provision was made for a redistribution of taxes
from the State to local governments threatened a
considerable disruption in the delivery of public
services. However, given the diverse objectives to
be served and differences of interests among
voters. a comprehensive approach may not be
proven politically feasible. Moreover. the State
did redirect substantial revenues to local government. Viewed in this light. Proposition 13 was
successful in liquidating the State surplus.

II. Expenditure Impacts

More than anything else. Proposition 13 has
been interpreted as a measure to reduce the level
and control the growth of government spending.
In this section. we offer quantitative estimates of

the expenditure impacts of the amendment in both the short and medium term. It will be seen that the pre-election estimates were grossly exaggerated, and that Proposition 13's impact on the size of California's public sector has been relatively modest. (For those readers who wish to skip the sometimes complex detail, the main conclusions are summarized in the last part of this section.)

Early estimates of impact

As noted earlier, the Jarvis-Gann Amendment initially had been expected to reduce local-government property-tax revenues by 57 percent ($7 billion) in fiscal year 1978-79. This would imply a 23-percent reduction in local expenditures, allowing for the fact that the property tax produced 40 percent of all local revenues. A reduction of such magnitude was not required, however, because the State government, by liquidating some of its surplus, allocated $4.1 billion in direct assistance and $0.9 billion in emergency loans to local governments. Actually, the State relief package amounted to only $4.1 billion, since no local units availed themselves of the loan funds, which would have required repayment in any case. With the $4.1 billion in hand, local governments faced a projected revenue shortfall of $2.9 billion in the first year after the passage of Proposition 13—which implies a 9.5-percent reduction in total expenditures.

An across-the-board cut of 9.5 percent would appear to be manageable, although somewhat painful. However, the problem is complicated by the fact that a large fraction of local expenditure is outside the control of local authorities, because of Federal or State mandates and/or grant funds which are not fungible. Consider for example, public welfare. Half of the welfare program's support comes from the State, and support levels and eligibility requirements are determined by Congress and the State Legislature. Hence, the major discretion left to the localities lies with administration, which amounts to less than 5 percent of total welfare outlay.[18] And efforts to trim administration may backfire, because payments to ineligible households could increase without proper supervision. The problem is further complicated by the legislative requirement that local communities maintain the qual-

ity of police and fire services as a condition for receiving emergency State assistance.

For those reasons, uncontrollable expenditures may amount to as much as 60 percent of local budgets. Hence, the remaining 40 percent would have to bear the full brunt of the $2.9-billion revenue shortfall. This would involve cuts of nearly 25 percent—not 9.5 percent—so that serious disruptions could be expected to follow.

Despite these somber circumstances, local-government employment dropped by only 7,000 workers during July, the first month of operation under Jarvis-Gann.[19] With a $2.9-billion shortfall, local employment presumably eventually would have had to drop by 80,000, more than ten times what actually occurred. (Even though the 7,000 drop reflects only the first month under the amendment, its permanent character would require much of the adjustment to be made early.) While local governments undoubtedly have some flexibility in substituting workers for other inputs, reducing overtime, etc., a discrepancy of 73,000 could not be due to such factors. Rather, the discrepancy must be explained in terms of an error in the official projection—in other words, the $2.9-billion figure is a gross exaggeration of the local-government revenue gap.

Impact on existing service levels

There are two ways to estimate Proposition 13's public-expenditure impact. The first is to compare public-service levels with those which had prevailed in fiscal year 1977-78, the year prior to implementation of the amendment. This comparison would help measure the magnitude of the disruption in the flow of public services resulting from the action. A second approach is to compare public services with what they would have been in the absence of Proposition 13, which should enable us to discern the expenditure impact of the amendment. Clearly the two measures will be the same if the level of public services remains constant over time. However, some growth in public services has been occurring and can be reasonably expected to continue into the future. For these reasons, both measures are examined below.

First, consider the impact on the existing level of public services. Between the 1977-78 and 1978-79 fiscal years, Proposition 13 was expected to reduce local-government revenues by $6,048 million (Table 4). From this must first be subtracted the State relief package of $4,100 million. But a second adjustment must be made for the fact that officials underestimated actual property-tax collections for 1978-79. Because of the rollback in assessments required by the amendment, officials projected the growth of assessments at only 1.3 percent, as compared to the 12.5 percent which would have been expected in the absence of Proposition 13.[20] In fact, fiscal 1978-79 assessments increased by a healthy 9 percent.

This discrepancy reflected the fact that, despite a three-year reassessment cycle, many properties had been underassessed relative to their 1975-76 values as late as the Spring of 1978, when the rolls for the 1978-79 fiscal year were taken. Furthermore, because of the assessment lag, many of the properties transferred during the 1975-78 period had not been reassessed at their value at time of sale. Since market values had escalated rapidly during this period, the degree of underassessment would be considerable. In

Table 4
Reduction in the Average Level of Local Public Services Caused by Proposition 13
($ millions)

Changes in Local Revenues
Caused by Proposition 13

1977-78 Property Tax Collection	$11,452	
1978-79 Officially Estimated Property	5,404	
Tax Collections		
Net Change		$6,048
Adjustments		
State relief	4,100	
Additional Property Tax Revenue	405	
Due to Higher Assessments		
Total		4,505
Projected Increase in Other Revenues		1,716
1977-78 to 1978-79		
Net Change in Revenues		173
Changes in Revenue Necessary to Maintain		
1977-78 Service Levels		
.08 × 1977-78 Expenditure	2,288	
Less Wage Share (55%)	1,258	1,030
Revenue Deficiency	857	
Percent Revenue Deficiency	2.8%	

both such cases, Proposition 13 allows assessors to adjust prevailing assessments for past errors—and as a result, a large number of properties showed higher assessments after Jarvis-Gann passed than they would have in its absence.[21] Consequently, property-tax revenues in fiscal 1978-79 will be $405 million higher than initially projected.[22]

A further adjustment must be made to allow for the growth of non-property tax revenues. Since the latter are not directly affected by the amendment, we assume that they will grow by 10 percent between 1977-78 and 1978-79—their average rate of growth since 1974-75.[23] This will produce an additional $1,716 million for use in 1978-79. Thus, the net change over the year in *total* local government revenue amounts to $173 million.

To complete this calculation, we must compute the growth of revenues which would have been necessary to sustain 1977-78 public-service levels. With an 8-percent expected rate of inflation, a revenue increase of $2,288 million would be necessary to maintain services. However, as part of its relief measure, the State Legislature prohibited cost-of-living adjustments for local-government employees, so that extra revenues would be needed only for the increased costs for materials and supplies. Since wages comprise 55 percent of total expenditures, the requisite increase is only $1,030 million.[24] Thus, the overall revenue deficiency is $857 million ($173 million less $1,030 million), or 2.8 percent.

It could be argued that the wage freeze will have to be made up sooner or later, and should therefore be excluded from consideration. This objection would be valid if local governments purchased labor services on competitive markets. However, wages in California's public sector run 23 percent above the national average,[25] while wages in its private (manufacturing) sector run only 9 percent above the national average. It would seem, therefore, that California's public-sector workers could live with a one-year wage freeze, because their wages are considerably above those dictated by a free market.

In summary, Proposition 13's actual effect was only a 2.8-percent reduction rather than the 23-percent initially-estimated shortfall in local-government revenues. Even allowing for the fact that mandated programs pushed the brunt of the adjustment upon 40 percent of local governments' budgets, the implied reduction amounted to 7.0 percent for those activities subject to cuts. Such an adjustment would seem to be achievable without major disruptions. And since many local governments responded to the revenue shortfall by imposing new schedules of fees, much of the remaining reduction may yet be avoided.[26]

The employment data cited above are consistent with this finding of only small impact of the Jarvis-Gann amendment on the level of public services. Further support is provided by the budget of the City and County of San Francisco. Although accounting procedures make year-to-year comparisons difficult, San Francisco's total budget showed only an $8-million decline, to $823 million, for fiscal 1978-79. Moreover, the budget for permanent employees' salaries remained unchanged from a year earlier—implying no layoffs. Furthermore, the City rescinded several emergency tax measures adopted at the time the amendment was first passed—which would hardly imply fiscal distress. Finally, there is some evidence that the City actually budgeted a considerable surplus for the year.[27, 28]

Impact on 1978-79 service levels

To determine the amendment's impact on 1978-79 planned local expenditures, we must calculate the loss of local revenue caused by Proposition 13 plus any State-mandated expenditure cutbacks (Table 5).[29] According to official estimates, the 1978-79 property-tax revenue loss amounts to $12,448 million, but from this we subtract State relief and the property-tax receipts not officially anticipated. The resulting figure, $2,469 million, is thus a first approximation of the reduction in local-government revenues from what would have prevailed without the amendment.

This figure overstates the impact on public services, however, because it fails to allow for the wage freeze imposed by the State Legislature. This action freed up funds which could be used for other purposes, and is thus tantamount to a State grant to local governments of an amount equal to the wage savings. Hence, it must be subtracted from the revenue shortfall. This yields a net reduction in public services of $1,281 million from the level that would have prevailed

Table 5
Local Public Expenditure Before and After Proposition 13 (1978-79)
($ millions)

Changes in Local Revenues Caused by Proposition 13		
Officially Estimated 1978-79 Property Tax Collections		$12,448
Officially Estimated 1978-79 Property Tax Collections Under Proposition 13		5,404
		7,044
Less:		
State Relief	4,100	
Additional Property Tax because of Higher Assessments	405	
Savings because of Prohibition on Cost-of-Living Increases	1,258	
TOTAL		5,763
Net Revenue Shortfall		1,281
Projected 1978-79 Local Revenue		31,473
Percent Net Revenue Shortfall		4.0%

without Jarvis-Gann—only a 4.0 percent shortfall from projected 1978-79 revenues. That cutback seems modest, indeed, when compared with the figures seen in the popular press—or when compared with what Proposition 13's supporters had hoped to achieve.

Future service-level impacts

Even though the first-year expenditure impact is minimal, it could be argued that Proposition 13 will still have a major impact in subsequent years. This view is based upon several considerations: (1) the State relief package was for a single year only; (2) the State surplus from which existing relief was drawn will be depleted in future years; and (3) the amendment's restrictions on assessments will inhibit the future growth of property-tax receipts.

A crucial question concerns the magnitude of surplus State funds, which helps determine the availability and the extent of future State assistance. Some analysts believe only modest amounts will be available, especially since the surplus available to the State Legislature in July 1978 was the result of several years' accumulation. However, there is ample reason to believe that the State could continue or even *increase* existing levels of assistance without increasing tax rates. To analyze this possibility, we project the State surplus under two alternative sets of assumptions about the growth of personal income and State relief. The first assumes growth rates of 12 percent and 10 percent, respectively; the second uses 10 percent and 8 percent.

How valid are these assumptions? While 12-percent personal-income growth is slightly higher than the 11 percent experienced over the past five years, the recent upsurge in inflation makes such an assumption quite plausible. The 10-percent growth in aid, on the other hand, would correspond to the pre-Proposition 13 average growth of property-tax receipts. If State aid grows at a 10-percent rate, therefore, any reduction in the growth of local expenditures would be the result of the failure of *locally* raised revenues to keep pace with the growth they would have experienced without the amendment. The second set of assumptions is more conservative. The 10-percent personal-income growth figure has been surpassed every year since 1973, and the 8-percent growth of State aid would do nothing more than maintain the *real* value of relief under present inflationary conditions. '

State expenditures are assumed to grow at the rate of personal income, while revenues grow at the same rate multiplied by the revenue elasticity, following the procedure used for Table 5. However, we must also adjust for two post-Proposition 13 developments—the one-time-only tax cut of $1 billion, and the indexation of income-tax brackets for the first three percentage points of inflation. Hence, we reduce the elasticity of the income tax from 1.7 (as in Table 5) to a figure of 1.5, and thus obtain a total State revenue elasticity of 1.166.

Under the first set of assumptions, therefore, the State can adequately fund the program without an increase in tax rates (Table 6).[30] Although annual expenditures would exceed revenues between 1978-79 and 1984-85, the carryover 'surplus would be sufficient to fund the deficits—and thereafter, annual revenues would begin to exceed expenditures. Under the second set of assumptions, cumulative deficits would begin to emerge in the mid-eighties, but the $170-million deficit in 1984-85 would amount to only .006 percent of State revenue and 2.6 percent of the State relief program. Since the deficit would disappear by the following year, the program appears to be fundable.

Whether or not the State can offset a constant proportion of local-government property-tax losses, then, hinges critically upon the growth of

Table 6
Projected Surplus of the State of California,*
1978-79 to 1986-87
($ millions)

Fiscal Year	Assumption A		Assumption B	
	Yearly Surplus	Cumulative Surplus	Yearly Surplus	Cumulative Surplus
1978-79	$1,800a	$2,000	$1,800a	$2,000
1979-80	468	1,532	516	1,484
1980-81	427	1,105	474	1,010
1981-82	372	733	420	590
1982-83	298	435	354	236
1983-84	203	232	271	35
1984-85	83	149	170	205
1985-86	65	214	49	254
1986-87	n.c.	n.c.	96	158

Assumption A: 12-percent growth of State personal income and 10-percent growth of State aid.

Assumption B: 10-percent growth of State personal income and 8-percent growth of State aid.

n.c.   Not calculated

a Reflects a $1-billion tax cut for 1978-79 only.

*Source: see derivation in text.

personal income. If this growth is as high as 12 percent, the State can meet its objective without an increase in statutory tax rates. If, on the other hand, income growth is only 10 percent, aid can grow at only 8 percent per year. In other words, relief would fall 2 percentage points below the level necessary to keep local public expenditures growing at the rate which would have prevailed in the absence of Proposition 13.[31]

Another crucial question concerns the potential problems caused by the amendment's 2-percent annual limit on property reassessments (unless the property is transferred). On its face, this might seem to limit property-tax revenue to 2-percent annual growth, but such is not the case. The growth of property-tax receipts will reflect the degree of underassessment as of 1978-79, the rate of increase of property values, the turnover rate of existing property, and the rate of new construction.

Consider, first, the growth of residential-property assessments. As the appendix shows, aggregate assessments for existing houses could grow at a rate equal to 90 percent of the underlying appreciation rate of housing prices in the *first* year following the reassessment limitation. Moreover, in subsequent years, assessments could continue to increase until reaching the appreciation rate. Thus, if housing values are increasing at a 10-percent annual rate, the assessed value of the housing stock in place during 1978-79 will grow by 9 percent in 1979-80. These results are based on two assumptions, both of which conform with recent experience—a 25-percent initial under-assessment of the existing housing stock, relative to its 1978-79 value, and a 15-percent annual turnover rate of existing housing.[32]

The rapid increase in the assessed value of the existing housing stock reflects the much larger (although less frequent) reassessment of homes under the amendment. For example, if a house is sold every seven years and housing prices grow at 10 percent per year, the assessed value of such a house will double at the time of sale. If, on the other hand, the house were assessed annually, the increase in assessment would be only 10 percent each year, leading to the same result over time. Thus, Proposition 13 would cause a much smaller reduction in the growth of the assessed

value of existing homes than perhaps some of its framers intended. We must also consider the growth caused by new construction, which amounts each year to between 2 and 4 percent of California's existing housing stock. If housing prices rise 10 percent per year, which is modest by recent standards, the total residential-property tax base will then increase by 11 to 13 percent per year, not much below its recent performance.

The situation is much different with non-residential properties, which are transferred much less frequently than housing. Hence, the taxable base for this class of property probably will grow at about the 2-percent allowable annual rate, plus any growth due to new construction, which normally accounts for about 2 percent of the existing stock. Thus, we could expect the non-residential property tax base to rise about 4 percent annually.

The *total* property-tax base, given our assumptions about the growth of the (relatively comparable) residential and non-residential components, could increase annually by 7½ percent to 8½ percent—say 8 percent. This is only 2 percentage points below what would have been expected without Proposition 13. But this gap will now pose a much less serious problem than before, because the property tax now accounts for only 20 percent of total local-government revenues, as compared with 40 percent in the pre-amendment period. This means that the annual revenue shortfall caused by the reassessment provision should amount to only 0.4 percent—scarcely a startling effect.

Under our assumption of 10-percent annual growth in state aid, the reduction in the growth of public expenditure would reflect the reassessment provision alone—only 0.4 percent. But with 8-percent annual growth in state aid, the total reduction will be 0.7 percent.[33] By either standard, the reduction appears insignificant in relation to the 10-percent anticipated annual growth in local public expenditures.

Overall impact

Altogether, Proposition 13 has had, and will probably continue to have, only minor effects upon the size of California's public sector. Public-service levels in 1978-79 are only about 2.8 percent below those prevailing in the year before the amendment took effect—or only about 4.0 percent below if allowance is made for increases in public services which would have occured in the absence of Jarvis-Gann. The future expenditure effect, on the other hand, will hinge largely upon what happens to the State relief program. Since the State will probably continue to amass surpluses, it will probably continue to make aid available to local governments. The major source of expenditure constraint, however, will be the slowdown in the growth of property-tax revenues. But even this shortfall should amount to only 0.4–0.6 percent of the total revenue requirement of local governments. And in view of the availability of other revenue sources—such as charges, fees, and wage taxes—even this minor shortfall could be resolved.

Two caveats are in order, however. First, our calculations were done entirely at the aggregate level, whereas some individual government units could experience considerable reductions in expenditure. Secondly, no allowance was made for the possibility of recession. A major recession could wipe out much of the carryover surplus which is providing the funding for the State relief program. However, even during the 1975 recession, California personal income grew by 10½ percent—which is above our minimum-growth assumption. This reflected the inflation which kept nominal incomes rising in the face of recession. Since substantial inflation could continue for the next four or five years, even the occurrence of a recession during this period need not invalidate our conclusions.

III. Tax Structure Impact

In contrast to Proposition 13's relatively minor impact upon the level of government expenditure, it will have a substantial impact upon the state-and-local tax structure, and also upon the distribution of revenue-raising responsibility between the State and local governments (Table 7). The local share of total revenues in 1978-79 drops 12 percentage points, to 37 percent, as a result of the amendment. (In contrast, the national average share was 46 percent in 1975-76.) This understates the extent of the

actual reduction, however, because without the amendment the State would probably have taken steps to liquidate its surplus. With a $4.1-billion reduction in the surplus—the actual amount of local relief—the local share of state-local revenue would have been considerably higher, so by that standard Proposition 13 lowered the local share by nearly 20 percentage points. And the situation is even more dramatic for specific local functions. For example, the share of education financed locally drops from

Table 7
State-Local Division of Revenue Raising Responsibility
in California, 1978-79

	Source of Total Own-Source Revenue ($ millions)			Share of Elementary and Secondary Education Costs	
	Without Amendment				
	Without Tax Reduction	With Tax Reduction*	With Amendment	Without Amendment	With Amendment
	(1)	(2)	(3)	(4)	(5)
Local	$16,983 (49%)	$16,983 (56%)	$10,483 (37%)	52%	28%
State	17,675 (51%)	13,575 (44%)	17,675 (63%)	n.c.	n.c.
Total	34,658	30,558	28,158		

n.c. Not calculated

*Assumes $4.1 billion in State tax reduction.

Source: U.S. Bureau of Census, *Government Finances,* and estimates by the author.

52 percent to 28 percent because of the amendment,[34] placing California below all but six other states in this regard.[35]

Political theory suggests that the control of public expenditure ultimately rests with the body which is responsible for raising the revenue. If this is correct, Proposition 13 will lead to a major shift towards State control. The prohibition against employee cost-of-living increases and against reductions in public safety may be just the tip of the iceberg for future state interventions. Local control or "home rule" could become a thing of the past in California.[36] Any judgment here, however, must remain in the realm of speculation. Our experience with Federal Revenue Sharing has shown that revenue-raising and expenditure authority can at least sometimes be kept separate.

Less uncertainty surrounds the tax-structure consequences of Proposition 13, which tends to substitute State tax sources for the local property tax. More specifically, in the absence of this measure, the State probably would have cut income taxes.[37] Since the income tax tends to be more progressive than the property tax, such a substitution presumably would have favorable equity consequences.[38]

Again, given the fact that income-tax reduction was the major alternative to Jarvis-Gann, areas which are relatively property intensive should now gain relative to those areas which are income intensive. Since cities and rural areas have a larger share of the statewide property-tax base than of the income-tax base, taxes consequently would be shifted towards the suburbs. Given the poor fiscal condition of many central cities, such a shift would provide welcome relief.

Further relief for fiscally disadvantaged jurisdictions should come from a little-noticed feature of the State relief measure, which allocates

relief roughly in proportion to previous property-tax collections.[39] Because of the massive reduction in property-tax receipts, it was necessary to specify how the remaining revenues from this source were to be allocated. Basically, the State Legislature decided to allocate these proceeds among counties in proportion to their total assessed valuation. This precluded inter-county tax transfers. Within each county, however, tax proceeds were divided roughly in proportion to previous property-tax collections; i.e., each local unit suffered the same percentage revenue loss. If this arrangement is continued, therefore, *future* increases in assessable base will be shared by all units within a jurisdiction.

In effect, California has developed a system of tax-base sharing similar to that in operation in the Minneapolis-St. Paul area, whereby increments to the metropolitan tax base are shared by all local units within the urban area. (However, the Twin City program is on a metropolitan rather than county basis.) Base sharing has been widely touted as a technique to cope with the adverse fiscal consequences of suburbanization, so that a central city does not suffer revenue losses if its tax base moves to the suburbs.[40] Moreover, the city reaps part of the benefit of whatever net growth occurs in the metropolitan area. Perhaps unwittingly, therefore, California with Proposition 13 has radically changed fiscal relationships in its metropolitan areas.[41]

In summary, the adoption of Proposition 13 may profoundly affect the system of governance of California. On the one hand, it could lead to a substantial loss in local control, while on the other, it could significantly affect fiscal relationships within metropolitan areas. Finally, it should increase the equity of California taxes, among persons and among political jurisdictions.

IV. Summary and Conclusions

This paper has shown that the emergence of the Jarvis-Gann Amendment cannot be attributable to a single cause, but rather to several different forces. First was a high and growing state-local tax burden during a period when similar burdens in other parts of the country were levelling off. Second was a substantial shift in the distribution of property-tax burdens towards homeowners at

a time when inflation was already causing budgetary problems for many households. Lastly was the emergence of a significant State surplus which, if left unchecked, would have grown to unreasonable proportions.

Each of these factors contributed to the different perspectives which voters had of the measure. By placing a ceiling on the property-tax rate, restricting the growth of assessments, and increasing the political majorities required for new taxes, the amendment promised to restrict the size and growth of the public sector. By focusing tax reduction upon property taxes, it provided the relief sought by homeowners. And finally, by placing local governments in an intolerable fiscal situation, it forced the State to liquidate much of its surplus.

Proposition 13 apparently has achieved two of its objectives—reduction of property taxes and liquidation of state surpluses—but to date it has had only a minimal effect upon the growth of public expenditures. In its first year, it required only a 2.8-percent reduction in the average level of public services; in the near future, barring a major recession, it may have little effect unless the State withholds the relief it can afford and which it seems already committed to provide.

In effect, then, Proposition 13 emerges primarily as a tax-reform measure—one which shifts the emphasis from the property tax to the income tax. Moreover, by shifting a major portion of local revenue-raising responsibility to the State, the amendment may seriously erode local control. The measure has also had some unintended consequences for fiscal relations at the local level, since the property taxes that remain are to be shared on a county-wide basis. This will tend to augment the resources of fiscally weak governments at the expense of the more affluent.

These unintended consequences aside, Proposition 13 emerges as a unique California phenomenon. The combination of factors which gave it birth are unlikely to be matched in any other state. The same can be said of its consequences. The existence of a significant State surplus has mitigated its potentially disruptive impacts upon the delivery of public services. This carries an important lesson for other states that have been considering measures similar to Proposition 13. Unless a considerable surplus already exists somewhere in their state-local system, they cannot expect to match the relatively smooth transition experienced by California. Without such a surplus, their citizens and public officials must be prepared to face considerable disruptions in the flow of public services.

Appendix
Behavior of Residential Investment

Let $V(t)$ be the market value of a home whose assessed value at $t = (T\text{-}1978) = 0$ is equal to $k\%$ of its true market value. Furthermore, assume homes appreciate at the constant rate $g\%$ per year, so that

$$V(t) = V(0)(1 + g)^t \qquad (1)$$

Under Proposition 13, the assessed value of such a home is equal to

$$A(t, u) \begin{cases} = (1.02)^{t-u} V(u) & \text{if } u \geqslant 1 \\ = (1.02)^t \, kV(0) & \text{if } u = 0 \end{cases} \qquad (2)$$

where u is the year of the last sale of the home. Let the probability that a home is sold during a given year be given by $s(t)$, and assume that $s(t) = s$, for all t. Then the probability that, at time t, the house would have last been sold $(t - u)$ periods earlier is given by

$$p(t, u) \begin{cases} = s(1 - s)^{t-u} & \text{if } u \geqslant 1 \\ = (1 - s)^t & \text{if } u = 0 \end{cases} \qquad (3)$$

The *expected* assessment of the home at time t is given by

$$A(t) = \sum_{u=o}^{t} p(t, u)A(t, u). \qquad (4)$$

Morever, since

$$p(t - 1, u) = (1 - s)^{-1} p(t, u) \qquad (5)$$

$$A(t - 1, u) = (1.02)^{-1} A(t, u) \qquad (6)$$

we can express (4) as

$$A(t) = (1.02)(1 - s)A(t - 1) + sV(0)(1 + g)^t, \qquad (7)$$

which is a first-order linear differential equation.

Assume there are two classes of residential property which differ only in their ratio of assessed value to market value. The first class, denoted by the subscript 1, has an initial assessment ratio of 1, while the other, denoted by 2, has an initial ratio of k. Then the expected aggregate assessed value is

$$B(t) = [wA_1(t) + (1 - w)A_2(t)] \cdot N \qquad (8)$$

where w is the share of homes in class 1 and N is the number of homes. For convenience we normalize so that $N = 1$.

Using (7), we can express (8) as

$$B(t) = (1.02)(1 - s)B(t - 1) \\ + sV(0)(1 + g)^t \qquad (9)$$

which has the solution

$$B(t) = [B(0) - (\frac{bz}{z - a})]a^t + (\frac{b}{z - a})z^{t+1} \qquad (10)$$

where

a = $(1.02)(1 - s)$
b = $sV(0)$
z = $(1 + g)$

Now let us normalize B such that

$$B(0) = wA_1(0) + (1 - w)A_2(0) \\ = wV(0) + (1 - w)kV(0) \\ = 1 \qquad (11)$$

Then

$$V(0) = \frac{1}{w + (1 - w)k} = \frac{1}{r} \qquad (12)$$

where r is the aggregate assessment ratio at $t = 0$.

Substituting from (11) and (12) into (10), and setting $t = 1$, we obtain

$$B(1) = \frac{1}{z - a}[z(1 - \frac{r}{s}) - a^2 + \frac{r}{s}z^2] \qquad (13)$$

Since we have set $B(0) = 1$, (11) represents one plus the growth rate of the aggregate assessments for the first year. Choosing $s = .15$, $g = .1$, and $r = .75$, yields $B(1) = 1.087$. With $r = .74$, $B(1) = 1.09$.

It remains to examine the subsequent growth of B(t). Clearly, if $1 + g > (1 - s)(1.02)$, which is to be expected,

$$\lim_{t \to \infty} \frac{B(t) - B(t - 1)}{B(t - 1)} = g$$

Moreover, it is easy to show that if the same condition holds

$$\frac{d\left[\frac{B(t)}{B(t - 1)}\right]}{dt} > 0.$$

Table A.1
State and Local Taxes
as a Percent of
Personal Income, 1957-78

Year	California	Other U.S.	Difference
	(1)	(2)	(1-2)
1957	9.31	8.14	1.17
1962	10.46	9.32	1.14
1963-64	12.07	10.13	1.94
1964-65	11.98	10.24	1.74
1965-66	12.47	10.43	2.04
1966-67	11.98	10.32	1.66
1967-68	13.37	10.49	2.88
1968-69	13.71	10.91	2.80
1969-70	13.38	11.44	1.96
1970-71	13.73	11.66	2.07
1971-72	14.94	12.42	2.52
1972-73	14.91	12.71	2.20
1973-74	14.01	12.16	1.85
1974-75	14.59	12.00	2.59
1975-76	14.89	12.17	2.72
1976-77	15.78 c	12.38 a	3.40
1977-78	15.96 c	12.11 a	3.85
1978-79	15.97 c	11.93 b	4.04
1978-79	12.64 d	11.93 b	0.71 d

Source: U.S. Bureau of Census, *Government Finances*

a Based on U.S. Commerce Department estimates, reported in *Survey of Current Business*.

b Same as a, but first quarter 1978 used to project entire year.

c 1976-78 tax receipts based on author's estimates using California State Comptroller Reports. Personal income for 1978 from *Economic Report of the Governor*, 1978.

d After Proposition 13.

Table A.2
Property Taxes as a
Percent of Personal Income,
1957-78

Year	California (1)	Other U.S. (2)	Difference (1-2)	Year	California (1)	Other U.S. (2)	Difference (1-2)
1957	4.39	3.61	.70	1970-71	6.75	4.49	2.26
1962	5.61	4.17	1.44	1971-72	7.11	4.65	2.46
1963-64	6.04	.4.41	1.63	1972-73	7.02	4.58	2.44
1964-65	5.93	4.43	1.50	1973-74	6.28	4.30	1.98
1965-66	6.26	4.44	1.82	1974-75	6.27	4.25	2.02
1966-67	6.16	4.28	1.88	1975-76	6.41	4.29	2.12
1967-68	6.19	4.21	1.98	1976-77	6.56a	4.18b	2.38
1968-69	6.33	4.26	2.07	1977-78	6.44a	4.09b	2.35
1969-70	6.27	4.36	1.91	1978-79	6.32a.c	3.97b	2.35

Source: U.S. Bureau of Census, *Government Finances*   b Estimated using U.S. Commerce Dept. data.
a Estimated using State of California data on property-tax   c Without the passage of Proposition 13.
  collections.

Table A.3
Distribution of Net* Assessed Value and Property Tax Burden
on Single-Family Dwellings in California,
1964-65 to 1978-79

Period	Share of Total Net Assessed Value				Share of Property Taxes of Single-Family Dwellings (5)	Taxes on Single-Family Dwellings as a Percent of Personal Income (6)
	Single-Family Residences (1)	Other Residences (2)	Non-Residential (3)	State Assessedf (4)		
1964-65	34.8%	12.3%	40.8%	12.1%	36.2%	1.97%
65-66	34.5	12.6	41.4	11.5	34.8	2.01
66-67	34.0	13.3	41.8	10.9`	35.3	2.04
67-68	33.6	13.7	42.6	10.1	35.0	2.05
68-69a	34.0	13.8	42.6	9.7	35.4	2.11
69-70b	32.2	14.4	44.0	9.5	33.5	1.98
70-71c	33.5	14.8	42.9	8.8	34.8	2.24
71-72	33.7	14.5	43.8	8.1	35.0	2.37
72-73	34.0	13.9	44.4	7.6	35.2	2.35
73-74d	31.6	13.8	46.9	7.7	32.1	1.88
74-75e	32.9	13.4	46.4	7.3	33.9	1.98
75-76	35.2	13.2	44.7	6.9	36.2	2.16
76-77	39.5	12.9	41.0	6.6	40.4	2.48
77-78	41.0	12.6	39.6	6.7	42.2	2.53
78-79	43.0	12.6	38.3	6.4	44.3	2.60

* Net of exemptions
a First significant "open space" assessments.
b Introduction of $750 homestead exemption; 15-percent inventory exemption.
c With 30-percent inventory exemption.
d With $1,750 homestead exemption; 45-percent inventory exemption.
e With 50-percent inventory exemption.
f State-assessed property is mainly personal property of utilities. Beginning in 1964 and ending in 1974, the assessment ratio
  on this class was lowered until it reached the ratio applying to other classes.
Source: California Board of Equalization; author's estimates for years 1975-76 to 1978-79.

FOOTNOTES

1. This rate limitation does not apply to the debt service on outstanding debt.

2. This description of the Amendment is only meant to be suggestive. For a more thorough discussion see the Beebe article in this **Review.**

3. It is estimated that a levy of 1/4 percent would be necessary initially to service outstanding debt.

4. "Analysis of the Fiscal Impact of the Proposed Jarvis-Gann Amendment", **Report to the Bureau of the Budget to the Board of Supervisors,** San Francisco, March 1978. The unevenness of these cuts reflects the fact that not all services are equally funded by the property tax, as well as the existence of a myriad of State and Federal mandates.

5. U.S. Bureau of the Census, **Government Finances** in 1975-76.

6. This conjecture is rejected by the U.S. Congressional Budget Office, which using unpublished data concludes that tax burdens in California have been growing about the same rate as elsewhere. Curiously, a 67 percent difference in growth rates of tax burden is interpreted as a 2.2 percent differential (i.e., 5.5 percent vs 3.3 percent). See "Proposition 13: Its Impact on the Nation's Economy, Federal Revenues, and Federal Expenditures", Congressional Budget Office, July 1978.

7. U.S. Bureau of the Census, op. cit.

8. Ibid.

9. Ibid.

10. Since the homeowners' share of State personal income is unknown it was not possible to construct an index of homeowner tax burden per se. Nevertheless, if income shares were constant over the period, the 30 percent figure was a measure of the *increase* in homeowner burden.

11. Real Estate Research Council of Northern California, **Northern California's Real Estate Report,** Vol. 30/Number 1.

12. This figure for 1975 is the latest year for which national data is available. While the California number for that year is close to the national average, the recent upsurge in residential share in California is unlikely to be matched nationally because the boom in real estate prices was much more pronounced in California than elsewhere. Advisory Commission on Intergovernmental Relations, **Significant Features of Fiscal Federalism,** 1976-77, Vol. II, p. 106.

13. The term "at least" is used because the State's projections, from which our figures were drawn, have proved markedly conservative in the past.

14. **Economic Report of the Governor, 1978,** Sacramento, 1978, p. A-55.

15. To arrive at this figure, multiply the 11 percent by 1.7 to obtain the growth of Personal Income Tax receipts—18.7 percent. Since the latter accounts for 1/3 of total general revenue, the growth of total revenue is simply $(1/3 \times 18.7) + (2/3 \times 11.0) = 13.5$.

16. Although our argument has been couched in terms of taxes, it applies equally well to government expenditures because taxes and expenditure move together. An exception to the latter occurs after the 1977-78 fiscal year when substantial surpluses emerge. However, the gap between tax burdens in California and the rest of the U.S. had already opened substantially by 1977-78.

17. Another element which may have played a role is the Serrano decision on the finance of elementary and secondary education. To implement Serrano, the *State* had planned to redistribute property taxes from rich to poor districts. Such action was to begin in the fiscal year 1978-79, but because of Proposition 13's restriction on property tax receipts, it had to be tabled. One might argue that support for Proposition 13 came from those who saw the impending *State* action as eliminating the connection between their property tax payments and the level of educational services they received. It should be noted, however, that under the *State* plan, local overrides to increase educational expenditures were permitted. See **Analysis of the Budget Bill,** California State Legislature, Sacramento, 1978, p. 720.

18. The localities also have control over a modest General Relief Program. However, the amounts here are too small to warrant explicit discussion.

19. "Recent National, Regional and International Developments", Federal Reserve Bank of San Francisco, September 5, 1978.

20. Legislative Analyst, "An Analysis of Proposition 13: The Jarvis-Gann Property Tax Initiative", Sacramento, May, 1978.

21. Since the California Board of Equalization makes annual surveys of assessment ratios, one would have expected such widespread underassessment to show up in their data. However, figures for fiscal year 1977-78 only indicated underassessment of 8 percent in terms of *current* prices. See **Annual Report,** State Board of Equalization, 1976-77.

22. Total assessments for 1978-79 were $116.2 billion compared with the estimate of $108.1 billion. At a tax rate of $5 per $100 valuation, the extra $8.1 billion would yield $405 million.

23. Excluding Special Districts, for which data were unavailable, non-property tax receipts grew as follows: 1974-75—1975-76—12.6%; 1975-76—1976-77—10.2%; 1976-77—1978-79—20.7%.

24. The 55 percent wage share was taken from **Governmental Finances,** op. cit., p. 30.

25. U.S. Bureau of the Census, **Public Employment in 1976.**

26. A survey by the **Los Angeles Times** showed that California cities increased expenditure by 4.6 percent and counties by 5.3 percent over 1977-78 levels. By our estimates such increases were sufficient to maintain *real* 1977-78 spending levels. **Los Angeles Times,** October 1, 1978.

27. The City Auditor is quoted as saying that the City "would probably have a surplus of $51 million", **San Francisco Chronicle,** September 6, 1978.

28. The situation with the San Francisco Unified School District is similar. The budget for 1978-79 actually appears to be higher than for the preceding year.

29. Legislative Analyst, op. cit.

30. Of course, because of the progressivity of the income tax, effective rates increase.

31. This assumes locally raised revenue also grows at without-Amendment rates. Otherwise, the 2 percentage points is added to the gap left by the latter revenues. See below.

32. Study by San Mateo County Manager, May 8, 1978. While one would expect turnover rates to be reduced somewhat because reassessment is triggered by transfer, the effect is likely to be small. Most property transfers involve employment transfers, retirement, or death. Moreover, the maximum savings from maintaining ownership is 1 percent of the value of the home—a figure which may be small compared to the benefits of upgrading one's housing.

33. To arrive at this figure the shortfall in relief growth of 2 percentage points must be translated into a fraction of total local revenue. This is done by observing that State relief is 70 percent of the size of local property tax receipts. Hence, the shortfall in State relief is equivalent to a 1.4 percentage point shortfall in property tax receipts. Since property taxes constitute 20 percent of local revenues, we have a *revenue* shortfall of .28 percent because of State relief. The latter is then added to the reassessment result and rounded.

34. There is some reason to believe, however, that the figures in Table 7 may overstate the effects of the Amendment on education finance. In response to the Serrano decision the State had decided to redistribute property tax receipts among local school districts beginning with fiscal year 1978-79. Because of the limitation on the level of property taxes imposed by Jarvis-Gann, this action had to be shelved. Strictly speaking those funds which were to be redistributed should be counted as State as opposed to local funds. Unfortunately, estimates of the extent of such redistribution were not available at the time this paper was written.

35. Advisory Commission on Intergovernmental Relations, op. cit.

36. This home-rule effect of Proposition 13 is reinforced by the Serrano school finance decision, which requires greater uniformity of expenditures among school districts.

37. While any of the major State taxes could, in principle, be cut, the California Legislature has cut income taxes three times in the past decade. It seems reasonable, therefore, to view income taxes as the marginal instrument.

38. Recently, it has been argued that the incidence of the property tax rests upon the owners of capital. However, this outcome is based upon the premise of a nationally applicable property tax. Since the case at hand is restricted to a single state, its major consequences will be upon output and input prices, as the orthodox theory would predict.

39. An exception is with aid to education. Here relief was allocated according to a complex formula which reflected an attempt to equalize resources between school districts. See SB 154, California State Legislature, 1978.

40. Unless the suburb was located in another county. Note that city-counties such as San Francisco obtain no benefit from this provision.

41. Since the relief measure is for the first year only, it is conceivable that the State Legislature might change the distribution formula in future relief measures. For example, county property tax revenues could be divided among local units in proportion to a unit's share of aggregate assessments. Because the jurisdictional boundaries of many local units overlap, however, such an approach might produce nonsensical results. Moreover, if the objective of the relief was to minimize disruption of public service flows, the present allocation formula may be optimal.

29

THE LIMITATIONS OF TAX LIMITATION

Milton Friedman

Two down, 48 to go.

The approval on June 6, 1978, by the people of our largest state of Proposition 13—a tax limitation amendment to the California Constitution—has given great impetus to the grassroots movement that Governor Ronald Reagan began in that state five years ago when he sponsored Proposition 1.[1]

The first victory for those who believe that government does not have an open-ended claim on the incomes of Americans came in Tennessee three months ago (March 7, 1978) when the people of that state, by a two-to-one majority, approved an amendment to limit the "rate of growth" of state spending to the "estimated rate of growth of the state's economy."

Similar amendments will be on the ballot in a number of other states this fall, and the prospects now look very good for their adoption.

The Jarvis-Gann Amendment, Proposition 13, will limit property taxes in California to one percent of assessed valuation. It will restrict increases in assessed valuation to a maximum of 2 percent a year except when property changes hands. In addition, it will require a two-thirds vote of the legislature to raise other taxes. It is estimated that this amendment will cut property taxes by more than half—or by some $7 billion.

Jarvis-Gann, it must be said, has many defects. It is loosely drawn. It cuts only the property tax, which is by no means the worst tax. It does nothing to halt the unlegislated rise in taxes produced by inflation. Proposition 1 was a far better measure and a revised version will be needed even though Jarvis-Gann has passed. Yet I strongly supported Jarvis-Gann. It does cut taxes. It does raise obstacles to further increases in government spending. Those in favor of more government spending mounted an expensive fear

1. That proposal was preferable to the one adopted on June 6. It would have limited spending by the state government to a specified and slowly declining fraction of the personal income of the people of California. That amendment was narrowly defeated, as were similar amendments in two other states in recent years.

From Milton Friedman, "The Limiations of Tax Limitation," no. 5 *Policy Review* 7-14 (Summer 1978). Copyright 1978 by the Heritage Foundation.

campaign financed in large part by big business (which apparently allowed its own fear of the politicians in Sacramento to trigger its unerring instinct for self-destruction). In this media blitz, the state employees' union leaders (naturally the core of the opposition) predicted that state services would be drastically cut, that thousands of policemen and firemen would be dismissed, and so forth and so on.[2]

In fact Jarvis-Gann will not have the dire effects its opponents threatened. The California government has a surplus of some $3 billion to offset the $7 billion revenue reduction. The remaining $4 billion is roughly 10 percent of the state and local spending now projected for the next fiscal year. Is there a taxpayer in California (even if he is a government employee) who can maintain with a straight face that there is not 10 percent fat that can be cut from government spending without reducing essential services? Of course, the reallocation of revenues to finance the most essential services will not be an easy or pleasant task, but that, after all, is just what we pay our elected representatives for.[3]

Tax Limitation Laws Are Not "Undemocratic"

Which brings us to an important point of political philosophy. It is my view that it is desirable for the people to limit their government's budget, to decide how much in total they are willing to pay for their government. Having done this, it is desirable for them to delegate to their elected representatives the difficult task of dividing that budget among competing good proposals. The opponents of

2. In their column 'for *The Washington Post* on June 1, 1978, Rowland Evans and Robert Novak reported from Los Angeles that some politicians were claiming that the referendum was "a fight between the haves and the have-nots." Evans and Novak concluded that this view was "almost surely wrong." They explained that "On the contrary, the establishment—business, labor, the big newspapers, the academic community, civic groups and practically every important elected official—vigorously opposes the Jarvis amendment."

They went on to point out that "in contrast, the amendment's hardcore support comes from lower income homeowners who are going under because of oppressive taxes. Their ranks, oddly, are swelled by substantial numbers of school teachers and other government workers who are first and foremost taxpayers . . . State Senator Bill Greene, a black Los Angeles legislator, told us he is astounded how many of his constituents are voting for the measure."

3. It is not without interest that California has the highest paid state legislators in the nation.

tax limitation laws charge that we are being undemocratic in proposing to tie the hands of government. After all, they say, don't we elect our state representatives and our congressional representatives in Washington to handle the affairs of government? I believe that if we are going to be effective in passing tax limitation laws, we must understand and make other people understand that these referenda are far from being undemocratic. I believe that the real situation is precisely the opposite.

The problem we face is that there is a fundamental defect in our political and constitutional structure. The fundamental defect is that we have no means whereby the public at large ever gets to vote on the total budget of the government.

Our system is one in which each particular spending measure is treated separately. For any single spending measure, therefore, there is always a small group that has a very strong interest in that measure. All of us are parts of such small groups. We are not talking about somebody else. As Pogo used to say, "We have met the enemy and they are us."

The vested interests are not some big bad people sitting on money bags; the vested interests are you and me. Each of us is strongly in favor of small measures that will benefit us and each of us is not too strongly opposed to any one small measure that will benefit someone else. We are not going to vote anybody out of office because he imposes a $3 a year burden on us. Consequently, when each measure is considered separately, there is considerable pressure to pass it. The proposers have greater force than the opponents (who are often called "negative" or "obstructionists") and the total cost is never added up.

The purpose of tax limitation is to remedy that defect. It will enable us to say to the legislature, "We assign you a budget. Now it's your job to spend that in the most effective way." The effect of removing this defect is to enable special interests to work for the general interest instead of against it. This is because with a given total budget, a special group that wants a special measure has to point out the other budget items that can and should be reduced. Each item that people want is a good item. There is no pressure on Congress or on the legislature, or very little, to enact bad legislation. The problem is that there is an infinite number of good and desirable proposals and you have to have some device to limit the appetite and that's the function of tax limitation.

The next time somebody says that tax limitation is undemocratic, we should ask him whether that means he is against the First

Amendment of the Constitution. Because, after all, the First Amendment of the Constitution limits very clearly what Congress can do. The First Amendment says Congress shall make no laws interfering with the freedom of speech or the free exercise of religion. Consider what would happen if we didn't have that amendment. For any single measure restricting freedom of speech you might very well obtain a majority. I am sure there would be a majority to prevent the Nazis from speaking on the street corner. There might be a majority to prevent the Seventh Day Adventists or vegetarians from speaking—or any other little group you could name. But our Founding Fathers had the wisdom to roll it up into one and say we are not going to let each individual issue be decided separately by a majority vote. They said that we are going to adopt the general principle that it is not the federal government's business to restrict freedom of speech.[4] In the same way, what is being proposed today is the enactment of a principle that a government shall have a budget determined by the voters and that it will have to stay within that budget.

Government Spending Is the Real Problem

Right now total government spending—state, federal and local—amounts to 40 percent of the national income. That means that out of every dollar anybody makes or gets, forty cents is being spent for him by the bureaucrats whom he has, through his voting behavior, put into office. There is upward pressure on that percentage. The screws will be put on. The real problem for the future is to stop that growth in government spending. Those who are really concerned, who really are fiscal conservatives, should forget about the deficit and pay all their attention to total government spending. As we have seen, California and Tennessee have recently led the way toward the goal of a limit on government spending.

On the federal level, there have been moves to try to get a federal constitutional amendment providing for a balanced budget. I think, however, that is a serious mistake. It spends the energies of the right people in the wrong direction. Almost all states have a balanced budget provision, but that hasn't kept spending and taxes from going up. What we need on the federal level, as we need it on the state and local level, is not a budget-balancing amendment,

4. It was left to the states to deal with such problems as an immediate danger of violence, and so on.

but an amendment *to limit government spending as a fraction of income.*
Recently a task force of the Southern Governors' Conference, which
was headed by Governor James Edwards of South Carolina, has
worked extensively to produce a government spending limitation
amendment for the federal government.

Congressman Jack Kemp has been pushing for several years now
a so-called tax reduction bill (the Kemp-Roth Bill). I support this
bill since I believe that any form of tax reduction under any circumstances must eventually bring pressure to bear to cut spending.
Moreover, I believe some taxes do more harm than others. There
is no doubt that the method by which we collect taxes could be
rearranged so as to have a less adverse effect on incentives and
production. And, from this point of view, the Kemp-Roth Bill is
certainly desirable. We should be clear, however, that it is in reality
not a tax reduction bill; it is a proposal to change the form of taxes.
As long as high government spending remains, we shall have the
hidden tax of inflation. The only true tax cutting proposal would
be a proposal to cut government spending. To my knowledge, no
one in Washington has yet proposed a genuine tax cutting bill, not
President Carter, not the Democrats in Congress, not the Republi-
cans. Every single so-called "tax cut plan" still envisions a higher
level of government spending next year and consequently a higher
level of taxes, both overt and covert.

There is an important point that needs to be stressed to those
who regard themselves as fiscal conservatives. By concentrating on
the wrong thing, the deficit, instead of the right thing, total government spending, fiscal conservatives have been the unwitting hand-
maidens of the big spenders. The typical historical process is that
the spenders put through laws which increase government spending. A deficit emerges. The fiscal conservatives scratch their heads
and say, "My God, that's terrible; we have got to do something
about that deficit." So they cooperate with the big spenders in
getting taxes imposed. As soon as the new taxes are imposed and
passed, the big spenders are off again, and then there is another
burst in government spending and another deficit.

The true cost of government to the public is not measured by
explicit taxes but by government spending. If government spends
$500 billion, and takes in through taxes $440 billion, which are the
approximate figures of President Carter's estimated budget, who
pays the difference? Not Santa Claus, but the U.S. citizen. The
deficit must be financed by creating money or by borrowing from
the public. If it's financed by printing money, that imposes the

hidden tax of inflation in addition to the explicit tax. If it's financed by borrowing, then the government gets those resources instead of the private sector. In addition, there will have to be a higher level of taxes in the future to pay the interest or to pay back that debt. Essentially every current piece of wealth in the United States has a hidden tax imposed on it because of the future obligation to pay those extra taxes. In effect, what you have are two kinds of taxes: the open, explicit taxes and the hidden taxes. And what's called a deficit is a hidden tax.

I would far rather have total federal spending at $200 billion with a deficit of $100 billion than a balanced budget at $500 billion. The thing we must keep our eye on is what government spends. That's the measure of the amount of the resources of the nation that people cannot individually and separately decide about. It's a measure of the amount we turn over to the bureaucrats to spend on our behalf. I believe along with Parkinson that government will spend whatever the tax system will raise plus a good deal more. Every step we take to strengthen the tax system, whether by getting people to accept payroll taxes they otherwise would not accept, or by cooperating in enacting higher income taxes and excise taxes or whatnot, fosters a higher level of government spending. That's why I am in favor of cutting taxes under any circumstances, for whatever excuse, for whatever reason.

Tax Limitation Laws Are Stopgaps

We have to bear in mind that tax limitation laws are not cure-alls; they are temporary stopgaps. They are a way of trying to hold back the tide, until public opinion moves in the direction that those of us who believe in limited government hold to be desirable. Without the support of public opinion all the written laws or constitutions you can think of are fundamentally worthless. One has only to look at the results of trying to transplant versions of the American and British constitutions to other nations around the world. I believe, however, that there is a definite movement in public opinion toward greater skepticism of large-scale government programs. People are aware that they are not getting their money's worth through government spending. Among intellectuals, more and more scholars are coming to the conclusion that many government programs have not had the results intended by their supporters. In journals read by opinion-leaders (for instance, *Commentary, Encounter, Harper's, The Public Interest, The Washington Monthly*), this view is becoming more and more commonly expressed. However, it takes time for such ideas to be accepted by the politicians who, after all, are mostly followers and not leaders of public opinion.

Let me give an example of what I mean. For about 150 years since the birth of our government (until about the late 1920s) there was no general tendency for government spending to get out of hand. Despite the fact that the same pressures inherent in representative democracy were present through this period, state, local and federal spending was still about 10 percent of national income. For the past 40 years, however, there has been a considerable change in these percentages, to say the least. Except for the Income Tax Amendment, the constitutional provisions relating to the financing of government were essentially the same as they were in 1789 (and the income tax rate was quite low during this period). The essential difference was that before 1930 or so there was a widespread belief on the part of the public that government should be limited and that danger arose from the growth of government. President Grover Cleveland maintained, for instance, that while the people should support their government, the government should not support the people. President Woodrow Wilson remarked that the history of liberalism was the history of restraints on government power. Almost everyone then agreed that the role of government was to act as a referee and umpire and not as a Big Brother. Once this fundamental attitude of the public changed, however, constitutional restrictions became very much less effective against the growth of government. As we all know, the Supreme Court does follow the election returns (sometimes tardily) and most of the New Deal measures which were ruled unconstitutional by the Court in President Roosevelt's first administration were ruled to be constitutional in the second administration.

The interstate commerce clause as an excuse for federal action is a good case in point. At one time in our history there were transactions which were regarded by the Court and Congress as *intrastate* commerce, but it would take a very ingenious man today to find any transaction whatsoever that the Supreme Court would not declare to be part of *interstate* commerce. The federal government, basically as a result of this change in public opinion, is now allowed to take all sorts of actions that would have been held *by the public* to be unconstitutional sixty or a hundred years ago.

In the same way, I believe that the effectiveness of tax limitation laws will depend upon their acceptance by the great bulk of the public as part of our constitutional tradition.[5] My own view is that we are seeing a genuine trend in support of the basic philosophy that there should be definite limits on government spending; however, I also believe that such trends take time to solidify and in the meantime I regard tax limitation amendments as a stopgap measure to hold back the tide.

5. In addition, they will not by themselves prevent all further government intervention. Many of the worst kinds of government intervention do not involve much spending. Some examples are tariffs, or regulation of industry (ICC, FCC, FPC) or the controls on the price of natural gas which have done such tremendous harm in the energy area. All of those involve government intervention into the economy in which the spending element is very small.

30

PROPOSITION 13
Tax Reform's Lexington Bridge?

Daniel Orr

The overwhelming acclaim given to the Jarvis-Gann initiative, which permanently cuts real estate taxes through an amendment to the California constitution, has excited much comment and speculation among quick-answer analysts. In the left-vs-right scheme of things, there is despair that Proposition Thirteen is a massive repudiation of responsibility toward society's downtrodden (especially the young and the black) on the part of the selfish propertied, or there is ecstasy that at last the voracious termites who devour the American edifice are getting a first whiff of chlordane. Those with a cost-benefit orientation have asked whether Thirteen is a good way to achieve low taxes: the possibility exists that essential public services will be interrupted, and the hardship, confusion and turmoil will be great. The Machiavellians have suggested that the government establishment, in hope of securing an early repeal, will punish the voters and subvert the intent of Thirteen by deliberately focusing most of the spending reductions in areas where the harm therefrom is greatest. There is also speculation as to why Thirteen succeeded so overwhelmingly: is it a harbinger of strong public disaffection toward big government and a first step away from continued government growth, or it is simply a peculiar and isolated response to a too-rapid increase in one particular tax?

Most of these questions can in some degree be illuminated by an analysis of the effects of tax reform on the interests of private individuals, politicians and bureaucrats. Such an analysis predicts not only the ways that Thirteen will be digested within California during the coming months, it also suggests where and how further efforts to cut the size and importance of government will occur and the kinds of responses that those who oppose such cuts will offer. Where it all ends up — perhaps as a first step in a major move to limit the scope of government — will depend almost entirely on the effectiveness that tax reformers have in selling further necessary

From Daniel Orr, "Proposition 13: Tax Reform's Lexington Bridge?" no. 6 *Policy Review* 57-67 (Fall 1978). Copyright 1978 by the Heritage Foundation.

changes to the voting public, compared to the job of under-
mining, neutralizing or co-opting those changes that is done by
those who oppose a diminished role for government.

If we examine what Proposition Thirteen does, we quickly
see that it will not be easy to extend it outside of California.
California has a peculiar institution, the constitutional initiative,
whereby voters can directly amend the state constitution
through a simple majority vote, once an amendment has been
placed on the election ballot by a petition with a required
number of signatures. Proposition Thirteen is such an amendment. It stipulates four important things about real estate tax
assessments and real estate rates. Real estate in California
is assessed by elected assessors who, prior to Thirteen, regularly
updated these recorded values on the basis of prices paid for
comparable properties. Thirteen provides, first, that a real
estate parcel shall be currently reassessed at its fiscal 1975
level unless it has changed ownership since January 1, 1976,
in which case the most recent price paid is the basis of assessment. Second, the assessed value of a parcel can rise no more
than two percent per year, unless the parcel changes ownership. Third, the maximum real estate tax that can be collected
is one percent of the assessed value; and fourth, a two-thirds
majority of both houses of the legislature is necessary in order
to change these rules of taxation.

Again, features peculiar to California enter into those
provisions. Assessors are elected. They operate openly,
according to specific rules and are remarkably free from
corruption. There is a high degree of uniformity in the assessment of different parcels. All of this has contributed to a focus
of anger against the tax laws rather than against the assessors.
And California real estate, above almost everywhere else in
the nation, has been the object of vast appreciation in market
value. During 1974-78, it was not unusual for a residential
property to triple in market value in many of the larger cities
of the state. This appreciation is a response to general
inflation: construction labor and material costs have increased,
and speculators seeking to protect the purchasing power of
their wealth have looked upon California real estate as a good
inflation hedge.

In California it is common that certain locally-based and
locally-funded welfare programs are paid out of property tax
revenues. In addition, there is widespread public concern in
some urban school districts (including Los Angeles and San
Diego, the two largest in the state) about the use of school

revenues to pay for extensive programs of pupil transportation to achieve racial balance in individual schools. Thus, the rapid escalation in property taxes was not accompanied by any increase in the quantity or quality of property-related services, and in fact the taxes were seen by some voters as being used for purposes which are socially non-productive or even harmful.

Finally, there had been a good amount of publicity given to the fact that the State of California was enjoying a very significant budgetary surplus. Due in part to the effects of inflation on personal incomes and the sharply progressive structure of the California state income tax, revenue collections by the state were outrunning expenditures to such a degree that Governor Brown was contemplating buying the state its very own communications satellite (a program that would have been budgeted at a level near $5 billion).

The interaction of all of these factors in one time and one state assured the success of Thirteen. There was a mechanism to change the law which bypassed the potentially subversive processes of representative democracy. There was a tax on which to focus, which imposed a large, rapidly growing and highly visible burden on numerous voters,[1] and which conveyed benefits about which many voters felt doubtful or toward which they felt hostile. There was a general perception of glut in the government sector. In short, the ingredients are a mirror image of what is usually found when a program involving new or higher taxes is successfully *imposed* (voter isolation from the decision process, highly concentrated benefits to a group of active supporters, diffusion of costs over a broad base of taxpayers).

The Effects of Proposition Thirteen

The immediate consequences of Thirteen in California will be relatively trivial. Property taxes will be lower for everyone and much lower for property owners whose holdings antedate January 1, 1976. There will be a temporary disruption of some public services (a subject we will examine in more detail shortly). The real estate game will be changed in important ways: the widespread and popular practice of "trading up" — using the price appreciation in this house to

1. The importance of the *visibility* of the property tax to successful revolt is pointed out in James Buchanan's "The Simple Analytics of Proposition 13" (Center for Study of Public Choice, VPI, Blacksburg, Va., •unpublished).

make a down payment on that larger house — will in some degree be defeated due to the assessment increases which follow on trade. These consequences all are distributive. Windfall gains are scattered among all property owners and in part are offset by higher income taxes due to lower income tax deductions. To the extent that the "business climate" is improved and incomes increase, the level of public services can be maintained without the imposition of any additional taxes, if some mechanism is found for using those higher state income taxes to pay for services previously provided out of the property tax.

In fact, the transfer of tax revenues from the local level to the state and federal levels is the most ominous and potentially the most significant effect of Thirteen. There may be an accompanying change in the balance of power and responsibility among different levels of government, which can have extremely important consequences.

The foregoing analysis identifies several features which contributed to the success of Thirteen. That analysis illuminates the issue of whether Thirteen is an excessively cumbersome tool with which to trim government fat (as was eloquently contended by Walter Heller in the *Wall Street Journal* on June 2). We have a number of examples in recent years (dating back to the Hoover Commissions and the efforts of Senator Paul Douglas in the late 1940s and 1950s) to eliminate specific ineffective government programs by selective withdrawal of their funding. That approach has seldom been successful: scalpels cannot seem to penetrate the blubber. On the other hand, we have seen that bureaucracies can continue to function while accommodating themselves to draconian across-the-board slashes in their funding (many public universities in the late 1960s offer instructive examples). Thus, the claim that Proposition Thirteen was a heedless, hasty and heavy-handed substitute for careful and judicious trimming is almost totally without merit: that latter choice simply does not exist, and the true alternative to Thirteen was business as usual.

What of the concern that bureaucrats and politicians will violate the intent of Thirteen or destroy its spirit by cutting back on services that the community deems essential, while preserving functions, offices or agencies that are peripheral or unnecessary? Will there be a confrontation in which public officials (elected or civil service) seek to demonstrate that the costs of Thirteen are very high, in an effort to start a popular movement for reversal or repeal?

Such concerns are not entirely without foundation. One problem with a sweeping and broad-based mandate like Thirteen is that the chief source of information on the costs and benefits of various government functions must be the bureaucracy itself. The bureaucracy has a strong interest in existing programs, and that interest may not coincide with taxpayer interest. For example, certain programs such as job training or environmental impact studies carry significant matching funds from the federal government. Every dollar budgeted at the local level carries an expenditure multiplier, and most of that expenditure is of benefit to the bureaucracy. It follows that the local-level bureaucrats, whose recommendations of areas for expenditure cutting will in the short run probably be highly influential, will have a strong incentive to favor such programs at the expense of activities more widely regarded as essential, such as fire and police protection. That fact, however, is not decisive. Politicians at the local level have a strong incentive to impose cutbacks in a way that will meet voter approval. There are many local governments affected by Thirteen and because interest will be high, press coverage of performance will enable comparisons to be drawn by voters between "our" politicians and "their" politicians. Whether or not elected officials directly control the budgets of their jurisdictions, they will be aware that if "essential services" are cut by more in their jurisdictions than elsewhere, vigorous political competition is likely to ensue. Those bureaucrats whose funding recommendations coincide most closely with voter preferences among governmental activities will be chosen to guide the allocation process and will benefit in personal power, status and income thereby. Because of the existence of many similar local jurisdictions and the opportunities for comparison among them, the danger is minimized that a serious effort will be made to subvert Thirteen by the imposition of excessive service reductions. Thus, it appears that everyone, including politicians and other beneficiaries of large government, will stand to gain by appearing to seek "reform" in the spirit of Proposition Thirteen.

Will Proposition Thirteen Result in Lower Taxes?

But, while it may not be possible or feasible to overthrow
Thirteen by keeping bad programs and reducing good ones,
there is a danger that wolves will dress as sheep, and those who
hope that Thirteen augurs smaller government and lower
taxes will be defeated by a more subtle and devious approach.

When it became clear that Thirteen was a resounding success,
Governor Brown immediately jumped on the bandwagon.
His first public act was to state that he took the mandate
seriously and would work toward reform. Governor Brown is
a clever man and a Democrat, and the likelihood that he will
lead a serious movement to diminish the scope of government
is nil. What, then, can he be up to? There are several ways that
Thirteen's success can be turned to his advantage and can be
made to work toward greater power for the Governor's office
and for him personally. As we noted, the immediate consequence of Thirteen is to diminish the revenue-collecting
potential of counties and municipalities. The revenue-generating
potential of the state is, by contrast, enhanced, due to the
greater taxable income and purchasing power that Thirteen
leaves in private hands. This change can be used to induce
greater state control of programs which previously had been
controlled at the local level. It is possible to imagine a simple
transfer of revenues, no strings attached, from the state treasury
to the local authorities, as a means of offsetting the fiscal
impact of Thirteen. But that will not happen. It will be
proclaimed necessary to husband state financial resources and
to exercise control over the way they are used. It will be
pointed out that the size of the total tax take has shrunk, and
therefore tax dollars must be stretched farther to do more.
These points all will be true, at least temporarily, and their
consequences will be that state bureaucracy will expand,
but by less than all local bureaucracies combined contract;
and substantial new powers will be vested in state government.
Such a move is, of course, inimical to the frequently-voiced
goal of increasing the importance of political decision-making
at the local level. Competition and diversity among counties
and municipalities will decline.

But what happens if taxes which are levied at the state level
also come under tax-revolt scrutiny? The only state tax in
California which has the attributes of burdensomeness and
visibility, and hence the most logical candidate for drastic

cutting, is the state personal income tax (which is one of the nation's highest, operating at a rate of eleven percent on incomes above $31,000 for married couples). California has other sources of revenue, however. The state sales tax, currently six percent on all items except food purchased for home consumption, labor services and prescription medicines, can no doubt be extended to those uncovered items and raised a notch or two. An increase in state taxes on all types of fuels could probably find support on environmental grounds. In addition, there might be considerable popular support for pricing some of the more selectively used state services, such as the state park system and the extensive state-supported system of higher education, at rates much closer to the marginal cost of use, thereby cutting down on the state's tax subsidy of these activities.

Could a constitutional amendment directed at the state income tax be successful? Almost certainly it could, under the California initiative system. The consequences, paradoxically, might be greater investment, more employment, higher *per capita* disposable income and reduced *per capita* consumption of state-provided services in California. Should that eventuate, recourse to increases in other taxes would be less necessary. But even if the tax revolt carries forward to a point that revenue-generating capability at the state level of government is seriously impaired, and even if the revolt spreads among all fifty states, the task confronting the advocates of small government has only begun to surface. For the federal government has shown itself to be favorably disposed toward the idea of revenue sharing with the states, and the taxing power of the federal government at present completely defies revolt.

At the federal level, tax reduction measures directed at specific individual taxes can readily be accommodated, as the record of the past fifteen years suggests. Beginning in 1963, with the Kennedy tax cut, income tax rates have fluctuated considerably, but overall the rates are considerably lower than they were in 1962. Accompanying these rate reductions have been offsetting movements which have tended to increase individual tax payments and government control of spendable revenue. First, and most important, inflation has increased taxable incomes and moved individuals up into higher income tax brackets. (The processes which cause inflation also have served directly to increase the federal government's purchasing power.) Second, certain federal taxes, conspicuously including the capital gains tax, have increased dramatically. The general tax cuts have been motivated by the Keynesian theory of effective demand and the importance of expenditure, and the capital gains tax increases have been motivated by soak-the-rich egalitarian sentiments. Both changes illustrate a rather ominous proposition: federal tax policy can blow with any political wind. The federal government is in no formal way constrained in terms of the amounts that it collects, spends, or redistributes. Only political assessment of the voter tolerance of deficits constrains the government in power, and the experience of recent years suggests that the "myth" of budget balance is increasingly less persuasive to voters.

The federal government's first mighty weapon with which to defeat tax reform, then, is inflation. Possession of that weapon stems from its monopoly over the printing of money.

Promiscuous reliance on inflation to fund government programs, however, carries its own dangers. Voters may never truly learn that *only* the monetary authority has the ultimate power to affect price levels, but high and persistent rates of inflation may nonetheless elicit meat-ax voter responses against the political establishment. The federal government possesses a second and almost equally potent weapon with which to generate the revenues which will sustain government growth, namely, the value-added tax. This is a type of tax which heretofore has never been important in the United States. It is collected from businesses and its basis is the total sales of the business, less purchases from other businesses. The total taxes paid at different levels of manufacture are hidden in the prices of goods bought by consumers, even much more so than a sales tax would be were it quoted directly as a part of the price of a purchased article, because many different manufacturers may be involved. European countries which have relied heavily on the VAT have been able to keep income taxes at fairly modest levels compared to the U.S. — France, Switzerland[2] and Germany, for example, all have lower income tax rates than does the U.S., but bar higher goods prices due to VAT. But in the U.S. the VAT appears to be strictly a federal-level tool. Use of the VAT at the state level would be extremely difficult due to the competition among states to attract new

2.   Switzerland uses a turnover tax, a sales tax charged at every stage of manufacture. The VAT is ubiquitous in the Common Market.

industry. An attempt on the part of California to institute a VAT would no doubt lead such "anti-progressive" states as Texas or Tennessee to advertise a more favorable tax climate, thereby stultifying California's growth — and tax base.

The Bureaucrats' Counter-Revolution

Apparently, then, it is child's play to parry or co-opt the Jarvis-Gann spirit of tax revolt. The strategy comprises two parts: (1) transferring the responsibility of funding "essential" government expenditures to more central, more powerful, and more distant levels of government; and (2) instituting less visible forms of taxes from which to make those expenditures. The whole operation must of course be accompanied by a heavy barrage of rhetoric on the efficiency gains that will be realized by a more centralized provision of services: predictably, many rhapsodies are soon to be written on how wonderful it is to eliminate costly duplication.

This all means that proponents of smaller government will have to work very hard to sell their ideas. The nation's electorate has recently not been receptive to abstract arguments based on the general principle that government is too large. Rather, government has grown because the electorate has always seemed to be responsive to a "problems and solutions" approach: a problem is pointed out, and some solution or other, usually governmentally implemented, is proposed.

The appeal and success of the "problems and solutions" approach hangs on the creation of two strongly interested groups of sufficient size to assure adequate political support: a beneficiary group which stands to gain from a solution of the problem, and a group of bureaucrats and entrepreneurs who will be actively involved in implementation of the proposed solution, and whose wealth and power will thereby be enhanced. Success also depends on devising the proposed solution in such a way that no group of significant size is sufficiently harmed by it to offer serious opposition. It appears difficult, in prospect, to use this approach to reduce the size and scope of government. Can the idea be sold that the size of government is in itself a problem? Many self-interested groups, small and large, will converge in opposition to that idea, and those who still view government as the protector of the poor and oppressed will see it as an attempt to reinstitute slavery and illiteracy. Can individual programs be eliminated one by one on cost-benefit grounds? As we noted earlier, that approach has never succeeded, because of the diffusion of support and concentration of opposition.

A likely and unfortunate consequence of Proposition Thirteen-style tax reform, then, is a greater concentration of taxing and spending authority in the federal government, and a proliferation of new federal bureaus, scattered perhaps among the Departments of Treasury, HUD, HEW and Agriculture which are charged with allocating and monitoring the use of revenues which have been provided to the municipalities and countries. Certainly, Thirteen is not an agenda for full-scale reform. The net long-run impact on the individual taxpayer of all the adjustments and changes that Thirteen will induce will be higher taxes, less visible and hence less painful taxes, and a much larger federal interest in patterns of local expenditure.

As a specific agenda for tax reform, then, Proposition Thirteen is perverse. If a major objective of tax reform is to increase the efficiency of government spending (that is, to make it conform more closely to the preferences of taxpayers) then increased federal control is a big move in the wrong direction. If the objective is to make spending authorities more compliant in limiting the menu or portfolio of goods and services provided by government, the move again is in the wrong direction. People who are concerned about the growth of government (as Jarvis and Gann purport to be, and as many who voted for Proposition Thirteen probably are) would do well to consider the possibility that their June 6 triumph may have set back the date when serious, meaningful fiscal reform of the federal government can take place.

It is my own reformer's perspective that in order to protect against the twin ravages of inflation and unlimited growth of government, we need a constitutional amendment which drastically reduces the scope of federal spending and regulating activity, accompanied by a constitutionally imposed formula requiring a federal budget which would, under conditions of full employment, yield a modest surplus in every year. (In a given year defined to be less than full employment, a deficit is permissible; but the formula must show that if employment in that year were increased to the defined full employment level, the deficit would become a surplus.). If federal activities are to be constrained, it will be necessary to refer many necessary or desirable governmental functions back to the state and local levels. To the extent that Proposition Thirteen weakens the mechanisms of local government, that task is made more difficult.

The one enormously hopeful augury offered by Proposition Thirteen is that two-thirds of the voters in the nation's most populous state seized the chance to roll back taxes. This they did in the face of hysterical forecasts and threats of school and library closings, police and firefighter layoffs, garbage in the streets and on the beaches. The main task confronting tax reformers remains, however. It still must be shown that the reason those property taxes were too high and were growing too fast is to be found on Capitol Hill and that something can and must be done.

31

THE POTENTIAL FOR TAXPAYER REVOLT
IN AMERICAN DEMOCRACY

James M. Buchanan

ABSTRACT

The victory of Proposition 13 in California in 1978 does not necessarily provide evidence of a widespread "Taxpayers' revolt." The results may be explained by the particular institutional choice presented to the California voters. The ensuing discussion of the results on the "as if" presumption that a shift in taxpayer attitudes has occurred may be more important than the results themselves.

I. INTRODUCTION

As early as 1969, Treasury Secretary Joseph Barr warned of a "taxpayers' revolt." In the decade that followed, there seemed to be growing evidence of apparent taxpayer discontent.[1] Such discontent was easily understandable given the dramatic acceleration in the growth of government spending, and hence in real tax rates. However, almost all efforts to generate effective taxpayer resistance failed to gain momentum. The attempted organization of taxpayers' lobbies met with little success. Proposition 1 was soundly defeated in California in 1972. A comparable attempt met a comparable fate in Michigan in 1976. The task for analysis seemed to be that of explaining failure rather than success.

With Proposition 13 in California in June 1978, however, the tables seem to have been turned. The resounding electoral victory for the Jarvis-Gann initiative was widely interpreted as signalling the onset of a nationwide taxpayers' revolt. Politicians and opinion leaders at all levels of government seem to have shared this view. In late 1978, bureaucrats and their supporters, at all levels, were "running scared." The spillover effects of the Jarvis-Gann results extended far beyond California's borders, and hopes were raised that apparently uncontrollable governmental spending growth might be put in bounds.

Before lapsing into this euphoria, with which my own personal values would be quite consistent, it is obligatory on me as a professional economist to look at Proposition 13 somewhat more carefully, and to ask whether or not the California results necessarily reflect a basic shift in taxpayer attitudes. Can the Jarvis-

From James M. Buchanan, "The Potential for Taxpayer Revolt in American Democracy," 59(4) *Social Science Quarterly* 691-696 (March 1979). Copyright 1979 by the University of Texas Press.

Gann results be "explained" without reference to a fundamental change in tax-payer preferences?[2] The answer to this question is surely relevant for assessing the probable success of other tax-limit or spending-limit efforts as well as the probable or predicted ultimate impact of the punitive taxpayers' revolt on the magnitude and the growth of public spending at all governmental levels in the 1980s.

In this paper, I shall argue that the success of Proposition 13 can indeed be "explained" by institutional elements in the particular choice presented to California voters. Comparable results may not be predicted to emerge for more general tax-limit and spending-limit propositions. Furthermore, the scope and range for initiatives that might generate results comparable to those of Proposition 13 may be quite narrow. From this analysis I advance the prediction that the ultimate impact of Jarvis-Gann may be slight.

I should, however, emphasize the restrictiveness of the argument. I explain the success of Jarvis-Gann and predict the failure of the more general tax-limit proposals on the basis of an analysis of the institutional setting for fiscal choices. There is nothing in my argument which suggests that fundamental taxpayer attitudes have *not* changed. Perhaps they have done so, in which case the implications of Proposition 13 are much wider than my analysis suggests. And I should not overlook the prospect that the widespread discussion of the California results *as if* they signalled a new set of taxpayers' views may itself be instrumental in modifying attitudes. My emphasis is on the simpler point that appears to be over-looked in much of the discussion; the Jarvis-Gann results, in themselves, cannot be taken as evidence that 1978 was different from 1972 or 1976.

II. THE FREE RIDER PRINCIPLE AND THE BIAS TOWARD PUBLIC SPENDING

My argument to the effect that the defeat of Governor Reagan's Proposition 1 in 1972 and the victory of Proposition 13 in 1978 can be reconciled *without* any presumption of a shift in basic taxpayer attitudes between 1972 and 1978 relies on an application of the familiar free rider principle from public-finance theory. This principle is fully symmetrical. If the benefits of an action are concentrated and well-defined, while the costs are diffused and generalized, we can predict that individuals will, in many circumstances, take such action (e.g., dumping litter on the beach) without due regard to the costs involved. Conversely, if the costs of an action are concentrated and well-defined, while the benefits are diffused and generalized, we can predict that individuals will, in many circumstances, refrain from taking such action (e.g., picking up litter from the beach) because of a failure to take the benefits sufficiently into account. In the language of Pigovian welfare economics, there is a divergence between "private" and "social" marginal cost or marginal production in each of these cases.

An elementary proposition in public choice theory states that the same basic principle applies to the behavior of individuals as they participate in democratically organized governmental processes. The allegedly excessive influence of producer interests in modern regulatory bureaucracy is often explained by the relative concentration of regulatory benefits as against the diffusion of regulatory costs among consumers. The same principle operates in governmental fiscal choice. If the benefits of public spending programs are concentrated and well-identifed, either with respect to distinct groups of citizens, geographically, functionally, or otherwise defined, or with respect to distinct programs (e.g., education, health, highways) while the costs are diffused and generalized, we can predict that such programs will be undertaken in many circumstances without due regard to the costs. Conversely, if the costs of public spending (taxes) are concentrated and well-identified, while the benefits are diffused and generalized, we can predict that in many circumstances governmental fiscal outcomes will reflect failure to take benefits sufficiently into account.

The directional bias introduced into the decision process is determined by the institutional setting for fiscal choice. Normative inferences cannot be drawn as to whether or not overall levels of spending (and taxation) are "too high" or "too low" or "just about right" until some empirical estimates are made about the way fiscal choices are actually made in democracies. In our book, *The Calculus of Consent*,[3] Gordon Tullock and I suggested that, empirically, taxes tend to be more diffused and generalized than the benefits of public spending programs. Taxes are, in principle, supposed to be general in their application. And historically, constitutional law has reflected this norm. The United States Constitution requires that taxes be uniformly apportioned among the states, and a constitutional amendment was required even to allow for progression in the tax on personal incomes. The treatment of public spending is not at all symmetrical.[4] There is no legal norm that requires uniformity among persons, regions, or anything else in the distribution of spending benefits. And public spending programs, almost by their nature, yield benefits to specific "consumer" groups—to families with children to be educated, to farmers, to urban transit users, to Sierra club members, to research scientists, to welfare recipients (apart from all those who benefit more directly in their capacities as producers of public goods and services, public employees, contractors, etc.). From such an empirical assessment, and applying the principle noted, Tullock and I concluded that fiscal decisions in modern democratic governments tend normally to be biased in the direction of public spending, with general taxes being more or less residually set by budgetary requirements. As we noted in our analysis, however, modifications in the setting within which people are allowed to make fiscal decisions could reverse the directional bias.

The Jarvis-Gann initiative in California (Proposition 13) may have been successful only because it was formulated, either by deliberate design or as a result of fortuitous circumstances, so that the behavioral force of the free rider principle could be fully exploited. California voters were presented with an opportunity to make a fiscal choice in a setting where the asymmetry was the *reverse* of that which is normally operative in democratic governmental processes. To appreciate this, we need only look more carefully at the choice alternatives faced by the Californians on 6 June 1978. The rejection of Proposition 13 would have implied continued payment of very high and accelerating taxes on real property. These quite visible costs were matched against the imagined benefits from the anticipated continued growth in generalized public outlays. In sharp contrast to these costs and benefits of rejection, the approval of Proposition 13 promised identifiable and measurable increments to individuals' spendable funds. Voters were informed by proponents of the proposition as to the precise reductions in their annual property tax bills that approval would insure. On the other side, the costs of approval seemed to be measured by generalized threats to cut public spending. Voters could not possibly have made accurate estimates as to just what programs might be actually reduced and how much. And they paid little or no heed to the bureaucrats' scare tactics which threatened cutbacks in only the most highly favored programs.

Once the issue was posed as one of identified and measurable tax reductions against cuts in generalized public spending, the outcome may well have been predictable. The Jarvis-Gann results seem novel, but only because the choice setting faced by voters was reversed from that which has normally and traditionally described democratic procedures, whether in referenda or, more frequently, in legislative assemblies. The directional bias was shifted toward tax-reduction. The fact that these results seem so novel, and that they are so widely interpreted, by politicians and press alike, as marks of a genuine taxpayers' revolt, tends indirectly to confirm the claims of the general bias toward spending that we advanced in *The Calculus of Consent*. If, through the years, the mix among fiscal choice situations should have been more or less in balance as between those settings which pair off concentrated benefit programs against general taxes and those which pair concentrated tax costs against generalized benefits, we should have been able to observe public complaints that also were roughly balanced. We should have been able to point to general public-citizen complaints about ill-advised tax reductions (and budgetary cuts) with about the same frequency as general public-citizen complaints about excessively high spending (and taxes).

If my analysis here is correct, it carries important implications for the possible success of differing forms of tax-limit and spending-limit proposals. The earlier California initiative, Proposition 1, failed in 1972. My analysis suggests that it may have failed because it did not embody a choice setting that exploited the free rider principle. The central feature of Proposition 1 was the establishment of a specific relationship between allowable state spending (taxation) and levels and/or rates of growth in state income. Proposals containing this feature were under consideration in many states in 1978, and initial efforts were made to extend such features to a proposal for amending the United States Constitution.

To the economists who may serve as consultants to tax-limit groups, these "ratio type" proposals, which relate fiscal constraints to levels or rates of growth in incomes, are much more attractive than the blunderbuss type of Jarvis-Gann variety. For one thing, the primary objective may be that of limiting potential levels and growth rates of spending (and taxing). No current reductions may be promised, and this feature may seem to be politically attractive since it allows the dislocations and distortion incident upon budget cuts to be avoided. My analysis suggests, however, that ratio-type proposals may fail precisely because of their neutralizing features. If there are to be no current cutbacks in spending, and in taxes, there can be no concentrated and well-defined current benefits, by definition. There may be no prospect for organizing a supporting coalition of voters with the required intensity of interest. Apathy may replace active concern among those groups of voters who might be predicted to support fiscal limits.

At the same time, however, the voters whose interests are most directly threatened on the other side of the choice, those who are among the beneficiaries of public spending, either as direct producers (e.g., public employees) or as primary beneficiaries (e.g., recipients of direct transfer payments) may react to potential spending or tax limits with almost as much fervor as they will act against explicit proposals for budgetary cutbacks, à la Jarvis-Gann. Casual observation suggests that the opposition to Proposition 1 in 1972 was, if any-thing, more rather than less well organized than the opposition to Proposition 13 in 1978. Even without reference to the organization of opposing interests, however, the differences between the ratio-type of tax-limit and the type exem-plified in the Jarvis-Gann initiative are evident. The former makes no effort to exploit the free rider motivation of the taxpayer to offset the natural free rider motivation of the established interests in the fiscal status quo.

The analysis suggests that a genuine shift in basic taxpayer attitudes might be required to secure approval of tax-limit proposals of the ratio-type, a shift that was not required to secure approval of Proposition 13. If, as, and when other propositions like Proposition 1, embodying ratio-limits, are considered in various states in 1979 and 1980, a test of my hypothesis will be possible. If these ratio-type proposals are successful, we can assert without qualification that a "taxpayers' revolt" has occurred. My explanation would have been proved to be wrong.

The lesson of my analysis should be clear in a normative sense. Those political leaders and opinion leaders, who share a conviction that the modern govern-mental Leviathan is out of hand and must be controlled if anything resembling a free and liberal society is to continue to be viable, must reckon with the ubiquity and the power of the free rider principle in designing their proposals for con-stitutional reform, whether these be for tax-limits, spending-limits, or other types of constraints. They must recognize the potential of this principle for producing directional bias in fiscal choice settings, whether these be reflected in referenda or in the more complex processes of legislative assemblies.

In the best of possible worlds, directional biases in fiscal choices should, of course, be eliminated. General taxes should be levied to finance programs that yield general benefits. Unfortunately, we cannot live in such a world. And, given the historical record of this century where the choice setting has been dramatically biased toward public spending explosion, it is surely salutary that, on the one occasion of Proposition 13, the tables were turned around. The scope for tax-reducing bias seems limited, however. Property taxes, personal income taxes, and payroll taxes levied directly on workers' earnings, may offer the only prospects for tax-reduction proposals that can be translated directly into measurable dollar increments by voters and/or their legislative representatives, at either local, state, or national governmental levels. Indirect taxes, which for this analysis must include all levies on business firms, payroll taxes on employers, and inflation, cannot be used to the same purpose. (Should we wonder at the attractiveness of these taxes to the politicians?) By contrast, almost all spending programs of the modern welfare state will continue to carry with them concentrated and well-defined benefits to identifiable groups of constituents.

At the federal government level, proposals for the creation of major tax loopholes in the personal income tax may exploit some of the free rider potential. To be effective, such proposals must carry advantages to a well-identified and sufficiently large set of beneficiaries, and these advantages must be measurable in specific dollar estimates for tax relief. The tuition tax-credit proposals considered in 1978 may well be a case in point. My colleague, Gordon Tullock, has suggested that comparable support might be generated for a proposal that would allow for the deduction of certain insurance costs, notably those against crime, under the personal income tax. (The existing medical expenses deduction can, of course, be explained in this way.) As these few examples suggest, however, the range of prospects for fiscal choices biased toward tax reduction is extremely limited.

Until and unless there is a genuine shift in attitudes, until and unless the citizenry, generally, again acquires the wisdom of our 18th century founders, we must live with a general democratic bias toward public spending. If and when we can once again recognize that a primary purpose of political constitutions is to constrain the excesses of governments and governors, we may begin to take the steps necessary to maintain a viable free society. We may acquire such wisdom too late.

Personally, I am encouraged by the Jarvis-Gann results; I am even more encouraged by the spillover effects that these results have generated, both in discussion and in action. In a sense, my analysis in this paper is a warning to those who would read these results to suggest that the desired "constitutional revolution" is upon us. Jarvis-Gann can tell us more about how "our side" might win in the long and hard, but absolutely necessary, struggle for constitutional reform that must take place than it tells us about the sudden attainment of wisdom by the citizenry.

NOTES

1. In an early attempt to examine the prospects for a taxpayers' revolt, Marilyn Flowers and I concentrated on the formal setting within which such a movement might become politically effective. See, James M. Buchanan and Marilyn Flowers, "An Analytical Setting for a 'Taxpayers' Revolution,'" *Western Economic Journal*, 8 (1969): 349-59.

2. As George Stigler and Gary Becker have suggested, it should be obligatory on economists to exhaust the explanatory power of their analyses before resorting to shifts in tastes or preferences of individuals. See, George Stigler and Gary Becker, "De Gustibus Non Est Disputandum," *American Economic Review*, (1977): 76-90.

3. Ann Arbor: University of Michigan Press, 1962.

4. For a specific discussion of the basic asymmetry between the tax and spending sides of the budget, see, David Tuerck, "Uniformity in Taxation, Discrimination in Benefits: An Essay in Law and Economics" (Ph.D. Diss., University of Virginia, 1966).

32

TAXATION AND THE TAXPAYERS' REVOLT

Robert J. Lampman

This chapter is drawn from the opening lecture of a series on the topic "Proposition 13: An Answer or an Invitation to Chaos?" Its mission is to provide some introductory and background material that may be helpful in evaluating the phenomenal popularity of the tax limitation movement. In accord with that purpose, this chapter has the following structure: (1) recent trends in taxation; (2) efforts to limit property taxation; (3) the rise of social welfare spending; (4) taxes and benefits by income level; and (5) explanations for the tax revolt.

RECENT TRENDS IN TAXATION

Last year Americans paid $591 billion in taxes to their federal, state, and local govcernments. That amounts to over $2,500 per person and is equal to 38 percent of personal income, or 31 percent of the gross national product (GNP). Ten years earlier, in 1967, combined taxes were only $224 billion, an amount equal to 28 percent of a much smaller GNP. Federal taxes have changed relatively little as a share of GNP, but state and local taxes (including "charges") have surged from 8 percent of GNP in 1960 to 10 percent in 1967 and to 12 percent in 1977 (see Table 1). Our present tax rates are not the highest in the world. In fact, they are exceeded by tax rates in most of the other rich, democratic nations.

Some taxes have grown faster than others. At the state and local levels, the fastest growers have been income taxes, while the slowest grower has been the property tax. Among federal taxes, the most rapid growth has been registered by the social security tax, and the least by sales and excise taxes (see Table 2).

Wisconsin taxes have changed in a manner similar to that of all other states. The fastest growing tax has been the individual income tax; the slowest has been the property tax (see Table 3). Wisconsin is, and has long been, a high tax state. Its state and local taxes amount to about 14 percent of state personal income, compared to the national average of about 12.5 percent. On this basis, Wisconsin ranks tenth among the fifty states.

The 1950s and 1960s were characterized by a fiscal mismatch. The federal government had the revenue-raising capacity, and the states and localities

From Robert J. Lampman, "Taxation and the Taxpayers' Revolt." Unpublished manuscript, 1979.

TABLE 1

| | | Taxes as Percentage of GNP | |
Year	All Taxes	Federal Taxes	State and Local Taxes (including charges)
1960	27	19	8
1967	28	18	10
1977	31	19	12

TABLE 2

| | Taxes in Billions of Dollars | | Ratio of 1976 Taxes to 1966 Taxes |
	1966	1976	
State and Local Taxes and Charges (Total)	70	201	2.9
Property Tax	25	57	2.3
Sales Taxes	19	55	2.9
Individual Income Taxes	5	25	5.0
Corporate Income Taxes	2	7	3.5
All Other	19	57	3.0
Federal Taxes (Total)	134	314	2.3
Individual Income, Estate and Gift Taxes	58	137	2.4
Corporate Income Taxes	31	52	1.7
Sales and Excise Taxes	16	24	1.5
Social Security Taxes	29	101	3.4

had the need. The federal government has frequently cut income tax rates—holding individual income tax revenues to about 10 percent of personal income—and has given away large sums of money to state and local governments. In 1977 such grants totaled $66 billion. At the same time, states scrambled hard for new tax sources. Most without them introduced income or general sales taxes, and persistently raised tax rates. State and local government debt soared in the 1960s.

There have been signs that the fiscal mismatch is easing in the 1970s. With the notable exception of the recession years, 1974 and 1975, state governments have tended toward larger and larger surpluses since 1970. In 1977, all state and local governments combined ran a surplus of $29 billion. This is cited by federal fiscal planners as one of the reasons why the federal deficit had to be as large as $48 billion in that year. And it also suggests the possibility of tax reductions at the state and local levels. The underlying reasons for this remarkable change include the increase in federal grants, the more diversified tax structures of state governments, and a decline in the school-age population.

TABLE 3

	Taxes in Millions of Dollars		Ratio of 1976 Taxes
Wisconsin State and Local Taxes	*1966*	*1976*	*to 1966 Taxes*
Total	1,440	3,781	2.6
Property tax	576	1,263	2.2
Sales and excise taxes[a]	296	830	2.8
Individual income tax	320	960	3.0
Corporate income tax	92	190	2.1
All other	156	538	3.4

a. Including motor fuel tax.

TABLE 4

Wisconsin Property Tax Relief, 1977	*In Millions of Dollars*
1. School aids, general	503
2. Vocational education aids	38
3. Shared taxes	306
4. General property tax relief	210
5. Personal property tax relief	165
6. Machinery and equipment relief	29
7. Payments in lieu of taxes and for municipal taxes	5
8. Homestead tax credit (to individuals)	48
9. Total of Items 1-8	1,305
10. Payments to local governments for other programs	732
11. Revenues from major state taxes	2,413

NOTE: Item 9 is 54% of item 11.

EFFORTS TO LIMIT PROPERTY TAXATION

States have made strenuous efforts to keep local property taxes from rising precipitously. By increasing the sharing of state-collected taxes, and by state grants-in-aid to local governments and school districts, states drove the property tax down from 43 percent of all state and local revenues in 1960 to 28 percent in 1977. Moreover, states have made widespread use of tax credits to reimburse some businesses and homeowners for property taxes paid to local governments.

We can illustrate this point by reference to Wisconsin, where property tax revenue fell from 51 percent of all state and local revenues in 1960 to 32 percent in 1977. This was accomplished in part by the development of the "property tax relief" items listed in Table 4. These include school aids, shared taxes (taxes collected by the state but paid ut by formula to local governments other than schools), tax relief paid to local governments (items 4, 5, 6, and 7 in Table 4), and tax relief paid directly to individuals (item 8). These measures use up over half the revenues from the state-collected taxes. Further, other substantial amounts are paid to local governments to carry out such state-mandated programs as welfare and health care programs (item 10). This means that the

TABLE 5

Income Rank of Families, by Fifth	Income Limit in Current Dollars		Total Money Income (%)	
	1960	1976	1960	1976
Upper Limit				
Lowest	2,784	7,441	4.8	5.4
Second	4,800	12,400	12.2	11.8
Middle	6,364	17,300	17.8	17.6
Fourth	8,800	–	24.0	24.1
Highest	–	–	41.3	41.1
Lower Limit				
Highest 5%	13,536	37,047	15.9	15.6

state government devotes the greater part of its efforts to collecting taxes which are spent at the local level.

The various credits referred to above, along with the income tax deductibility of property taxes paid, mean that the property tax is less onerous than it might appear at first glance. This does not mean, however, that it is now justified on either ability-to-pay or benefits-received grounds. The value of real property, particularly in inflationary times, does not move in accord with the income of its owner. And a property owner may benefit from few of the services he or she pays for, particularly if the owner does not live in the jurisdiction where the property is located. The principal justification for the property tax—probably the only one that keeps it alive—is that it is virtually the only tax source local governments can manage. If the property tax goes, so goes the principle of autonomy for school districts, cities, and counties.

Property tax limitation movements flourished in the 1930s, and they have never died since. Gubernatorial candidates of all political persuasions found "property tax relief" a sure-fire issue. But protest against "intolerably high" property taxes continued almost no matter what was done at the state level. This protest rose to fever pitch in response to the recent unexpected surpluses in the current accounts of many state governments. Property tax limitation leaders quickly put in a claim for a lion's share of those surplus funds, but so did those who wanted relief of income or sales taxes, and those who wanted to spend more on state or local programs.

THE RISE OF SOCIAL WELFARE SPENDING

While the level and relative importance of several types of taxes have changed, there has been an equally dramatic shift in the uses for revenue. Here the big story is the rise of social welfare expenditures from 11 percent of GNP in 1960 to 21 percent in 1976. This was financed in part by a decline in national defense outlays from 9 to 6 percent of GNP. (One might say that the "health-education-welfare complex" has eclipsed what President Eisenhower identified as the "military-industrial complex.") It is perhaps unnecessary to point out that these social welfare expenditures are the main destinations of state and local taxes. Spending for economic development has been steady at about 5 percent of GNP, as has the 2 percent share for police and fire protection, sanitation, recreation, and "all other."

The ten-point increase in social welfare spending was divided up as follows: Two points went to education; four points, to expansions of social security cash benefits; and the remaining four points, to cash public assistance, health care, food stamps, and other in-kind benefits.

This social revolution was, of course, given impetus by President Johnson's Great Society and War on Poverty programs, but it continued unabated during the Nixon-Ford era. By 1976, social welfare expenditures were running at a rate of $331 billion. Cash benefits alone amounted to $157 billion. About half the cash benefits went to those who, in the absence of such transfer payments, would have been poor. But even so, 11 percent of the population, in contrast to 22 percent in 1960, remained below the income-poverty lines set by President Johnson. These lines turn around $3,000 of money income in 1962 prices for a family of four, but are adjusted for family size and changes in consumer prices. If we count food stamps, housing subsidies, and free health care (about half of which go to the poor) as income, then the percentage of all people who might be counted as poor was only 7 percent in 1976.

Social welfare expenditures also modify the distribution of income. Table 5 shows that the lowest fifth of families received 5.4 percent of total pretax income, including cash transfers, in 1976. This would have been about 2 percent if only pretransfer income were included, but about 8 percent if all noncash social welfare benefits, net of taxes paid, were included. If the latter procedure were followed, the overall inequality among the fifths of family would be somewhat smaller than shown in the table.

Also, it is at least arguable that there has been some decline over time in overall inequality of income. As shown in the table, the top fifth of families now get a somewhat smaller share, and the bottom fifth gets a somewhat larger share of the national total of money income than it did in 1960. Whether this trend remains after consideration of taxes and nonmoney income, adjustment for changing family sizes, and after taking account of the growing number of "unrelated individuals," is subject to some dispute. It is clearer that certain long-standing class or group differences in income have been modified in the postwar period. For example, the median income for black families increased from 52 to 62 percent that of white families, and the median income of Southerners, which used to be 78 percent of the national average, is now 89 percent. These examples support the impression of a trend toward equalization of income, and of consumption and satisfactions therefrom.

TAXES AND BENEFITS BY INCOME LEVEL

It is not possible to assign tax burdens with certainty by income level because taxes have a way of being shifted onto others by the business firms and landlords who are legally required to pay them. One of the best studies of this question is *Who Bears the Tax Burden?*, by Joseph A. Pechman and Benjamin Okner, published by The Brookings Institution. They assume that sales and property taxes are largely shifted to the consumer, that payroll taxes are borne by the worker, and that income taxes are largely borne by the earner and the dividend recipient. Following these conventional assumptions, they conclude that the overall tax system in 1966 was roughly proportional to income for most lower-income and so-called middle-income taxpayers.

The several parts of the tax system may be classified as having progressive and regressive properties. The progressive taxes—those that take a larger share of the income of the rich—include the individual and corporate income taxes and estate and inheritance taxes. Regressive taxes—those that take a larger share of the income of the nonrich—include property, sales, and payroll taxes. The federal tax system on balance is thought to be progressive, while the state and local tax systems are considered regressive. Wisconsin's tax system was found to have a regressive pattern by the Tax Impact Study Committee of 1958. More recently, the Advisory Commission on Intergovernmental Relations characterized Wisconsin's taxes as "mildly regressive." Currently, the State Department of Revenue is completing a study of 1974 tax burdens by income level.

There are numberous conflicting signals about how tax burdens may have changed for the several income classes in recent years. Lacking any better comprehensive information, however, we can update the conclusion of Pechman and Okner for 1966. Applying their findings to the taxes paid directly and indirectly by households in 1977 suggests that most taxpayers with up to about $40,000 of "broadly defined income" paid a combined tax rate of 35 percent. The top 5 percent of taxpayers, with incomes above $40,000 paid rates rising with income to well above the average rate of 38 percent. This largely proportional tax system with a progressive kick at the top end makes the posttax distribution of income only slightly less unequal than the pretax distribution.

The great middle class, which is variously defined as the middle 60 to 90 percent of the population, undoubtedly draws most of the direct benefits from social welfare expenditures. Their children are in school; their parents receive social security and medicare. But for every one of these programs, there is an income class which pays a higher amount in taxes to finance the program than it gets back in direct benefits. Ths "break-even point" varies with age and family size, but for nonaged persons without children in school it is probably somewhat below the median income of $16,000. For programs that do not provide separable benefits to specific individuals, like national defense and scientific research, we can assume that all persons share in the benefits in a fashion that does not affect the distribution of income. This means that many middle-class people, as well as the rich, are subsidizing programs for others, and doing so on the grounds that the indirect benefits—net of unwanted side effects—of improving the lot of the poor and making the country a better place to live are worth the sacrifice. In the recent past, they have been willing to devote a rising share of income to such purposes.

EXPLANATIONS FOR THE TAX REVOLT

The overwhelming vote in favor of Proposition 13 may be a message that the voters want not just to further limit the property tax, but to put a lid on social welfare spending. One can draw that same conclusion from the rough sledding encountered by President Carter's plans for welfare reform and national health insurance. Somewhat contradictory to this are the calls for expanding social welfare benefits and redirecting them to what may be identified as the upper reaches of the middle class. A prime example is the live proposal to extend the income cutoff for basic grants for college students from $15,000 to $25,000. Another example is the struggle to keep eligibility for so-called public service employment jobs open to members of nonpoor families. Still another example is the action last winter by Congress to extend the taxable earnings base and hence the base for calculating social security benefits from its present level of $16,500 to $31,800 in 1982. This means that maximum retirement benefits will rise faster than they otherwise would have.

These examples of "welfare for the middle class" can be matched by countless instances of tax relief for the middle class. These latter include the more generous exemptions adopted in 1976 for estate and gift taxes, income tax credits for child care expense that reach those earning up to $30,000, efforts in several states to advance the cutoff for property tax credits to those with $25,000 of income, and the Steiger plan to reduce tax rates on capital gains. In all these examples, lower-income groups are called upon to help finance benefits for upper- and middle-income people.

Whether the California vote for less spending or the request for more spending and tax relief for the middle class is the dominant message, the portent is the same—a limit at or below present rates of redistribution toward the lower-income groups.

It is possible that this mood is only a temporary one brought on by the recent experience with recession, slow growth in production and income, and a high rate of inflation. It is no doubt easier for people to pay higher tax rates when they are confident that real incomes are rising. Inflation is a great redistributor of income and of capital gains, but it is to rationally planned redistribution what witchcraft is to true religion. There is no good evidence that the middle class has suffered more from the current inflation than either the rich or the poor. However, the fear and insecurity inflation breeds may be what has generated the wish to slow down the growth of taxes and spending on what are still thought of as valid public purposes. According to this theory, economic adversity has made the American public even more conservative than they generally are. When the economy returns to normal, taxpayers may return to the pattern of accepting higher tax rates.

Somewhat related to the above is the idea, well-developed by John Shannon, that the tax limitation movement was triggered by voter surprise at discovering that their taxes had gone up. He attributes this to the facts that: with inflation, income tax revenues rise faster than income unless tax rates are reduced; property tax revenues may behave in similar fashion; and local tax rates may be pushed up by decisions made at state or federal levels. He sees the ways to eliminate this element of surprise in indexing the income tax to adjust for inflation, requiring full prior notification of plans to raise property tax bills, and prohibition of mandates without compensation by senior governments (*Intergovernmental Perspective*, Summer 1978).

An alternative explanation for the apparent change of mood—and one that is more consistent with a premanent shift—is that the median voters have carefully surveyed the situation and have concluded that the extra direct and indirect benefits to them of further increases in spending do not match the pain and sacrifice of giving up a larger share of income in taxes. That is to say, they have satisfied their taste for redistribution by the shift from 11 to 21 percent of GNP for social welfare expenditures. Or to state it another way, it may be that the new generation has less taste for redistribution than did its predecessor. Perhaps the harder thing to explain is the shift in tastes that was responsible for the unusually rapid growth of redistributive activity of the preceding fifteen years.

Historians are hard put to explain why some Western countries have moved more rapidly than others in developing what is commonly referred to as a welfare state. Today, most of the other rich, democratic nations spend considerably more than 21 percent of GNP for social welfare. But they approached those levels at different paces—and sometimes with longer pauses. Harold Wilensky, a Berkeley sociologists who is a keen observer of these international trends, sees us as moving toward the welfare state, but "with ill grace, carping and complaining all the way." He believes the current backlash is due to our reliance, in contrast to Sweden and Germany, on progressive taxes and property taxes on households. He concludes that "misguided enthusiasm for [these] painfully visible taxes will keep the country in turmoil without producing enough revenue to meet citizen demands." His remedy is greater use of payroll taxes, sales taxes, and the introduction of a federal value-added tax (Chicago *Tribune*, September 15, 1978).

A still different explanation for the tax revolt is that increasing numbers of voters may have been influenced by a new understanding of undesirable side effects of social welfare expenditures with respect to people's willingness to work, save, and invest. Economists emphasize that taxing and spending have not only redistributive but also efficiency effects. Perhaps the most extraordinary efficiency effect was the one predicted by USC's Arthur Laffer—namely, that Proposition 13 would so improve private investment in California that tax revenues at the new, lower rates would soon exceed those that would have been collected at the old rates.

William Schneider, writing in the current issue of *Politics Today*, reviews public opinion polls to demonstrate that most Americans have contradictory attitudes about government. They simultaneously favor less government and lower taxes, but not fewer government services. He asserts that while confidence in government has fallen drastically since the mid-1960s, there is "no evidence that Americans have turned against the idea that government should support the social welfare, provde services, help disadvantaged groups, and protect citizens from economic and social adversity." He explains the current tax revolt not as a "New Negativism" of the moddle class, as Vernon Jordan does, but as a coalition of high-status people who are opposed to government in principle and a low-status group who see government as hopelessly wasteful and inefficient.

The several theories used to explain the tax revolt emphasize one or more of the following as causal factors.

— the recent recession and current inflation

— satisfaction of the "taste for redistribution"

— concern about undesirable side effects of taxes and expenditures

— loss of confidence in government

SUMMARY

We have covered the following points.

— Taxes are high and rising.

— Property taxes have risen less than most other taxes.

— The main reason for increases in taxes is the rise of social welfare expenditures.

— These expenditures and the taxes to pay for them are redistributive toward the poor.

— The current tax revolt, which may be either short- or long-lived, is subject to alternative explanations relating either to particular taxes or to the outcomes of public expenditures. It may signal an important revision of the social contract expressed in government budgets. As such, it merits careful study.

33

THE ROLLER-COASTER INCOME TAX

Martin Anderson

If Niccolò Machiavelli himself had designed a tax system, it is doubtful he could have improved on ours. For any wise prince would want a tax system—like ours—that extracted the most tax revenues with the least awareness on the part of the citizens as to how much they were actually paying.

For the individual, the most important part of our tax system consists of taxes on income. These taxes are particularly important because, in the course of raising revenue for government, they also directly affect the incentive of the individual to work. The higher the tax rates, the less a worker keeps of what he earns. And the less he keeps, the smaller his incentive to create and produce goods and services.

Largely because of the different kinds of taxes on income, and the use of the withholding tax system, few people—even experts—are aware of how much tax is paid on income and, in particular, how the rate of tax varies with the level of income. Most of us seem to know, with a fair degree of accuracy, what our net pay is after deductions. But few could immediately recall how much tax they paid for, say, last month. And fewer still know what tax rate they would pay on additional income if their earnings increased.

There are good reasons for this state of affairs. First, we tend to think of income taxes as just *Federal* income taxes. This is reasonable to an extent, since the Federal income tax is by far the largest. But 42 states and the District of Columbia, as well as many cities, also tax earned income. The social security tax is also a tax on income. For many people, the combination of all these taxes adds up to considerably more than just the Federal income tax alone. The real income tax we pay is the sum of all the income taxes we pay to the government.

This article is based on the author's forthcoming book, Welfare: The Political Economy of Welfare Reform *(Hoover Institution Press).*

From Martin Anderson, "The Roller-Coaster Income Tax," no. 50 *The Public Interest* 17-28 (Winter 1978). Copyright © 1978 by National Affairs, Inc.

Second, we tend to think only of the published tax rates on "taxable income," which are progressive. We often neglect to calculate the effect of exemptions, deductions, and credits. It seems to be generally assumed that the Federal income-tax rate begins at 14 percent and rises smoothly to 50 percent on earned income—or to 70 percent for investment income. It doesn't: In recent years, income-tax exemptions, deductions, and credits have multiplied both in number and size. They now exert a powerful effect on actual tax rates paid, especially in the lower-income brackets. Actual tax rates on earned income are dramatically different from the impression given by the official tax tables.

Third, we tend to think in terms of the *average* tax rate—the total amount of taxes we pay divided by our total income. This is useful enough for some purposes. But in gauging the effect on income taxes on the incentive to work, the *marginal* tax rate is what matters: the varying tax rate that applies to each additional increment of earned income.

The Federal income tax and most state income taxes are supposed to be "progressive" over most of the income range. Generally speaking, if earnings increase, a higher rate of tax must be paid on the added amount of earnings. In the move to a higher income tax bracket, the tax rate changes *only* for the *additional* income earned in the higher bracket.

Fourth, many of us tend to focus our thoughts on income taxes only during March and early April. Automatic payroll deductions make paying taxes relatively painless over the course of the year. When it comes time to balance accounts in the spring, we are usually concerned only with how much more we will have to pay or how much we will "get back." We have been conditioned to think of taxes in terms of small incremental payments or returns, rather than total amounts.

The overall effect is a significant lack of knowledge about how high income taxes really are and how much they vary for different income groups. Of course, there are other taxes besides income taxes. But the taxes on earned income have the most powerful, direct effect on the incentive to produce. The higher they are, the greater the deadening effect on the productivity of workers.

The overall level of all taxes—income taxes, sales taxes, property taxes, and others— is also critically important. To a large extent the amount of taxes we pay determines the role government plays in our lives. The amount of all taxes in the United States has grown dramatically during the last 30 years. In 1950, taxes of all kinds were 25 percent of our net national product. By 1960, they were over 30 percent. By 1970, they were over 35 percent. It will not be a great surprise if we find that they are over 40 percent in 1980.

THE FAMILY'S TAX BURDEN

How high are the income tax rates paid by workers in the United States? How do they change as income changes? There is no way to answer these questions both completely and simply. Income taxes vary from andividual to individual and from family to family, depending on the size of the family, on the amount and kind of deductions taken, on the size of the earnings, and on the city and state of residence. However, we can get a reasonably clear idea of the magnitude of the income taxes by calculating what a typical family pays.

As an example, let us consider a family of four—a husband, a wife, and two children. Let us assume that the entire income of this family comes solely from wages and salaries and that the family files a joint return, takes the standard deduction, and lives in California. Let us further assume that the family pays only three major taxes on earned income: social security tax, Federal income tax, and state income tax.

In 1976, the social security tax rate was 5.85 percent, paid on all wage and salary income up to $16,500 a year. The marginal tax rate of 5.85 percent is constant over the entire range of income from $0 to $16,500. (See the second column of Table 1.)

The Federal income tax is a little more complicated. In 1976, *exemptions* from taxable income were $750 per person, regardless of the amount of earned income. The standard *deduction* on a joint return was $2,100 for all levels of income between $0 and $13,125. The deduction then rises gradually, reaching a maximum of $2,800 for earnings of $17,500 and above. For a family of four, the amount of income untaxed because of exemptions and deductions varies from $5,100 to $5,800, depending on the level of income.

The Federal income-tax rate on taxable earned income starts at 14 percent and gradually increases to 50 percent. After the amount of Federal tax *owed* is calculated there are tax credits that reduce the amount of tax that must be *paid*. In 1976, the *general tax credit* on Federal income taxes was $35 per person *or* 2 percent of taxable income, whichever was larger. For a four-person family taking the standard deduction, this mean a credit of $140 for incomes between $0 and $12,100. The general tax credit increased slowly after that, reaching its maximum value of $180 at $14,286 of earned income, and remaining constant at $180 for all higher incomes.

To complicate matters further, an *earned-income credit* was added to the Federal tax code in 1975 (though it was generally considered to be only a temporary addition). Though called a tax credit, it actually constitutes a welfare program using the tax system to give money to low-income families. This is how it works: The earned-income "credit" is 10 percent of earnings up to $4,000 a year. A family with no earnings receives no "credit." If its earnings are $1,000, it gets a "credit" of $100. But at that low level of earnings there are no taxes owed to the Federal government to which such a "credit" can be applied. So the Federal government reasons that it owes the family the amount of the "credit" and sends it a check for $100.

The earned-income "credit" increases to a maximum of $400 for earnings of $4,000, and then begins to decline. If the family has earnings of $5,000, the Federal government reduces the amount of the check to $300. If it makes $6,000, the check is $200; at $7,000, it is only $100. When earnings reach $8,000, the

TABLE 1

Marginal Income Tax Rates for a Typical Family of Four
in California (1976)

Annual Earned Income	Social Security Tax Rate	Federal Income Tax Rate	State Income Tax Rate	Overall Income Tax Rate
$1,000	6%[a]	−10%	−	−4%
2,000	6	−10	−	−4
3,000	6	−10	−	−4
4,000	6	−10	−	−4
5,000	6	10	−	16
6,000	6	10	−	16
7,000	6	23	−	29
8,000	6	26	−	32
9,000	6	17	−	23
10,000	6	19	−	25
11,000	6	19	9%	34
12,000	6	19	3	28
13,000	6	17	4	27
14,000	6	18	4	28
15,000	6	17	4	27
16,000	6	19	5	30
17,000	3	19	5	27
18,000	−	20	5	25
19,000	−	25	6	31
20,000	−	25	6	31
21,000	−	25	6	31
22,000	−	26	7	33
23,000	−	28	7	35
24,000	−	28	7	35
25,000	−	28	8	36
26,000	−	30	8	38
27,000	−	32	8	40
28,000	−	32	9	41
29,000	−	32	9	41
30,000	−	33	9	42
31,000	−	36	10	46
32,000	−	36	10	46
33,000	−	36	10	46
34,000	−	37	11	48
35,000	−	39	11	50
36,000	−	39	11	50
37,000	−	39	11	50
38,000	−	40	11	51
39,000	−	42	11	53
40,000	−	42	11	53

TABLE 1 (Continued)

Annual Earned Income	Social Security Tax Rate	Federal Income Tax Rate	State Income Tax Rate	Overall Income Tax Rate
41,000	–	42	11	53
42,000	–	43	11	54
43,000	–	45	11	56
44,000	–	45	11	56
45,000	–	45	11	56
46,000	–	46	11	57
47,000	–	48	11	59
48,000	–	48	11	59
49,000	–	48	11	59
50,000	–	48	11	59
51,000	–	50	11	61

a. All tax rates rounded to nearest full percent.

earned-income "credit" is phased out completely. The combined effect of exemptions, deductions, and credits of one sort or another is to eliminate any Federal income tax on earned incomes below $6,900 a year. The earned-income "credit" is thus nothing but a negative income tax. But since truth-in-labeling laws do not apply to the government's own legislation, the earned-income "credit" was mislabeled when it was originally enacted.

There are some curious features of the earned-income tax credit. Perhaps the original idea was to redistribute more income from upper- and middle-income taxpayers to low-income workers, by more than offsetting the effect of the social security tax. The "credit" does accomplish this, but in doing so it violates a basic principle of welfare. For earnings up to $4,000, the amount of the check from the government is *inversely* proportional to need: The more a family earns, the more welfare it gets.

Perhaps the intent of the "credit" was to encourage the low-income population to work. It does provide some incentive, at least for those contemplating working for $4,000 a year or less. But in order to phase out the $400 "bonus" incomes between $4,000 and $8,000 a year, it is necessary to impose, in effect, an additional marginal tax of 10 percent on all earnings above $4,000. And this has a very critical effect on work incentives.

Perhaps the original intent was to pave the way for a full-fledged negative income tax by smuggling the principle quietly into the tax code. This attempt has been successful, to some extent, but the "credit"—with its rising and falling subsidy—is such a strange and twisted version of the negative income tax that it really adds nothing to our understanding of the possible consequences of a genuine negative income tax.

One thing the earned-income "credit" does do, which clearly was not intended, is to provide a tidy government subsidy to employers who pay low wages. Employers in low-wage industries will not take long to realize that any employee earning $4,000 annually will also receive a government check for an additional $400. Maybe employers will ignore this government "bonus" when they set pay scales. But maybe they won't.

The combined effect on all these exemptions, deductions, and credits on the Federal income-tax rate can be seen in the third column of Table 1. We now have a *negative* income-tax rate of 10 percent on all earnings below $4,000. As the earned-income "credit" begins to decline when earnings exceed $4,000, the marginal tax rate jumps abruptly *by 20 percentage points*—from minus 10 percent to plus 10 percent. We don't really know much about the effects of imposing such a large, sudden tax-rate increase on the earnings of a low-income worker. But it probably does not do too much for his incentive to better himself.

As the family's annual earnings rise over $6,100, the regular Federal income tax rate takes effect, and the marginal tax rate jumps another 13 percentage points and then continues to rise. The Federal income tax rate on the additional $1,000 earned between $6,000 and $7,000 is 23 percent. For the $1,000 earned between $7,000 and $8,000, it is 26 percent. After the earned-income "credit" is phased out at $8,000, the Federal rate drops sharply back to 17 percent for the next $1,000 increment of earned income. It then reverses and rises smoothly until it flattens out at 50% for all earned income over $49,800 a year.

California's income tax was chosen to represent a typical state system. (Although California is the largest state, 11 other states have marginal income tax rates that equal or exceed California's.) In 1976, the standard *deduction* for a joint return in California was $2,000. An *exemption credit* of $25 for each parent and $8 for each child was allowed, making a total exemption credit of $66 for a family of four.

California also has a special *low-income credit* of $80 for families with incomes up to $10,000 a year. The effect of this low-income credit is similar to that of the Federal earned-income "credit." A typical family of four does not pay any income tax in California until its earnings exceed $10,000. Because of the manner in which the low-income credit is phased out, California's marginal income-tax rate on earnings between $10,000 and $11,000 a year is surprisingly high, 9 percent (see the fourth column of the table). The tax rate then drops sharply to 3 percent for the next $1,000 increment of earnings, rises gradually, and finally peaks at 11 percent for earnings over $33,000.[1]

The three major taxes on income—the social security tax, the Federal income tax and the state income tax—all combine to determine the overall marginal tax rate on earned income. The results are summarized in the fifth column of Table 1.

THE ROLLER-COASTER RIDE

Using the table, we can follow our typical family through a series of pay raises. Assume first that the husband works about half time and makes $4,000. Social security taxes are $234, and the Federal government sends the family a check for $400. On balance, the government pays the family $166, making its total income $4,166. The "tax rate" is a *negative* 4 percent.

Next year, the husband accepts the opportunity to increase his working hours by 50 percent. His income before taxes and subsidies jumps to $6,000, and he feels pretty good: After all, he has increased his income by half. But has he really? He now earns $6,000. Social security taxes have increased to $351. But his Federal "credit" has been reduced to only $200. By working more, he receives less from the Federal government, and this decreases his income, just as an increase in taxes would. The family must now *pay* the government $151 in net taxes. Thus its net income is now $5,849—$1,683 more than it was when their earned income was $4,000. Earnings have increased by $2,000, but spendable income has increased by only $1,683. The effective tax rate on the additional $2,000 of earnings is 16 percent.

Then suppose the husband is offered a better job, with longer hours, that pays $8,000 a year. Undaunted, he accepts. Social security taxes increase to $468. No more checks are mailed to the family from Washington. Instead, the Internal Revenue Service requires him to *pay* $292 in Federal income taxes. The total tax bill has increased to $760. The family's net income rises to $7,240. If the family begins to get an uneasy feeling that the additional $2,000 of income does not seem to go quite as far as expected, the feeling would be justified. When the father's earnings were $6,000, the family's net income was $5,849. Now the net income is $7,240—an increase of only $1,391. The effective marginal tax rate on the added income from the new job is *over 30 percent*. (There once was a time not very long ago when income tax rates like these applied only to people in *high*-income brackets).

The husband's job prospects continue to improve. He learns his job well, works hard, and is soon earning an additional $2,000 a year. The family's financial situation is a little brighter now, because the mysterious workings of our income-tax system *lower* the tax rate. On the family's earnings of $10,000, the social security tax is now $585, and the Federal income tax has increased to $646. There is still no state income tax to pay. The family's net income is $8,769— an increase of $1,529. For this $2,000 of additional earnings the income-tax rate is slightly over *23 percent*. The husband may feel, if he did the calculations, that it is somewhat odd that he should be paying a lower rate of tax on higher levels of income. The taxpayer's lot, however, is not to reason why, but to pay.

The husband is then offered overtime work and accepts. Income before taxes increases by $1,000. The social security tax becomes $644; the Federal income tax is $836. And now the state of California wants a contribution— $94, to be exact. The family's net spendable income is $9,426, only $657 more than it was before the husband started working overtime. Perhaps he would have reconsidered if he had realized that the tax rate on that $1,000 of overtime pay would be over *34 percent*.

Let us briefly review the experience of our typical family. When its earned income was less than $4,000, the marginal tax rate was a *negative* 4 percent. For the next $2,000 of income, it jumped to a *positive* 16 percent. For the next $2,000 it was over 30 percent. On the next $2,000 the marginal tax rate *dropped* to 23 percent. And then it bounced back up to over 34 percent for the next $1,000 of earnings.

Moving on to higher levels of earned income, the family probably becomes increasingly mystified. Between $11,000 and $13,000 the marginal tax rate is 27 percent, a *fall* of 7 percentage points (see the fifth column of the table). Between $13,000 and $14,000, the tax rate then *rises* slightly to 28 percent. Between $14,000 and $15,000 it *falls* slightly to 27 percent. Between $15,000 and $16,000, it again *rises* to 30 percent. After the family's income passes the $16,500 mark, it stops paying social security taxes.[2] Although both Federal and state tax rates continue to rise, the net effect is that the overall tax rate on income between $16,000 and $18,000 *falls* by four percentage points to 26 percent.

After the $18,000 income level has been passed, the roller coaster course of the marginal income-tax rate ends. On the next $3,000 of income, the marginal tax rate *rises* to 31 percent—and continues to rise smoothly until it reaches its maximum rate of 61 percent for all earned income in excess of $49,800 (see the fifth column of Table 1).

AN UNCONSCIONABLE SYSTEM

The income tax in the United States is widely believed to be a tax whose marginal rate starts low, and rises evenly with increasing income. But tinkering with the income tax system to achieve social welfare objectives rather than to raise revenues has essentially destroyed this feature over a wide and critical range of income. To make the marginal income tax rate *negative* for the first $4,000 of income, and to hold it at 16 percent for the next $2,000, it was necessary to increase sharply the tax rate on income between $6,000 and $8,000.

The combined effect of Federal and state income taxes—with all their exemptions, deductions, and credits—and the social security tax *is a marginal income tax rate that averages 28 percent for the entire range of income between $6,000 and $18,000 a year.* While there are sharp fluctuations within this range, a trend line statistically fitted to the data points is essentially flat. Only when income exceeds $18,000 a year does the marginal tax rate begin its expected steady, upward climb.

In Chart 1, the marginal income-tax rates are plotted for the family of four in our example. What is especially interesting, and dismaying, is the shape of the plotted tax rate schedule for earned incomes below $18,000. The most steeply increasing part of the marginal tax rate curve lies between $4,000 and $8,000 of income. Flat and negative for the first $4,000 of income, it suddenly thrusts upward—rising 36 percentage points over only $4,000 of additional income.

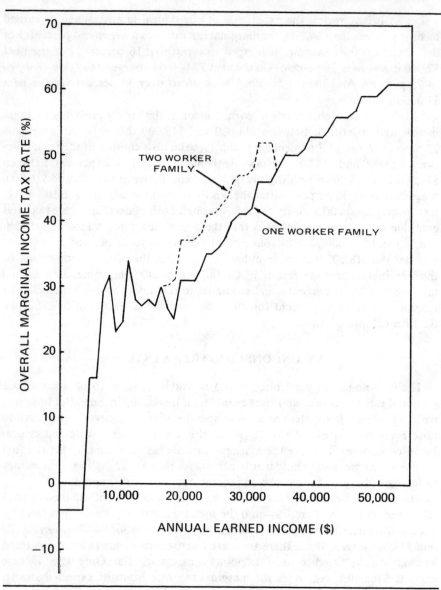

Chart 1: **Marginal Income Tax Rates for a Typical Family of Four in the United States (1976)**

It is hard to believe we did this on purpose—that we intentionally saddled with the highest rate of increase in the marginal tax rate that part of our labor force perhaps most sensitive to disincentives. We should not be surprised if some of these workers became reluctant to increase, or even maintain, their work effort.

The nonsensical nature of our income tax rates becomes even clearer between $8,000 and $10,000. Within this short range it suddenly reverses—the more you earn, the lower your marginal tax rate. When the California state income tax takes effect between $10,000 and $11,000, the marginal income-tax rate again reverses itself and jumps sharply to 34 percent. This pattern, of course, is peculiar to families living in California. But the odds are good that other state income taxes (and city income taxes) would produce similar results in many cases.

Over the next $7,000 of earned income—between $11,000 and $18,000—the marginal tax rate reverses once more and moves jaggedly downward. Within this income range lie many middle-income families. Their overall marginal income-tax rate, at least for those who take the standard deduction, is high and *declines* with increasing income. And this would be true even in a state with no income tax.

After earnings exceed $18,000, the marginal income-tax schedule assumes the more familiar pattern of a consistent, rising rate, assuming that the standard deduction is taken. But as incomes move into these ranges, the likelihood that a family will itemize deductions increases with increasing income.

The typical family of four in our example is, of course, not representative of *all* American families. For families that itemize deductions, the marginal tax rates can be lower, but the tax situation is much more complicated. The marginal income-tax rate for the family that itemizes deductions depends on the number and size of their deductions—for such items as state and local income taxes, mortgage interest, sales taxes, medical expenses, and charitable contributions. There can thus be even more bizarre variations in the size of the marginal tax rate on income. Some people live in states where the state income-tax rate is lower than in California. In some states it is higher; and in others there is no income tax. There are also those unlucky souls who live in places like New York City and pay a fourth major tax on income.

The income-tax situation is undeniably complex. It is reasonably clear what happens to a family making less than $18,000 a year and lacking the inclination or sophistication to puzzle out and itemize deductions—or lacking enough deductions to make it worthwhile to itemize them. For most of these families, marginal income-tax rates are high and inconsistent—and confusing.

The effect of our efforts to use the tax system to accomplish social goals, such as giving money to those with low incomes and trying to increase their incentive to work, has had serious and apparently unforseen side effects.

Income tax rates in the United States have now risen so high for so many people that we should be seriously concerned with the effect of these high tax rates on national productivity. The combined tax on income is now far too high. It should be lowered across the board.

The shape of the marginal tax-rate schedule has been so distorted that a graph of the rates looks like the course followed by a roller coaster. The up-and-down nature of the income-tax rates raises unanswerable questions about the equity of our tax system. Why should someone whose income increases from $7,000

$8,000 pay a tax of 32 percent on an increase of $1,000 in his income, while some-one making $17,000 pays only 25 percent on a $1,000 increase in his income?

If the marginal tax-rate structure that results from the interaction of all deductions, exemptions, and credits had been spelled out in one comprehensive reform plan, it would have been dismissed as self-evident nonsense. But the nonsense is not self-evident: It is masked today by the variety and complexity of our income-tax system. We have an embarrasing system that should be corrected as soon as possible before its distorting effects become permanently established in our society. As it now works, the income-tax system is unconscionable.

NOTES

1. California has one other small tax on earned income, the Disability Insurance Tax, which is 1 percent of all earnings up to $11,400.

2. It should be noted that the social security tax is significantly higher for two-worker families, an increasingly large segment of the working population. If both husband and wife work, each pays social security taxes on *all* personal income up to $16,500. If their earnings are approximately equal, the family would pay social security taxes on all earned income up to $33,000 a year. The result for that two-worker family is an increase of six percentage points in the marginal income-tax rate on all income between $16,500 and $33,000 a year (see the dotted line in Chart 1). In order to keep our example as simple as possible, it has been assumed that only one member of the family works.

34

THE ROLLER-COASTER INCOME TAX—
WISCONSIN STYLE

*W. Lee Hansen**

A recent paper by Anderson[1] indicates that federal attempts to reduce the tax burden on low income-tax units, in combination with social security and state (in his illustration, California) income taxes, have produced a "roller-coaster" pattern of marginal tax rates, a pattern that defies not only common sense but also the basic tenets of tax reform. Knowing that Wisconsin has attempted to do the same thing through alterations in its tax structure, I thought the rollar-coaster effect might be even greater than in California. This note extends the Anderson analysis to Wisconsin. It begins with a review of Anderson's results, compares the findings for California and Wisconsin in 1976, projects the effects to 1981 and 1987 to reflect already legislated changes in social security,[2] and then traces changes for Wisconsin from 1967 to 1976. Throughout the paper, income refers to earned income rather than adjusted gross income.

Here is a recapitulation of Anderson's results. The roller-coaster effect is reflected by multiple peaks and troughs in the overall federal marginal tax rates (column 3).[3] This pattern is produced by the superimposition of the general tax credit and the earned-income credit on the rate structure for federal taxes, the results of which are shown in column 2. Peaks appear at the $7,000, $9,000-$11,000, $13,000, and $15,000 brackets, with troughs at $8,000, $12,000, $14,000, and $16,000 brackets. However, the oscillations are relatively minor beyond $11,000.

California's tax structure (column 4) gives the roller-coaster added zip with its high initial marginal tax rate of 9% at the $10,000 bracket. This is followed immediately by a much lower rate of 3% at the $11,000 bracket. After that, there is a slow progressive ride upward to $33,000. The pattern for the combined California and federal tax rates (column 5) reveals two exceptional peaks at the $7,000 and $10,000 brackets—levels not attained again until income reaches $21,000.

---

*Professor of Economics and Education Policy Studies, and Fellow of the Institute for Research on Poverty. The author is indebted to Lou Ann Karter for her research assistance and to Robert J. Lampman for his comments.

From W. Lee Hansen, "The Roller-Coaster Income Tax—Wisconsin Style." Unpublished manuscript, 1979.

TABLE 1

Marginal Income Tax Rates for a Typical Family of Four in California (1976) and Wisconsin (1976)

Annual Earned Income Brackets	Federal 1976			California 1976		Wisconsin 1976		Wisconsin Overall State and Federal Income Tax Rate Based on 1977 Social Security Changes	
	Social Security Tax Rate	Federal Income Tax Rate	Overall Federal Income Tax Rate	California Income Tax Rate	Overall State and Federal Income Tax Rate	Wisconsin Income Tax Rate	Overall State and Federal Income Tax Rate	1981	1987
	(1)	(2)	(3)	(4)	(5)	(6)	(7)	(8)	(9)
$0-1000	6%a	-10%	-4%	—	-4%	0%	-4%	-3%	-3%
1000-2000	6	-10	-4	—	-4	0	-4	-3	-3
2000-3000	6	-10	-4	—	-4	0	-4	-3	-3
3000-4000	6	-10	-4	—	-4	4	0	1	1
4000-5000	6	10	16	—	16	16	32	33	33
5000-6000	6	10	16	—	16	17	33	34	34
6000-7000	6	23	29	—	29	17	46	47	47
7000-8000	6	26	32	—	32	12	44	45	45
8000-9000	6	17	23	—	23	7	30	31	31
9000-10000	6	19	25	—	25	7	32	33	33
10000-11000	6	19	25	9%	34	7	32	33	33
11000-12000	6	19	25	3	28	8	33	34	34
12000-13000	6	17	23	4	27	7	30	31	31
13000-14000	6	18	24	4	28	10	34	35	35
14000-15000	6	17	23	4	27	11	34	35	35
15000-16000	6	19	25	5	30	11	36	37	37
16000-17000	3	19	22	5	27	11	33	37.	37
17000-18000	—	20	20	5	25	11	31	38	38
18000-19000	—	25	25	6	31	11	36	43	43
19000-20000	—	25	25	6	31	11	36	43	43

TABLE 1 (Continued)

Annual Earned Income Brackets	Federal 1976			California 1976		Wisconsin 1976		Wisconsin	
	Social Security Tax Rate	Federal Income Tax Rate	Overall Federal Income Tax Rate	California Income Tax Rate	Overall State and Federal Income Tax Rate	Wisconsin Income Tax Rate	Overall State and Federal Income Tax Rate	Overall State and Federal Income Tax Rate Based on 1977 Social Security Changes 1981	1987
	(1)	(2)	(3)	(4)	(5)	(6)	(7)	(8)	(9)
20000-21000	—	25	25	6	31	11	36	43	43
21000-22000	—	26	26	7	33	11	37	44	44
22000-23000	—	28	28	7	35	11	39	46	46
23000-24000	—	28	28	7	35	11	39	46	46
24000-25000	—	28	28	8	36	11	40	47	47
25000-26000	—	30	30	8	38	11	41	48	48
26000-27000	—	32	32	8	40	11	43	50	50
27000-28000	—	32	32	9	41	11	43	50	50
28000-29000	—	32	32	9	41	11	43	50	50
29000-30000	—	33	33	9	42	11	44	49	51
30000-31000	—	36	36	10	46	11	47	47	54
31000-32000	—	36	36	10	46	11	47	47	54
32000-33000	—	36	37	10	46	11	48	48	55
33000-34000	—	37	37	11	48	11	48	48	55
34000-35000	—	39	39	11	50	11	50	50	57
35000-36000	—	39	39	11	50	11	50	50	57
36000-37000	—	39	39	11	50	11	50	50	57
37000-38000	—	40	40	11	51	11	51	51	58
38000-39000	—	42	42	11	53	11	53	53	60
39000-40000	—	42	42	11	53	11	53	53	60

TABLE 1 (Continued)

Annual Earned Income Brackets	Federal 1976			California 1976		Wisconsin 1976		Wisconsin	
	Social Security Tax Rate	Federal Income Tax Rate	Overall Federal Income Tax Rate	California Income Tax Rate	Overall State and Federal Income Tax Rate	Wisconsin Income Tax Rate	Overall State and Federal Income Tax Rate	Overall State and Federal Income Tax Rate 1981	Overall State and Federal Income Tax Rate Based on 1977 Social Security Changes 1987
	(1)	(2)	(3)	(4)	(5)	(6)	(7)	(8)	(9)
40000-41000	—	42	42	11	53	11	53	53	54
41000-42000	—	43	43	11	54	11	54	54	54
42000-43000	—	45	45	11	56	11	56	56	56
43000-44000	—	45	45	11	56	11	56	56	56
44000-45000	—	45	45	11	56	11	56	56	56
45000-46000	—	46	46	11	57	11	57	57	57
46000-47000	—	48	48	11	59	11	59	59	59
47000-48000	—	48	48	11	59	11	59	59	59
48000-49000	—	48	48	11	59	11	59	59	59
49000-50000	—	48	48	11	59	11	59	59	59
50000-51000	—	50	50	11	61	11	61	61	61

SOURCE: Columns 1, 2, 4, and 5 from Anderson's paper. Column 3 is simply the sum of columns 1 and 2. Columns 6, 7, 8, and 9 calculated by author.
a. All tax rates rounded to nearest full percent.
*Indicates total taxes are negative, based on homestead tax credit of up to $428.

Wisconsin's tax structure offers several additional twists (column 6). The state income tax structure itself provides a smooth rise (but steeper than California's) in marginal tax rates; successive marginal tax rates of 1, 4, 5, 6, 6, and 7% occur for the $3,000 through $8,000 income brackets. The addition of its circuit-breaker property tax relief program provides a maximum credit of $428 that nearly reaches the $4,000 income level;[4] the credit then begins to diminish but is still sufficient to offset the positive tax up through the $5,000 income bracket. However, the combination of the circuit-breaker's substantial marginal benefit reduction rates of 3, 11, 12, 11, 6, and 0% for the $3,000 through $8,000 income brackets, and the regular rate structure, produce surprisingly high marginal tax rates across the $4,000 through $8,000 income brackets.

The resulting roller-coaster combination of state and federal rates is shown in column 7. With the high federal rates in the $6,000 and $7,000 income brackets, Wisconsin taxpayers get a harrowing ride as the overall marginal tax rate hits 46% for the $6,000 income bracket and 44% for the $7,000 income bracket. This is followed in the next bracket by a sharp drop to 30%, then by a slow but irregular rise until the pattern smoothes out at the $18,000 income bracket.

The net result for Wisconsin taxpayers as compared to those in California is a considerably steeper and more erratic pattern of marginal tax rates. The erratic pattern is the result of attempts by both the federal government and the State of Wisconsin to reduce the tax burden on lower income tax units. Wisconsin's Homestead Tax Credit Program has numerous virtues, but the pattern of marginal tax rates it helps to produce leads to high marginal tax rates at fairly low levels of income, and to notches that could have adverse effects on work incentives.

What changes can be expected by 1981 and 1987 given already legislated social security changes and an assumption that the federal and state tax structures remain unchanged? This information is provided in columns 8 and 9 of Table I which capture the impact of the approximately one-percentage point increase in the social security tax and the increase in the wage base to $29,700 in 1981 and to $40,200 in 1987. The same roller-coaster effect noted for Wisconsin in 1976 prevails except that the discontinuity at the $16,000 and $17,000 income brackets disappears only to reappear at the $29,000 and $30,000 brackets in 1981 and at the $41,000 bracket in 1987.

What changes have occurred over the past decade in the overall marginal tax rates faced by Wisconsin taxpayers? Columns 1 through 5 in Table 2 provide comparable data from 1967. These data ignore the effect of the Homestead Relief Credit Program which in 1967 was restricted to elderly taxpayers over age 65, had a maximum credit of $223, and provided no credits to anyone whose income exceeded $3,500; it should also be noted that the percentage of eligibles participating was still quite low because the program was new. No comparable roller-coaster effect is evident. The only ripple in the overall federal tax results from the social security wage base cutoff; this produces a sudden downward displacement of the overall marginal rates (column 3) beginning at the $6,000

TABLE 2

Marginal Income Tax Rates for a Typical Family of Four
in Wisconsin (1967)

Annual Earned Income Brackets	Federal 1967			Wisconsin 1967	
	Social Security Tax Rate	Federal Income Tax Rate	Overall Federal Income Tax Rate	Wisconsin Income Tax Rate	Overall State and Federal Income Tax Rate
	(1)	(2)	(3)	(4)	(5)
$0-1000	4%	0%	4%	0%	4%
1000-2000	4	0	4	3	7
2000-3000	4	.4	4.4	3	7.4
3000-4000	4	14	18	4	22
4000-5000	4	15	19	4	23
5000-6000	4	16	20	5	25
6000-7000	–	15	15	5	20
7000-8000	–	17	17	5	22
8000-9000	–	17	17	6	23
9000-10000	–	17	17	6	23
10000-11000	–	19	19	8	27
11000-12000	–	21	21	8	29
12000-13000	–	22	22	9	31
13000-14000	–	22	22	9	31
14000-15000	–	22	22	10	32
15000-16000	–	24	24	10	34
16000-17000	–	25	25	10	35
17000-18000	–	25	25	10	35
18000-19000	–	25	25	10	35
19000-20000	–	27	27	10	37
20000-21000	–	28	28	10	38
21000-22000	–	28	28	10	38
22000-23000	–	28	28	10	38
23000-24000	–	30	30	10	40
24000-25000	–	32	32	10	42
25000-26000	–	32	32	10	42
26000-27000	–	32	32	10	42
27000-28000	–	34	34	10	44
28000-29000	–	36	36	10	46
29000-30000	–	36	36	10	46
30000-31000	–	36	36	10	46
31000-32000	–	38	38	10	48
32000-33000	–	39	39	10	49
33000-34000	–	39	39	10	49
34000-35000	–	39	39	10	49
35000-36000	–	41	41	10	51
36000-37000	–	42	42	10	52
37000-38000	–	42	42	10	52
38000-39000	–	42	42	10	52
39000-40000	–	44	44	10	54

TABLE 2 (Continued)

Annual Earned Income Brackets	Federal 1967			Wisconsin 1967	
	Social Security Tax Rate	Federal Income Tax Rate	Overall Federal Income Tax Rate	Wisconsin Income Tax Rate	Overall State and Federal Income Tax Rate
	(1)	(2)	(3)	(4)	(5)
40000-41000	–	45	45	10	55
41000-42000	–	45	45	10	55
42000-43000	–	45	45	10	55
43000-44000	–	47	47	10	57
44000-45000	–	48	48	10	58
45000-46000	–	48	48	10	58
47000-48000	–	49	49	10	59
48000-49000	–	50	50	10	60
49000-50000	–	50	50	10	60
50000-51000	–	50	50	10	60

SOURCE: Calculated by author.

income bracket. This is followed by a smooth upward progression thereafter. The state income tax also shows a smooth upward pattern of marginal rates (column 5). The resulting pattern of marginal rates for the overall state-federal tax system is relatively smooth except for the displacement already noted. Of course, in comparing the 1967 and 1976 marginal tax rates it should be recalled that on average family incomes increased about 80%; thus, the 1967 marginal tax rate for the $4,000 bracket is roughly equivalent to the 1976 rate for the $7,000 bracket.

This is not the entire story, since only a limited number of taxes are considered here: social security taxes, federal and state income taxes, the federal earned income credit, and the Wisconsin Homestead Tax Credit. There are other programs with significant benefit reduction rates in the social security earnings test: AFDC, SSI, food stamps, BEOG, child-care, unemployment insurance, and so forth.

The results presented here raise some interesting questions. First, how serious is the "roller-coaster" effect on work incentives? Much of the discussion of welfare reform has centered on estimating the adverse impact of high marginal tax rates on work incentives. Are the variations reported here great enough to be of comparable concern? Second, to what extent do the benefits of providing tax relief for low income units exceed whatever disadvantages may result from the disincentive effects these benefits create? This may be an unanswerable question, but it certainly deserves examination. Third, to what extent might it have been wiser to reduce tax rates to zero at the lower income levels rather than try to achieve roughly comparable reductions indirectly via the Homestead Tax Credit

Program? Had California started with a 2% rather than a 9% rate for the $10,000 bracket, the state would have made only a minimal contribution to the roller-coaster effect. Why does Wisconsin not follow this approach? And fourth, to the extent that high marginal tax rates are believed to affect work incentives at lower income levels, what kinds of effects are they likely to produce at higher income levels where marginal tax rates equal and then exceed by a considerable margin the high 46 and 44% rates for the $6,000 and $7,000 income brackets?

NOTES

1. Martin Anderson, "The Roller-Coaster Income Tax," *The Public Interest* (Winter 1978), pp. 17-28.

2. As nearly as possible the methods I followed parallel those of Anderson. For greater clarity I have identified the income brackets rather than merely referring to the top of each bracket, as was done by Anderson in his paper.

3. All federal tax rates are based on use of the standard deduction.

4. We ignore here differences in the income definition used in the Homestead Tax Credit Program; the definition is much more inclusive than the definition of taxable income.

Section
VIII

Education Financing
and
Desegregation

35

EDUCATION

David W. Breneman

THE PRESIDENT'S 1979 education budget, in marked contrast to its recent predecessors, proposes substantial spending increases and several new initiatives. Although it may be premature to talk with certainty about the new administration's education policy, the budget is, in fact, the single most important policy statement. In addition, several events of the last year contributed to the accumulation of decisions and actions that collectively constitute policy: (1) expiring legislation provided an opportunity for the administration to develop reauthorization proposals for most elementary and secondary education programs; (2) congressional interest in tuition tax credits forced a review of existing student aid policy in a search for alternatives; and (3) President Carter's decision to create a department of education gave rise to active investigation of reorganization options. This chapter examines each of these topics together with the 1979 budget request in order to form a tentative judgment on the nature and direction of the Carter administration's education policy.

Elementary and Secondary Education

Table 4-1 presents federal outlays for elementary and secondary education programs. Most of the programs are administered by the

Many individuals in federal agencies provided the author with information and assistance in preparing this chapter; special thanks are due Mary Moore, Michael O'Keefe, Elizabeth Reisner, and Marshall Smith. Mara O'Neill provided research assistance for all budget tables, and Joseph Minarik, James McClave, and Laurent Ross prepared the tuition tax credit estimates from the Brookings MERGE file.

Table 4-1. Federal Outlays for Elementary and Secondary Education, by Program, Selected Fiscal Years, 1965–79

Millions of dollars

Program	1965	1969	1973	1975	1977	1978[a]	1979[a]
Office of Education	548	2,195	3,044	3,924	4,087	4,533	5,243
Compensatory education (title I)[b]	...	1,073	1,820	1,960	1,930	2,129	2,580
Education for the handicapped	...	54	106	151	247	366	560
Emergency school aid	...	...	41	216	241	281	305
Bilingual education[c]	...	...	30	63	89	109	130
Impact aid	349	398	580	619	765	810	781
Vocational education	95[d]	154	355	375	393	417	458
Other	104	516	112	540	422	421	429
Head Start[e]	5	350	373	426	458	536	566
Other[f]	320	374	487	667	741	839	956
Total except food	**873**	**2,919**	**3,904**	**5,017**	**5,286**	**5,908**	**6,765**
School milk and child nutrition[g]	263	336	1,298	1,832	2,792	2,811	2,699
Total	**1,136**	**3,255**	**5,202**	**6,849**	**8,078**	**8,719**	**9,464**

Sources: *Special Analyses, Budget of the United States Government, Fiscal Year 1979,* and preceding issues, except as indicated in notes.

a. Estimates by Office of Management and Budget as reported in *Special Analyses . . . 1979.*
b. Authorized by the Elementary and Secondary Education Act of 1965 (ESEA), title I.
c. Data from the Office of Bilingual Education.
d. Author's estimate, based on data from the Office of Education.
e. Head Start was first administered by the Office of Economic Opportunity. In July 1969, it was delegated to the Department of Health, Education, and Welfare, Office of Child Development. Until 1975 the money was still appropriated to the OEO before going to HEW. In 1975 and 1976 it was funded through HEW. In mid-1977, Head Start became a separate bureau in the newly formed Administration for Children, Youth, and Families under HEW's Office of Human Development Services.
f. Includes overseas dependents' education administered by the Department of Defense; Indian education administered by the Bureau of Indian Affairs, Department of the Interior; science education administered by the National Science Foundation; and other HEW programs.
g. Administered by the Department of Agriculture.

Office of Education, Department of Health, Education, and Welfare (HEW). The exceptions are the Head Start program, under the Administration for Children, Youth, and Families, and child nutrition programs (school breakfast and lunch), administered by the Department of Agriculture. The school breakfast and lunch programs are not strictly education programs; a strong case can be made for classifying them as welfare programs or even as aid to agriculture. Because of their size (nearly $2.8 billion in 1977), their inclusion as education programs would seriously affect total costs; in what follows, spending on these programs is reported separately.

Before 1965, federal support for elementary and secondary education was primarily impact aid to school districts burdened by the presence of federal installations (enacted in 1950), vocational education (authorized by legislation in 1917, and by the Vocational Education Act of 1963), Defense Department support of overseas schools for dependents, and National Science Foundation support for science education. The Elementary and Secondary Education Act of 1965 (ESEA) marked the beginning of a larger federal role in elementary and secondary education, and this act, with its numerous titles, is the principal charter of Office of Education programs. Other important legislation is the Emergency School Aid Act (1972) and the Education for All Handicapped Children Act of 1975. Since 1965 the federal share of public school revenues (including child nutrition) has been roughly 8 percent.[1] State and local governments provide the balance of support; in the 1975–76 school year, states paid 44 percent and local governments 48 percent.[2]

Federal Goals

Nearly two-thirds of federal educational appropriations provide supplemental or compensatory education services for youngsters who are educationally disadvantaged. The largest single program, title I of the Elementary and Secondary Education Act, provides money to states and to school districts based on the number of students from low-income families. The schools use the money for compensatory education services (specialized reading classes, individu-

---

1. W. Vance Grant and C. George Lind, *Digest of Education Statistics, 1976 Edition* (Government Printing Office, 1977), p. 71.
2. Federal general-revenue sharing funds to public schools are included in these figures as state funds. The Congressional Budget Office estimates that the federal share is between 9 and 10 percent when these funds are counted as federal dollars.

alized instruction, paraprofessional teacher aides) for youngsters who are well below the grade level in their work. Bilingual education (ESEA title VII) is aimed at children for whom English is a second language and is intended to help them develop proficiency in English. In the programs for the handicapped, federal dollars supplement state and local outlays to help ensure that all handicapped children have available to them a free appropriate public education. Emergency school aid money helps cover costs associated with school desegregation and is intended to aid those children who must overcome the educational disadvantages of minority-group isolation. Head Start is a preschool program that provides a wide range of social services—including education—to children from low-income families. The principle underlying all of these programs is the provision of additional or different educational resources to help equalize educational opportunities.

Although pressed by groups such as the National Education Association, the federal government provides no general-purpose support for school district operating expenses. Impact aid comes closest, but its purpose is to assist districts that have lost property tax revenue or have suffered extra expenditures because of the presence of federal installations or activities. Nearly 4,000 school districts are eligible for impact aid payments in the 1979 fiscal year. Federal dollars also underwrite the purchase of curricular materials and services, strengthen state and local education agencies, underwrite demonstration projects and other forms of educational innovation, and support educational research. The National Institute of Education, created in 1972, supports and coordinates federal educational research and development.

In sum, the federal government has focused primarily on the special educational needs of disadvantaged groups not well served by ordinary school programs. Existing programs cover these purposes rather comprehensively, and costly new programs are unlikely to be developed until a new—or broader—federal role in elementary and secondary education has been articulated and accepted.

The 1979 Budget

Table 4-2 presents the administration's budget proposal for elementary and secondary education for fiscal 1979, together with four benchmarks: 1977 appropriations, the Ford administration's 1978

budget, the Carter administration's 1978 budget, and 1978 appropriations.[3] President Ford's 1978 budget called for a cut of nearly
11 percent in Office of Education programs. President Carter requested approximately the 1977 appropriation, primarily by adding $350 million to title I funds. Ford's proposed cut of nearly $400
million in impact aid was left in the Carter budget, however, with
the large increase in ESEA title I offered as a quid pro quo. Congress raised the title I increase another $100 million and restored even
more than the $400 million to impact aid. In addition, Congress in-
creased funds for education for the handicapped by $100 million and
made numerous smaller increases in other programs, producing a
1978 Office of Education appropriation of $5.8 billion, a 16 percent
increase over Carter's revised budget. Combined with other agency
programs, total federal appropriations for elementary and secondary
education (excluding child nutrition) in 1978 were $7 billion, 16
percent above the 1977 level.

Perhaps chastened by this initial experience with congressional independence, the administration has requested a 15 percent increase
in current dollars for Office of Education programs in 1979. Impact
aid is still slated for a reduction (the budget requests $780 million),
but this time the administration seeks to reform the program selectively (in ways discussed later in this chapter).

The budget includes $804 million for state grants under the Educa-
tion for All Handicapped Children Act (Public Law 94-142), an
increase of $269 million, or 50 percent, over the 1978 appropriation
but substantially less than the estimated $1.3 billion authorized for
1979. The law provides for federal payments based on the number of
handicapped[4] children receiving special services in each state (up to a
maximum of 12 percent of the school-age population), multiplied by
a percentage of the national average per-pupil expenditure. This percentage increases from 5 percent in 1977 to 10 percent in 1978, 20
percent in 1979, 30 percent in 1980, and 40 percent in 1981 and be-

---

3. Data in tables 4-1 and 4-2 are not comparable because the first records outlays
while the second records appropriations (budget authority). Apart from administrative problems that can cause the two to differ, forward funding accounts for the main
discrepancies. Forward funding (one year's appropriation spent in the following
year) allows school administrators to plan on a certain amount of federal dollars.
Most of the large elementary and secondary education programs, with the exception
of impact aid and emergency school aid, are forward-funded.

4. The term covers seven categories of disability, and each category includes
conditions ranging from mild to severe.

Table 4-2. Federal Budget Authority for Elementary and Secondary Education, by Program, Fiscal Years 1977-79

Millions of dollars

Program	1977 appropriations	1978 Ford budget	1978 Carter budget	1978 Appropriations	1979 budget
Office of Education	4,986	4,449	4,966	5,771	6,643
Compensatory education (title I)[a]	2,285	2,285	2,635	2,735	3,379[b]
Education for the handicapped	469	470	520	693	972
State grants	315	315	365	535[c]	804
Other	154	155	155	158	168
Emergency school aid	292	275	295	310	333
National and state grants	257	240	260	275	290
Training and advisory services[d]	35	35	35	35	43
Bilingual education	115	90	135	135	150
Follow Through	59	45	59	59	35
Indian education	57	45	45	60	76
Vocational education[e]	393	385	385	418	414
Impact aid	793	395	395	839	780
A children[f]	272	292	296	298	...
B children[f]	342	0	0	345	...
Total	614	292	296	643	655[g]
Disaster assistance	...	...	...	39	12
Other	154	78	74	127	80
Construction	25	25	25	30	33
School libraries and institutional resources[h]	157	154	154	168	168
Support and innovation grants[i]	194	194	194	198	197
Special projects and training	93	90	99	101	105
Other	79	21	50	55	34
Other federal support	1,048	1,124	1,160	1,244	1,384
Head Start	475	475	485	625	680
National Institute of Education	70	109	109	90	100
Special institutions[j]	21	25	25	23	26
Indian education[k]	237	245	271	249	271
Overseas dependents' education[m]	245	270	270	257	307
Total except food	**6,034**	**5,573**	**6,126**	**7,015**	**8,027**
School milk and child nutrition[n]	2,986	2,391	2,621	2,932[p]	2,835
Total	**9,020**	**7,964**	**8,747**	**9,947**	**10,862**

Sources: Department of Health, Education, and Welfare, Office of Education, "FY 1979 Preliminary Request," unpublished data; *The Budget of the United States Government, Fiscal Year 1979—Appendix*, and preceding issue; and staffs of respective agencies.

a. Authorized by ESEA, title I.

b. This figure includes $400 million that proposed new legislation would direct to areas with high concentrations of title I children.

c. Includes $70 million carried forward from fiscal year 1977.

d. Authorized by the Civil Rights Act of 1964, title IV.

e. Author's calculations based on estimate that the elementary and secondary share of federal occu-

yond. Total federal outlays authorized under this program depend, therefore, on these percentages, on average per-pupil expenditures, and on the number of handicapped children identified and served. The $1.3 billion figure cited is based on $334 per child (20 percent of an estimated 1977–78 national average per-pupil expenditure of $1,670) for an estimated 4 million handicapped children.

Of all existing federal education programs, education for handicapped children has the most potential for explosive growth; an estimate of authorized outlays for school year 1982–83 under the existing formula is $3.9 billion.[5] The administration's 1979 request is less than authorized because the program is not a fixed entitlement but is subject to annual appropriation; $804 million is equivalent to $201 per child (assuming 4 million is an accurate estimate), or roughly 12 percent of estimated national average per-pupil expenditure.

Consistent with the administration's expressed interest in providing aid for the disadvantaged, the existing title I program is budgeted at nearly $3 billion and Head Start at $680 million, both 9 percent increases in current dollars over 1978 appropriations. In addition, the budget includes a $400 million targeting provision (a new part C of ESEA title I) to provide extra resources for high-poverty urban and rural districts. Under this provision, districts would receive support based on the number of enrolled students counted under the title I formula in excess of (1) 20 percent of district enrollment or (2) 5,000 students.[6] The 20 percent threshold will tend to channel

5. Congressional Budget Office, unpublished estimate. All estimates relating to this act are subject to considerable uncertainty, for reasons discussed in the next section.

6. Discussion of this provision within the Department of Health, Education, and Welfare predates President Carter's search for an "urban initiative," so it would be wrong to describe the $400 million as a recently developed education component of that initiative.

Table 4-2 notes *(continued)*

pational and vocational education budget is 57 percent.

f. An A child is a school child with a parent who works *and* lives on federal property. A B child is a school child with a parent who works *or* lives on federal property.

g. The 1979 budget does not disaggregate A and B children. However, data from the staff of the Assistant Secretary for Planning and Evaluation, HEW, show that $80 million is for the hold-harmless provision (for introducing formula changes gradually), and $85 million is determined by the number of children whose parents work or live in public housing.

h. Authorized by ESEA, title IV-B.

i. Authorized by ESEA, title IV-C.

j. Author's estimates.

k. Administered by Bureau of Indian Affairs.

m. Administered by Department of Defense.

n. Administered by Department of Agriculture.

p. Includes $274 million available from a special fund created to strengthen agricultural markets.

money to poor, rural districts, while the 5,000 student threshold will favor large, urban districts with high poverty levels. The rationale for providing high-poverty rural districts with extra dollars is that such districts are often located in states with low average per-pupil expenditures, meaning that fewer dollars per eligible student go to those areas under the title I formula. The arguments for spending additional dollars in large, high-poverty, urban districts are based on the high cost of educating large numbers of disadvantaged students (costs are said to rise disproportionately because of educational and behavioral problems that accompany large numbers), and on the general financial problems facing many central cities and their school districts. Since the amounts appropriated have never been sufficient to fund the program fully, many eligible children have not been helped.[7] The likely effect of the targeting provision, therefore, will be to serve more children rather than to increase resources per child.

Legislative Reauthorization

The Elementary and Secondary Education Act of 1965, as amended, expires on September 30, 1978, as do the Indian Education Act and legislation authorizing impact aid. As a consequence, the administration last year thoroughly reviewed and analyzed virtually all federal elementary and secondary education programs to prepare its reauthorization proposals. With the exception of the title I targeting provision and the reform of impact aid, the effects of the administration's reauthorization proposals will first be seen in the 1980 budget.[8]

ESEA TITLE I. The potentially most divisive issue in reauthorization is the title I allocation formula, which determines how funds are distributed among and within the states.[9] Currently, the dollars are allocated through successive jurisdictions to the schools on the basis of economic data, such as poverty counts and average per-pupil expenditure in the state; within schools, however, the children with the

7. The Committee for Full Funding of Education Programs estimates that 58 percent of eligible children received title I services in 1977. See *EFFORT: Education Full Funding Organization Report,* vol. 5 (November 15, 1977), pp. 4–5.

8. This chapter's emphasis on the budget explains the absence in this discussion of the administration's much-publicized efforts to improve basic skills. This shift in educational policy is embedded in several legislative proposals (particularly for ESEA titles II, III, and IV), but is largely one of changed program focus, administrative procedure, and targeting of existing funds. From the standpoint of educational philosophy and administration, these proposals are of considerable interest; however, virtually no new budget authority is involved.

9. For a concise description of the current formula, see National Institute of Education, *Title I Funds Allocation: The Current Formula* (NIE, 1977), pp. 103–11.

greatest educational need, regardless of family income, receive the services. These dual criteria (poverty and educational need) have caused much debate and confusion about the purpose of title I, for although low income and low achievement often coincide, they are by no means the same. Prompted by this apparent ambiguity, Congressman Albert H. Quie (Republican, Minnesota) has again introduced a bill that would drop the economic indicators from the formula and would base allocation solely on educational need. If enacted, the distributional consequences of this proposal cannot be determined accurately because the necessary student achievement data are not available; however, as many as twenty-three states might experience changes of over 15 percent in their share of funds.[10]

Assuming that economic indicators will continue to be used (as seems likely), a second issue is whether to update the poverty data by supplementing the 1970 census information with data from the 1976 Survey of Income and Education (SIE).[11] This survey produced evidence that a substantial geographic redistribution of poor children occurred between 1969 and 1975. If the 1970 census data were thus updated, southern states (with the exception of Florida) would lose title I funds to the industrial states in the Northeast, Middle Atlantic, and Great Lakes regions.[12]

Neither the administration nor the Congress want to precipitate a formula fight as part of the reauthorization. Consequently, alleged shortcomings of the SIE data are being given as reasons for not updating the formula. It seems unlikely, however, that representatives from states that would benefit from the use of more recent data (particularly those in the Northeast) will miss this opportunity to try to capture more federal dollars for their states. Furthermore, assuming that the new data are broadly accurate, not to use them would be irresponsible. As a practical matter, it is sensible to begin adjusting now to the changing distribution of poverty, rather than wait for the

10. "Statement of Paul T. Hill, Director, Compensatory Education Study, National Institute of Education" (testimony before the Subcommittee on Elementary, Secondary, and Vocational Education of the House Committee on Education and Labor, November 1, 1977; processed), p. 17.

11. A description of SIE can be found in U.S. Bureau of the Census, *Current Population Reports,* series P-60, no. 108, "Household Money Income in 1975, by Housing Tenure and Residence, for the United States, Regions, Divisions, and States (Spring 1976 Survey of Income and Education)" (GPO, 1977), pp. 1–3.

12. For example, an HEW simulation using SIE data for 1978 title I allocation yielded the following percentage changes: Illinois,+ 29; Michigan, +13; New Jersey, +23; Pennsylvania, +10; Florida, +31; Louisiana, −24; Mississippi, −20; Virginia, −20; and South Carolina, −18.

1980 census and a probably much larger and more difficult redistribution.

In theory, changing the formula through either of these alternatives would have no effect on the level of appropriations, but in practice—under a fixed budget—a change in formula would create losers, violating that informal rule of the American political system, "Do no direct harm."[13] For this reason, Congress seems to be moving toward a two-tiered formula that would not change the allocation of the first $2.8 billion (the size of the 1978 appropriation) but would change the distribution of funds in excess of that amount. This approach is appealing politically because no state would lose money compared to 1978, while the incremental funds would be allocated to reflect the shifting concentration of poverty.

Other title I reauthorization issues with potential budget impact are the part C targeting provision and a proposed part B for incentive grants to encourage the creation and expansion of state compensatory education programs. In the 1976 fiscal year, seventeen states spent a total of $364 million of their own funds on compensatory education, nearly 40 percent of the title I funds received by those states. To encourage growth of these programs, the administration proposes to match every two state dollars spent on compensatory education with one federal dollar.[14] Although administrative and conceptual problems remain, this proposal exemplifies the administration's policy of using matching funds to encourage states and localities to help achieve federal education goals.

IMPACT AID. In recent years, evaluations of impact aid have identified several features of the program that need reform:[15]

1. Payments are made for children who are not a federal burden.

2. Payments are made to wealthy districts minimally affected by federal activity.

13. Charles L. Schultze, *The Public Use of Private Interest* (Brookings Institution, 1977), p. 23.

14. Under this proposal, only state dollars spent on title I eligible schools and children would be counted for matching federal dollars. Federal payments would also be limited to a percentage of each state's title I, part A entitlement. Thus only $88 million is estimated to be eligible for matching federal funds in the 1979 fiscal year. Recent congressional action indicates that these limitations may be rejected.

15. See Harold A. Hovey and others, *School Assistance in Federally Affected Areas,* House Committee on Education and Labor, 91:2 (GPO, 1970); and Comptroller General of the United States, *Assessment of the Impact Aid Program* (General Accounting Office, 1976).

3. Payments are based on methods (particularly the use of comparable districts) that are imprecise and subject to abuse.

4. Payments sometimes increase rather than reduce financial inequities among school districts.

Successive administrations have tried to reform the program by eliminating from budget requests certain payments, such as that for B children (those whose parents live or work on federal property). Both the Ford and Carter administrations used this approach in their 1978 budgets. As always, Congress appropriated far more for impact aid than was proposed.

The Carter administration's reauthorization proposal is more finely tuned. Its major provisions are listed below.[16]

1. Payments for children whose parents are employed on federal property outside the county in which the school district is located would be eliminated. (These children clearly do not represent a loss to their districts, since their parents pay local property taxes.)[17]

2. The school district must absorb the full educational cost of federally connected children if they constitute less than 3 percent of the district's nonfederal enrollment. (Three percent is the national average of federally connected children in school districts. The purpose of this absorption provision is to end the many small payments that go to minimally affected districts, a change that would eliminate an estimated 2,400 districts from the program.)

3. Payments for children in public housing remain at the 1978 level of $85 million. (HEW wanted to end these payments on the ground that these children do not represent a federal burden of the type that impact aid was designed to ease. That proposal was rejected within the White House, and instead payments for students were to be kept at this level for two years and then phased out.)

4. The program would be shifted to forward funding.

These reforms would save an estimated $76.4 million in 1979 and, by 1983, depending on payments for public-housing students, more than $300 million a year. Early indications suggest that the proposals will not survive congressional review; the absorption provision is particularly vulnerable, since it is an assault on the principal pork-

16. Other provisions change the method of calculating the local contribution rate, modify the hold-harmless provisions, and eliminate the tier system of payments.

17. 1974 legislation eliminated payments for children whose parents work on federal property in another state and reduced payments for those out of the county.

barrel feature of the program. Nonetheless, the administration has offered a serious and well-reasoned reform package, and its fate will be a good test of congressional responsiveness.

EDUCATION FOR HANDICAPPED CHILDREN. Although the authority for grants to states for educating handicapped children is not expiring, it has figured prominently in the administration's review of education programs. First, it is enmeshed in significant ways with legislation that is expiring. Second, its potentially explosive growth could easily dominate the education budget in future years, and the administration has been forced to consider alternatives to the funding levels currently authorized.

Before the enactment of Public Law 94-142, set-asides and other provisions for handicapped children were incorporated in existing programs, including ESEA titles I and IV, impact aid, vocational education, and Head Start. Recent annual outlays under these set-asides and special provisions have been over $200 million. There is an opportunity now to rationalize and consolidate the old programs with the new law and to eliminate overlap. However, until appropriations under the new law grow substantially, consolidation may not be politically possible. For example, the administration considered proposing the transfer of ESEA title I state-operated programs for handicapped children into the new program but backed away when the political opposition became evident.[18]

For a program of such high potential cost ($3 billion to $4 billion by the early 1980s), remarkably little is known with certainty about the number of handicapped children by type and severity of handicap or about the costs of providing each with an appropriate public education. The U.S. Office of Education's Bureau of Education for the Handicapped has estimated that as many as 8 million children under the age of twenty-one are handicapped, 6 million of them school age. However, during school year 1976–77, only about 3.5 million children received aid through the new program, and, counter to expectations, very few more were reported in October 1977. An important part of the rationale for large federal payments is the assumption that many thousands of handicapped children are not being served,

18. Constituent groups argue, probably correctly, that education for the handicapped receives more money from the two discrete programs than it would from a consolidation, particularly since the ESEA program is fully funded "off the top" of the title I appropriation.

and that the new law will result in their being identified and provided with costly new programs. If the number of additional handicapped children turns out to be substantially less than predicted, appropriations will almost surely remain well below authorized levels, for not only will the number of eligible children be smaller than predicted, but the sizable new burden that the law was thought to place on school districts will not have materialized.

Complicating predictions further are the uncertain incentive effects of the law. The federal government pays what amounts to a bounty for each handicapped child identified and provided with the requisite educational program. Since the payment is not related to the actual cost of the education, some have feared that school districts would concentrate primarily on identifying children with very mild or questionable handicaps, whose educational needs the federal payment would cover in full. Uncertainty over funding levels in the program may offset this tendency, however, for once a student is identified as handicapped, the necessary supplemental services must be provided, regardless of the size of the federal payment.[19] Since the provision of a free, appropriate public education for all handicapped children becomes a requirement of law after September 30, 1978, the reports filed by states in October 1978 should be better indicators of the eventual size of the eligible population.

Another curious feature of the law deserves mention. Although it imposes its heaviest costs on state and local governments now, the federal share of the costs begins low and continues growing until 1982, when outlays are authorized at 40 percent of average per-pupil expenditures. Prompted by this incongruity, some administration officials during 1977 briefly considered reversing the payment schedule, providing as much as 40 percent of per-pupil expenditure in fiscal year 1979 (or even 1978), and scaling the payment down year by year. Estimation of the 1978 cost—$2.2 billion—ended serious consideration of this "front-loading" strategy. The result, however, is a payment schedule curiously out of synchronization with costs, which may lead to some questioning of the need for escalating payments after 1978.

A further problem with the legislation is that the entitlement formula does not reflect the large differences in costs associated with the various types and severity of handicap. Not being grounded in any

19. In this respect, Public Law 94-142 is also a civil rights law.

rational fashion on the actual educational costs, the formula is certain to be questioned as the size of entitlements grows. In particular, if the majority of newly identified children are minimally handicapped (as seems likely), questions are bound to be raised about why federal payments per eligible student should exceed (or even equal) ESEA title I payments.

These factors combine to make forecasts of future outlays for the education of handicapped children subject to great uncertainty. There is clearly a need to develop a better rationale for the level of federal assistance to the states, but it is difficult even to discuss that subject intelligently in the face of so much uncertainty about the basic facts. As experience with the program grows, Congress and the administration will have to reach a more rational policy for federal payments. In the meantime, appropriations will surely increase, though they will probably fall ever more behind the large sums authorized.

Future Initiatives

The Congressional Budget Office has identified three areas for possible expansion of the federal role in elementary and secondary education:[20] (1) school finance reform, (2) universal preschool, and (3) general aid to education (for example, the National Education Association's proposal to increase the federal share of school expenditures from 8 to 33 percent). Within the administration, there is discussion of a career incentives act and a community school act. Of these various possibilities, school-finance reform is most likely to be considered soon. Congressman Carl D. Perkins (Democrat, Kentucky), chairman of the House Committee on Education and Labor, introduced a bill authorizing federal incentive payments to states working to equalize school financial resources. Hearings on this bill served to stimulate interest in the topic; the 1979 budget includes $2 million to study the potential federal role in school finance reform. Possible results might be (1) modification of categorical programs so that they help, rather than hinder, state attempts at reform, and (2) a new federal program to encourage more equitable financing of elementary and secondary education both within and among states. It seems highly unlikely that

20. Congressional Budget Office, *Elementary, Secondary, and Vocational Education: An Examination of Alternative Federal Roles* (GPO, 1977), pp. 40–46. In addition, the Senate Finance Committee recently approved a bill that would provide tuition tax credits for families that send children to private elementary and secondary schools. The bill is discussed later in this chapter.

substantial new federal expenditures for this purpose will be made in the next three to five years, however, unless the Supreme Court reconsiders *San Antonio* v. *Rodriguez* (1973), in which it held (by a five to four decision) that interdistrict expenditure disparities did not violate the Constitution.

Postsecondary Education

The federal role in postsecondary education is in many ways more complex and difficult to analyze than it is at the elementary and secondary level. Over 400 separate legislative provisions govern the flow of federal dollars to postsecondary students and institutions, and virtually every federal agency provides some form of support. While HEW provides more money than any other agency, its programs do not dominate the federal connection with higher education as they do at the elementary and secondary level. The education division shares the limelight with the Social Security Administration (which dispenses over $1 billion annually in student benefits) and with the Public Health Service, which underwrites health professionals' education, biomedical research, graduate training in biological and behavioral sciences, and numerous related educational activities.

Because postsecondary programs are so widely dispersed throughout the government, it makes little sense to talk of a comprehensive higher-education policy. It is at the level of the component elements —undergraduate student aid, research, veterans' education benefits —that decisions are made. The cumulative effect of these decisions on the nation's colleges, universities, and other postsecondary institutions is largely unplanned, since the institutions and the higher education system are rarely the subject of policy analysis and debate.

Table 4-3 presents federal expenditures for postsecondary education for selected years since 1965, organized under three categories: payments to students, payments to institutions, and tax expenditures. By the 1977 fiscal year (the most recent year for which outlays are reasonably definite), expenditures under these three groupings totaled almost $14 billion, with over $7 billion spent as aid to students, over $4 billion as payments to institutions (largely for research), and $2 billion dispensed indirectly as education-related tax expenditures. In comparison with federal outlays for elementary and secondary education (table 4-1), federal expenditures for postsecon-

Table 4-3. Federal Outlays and Tax Expenditures for Postsecondary Education, by Program, Selected Fiscal Years, 1965–79
Millions of dollars

Program	1965	1969	1973	1975	1977	1978[a]	1979[a]
Payments to students	502	1,687	4,195	6,913	7,321	7,522	8,097
Basic educational opportunity grants	...	...	...	342	1,387	1,534	2,094
Campus-based aid[b]	131	373	829	844	865	1,033	1,099
Guaranteed loans	27	44	206	335	344	559	628
Health training and other HEW aid	206	219	283	440	303	303	309
Social security student benefits	...	366	638	840	1,181	1,338	1,505
Veterans' education benefits	43	590	2,016	3,479	2,802	2,316	2,009
Reserve Officer Training Corps and other military training[c]	42	27	113	532	330	333	349
Other	53	68	110	101	109	106	104
Payments to institutions	1,467	2,750	3,493	3,613	4,421	4,719	5,106
Research and development conducted at colleges and universities	934	1,426	1,888	2,228	2,702	3,061	3,339
Programs for disadvantaged students and aid to developing institutions	...	...	85	230	130	184	226
Vocational education[d]	57	121	160	137	166	176	193
Special institutions	20	38	79	89	99	112	126
Grants and loans for facilities (except health)[e]	225	597	159	73	13	56	54

Health facilities and resources and other HEW aid	58	405	554	682	874	672	683
Service academies and other defense education[f]	117	59	289	71	326	338	366
Other[g]	57	104	279	103	111	120	119
Total outlays	**1,969**	**4,437**	**7,688**	**10,526**	**11,742**	**12,241**	**13,203**
Tax expenditures	n.a.	n.a.	n.a.	**1,770**	**2,015**	**2,105**	**2,220**
Exclusion of scholarships and fellowships	n.a.	n.a.	n.a.	200	245	295	330
Parental personal exemptions for students aged 19 and over	n.a.	n.a.	n.a.	670	750	770	790
Deductible personal contributions	n.a.	n.a.	n.a.	440	525	585	645
Deductible corporate contributions	n.a.	n.a.	n.a.	205	235	255	285
Exclusion of veterans' benefits	n.a.	n.a.	n.a.	255	260	200	170

Sources: *Special Analyses, Budget of the United States Government, Fiscal Year 1979*, and preceding issues; 1979 figures updated by HEW.

n.a. Not available.

a. Estimated by Office of Management and Budget as reported in *Special Analyses . . . 1979*.

b. Components vary over the years but include educational opportunity grants, national defense student loans (supplemental educational opportunity grants and national direct student loans, respectively, after 1972), work-study program, and incentive grants for state scholarships (after 1974).

c. Administered by the Department of Defense.

d. 1965 and 1969 outlays estimated from data provided by the staff of the Office of Education.

e. 1979 amount includes $10 million for renovation grants to institutions for removing architectural barriers to handicapped students.

f. 1969 amount is not comparable to 1965 because the reporting format of the *Special Analyses* changed between those years; in 1975 a larger share of Defense Department education outlays were counted as student assistance. However, total outlays are comparable.

g. In 1973, other Office of Education and HEW programs were lumped into a general category; hence the large size of this figure relative to other years.

dary programs are large; this is, in part, attributable to the higher per-capita costs of postsecondary education and to the broader purposes served (for example, research support). While the federal share of total public outlays for elementary and secondary education hovers around 8 percent, the comparable figure for postsecondary education is over 45 percent.[21] Because federal support for higher education is provided by many agencies and is a relatively more important part of higher education than of elementary and secondary education budgets, the higher-education community has generally been ambivalent, if not opposed, to versions of the proposed department of education that would be limited essentially to HEW's education division.

Federal Goals

Before World War II, federal involvement in higher education was virtually nonexistent. After that war, the Servicemen's Readjustment Act of 1944—the GI bill of rights—made a college education possible for many thousands of veterans, and the creation of the National Science Foundation in 1950 stimulated federal support for university-based research. In the years immediately following the Soviet Union's 1957 launching of Sputnik, Washington concentrated its efforts in higher education on graduate education and research, particularly in the sciences and engineering; the National Defense Education Act of 1958 was one manifestation of this interest. These defense- and space-related education activities declined in priority as the 1960s waned and were replaced by civil rights, antipoverty, and equal educational opportunity issues. These concerns led to an emphasis on undergraduate student aid, awarded on the basis of financial need rather than academic merit and designed to ensure access to some form of postsecondary education for all who sought it.[22] These early student aid programs (educational opportunity grants, college work-

21. Calculated from data reported by the National Center for Education Statistics; Joseph D. Boyd, *National Association of State Scholarship and Grant Programs, 1976–77 Academic Year* (Deerfield, Ill.: NASSGP, n.d.); and *Special Analyses, Budget of the United States Government, Fiscal Year 1978.* The $2 billion in tax expenditures (see table 4-3) were not included. Some of the money does not accrue to the institutions; for example, a significant portion of GI bill and social security benefits are used for living expenses.

22. The Higher Education Act of 1965 created undergraduate educational opportunity grants; this act as amended provides the framework for most postsecondary education programs administered by HEW's education division.

study) provided grants to campuses for distribution to eligible students; these programs, together with direct student loans, still exist as campus-based aid programs. After tumultuous debate, Congress passed amendments in 1972 providing for direct aid to low-income undergraduates—basic educational opportunity grants. With appropriations of more than $2 billion for the 1978 fiscal year, basic grants have become the foundation of government student aid.[23]

In 1965, Congress amended the social security legislation to continue payments past the age of eighteen, up to the twenty-second birthday, for recipients' children who were full-time students and unmarried. This amendment was understandable for the time; other student aid programs were few and the problems of financing social security were less pressing. A decade later, the Ford administration questioned the need for these payments in light of expanded student aid programs and proposed (unsuccessfully) to phase them out. As other student aid programs grow, the rationale for social security education benefits will become less compelling. Nonetheless, the program's future seems politically secure.

The GI bill, managed by the Veterans Administration, is one of the largest student aid programs, with outlays of almost $3 billion in the 1977 fiscal year. When it was reinstated in 1966, it served as a type of deferred compensation and recruiting lure, but the advent of the more highly paid volunteer army largely undermined that rationale. For that and other reasons, the Ninety-fourth Congress changed the program for those enlisting after December 31, 1976, into one that requires each veteran to set aside money from salary for educational purposes, to be matched by federal dollars on a two-to-one basis. It is too early to know what effect this new legislation will have; in the meantime, the older program remains in effect until 1989, since those who enlisted before the change retain their eligibility for ten years after discharge. The number of eligible veterans has already begun to decline, however, and payments under the old GI bill will drop substantially over the next decade.

Two loan programs—national direct student loans and guaranteed student loans—round out the major federal student aid programs.

23. The former educational opportunity grants were renamed supplemental educational opportunity grants. The amendments also created the much smaller state student incentive grant program, which provides federal matching funds for states that establish or expand direct student aid programs.

The first dates from the National Defense Education Act of 1958 and the second from the Higher Education Act of 1965. Direct student loans are administered by the campuses, with 90 percent of the loan capital provided each year by the federal government. Loans are allocated on the basis of student financial need, with interest fully subsidized while the student is enrolled and heavily subsidized during repayment (the student pays 3 percent interest). The guaranteed loan program was legislated as an alternative to a tuition tax credit under serious consideration in the Senate in 1964. The Treasury Department, worried then as now by the enormous drain on revenues a tax credit would mean, took the lead in formulating a loan program to help middle-income families finance college costs. Financial need is not a criterion for eligibility, although interest subsidy is linked to income; students from families with less than $31,000 in adjusted gross income receive full interest subsidy while enrolled and pay 7 percent interest during repayment. Unlike direct loans, there is no federal capital contribution, for banks and other commercial lenders make the loans; federal outlays are necessary for interest subsidies and to reimburse lenders for loan defaults. In the 1977 fiscal year, $310.5 million in capital was provided for direct loans, and $367 million was appropriated for interest subsidies and loan defaults for guaranteed loans.

As is true of its role in elementary and secondary education, the federal government does not provide general-purpose institutional support for colleges and universities, for the financial health of institutions has never been accepted as an explicit federal obligation. Outlays listed in table 4-3 under "payments to institutions" are mainly for research. The federal government relies heavily on universities for basic research; in recent years, roughly half of federal basic research outlays have been spent on university research. Since most research grants and contracts are awarded competitively, guided by peer review, federal research money is concentrated in the leading institutions; the top one hundred recipients consistently garner about 85 percent of the funds.

The remaining federal payments to institutions are for specialized purposes, such as payments to medical schools for support of health manpower training and related activities, Defense Department support for military academies and reserve officer training, and Office of Education support for developing institutions. The latter program, financed at $120 million in 1978, provides direct support for small, struggling colleges, with over half of the money allocated to predominantly black private colleges, located mostly in the South.

Finally, through a variety of provisions in the tax code, the Treasury forgoes an estimated $2 billion in revenue to support activities that directly and indirectly benefit colleges and universities or their students and faculty. Various forms of income (scholarships, fellowships, GI benefits) are not taxed; parents are allowed to claim the dependent's exemption for college students, even if the student's earnings exceed the amount that would normally disqualify him or her for the exemption; and personal and corporate gifts to colleges and universities are treated as charitable deductions. The Congress is currently considering a tuition tax credit, whose lost revenues could easily surpass existing education-related credits and deductions.[24]

The 1979 Budget

Table 4-4 displays recent appropriations and presidential budgets. In a sense, there are two 1979 budgets, since the President requested additional budget authority of $1.2 billion for student aid in February, less than three weeks after the budget was released. To avoid confusion, I refer to the original as the January budget and to the enlarged version as the February budget. Since the additional $1.2 billion request was prompted by the administration's desire to head off congressional enactment of a tuition tax credit, discussion of the credit and the administration's counterproposal is deferred to the next section.

As was true of elementary and secondary education, Ford's 1978 budget request was well below 1977 appropriations, Carter raised budgets of selected programs, and Congress appropriated still more. The 1979 February budget calls for $14.4 billion for expenditure programs, up from Carter's 1978 request of $12.4 billion and congressional 1978 appropriations of $12.9 billion. The February budget is best understood when the prior year's transition budget and the momentum for middle-income aid (which prompted the additional $1.2 billion request) are recalled.

24. For a thorough discussion of tax provisions aiding education, see Emil M. Sunley, Jr., "Federal and State Tax Policies," in David W. Breneman and Chester E. Finn, Jr., eds., *Public Policy and Private Higher Education* (Brookings Institution, 1978).

Table 4-4. Federal Budget Authority for Postsecondary Education, by Program, Fiscal Years 1977–79
Millions of dollars

Program	1977 appropriations	1978			1979	
		Ford budget	Carter budget	Appropriations	January budget	February budget
Payments to students	**7,857**	**6,616**	**7,743**	**8,078**	**8,159**	**9,369**
Office of Education	3,294	2,434	3,044	3,788	4,043	5,253
Basic opportunity grants	1,904[a]	1,844	2,070	2,160	2,177	3,167
Supplemental opportunity grants	250	0	240	270	270	270
Work-study	390	250	390	435	450	600
Direct student loans[b]	323	15	15	326	304	304
State student incentive grants	60	44	44	64	77	77
Student loan insurance fund and guaranteed loans[c]	367	281	281	530[d]	751	821
Graduate and professional opportunity grants	...	...	4	3	8	8
Health professions graduate student loan insurance					6	6
Health training[e]	249	214	231	300	251	251
Social security student benefits[f]	1,181	1,078	1,238	1,338	1,505	1,505
Veterans' benefits[f]	2,802	2,573	2,913	2,316	2,009	2,009
Reserve Officer Training Corps and other military training[g]	331	317	317	336	351	351
Payments to institutions	**4,401**	**4,420**	**4,634**	**4,832**	**5,043**	**5,043**
Office of Education	464	378	463	538	539	539
Programs for disadvantaged students	85	73	70	115	115	115
Aid to developing institutions	110	110	120	120	120	120

Language training and area studies	18	10	16	18	18	18
Construction[b]	3	7	7	12	82	82
Renovation grants	..	..	..	..	50	50
Interest subsidy and other loans	3	7	7	12	32	32
Strengthening research libraries	..	..	..	5	5	5
Other library resources[i]	20	10	19	20	0	0
Vocational education[i]	161	158	158	171	170	170
Other	67	10	73	77	29	29
Special institutions[j]	94	109	109	111	122	122
Health facilities and resources[e]	539	251	380	507	401	401
Improvement of postsecondary education	12	14	14	12	14	14
Lifelong learning	..	..	..	..	5	5
Other HEW	22	27	27	24	27	27
Service academies and other defense education[g]	328	346	346	341	369	369
Research and development conducted at colleges and universities	2,942	3,295	3,295	3,299	3,566	3,566
Total	12,258	11,036	12,377	12,910	13,202	14,412

Sources: *Higher Education Daily, Supplement*, vol. 6 (January 24, 1978), and vol. 5 (January 21, 1977); *The Budget of the United States Government, Fiscal Year 1979—Appendix*, and preceding issue; *Special Analyses, Budget of the United States Government, Fiscal Year 1979*, and preceding issue; Office of Management and Budget, *Fiscal Year 1978 Budget Revisions, February 1977* (GPO, 1977); unpublished data from Social Security Administration, Veterans Administration, American Association for the Advancement of Science, and HEW, Division of Education Budget Analysis; and author's estimates as noted. Figures are rounded.

a. Includes a supplemental grant of $211 million used in 1976 but carried over into the 1977 accounts.
b. Primarily capital contributions; for example, the 1979 figure of $304 million includes $286 million in capital contributions. The $15 million in 1978 was for prior year's loans that were forgiven because of special service.
c. In 1978 the guaranteed student loan program was absorbed into and replaced by the student loan insurance fund.
d. Includes a proposed supplemental grant of $239 million as a result of cost increases.
e. Author's estimates, based on data from the Office of Management and Budget.
f. Outlays rather than budget authority most accurately reflect administration and congressional intent for these entitlement programs.
g. Administered by the Department of Defense. Author's estimates based on data from OMB.
h. Authorized by Higher Education Act, title VII.
i. Author's estimates. Assumes that the higher-education share of federal occupational and vocational education budget is about 23 percent.
j. Author's estimates.

Ford's 1978 budget called for $1.844 billion for basic opportunity grants, an amount that would have limited the maximum award to $1,400, even though Congress had authorized grants up to $1,800 in the 1976 amendments. In addition, Ford requested no money for either supplemental opportunity grants or direct student loans, arguing that basic grants, college work-study, and guaranteed student loans provided sufficient coverage. Carter raised the basic grant request to $2.07 billion (an amount estimated to allow full funding with a $1,600 maximum grant), requested $240 million for supplemental opportunity grants, and raised college work-study from $250 million to $390 million, but left direct loans unchanged on the ground that they were redundant. This heavy-handed approach to student-loan reform was no more effective than the comparable attempt with impact aid, for Congress promptly appropriated $311 million for direct loans.

The January 1979 budget raised the maximum basic grant to $1,800 but kept the total request virtually unchanged at $2.18 billion. That was possible because, even though the higher maximum grant would have raised the average award from roughly $900 to $990, it was estimated that the number of recipients would drop by nearly 200,000, from 2.4 million to 2.2 million students. Increases in nominal family incomes were projected to rise faster than the cost of living, thereby reducing the number of eligible students. The program's inflation adjustment is not sufficient to offset the annual growth in family incomes.

Although touted as expanding aid to middle-income families, the two changes proposed for basic grants in the January budget (raising the ceiling to $1,800 and increasing the asset exclusion in the family contribution formula from $17,000 to $25,000) would do little in that regard. Of the $2.18 billion requested, it was estimated that less than $140 million (approximately 6 percent) would go to recipients from families with incomes over $16,000, a minimal change from the preceding year. To use the basic grant program to help large numbers of middle-income families, the government would need to reduce the expected family contribution by changing either the income assessment rates or the family-size offset schedule, and neither change was proposed in the January budget.[25]

25. See footnote 35 for an explanation of these terms.

The three campus-based student aid programs and the state student-incentive grant program were budgeted in January at essentially 1978 appropriation levels, meaning a cut in real terms roughly equal to the inflation rate. Having learned from last year's experience that to try to restrict funding of direct student loans is futile, the President requested a $286 million capital contribution (the first time in seven years that a President has requested money for that program). The one new student aid program of 1977, graduate and professional opportunity fellowships for minorities and women, increased from $3 million to $8 million, an amount more than offset, however, by the proposed termination of fellowships for public service and mining.

Interest subsidies and loan defaults under the guaranteed loan program are paid from the recently established student loan insurance fund. Although only $281 million was initially requested for the 1978 fiscal year—because more than $230 million of unobligated funds were carried over from the previous year—$239 million more was eventually appropriated to meet the estimated $737 million required. Rising interest rates had raised the special allowance paid to lenders by roughly 1.5 percentage points, and 1976 legislative changes increased the federal government's share of the costs incurred by state guarantee agencies. The January budget anticipates expenditures at the 1978 level, including $530 million in interest subsidies and nearly $220 million in net default payments. That outlays on guaranteed loans are now second in size only to basic grants among Office of Education student aid programs is particularly ironic, since the program's original appeal was that federal outlays would be minimal.

The budget includes $1.5 billion in outlays for social security education benefits, an increase of nearly $170 million over the 1978 expenditure level. As mentioned earlier, the Ford administration had sought to phase out these benefits over four years, a decision that the Carter administration reversed but, instead, proposed to limit to amounts no larger than the maximum basic grant. Congress rejected this proposal for 1978, but the administration has advanced it again, expecting it to reduce outlays by $131 million.

Although the GI bill is an entitlement for those enrolled in eligible programs, the Ford administration found a way to cut its 1978 budget by proposing that eligibility be reduced from ten to eight years after discharge, a change that would have saved over $300 million in 1978 alone. The Carter administration rejected that proposal and projected outlays of $3.8 billion for 1978 education benefits, of which an estimated $2.9 billion were for postsecondary education. Actual 1978 expenditures are nearly $600 million lower, for reasons that are not clear. One possible explanation is that the Veterans Administration's closer monitoring of the satisfactory progress rule and similar administrative changes reduced the incentive for institutions to recruit veterans. The projected decline in 1979 payments to $2.0 billion reflects the steady drop in eligible Vietnam-era veterans, as well as the proposal to eliminate payments for general flight training and correspondence schools, which is estimated to save $100 million.

Most of the relatively small programs of institutional assistance in the Office of Education are budgeted at the 1978 appropriation level. The major breakthrough from the higher education community's standpoint is a $50 million request to help colleges and universities offset the cost of removing architectural barriers in complying with regulations governing nondiscrimination against handicapped persons. The President's budget refers to this initiative as a loan program under the higher education facilities loan and insurance fund, while HEW's budget-briefing materials claim it as a grant program under title VII of the Higher Education Act as amended. This confusion apparently reflects last-minute debates between HEW and the Office of Management and Budget (OMB), with HEW favoring the grant, OMB the loan approach. Arguments favoring grants stress the absence of an investment objective in complying with the regulations, while loan proponents argue that grants might encourage unduly zealous (and expensive) forms of compliance, which loans would discourage. The indecision apparent within the executive branch and the last-minute nature of the request suggest a need for Congress to examine this item closely. The potential costs of this program are enormous, not to mention those associated with making college buildings both energy-efficient and in compliance with federal health and safety laws.[26]

The administration's budget for basic research (the part of the R&D budget of greatest concern to universities) continues the real

26. HEW also plans a 1978 supplemental appropriation of $30 million for loans under the higher education facilities and loan insurance fund for assistance in complying with federally mandated programs.

growth that began again in the 1976 fiscal year, following nearly a decade of decline. Between 1967 and 1975, budget authority for basic research dropped by more than 20 percent in constant dollars,[27] and the real growth that began again under President Ford and continues under President Carter will only manage to regain 1967 levels (in constant dollars) by the 1979 fiscal year.[28] Specifically, the 1979 budget requests $3.6 billion for basic research, an increase of nearly 11 percent over 1978. Basic research is given favored treatment over applied research and development, for the total R&D budget of $27.9 billion is up by just 6.1 percent, barely keeping pace with inflation. The budget provides roughly an 8 percent increase in research and development at colleges and universities, rising from $3.30 million to $3.57 billion.

Tuition Tax Credits and the Middle-Income "Squeeze"

One issue dominated higher-education discussion last year—the financial squeeze facing middle-income families with children in college. Political pressure for some type of aid for middle-income families reached a near-fever pitch during late 1977 and early 1978, expressing itself initially in a congressional push for education tax allowances. Over one hundred bills for tax credits, deductions, or deferrals were introduced in the Ninety-fifth Congress,[29] and one (S. 311), sponsored by Senator William V. Roth, Jr. (Republican, Delaware), was tacked onto the Senate's social security bill and was removed by the conference committee only after steadfast resistance by several House conferees. Treasury and HEW officials testified against the tax expenditure approach to aiding middle-income families, and an HEW task force began work in late 1977 to develop

27. Willis H. Shapley, Don I. Phillips, and Herbert Roback, *Research and Development in the Federal Budget, FY 1978* (American Association for the Advancement of Science, 1977), pp. 30–36. These annual reports sponsored by AAAS provide thorough analyses of each year's R&D budget, including its impact on colleges and universities.

28. President Ford's final budget message stressed basic research and development as one of two areas where he had requested real growth in expenditures, but even those increased requests left the 1978 level more than $100 million below 1967 in 1972 dollars. Ibid., p. 33.

29. *Report on Hearings before the Task Force on Tax Expenditures, Government Organization, and Regulation on College Tuition Tax Credits,* prepared for the House Committee on the Budget (GPO, 1977), pp. 35–37.

an alternative. The administration argued that extending and modifying current student aid programs would be more efficient and more equitable than a tax credit in directing aid to families with the greatest relative need. Although the January budget did not contain specific aid for middle-income families, HEW officials claimed that $700 million in the allowance for contingencies was for additional student aid.

By early February, members of Congress opposed to tax credits began to doubt that the administration would produce its counterproposal in time. Senator Claiborne Pell (Democrat, Rhode Island), chairman of the education subcommittee of the Human Resources Committee, introduced a bill—the college opportunity act—to extend basic grants (at a cost of $1.2 billion) to an estimated 1.5 million students whose families earn up to $25,000. Congressman William D. Ford (Democrat, Michigan), chairman of the postsecondary education subcommittee of the Education and Labor Committee, consulted with representatives of the higher education associations and developed a bill for middle-income student assistance that he was prepared to introduce with or without administration support.[30] Suddenly, all assumptions about student aid expenditures (and purposes) were shattered, as members of the authorizing committees sought to derail tuition tax credits with vast (and hastily developed) increases in direct-aid programs.[31] The administration's sluggishness had nearly removed it from participation, and the opportunity to review student aid legislation with care before the 1980 reauthorization was being jeopardized by the middle-income backlash.

As the February budget shows, the administration managed to assert its role by requesting $1.2 billion for student aid programs, most of it for basic grants. Tax credit proposals still have many supporters in Congress, however, and the outcome will not be known until later this year when budget realities have been considered and

30. Budget amounts considered by Congressman Ford ranged between $1.2 billion and $2.0 billion. It was assumed that direct outlays would have to be roughly the same as the revenue loss under tax credits for the bill to be seriously considered. The administration's promised $700 million was dismissed as too small to be a serious alternative.

31. Apart from the merits of direct expenditures over tax credits, competition between committees was also involved, since tax legislation is the province of the Senate Finance Committee and the House Ways and Means Committee, while most student aid programs are governed by the Senate Human Resources Committee and the House Education and Labor Committee.

final tallies taken. Tax credits may be defeated, but the cost of that defeat will be far more expensive than the administration had originally hoped. Furthermore, until the outcome is known, it will be virtually impossible for HEW to develop legislative proposals for postsecondary reauthorizations since the shape—and purpose—of existing student aid programs will be in flux.

What are the issues and arguments that underly this emotion-laden debate? As is true of costs for virtually all goods and services in the last decade, college costs have risen sharply; for some campuses, tuition, room, and board for a year's schooling exceed $7,000, and families with more than one child in college face a particular burden. Often overlooked is the fact that median family incomes have also risen sharply during these years, generally outpacing the growth of college costs.[32] But even if the absolute burden of financing a college education has not changed dramatically, the *relative* burden has shifted against families whose incomes are too high to qualify for need-based student aid. For such families, college is no easier to finance now than it was ten years ago, while the large increases in need-based student aid have helped many low-income families finance an education that would have been totally out of reach before.

Much of the political pressure arises from this relative deterioration in the position of middle-income families, and Congress and the administration have clearly responded to this newfound student-aid constituency. The debate centers on the form such aid should take. Tax credits can be designed in endless variations, and it is impossible to analyze all of their features here; however, most versions provide a flat amount (say $250) to be subtracted from tax liability if net tuition charges of at least that amount have been incurred.[33] Table 4-5 presents an estimate of the cost and distribution of a $250 credit, similar to that proposed by Senator Roth. If the credit were nonrefundable, families with adjusted gross incomes below $10,000 would receive only 8.6 percent of the benefits, while those with adjusted gross incomes above $25,000 (representing roughly 14 percent of all families) would receive nearly 45 percent of the total. Less

32. See Breneman and Finn, eds., *Public Policy and Private Higher Education:* chapter 1 for data on family income and college costs; chapter 3 for a detailed analysis of the middle-income squeeze.

33. Low-income families that do not have $250 in tax liability would not receive the benefit of the credit unless it was refundable; that is, paid as a negative income tax.

Table 4-5. Distribution of Annual Costs of $250 Tuition Tax Credit for Undergraduate Students, Nonrefundable and Refundable Versions, by Adjusted Gross Income of Family[a]

Income class (dollars)	Distribution of population (percent)	Nonrefundable tax credit			Refundable tax credit		
		Cost (millions of dollars)	Distribution (percent)	Cumulative distribution (percent)	Cost (millions of dollars)	Distribution (percent)	Cumulative distribution (percent)
0–4,999	27.1	34.9	2.5	2.5	432.6	22.8	22.8
5,000–9,999	16.6	85.9	6.1	8.6	151.8	8.0	30.9
10,000–14,999	17.8	166.1	11.8	20.4	185.1	9.8	40.6
15,000–19,999	15.2	257.9	18.3	38.7	262.0	13.8	54.5
20,000–24,999	9.5	230.3	16.4	55.1	230.4	12.2	66.6
25,000–34,999	8.7	342.6	24.4	79.5	342.7	18.1	84.8
35,000–49,999	3.2	182.5	13.0	92.5	182.6	9.6	94.4
50,000 and above	1.8	106.2	7.5	100.0	106.2	5.6	100.0
Total	100.0	1,406.4	100.0	...	1,893.4	100.0	...

Sources: Brookings 1970 MERGE file projected to 1977; and estimates from the Congressional Budget Office of the family income distribution of the undergraduate population, based on the Survey of Income and Education.

a. No attempt was made to net out student aid in determining eligibility for the credit. Estimates allow full credits for all full-time students and one-third credits to all part-time students.

than half (46.5 percent) of total benefits would go to families in the middle-income range of $10,000–$25,000. Cost to the Treasury is estimated at $1.4 billion; it would rise sharply if the size of the credit were increased.

A refundable credit would be less regressive, reducing the proportion of the total benefit going to families with incomes over $25,000 from 45 to 33 percent. The price tag for this improvement in equity would be roughly $500 million, raising the total cost to nearly $1.9 billion.

Although a tax credit has little to commend it on equity grounds, would it offset that flaw by encouraging increased investment in education or by altering the choice between low-priced public and high-priced private institutions? Unfortunately, research supports neither of these possibilities. Although the college enrollment decision is responsive to price changes, most estimates indicate that the tuition elasticity is substantially less than 1.0, meaning that a given percentage fall in price does not produce a comparable percentage increase in demand. In particular, the price responsiveness of higher-income families (the group that receives the bulk of benefits under most tax credit schemes) has been estimated to be highly inelastic. Consequently, a $250 nonrefundable tax credit would induce very little increased college enrollment and instead would simply be pure tax relief to most families.[34]

Nor would such a credit help struggling private colleges by reducing their costs relative to state-supported institutions, since it applies to the *first* $250 in tuition paid. With the exception of the California community colleges, virtually every public institution in the land charges at least $250 in tuition, and thus most families would receive the full value of the credit regardless of the college attended; the tuition gap between public and private colleges would not be reduced. If that were the public purpose, one could devise an effective tax credit by excluding the first $500 or $1,000 of tuition, so that only those attending high-priced institutions would benefit. That type of credit would influence choice, since the benefit would depend on the price of the college attended, but the very features that make it

34. Of course, there would be no tax relief if the credit led to offsetting tuition increases. See Michael S. McPherson, "The Demand for Higher Education," in Breneman and Finn, eds., *Public Policy and Private Higher Education*, for a thorough review of the demand literature, and Emil M. Sunley, Jr., "Federal and State Tax Policies," ibid., for further analysis of tax credits.

Figure 4-1. Basic Grants^a for College Students by Annual Family Income, under 1978 Program and Carter and Senate proposals^b

Figure 4-1. Basic Grants[a] for College Students by Annual Family Income, under 1978 Program and Carter and Senate proposals[b]

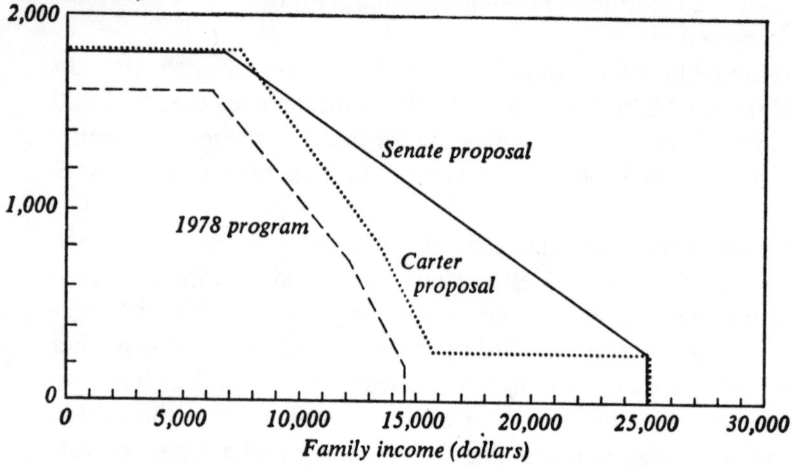

a. Assumes a family of four with one parent working, no unusual expenses, no contribution from assets, no unreimbursed tuition offset, filing a joint income-tax return, and with one child in college at a cost of at least $3,600.

b. See text for details of Carter and Senate proposals.

effective reduce its attractiveness politically, and proposals of this ilk are not likely to be enacted.

The main features of the administration's counterproposal and the Senate's college opportunity bill are illustrated in figure 4-1. Of the $1.2 billion added in the administration's budget, $1.0 billion is for basic grants. The January budget raised the maximum award from $1,600 to $1,800 and liberalized the treatment of assets. The February budget added $750 to the family-size offset (the amount of income from which no contribution to college costs is assessed) which, in combination with the larger maximum grant, increased awards for those with incomes between $8,000 and $16,000 by as much as $200; it also added a flat $250 grant for students from families with incomes from $16,000 to $25,000 and liberalized the program's treatment of independent students.[35]

35. Eligibility for basic grants is calculated as follows: applicants fill out a financial statement listing family income and assets. Adjustments for federal tax payments and living costs (the family-size offset) produce a figure called discretionary net income. Income assessment rates of 20 percent on the first $5,000 of discretionary net income and 30 percent on amounts above $5,000 are applied to determine the family contribution to education costs. This amount is subtracted from the maximum grant to determine the actual award. A similar procedure is applied to assets. Thus, basic grants can be given to higher-income families by raising the family-size offset, by lowering income assessment rates, or by liberalizing asset treatment.

If the administration's February budget for basic grants were enacted, more than $300 million of the additional money would go to those with incomes below $16,000, and nearly $700 million would go to families in the $16,000–$25,000 range, largely through the $250 flat grants. Approximately 250,000 additional students would be added to the program through changes in the family-size offset and the liberalized treatment of independent students,[36] while as many as 2.8 million additional students would be covered by the $250 grants. The bulk of the benefits, therefore, would go to the higher-income families added to the program. (The February proposal also extends the interest subsidy on guaranteed student loans to families with adjusted gross incomes up to roughly $47,000.)

How does the administration's February proposal compare with a nonrefundable $250 tax credit? First, it is less regressive, in that grant benefits stop at incomes of $25,000. On the other hand, it does little for dependent students from the lowest income families (under $8,000). Their principal gain in 1979 is the $200 increase in the maximum grant, an increase authorized by Congress in 1976 and proposed in Carter's January budget. Thus, for the lowest income levels, the February proposal confers little benefit, except for liberalizing treatment of independent students and increasing work-study funds (see table 4-4). The flat $250 payment for students from families making $16,000–$25,000 a year violates the income-related principle on which the program was founded, for surely if a family earning $25,000 needs a $250 grant, a family earning $16,000 needs even more. In short, the administration's proposal is essentially equivalent to a nonrefundable $250 tax credit with a cap on eligibility at $25,000 income. Seen in this light, the proposal is not "the greatest higher education initiative since the G.I. bill enacted 30 years ago."[37] If it were politically possible to cap a $250 tax credit at the $25,000 income level and prevent the credit from being steadily increased, one might even prefer the credit on grounds of administrative efficiency.

The Senate's college opportunity proposal (see figure 4-1) remedies one of the obvious deficiencies in the administration's proposal by maintaining the link between grant size and family income. This

36. The change in the family offset schedule increases the amount of the grants to students already in the program but receiving less than the maximum grant. It also adds new students in higher income brackets.

37. Attributed to HEW Secretary Joseph A. Califano, Jr., *Higher Education Daily*, vol. 6 (February 10, 1978), p. 1.

is achieved by lowering the assessment rate levied against discretionary net income to 10.5 percent, thereby producing a steadily declining grant up to the $25,000 income level. Thus, a family with $15,000 income would receive a grant of roughly $1,075, while a family with $23,000 income would receive approximately $435 in grant assistance. Assuming that the middle-income squeeze is a real problem, the Senate's bill has the merit of concentrating aid at the lower end of the middle-income range, at a cost of roughly $200 million more in basic grant expenditures than under the administration's proposal. The companion bill in the House was modified in late February to be similar to the Senate's proposal, meaning that the administration's version has been effectively rejected.

Although the details of the various direct assistance programs are important, there are much greater stakes involved in heading off a tax credit for college tuition, for a successful counterproposal should ensure the defeat of the Packwood-Moynihan tuition tax credit bill. Sponsored by Senators Robert Packwood (Republican, Oregon) and Daniel P. Moynihan (Democrat, New York) and introduced with forty-one cosponsors, this bill would provide a refundable tax credit (up to $500) equal to 50 percent of tuition paid for any individual paying tuition for higher education (including graduate study), vocational education, or accredited and tax-exempt elementary and secondary education. When fully implemented it would cost an estimated $4 billion to $4.7 billion. Senator Moynihan's goal is to prevent a state monopoly in education, particularly elementary and secondary education, by providing aid to parents sending children to private (including parochial) elementary and secondary schools. The sponsors believe that the courts will not rule this form of aid to church-related schools unconstitutional, since such schools are only a small part of all eligible institutions.

The stakes riding on this legislation are much more than the billions of dollars in cost—far more significant is the challenge to the system of public elementary and secondary schools. Unlike the $250 college tuition tax credit, which would have little effect on the choice of college, the Packwood-Moynihan credit could be expected to influence choice between public and private school. Not only is the credit larger, but it would cover a significant fraction of the cost of private elementary or secondary schooling. Its enactment might well prompt the more concerned and more affluent parents to abandon the public schools, helping to further the separation of public and private schools along economic class lines. (Since the credit covers only 50 percent of tuition, private schools would still be out of the reach of most poor parents.) Having left the public schools, many parents would be less likely to support bond issues and property tax increases earmarked for them, thereby hastening their decline.

Some supporters of the Packwood-Moynihan bill have likened tax credits to educational vouchers, arguing that increased competition from private schools will help to improve public schools. The counterargument is that tax credits would simply subsidize the withdrawal of the most vocal and concerned parents, thereby removing the strongest source of pressure for improvement in the public schools.[38] Regardless of one's view on the relative merits of competition versus working from within to maintain the vitality of institutions, the Packwood-Moynihan tax credit is not as equitable as a pure voucher system, since the benefits of the credit would be limited to those families able to pay 50 percent of tuition costs. By contrast, a voucher system would provide each student with an amount of money to spend on education equal, for example, to existing public expenditures per pupil.[39] One of the principal failings of the Packwood-Moynihan tax credit as social policy is that it would preserve an effective state monopoly in education for one group of citizens (the poor) while helping to undermine the one benefit that a state monopoly would have— the participation and involvement of all citizens, rich and poor alike. Those who believe in the value of educational diversity and competition at the elementary-secondary level should, on grounds of equity, advocate educational vouchers rather than tuition tax credits.[40]

A Department of Education?

During the election campaign, Jimmy Carter endorsed a department of education at the cabinet level, which the politically active National Education Association wants. During 1977, a reorganiza-

38. For an analysis, see Albert O. Hirschman, *Exit, Voice, and Loyalty: Responses to Decline in Firms, Organizations, and States* (Harvard University Press, 1970).

39. Some versions of the voucher proposal would provide larger payments to students from low-income families.

40. In February 1978, the Senate Finance Committee passed a phased-in version of the Packwood-Moynihan proposal.

tion task force within the Office of Management and Budget studied the issue and presented three options to the President. The most far-reaching called for a department of education and human development, embracing not only most of the programs discussed in this chapter but others such as the Labor Department's youth-oriented training programs. The second option described a more modest department, limited largely to the current education division of HEW plus activities such as the National Science Foundation's science education programs and Housing and Urban Development's college housing program. The final option, advocated by HEW Secretary Joseph Califano, would have upgraded HEW's education division, making its head an undersecretary and increasing the number of assistant secretary positions. Although the President did not endorse any option then, he reaffirmed his commitment in the State of the Union address on January 19, 1978, and instructed the task force to work on the details with congressional staff members (Senator Abraham A. Ribicoff, Democrat, Connecticut, had independently introduced a bill to create a department of education).

The dilemma is that only a comprehensive department will draw together the many education functions scattered throughout the government, but such a department may be politically impossible to create.[41] A broad department might include, in addition to the education division, such HEW programs as Head Start, vocational rehabilitation, and the Administration for Native Americans (all from the Office of Human Development Services), and health professionals' education (from the Health Resources Administration); the Veterans Administration's GI bill;[42] the Interior Department's Indian education program (from the Bureau of Indian Affairs); Labor Department's Job Corps and other youth training programs; the Defense Department's overseas dependents education program; the National Science Foundation's science education programs; and the entire National Foundation for the Arts and Humanities. However, the active constituencies of most of these programs will resist their transfer into an education department. The changes would also play havoc with the cognizant congressional committees, generating resistance

41. In addition, there are administrative obstacles. For a thorough discussion, see Rufus E. Miles, Jr., *A Cabinet Department of Education* (American Council on Education, 1976).

42. This shift was never seriously considered by the reorganization task force.

from that source as well. In the absence of a compelling reason (and few argue that an urgency exists comparable, for example, to the need for a department of energy), there is little political advantage for the President in pursuing this option—but many political pitfalls.

The second option is a modest department formed largely from Office of Education programs. But the relevant question is, Why bother? It would not provide the benefits of greater coordination or centralized control but would simply add another cabinet officer seeking the President's ear. Some argue that cabinet status is necessary to ensure larger appropriations for education programs, but the 1979 budget belies that view, for surely education was as generously treated in this year's budget as any of its supporters could hope.[43] In short, if a President wants to spend heavily on education, the structure does not stop him; if he does not want to, a secretary of education is unlikely to sway him.

A further issue is what happens to "health" and to "welfare" when "education" is removed. Is it reasonable to think that the health industry will rest content at the subcabinet level if education has gained a seat in the cabinet? And can a department of welfare (or income maintenance) be far behind a department of health? This reasoning suggests that pressure for proliferating cabinet departments is likely to result from granting cabinet status to any activity that does not absolutely require it. Although campaign pledges should not be dismissed lightly, honoring them should not take priority over clear-headed analyses of their implications.

What can be said on behalf of change is that a clear need exists to reorganize the education division of HEW. The position of assistant secretary for education (ostensibly the highest ranking education official) is simply untenable, for the commissioner of education has virtually all program and budget authority. The one resource in the assistant secretary's office is the policy development staff, but it is wasteful not to have that staff working directly for the official who has operating and budget responsibility for the programs. Whenever competent and ambitious people occupy these two positions, competition and jurisdictional disputes are sure to ensue and the result is often poor policy formulation. Clarifying lines of authority and improving the policy process within the education division would be

43. Some observers believe, however, that Secretary Califano strongly advocated the large education budget to undercut that argument for a separate department.

a sound first step in reorganization. With one official clearly in charge, less time would be spent in bureaucratic scuffles and more on program management and improvement. Elevating that person to the rank of undersecretary would enhance the status of the position and signify that a meaningful change had taken place.

In April, the administration testified in favor of a department with a heavy emphasis on elementary and secondary education. It would include all of HEW's education division plus most programs listed in table 4-1 but no other major postsecondary programs. Congressional failure to enact this limited version would be more damaging to the President than to education.

A Glance Ahead

Based on the preceding discussion, it is possible to make rough estimates of future federal education outlays and to compare them with OMB's projections. Table 4-6 presents aggregate federal education outlays, actual or estimated, for 1965–83. Education outlays as a percent of the budget hit a high of 4.8 percent in 1971 and stayed near that level through 1976. That figure dropped sharply in 1977 and 1978, to a low of 3.9 percent, largely reflecting President Ford's lean education budgets.[44] Because of forward funding, the effect of President Carter's 1979 request (if enacted) will show up mainly in 1980 outlays, when education is estimated at 4.1 percent of the budget. Based on foreseeable trends, education's share is projected to decline steadily through 1983.

The projections are based on separate estimates for seven large programs (or areas of support): ESEA title I, education for the handicapped, impact aid, GI bill, social security education benefits, basic opportunity grants, and research and development conducted at colleges and universities. All other components of the education budget are projected to increase between 6 and 7 percent a year.

For ESEA title I, the targeting provision is assumed to remain at $400 million, while part A is assumed to grow at roughly 7 percent a year, in line with the Congressional Budget Office current-policy projections. Outlays for education for the handicapped are conservatively projected to increase to $1.6 billion in 1983, while the adminis-

44. Remember that most large education programs are forward-funded, so that outlays reflect the previous fiscal year's appropriations.

Table 4-6. Federal Outlays for Elementary and Secondary Education and Postsecondary Education, Actual and Projected, Fiscal Years 1965–83

Fiscal year	Outlays (billions of dollars)			Percent of total federal outlays[a]		
	Elementary and secondary[b]	Post-secondary[c]	Total	Elementary and secondary	Post-secondary	Total
1965	0.9	2.0	2.9	0.74	1.63	2.37
1966	2.0	2.8	4.8	1.45	2.03	3.48
1967	2.7	3.7	6.3	1.76	2.42	4.11
1968	3.0	4.4	7.4	1.68	2.46	4.14
1969	2.9	4.4	7.4	1.57	2.38	4.01
1970	3.6	5.1	8.8	1.83	2.59	4.48
1971	3.9	6.2	10.1	1.84	2.93	4.78
1972	3.8	6.6	10.3	1.64	2.85	4.44
1973	3.9	7.7	11.6	1.58	3.12	4.71
1974	4.1	8.1	12.1	1.53	3.02	4.51
1975	5.0	10.5	15.5	1.54	3.23	4.78
1976	4.8	12.6	17.3	1.31	3.44	4.72
1977	5.3	11.7	17.0	1.32	2.91	4.23
Projections[d]						
1978	5.9	12.2	18.1	1.28	2.64	3.92
1979	6.8	13.2	20.0	1.37	2.65	4.02
1980	7.9	14.2	22.1	1.46	2.63	4.09
1981	8.5	14.7	23.2	1.44	2.49	3.93
1982	9.2	15.4	24.7	1.40	2.35	3.77
1983	10.0	16.3	26.3	1.39	2.26	3.64

Sources: For 1965–78, *Special Analyses, Budget of the United States Government, Fiscal Year 1979*, and relevant preceding issues; for projections, see note d. Figures are rounded.
a. Total federal outlays for 1978–80 are official budget estimates; for 1981–83, outlays are assumed to be 21 percent of projected gross national product.
b. Excludes school breakfast and lunch programs.
c. Excludes tax expenditures.
d. 1978, see source note; 1979, *Special Analyses . . . 1979* and updated figures from staff of HEW, Division of Education Budget Analysis; 1980–83, author's calculations based on data from the Congressional Budget Office and HEW staff.

tration's reform of impact aid is assumed to be unsuccessful, yielding outlays of about $1.1 billion in 1983.

Projected GI bill expenditures are somewhat firmer, since the number of eligible veterans is known; these outlays for postsecondary education fall to an estimated $1.1 billion by 1983. Social security benefits are also more predictable; they will increase to an estimated $1.9 billion for postsecondary education by 1983 on the assumption that the administration will not be successful in capping the maximum benefit to coincide with basic grants. By contrast, future outlays for

Table 4-7. Federal Outlays for Selected Elementary and Secondary and Postsecondary Programs, Estimates by Author and by Office of Management and Budget, Fiscal Years 1977–83

Millions of dollars

Program	1977	1978	1979	1980	1981	1982	1983
Author's estimates	**6,888**	**7,944**	**9,438**	**11,155**	**11,917**	**12,912**	**14,018**
Elementary and secondary education (ESEA)	2,352	2,574	3,031	3,617	3,796	3,992	4,216
Impact aid	765	810	838	903	962	1,030	1,105
Education for the handicapped	247	366	560	846	1,058	1,300	1,590
Vocational education[a]	559	593	651	692	736	787	843
Postsecondary student aid and institutional support	2,965	3,601	4,358	5,097	5,365	5,803	6,264
Office of Management and Budget estimates	**6,878**	**7,971**	**9,131**	**10,139**	**10,465**	**10,528**	**10,517**
Elementary and secondary education (ESEA)	2,352	2,574	3,031	3,550	3,719	3,771	3,787
Impact aid	765	810	780	762	786	783	783
Education for the handicapped	249	367	562	850	961	978	960
Vocational education[a]	559	593	651	599	591	588	588
Postsecondary student aid and institutional support	2,953	3,627	4,107	4,378	4,408	4,408	4,399

Sources: *Special Analyses, Budget of the United States Government, Fiscal Year 1979*, Office of Management and Budget, unpublished data.
a. Adult education is excluded.

basic grants are extremely uncertain, since the outcome of middle-income student aid versus tuition tax credits is not settled. My projections assume enactment of the student aid proposal and increases of $200 million in subsequent years.[45]

Grants for research and development at colleges and universities are estimated to increase at 7 percent a year. This figure allows for modest growth but not at recent rates.

Table 4-7 compares my estimates with OMB current-service projections for several programs where large discrepancies exist between the two. In elementary and secondary education, projections for title I (including the targeting provision) differ by more than $400 million in 1983, primarily because the Office of Management and Budget projects virtually no growth after 1981. Impact-aid figures differ by more than $300 million in 1983, largely because my estimate assumes that the reform proposals are not adopted. The 1983 figures for education for the handicapped differ by $630 million, again because OMB projects no growth after 1981.

The Office of Management and Budget combines occupational, vocational, and adult education in a single category, while my figures exclude adult education. When the adult education component is subtracted from OMB figures as in table 4-7, the projections for 1983 differ by over $250 million, again because OMB projects virtually no growth for this program.

For higher education, OMB projects student aid and institutional support as a single category composed largely of Office of Education programs.[46] My estimates are grouped in table 4-7 to be consistent with the OMB category. The main reason my 1983 estimate is $1.9 billion above the OMB estimate is that the OMB projections were made before the middle-income student initiative was announced in February.

In the programs in table 4-7 alone, the difference between the two projections for 1983 is $3.5 billion. Of course, the OMB figures are not meant to be forecasts; mine are. In that sense, the two are not comparable. My estimates incorporate assumptions about congres-

45. Although HEW officials and several congressmen have reportedly discussed an additional $800 million in middle-income relief for the 1980 fiscal year, that increase is not included in these projections.

46. This category should not be confused with payments to institutions, table 4-3, which is largely R&D outlays; OMB does not project total federal R&D outlays as a separate category.

sional appropriations which, if roughly accurate, reduce discretionary space in the 1983 budget by at least $3.5 billion.

Even though projections must be taken with a grain of salt (for example, few observers could have forecast in mid-1977 that the middle-income squeeze would produce a request for $1.2 billion in additional budget authority for 1979), the figures in table 4-6 describe two seemingly robust trends: (1) the greater growth potential in elementary and secondary education programs than in postsecondary programs (that is, by 1983, their ratio is projected to be 1:1.6, while it was closer to 1:2 during much of the 1970s); and (2) the virtual certainty that education will not regain the 4.8 percent share of the budget that it enjoyed briefly during the early 1970s. In future years, education seems destined to yield budget space to other outlays or to tax cuts.

36

TUITION TAX CREDIT PROPOSALS
An Economic Analysis of the 1978 Packwood/Moynihan Bill

E. G. West

The late 1970s are witnessing a flurry of new activity to revitalize American education. The required new stimulus, it is widely believed, can come only through the increase of educational choices, the reduction of the monolithic bureaucracies in education, the encouragement of genuine competition, and the acceptance of innovation and greater flexibility. Parents have been using their own initiative to seek legal alternatives to public schools that would not infringe upon the compulsory education statutes. The latest reports to the Department of Health, Education and Welfare suggest that in some towns the public schools and high schools are the most dangerous places for young people to be. Not waiting for such official pronouncements, parents have for many months been taking their own actions. This new mood among many parents has given rise to a rash of "learning exchange networks," travel study programs, independent home-study courses, tutorial instruction, and small, nonpublic "family" schools.

Previously such attempts have failed in most cases because public school administrators have succeeded in arguing that the education provided through alternative channels was not "equivalent" to that of the public school. Today the courts seem to be less impressed by such "equivalency" tests; this is probably due to the accumulating evidence of public school failure.

The frustration of parents was recently neatly summed up in a case heard in Maine in which a criminal action had been brought against a mother who refused to send her child to a local public school and was using the alternative "home-study educational program." The parent, complaining of the monopolistic nature of compulsory public schooling, asserted:

> We are forced to accept this service whatever our opinion of the quality of the service may be. Not only is there no alternative available but we are not even allowed to refuse the State offers if we don't like it . . . .

From E. G. West, "Tuition Tax Credit Proposals: An Economic Analysis of the 1978 Packwood/Moynihan Bill," no. 3 *Policy Review* 61-75 (Winter 1978). Copyright 1978 by the Heritage Foundation.

Why does the burden of proof have to rest on the parents, to show that they can teach their children? I am trusted to provide adequate food, shelter, clothing and medical care for my children without any direction or supervision from the State . . . Why can't I be trusted to educate them also?

The parents have the ultimate responsibility for raising the children, whose time and energy is being appropriated and who bear the ultimate consequences of educational failures. It is not reasonable to deal out the responsibility to the parents, the consequences to the children, and leave all the authority with the schools.

It is interesting that in this case the court dismissed the criminal action against this family. Similarly, the Vermont Supreme Court rejected, in 1976, criminal actions brought against several parents for sending their children to a school that was not approved by the state. The famous *Pierce* case of 1922 seems to be receiving a reappraisal in the courts and new discussion is being generated on the interpretation of the First Amendment.

But although the *Pierce* case decided half a century ago that the state could not compel students to be educated in public schools, for most parents there is a *de facto* compulsion in the sense that they cannot realistically afford an alternative since their money is pre-empted through educational taxes that finance one particular kind of school — the public school.

It is in this context that the new effort in 1978 to press legislation providing tuition tax credits seems to be a crucial event in the history of education and of public finance generally. Senators Bob Packwood (Republican - Oregon) and Daniel Moynihan (Democrat - New York) presented to the Senate in January 1978 a proposal aimed at stimulating diversity and excellence in education by attempting to partially overcome the inability of many parents to afford alternatives. Their bill would provide a tax credit, subtracted directly from the amount of taxes owed, for tuition expenses paid by an individual for himself, his spouse, or his dependents. The amount of this credit would be 50 percent of tuition payments up to a total credit of $500 per student. The credit would be refundable to low income taxpayers. This means that "if the taxpayer is entitled to a credit greater than the

amount of his tax liability, the difference will be refunded
to him in cash." The proposal, if adopted, would take effect
in January 1980.

Supporting their proposal, Packwood and Moynihan argued
that private elementary schools have lost 35 percent of their
enrollment in the last ten years. Private high school enrollment
around the country *rose* by 18 percent. The same kind of
experience was occurring in higher education; the tax credit
proposal was aimed at arresting the decline in this sector also.
The reasoning was the same; the authors argued that unless
this was done America would lose some of its pluralism and
diversity.

This article critically assesses the Packwood/Moynihan
proposal under the following three headings: first, the degree
of benefit to the children of low income families; second,
the total costs to the Treasury; third, the likely fate of the
legislation in the light of recent Supreme Court interpretations
of the First Amendment. I shall conclude that the supporters
of the legislation could make even stronger arguments for it
if they relied a little more on important, but elementary,
economic logic.

Benefits to Low Income Families

In recent years Congress has considered several bills to permit
federal tax deductions for individuals paying tuition at non-
public schools. Apart from the legal problems, experience has
shown that these bills have confronted considerable political
opposition. This is because tax *deduction* favors higher income
groups for it provides a benefit that varies positively with
income. Since the American income tax system is a
graduated one, a benefit gives a greater tax relief to a high-
income taxpayer than to a low-income taxpayer.

In an attempt to avoid this difficulty, later bills proposed
tax *credits* that gave an income-constant benefit. That is, the
creditable amount was subtracted from the taxpayer's bill,
not from his income. High and low income taxpayers were
to receive the same size benefits as long as both had precredit
liability equal to or in excess of the available credit. This
modification still faced a serious equity objection, however.
The new tax credit systems failed to provide assistance to low-
income families who had little or no income tax liability for

the credit to offset.

The outstanding feature of the Packwood/Moynihan proposal is that it completely avoids this objection. For this reason, this proposal constitutes the most persuasive and important tax credit plan that has appeared so far. The amount of the credit is 50 percent of tuition payments up to a total credit of $500 per student. But if the taxpayer is entitled to a credit greater than the amount of his tax liability, the difference will be refunded to him in cash. This must be interpreted to mean that where income tax liability is zero then non-income tax-payers will stand to qualify for tuition credits up to $500 per student. It is this provision that has a revolutionary potential for low-income groups. But there is a further point on the side of equity that has not been made in past discussions.

Most of the private schools in America have religious affiliations. As such they have been able to take advantage of the fact that contributions to them are deductible under the tax codes as they relate to charities in the broad sense of that term. Insofar as parents have been able to give "contributions" in lieu of tuition, they have already been receiving the *equivalent* of some tax credit. There is, indeed, some evidence that this has been happening.[1] Clearly this advantage has been made to the benefit of income taxpayers exclusively, and within the income tax paying group it has benefited the higher income individuals progressively. What the Packwood/Moynihan legislation will do is to spread the advantage to the poorer families which use private schools (and these are considerable in number), families which pay no income tax at all.

Finally, although the new proposal is very modest in the size of the tax credits, it will, nevertheless, present at the margin much more opportunity among the low income groups for choice. At present when they elect for private education, they have to pay their share of the public school taxes as well. This opportunity cost will now be offset by the extent of the tax credit — in other words the cost of using the private sector will

1.   R. D. Reischauer and R. W. Hartman, *Reforming School Finance*, (Washington, D.C.: The Brookings Institution, 1973, p. 143).

Donald A. Erickson and others, "Crisis in Illinois Nonpublic Schools," Final Research Report to the Elementary and Secondary Nonpublic Schools Study Commission, State of Illinois, (The Commission, 1971; processed).

be reduced. Hitherto the privilege of exercising meaningful choice in schooling has been largely concentrated in the hands of the rich. What the new proposal will do is provide "fairer shares in choice." And insofar as choice promotes competition the result will be an education that is more effective and less costly.

Costs to the Treasury

The proponents explain that their legislation will result, according to the Joint Committee on Taxation estimates, in a 1980 revenue loss to the Treasury of $4.7 billion. This calculation omits an important and elementary economic consideration. There is a consensus in conventional economics that monopoly increases costs and competition lowers them. In the absence of the tax credit legislation, or some alternative plan, most participants in the debate agree that in the long run the last vestiges of education in the private sector will virtually disappear. In this event the present near monopoly of publicly provided education will become a full monopoly. For this reason we can expect further increases in costs, and these have not been taken into account in the current reasoning.[2] Conversely, insofar as the tax credits promote choice and competition there will be a new downward trend in costs, not only in the private sector, but in the public sector also. This will mean, in turn, that even though the Treasury may lose a revenue of $4.7 billion, its need for expenditure on education up to, and even beyond, this figure may be less.

With respect to higher education, much depends on the trends in enrollments in the absence of the tax credit. All parties seem to agree that, if nothing is done, enrollments will decline with increasing severity because of the expected increases of costs. This, in turn, will mean a lower investment in professional skills, or what economists call "human capital." To the extent that other forms of human capital formation, such as on-the-job training, are imperfect substitutes for formal higher education, there will be just as much a break in economic growth as there would be if there were a check on *physical* capital expansion. Less growth means less income generated,

2. There is considerable evidence that private schools on the average are able to provide education equal or superior to that provided by the

and the latter implies less revenue for the Treasury. Thus, the eventual shortfall for the Treasury in the *absence* of tax credits could be even more than the $4.7 billion a year that Packwood and Moynihan claim to be the cost of their proposals.

Another key aspect of cost concerns possible changes in the whole structure of educational finance that the present Packwood/Moynihan proposal may bring. The present structure relies, to a significant degree, on student loans. The tax credit proposal comes at a time when the student loan system in America is at its lowest ebb in terms of efficiency. To the extent that the tax credit system begins to supersede the conventional loan system it could be an important source of cost saving for future years.

The source of the inefficiency in the American Federally Guaranteed Loan system is the unprecedented rate of defaults. Table 1 illustrates the growth in defaults over the last four years.

Table 1: The Growth of Defaults in U.S. Guaranteed Student Loans, 1974 to 1977

Fiscal Year	Claims on Defaulted Student Loans Paid by the Federal Government (in millions)	Amounts Collected Against Defaults (in millions)
1974	$55.2	$4.2
1975	71.7	7.6
1976 (15 months)	105.5	10.0
1977 (estimated)	148.8	8.7

Source: *Chronicle of Higher Education*, September 6, 1977.

public schools at lower cost. In the long run, therefore, the encouragement of private schools will mean a reduction in the costs of education to local governments and a reduction in the amount of federal aid sent to them. See, for instance, Robert G. Hoyt's recent article, "Learning A Lesson From The Catholic Schools," in the September 12, 1977 issue of *New York* magazine (p. 50). The author reports that in 64 parishes of Manhattan, 78% of the students were non-White and the majority of them were non-Catholic. The minority students in these Catholic schools have done better on standardized achievement tests. Most interesting of all was the large cost disparity between the Catholic and public schools; the

By the end of September 1977, the government was estimated to have paid out $436 million in claims from lenders and to have collected $33.8 million of bad debts. According to the recent study by the General Accounting Office, about one of every six of the $4.5 billion worth of loans made to over four million students under the Guaranteed Student Loan Program was not paid back after the students completed their schooling or withdrew. To "internalize" the cost of these growing defaults, or, in other words, to switch the burden of defaults from the taxpayer to the nondefaulting student class, would mean charging all student borrowers at a rate of interest well over 24 percent per annum! Clearly this program cannot continue in its present form, judging from its recent performance.

There seem to be two primary reasons why the loan system has failed. First, the banks have very little incentive to collect payments on loans once they are defaulted, since the federal government provides a substantial guarantee for payment of these loans. The incentive to default, meanwhile, is quite high and some students even declare bankruptcy in order to avoid repaying. The General Accounting Office's study illustrated the case of a psychiatrist earning about $31,500 a year who owed $8,700 including interest, and a professional basketball player earning $85,000 a year who owed $3,500 plus interest, both of whom never *began* to repay their educational loans.

When first proposed by economists in the early 1960s, it was planned that the loan system would use the already substantial machinery of the income tax establishment to collect interest and repayments. The incentives of individuals to default against the income tax authorities are likely to be considerably smaller than present incentives. (And bankruptcy

Catholic schools' annual per pupil cost is $462 while it costs the public schools $2,647 yearly to educate a child. Of course, private school teachers, especially nuns, receive lower salaries than do public school teachers. However, the main reason for the large differential would seem to be administrative costs. The Catholic schools in New York have one "downtown" administrator for every 600 students while the Board of Education central office has one administrator for every 234 students. Yearly administrative salaries for the Board of Education are at least $67 million; equivalent salaries for the Catholic system are only $250,000.

cannot be pleaded as an excuse for nonpayment of income tax.) What is interesting about the Packwood/Moynihan proposal is that it can be treated as a return to the philosophy of the loan system as originally intended and described — a system that does use the income tax machinery for collection. It is true that Packwood and Moynihan do not present their plan in such a light, and they speak of the facility as providing state *aid*. Nevertheless, the burden of their argument is that unless their proposal is adopted many students will not receive higher education, and ultimately the government will receive less in tax revenues. Conversely, if their tax credits are successful, users of their system will eventually "pay back" to the income tax authorities a higher volume of .tax revenues than they otherwise would. In this sense the Packwood/Moynihan plan can be regarded as a device that *stimulates* a loan system and moves in the direction of efficiency in "lending" in contrast to the present conventional loan system.[3]

It is not being argued here that the cost savings from the replacement of the present loan system would be sufficient to offset the $4.7 billion of cost that the sponsors of the bill estimate. One can foresee, however, no likely improvement in the present loan system and, if anything, defaults are likely to impose *increasing* costs. These can be expected to be of such a magnitude as to make the comparison of the two systems not without some significance.

Judicial Interpretation of the Tax Credit Bill

One possible problem with the tax credit bill, if it is passed by the Congress, must be anticipated. This is the question of

3.   Insofar as critics may argue that the provision of tax credits for *human* capital and not *physical* capital results in horizontal inequity, there is an argument for a special "graduate" tax on the accumulators of human capital. The Packwood/Moynihan legislation does not preclude this possibility from discussion. As Senator Moynihan observed (*Congressional Record*, September 26, 1977), the sponsors of the bill are "open to suggestions for modifying and improving it, and look forward to the careful consideration that it will receive as it moves through the Congress."

At the same time it should be remembered that the accumulators of physical capital are allowed certain tax privileges to encourage them to undertake "healthy" rates of growth. A tax credit for human capital, especially at the modest rates proposed in the present bill, might no more than offset the privileges for a physical capital formation.

constitutionality. Senator Moynihan gives considerable attention to this problem in his report to the Senate (*Congressional Record*, September 26, 1977). His argument can be strengthened considerably, again by demonstration of some economic reasoning.

The possible constitutional difficulty with the proposal according to some critics is that, because the plan provides credits that- are refundable (e.g., to individuals who don't earn enough to qualify for income tax), the plan will be transformed into one of tuition reimbursements. These are direct payments that can be spent in parochial schools, and as such they will be regarded as "aid to religion." Again, even without rebates, income tax credits may not be acceptable to the courts because if credits were restricted to parents with children in schools that conformed to government regulations, such regulations would involve "excessive entanglement" (to use the Supreme Court's current terminology) between Church and State. On the other hand, if the credit were available without such regulations the courts would have no evidence that public aid was not being employed to finance the religious component of parochial schooling.

Some experts have replied that since tax credits represent aid to the parents, not to the school or religious organization, they should not be regarded as unconstitutional. If, moreover, the credit is limited to a fraction of tuition paid, it can be argued that it finances only the secular portion of the education.

The fact is that the recent *Nyquist* case refused to allow the distinction of family-directed aid from denominational school-directed aid. Moreover the *Nyquist* court appeared to view any attempt to show that the public subsidy financed only the secular part of education as being fraught with almost insuperable "entanglement" difficulties.

In his response to the Supreme Court's latest stance, Senator Moynihan relies on the argument that the Court itself is wrong in its interpretation of the Constitution. Many (including the present writer) will sympathize with this argument that (historically interpreted) the First Amendment attempted primarily to insure against a national state religion. Some will also sympathize with his claim that tax credits provide modest amounts of aid anyway, and will protect a pluralistic system that was intended by the Founding Fathers.

Senator Moynihan's argument, however, would be more persuasive if he had focused on the Free Exercise Clause of the First Amendment, instead of the Establishment Clause. The Free Exercise Clause states that Congress, in its attitude toward religion, shall make no law "prohibiting the free exercise thereof." The fact is that a system that taxes everybody to support a public school system *prohibits in some degree* the ability of those parents who want to patronize parochial schools from making use of their right to do so. Under such a system, whenever the parent chooses a parochial school he forgoes the opportunity of receiving a "free" education in the government sector. The forgoing of this opportunity, to the economist at least, is the very essence of the term "cost." In other words, a public sector, so financed, automatically imposes *costs* on the private and parochial sector. As such it cannot be denied that the result is some degree of prohibition of religious education and therefore of religion.

Senator Moynihan defends his tax credit system on the grounds that *aid* to parochial schools is legitimate in the strictest historical interpretation of the First Amendment. To the extent, however, that the so-called "aid" is nothing but a return of the parochial taxpayers' public contributions, the correct viewpoint is that a previous "prohibition" affecting the religious sector is cancelled out. It represents the deletion of a previous error rather than a provision of a (debatable) right to *state* help.

Some will argue that, in the case of those who qualify for no income tax but receive the tax credit for education, the state, in the sense of other taxpayers, is indeed involved. Such an argument, however, can be firmly rebutted. First, income tax is not the only revenue source to finance education. Revenues flow from several types of taxes including sales taxes and property taxes which are particularly regressive. It is not unreasonable, therefore, to view the refunded credit to persons who do not qualify for income tax as a refund offsetting other taxes that they pay. Moreover, because a person does not pay income tax in the current period, this is not to say that he will not pay it in future periods of his lifetime. Indeed, the economically correct way to view the individual taxpayer's contribution to education is as a contribution from his *lifetime* income. Over his lifetime he will go through several stages of income levels and social positions. He or she will pay indirect taxes at all of these stages. After leaving school the individual will pay taxes of various kinds on his earnings. When married, but before having children, the individual will contribute probably to direct as well as indirect taxes. When children arrive, the pre-school period of their lives will coincide with continuing tax payments by their parents. The same tax payments will continue through the school age and after.

Table 2 shows one recent piece of investigation on the distribution of costs of public school systems. It revealed that people in the very poorest family income categories were paying nearly 8 percent of their annual incomes in education taxes. Table 3 produces the absolute dollar contributions of families in different income groups. These figures, it should be remembered, related to the 1960 census year. To make them representative of present day conditions we would have to multiply by a considerable inflation factor. Using this table, I have estimated elsewhere that a poor family contributes a total undiscounted lifetime contribution in education taxes of $7,380. We have to remember, also, that the poor typically receive an education that is of a shorter duration than others. So while their cost contributions are lower than average so are their benefits. It is, therefore, not clear that they are not contributing enough to finance their educations entirely.

Finally, it may be retorted that if the burden of our argument is that each individual family pays for its own education through its lifetime taxes, then the correct response of government is to withdraw from education entirely rather than provide tax credits. This, however, does not necessarily follow. The fact that we argue that so far there has been no demonstration that the typical individual family does not pay for its education over its lifetime does not necessarily mean that the same family could obtain the same funds without intervention. It could indeed do this if there were a perfect capital market. In this case the family would pledge its future income and borrow money accordingly. Insofar as there are serious capital market imperfections, however, and some economists argue strongly that this is the case, it is possible that the government can provide the equivalent of a capital market via the tax process. The resultant government facility is a *financial* one rather than an educational one. Individuals would receive financial facilities in the same way as they receive help in the purchase of long-lasting durables such as houses. The important point remains that when the individual family is viewed as spending *its own money* through a simulated loan

Table 2: Distribution of Taxes Supporting Public Education
(as a percent of income) 1960 Census Year:

(Family Income)

	Under $2000	2000- 2999	3000- 3999	4000- 4999	5000- 5999	6000- 6999	7000- 7999	8000- 8999	10,000- 14,999	15,000 +
All Taxes										
Whites	7.83	4.72	4.00	3.69	3.37	3.00	2.53	2.14	2.14	2.63
Non-Whites	7.73	4.16	3.45	2.87	2.61	2.55	2.48	2.83	3.08

Source: W. Norton Grubb, "The Distribution of Costs and Benefits in an Urban Public School System," *National Tax Journal*, Vol. XXIV, No. 1, March 1971, Table I.

Table 3: Absolute Dollar Contributions of Whites to Public Education (approx.)

(Family Income)

$2000	2000- 2999	3000- 3999	4000- 4999	5000- 5999	6000- 6999	7000- 7999	8000- 8999	10,000- 14,999
$117	$118	$140	$166	$197	$219	$225	$215	$268

Source: Calculations made of percentage in Table 2 applied to median income of each column.

plan, one can no longer complain that it is relying on *public* funds, or that those funds are *aiding* religion or anything else.

Finally, the possibility remains that *some* individual families will be net receivers from the system; that is, they will receive more in benefits than their lifetime education tax contributions. A loan system of the income-contingent kind, however, will have the same effect *ex post*. When people join such a plan they are uncertain of their future income prospects. They will probably agree to some kind of "insurance" element built into the plan so that should it turn out that they are more prosperous than expected they will contribute more to the revolving loan fund than people in the opposite position. They will do this *ex ante* with the balancing benefit that, should their income earnings fall below those expected, they will enjoy the "insurance" of contributions from others. Again, this is a financial system, not an educational one.

In any case, even if some families do receive more in benefits than they have contributed it is almost impossible to conceive of a family that pays less tax contributions from its lifetime income than the modest amounts of tax credit that are involved in the Packwood/Moynihan bill.

Summary and Conclusion

There is more economic justice in the Packwood/Moynihan bill than the authors realize. In America *everybody* pays taxes including the poorest. The bill provides an opportunity for poor people to retrieve some part of their education taxes and spend it directly. This gives them the extra advantage of exercising choice. Hitherto, choice has been concentrated in the higher income sectors. The Packwood/Moynihan proposal will promote "fairer shares in choice" in education.

Hitherto, middle class families using parochial schools have been able to take advantage of their status as charitable institutions. Contributions to charitable institutions are tax deductible. Some parents have managed to arrange a *quid pro quo* with parochial schools so that their contributions are received in lieu of fees. In this way *income taxpayers* who use parochial schools have been at an advantage compared with poorer users who do not pay income tax. The Packwood/Moynihan legislation will equalize the tax advantages among all income groups who use parochial schools.

The calculation of the bill sponsors of a cost to the Treasury of $4.7 billion in 1980 is a gross overestimate. First, insofar as their proposal will stimulate competition, and since competition is generally acknowledged to put downward pressure on costs, some part of the revenue loss anticipated will be offset by a decrease in necessary expenditures for education. Second, in the absence of a tax credit scheme the consensus is that enrollments in higher education will fall. This means a lower formation of human capital. In turn, this implies a lower rate of growth of the national product. A lower national product, however, means a smaller tax base. The Treasury could end up losing several billion dollars on this account, and the Packwood/Moynihan proposal should be costed on the basis of an alternative revenue scenario that takes a reduced tax base into account.

The proposal could, next, substantially reduce another important cost in the higher educational system — the cost of increasing student loan default rates. Student loan defaults have been increasing because of inadequate incentives to the banks to police the offenders, and also because there are high incentives to student borrowers to default. The Packwood/Moynihan Tax Credit Scheme could stimulate a loan system that uses the income tax machinery as the collection device. This will cut down the incentive to default and the cost of administration of such a "loan scheme" would be much lower than the present loan system.

Stronger arguments could be made in support of the bill with respect to its constitutionality. If the focus is placed on the Free Exercise Clause of the First Amendment, the imposition of general taxes upon non-users of the public system can be interpreted as prohibiting in degree the activities of voluntarily chosen religious schools. What a tax credit scheme does is to focus on the fact that individuals themselves contribute the "public funds" in the first place. The receipt of a tax credit can then be argued to be the cancelling out of a previously prohibited act of government against parochial schools. The tax credit can also be viewed as an attempt by government to provide a *financial* facility. In the absence of efficient capital markets to allow families to borrow money on pledges of their future incomes, the government may well be able, through the use of its income tax machinery, to provide the equivalent of such a loan market. But this, to repeat, is a *financial* facility and not an educational one. The constitutionality of the Packwood/Moynihan legislation, therefore, could not be on firmer ground.

37

TUITION TAX CREDITS
A Social Revolution

Thomas Sowell

The Packwood-Moynihan tuition tax rebate legislation is, as Professor E. G. West aptly calls it, "a crucial event in the history of education."[1] Its "revolutionary potential for low-income groups"[2] has been missed by most other commentators and critics and deserves further exploration.

Why is this bill so important — and to whom? It is most important to those who are mentioned least: the poor, the working class, and all whose children are trapped in educationally deteriorating and physically dangerous public schools. Few groups have so much at stake in the fate of this bill as ghetto blacks. To upper-income families with children in college, the maximum $500 tax relief is hardly of decisive importance, when annual college costs range up to ten times that amount. The campaign of misrepresentation by the education establishment has depicted the affluent as the chief (or sole) beneficiaries, when in fact the opposite is nearer the truth. There are many times more students in elementary and secondary schools than in college, and among those children enrolled in pre-college private institutions, there are more whose parents earn from $5,000 to $10,000 a year than those whose parents are in *all* the brackets from $25,000 on up.

Even the current enrollees in private education are not primarily the affluent. The average family income of private elementary and secondary school children is about $15,000. But since the whole purpose or effect of the tuition tax rebate is to extend to others the opportunity for private education, the question is not so much who *now* goes to private school, but who *could* go after this legislation is in effect. No doubt those who went to college in past generations, before the

1. E. G. West, "Tuition Tax Credit Proposals: An Economic Analysis of the 1978 Packwood/Moynihan Bill," *Policy Review*, Winter 1978, p. 62.
2. *Ibid.*, p. 64.

From Thomas Sowell, "Tuition Tax Credits: A Social Revolution," no. 4 *Policy Review* 79-83 (Spring 1978). Copyright 1978 by the Heritage Foundation.

G. I. Bill and other educational subsidies, were far more affluent than the general population, but to object to the G. I. Bill as aid to the affluent would be to miss the whole point — that it extended a privilege previously enjoyed by a few into an opportunity open to millions more. That is precisely what this bill does. That is precisely why it is being opposed and misrepresented by those whose jobs, pensions, and power derives from the public school bureaucracy.

Most Private Schools Less Expensive Than Public

While $500 does not begin to cover college costs, it does cover all or most of the cost of sending a child to many private day schools. Most of those private schools are not the expensive Andover or Exeter stereotypes, but rather schools costing a fraction of the tuition they charge — and having costs per pupil that are a half, a third, or a fifth of the per pupil cost in the public schools. It is not uncommon for Catholic parochial schools costing a few hundred dollars a year to have test scores higher than public schools in the same neighborhoods with per pupil costs well over a thousand dollars. One of the misrepresentations by opponents of the tuition tax rebate is that it would cost billions of dollars. They are talking about Treasury disbursements, which may be politically important. What is *economically* important is that a shift of students to lower-cost private schools can *save* billions of dollars for society as a whole.

Most of the private schools do not have the runaway pay scales or plush pensions that teachers' unions have extracted from politicians handing out the taxpayers' money. Few parochial schools are surrounded with tennis courts or contain many of the other expensive amenities or status symbols that add little to the education of children, but which have become part of the fringe benefits of public school administrators. Indeed, most private schools have far fewer administrators per hundred pupils, which is no small part of the reason for their lower costs or for the opposition of public school administrators to allowing parents a choice of where to send their children.

The crux of the controversy over this bill is *choice* and *power*. If parents are given a choice, public school officials will lose the monopoly power they now hold over a captive audience. That monopoly power is greatest over the poor, but it extends to all who cannot afford to simultaneously pay taxes for the public schools and tuition at a private school. Public schools in affluent neighborhoods where parents already have that option must pay some attention to those parents' wishes and be responsive. But parents in poorer neighborhoods and ghettoes have no such leverage to use to get attention, response or even common courtesy. The mere prospect of being able to remove their children to private schools changes all that. In other words, the benefits of the availability of tuition tax credit do not end with those who take advantage of it, but extend to those who keep their children in the public schools and never collect a dime from the Treasury — but whose children's needs now have to be taken seriously by public school officials no longer insulated or assured of a captive audience.

Much has been made of the fact that most of the enrollment in private elementary and secondary schools is in Catholic parochial schools. Like many other statements about the situation before this bill is passed, it is far from decisive in determining what the situation will be afterwards. The government is constantly overestimating the revenues to be gained from imposing a given tax by assuming that the pre-tax situation will continue unchanged except for the collection of the tax. In the same way, some are now assuming that the social, economic, and religious composition of families with children in private schools will remain unchanged after a subsidy that will put such education within reach of tens of millions of other people. Moreover, not all of the children enrolled in Catholic schools are Catholic. In urban ghettoes, especially, it is not uncommon for many Protestant black families to send their children to Catholic schools, as an escape from ineffective and dangerous public schools. About 10 percent of the ghetto youngsters in Chicago are in parochial schools. In some places, a majority of the enrollees in a Catholic school are non-Catholic. A parochial school can be a social service activity, like a denominational hospital that does not limit its medical care to co-religionists.

The Constitutional Issue

The Constitutional ban on government support for religious establishments raises legalistic issues for legislation whose initial impact may be more pronounced on Catholics. The First Amendment, as written, would not prohibit tax rebates for individuals to do with as they please and the G. I. Bill is used at Catholic colleges and universities, but the Supreme Court has sometimes drawn an arbitrary line between higher and pre-college education and made the Constitution more restrictive on the latter. However, the uncertain course of the Supreme Court in this area in recent years and some evidence of at least a pause in the trend toward judicial policymaking under the guise of interpretation leaves reason to hope that extremist extensions of the "separation of church and state" doctrine will not nullify a bill that offers major benefits to all segments of the population. As things·stand now, there is no Constitutional limitation on an individual's choice to donate money received from the government — whether as salary, tax refund, or Social Security benefits — to a religious organization. To say that the individual cannot choose to *buy* an educational service from the same religious organizations with money originating from the government seems inconsistent at best.

Another red flag to many is the possible effect of parental choice on racial integration. Visions of "segregation academies" are sometimes invoked (even though the tuition tax rebates cannot be used for any institution practicing racial discrimination). Quite the contrary is the case. In most of the nation's largest urban public school systems, there are not enough whites left to integrate, so any further racial integration in such places may be achievable only by the voluntary movement of black children into private schools. But even this is objected to by some "liberals," because blacks who take this opportunity to get ahead and leave the ghetto public schools would leave behind only the children of "the least educated, least ambitious, and least aware."[3] In other words, black parents who want to make a better future for their children must be stopped and their children held hostage in the public schools until such indefinite time as all other people in the ghetto share their outlook. Ethnic minorities in the past rose out of the slums layer by layer, but for blacks it must be all or none! This arrogant treatment of millions of other human beings as pawns or guinea pigs would be impossible when parents have individual choice. That is precisely why both the education establishment and the social tinkerers are opposed to it.

3. "Kissing Off the Public Schools," *The New Republic*, March 25, 1978, p. 6.

TUITION TAX CREDITS
Other Benefits

Walter E. Williams

"Tuition Tax Credit Proposals," by Professor E. G. West, which appeared in *Policy Review* (Winter, 1978) is an insightful discussion of several important educational problems that could be solved in part by the passage of the Tuition Tax Credit bill sponsored by Senators Packwood and Moynihan. In this note I would like to briefly comment on some other educational issues, not raised by Professor West, upon which the Packwood-Moynihan bill could have a favorable effect.

Diversity in Education

People exhibit different preferences for a host of goods and services produced in the United States, preferences influenced by factors such as culture, religion, education and income. In order to resolve or minimize conflict there must be cooperation without conformity; that is, to the extent possible, there must be a variety of goods and services so that people can choose freely in the manner dictated by their preferences. A large, robust private sector increases the likelihood that there will be cooperation without conformity, through the natural evolution of producers of goods and services who specialize in catering to different tastes. In other words, my purchase of an automobile with a rotary engine does not require that I coerce my neighbors to purchase such an automobile.

A state monopoly in the production of a good or service enhances the potential for conflict, through requiring uniformity; that is, its production requires a *collective* decision on many attributes of the product, and once produced, everybody has to consume the identical product whether he agrees with all the attributes or not. State monopolies in the production of education enhance the potential for conflict by requiring conformity on issues of importance to many people. For example, prayers in school, ethnic history, saluting the flag and educational tracking are highly controversial issues which have received considerable court attention and have resulted in street fighting and heightened racial tensions. With

From Walter E. Williams, "Tuition Tax Credits: Other Benefits," no. 4 *Policy Review* 85-89 (Spring 1978). Copyright 1978 by the Heritage Foundation.

a larger non-public education sector and hence more diversity in education, parents who, for example, wanted prayer reading could realize this preference by simply enrolling their child in such a school. They would not be required to either lobby for laws requiring all schools to present prayers or to pay a tariff to opt out of the public school system.[1]

Racial Desegregation

One criticism of the Tuition Tax Credit bill is that it will promote racial homogeneity in our school systems. In fact, for the most part, schools across the country are already racially homogeneous and according to the U.S. Civil Rights Commission they are becoming more so. Contrary to the statements made by its critics, the Tuition Tax Credit may *reverse* this trend not only in education ·but in other areas of life as well. This result will be achieved through higher quality education in cities which will follow from market competition encouraged through the Tuition Tax Credit. With higher quality education available in cities, middle-class, predominantly white families will have reduced incentives to flee to the suburbs as a way of insuring good education for their children. It is noteworthy to recognize that the flight to suburbia in search of better schooling is becoming less of an exclusively white phenomenon. Blacks are fleeing the cities in unprecedented numbers.[2]

The Tuition Tax Credit bill would create the possibility of school integration in a way that school integration decrees do not — through people *voluntarily* pursuing what they believe to be in their own best interests. The use of the courts to promote racial heterogeneity and cooperation in our school

1. Tariff is an appropriate word here because parents who choose to send their children to non-public schools must pay tuition *plus* continue to pay for public schools. This has disincentive effects similar to international tariffs which protect and preserve relatively inefficient producers from competitive forces.

2. The number of blacks living in suburbs between 1970 and 1974 has increased by 550,000, over 11 percent of the net (4,600,000) migration to the suburbs. See: U.S. Department of Commerce, Bureau of Census, *Current Population Reports*, Series P-23, No. 55, "Social and Economic Characteristics of the Metropolitan and Non-Metropolitan Population: 1970-1974." (Washington, D.C.: U.S. Government Printing Office, 1975), p. 1.

systems can be called nothing less than a dismal failure.

Enhanced Educational Opportunity for Minorities

Clearer than its impact on school desegregation is the Tuition Tax Credit bill's effect on the quality of education. The fact that a grossly inferior education is received by most black children has been chronicled in the news media, professional publications and elsewhere. Test performance scores show that the great majority of black children are three to five years behind the national norm. These facts make meaningless the argument advanced by the critics of the Tuition Tax Credit, that if it were enacted there would be a ground swell of fly-by-night, poor quality schools which would exploit the poor.

Black parents, educated or not, can discern high and low quality education. This is evidenced by the fact that many black (as well as white) parents have given false addresses so that their children could attend better schools outside of their districts. The recent surge in the number of non-Catholic black parents sending their children to Catholic schools and the increased number of community and Islamic schools in black ghettos all point to the fact that black parents who want higher quality education for their children *and* have the financial resources seize the opportunity to opt out of the public school system. What the Tuition Tax Credit will do is enable more parents, black and white, who are dissatisfied with public education, to obtain a better and more productive life for their children.

Costs

Professor West and others have evaluated the costs of the proposed Tuition Tax Credit in terms of its impact on the federal budget — a particularly narrow view of costs and benefits of the proposed legislation. The social cost of education is the amount of resources that the society gives up. The cost is seriously understated if in our general view we exclude state and local expenditures. This everyone knows. However, the social cost has not so far entered the debate on the Tuition Tax Credit.

Many non-public schools educate youngsters at costs that are only a small fraction of the cost of public schools.

Many parochial schools charge an annual tuition of $600.00 and there are Islamic and community schools which charge similar tuitions. On the other hand, the per child cost of education in some metropolitan school systems approaches $3,000.00. Old or new mathematics tells us that if we *reduce* the number of children receiving a $3,000 per year, poor quality education and *increase* the number of children receiving a $600.00 higher quality education, the nation as a whole will benefit by reduced educational expenditures and better education.[3]

Therefore, a broader assessment of costs would consider the likely reduction of educational expenditures at the state and local levels which would be the ultimate result of fewer children attending public schools. Tax credits will provide freer choice and as Professor West comments, ". . . insofar as choice promotes competition the result will be education that is more effective and less costly."

The Prospects for Public Schools

The prediction that Tuition Tax Credits would lower the number of children attending public school has given rise to the argument that this tax measure would contribute to the destruction of public schools. This perhaps is the most revealing confession of the opponents of the Packwood-Moynihan bill, who are mostly members of the public education establishment. This position does not differ from one which says that if parents were given freedom of choice many would opt out of the public school system. In other words, the public education establishment is saying that if their state-granted monopoly powers are reduced, the schools run by them will be destroyed.

Destroyed is obviously too strong a word, because many, many public schools are doing an excellent job of educating America's youth. These are schools which satisfy parents and would not be threatened by increased competition. The schools that *would* be threatened by the reduction of monopoly powers are those public schools failing to do a job at least as good as their nearby competitors. These schools, for the most

---

3.   For an important study of "islands" of black academic excellence, see Thomas Sowell, "Patterns of Black Excellence," *The Public Interest* (Spring, 1976), pp. 26-58.

part, are those in inner cities that produce a product *grossly* inferior to their non-public counterparts. If such schools go out of business (become unattended), such an outcome is consistent with market efficiency and enhanced social welfare: the inefficient producers are weeded out and replaced by efficient producers.

Conclusion

At the heart of the problem in public education is a system of educational delivery which creates a perverse set of incentives for all parties involved. At the core of the perverse incentives is the fact that teachers get paid and receive raises whether or not children can read and write; administrators receive their pay whether or not children can read or write. Children (particularly minority children) receive grade promotions and diplomas whether or not they can read and write.

The individual parent who is poor is helpless in such a setting. It is quite difficult for the individual parent or group of parents to effectively force the public school system to produce a higher quality education. The benefit of the Tuition Tax Credit is that it enhances the possibility for the individual parent to *fire* the school providing poor services and to enroll his child in some other school providing better services. The Packwood-Moynihan bill promises to give low-income parents at least some of the powers that their higher-income counterparts have, namely a greater role in determining educational alternatives for their children.

38

THE DEMOGRAPHIC IMPACT
OF SCHOOL DESEGREGATION POLICY

Karl E. Taeuber and Franklin D. Wilson

In a courtroom in Dallas in March 1976, a federal judge heard testimony from sociologists retained by each party in a remedy hearing on school desegregation.[1] The expert witness for the school district presented an analysis showing that full desegregation with extensive busing would spur rapid and sustained white flight, quickly turning the public schools into a system serving primarily black and Mexican American children. The school district proposed a limited desegregation plan that it claimed would avoid excessive white flight and thus permit the maximum feasible amount of desegregation. The plaintiffs opposed a plan that preserved a substantial amount of uniracial schooling. Their expert took issue with the unpublished and incomplete analysis of the other expert, and presented unpublished and incomplete evidence that showed no consistent relation between desegregation and white flight. The judge reached his decision only a few days after the conclusion of hearings.[2] He expressed dismay at his inability to resolve "the battle of the sociological experts." But he accepted a limited plan that had as one of its perceived virtues the avoidance of massive white flight.

Social science research on white flight is becoming a growth industry, but it has yet to return significant policy dividends. The judge was right to express bewilderment. Despite the recent flurry of studies, there is as yet little scholarly consensus.[3] The news media have publicized particular experts who are willing to express policy conclusions, and protagonists have seized upon those scholars willing to present evidence in judicial or legislative hearings. Presentation of evidence in scholarly publications is increasing, but cumulation of trustworthy evidence occurs at a glacial pace. Our purpose here is to indicate certain complexities in the study of white flight that make it extraordinarily difficult to

This paper is one in a series, "Studies in Racial Segregation," supported by funds granted to the Institute for Research on Poverty at the University of Wisconsin by the Department of Health, Education and Welfare pursuant to the provisions of the Economic Opportunity Act of 1964, by Contract No. HEW-100-76-0196 from the Assistant Secretary for Planning and Evaluation, DHEW, and by Grant No. 5 RO1 MH 27880-02 from the Center for Studies of Metropolitan Problems, NIMH. Data acquisition and processing were supported in part by Population Research Center Grant No. 5PO1-HD-0-5876 awarded to the Center for Demography and Ecology of the University of Wisconsin by the Center for Population Research of the National Institute of Child Health and Human Development. Conclusions and interpretations are the sole responsibility of the authors.

analyze, and to suggest some data sources and modes of analysis that should prove helpful.

The redistribution of metropolitan population has long been affected by a variety of governmental actions, among which central city school desegregation actions are a recent addition. The call for a coherent national policy on population distribution is a recurring one in the United States (and many other nations), but the United States has been no more successful at developing a distribution policy than it has been at developing a comprehensive population growth policy or an integrated national urban policy.[a] Massive suburbanization of the white population is a fundamental feature of twentieth-century social change. It has been spurred by numerous governmental actions, often in ways not fully anticipated. At the federal level, public housing, slum clearance, highway construction, urban renewal, transformation of residential mortgage markets, public assistance regulations, facility location, and other programs, together with pervasive racial discrimination in the conduct of each, all contributed to shaping the current urban crisis and its racial dimensions. State and local governmental actions similarly contributed. Inactions at each level of government in the regulation of private racial discrimination (redlining, restrictive covenants, and so forth) may also be cited. ·

Interest in school desegregation as a possible contributing cause of the suburbanization of white families has not developed out of a broad concern for a coherent distribution policy, but springs rather from political maneuvering over school desegregation policy. The narrow policy framework within which questions about white flight have been posed is one explanation for the narrowness of the social science research on this topic. We believe a broader perspective is both feasible and more enlightening.

Varieties of White Flight

In its decision mandating implementation of school desegregation with "all deliberate speed," the Supreme Court ruled that "the vitality of these constitutional principles cannot be allowed to yield simply because of disagreement with them."[4] The Court did not then recognize the ingenuity that would be displayed in devising ways to inhibit application of these principles. In the 1960s and early 1970s the Court struck down one after another technique of delay and evasion. As public school systems increasingly desegregated their formal operations, avoidance of central city public schools became one of the most effective techniques by which individual white families could evade "unyielding" constitutional principles.

The immediate objective of most school desegregation programs is to effect a redistribution of pupils among schools. Although school districts have the

---

[a]For a discussion of the institutional and political factors inhibiting policy development, see chapter 6 by James L. Sundquist.

authority to assign pupils to specific public schools, not all of the pupils need attend as directed. In the early stages of desegregation in many districts, a simple boycott disrupted the intended attendance patterns. Usually organized for the purpose of keeping white children out of racially mixed schools or off the buses, boycotts and the agitation that often accompany them could induce such fear and concern among black parents that minority as well as white enrollments were diminished. Under local compulsory attendance laws and with the continued high valuation by the public of universal education, boycotts have invariably been temporary phenomena. Their effectiveness, however temporary, suffices to demonstrate that a carefully devised desegregation plan can, upon implementation, result in a greatly diminished and still totally segregated pupil enrollment.

The transfer of pupils from public to private schooling is another constitutionally permissible form of white evasion of public school desegregation. Many hastily organized and poorly financed "segregation academies" have proved to be only somewhat less temporary than school boycotts. In a few school districts, with Memphis a leading example, large-scale private educational systems have persisted for several years. Previously existing parochial schools, especially in cities with a large Catholic population, have also received recruits from public schools. In some districts, with Boston a prime example, religious authorities have sought to avoid use of parochial schools as a haven for white flight from desegregation. In other districts new pupils have been welcomed, if only covertly, as the basis for overcoming problems associated with a steadily declining enrollment.

The most permanent type of white flight is movement to another school district. If the district undergoing desegregation is the central city of a metropolitan area, there may be many suburban districts that offer schooling with few or no minority pupils. Nearly all northern suburban districts and many southern suburban districts have an overwhelmingly white enrollment. Their schools are nearly uniracial even if the suburban district has implemented its own desegregation plan.

Residential mobility to escape undesirable effects of a desegregation plan may be possible within a city. A change of residence may permit a family's children to attend a nearby school or a racially unbalanced school, depending on the details of the plan and its completeness. In other situations, moving may be of little effectiveness as flight from desegregation. In Florida, for example, school districts are county-wide, most counties contain a sizable proportion of black pupils, and all counties have desegregation plans in operation.

A Cohort Perspective on Enrollment Changes

Most studies of white flight from school desegregation have taken as their index a measure of change in the enrollment of white pupils in public school systems.[5]

The energy that has been put into assembling data and undertaking complex multivariate time-series analyses has not been matched by sufficient attention to the key variable. The change in white enrollment from one year to the next is a composite reflection of several types of change. In standard demographic parlance, it is a measure of "net" change rather than "gross" change. Use of net change glosses over the separate types of change and conceals information that would be revealed by appropriate specific measures.

To illustrate the limitation imposed by using net enrollment change as an index of white flight, consider any central city school district. Each year some families move to the city and some from the city, and some pupils transfer from public to private school or the reverse. Each year some pupils graduate from high school or drop out at an earlier stage, and others first enroll in kindergarten or first grade. Assume that this normal flow of pupils into and out of the public schools amounts to a 10 percent annual turnover in white pupils. Each year about 10 percent of the pupils from the previous year do not return and about 10 percent of the pupils are new to the system. Now assume that a desegregation program is begun, and that as a result of public controversy the supply of new white pupils dries up. No white parents moving to or within the metropolitan area locate so that they have to enroll their children in the desegregated system, and no five or six year olds enroll for the first time. Even if all of the pupils in the public school system comply fully with the desegregation action, there will be an annual percent decline in white enrollment. There is in this hypothetical situation a strong demographic response to school desegregation. To label that response white flight rather than white avoidance encourages a simplistic misidentification of the process.

Most studies of white flight have been sensitive to the problem of demonstrating that postdesegregation enrollment changes differ from predesegregation enrollment changes, but have overlooked the possibility of identifying separately any of the components of change. A diagram of the main linkages between desegregation actions and enrollment changes is given in figure 11-1. A desegregation action can affect aggregate enrollment by its influence on migration or private school enrollment. (The diagram simplifies by omitting the possibility of an effect on dropout rates, on annexation to or from the school district, on the pattern of interdistrict pupil changes, or on schools, grade spans, and special students included in the district enrollment court.) A change in pupil migration patterns may take several forms, as suggested in the hypothetical example of a district with a 10 percent turnover rate: (1) parents of currently enrolled pupils may move to another district; (2) parents of preschool children or potential parents may leave the district (note that parents may fit in categories (1) and (2) simultaneously); or (3) parents or potential parents who live in other districts and might have moved to the desegregated district may decide not to do so. An increase in enrollment in private schools may occur from: (1) an increased rate of transfer of pupils from public schools; (2) higher-

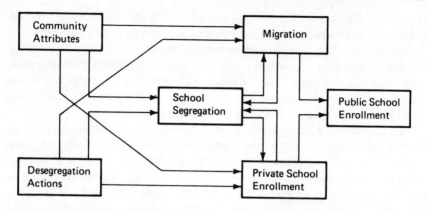

Figure 11-1. Model of School Enrollment Responses to Desegregation Actions

than-expected rates of enrollment of new pupils in private rather than public schools; or (3) lower-than-expected rates of transfer of pupils from private to public schools.

The second set of three modes of desegregation action affecting enrollment patterns was couched in terms of higher or lower enrollments than expected; the first set could have been phrased in similar conditional terms. Each of the distinct enrollment effects occurs in the "normal" course of events in the absence of desegregation actions. To identify the causal effects suggested by figure 11-1 requires a complex analysis of trends and the determinants of deviations from trends. Much enrollment change arises from causes other than desegregation actions. Unless these are well specified and well measured, there is a severe danger of overinterpretation of the impact of desegregation actions. The greater the reliance on aggregate measures of net change rather than on disaggregated or gross measures of specific components of change, the greater the interpretive difficulties.

Many of the analytic problems we have raised are not subject to resolution with the kinds of data generally available, nor are they all soluble within the techniques of contemporary social science. We shall return to these issues later, but first we wish to indicate that simple improvements in the measurement of enrollment change are feasible with data that often are available, and that these simple improvements may increase the interpretability of desegregation analyses.

The task of describing and assessing components of change in public school enrollment is formally similar to tasks routinely encountered in demographic studies of population change. Demographers have developed a variety of techniques for assessing components of change. One of the most powerful is cohort analysis. A cohort is a group of people defined on the basis of some common event during an initial period (for example, being born in year T). Cohort members are traced through succeeding years as they are exposed to the risk of sequential events (in the most elementary demographic example, the risk of death, which may be viewed as one form of departure from the initial population). The entrance of children into grade 1 of a public school district may be used as the defining event for a cohort. In a school population unaffected by migration, failure, mortality, and other changes, the number of pupils in grade 2 in year $T + 1$ should equal the number initially observed in grade 1 in year T. In fact, of course, there will be additions to and subtractions from the initial cohort that alter the numbers observed year by year. And if our data source is enrollment data rather than longitudinal information on the schooling and residential experience of each individual child, then we cannot identify all of the components of change nor exploit the full potential of cohort analysis. But administratively gathered data do permit a partial cohort analysis that improves upon analysis of aggregate net enrollment change. We shall illustrate the technique with published data from annual reports of the State Department of Education of Louisiana.

In Louisiana, public education is organized by parishes (counties). The East Baton Rouge Parish School District serves the population of the Baton Rouge metropolitan area (as defined at the time of the 1970 census). The Shreveport metropolitan area is served by the Bossier Parish and Caddo Parish School Districts, and we have combined data for these two parishes. Data for these school districts are displayed in tables 11-1 and 11-2. Each of these districts implemented a partial desegregation program in fall 1970.

In table 11-1, selected enrollment data for the years 1968 to 1975 in the East Baton Rouge Parish School District are organized to permit tracing the enrollment history of cohorts. The cohorts are identified by the year in which the pupils who progressed normally entered first grade. The first row of the table refers to the cohort of white pupils that entered first grade in fall 1961. We first observe them in this data set in fall 1968, when they are in eighth grade. They numbered 3,319 when the official enrollment count was made. In fall 1969, the official enrollment count of white ninth grades was 3.9 percent greater. The tenth grade count, in fall 1970 (upon implementation of the partial desegregation plan) was 5.5 percent lower than the year before. Between tenth and eleventh grades, this cohort experienced a net loss of 8.9 percent of its members. Throughout the table, the first entry for each row shows the size of the cohort of white pupils when it first appears in this data set, and subsequent entries in each row show the percentage change in enrollment from the previous year.

The principal question for which these data were assembled is whether grade by grade changes in white public school enrollment are associated with the implementation of a desegregation program. In table 11-1 and in table 11-2 the entries in the 1970 column are uniformly negative and are among the largest negative percentages in each row. Each cohort experienced a large loss in the year of desegregation.

Another question raised in the white flight literature is whether an apparent

Table 11-1

Initial Public School Enrollment and Annual Percent Change, for Selected Cohorts of White Pupils, East Baton Rouge Parish School District: Fall 1968 to Fall 1975

Cohort and Grade[a]		1968	1969	1970[b]	1971	1972	1973	1974	1975
1961	8th	3319	3.9	−5.5	−8.9	−2.5			
1962	7th	3678	−2.0	−4.3	−0.9	−11.8	−0.4		
1963	6th	3549	6.9	−9.2	4.9	2.8	−10.1	−18.6	
1964	5th	3362	1.6	−0.6	−1.6	−0.1	0.1	−16.1	3.3
1965	4th	3623	0.6	−6.3	3.9	−1.9	2.4	−5.7	−1.5
1966	3rd	3625	0.8	−7.7	3.3	−3.2	0.1	5.9	7.0
1967	2nd	3680	−0.9	−5.4	−0.3	0.2	7.6	7.9	7.2
1968	1st	3734	−1.7	−6.4	0.8	−2.3	1.6	−4.4	18.7
1969	1st		3650	−10.2	1.3	0.3	2.1	−4.5	9.5
1970	1st			3410	−1.3	−0.7	2.0	−7.2	6.4
1971	1st				2947	−0.2	1.9	−7.5	8.7
1972	1st					2931	1.9	−8.6	8.1
1973	1st						3111	−8.4	8.4
1974	1st							2988	9.5

Source: Annual Reports of the State Department of Education of Louisiana.

[a]Cohorts are identified by year (Fall) that most entered 1st grade. Grade identified is that at time of first observation in this data set (Fall 1968 or later).

[b]A large-scale pupil desegregation plan was implemented in Fall 1970.

first year white enrollment loss is matched by unusually high losses for several succeeding years, whether the pattern for subsequent years returns to "normal," or whether there is a drift back to public schools of some of those who left the first year. Examination of experience in the years after 1970 shows an erratic pattern of gains and losses for the East Baton Rouge cohorts, and an inconsistent pattern of small declines for the Bossier/Caddo cohorts.

The data in tables 11-1 and 11-2 provide other opportunities for browsing to discern patterns in enrollment trends. In both tables there are substantial enrollment declines associated with the transition from tenth to eleventh grades; perhaps this reflects dropouts of children exceeding compulsory attendance ages. The numbers at the bottom of each column show the size of the successive cohorts entering first grade. These numbers display a general downward trend. We cannot determine from these data how much of this downward trend is accounted for by previous fertility declines and the consequent annual declines in the number of children in each parish reaching age six, how much stems from increasing utilization of private schooling, and how much reflects migration patterns of families with young children.

Table 11-2
Initial Public School Enrollment and Annual Percentage Change for Selected
Cohorts of White Pupils, Bossier and Caddo Parish School Districts (combined):
Fall 1968 to Fall 1975

Cohort and Grade[a]		1968	1969	1970[b]	1971	1972	1973	1974	1975
1961	8th	3944	−1.6	−6.9	−9.8	−8.1			
1962	7th	4069	−3.3	−5.3	−4.2	−6.9	−9.5		
1963	6th	4127	−1.1	−9.9	2.7	−3.8	−7.4	−7.6	
1964	5th	4064	−2.7	−6.4	−3.3	7.1	−6.8	−7.2	−9.5
1965	4th	4232	−4.2	−6.6	−5.0	1.4	3.4	−3.2	−8.2
1966	3rd	4305	−4.9	−9.4	−3.3	0.4	−2.5	5.6	−3.0
1967	2nd	4207	−4.0	−10.1	−3.2	−0.4	−0.3	−1.2	7.8
1968	1st	4580	−9.1	−11.1	−2.9 .	−2.0	−2.0	−1.6	−0.7
1969	1st		4284	−12.6	−3.6	−1.4	−4.5	1.6	−1.7
1970	1st			3525	−4.8	−1.8	−4.0	0.2	−0.6
1971	1st				3026	−3.0	−3.6	0.7	−3.4
1972	1st					2725	2.0	1.7	−3.5
1973	1st						2590	0.4	0.0
1974	1st							2780	−2.8

Source: Annual Reports of the State Department of Education of Louisiana.

[a]Cohorts are identified by year (Fall) that most entered 1st grade. Grade identified is that at time of first observation in this data set (Fall 1968 or later).

[b]A large-scale pupil desegregation plan was implemented in Fall 1970.

Annual counts of enrollment by grade are often produced and used in educational administration. Standard computer programs have been prepared to permit use of such data in projecting future enrollments.[6] It is common experience that these numbers and the associated grade-to-grade transition rates fluctuate in erratic patterns. One expert recommends using a ten-year trend to establish a base from which to make a projection..[7] Clearly the task of establishing "normal" trends from which to identify deviations attributable to school desegregation actions is extraordinarily difficult. If it is assumed that parental flight responses may occur during the period that desegregation is a controversial issue before any action has been taken, at the time of actions, and for some years following, identification of effects would require extraordinarily rich data sources and ingenious and meticulous statistical methodology.[8]

Flight to Where

If pupils flee from public schools in a desegregating district, they must alight in some other school system. One way to work the puzzle of interpreting complex enrollment trends in the desegregating district is to find evidence of complementary enrollment trends in private schools or adjoining districts. Of course, it is not necessarily any easier to identify unusual enrollment increases in suburban districts than it is to identify unusual enrollment declines in a central city district. Indeed, for those central city districts in which the number of white public school pupils declined greatly before desegregation, use of enrollment data to identify destinations of fleers may be much harder. A 10 percent decline in public school whites in the central district may represent only a 2 or 3 percent rise in public school whites in suburban districts. If the suburban territory is divided into many small school districts, the enrollment in each may be too small and trends too erratic for reliable interpretation.

To illustrate the utility of pairing outflow with inflow data, we may use the Louisiana districts. Because these are metropolitan districts, the principal destination of white fleers from public schools must have been private schools. (Unfortunately for our example, each of these metropolitan areas has been expanding into adjoining parishes, and the formal definitions of the Standard Metropolitan Statistical Areas have been altered since 1970 to include additional parishes. To keep our example simple, we ignore this real-world complication.)

Annual data on private school enrollments, by race and grade, are provided in the annual reports of the State Department of Education of Louisiana. To permit a summary comparison of public and private enrollment trends, without sacrificing all of the benefits of the cohort approach, we have summed together data for five cohorts, those that were in first through fifth grade in fall 1968 (seventh through eleventh grades in fall 1975). Public and private school totals are arrayed side by side in table 11-3. The first pair of data columns shows the aggregate enrollment in the five-grade span for each year, 1968 to 1974. The middle columns present the annual numerical changes in enrollment, and the final columns present the change figures as percentages.

During the years 1968-1975 public school enrollments for these cohorts were generally declining. Private school enrollments increased to a peak in 1970 and subsequently declined. We must examine the middle columns for evidence of complementarity in public and private enrollment trends. The most striking result is the change accompanying the partial desegregation in Bossier/Caddo from 1969 to 1970. Public enrollment for our cohorts declined by 1,879 and private enrollment increased by 1,822. The prima facie case for a significant white flight to private schools could not be stronger. But there is more than just this one piece of evidence, and the other pieces do not fit so easily into a white flight interpretation. The year prior to desegregation in Bossier/Caddo also reveals a matched transfer from public to private schooling, of a large magnitude. The second year after desegregation there is an increase in public enrollment and a somewhat greater decrease in private enrollment. Is this evidence of a return to the public system once desegregation is implemented successfully? No other year shows such a pattern, and the last two annual observations reveal declining enrollments in both public and private schools.

The data in table 11-3 for East Baton Rouge contain evidence of a

Table 11-3
Annual Change in Enrollment of Selected Cohorts of White Pupils in Public and Private Schools, East Baton Rouge Parish and Bossier and Caddo Parishes (combined): Fall 1968 to Fall 1975

School Year (Fall)	Initial Enrollment		Changes in Enrollment			
			Number		Percent	
	Public	Private	Public	Private	Public	Private
	East Baton Rouge Parish					
1968 to 1969	18,024	4,581	14	−135	0.1	−2.9
1969 to 1970	18,038	4,446	−969	459	−5.4	10.3
1970 to 1971	17,069	4,905	254	−378	1.5	−7.7
1971 to 1972	17,323	4,527	−14	−242	−0.1	−5.3
1972 to 1973	17,309	4,285	434	−379	2.5	−8.8
1973 to 1974	17,743	3,906	−1,382	−638	−7.8	−16.3
1974 to 1975	16,361	3,268	808	107	4.9	3.3
	Bossier and Caddo Parishes					
1968 to 1969	21,388	1,205	−1,084	1,008	−5.1	83.7
1969 to 1970	20,304	2,213	−1,879	1,822	−9.3	82.3
1970 to 1971	18,425	4,035	−749	−71	−4.1	−1.8
1971 to 1972	17,676	3,964	251	−378	1.4	−9.5
1972 to 1973	17,927	3,586	−341	124	−1.9	3.5
1973 to 1974	17,586	3,710	−309	−411	−1.8	−11.1
1974 to 1975	17,277	3,299	−568	−427	−3.3	−12.9

Source: Annual Reports of the State Department of Education of Louisiana.
Note: Enrollment figures for all years are for those cohorts present in 1st through 5th grade in Fall 1968 (identified in tables 1 and 2 as the 1964 through 1968 cohorts).

public-to-private transfer upon implementation of desegregation and a subsequent return movement, but again there is much other evidence not so readily interpreted. The public school loss with desegregation is twice the size of the private school gain. The subsequent pattern of return from private to public schooling shows up in the first and third years after desegregation, but not in the second year.

In East Baton Rouge Parish, 20 percent of white pupils in these cohorts attended private schools in fall 1968. This increased to 22 percent with desegregation, but had dropped back to 17 percent by 1974 (a drop that may reflect a general tendency to utilize private schooling more during the early grades when children are younger and costs are lower). In Bossier/Caddo Parishes, only 5 percent of white pupils in these cohorts attended private schools in fall 1968, and this increased in two years to 18 percent. By 1974 this had dropped only to 16 percent.

Enrollment data collected by governmental agencies cannot be expected to provide complete information on where parents flee to when desegregation occurs. Longitudinal data for individual pupils seem, in principle, to be needed. Such data are difficult and expensive to collect, and the only extant body of repeated interviews of parents in a district undergoing desegregation is the Boston study.[9] Alas, even this massive body of data has proven intractable to simple analysis of white flight, and no unambiguous findings have yet been reported.

Identifiability of Desegregation Effects

During the Dallas desegregation remedy hearings, a sociologist testified about the ambiguities in the evidence for desegregation-induced white flight. During the morning recess he was corralled by two persons who presented themselves as living proof that white flight exists. In a search for other living proof, we present in tables 11-4 and 11-5 sample survey data on the "main reason" given by white heads of households with school-age children for moving from the central city to elsewhere in the metropolitan area. These data are from the Annual Housing Survey, a recently inaugurated innovative program sponsored by the Department

Table 11-4
Percentage Giving Each Main Reason for Moving from the Central City to the Suburbs, White Households with School Age Children, Selected Metropolitan Areas: 1974 to 1975

Metropolitan Area	Employment	Family	Housing	Neighborhood	Schools	Other
Minneapolis-St. Paul	8.7	9.1	36.5	0.0	0.0	45.7
Newark	0.0	13.6	43.2	26.8	0.0	16.4
Phoenix	28.6	0.0	29.1	14.5	0.0	27.8
Pittsburgh	13.4	13.1	33.3	6.4	7.2	26.6
Boston	0.0	17.3	41.4	23.2	5.7	12.4
Detroit	22.7	8.7	36.4	23.3	4.3	4.6
Anaheim	8.2	8.1	39.9	15.9	7.8	20.1
Albany	0.0	4.9	50.0	24.4	4.9	15.8
Dallas	24.1	11.2	32.2	0.0	3.7	28.8
Fort Worth	14.9	6.5	32.3	18.8	15.3	12.2
Los Angeles	0.0	13.7	34.0	19.4	6.3	26.6
Washington	13.1	25.6	49.6	0.0	0.0	11.7

Source: U.S. Bureau of the Census, Annual Housing Survey for Metropolitan Areas, 1974/75.
Note: Each row sums to 100 percent.

Table 11-5
Percentage Giving Each Main Reason for Moving from the Central City to the Suburbs, White Households with School Age Children, Selected Metropolitan Areas: 1975 to 1976

Metropolitan Area	Employment	Family	Housing	Neighborhood	Neighborhood Racial Change	Schools	Other
Atlanta	11.5	4.5	56.8	6.8	2.2	0.0	18.2
Chicago	7.5	14.6	26.8	10.7	14.7	3.6	22.1
Philadelphia	0.0	36.9	36.9	8.9	0.0	8.6	8.7
San Francisco	0.0	10.8	22.5	45.1	0.0	10.6	11.0
Paterson	0.0	49.8	50.2	0.0	0.0	0.0	0.0
Rochester, NY	0.0	15.6	54.7	11.1	3.7	3.6	11.3
Miami	7.0	30.6	28.0	3.4	3.2	0.0	27.8
Cincinnati	9.1	36.3	32.3	4.6	4.7	0.0	13.0
Columbus, OH	22.5	30.1	34.7	4.3	0.0	4.1	4.3
Milwaukee	5.9	12.2	37.7	18.4	0.0	0.0	25.8
New Orleans	6.6	24.0	31.7	0.0	6.6	6.2	24.9
Kansas City	0.0	13.1	62.7	0.0	0.0	0.0	24.2
San Bernardino	14.5	4.5	47.7	9.0	0.0	0.0	24.3
San Diego	6.8	0.0	40.2	26.7	0.0	0.0	26.3
Portland, OR	5.3	7.3	43.7	10.1	0.0	4.9	28.7

Source: U.S. Bureau of the Census, Annual Housing Survey for Metropolitan Areas, 1975/76.
Note: Each row sums to 100 percent.

of Housing and Urban Development and conducted by the Bureau of the Census. Each year a subset of the nation's largest metropolitan areas is oversampled so that data for those individual areas can be reported in addition to national estimates.

Results for the metropolitan areas included in the 1975 and 1976 surveys are presented in tables 11-4 and 11-5. In each year, the interviewer was instructed to write all reasons mentioned and to mark the main reason. Reasons were subsequently coded into a specific set of about thirty categories, which we have collapsed into the groupings shown in the column headings. There was one change in coding of particular interest to us. In 1975, "neighborhood" was a single category, while in 1976 it was subdivided into "neighborhood over-crowded," "change in racial or ethnic composition of neighborhood," and "wanted better neighborhood." In both years, "schools" was a single coding category.

Housing considerations—needed larger house or apartment, wanted to own or rent, wanted better house, wanted residence with more conveniences, and so forth—dominate as the main reason for a suburban move. Family reasons—

change in marital status, change in size of family, wanted own household, moved to be closer to relatives—were cited frequently in many metropolitan areas. Employment reasons include job transfer or change and commuting reasons. The "other" category in the tables includes displacement by urban renewal, highway construction, fire, or disaster, along with a few miscellaneous categories.

The reasons of principal interest in the study of white flight from desegregation are "schools" and "neighborhood." The percentage of families indicating schools as the main reason for moving to the suburbs is small, ranging from zero for twelve of the twenty-seven places to above 10 percent for only two. Both Fort Worth and San Francisco have school desegregation programs, with a major implementation occurring one year and four years prior to the housing survey, respectively. Even in Boston with its history of bitter and sustained public controversy over desegregation, schools are cited as the main reason for moving by only 6 percent of white families who moved to the suburbs.

Perhaps white parents are reluctant to cite schools because that might tend to identify them as prejudiced. Judging from the public controversy in many cities, and from the national turmoil over busing, we would expect "schools" to be regarded by most whites as a legitimate and respectable answer. In the 1976 survey, neighborhood racial change was singled out as a separate category; it was cited by 15 percent of Chicago area movers (Chicago did not yet have a desegregation plan) and a much lower percentage of families in five other places. Wanting a "better neighborhood" may entail racial considerations, even if unspoken. Neighborhood reasons are relatively common for some metropolitan areas and infrequent for others. Unfortunately for simple interpretation, the search for better neighborhoods has been a motivating force for suburbanization for many decades, and hence cannot be regarded with any confidence as an indicator of racial concerns. To the extent that racial concerns are subsumed in broader reasons such as wanting a better neighborhood or better house, the racial considerations may reflect white flight from black neighbors—a process that has also been an active suburbanizing force for many decades—rather than a direct or immediate concern with school desegregation. Indeed, the opinion that suburban schools are better than city schools predates the controversy over desegregation.

Surveys designed more specifically to tap sentiments toward school desegregation could provide better information for our purposes than is available from the Annual Housing Survey. Even if such data were available, the analyst would be faced with a difficult task of inferring motivation. There are many reasons for moving to the suburbs and each family may have a mixture of motives. In this sense the behavior of most families is "overdetermined." If a concern with desegregation is identified as one reason among a larger set of reasons, how is it possible to specify whether it is one more straw on the pile or the straw that broke the back of residential inertia? Self-perceptions of motivation and public opinion polling on reactions to school desegregation are informative, but they do not provide a simple solution to the task of identifying desegregation effects.

Any specific effects of desegregation actions taken by a school district on migration patterns within, to, or from that district, occur in a context of many other political, social, economic, and psychological forces. National concern over white suburbanization and black ghettoization predates the recent decade of controversy over urban school desegregation, and the scholarly literature on the causes of these residential transformations is enormously rich and complex. Trends in public and private school enrollment have also been analyzed, incorporating such causes as trends in the birthrate, city-suburb and white-black differentials in fertility, the changing role of parochial education and of Catholicism in American life, the declining availability of nuns as teachers, educational finance, increasing educational attainment of parents, changing parental perspectives on the constituents of quality education, and many more.

To identify a specific impact of desegregation actions on public and private school enrollment and on the residential distribution of racial groups, we must be able to demonstrate either that the changes in these variables could not have occurred as they did in the absence of desegregation actions, or that some temporal or spatial variation in these processes can be attributed statistically to variations in desegregation actions. The first alternative can be dismissed, for racial enrollment and residential patterns clearly can and do change enormously in the absence of desegregation actions. Thus the task of identifying the impacts of desegregation actions requires sophisticated multivariate analysis.

If the effects of a desegregation action are direct and large, it should be feasible to disentangle their influence from the milieu of other forces. David Armor's recent work purports to demonstrate such a consistent pattern of massive white flight (when there is extensive mandatory busing in large districts with substantial minority populations and developed suburbs to accommodate residential flight) that no entanglement of other forces could possibly account for the results.[10] Gary Orfield's conclusion is similar to ours, that "to firmly establish any argument about white flight one would need some kind of general theory of urban racial change."[11]

Most studies of white flight, even when they have incorporated some kind of multivariate model, have been ineffective in controlling for the full range of known factors that should form part of a general theory of urban racial change.[12] Consider the two most noteworthy published studies. Coleman, Kelly, and Moore estimated equations in which changes in white public school enrollment were evaluated as a function of change in school segregation, number of pupils in the district, proportion black, segregation between districts in the metropolitan area, region, and certain interaction terms.[13] Farley added variables reflecting the metropolitan residential structure (city/suburb housing ratio, percentage of homes built before 1940, population density) and economic structure (white unemployment rate).[14] Neither study included measures of the administrative structure of school districts, the fiscal situation of municipalities and school districts, social and physical characteristics such as crime rates, fire and bond ratings, history of racial disturbances, and other such components of a general theory of urban racial change. In both studies the variable to be explained was aggregate net change in white public school enrollment, and desegregation action was characterized by a single measure (decline in the value of a segregation index). Orfield's mandate has not yet been fulfilled.

A Policy Research Agenda

Much social science research on contemporary society can be regarded to some degree as policy analysis. Narrowly focused evaluation research obviously seeks to influence policy choice, but even general social research is often carried out in the hope that better understanding of social change will enhance the design and implementation of social policy. In the case of school desegregation and white flight, neither is prime cause or consequence of the other. There are many reasons for undertaking school desegregation, and white flight is but one of many outcomes in need of assessment. There are many facets to white flight, and each has a number of causes. Many of these are the direct or indirect consequence of governmental policies of diverse sorts beyond the explicitly educational. As students of urban racial patterns in migration, housing consumption, residential location, and schooling, we can design an array of further studies of the demographic impacts of school desegregation. Some of these would be considered policy analysis only to the extent that they help set a realistic social context for the policy discussion, whereas others respond more directly to questions that legislators, judges, school board members, and citizens think need answering. We shall describe a few prospective studies to illustrate the range of types of policy relevance.

What is the response of white families to the presence of minority pupils in communities that have not implemented desegregation programs? The literature on residential succession abounds with instances of neighborhood racial turnover.[15] How are residential change and school change linked in this process? Can annual racial enrollment data provide a richer data resource for neighborhood turnover studies than is available from decennial census data? Is there anything distinctive about the presumed white flight from desegregation that is not already embraced in the white avoidance of "changing" neighborhoods and schools? Why should a concern with white flight lead to a policy focus on school desegregation rather than on racial functioning of the metropolitan housing market, economic shifts between cities and suburbs, and the like?

Somewhat less far-reaching would be studies differentiating the private school and migration components of white flight. Moving one's children to private schools is much less permanent than moving one's family to the suburbs, and does not entail the same range of fiscal and residential impacts on the city. Further knowledge is needed of the circumstances under which existing or new private school systems serve as havens, and of the circumstances that are conducive to a return to public schooling.

The white population has been treated throughout our discussion as an undifferentiated aggregate. The socioeconomic differentiation within the white population is of great concern in the assessment of policy implications. Socioeconomic activity in private school enrollment and residential relocation is to be expected, yet has been ignored in most studies.[16] The socioeconomic selectivity of the response bears on the degree of conflict between seemingly independent federal policies. Urban development policy is concerned with attracting and retaining middle class persons as central city residents, with the avowed aim to alleviate the fiscal crisis of the cities and to reduce the city/suburb racial separation. To what extent is the federal effort to improve the education of city residents through desegregation working at cross-purposes with other urban policy goals? Within the domain of education, what are the potential conflicts in methods and aims between (1) desegregation actions that seek to disperse pupils according to race, (2) educational assistance programs aimed at schools with concentrations of disadvantaged children, and (3) programs designed to meet the special needs of non-English-speaking children and others of minority ethnic identification?

The attempt to use studies of white flight as a specific basis for changing public policy on school desegregation reached a peak in 1975 with extensive press coverage given to statements by James S. Coleman. There has been controversy over the methodology of the study conducted by Coleman and his colleagues, but let us ignore shortcomings of the research and consider two of his primary conclusions:

The effect of desegregation on white loss has been widely different among different cities where desegregation has taken place.

Because, insofar as we can estimate, the loss of whites upon desegregation is a one-time loss, the long-term impact of desegregation is considerably less than that of other continuing factors. The continuing white losses produce an extensive erosion of the interracial contact that desegregation of city schools brings about.[17]

The second of these conclusions might have been used as the rationale for undertaking broader-based research of the type we have presented and proposed. The import of this conclusion was largely overlooked in the effort to reach immediate specific policy conclusions regarding school desegregation.

The first of these conclusions is even more intriguing, for it has also been largely overlooked but pertains directly to the information needed for appropriate policy modification. The most immediately pertinent policy research on demographic impacts of school desegregation actions would be identification of the sources of differentials in the impacts. Of particular interest is whether the character of the desegregating agent (court, HEW, state, school district) or of the desegregation action affects the demographic impact. Katzman's review of a few case studies suggests that these policy choices do not affect the outcome,[18] but Armor's previously cited report suggests that the agent and the action are of fundamental import.[19] If it could be demonstrated that some controllable features of the desegregation process had a significant effect on the demographic impact—for example, the number of schools affected, the speed of implementation, the specific techniques used, the character of community education about the plan, reliance on court order or other federal pressure—then educational administrators could better plan to desegregate and avoid or minimize white flight.

Press coverage of Coleman's research and even subsequent scholarly research focused on the finding of an average effect of school desegregation on white enrollment. No judge, superintendent, or school board really cares much about average effects. They seek to discern what choices within their power can make the outcome of their actions more favorable. If social research is to aid in resolving America's continuing racial dilemma, its protagonists should seek to increase the stock of information about the effects of alternative policy choices. Otherwise the battles of the sociologists will continue to be dismissed in favor of personal intuition.

Notes

1. One of us (K.T.) testified as an expert witness for the plaintiffs.
2. *Tasby* v. *Estes*, 416 F. Supp. 644 (1976).
3. See, for example, Charles T. Clotfelter, "School Desegregation, 'Tipping,' and Private School Enrollment," *The Journal of Human Resources* 11 (December 1975):28-50; James S. Coleman, Sara D. Kelly, John A. Moore, *Trends in School Segregation*, 1968-73, (Washington, D.C.: Urban Institute Paper 722-03-01, 1975); Michael W. Giles, Everett F. Cataldo, Douglas S. Gatlin, "White Flight and Percent Black: The Tipping Point Re-examined," *Social Science Quarterly* 56 (June 1975):85-92; Reynolds Farley, "Can Governmental Policies Integrate Public Schools?" (Paper presented at the Annual Meeting of the American Sociological Association, New York City, September 1, 1976); Thomas F. Pettigrew and Robert L. Green, "School Desegregation in Large Cities: A Critique of the Coleman 'White Flight' Thesis," *Harvard Educational Review* 46 (February 1976):1-53; David J. Armor, "Declaration of David J. Armor," *Carlin et al.* vs. *San Diego Board of Education* (San Diego, 1977); Martin T. Katzman, *The Quality of Municipal Services, Central City Decline and Middle Class Flight* (Boston: Department of City and Regional Planning, Harvard University, 1977).

4. *Brown* v. *Board of Education*, 349 U.S. 294 (1954).

5. Coleman, Kelly, and Moore, *Trends in School Segregation*; Christine Rossell, "School Desegregation and White Flight," *Political Science Quarterly* 90 (Winter 1975/76):675-695; Armor, "Declaration of David J. Armor."

6. Donald N. McIsaac, Dennis W. Spuck, and Lyle Hunter, "Enrollment Projections: ENROLV2," Department of Educational Administration, University of Wisconsin, September 1972.

7. Ibid., p. 2.

8. Armor, "Declaration of David J. Armor."

9. J. Michael Ross, "Changes in Public Preference for Alternative School Desegregation Policies: Theoretical Formulations" (Paper presented at the Annual Meeting of the American Sociological Association, 1976). See also D. Garth Taylor and Arthur L. Stinchcombe, *The Boston School Desegregation Controversy*, Draft Report (Chicago: National Opinion Research Center, 1977).

10. Armor, "Declaration of David J. Armor."

11. Gary Orfield, "White Flight Research: Its Importance, Perplexities and Possible Policy Implementations." *Symposium on School Desegregation and White Flight* (Notre Dame, Ind.: Center for Civil Rights, 1975), pp. 48-49.

12. Katzman, *Quality of Municipal Services.*

13. Coleman, Kelly, and Moore, *Trends in School Segregation.*

14. Farley, "Can Government Policies Integrate Public Schools?"

15. Howard Aldrich, "Ecological Succession in Racially Changing Neighborhoods, A Review of the Literature," *Urban Affairs Quarterly* 19 (March 1975):327-348.

16. A study reported by Giles, Gatlin, and Cataldo does deal with the class issue as it relates to forms of protest against school desegregation. Michael W. Giles, Douglas S. Gatlin, and Everett F. Cataldo, "Racial and Class Prejudice: Their Relative Effects on Protest Against School Desegregation," *American Sociological Review* 41 (April 1976):280-288.

17. Coleman, Kelly, and Moore, *Trends in School Segregation*, p. 79.

18. Katzman, *Quality of Municipal Services*, chapter 3, p. 28.

19. Armor, "Declaration of David J. Armor."

39

DESEGREGATION AND BLACK ACHIEVEMENT
A Review of the Research[a]

ROBERT L. CRAIN[b] AND RITA E. MAHARD[c]

INTRODUCTION

The effect of desegregation on the performance of black and white students on achievement tests has received an undeserved emphasis in the desegregation literature. There are over a hundred studies of achievement test performance following desegregation. When this is contrasted with the number of studies on other aspects of desegregation, the emphasis is embarrassing—even more embarrassing when the justification for this research is considered. In part, research on the effects of desegregation on achievement test scores is undertaken in the belief that the major problem facing minorities—especially blacks—in this society is their lack of cognitive ability. This argument has been virtually demolished by recent analyses indicating that only a small proportion of the difference in income between blacks and whites can be related statistically to racial differences in cognitive performance.[1] Nevertheless, the emphasis on achievement test scores continues.

The performance of blacks on achievement tests is also of concern because for seventy-five years the lower performance of blacks on such tests has been used to support beliefs in their racial inferiority. Furthermore, it is likely that many black as well as white elites still subscribe to the theory that one can measure the economic productivity and, for that matter, the moral worth of human beings in terms of whether they can state correctly the Pythagorean theorem, add two improper fractions, or select the answer on a multiple choice battery that indicates they have properly decoded a paragraph about the nesting habits of bluebirds. Even assuming that achievement test performance is important, it is still questionable whether factors like the *rate* of change in cognitive performance between the ages of seven and nine will have any great bearing on a student's ability to perform cognitive tasks as an adult.

Although there are good reasons not to overemphasize the importance of achievement test performance, a review of the research literature is still worthwhile. All else being equal, it is probably better to obtain a high score on a test than a low score. The fact that students at a

From Robert L. Crain and Rita E. Mahard, "Desegregation and the Black Achievement: A Review of the Research," 42(2) *Law and Contemporary Problems* (forthcoming). Copyright © 1978 by The Institute of Policy Sciences and Public Affairs, Duke University.

particular school score well may indicate that the school has done a good job of making students want to learn and to do well on tests, which in the long run may be as important as what they actually learn.

One clear answer has already emerged from the research literature on desegregation: virtually every writer on the subject has agreed that the test performance of white students is unaffected by school desegregation.[2] It is safe to assume this issue is settled, at least until some dramatic new research is done; accordingly, the effect of desegregation on the achievement test scores of whites is ignored in this article.

Researchers and writers find it harder, however, to agree on the effect of desegregation on black student achievement, and many argue the merits of desegregation policy on the basis of differing interpretations of the research in this area. The future of desegregation policy will not and should not be determined by test scores, nor will the Supreme Court reverse the *Brown*[3] decision simply because the test scores of black students have not improved as quickly as society thinks they should. Nevertheless, a clearer understanding of the research on desegregation's effects on achievement may have some impact on policy matters. More important, an analysis of existing research suggests optimal strategies for desegregation—for example, at which grade levels desegregation is more likely to have a positive effect on the test scores of blacks.

I

THE RESEARCH STUDIES REVIEWED

A. Studies of "Natural" versus "Intentional" Desegregation

The major input-output analyses of achievement test performance, including the frequently cited *Coleman Report*,[4] are not reviewed in this article for two reasons. First, a good review of this material is now being completed and there seems no reason to duplicate it.[5] Second, the issues studied in this type of research are somewhat different from those in the other studies, so it is useful to keep them separate. The input-output research focuses on school racial composition rather than the type of desegregation as the independent variable. Most of the racially mixed schools in the United States result from what is sometimes called natural desegregation: the assignment to neighborhood schools of students from mixed neighborhoods or from adjoining segregated neighborhoods. Therefore, the input-output studies are evaluating the effect of long-term desegregation, unaffected by public controversy or any impact of busing. In contrast, the other studies of desegregation have, almost without exception, been undertaken during the first two years after a desegregation plan has been implemented. Intentional and natural desegregation are in the long run probably indistinguishable, but the impact of the first two years of intentional desegregation may be different from long-term natural desegregation effects.

A recent review of the input-output studies concludes that there is no relationship between white academic performance and school racial composition, and that, with one exception, black achievement test performance is higher in predominantly white schools.[6] One input-output study of a very large sample—the National Longitudinal Study (NLS) of the 1972 high school senior class[7]—has examined the relationship between school racial composition and black achievement in the North and the South separately.[8] Analysis of the Northern data shows a significant positive relationship between the percentage of white students attending the school and black achievement. However, in the South, black students who attend predominantly white schools do not have higher achievement scores than those who attend all-black schools.[9] The difference in achievement scores between those who attended all-black and those who attended predominantly white schools is shown in Table 1.

The foregoing input-output studies present some methodological problems, including that of how to control for background factors. In most of these studies, the black students who attend predominantly white schools are of higher socioeconomic status than those in segregated schools. When this is the case, the use of a pretest score or a measure of socioeconomic status as a control does not remove all of the differences in achievement related to background. There are various potentially helpful statistical techniques, but ultimately the only answer is perfect measurement of all variables, which is of course impossible. A second problem is that of bias due to self-selection. If black parents who move into integrated neighborhoods are more motivated to advance the achievement of their children than parents who remain in segregated neighborhoods, a bias is introduced that cannot be easily eliminated.[10]

Despite these methodological difficulties, the consistent finding of these input-output studies, which use a variety of methodologies and analyze a variety of data sets, is that black achievement is higher in predominantly white schools. These analyses of so-called natural desegregation fulfill a function that no evaluation of a particular desegregation plan can duplicate. Even the most carefully designed evaluation provides information about only one school system and the ef-

TABLE 1

BLACK SCHOOL-LEVEL ACHIEVEMENT TEST SCORES BY HIGH SCHOOL
PERCENTAGE WHITE AND REGION, STATISTICALLY CONTROLLED FOR
SOCIOECONOMIC STATUS (SES) AND SCHOOL DISTRICT SIZE

	South School Percent White		North School Percent White	
	0%	90%	0%	90%
Mean Black Achievement	41.63	41.90	42.30°	45.99°

° $p < .05$

NOTE: Percentages are derived from a regression equation in which mean black SES, school district size, and school percentage white are used to predict mean black achievement. Black achievement is reported in standard scores (*i.e.*, $\overline{X} = 50$, $\sigma = 10$), and achievement scores are computed from the equations by entering 0% and 90% as values of percent white.

Source: Crain & Mahard, *School Racial Composition and Black College Attendance and Achievement Test Performance*, 51 SOC. OF EDUC., April 1978, at 88.

fects of the first year or two of desegregation. Input-output studies, on the other hand, can measure the long-term effects of desegregation, and in the case of two such studies, provide averages of such effects across a large number of districts.[11]

The conflict over the effects of desegregation will not be resolved by further input-output studies not only because of the methodological problems already noted, but also because of the failure to agree upon how large an effect must be before it can be considered positive.[12] If the standard is *closing* the black-white achievement gap, then desegregation has failed.[13] But we think this is an unreasonable standard; the black-white achievement gap will not disappear overnight. Assuming that the relationship between racial composition and achievement found by these input-output studies is not due to methodological error, it seems absurd to dismiss desegregation on the basis that it will raise black student achievement by "only" one grade level (which makes it a more effective tool for improving black student academic performance than any curriculum innovation or other educational treatment yet devised by educators and researchers).

A review of studies of particular desegregation plans will complement the review of input-output studies now underway.[14] Analyses of desegregation plans can sometimes control for differences in socioeconomic status and for self-selection more carefully than the input-output studies can. Also, if the input-output studies are correct in indicating a long-term positive effect of desegregation on black achievement, it is worthwhile to analyze the process by which that long-term effect is attained. Finally, a comparison of different desegregation plans can provide information on which strategies are most effective.

The short-term desegregation evaluations do not show results as consistently positive as those found in the long-term studies, in part because they are not as methodologically sound. But we also suspect that if desegregation occurs under certain conditions, the short-run effects will not be positive. Student performance can be affected by community conflict, by school desegregation that is not reinforced by neighborhood integration, and by the racial attitudes of black and white students and staff. For example, desegregation may have a short-term negative effect if teachers do not adapt their teaching methods to their new students, or if black students do not make the transition to a white school easily and are upset by racial issues or simply by the change in schools. Thus, a review and comparison of various studies of specific desegregation plans should indicate which characteristics of desegregation plans are most likely to result in immediate positive achievement effects. This question is the primary motivation for this analytical review.

B.   The Sample of Studies Reviewed

The authors have identified approximately 100 studies of the effects of desegregation and black achievement. Of these 100 studies, 41 were obtained and reviewed by the authors,[15] and 32 have been reviewed by either Nancy St. John[16] or Meyer Weinberg[17] in their earlier reviews of the desegregation research literature, making a total of 73 studies analyzed in this article.[18] This sample is limited to studies of specific desegregation plans. Studies of school integration resulting from residential integration are ignored on the assumption that they provide no more information than the generally better quality input-output studies do.

This article owes a great debt to the extensive bibliography prepared by Meyer Weinberg.[19] However, even this bibliography is incomplete. There is surprisingly little overlap between the St. John and Weinberg bibliographies, suggesting that the eighty-seven citations culled from Weinberg for this study may be as little as one-half of the available literature. Even after the inadequate studies and those that duplicate other reports are eliminated, there may be as many as 200 studies in the United States. This is a fugitive literature. Of the forty-one studies the authors have obtained, only sixteen are published in scholarly journals and books. The remainder are unpublished reports and doctoral dissertations.[20]

For the purposes of this review of the research, each of the seventy-three studies that comprised the sample was coded according to the following:

1. The demographic characteristics of the community.
2. The type of desegregation plan.
3. The methodology used in the research.
4. The racial composition of schools before and after desegregation.
5. The grade levels of desegregated students.
6. The direction of the achievement effect, and its magnitude expressed as change in either grade equivalents or standard scores, and reports of any interaction effects in the data (*e.g.*, a finding that desegregation effects are stronger at one grade than another).
7. The presence of special programs to improve the quality of education or to prepare students or staff for desegregation.
8. The source of research funding, the position held by the researchers, and the form of publication.

The strategy of this ongoing study is to examine the relationship between achievement and the type of desegregation plan, the degree of school or staff preparation for desegregation, and the characteristics of the students involved. An important aspect of the study will be to test hypotheses about bias (for example, whether academic researchers fail to publish negative findings). In the present article, only two questions are addressed:

1. What is the average effect of desegregation on black achievement?

2. What are the effects of age of student, region of the country, and voluntary versus mandatory pupil reassignment on black achievement?

Of the seventy-three research studies analyzed for this article, forty find that desegregation has a positive effect on black achievement, and only twelve show a negative result: positive findings outnumber negative findings by a ratio of three to one. The agreement between these studies and the input-output research is encouraging, although some will undoubtedly argue that the achievement gains are usually small compared to the size of the overall black-white achievement gap. No comprehensive statement can be made about the magnitude of these effects of desegregation, since many of the studies do not provide sufficient information to permit the effects to be converted into either standard score differences or grade equivalents.

The forty-one studies reviewed by the authors are a biased sample of the seventy-three, since they include somewhat fewer studies with positive findings and more studies with negative results than are found in the thirty-two studies reviewed by St. John or Weinberg. This is partly because we have interpreted some small differences as negative rather than as zero. A comparison of the results of the studies reviewed by the authors with the results of those reviewed by Weinberg and St. John is given in Table 2.

C. Methodological Issues

Optimum evaluation research follows the experimental model. The experiment is as simple as it is effective, consisting of only three basic steps. First, the population is randomly divided into two groups. Second, a treatment is administered to one of the two groups and not the other, and third, a measurement is made. If there is a difference between the two groups at the end of the experiment, the difference can almost always be assumed to have been caused by the treatment. One serious problem with applying the experimental model to desegregation is that the treatment in this case is of thirteen years duration and no one thus far has been willing to wait that long to publish his results. There are also serious questions about whether the standardized achievement test is the correct measure of cognitive outcomes.

Experimental research can be hard to execute—in some cases, impossible. A mandatory desegregation plan that reassigns every student cannot normally be designed to exclude some students randomly. But there are many cases when experimental design is possible, and at least two studies have used one. The two designs differed only slightly. In both cases, black students in an inner-city school system volunteered to attend predominantly white schools in the suburbs. In the first study, by Mahan and Mahan,[21] a group of inner-city classrooms was identified, and twelve classrooms were selected by a table of random numbers.[22] A subsample

TABLE 2

NUMBER OF STUDIES WITH POSITIVE, ZERO, OR NEGATIVE EFFECTS ON DESEGREGATION
REVIEWED BY THE AUTHORS OR BY ST. JOHN AND WEINBERG

		Reviewer of Studies				
		C + M[a]	St. J.[b]	W[c]	W + St. J.[d]	Total
Effect:	Positive	19	8	7	6	40
	Zero	12	1	3	5	21
	Negative	10	1	0	1	12
Total		41	10	10	12	73
% Positive		46%	80%	70%	50%	55%

  [a] Studies reviewed by the authors.
  [b] Studies not received by the authors at press time but reviewed by Nancy St. John, in
N. ST. JOHN, SCHOOL DESEGREGATION: OUTCOMES FOR CHILDREN (1975).
  [c] Studies not received by the authors at press time but reviewed by Meyer Weinberg, in
M. WEINBERG, MINORITY STUDENTS: A RESEARCH APPRAISAL (1977).
  [d] b + c.

of the unselected classrooms was used as the control group. Parents of
the treatment group were notified, and their cooperation was requested.
Ninety-six percent of the parents agreed to permit their child to attend
suburban schools. Thus, although this was a voluntary project, for research purposes it differed little from a mandatory reassignment except
for the 4 percent who refused. The second study, by Zdep,[23] is more
conventional: parents were asked if they wanted to send their children
to suburban schools voluntarily, and a random sample of treatment and
control students was selected from among the volunteers. Refusing some
volunteers was possible in this case because the suburban school was only
willing to accept a limited number of students.[24]

When a true experimental design cannot be employed, the next best
alternative is a study in which an approximation of a random process
has occurred. The best example of this is the research of Schellenberg
and Halteman in Grand Rapids, Michigan.[25] In this case, students were
reassigned from inner-city schools to white suburban schools to relieve
overcrowding, and the students designated for reassignment were those
who lived in areas farthest from their neighborhood schools. Schellenberg and Halteman argued that there was no reason to assume that
students who lived in the same general residential area differed in any
significant way. In effect, the control group consisted of those who lived
a few blocks nearer their local school than the experimental (bused)
group had.[26] A similar argument can be made with regard to Evans's research on desegregation in Fort Worth.[27] A map of the Fort Worth
desegregation plan indicates that the areas included in the plan are
widely scattered throughout the city and seem to have been chosen
mainly for geographical reasons rather than because of any student
characteristics.

A considerably weaker design is the conventional longitudinal design
with students matched on pretest scores or on socioeconomic status. One
problem is that in a voluntary plan there is a serious possibility of self-
selection bias. This is especially true if the volunteers represent only a
small fraction of the total student population available. Students attending desegregated schools are more likely to have parents who are in-

terested in desegregation, or interested in their child's school perform-ance, or simply more likely to have heard about the plan. Various devices have been used to match students to an artificial control group under these circumstances, but none of these techniques are infallible. Walberg[28] and Armor[29] each evaluated the Boston METCO Plan[30] using siblings of the transferred students as the control group. The argument for sibling matching is that home environment factors and the gene pool are controlled. But this may not be a good solution, since sibling controls virtually maximized the possibility of self-selection bias. Parents chose to bus one of their children but not another. Presumably they did so be-cause of feelings about the differences between their children. We do not know whether the parents would usually select the child most likely to succeed in school or the child having the most difficulty. In either case, a bias has been introduced.

A second problem with research studies that use the conventional longitudinal design also confronts the input-output studies:[31] if the two groups are not identical in social class or ability, the use of a pretest score or a measure of socioeconomic status as a control will not eliminate these differences entirely. A final problem with all studies using control groups is that a control group may not exist. Again, one can take des-perate measures, though they may be ineffective or self-defeating. For example, Carrigan, in her study of school desegregation in Ann Arbor, Michigan,[32] used as her control group black students who were not reas-signed for desegregation purposes. Unfortunately for the research, the reason they were not reassigned is that they were already attending a school that was 50 percent white.

Cross-sectional studies that do not use pretests but instead use black students attending a segregated school as a control are also possible. These have a disadvantage compared to longitudinal studies in that measures of socioeconomic status are not as good at predicting achieve-ment as are pretest achievement scores. Consequently, the cross-sectional studies have a weaker control variable. Their advantage is that they are lower in cost, lend themselves to studies across a number of school dis-tricts simultaneously, and permit the researcher to administer the achievement test, thereby controlling the testing situation.

While it is possible to study the effects of desegregation without a control group comprised of black students who attend segregated schools, the absence of such a control group makes the research prob-lems more critical and complex. Districts in which all students are reas-signed to desegregated schools must be analyzed by comparing the per-formance of the reassigned black students with that of a cohort, with that of white students, or with national norms. A cohort study seeks to determine whether black students in a particular grade after reas-signment are performing better or worse than black students who were in the same grade before desegregation, that is, in an earlier cohort. The necessary assumption is that the students in the two cohorts are similar—that there has been no external trend in the student population over time. More importantly, the cohort study design assumes there is no difference in the testing conditions between the two years. These conditions obviously were not met in at least some of the studies reviewed for this article. Aberdeen's study of the effect of the desegregation of the Ann Arbor schools found a decline in achievement test scores over time.[33] However, Carrigan's analysis of the same data showed that in one year IQ scores of black students in the school district jumped nearly five points.[34] It is doubtful whether either the increase in the IQ scores or the decline in achievement test scores should be trusted. A reanalysis of data from Evanston, Illinois showed that while black achievement scores declined steadily after desegregation, there was a similar decline in the scores of white students, suggesting that something other than desegregation was involved.[35]

The weakest possible research design involves a comparison of the post-desegregation achievement scores of black students with those of white students in the same district or with national norms. In the latter case, this may mean merely a comparison of the test scores of the black students with those of a virtually unknown and probably nonrandom sample used by the test manufacturer. Even under the most careful statistical controls, it is difficult to interpret the results of such comparisons. For example, Perry's study of the talented black students who received scholarships to elite private schools under the ABC (A Better Chance) Program in Boston, found that black achievement scores did not go up.[36] Perry compared black and white students who attained the same scores on their ninth grade tests. When both groups were tested in the twelfth grade, however, the black students performed less well than their white classmates did. Perry was, of course, well aware of the inadequacy of this evidence, given that, under normal conditions, the black-white achievement gap increases with age.[37]

It must not be assumed that methodological weaknesses in a study always tend to produce false positive results. If the methodological weakness is the inability to control adequately for sharply differing pretest conditions between the treatment and the control group, pretest differences are likely to persist, producing a false positive or negative result. If the error is inadequate control for either the known independent national decline in achievement occurring over the past few years, or the known increase with age in the achievement gap between blacks and whites, then a false negative result is more likely. Of the three studies that compared black to white achievement, only one produced a positive result.[38] Of five studies that compared black student performance after desegregation with national norms, three found negative results.[39] The same pattern occurs with the cohort studies. Only three of the eight cohort studies that compared black performance after desegregation to the performance of students in the same grade before desegregation found a positive outcome.[40] In other words, the studies that compare the performance of reassigned black students with that of a cohort, or that of white students, or with national norms produced half of the negative findings in the forty-one studies reviewed by the authors, but only one-third of the positive findings.

In reviewing the forty-one studies, the strongest methodological test was extracted from each study. Frequently, several different tests of the achievement effect were done; the one we judged to be the strongest design is reported. For example, if the study reported a comparison of the achievement of desegregated black students both with national norms and with that of a previous cohort, the latter design is used in this analysis. In some cases, the stronger design was flawed, and a theoretically weaker design was considered to be the better. For example, we discarded Carrigan's control group in our analysis because it consisted of black students attending a biracial school and used her cohort comparison instead.[41]

D.   General Comments on the Sample and on School Desegregation Research

There are a number of excellent studies included in this review of the research that merit recognition. The Mahan and Mahan study of the Hartford Experiment[42] and the Zdep study of Newark and Verona, New Jersey,[43] are carefully executed research designs. The Teele study of Operation Exodus in Boston is impressive because of the author's attempts to outwit an intractable environment and produce a successful evaluation where most people would have given up.[44] Another study that deserves attention is Schellenberg and Halteman's analysis of desegregation in Grand Rapids, Michigan, because more than any other study, it shows an attention to the logic of the control group comparison where randomization is absent.[45] The Evans analysis of Fort Worth[46] and the evaluation of Goldsboro by Mayer, King, Borders-Patterson, and McCullough[47] are outstanding because of the completeness of the data—even maps of the desegregation plan are included. The Goldsboro report analyzes the desegregation planning process, community reaction, the logistics of the desegregation plan, staff preparation, reactions of students to each other, and changes in teaching methods. It is not irrelevant to note that the four authors of this most comprehensive single evaluation of desegregation are a white professor of city planning, a black sociologist, a black testing expert, and a white psychologist. The diversity of race and disciplines is no doubt important to good research.

The experimental tradition in psychology has been a source of both the strengths and the weaknesses of desegregation research. That tradition has provided a sophisticated methodology for desegregation research, but in going from the laboratory to the real world we have lost control of the intervention. No two desegregation plans are alike; there is little reason to expect a uniform treatment effect of desegregation. The common error of this research can be stated in six words: Desegregation is not an educational treatment.

The authors of this article believe this explains why so many of the aspects of desegregation plans that need to be examined are not discussed in these studies. One problem is the absence of studies of the effects of desegregation past the second year. In general, however, our dissatisfaction stems not from the inadequacies of the design but from the inadequacy of the research reporting. For example, it would be useful to know if there is an optimal racial composition for the desegregated school, but three-quarters of the studies do not report the racial composition of the schools either before or after desegregation. It would be useful to know the relationship of different socioeconomic mixes to the impact of desegregation on achievement; again, there are usually no data. There is almost never any information on the school curriculum, staff racial composition, teacher attitudes, staff preparation, special school programs, or community reactions included in the evaluations of desegregation effects. Data on teacher racial behavior would seem to be especially important since several recent studies have suggested that the negative racial attitudes and behaviors of teachers have a harmful effect on black student attitudes and achievement.[48]

II

FACTORS INFLUENCING THE SUCCESS OF DESEGREGATION PLANS

A.   The Effect of Region

A clear regional pattern, shown in Table 3, is demonstrated by the forty-one studies reviewed for this article. Two-thirds of the Southern studies show positive outcomes, compared to only 35 percent of the Northern studies. This result is tentative, at best, since it is not supported by the data from the thirty-two other studies that St. John and Weinberg have reviewed. The studies reviewed by St. John and Weinberg also showed significant positive gains in the South, but differed from the forty-one studies we reviewed in that they also showed a generally positive outcome in the North. It is possible that when these thirty-two other studies are combined with the studies we reviewed, the North-South difference indicated by our analysis will be greatly reduced.

It is safe to conclude at this point, however, that the short-term impact of desegregation in the South is not a negative one. Ten of the fifteen Southern studies in the sample indicated that desegregation produces short-term positive gains. Analysis of the five deviant studies showed them to have more methodological weaknesses than did the ten studies showing positive results. Among the studies indicating that desegregation has a short-term negative impact on black student achievement is Stallings's 1955 study of Louisville[49] after the first year of desegregation, which found that black students who chose to remain with black teachers gained more than the blacks who did not so choose.

TABLE 3

OVERALL DESEGREGATION EFFECTS OF REVIEWED STUDIES, BY REGION

		Region		
		North	South	Total
Effect:	Positive	9	10	19
	Zero	11	1	12
	Negative	6	4	10
Total		26	15	41
% Positive		35%	67%	46%

But scores of both groups went up compared to the preceding year, as did white students' scores;[50] it is hard to argue that desegregation has a negative effect when scores go up. Justin and Thabit[51] found a decline in the test scores of black students after desegregation in Florida, but this study involved a cohort comparison and was accompanied by a white decline as well—a result exactly the opposite of that found by Stallings. These results suggest that the test situation may have changed or that there was a general secular decline in performance at the same time, independent of desegregation. Felice's study of Waco, Texas,[52] found a negative impact on achievement, but his sample was small (only fifty-five students in the control group). In addition, although his control group was matched to the treatment group in terms of their previous achievement levels, they were mismatched on age, grade, and sex, which may have influenced the results. Fortenberry's study of desegregation in Oklahoma,[53] limited to the eighth and ninth grades, was apparently ambushed by unusual differences in the curriculum provided in the black and white schools.[54] Of the five studies showing non-positive results, only a study of Dade County desegregation,[55] which found a decline in the achievement of black students who were reassigned to white schools. Much of the apparent loss due to desegregation can be attributed to a gain over time among black students in segregated schools.

The ten Southern studies that found positive results seem stronger methodologically. These include the two Forth Worth studies[56] and the study by Mayer and his co-workers.[57]

The proposition that methodological differences account for some of the negative results in the Southern studies can be tested in one other way. There is evidence that evaluations done at the end of the first year of desegregation, three obtained negative results;[58] of the seven done at the end of the second year or later, six were positive.[59] Therefore we can hypothesize that the Southern results would be even more positive if all the evaluations had been done after the second year.

These data indicate that desegregation in the South has resulted in consistently positive outcomes, a finding in accord with the findings of the Northern input-output studies of school racial composition.[60] It is not, however, consistent with the input-output analysis of the National Longitudinal Study's Southern data, which showed that black students who attended predominantly white schools did not have higher achievement scores than those who attended all-black schools.[61] This discrepancy can be explained by the fact that the National Longitudinal Study data are on twelfth graders only. These students had experienced only two or three years of desegregation in 1972. It is widely believed, however, that desegregation may not show positive effects until a longer period of time has elapsed. It is also frequently argued that desegregation, to be successful, should occur in the early grades,[62] yet few black seniors attending a Southern high school in 1972 were likely to have attended desegregated elementary schools. All of this suggests that there was insufficient time for positive effects to appear when the 1972 survey was undertaken. This conclusion is supported by the findings of the 1976 National Assessment of Educational Progress, which found that between 1969 and 1973 the achievement of Southern black nine-year-olds went up, while the achievement of nine-year-olds for the nation as a whole declined.[63] The white-black achievement gap decreased for this age group in the South but not for thirteen- or seventeen-year-olds. The achievement gap increased for nine-year-olds in the North. At the same time, the achievement levels of Southern whites did not increase over those of Northern whites.[64] We do not know if the increase in the achievement levels of black nine-year-olds is due to desegregation, although the first substantial desegregation of the South occurred during that time.[65] At about the same time, the quality of schooling available for blacks generally in the South also improved. But if this gain is attributable to desegregation, the fact that it occurred for young students but not for the older ones reconciles the positive findings of the Southern desegregation evaluations with the NLS results in the South.

There is some evidence that desegregation increases black achievement in the long run as well as in the short run—at least in the South and in the early grades. The important questions are how desegregation raises achievement, to what extent it does, and what kinds of desegregation plans are most effective. These questions can best be considered together, since knowing that a certain type of plan is effective can provide clues to why desegregation works.

B.   Grade Level at Which Desegregation First Occurs

Although most of the conclusions drawn from our review of the desegregation research are debatable, on one aspect the results are clear and unmistakable: the earlier the grade at which desegregation occurs, the more positive the impact on achievement. Of the studies we have reviewed, fourteen showed a more positive impact on the achievement scores of students desegregated in earlier grades than on those desegregated in the later grades.[66] Only three found the opposite effect. Beker's study in Syracuse[67] used a tiny sample—his total control group contained only twenty-three students, which could hardly be sorted by grade and produce meaningful results. Evans's study of the first year of desegregation in Fort Worth also found a greater achievement gain in the higher rather than the lower grades,[68] but his own follow-up study a year later reversed this conclusion.[69] The Dade County study also found larger achievement gains in the upper grades than in the lower grades, but this seems to be explained not by the high performance of upper-grade students assigned to white schools, but by a rather dramatic drop in the performance of the upper-grade students remaining in the segregated schools.[70] The achievement of these segregated black students decreased by about a third of a year in comparison with the preceding year's class even though black achievement in other grades went up. The fourteen studies indicating greater achievement gains in the earlier grades are methodologically stronger than these three studies.[71] Even some studies whose overall effects were zero show positive results in the early grades.[72] St. John and Weinberg report three other studies in which stronger results occurred in the lower grades.[73] Both reviewers have concluded that desegregating the early grades is preferable to desegregating older students.[74]

As a further test of the hypothesis, we related the impact of desegregation on achievement reported in the different studies to the grades that were tested. The results of this analysis support the conclusion that desegregation in the early grades is more successful in terms of achievement gains than is desegregation in later grades. Of twelve studies of desegregation undertaken at the junior high school and high school level,[75] five showed negative effects,[76] while none of ten studies of desegregation undertaken in the first and second grades showed negative results.[77] Data showing the relationship between achievement outcomes and grade level at which desegregation occurred are given in Table 4 for the sample of forty-one studies we reviewed, as well as for twenty-one additional studies for which Weinberg and St. John provided data by grade level. All three sets of studies support the hypothesis.

The critical point, as indicated by the data presented in Table 4, is at the second or third grade, since only twelve of the twenty-four studies of desegregation that occurred in grades three or four showed positive achievement results.[78] These grades are at the center of an age range that Inbar has called the "vulnerable age."[79] His study of persons migrating to Israel indicated that those who migrated between the ages of six and eleven were less likely later to attend college than those who came at either younger or older ages.[80] This result was replicated by the same researcher using data on migration to Canada and regional migration within the United States.[81] A similar pattern was found for blacks who migrated from the South to the North at this age.[82] As early as 1953, the theory was propounded that the elementary school years are an important period for establishing social relationships, so that social relationships should not be disrupted during this time.[83] If this theory is correct, the social migration that occurs as a result of desegregation may have effects analogous to geographic migration.

It has been frequently urged that desegregation begin in the early grades. It is gratifying to see empirical evidence support the conventional wisdom so clearly—although if the Inbar finding is pertinent, even third grade may not be early enough.

TABLE 4

GRADE FIRST DESEGREGATED RELATED TO ACHIEVEMENT OUTCOMES

Studies of Southern Desegregation Reviewed by the Authors

Average (Mean) Grade First Desegregated

	1–2	3–4	5–6	7–9	10–12	TOTAL
Positive	2	3	2	2	1	10
Zero	0	0	1	0	0	1
Negative	0	1	1	1	1	4
Total	2	4	4	3	2	15 $(\gamma = .40)$
Percent Positive	100%	75%	50%	67%	50%	

Studies of Northern Desegregation Reviewed by the Authors

Average (Mean) Grade First Desegregated

	1–2	3–4	5–6	7–9	10–12	TOTAL
Positive	3	3	3	0	0	9
Zero	2	7	1	1	0	11
Negative	0	3	1	2	0	6
Total	5	13	5	3	–	26 $(\gamma = .36)$
Percent Positive	60%	23%	60%	0%	–	

Additional Studies Reviewed by Weinberg and/or St. John

Average (Mean) Grade First Desegregated

	1–2	3–4	5–6	7–9	10–12	TOTAL
Positive	3	6	5	1	0	15
Zero	0	1	5	0	2	8
Negative	0	0	1	0	1	2
Total	3	7	11	1	3	25 $(\gamma = .77)$
Percent Positive	100%	86%	45%	100%	0%	

NOTE: Only 25 of 32 studies reviewed by Weinberg and/or St. John appear in this table; the reviewer did not indicate the grade level at which desegregation occurred in the other 7 studies.

C. Curriculum Factors

St. John argues that achievement gains as a result of desegregation are more likely to occur in mathematics than in reading.[84] Of the forty-one studies we reviewed, ten show this to be the case.[85] Only three studies find stronger effects in reading than in mathematics. However, these three studies cannot be dismissed so easily, since they represent some of the methodologically best desegregation studies undertaken.[86] The general rule seems to be that achievement gains are specifically related to curriculum. Where there is a marked difference in part of the curriculum of the sending and of the receiving schools, achievement changes—sometimes dramatic ones—will occur in that subject. It may be true that mathematics is usually easier to learn in most desegregated schools, but this may be because of curriculum differences and not a necessary consequence of racial interaction.[87] One of the best examples of this is seen in the experiment undertaken by Zdep.[88] The first-grade students randomly assigned to white suburban schools raised their achievement scores in mathematics three grade levels more than their segregated counterparts.[89] At the same time the second graders in the desegregation experiment lost nearly half a grade level compared to their segregated counterparts.[90] Zdep noted, however, that the suburban schools used a high quality modern math curriculum for which the transferring second graders had an inadequate background. The most dramatic example of what is probably a curriculum effect appears in ample of what is probably a curriculum effect appears in Williams's evaluation of a desegregation program in a Florida county.[91] The segregated secondary school was a six-year consolidated school with only 100 students per grade and only thirty teachers in the school. Williams noted that the curriculum was "not comprehensive." Half of the black students transferred at the end of the ninth grade to the white high school, which was much larger and had what Williams called a "fully comprehensive" high school program. The pretest administered in the ninth grade showed the transferring and control students to have the same verbal and quantitative IQ scores and achievement levels. The posttest, administered in the twelfth grade, showed the verbal IQ scores to be the same for both groups, but indicated that the quantitative IQ scores of the desegregated group had gone up a little over one and one half grade levels.[92] In achievement, their English-language skills had increased nearly three grade levels and their performance in social studies, math, and science had increased by a little less than one and one half grade levels or more.[93] Thus the desegregated students had all gained an average of two to three additional grades in achievement in three years. In other words, their rate of growth was more than double that of the segregated students, with no change in verbal IQ. The only plausible explanation for such extreme gains is that the white "comprehensive" high school had a markedly better curriculum.

Another study showing rather dramatic results that seem to be unexplainable except as a curriculum effect is Fortenberry's study of Oklahoma City.[94] His is one of the Southern studies that shows no positive overall effect of desegregation. The study does, however, show marked differences in individual subject matter areas. His control and treatment groups were matched on the basis of a sixth-grade achievement test. By the ninth grade, the desegregated students had declined seven-tenths of a grade in reading ability compared to the students in the control group. This is a disturbing result, but it becomes especially intriguing in view of the fact that these same desegregated students went up 1.2 grade levels in language arts. Obviously, these tests are not measuring a single verbal skill; the black school must have been doing a better job teaching reading, but not the mechanics of writing.

In general, where there are radically different curricula, desegregation can have sharply different effects in specific subject matter areas. In most studies of elementary school desegregation, this will generally appear as greater achievement gains in mathematics for desegregated students. In high school, it may appear in any of a variety of subject matter areas. The remarkable results of the desegregation program in Brevard County, Florida, as found by Williams,[95] can only be reconciled with the absence of any significant achievement differences between most segregated and desegregated Southern high schools as a result of desegregation, as indicated by the NLS analysis, by arguing that most of the woefully inadequate small segregated high schools of the South, located mostly in rural areas, had been closed in 1972. The Southern black students in segregated schools surveyed by the NLS cannot have been attending schools like the one Williams studied.

D.   Voluntary and Mandatory Plans

Desegregation plans were analyzed for this article according to whether the black students were mandatorily reassigned for desegregation or were volunteers. The results of this analysis are shown in Table 5. The twenty-six Northern studies that we reviewed show a definite pattern—achievement gains are more likely to occur when reassignment is mandatory. Only two positive results among the eleven studies of Northern voluntary plans were found,[96] while of fifteen studies of Northern mandatory plans, seven showed positive results.[97] The St. John and Weinberg studies that we have not yet reviewed show a similar pattern: voluntary plans are evaluated positively in nine of twelve studies, but mandatory plans show positive results seven times out of eight.[98]

A methodological analysis of the exceptions was undertaken. Of the eleven voluntary plans, the two voluntary plans that produced positive results were those analyzed by Zdep[99] and Teele.[100] There are peculiar aspects of each study that might explain the aberrant results, although

TABLE 5

VOLUNTARY AND MANDATORY PLANS IN NORTHERN SCHOOL DISTRICTS
RELATED TO ACHIEVEMENT OUTCOMES

Review Sample

	Voluntary	Mandatory	Total
Positive	2	7	9
Zero	5	6	11
Negative	4	2	6
Total	11	15	26
Percent Positive	18%	47%	35%

$\gamma = .54$

St. John/Weinberg Sample

	Voluntary	Mandatory	Total
Positive	9	7	16
Zero	2	1	3
Negative	1	0	1
Total	12	8	20
Percent Positive	75%	87%	80%

$\gamma = .42$

Review Sample Using Only Longitudinal Designs
With Black Control Group

	Voluntary	Mandatory	Total
Positive	1	4	5
Zero	3	2	5
Negative	2	0	2
Total	6	6	12
Percent Positive	17%	67%	42%

$\gamma = .85$

the peculiarities are not methodological. The Zdep study used random assignment. Although the Teele study is methodologically weak, because the Boston School Committee refused to allow the researcher access to a control group, Teele did a brilliant job of, to use his phrase, "patching up" the study.[101] Both studies have some unusual aspects, however. The Zdep study involved a very strong quality of schooling effect, since the black students who remained in segregated schools were on half-day sessions due to overcrowding. This might explain a portion of the very large increase in achievement found for the desegregated students, who gained nearly three grade levels in the first and second grade overall.[102]

In addition, both experiments had a somewhat unusual method for recruiting volunteers. The voluntary-mandatory distinction in these studies is a continuum. Programs vary from highly voluntary plans, where only a small number of students select the plan (such as in the ABC Program of sending black students to prep school),[103] all the way to a virtually mandatory plan such as that analyzed by Mahan and Mahan, in which 96 percent of the parents agreed to "volunteer."[104] Zdep's design is almost identical to the Mahans', except that permission slips were requested before reassignment rather than after.[105] Zdep does not give the exact number of parents who agreed to reassignment, but it is at least 50 percent.[106] If a very large number of parents agreed to reassignment, then for all practical purposes the plan is identical to a mandatory plan. The Teele study is also different from most voluntary plans in that the volunteers were recruited not by the school district but by a private black parents' organization, Operation Exodus.[107] An open enrollment plan in the North run by public school authorities appeals to a certain type of parent. Operation Exodus, which had an ideological community organization behind it, may have reached a very different set of parents.

Among the nine voluntary studies that did not find positive effects, there are several of good quality. The Fox study of open enrollment in New York City, which has a large sample size, found that students who volunteered for reassignment did not do as well as those who stayed behind in segregated schools.[108] Two voluntary programs in Syracuse,[109] the two evaluations of METCO,[110] Wolman's evaluation in New Rochelle,[111] and the Thompson and Dyke evaluation in Rochester[112] also found no achievement gains resulting from desegregation. Two other studies are less useful since they dealt with private school populations: Perry's study of ABC,[113] which is clearly not comparable to any public school program, and Gardner's analysis of open enrollment in the Chicago Catholic School System.[114] The most that can be said here is that there seem to be some conditions under which voluntary programs are not successful.

A methodological analysis of the Northern mandatory studies indicates that the studies that obtained positive results are methodologically superior to those that did not. Of the fifteen Northern mandatory studies, eight do not show positive results, but seven of those eight have characteristics that weaken their conclusions. Aberdeen's study of desegregation in Ann Arbor, Michigan shows negative results, but he used national norms as the standard, and in the middle of the evaluation the school district changed the test it was using.[115] Carrigan's study of Ann Arbor used black students attending an integrated school as the control group.[116]

The problems inherent in cohort analysis[117] also plague the evaluations of the Riverside, California desegregation.[118] Gerard and Miller attempted to use a segregated control group, since one of the elementary schools in the district was desegregated in two stages, with half the students remaining behind for the first year. Thus, a comparison of the two halves of the student body, where, according to Gerard and Miller, there was no reason to believe that the two groups differed, shows the impact of an additional year of desegregation on one group but not on the other. However, the elementary school was entirely Mexican American, and consequently the evaluation is not comparable to studies of black-white desegregation. Fortunately, Gerard and Miller tabulated the data for blacks and Mexican Americans separately, which made it possible for us to construct a cohort evaluation for blacks. The cohort evaluation indicates no gain in achievement, but there is no information as to the sort of trends in achievement test administration that occurred independently of desegregation, what trends occurred in the composition of the district, or whether the various tests used at various times are exactly comparable. The Kurtz reanalysis of Evanston data,[119] using a cohort design, also failed to produce positive results, but since he found that white as well as black scores were declining, the outcome is suspect. A cohort evaluation of Berkeley school desegregation is ambiguous, since although there was no change in achievement overall, the effects were positive in the lower grades.[120] Both St. John and Weinberg reviewed other studies of Berkeley that showed positive outcomes.[121] An evaluation in White Plains, which showed no significant effects, was based on a very small sample (treatment and control groups together amounted to sixty-nine students).[122]

In sum, it seems reasonable to discount heavily these seven studies of five cities.[123] Thus, of the eight studies of Northern mandatory plans that do not show positive results, only the one by Schellenberg and Halteman seems to be a carefully designed study of good quality, with an adequate control sample.[124]

The seven studies that found positive results in Northern mandatory desegregation plans seem much stronger.[125] Four of these use adequate control groups. The Syracuse study is based on a single school,[126] but the Buffalo study,[127] a study of the Sacramento school system,[128] and a study of the Hartford Experiment[129] used students from several schools. We systematically tested the hypothesis that the studies with positive findings are stronger methodologically than those with negative findings. The Northern studies that were longitudinal designs using a black control group were analyzed separately. These twelve studies, presented at the bottom of Table 5, show a stronger correlation between achievement outcomes and whether the plan is mandatory or voluntary. Four of the six mandatory studies show positive results, while only one of the six voluntary studies does.

On the whole, the evidence suggests that there is a significant correlation between mandatory assignment and positive achievement outcomes.[130] We are reluctant to recommend policies based on a finding so clearly counterintuitive, other than to suggest caution on the part of those recommending voluntary desegregation plans for blacks over mandatory plans and denouncing mandatory busing as an especially evil form of desegregation.

There are several possible explanations for the foregoing results. The obvious explanation is that the volunteering blacks are more talented than those that choose to remain in segregated schools, and that the desegregated blacks do not improve because they were doing well before desegregation. But this does not fit the data; volunteers generally do not have higher pretest scores. The opposite seems more plausible: elementary school students are volunteered for desegregation programs by their parents not because their children are doing well in segregated schools, but because they are doing poorly. Why reassign a student who is happy in school? Is it not more likely that in a program like METCO, parents will select the child who is doing badly in school, rather than the sibling who is doing well?[131] But doing well in school is partly, or perhaps largely, a matter of adaption to bureaucratic structure and to authority. Transferring to a white school requires even more adaptation, and it may be that the least adaptive students were volunteered to make this transition. While this hypothesis does not make as much sense for secondary school students, none of the studies of voluntary plans involved secondary school students except the study of the prep school ABC Program.[132] Presumably, most secondary student volunteers are not motivated to change schools because they are doing badly where they are, but because they want to enhance their chances of going to college. This suggests the possibility of a positive self-selection bias in secondary school and a negative bias in elementary school. If this hypothesis is correct, then positive effects should occur for students transferring to predominantly white schools at the secondary level, or during kindergarten and first or second grade (before the average child has established an academic record on which a parent could base a decision). This hypothesis receives some support from the data, since the only studies of voluntary desegregation at kindergarten or first grade are Zdep's,[133] which found positive effects, and Wolman's,[134] which found the strongest effects at kindergarten, although the upper grades showed nonsignificant differences. St. John reports on two other studies of voluntary desegregation, one for kindergarten through second grade and one for second grade only, both of which show positive effects.[135]

The hypothesis that the least adaptive elementary school students will be volunteered does not seem plausible for the South, however. One would hardly expect a Southern black parent whose child was doing poorly in school to believe that he would be happier in a white school. It seems reasonable to argue that Southern pioneering parents were motivated mainly by ideological concerns. If this was the case, the lack of positive results from studies of voluntary desegregation in the South cannot be explained. The desegregated students are not doing as well as others who refused the opportunity to transfer, but they might have done worse than the nonvolunteers if they had remained in the segregated school. If so, there is a methodological error in the design, since the control group does not match the treatment group. The second possibility is that the students who refused to transfer would have benefited from desegregation while those who volunteered did not; this is an aptitude-treatment interaction effect.

Another hypothesis to explain the lack of positive outcomes from voluntary plans is that no one would have benefited from desegregation in such cases. We suspect that when the plan is voluntary, there is very little pressure on the receiving schools to adapt to the incoming students. The principal, teachers, and central administration may feel that if students are volunteering to transfer to their school, the school must be a good one and there is no reason to change. In contrast, mandatory desegregation often involves staff desegregation, in-service training of teachers, and curriculum changes. The new black teachers in the desegregated school may become spokesmen for the black students, and the community attention on the schools may make teachers and administrators feel that their student body has changed in some important ways, requiring the school to accommodate itself to this change. All of this activity may make mandatory desegregation work better than voluntary desegregation.

The final hypothesis is related to the theory of the impact of disrupting social relationships.[136] If migration has unfortunate effects because it disrupts the newly forming social bonds of the elementary school child, then voluntary desegregation will disrupt this pattern more than a mandatory reassignment. In a mandatory plan, a black student either moves with many of his classmates to a classroom in a white school, or remains with many classmates while whites are brought into his school. In either case, the result is less disruptive than if he volunteers to move and leaves most of his classmates behind.

These hypotheses are tentative. We do not recommend that voluntary plans be terminated in Northern elementary schools on the basis of these data. But there are some recommendations that seem reasonable to make about voluntary desegregation plans instituted in the North:

1. Voluntary desegregation programs should begin in kindergarten or first grade.
2. Vigorous promotion efforts should be made to recruit as many volunteers as possible to minimize possible self-selection bias and create a critical mass of transferring students.

3. School faculty and staff should be permitted to recommend intensive remedial work for students who seem to have serious problems in school.
4. Receiving school staffs should be desegregated, and the receiving schools should be encouraged to use desegregation as an opportunity to achieve needed reforms in the school program.

IV

SUMMARY: WHAT CAN BE SAID ABOUT DESEGREGATION AND ACHIEVEMENT?

The best studies of the effects of school desegregation on the achievement of black students have in common a recognition of an important fact about desegregation—that desegregation is not a laboratory-controlled experiment that is identical in Jacksonville, Florida and in Berkeley, California. Every case is different, and identical results should not be expected. Thus one answer to the question, What is the effect of desegregation on achievement? is that sometimes it works and sometimes it doesn't. But this is true of any intervention. Can anything more be said? The answer seems to be yes, but it is important to frame the question carefully. If the question is, Has desegregation resulted in improved achievement for blacks? the answer hardly needs study, since desegregation has resulted in the closing of many inadequate segregated schools in both the North and the South. If the question is, Will desegregation in the future improve the achievement of black students? the answer seems to be yes, with perhaps some reservations.

Pooling the data from the forty-one studies reviewed by the authors and the thirty-two studies reviewed by St. John and Weinberg, thirty-nine studies of desegregation plans involving mandatory assignment of black students have been identified in both the North and the South. Twenty-four of these evaluations report achievement gains, and five show losses—a four-to-one ratio favoring positive outcomes. The average gain in achievement (on the few studies where we have been able to code quantitative data) is around one-half of a grade-equivalent change in the first one or two years. The input-output studies show somewhat larger differences.

A policymaker will not be satisfied with this answer, however. He may ask, "Which is the most effective way to raise the achievement levels of black students—through desegregation or through improving the quality of education in segregated schools?" Here the answer is probably that both approaches are effective; not enough research has been done to determine which is more effective. If the policymaker then asks, "Are the gains in black achievement resulting from desegregation worth the social and political cost?" the question has no scientific answer, and becomes a matter of values.

We have stressed the differences between these various questions in order to suggest that the contradictory statements made by social scientists reflect not only disagreement about the data, but disagreement about the question being asked. The best examples of this confusion are the statements made about desegregation's impact on the achievement gap. Certainly differences between black and white achievement are interesting, but the idea that black achievement is only worth having if it erases the gap seems to be based on a confused idea of the policy issues. There is also confusion about the sorting out of the direct and indirect effects of desegregation. For example, are the Zdep[137] and Williams[138] studies a fair test of desegregation's effects, since in one case the black school used as the control was hopelessly overcrowded and in the other case had an inadequate curriculum? The answer is certainly yes, since desegregation was the policy instrument that provided uncrowded schools and adequate curricula for these blacks. This does not mean that desegregation always means movement from a poor educational situation to a better one, which is why other studies do not show effects similar to these two. Both the Zdep and Williams studies recorded black achievement gains of from one and one half to three grade levels in two to three years.[139] More typical positive results are on the order of a little over half a grade level.[140]

Part of the confusion surrounding desegregation research arises because academics have frequently not viewed desegregation from a policymaking viewpoint. They have been too fascinated by what is intellectually the most interesting question: All else being equal, will the mixing of races alone result in higher black achievement? That question cannot be answered, because in the real world desegregation is never an "all else being equal" situation. Desegregation sometimes results in better curricula or facilities; it often results in blacks having better trained or more cognitively skilled teachers; it is frequently accompanied by a major effort to upgrade the quality of education; and it almost always results in socioeconomic desegregation. When desegregation is accompanied by all of these factors, it should not be surprising that there are immediate achievement gains half to two-thirds of the time. This suggests that desegregation is sufficient but not necessary to obtain these gains, since there are other ways to achieve curriculum reform or better teaching if the political will is present.

The presence of all these complicating factors makes it difficult to determine exactly why desegregation has beneficial achievement effects when it does, and why it sometimes fails to produce these effects. Various writers have argued that desegregation is most successful in raising achievement when it results in one or more of five favorable conditions:

1. Black students have transferred to schools that have better facilities and better teaching.
2. The expectations to which blacks are held are higher in their new schools.

3. The newly desegregated schools have undergone a flurry of in-service preparation for teachers and have adopted new curricula.
4. Black students are influenced by higher-status college-bound white peers with better study habits and less rebellious attitudes toward school.
5. Black students develop a greater amount of self-confidence from discovering that they can cope, both socially and academically, in a white environment.

However, it is easy to imagine a desegregated situation where none of these five conditions occurs. Thanks to Title I of the Elementary and Secondary Education Act[141] and the national concern about black achievement, many all-black schools have excellent facilities and staff. The white receiving schools may have teachers who are lazy or unconcerned, or whose training is obsolete. They may hold unfavorable attitudes toward blacks and express this in the low expectations they set for black students. The school may be unwilling to adapt to the new situation. Race relations may be so poor that peer effects across races cannot occur, and black students may develop a sense of futility.

Between these two extremes are more complex cases, when one or another of these favorable factors appears, while others do not. For example, what achievement effects can be expected in schools that are desegregated but predominantly black? If the white minority is bused into the school, the school administration may go to great lengths to strengthen the curriculum and modernize the facilities. On the other hand, if the white minority is a low-income group living near a black neighborhood, the school may be perceived as a slum school and treated as one, so that few significant reforms may result. As we begin to tease out the possibilities, we can see that the pattern of interaction effects is very complex.

In future research, the authors of this interim report plan to search for these higher-order relationships to answer some of the following questions:

1. What is the optimal racial composition of a desegregated school?
   a. Does this differ for different socioeconomic mixes?
   b. Does the optimum change during the first few years of the plan?
2. What is the impact of desegregation over time? Are achievement effects cumulative, or is there a "honeymoon" followed by a crisis?
3. What is the impact on desegregation of white and black student socioeconomic status? Is there an optimal difference between the socioeconomic backgrounds of black and white students brought together by desegregation for producing achievement gains?

We suspect that if these questions can be answered we will be closer to knowing why desegregation raises black achievement in the short run (as it often appears to do) and in the long run (which apparently it almost always does). We should certainly know why it fails in the short run, which also happens. We do not believe that research will ever tell us whether desegregation is "good" or "bad," since this is more a matter of values than of data.

Appendix I

List of Studies Reviewed by the Authors

† Aberdeen, Frank D. "Adjustment to Desegregation: A Description of Some Differences Among Negro Elementary School Pupils." Ed.D. dissertation, University of Michigan, 1969. University Microfilms Order No. 70-04025.

‡ Anderson, Louis V. "The Effect of Desegregation on the Achievement and Personality Patterns of Negro Children." Ph.D. dissertation, George Peabody College for Teachers, 1966. University Microfilms Order No. 66-11237.

* Armor, David J. "The Evidence on Busing." *The Public Interest* 28 (1972), pp. 90–126.

Baltzell, D. Catherine. "Rapid Desegregation and Academic Achievement in a Large Urban School District." Paper presented at the annual meeting of the American Education Research Association, April 1974, in Chicago, Illinois. ERIC Document No. 090 282.

Beers, Joan S., and Reardon, Francis J. "Racial Balancing in Harrisburg: Achievement and Attitudinal Changes." *Integrated Education* 12 (1974), pp. 35–38.

* Beker, Jerome. "A Study of Integration in Racially Imbalanced Urban Public Schools—A Demonstration and Evaluation." Final report to the Syracuse University Youth Development Center, Syracuse, New York, May 1967. Mimeographed.

Bondarin, Arley. "The Racial Balance Plan of White Plains, New York." Report to the Center for Urban Education, New York, New York, 1970. ERIC Document No. 012 710.

‡ Carrigan, Patricia M. "School Desegregation via Compulsory Pupil Transfer: Early Effects on Elementary School Children." Ann Arbor, Michigan: Ann Arbor Public Schools, September 1969. ERIC Document No. 036 597.

Clark County School District. "Desegregation Report." Las Vegas, Nevada: Clark County School District, July 1974. ERIC Document No. 106 397.

§ Dambacher, Arthur D. "A Comparison of Achievement Test Scores Made by Berkeley Elementary Students Pre and Post Integration Eras, 1967–1970." Mimeographed. Berkeley, California: Berkeley Unified School District, 1971.

† Denmark, Florence L. "The Effect of Integration on Academic Achievement and Self-Concept." *Integrated Education* 8 (1970), pp. 34–41.

* Dressler, Frank J. "Study of Achievement in Reading of Pupils Transferred from Schools 15 and 37 to Peripheral Schools to Eliminate Overcrowding, to Abandon an Obsolete School, and to Achieve a More Desirable Racial Balance in City Schools." Mimeographed. Buffalo, New York: Buffalo Public Schools, Division of Curriculum Evaluation and Development, March 1967.

Evans, Charles L. "Short-term Desegregation Effects: The Academic Achievement of Bused Students, 1971–72." Fort Worth, Texas: Fort Worth Independent School District, 1973. ERIC Document No. 086 759.

Evans, Charles L. "Integration Evaluation: Desegregation Study II—Academic Effects on Bused Black and Receiving White Students, 1972–73." Forth Worth, Texas: Fort Worth Independent School District, 1973. ERIC Document No. 094 087.

Felice, Lawrence G. "The Effects of School Desegregation on Minority Group Student Achievement and Self-Concept: An Evaluation of Court-Ordered Busing in Waco, Texas." Waco, Texas: Research Development Foundation, 1974. ERIC Document No. 094 096.

* Fortenberry, James H. "The Achievement of Negro Pupils in Mixed and Non-Mixed Schools." Ed.D. dissertation, University of Oklahoma, 1959. University Microfilms Order No. 59-05492.

* Fox, David J., Stuart, Colleen, and Pitts, Vera. "Services to Children in Open Enrollment Receiving Schools: Evaluation of ESEA Title I Projects in New York City, 1967–68." Mimeographed. New York, New York: New York Center for Urban Education, December 1968. ERIC Document No. 034 004.

* Frary, Robert B., and Goolsby, Thomas M. "Achievement of Integrated and Segregated Negro and White First Graders in a Southern City." *Integrated Education* 8 (1970), pp. 48–52.

* Gardner, Burleigh B., Wright, Benjamin D., and Sister Rita Dee. "The Effect of Busing Black Ghetto Children into White Suburban Schools." Archdiocese of Chicago, Illinois: Chicago Catholic School Board, July 1970. ERIC Document No. 048 389.

† Gerard, Harold B., and Miller, Norman. *School Desegregation: A Long-Term Study*. New York: Plenum Press, 1975.

Justin, Neal E., and Thabit, Judy. "Black and White Achievement Before and After Integration," *Intellect* 102 (1974), pp. 458–59.

Kurtz, Harold. "An Independent Assessment of 'Integration in Evanston, 1967–1971: A Longitudinal Evaluation': A Report on the Educational Consequences of Desegregation in District 65 of Evanston, Illinois." U.S., Congress, House, Committee on the Judiciary, Subcomm. No. 5, 92d Cong., 2d Sess., 1972, pp. 1436–43.

§ Mahan, Thomas W., and Mahan, Aline M. "The Impact of Schools on Learning: Inner-City Children in Suburban Schools." *Journal of School Psychology* 9 (1971), pp. 1–11.

Mayer, Robert R., King, C., Borders-Patterson, A., and McCullough, J. *The Impact of School Desegregation in a Southern City*. Boston: D.C. Heath, 1974.

Maynor, Waltz, and Katzenmeyer, W. G. "Academic Performance and School Integration: A Multi-Ethnic Analysis." *Journal of Negro Education* 43 (1974), pp. 30–38.

* Perry, George A., and Kopperman, N. "A Better Chance: Evaluation of Student Attitudes and Academic Performance, 1964–1972." Boston: A Better Chance, 1973. ERIC Document No. 075 556.

‡ Prichard, Paul N. "The Effects of Desegregation on Student Success in the Chapel Hill Schools." *Integrated Education* 7 (1969), pp. 33–38.

‡ Sacramento City Unified School District. "Focus on Reading and Mathematics 1970–71: An Evaluation Report on a Program of Compensatory Education, ESEA Title I. Sacramento, California: Sacramento City Unified School District, July 1971.

Schellenberg, James, and Halteman, John. "Bussing and Academic Achievement: A Two-Year Follow Up." *Urban Education* 10 (1976), pp. 357–65.

Singer, Harry. "Effect of Integration on Achievement of Anglos, Blacks, and

Mexican-Americans." Paper presented at the annual meeting of the American Education Research Association, March 3–6, 1970, in Minneapolis, Minnesota. ERIC Document No. 041 975.

* Stallings, Frank H. "A Study of the Immediate Effects of Integration on Scholastic Achievement in the Louisville Public Schools." *Journal of Negro Education* 28 (1959), pp. 439–44.

† Stephenson, Robert, and Spieth, Phillip. "Evaluation of Desegregation 1970–1971." Miami, Florida: Dade County Public Schools Department of Program Evaluation, June 1972. ERIC Document No. 070 792.

† Syracuse City School District. "Study of the Effect of Integration—Croton and Edward Smith Elementary School Pupils." In *Hearing Held in Rochester, New York, September 16–17*. U.S. Commission on Civil Rights, 1966, pp. 327–28.

† Syracuse City School District. "Study of the Effect of Integration—Washington Irving and Host Pupils." *Hearing Held in Rochester, New York, September 16–17*. U.S. Commission on Civil Rights, 1966, pp. 323–36.

† Teele, James E. *Evaluating School Busing: A Case Study of Boston's Operation Exodus*. New York: Praeger, 1973. ERIC Document No. 083 334.

† Thompson, Carolyn E., and Dyke, Frances L. *First Interim Evaluation Report: Urban-Suburban Pupil Transfer Program 1971–1972*. Rochester, New York: Rochester City School District, August 1972. ERIC Document No. 068 609.

‡ Walberg, Herbert J. *An Evaluation of an Urban-Suburban School Busing Program: Student Achievement and Perception of Class Learning Environment*. Paper presented at the annual meeting of the American Education Research Association, February 1971, in New York, New York. ERIC Document No. 047 076.

‡ Williams, Frank E. "An Analysis of Some Differences Between Negro High School Seniors from a Segregated High School and a Nonsegregated High School in Brevard County, Florida." Ed.D. dissertation, University of Florida, 1968. University Microfilms Order No. 69-17050.

‡ Wolman, T.G. "Learning Effects of Integration in New Rochelle." *Integrated Education* 2 (1964), pp. 30–31.

§ Zdep, Stanley M. "Educating Disadvantaged Urban Children in Suburban Schools: An Evaluation." *Journal of Applied Social Psychology* 1 (1971), pp. 173–8.

* Referenced by St. John
† Referenced by Weinberg
‡ Referenced by St. John and Weinberg
§ St. John and Weinberg cite different versions of the same study
  Evans's 1971–72 and 1972–73 studies were coded separately.
Mayer's ninth grade had no control group and consequently was coded separately.

APPENDIX II

STUDIES NOT RECEIVED BY PRESS TIME BUT REVIEWED BY ST. JOHN

Archibald, David K. "Report on Change in Academic Achievement for a Sample of Elementary School Children: Progress Report on METCO." Mimeographed. Roxbury, Massachusetts, 1967.

Clinton, Ronald R. "A Study of the Improvement in Achievement of Basic Skills of Children Bused from Urban to Suburban School Environments." Master's thesis, Southern Connecticut State College, 1969.

Danahy, Ann H. "A Study of the Effects of Bussing on the Achievement, Attendance, Attitudes, and Social Choices of Negro Inner-City Children." Ed.D. dissertation, University of Minnesota, 1971. University Microfilms Order No. 72-14285.

Heller, Barbara R. "Project Concern: Westport, Connecticut." New York: Center for Urban Education, June 1972.

Jonsson, Harold A. "Report of Evaluation of ESEA Title I Compensatory Activities for 1966–67. Mimeographed. Berkeley, California: Berkeley Unified School District, 1967.

Laird, Mary, and Weeks, Grace. "The Effect of Bussing on Achievement in Reading and Arithmetic in Three Philadelphia Schools." Mimeographed. Philadelphia, Pennsylvania: School District of Philadelphia, Division of Research, 1966.

McCullough, James S. "Academic Achievement Under School Desegregation in a Southern City." Mimeographed. Chapel Hill, North Carolina: Department of City and Regional Planning, University of North Carolina at Chapel Hill, January 1972.

Rentsch, George J. "Open-Enrollment: An Appraisal." Ed.D. dissertation, State University of New York at Buffalo, 1967. University Microfilms Order No. 67-11516.

Rock, William C. "A Report on a Cooperative Program Between a City School District and a Suburban School District." Rochester, New York, June 28, 1968.

Shaker Heights School Board. "An Interim Evaluation of the Shaker Schools Plan." Mimeographed. Shaker Heights, Ohio: Shaker Heights School Board, February 1972.

APPENDIX III

STUDIES NOT RECEIVED BY PRESS TIME BUT REVIEWED BY WEINBERG

Bowman, Orrin H. "Scholastic Development of Disadvantaged Negro Pupils: A Study of Pupils in Selected Segregated and Desegregated Elementary Classrooms." Ph.D. dissertation, State University of New York at Buffalo, 1973. University Microfilms Order No. 73-19176.

Brooks, Bernice D. "A Study of Ninety-five Children Traveling by Bus to a K–5 School as Part of the Open Enrollment Program in a Large Urban School System." Ed.D. dissertation, Columbia University, 1969. University Microfilms Order No. 71-08957.

Clark, El Nadal. "Analysis of the Differences Between Pre- and Post-Test Scores (Change Scores) on Measures of Self-Concept, Academic Aptitude, and Reading Achievement Earned by Sixth Grade Students Attending Segregated and Desegregated Schools." Ed.D. dissertation, Duke University, 1971. University Microfilms Order No. 72-00307.

Howell, William L. "The Correlates of Change in School Integration With the Academic Achievement of Eighth Grade Students." Ph.D. dissertation, University of South Carolina, 1972. University Microfilms Order No. 72-18153.

Moore, Louise M. "The Relationship of Selected Pupil and School Variables and the Reading Achievement of Third-Year Primary Pupils in a Desegregated School Setting." Ed.D. dissertation, University of Georgia, 1971. University Microfilms Order No. 72-11018.

Samuels, Ivan G. "Desegregated Education and Differences in Academic Achievement." Ph.D. dissertation, Indiana University, 1958. University Microfilms Order No. 58-02934.

San Francisco Unified School District. "Evaluation of San Francisco Unified School District Desegregation Data from Integration 1971–1972." San Francisco, California: San Francisco Unified School District, 1972.

Savage, LeMoyne W. "Academic Achievement of Black Students Transferring from a Segregated Junior High School to an Integrated High School." Master's thesis, Virginia State College, 1971.

Scott, Wayne. *A Study of Bused and Non-Bused Children*. Grand Rapids, Michigan: Grand Rapids Public Schools, June 1970.

Starnes, Thomas A. "An Analysis of the Academic Achievement of Negro Students in the Predominantly White Schools of a Selected Florida County." Ed.D. dissertation, University of Southern Mississippi, 1968. University Microfilms Order No. 68-14712.

APPENDIX IV

STUDIES NOT RECEIVED BY PRESS TIME BUT REVIEWED
BY ST. JOHN AND WEINBERG

Banks, Ronald, and Di Pasquale, Mary E. "A Study of the Educational Effectiveness of Integration." Buffalo, New York: Buffalo Public Schools, January 1969.

Bryant, James C. "Some Effects of Racial Integration of High School Students on Standardized Achievement Test Scores, Teacher Grades and Drop-Out Rates in Angleton, Texas." Ed.D. dissertation, University of Houston, 1968. University Microfilms Order No. 69-00768.

Graves, Marian F., and Bedell, Frederick D. "A Three-Year Evaluation of the White Plains Racial Balance Plan." Mimeographed. White Plains, New York: Board of Education, October 1967.

Griffin, Jack L. "The Effects of Integration on Academic Aptitude, Classroom Achievement, Self-Concept, and Attitudes Toward the School Environment of a Selected Group of Negro Students in Tulsa, Oklahoma." Ed.D. dissertation, University of Tulsa, 1969. University Microfilms Order No. 69-17923.

Hsia, Jayjia. "Integration In Evanston, 1967–1971: A Longitudinal Evaluation." Evanston, Illinois: Educational Testing Service, August 1971. ERIC Document No. 054 292.

Klein, Robert S. "A Comparative Study of the Academic Achievement of Negro Tenth Grade High School Students Attending Segregated and Recently Integrated Schools in a Metropolitan Area of the South." Ph.D. dissertation, University of South Carolina, 1967. University Microfilms Order No. 67-15565.

Marcum, Roger B. "An Exploration of the First-Year Effects of Racial Integration of the Elementary Schools in a Unit School District." Ed.D. dissertation, University of Illinois at Urbana-Champaign, 1968. University Microfilms Order No. 69-10784.

Moorefield, Thomas E. "The Bussing of Minority Group Children in a Big City School System." Doctoral dissertation, University of Chicago, 1968.

Rochester City School District. "Final Report: A Three-Year Longitudinal Study to Assess a Fifteen-Point Plan to Reduce Racial Isolation and Provide Quality Integrated Education for Elementary Level Pupils." Rochester, New York: Rochester City Schools, September 1970. ERIC Document No. 048 428.

Samuels, Joseph M. "A Comparison of Projects Representative of Compensatory; Busing; and Non-Compensatory Programs for Inner-City Students." Ph.D. dissertation, University of Connecticut, 1971. University Microfilms Order No. 71-14252.

Slone, Irene W. "The Effects of One School Pairing on Pupil Achievement, Anxieties, and Attitudes." Ph.D. dissertation, New York University, 1968. University Microfilms Order No. 68-11808.

Wood, Bruce H. "The Effects of Bussing Versus Non-Bussing on the Intellectual Functioning of Inner City, Disadvantaged Elementary School Children." Ed.D. dissertation, University of Massachusetts, 1969. University Microfilms Order No. 69-05186.

NOTES

a. Research was supported by the National Review Panel on School Desegregation Research, through funding provided by the Ford Foundation, the National Institute of Education, and Duke University; and by NIE grant G-78-0150, Ronald Henderson, project officer. The assistance of Karen Mokrzycki, Lida Nash, Barbara Neff, and Reginald Van Driest, research librarians of the Rand Corporation, is gratefully acknowledged. We wish to thank Christine Rossell for her thoughtful commentary.

b. Senior Social Scientist, The Rand Corporation; presently, Academic Visitor, The London School of Economics.

c. Assistant Social Scientist, The Rand Corporation.

1. *See* C. JENCKS, M. SMITH, H. ACLAND, M. BANE, D. COHEN, H. GINTIS, B. HEYNS, & S. MICHELSON, INEQUALITY 81 (1972).

2. Only a few studies have found that test scores of white students improved after desegregation. *See, e.g.,* Stallings, *A Study of the Immediate Effects of Integration on Scholastic Achievement in the Louisville Public Schools,* 28 J. NEGRO EDUC. 439, 442–43 (1959); R. MAYER, C. KING, A. BORDERS-PATTERSON, & J. MCCULLOUGH, THE IMPACT OF SCHOOL DESEGREGATION IN A SOUTHERN CITY 87–94 (1974). A few others found that the test scores of white students declined. *See., e.g.,* D. Catherine Baltzell, Rapid Desegregation and Academic Achievement in a Large Urban School District (paper presented at the annual meeting of the American Education Research Association, April 1974, in Chicago, Illinois) (ERIC Document No. 090 282); Justin & Thabit, *Black and White Achievement Before and After Integration,* 102 INTELLECT 458 (1974); Kurtz, *An Independent Assessment of "Integration in Evanston, 1967–1971: A Longitudinal Evaluation": A Report of the Educational Consequences of Desegregation in District 65 of Evanston, Illinois, Hearings on School Busing, Part 3, Before the House Comm. on the Judiciary, Subcomm. No. 5,* 92d Cong., 2d Sess., 1436, 1437 (1972). The majority, however, found no significant change. *See, e.g.,* N. ST. JOHN, SCHOOL DESEGREGATION: OUTCOMES FOR CHILDREN (1975), listing 23 studies of white achievement after desegregation, of which only 5 show consistent effects (2 positive, 3 negative).

3. Brown v. Board of Educ., 347 U.S. 483 (1954).

4. J. COLEMAN, E. CAMPBELL, C. HOBSON, J. MCPARTLAND, A. MOOD, F. WEINBELD, & R. YORK, EQUALITY OF EDUCATIONAL OPPORTUNITY (1966) [hereinafter cited as COLEMAN REPORT].

5. G. BRIDGE, C. JUDD, P. MOOCK, THE DETERMINANTS OF EDUCATIONAL OUTCOMES: THE EFFECTS OF FAMILIES, PEERS, TEACHERS, AND SCHOOLS (forthcoming).

6. *Id.* The one exception involves a California school district where a negative effect was found for students who went to predominantly white junior high schools from black elementary schools, but a positive effect for those black students who had attended predominantly white elementary schools before entering junior high school. Winkler, *Educational Achievement and School Peer Group Composition,* 10 J. HUMAN RESOURCES 189, 198–99 (1975). This finding suggests that delaying desegregation until the sixth grade is dysfunctional. *See* discussion *infra* at [19-21].

7. National Longitudinal Study of the High School Graduating Class of 1972, described in W. FETTERS, NATIONAL LONGITUDINAL STUDY OF THE HIGH SCHOOL CLASS OF 1972: COMPARATIVE PROFILES ONE AND ONE-HALF YEARS AFTER GRADUATION (1975) [hereinafter

cited as W. Fetters, National Longitudinal Study]. *See also* McPartland, *Desegregation and Equity in Higher Education and Employment: Is Progress Related to the Desegregation of Elementary and Secondary Schools?*, 42 Law Contemp. Prob., Summer 1978, at [15-17] for a discussion of the study. The NLS surveyed 23,000 students in 1,000 schools.

8.   Crain & Mahard, *School Racial Composition and Black College Attendance and Achievement Test Performance*, 51 Soc. of Educ., April 1978, at 81, 86–88.

9.   *Id.*

10.   The analysis of the NLS data, *supra* note 7, by Crain and Mahard found no evidence that the higher achievement of Northern blacks who attended predominantly white schools compared to those who attended all-black schools was a result of self-selection. Crain & Mahard, *supra* note 8, at 90–98. However, the problem of self-selection bias requires more work.

11.   Coleman Report, *supra* note 4; W. Fetters, National Longitudinal Study, *supra* note 7.

12.   For these reasons we think no more than a small part of the current conflict will be settled by publication of the analyses undertaken by G. Bridge, C. Judd, & P. Moock, *supra* note 5.

13.   One study has concluded that the *Coleman Report* indicated that no more than one-fifth of the black-white gap in achievement will be eliminated as a result of desegregation. Cohen, Pettigrew, Riley, *Race and the Outcomes of Schooling*, in On Equality of Educational Opportunity 343, 358 (Mosteller, Moynihan eds. 1972).

14.   *See* G. Bridge, C. Judd, & P. Moock, *supra* note 5.

15.   The 41 studies represent data from 35 desegregation plans by 38 different authors. Two different authors study the same plan in three cases: Armor, *The Evidence on Busing*, 28 Pub. Interest 90 (1972) and Herbert Walberg, An Evaluation of an Urban-Suburban School Busing Program: Student Achievement and Perception of Class Learning Environment (paper presented at the annual meeting of the American Education Research Association, February 1971, in N.Y., N.Y.) (ERIC Document No. 047 076); Jayjia Hsia, Integration in Evanston, 1967–1971: A Longitudinal Evaluation (Educational Testing Service Report, August 1971) and Kurtz, *supra* note 2; F. Aberdeen, Adjustment to Desegregation: A Description of Some Differences Among Negro Elementary School Pupils (1969) (unpublished Ed.D. dissertation, University of Michigan) and Patricia Carrigan, School Desegregation via Compulsory Pupil Transfer: Early Effects on Elementary School Children (report to Ann Arbor Public Schools, September 1969) (ERIC Document No. 036 597). In three other cases, a study was treated as two separate studies, once because different methodologies were used at different grade levels, R. Mayer, C. King, A. Border-Patterson, & J. McCullough, *supra* note 2; and twice, because different results were obtained in different schools or in different years of a continuing evaluation, Charles Evans, Short-term Desegregation Effects: The Academic Achievement of Bused Students, 1971–72 (report to Fort Worth Independent School District, 1973) (ERIC Document No. 086 759) [hereinafter cited as Short-term Desegregation Effects], Charles Evans, Integration Evaluation: Desegregation Study II—Academic Effects on Bused Black and Receiving White Students, 1972–73 (report to Fort Worth Independent School District, 1973) (ERIC Document No. 094 087) [hereinafter cited as Integration Evaluation], Syracuse City School District, *Study of the Effect of Integration—Croton and Edward Smith Elementary School Pupils*, in U.S. Comm'n on Civil Rights, Hearing Held in Rochester, New York, September 16–17 (1966) [hereinafter cited as Syracuse City School District, *Croton and Edward Smith Elementary School Pupils*], and Syracuse City School District, *Study of the Effect of Integration—Washington Irving and Host Pupils*, U.S. Comm'n on Civil Rights, Hearing Held in Rochester, New York, September 16–17 (1966) [hereinafter cited as Syracuse City School District, *Washington Irving and Host Pupils*].

16.   N. St. John, *supra* note 2.

17.   M. Weinberg, Minority Students: A Research Appraisal (1977).

18.   These studies, reviewed by Weinberg, St. John, or the authors, are listed in the appendixes.

19.   M. Weinberg, *supra* note 17.

20.   Many of these studies are not available in the ERIC library.

21.   Mahan & Mahan, *The Impact of Schools on Learning: Inner-City Children in Suburban Schools*, 9 J. Sch. Psych. 1, 3 (1971).

22. To help the study's legitimacy, the lottery was conducted by minority leaders.

23. Zdep, *Educating Disadvantaged Urban Children in Suburban Schools: An Evaluation*, 1 J. APPLIED SOC. PSYCH. 173, 174–76 (1971).

24. Both studies used achievement test scores obtained prior to assignment to the white suburban schools. This control on achievement scores prior to desegregation eliminated a good deal of variance in the dependent variable, meaning that effects were more likely to be significant with this small sample size. However, a pretest is not necessary; a cross-sectional analysis is sufficient when students are randomly selected. *See* D. CAMPBELL & J. STANLEY, EXPERIMENTAL AND QUASI-EXPERIMENTAL DESIGN FOR RESEARCH 2 (1966).

25. Schellenberg & Halteman, *Bussing and Academic Achievement*, 10 URB. EDUC. 357 (1976).

26. *Id.* at 360.

27. Charles Evans, Short-term Desegregation Effects, *supra* note 15; Charles Evans, Integration Evaluation, *supra* note 15.

28. Herbert Walberg, *supra* note 15.

29. Armor, *supra* note 15.

30. The voluntary METCO program was begun in 1966 to bus black students of all grade levels from predominantly black city schools in Boston to predominantly white middle-class schools in the suburbs. The control group consisted of siblings of the bused students who were matched with the bused students by sex and grade level.

31. *See* discussion in text at note 10, *supra*.

32. Patricia Carrigan, *supra* note 15, at 21.

33. F. Aberdeen, *supra* note 15.

34. Patricia Carrigan, *supra* note 15, at 108.

35. Kurtz, *supra* note 2.

36. B. Perry N. Kopperman, A Better Chance: Evaluation of Student Attitudes and Academic Performance, 1964–1972 (1973) (ERIC Document No. 075 556).

37. Perry attempted to construct a control group of black applicants who were not admitted to the program because of limited space, but he was unable to find sufficient numbers of such students.

38. The study showing a positive result is Denmark, *The Effect of Integration on Academic Achievement and Self-Concept*, 8 INTEGRATED EDUC. 34 (1970). The other two studies show a constant black-white achievement difference before and after desegregation. Beers and Reardon argue that this result should be interpreted as a positive effect, given that racial differences in achievement levels usually increase with age. Beers & Reardon, *Racial Balancing in Harrisburg: Achievement and Attitudinal Changes*, 12 INTEGRATED EDUC. 35 (1974); Harry Singer, Effect of Integration on Achievement of Anglos, Blacks, and Mexican-Americans (paper presented at the annual meeting of the American Education Research Association, March 3–6, 1970, in Minneapolis, Minnesota) (ERIC Document No. 041 975).

39. F. Aberdeen, *supra* note 15; B. Perry & N. Kopperman, *supra* note 36; Carolyn Thompson & Frances Dyke, First Interim Evaluation Report: Urban-Suburban Pupil Transfer Program 1971–1972 (report to Rochester City School District, August 1972) (ERIC Document No. 068 609) found negative results. Two studies found black students gaining ground with respect to national norms. Maynor & Katzenmeyer, *Academic Performance and School Integration: A Multi-Ethnic Analysis*, 43 J. NEGRO EDUC. 30 (1974); R. MAYER, C. KING, A. BORDERS-PATTERSON, J. MCCULLOUGH, *supra* note 2.

40. Among the eight cohort studies are two with negative results: Justin & Thabit, *supra* note 2; Kurtz, *supra* note 2. Three produced results of zero: Patricia Carrigan, *supra* note 15; Arthur Dambacher, A Comparison of Achievement Test Scores Made by Berkeley Elementary Students Pre and Post Integration Eras, 1967–1970 (mimeographed report for Berkeley Unified School District, 1971); and H. GERARD & N. MILLER, SCHOOL DESEGREGATION: A LONG-TERM STUDY (1975). Three studies produced positive results: Prichard, *The Effects of Desegregation on Student Success in the Chapel Hill Schools*, 7 INTEGRATED EDUC. 33 (1969); J. TEELE, EVALUATING SCHOOL BUSING: A CASE STUDY OF BOSTON'S OPERATION EXODUS (1973) (also ERIC Document No. 083 334); and Clark County School District, Desegregation Report (Clark County School District report, Las Vegas, Nevada, July 1974) (ERIC Document No. 106 397).

41. *See* text at note 32 *supra*.

42. Mahan & Mahan, *supra* note 21.
43. Zdep, *supra* note 23; M. WEINBERG, *supra* note 17, at 122.
44. J. TEELE, *supra* note 40.
45. Schellenberg Halteman, *supra* note 25.
46. *See* note 27, *supra*.
47. R. MAYER, C. KING, A. BORDERS-PATTERSON, & J. McCULLOUGH, *supra* note 2.
48. *See, e.g.*, R. CRAIN, SOUTHERN SCHOOLS: AN EVALUATION OF THE EFFECTS OF SCHOOL DESEGREGATION AND OF THE EMERGENCY SCHOOL AID PROGRAM (National Opinion Research Center Report Nos. 124A, 124B, October 1973) (ERIC Document Nos. 085 426, 085 427); J. Coulson, D. Ozenne, S. Hanes, C. Bradford, W. Doherty, G. Duck, & J. Hemenway, The Third Year of Emergency School Aid Act (ESAA) Implementation (March 1977) (ERIC Document No. 154 952); G. FOREHAND, M. RAGOSTA, D. ROCK, CONDITIONS AND PROCESSES OF EFFECTIVE SCHOOL DESEGREGATION (1976) (ERIC Document No. 131 155); J. WELLISCH, R. CARRIERE, A. MACQUEEN, & G. DUCK, AN IN-DEPTH STUDY OF EMERGENCY SCHOOL ASSISTANCE ACT SCHOOLS 1975–1976 (1977) (ERIC Document No. 133 361); Felice, The Effects of School Desegregation on Minority Group Student Achievement and Self-Concept: An Evaluation of Court Ordered Busing in Waco, Texas (1974) (ERIC Document No. 094 096); and H. GERARD & N. MILLER, *supra* note 40.
49. Stallings, *supra* note 2, at 439, 443.
50. *Id.*
51. Justin & Thabit, *supra* note 2.
52. Felice, *supra* note 48.
53. James Fortenberry, The Achievement of Negro Pupils in Mixed and Non-Mixed Schools (1959) (unpublished Ed.D. dissertation, University of Oklahoma).
54. *See* discussion *infra* at [22–23].
55. Robert Stephenson and Phillip Spieth, Evaluation of Desegregation 1970–1971 (Dade County Public Schools Department of Program Evaluation report, June 1972) (ERIC Document No. 070 792) [hereinafter cited as Dade County Evaluation].
56. Charles Evans, Short-term Desegregation, *supra* note 15; Charles Evans, Integration Evaluation, *supra* note 15.
57. R. MAYER, C. KING, A. BORDERS-PATTERSON, & J. McCULLOUGH, *supra* note 2.
58. The studies conducted at the end of the first year of desegregation that obtained positive results are: D. Catherine Baltzell, *supra* note 2; Charles Evans, Short-term Desegregation, *supra* note 15; Frary Goolsby, *Achievement of Integrated and Segregated Negro and White First Graders in a Southern City*, 8 INTEGRATED EDUC. 48 (1970); and Maynor & Katzenmeyer, *supra* note 39. Three other one-year studies found negative results: Justin & Thabit, *supra* note 2; Stallings, *supra* note 2; and Dade County Evaluation, *supra* note 55.
59. Among studies done at the end of two or more years of desegregation, only Felice's presents negative results. Felice, *supra* note 48. Positive results are reported in: Louis Anderson, The Effect of Desegregation on the Achievement and Personality Patterns of Negro Children (1966) (unpublished Ph.D. dissertation, George Peabody College for Teachers); Charles Evans, Integration Evaluation, *supra* note 15; R. MAYER, C. KING, A. BORDERS-PATTERSON, & J. McCULLOUGH, *supra* note 2 (also in the results from Mayers's study of the ninth grade students, which we coded separately because it had no control group); Prichard, *supra* note 40; and Frank Williams, An Analysis of Some Differences Between Negro High School Seniors from a Segregated High School and a Nonsegregated High School in Brevard County, Florida (1968) (unpublished Ed.D. dissertation, University of Florida). The one study that obtained a zero result, James Fortenberry, *supra* note 53, did not specify the duration of desegregation. The gamma between years of desegregation at posttest and desegregation outcomes is +.55.
60. *See* discussion at text accompanying notes 6–9, *supra*.
61. Crain & Mahard, *supra* note 8, at 86–88.
62. *See* discussion *infra* at [19–21]. One study goes even further and suggests that it is actually detrimental to the achievement of black students if their first desegregation experience does not occur until after the sixth grade. Winkler, *supra* note 6, at 189, 202.
63. S. Johnson, Update on Education: A Digest of the National Assessment of Educational Progress (Education Commission of the States report, 1975) (ERIC Document No. 013 381).

64. *Id.*

65. Until the Supreme Court's decision in Green v. New Kent County School Bd., 391 U.S. 430 (1968), followed by Alexander v. Holmes County Bd. of Educ., 396 U.S. 19 (1969) and Carter v. West Feliciana Parish School Bd., 396 U.S. 290 (1970), little more than token desegregation had occurred in the South. *See* Read, *Judicial Evolution of the Law of School Integration Since Brown v. Board of Education*, 39 LAW & CONTEMP. PROB., Winter 1975, at 7, 28–32.

66. The fourteen studies are: Louis Anderson, *supra* note 59; D. Catherine Baltzell, *supra* note 2; Clark County School District, *supra* note 40; Arthur Dambacher, *supra* note 40; James Fortenberry, *supra* note 53; Justin & Thabit, *supra* note 2; Kurtz, *supra* note 2; Mahan & Mahan, *supra* note 21; Maynor & Katzenmeyer, *supra* note 39; B. Perry & N. Kopperman, *supra* note 36; Schellenberg & Halteman, *supra* note 25; Wolman, *Learning Effects of Integration in New Rochelle*, 2 INTEGRATED EDUC. 30 (1964); and Zdep, *supra* note 23.

67. Beker, A Study of Integration in Racially Imbalanced Urban Public Schools—A Demonstration and Evaluation (mimeographed final report, Syracuse University Youth Development Center, Syracuse, N.Y., 1967) (ERIC Document No. 012 710).

68. Charles Evans, Short-term Desegregation Effects, *supra* note 15.

69. Charles Evans, Integration Evaluation, *supra* note 15.

70. Dade County Evaluation, *supra* note 55. The achievement levels of the control group declined by about a third of a year more than the preceding year's class, even though black achievement in other grades went up.

71. In particular, see Mahan & Mahan, *supra* note 21; Zdep, *supra* note 23; and Schellenberg & Halteman, *supra* note 25.

72. Examples are: Arthur Dambacher, *supra* note 40; James Fortenberry, *supra* note 53; Schellenberg & Halteman, *supra* note 25; and Wolman, *supra* note 66.

73. Rochester City School District, A Three-Year Longitudinal Study to Assess a Fifteen-Point Plan to Reduce Racial Isolation and Provide Quality Integrated Education for Elementary Level Pupils (Rochester City School District report, Rochester, N.Y., September 1970) (ERIC Document No. 048 428); Shaker Heights School Board, An Interim Evaluation of the Shaker Schools Plan (mimeographed, Shaker Heights School Board, Shaker Heights, Ohio, February 1972); and Ivan Samuels, Desegregated Education and Differences in Academic Achievement (1958) (unpublished Ph.D. dissertation, Indiana University).

74. N. ST. JOHN, *supra* note 2, at 77–78 M. WEINBERG, *supra* note 17.

75. Dade County Evaluation, *supra* note 55; Felice, *supra* note 48; Maynor & Katzenmeyer, *supra* note 39; R. MAYER, C. KING, A. BORDERS-PATTERSON, & J. MCCULLOUGH, *supra* note 2; Frank Williams, *supra* note 59; Armor, *supra* note 15; B. Perry & N. Kopperman, *supra* note 36; Herbert Walberg, *supra* note 15; Lemoyne Savage, Academic Achievement of Black Students Transferring from a Segregated Junior High School to an Integrated High School (July 1971) (unpublished Master's thesis, Virginia State College); Robert Klein, A Comparative Study of the Academic Achievement of Negro Tenth Grade High School Students Attending Segregated and Recently Integrated Schools in a Metropolitan Area of the South (1967) (unpublished Ph.D. dissertation, University of South Carolina); James Bryant, Some Effects of Racial Integration of High School Students on Standardized Achievement Test Scores, Teacher Grades and Drop-Out Rates in Angleton, Texas (1968) (unpublished Ed.D. dissertation, University of Houston); and James McCullough, Academic Achievement Under School Desegregation in a Southern City (mimeographed report, Department of City and Regional Planning, University of North Carolina at Chapel Hill, January 1972).

76. Dade County Evaluation, *supra* note 55; Felice, *supra* note 48; B. Perry & N. Kopperman, *supra* note 36; Herbert Walberg, *supra* note 15; and James Bryant, *supra* note 75.

77. Louis Anderson, *supra* note 59; Frary & Goolsby, *supra* note 58; Beker, *supra* note 67; Clark County School District, *supra* note 40; Frank Dressler, Study of Achievement in Reading of Pupils Transferred from Schools 15 and 37 to Peripheral Schools to Eliminate Overcrowding, to Abandon an Obsolete School, and to Achieve a More Desirable Racial Balance in City Schools (March 1967) (mimeographed report, Buffalo Public Schools Division of Curriculum Evaluation and Development, Buffalo, New York); H. GERARD & N.

MILLER, *supra* note 40; Zdep, *supra* note 23; Barbara Heller, Project Concern: Westport, Connecticut (June 1972) (Center for Urban Education report, N.Y., N.Y.); William Rock, A Report on a Cooperative Program Between a City School District and a Suburban School District (June 28, 1968) (Rochester, N.Y.); and Joseph Samuels, A Comparison of Projects Representative of Compensatory; Busing; and Non-Compensatory Programs for Inner-City Students (1971) (unpublished Ph.D. dissertation, University of Connecticut).

78. The twelve showing positive results are: D. Catherine Baltzell, *supra* note 2; Charles Evans, Short-term Desegregation, and Integration Evaluation, *supra* note 15; R. MAYER, C. KING, A. BORDERS-PATTERSON, & J. McCULLOUGH, *supra* note 2; Denmark, *supra* note 38; Mahan & Mahan, *supra* note 21; Syracuse City School District, *Washington Irving and Host Pupils*, *supra* note 15; Jayjia Hsia, *supra* note 15; Irene Slone, The Effects of One School Pairing on Pupil Achievement, Anxieties, and Attitudes (1968) (unpublished Ph.D. dissertation, New York University); Bruce Wood, The Effects of Bussing Versus Non-Bussing on the Intellectual Functioning of Inner City, Disadvantaged Elementary School Children (1969) (unpublished Ed.D. dissertation, University of Massachusetts); Ann Danahy, A Study of the Effects of Bussing on the Achievement, Attendance, Attitudes, and Social Choices of Negro Inner-City Children (1971) (unpublished Ed.D. dissertation, University of Minnesota); Harold Jonsson, Report of Evaluation of ESEA Title I Compensatory Activities for 1966–67 (1967) (mimeographed report, Berkeley Unified School District, Berkeley, California); and Ronald Clinton, A Study of the Improvement in Achievement of Basic Skills of Children Bused from Urban to Suburban School Environments (1969) (unpublished Master's thesis, Southern Connecticut State College).

The other twelve are: Justin & Thabit, *supra* note 2; Patricia Carrigan, *supra* note 15; Arthur Dambacher, *supra* note 40; Arley Bondarin, The Racial Balance Plan of White Plains, New York (Report to the Center for Urban Education, N.Y., N.Y., 1970) (ERIC Document No. 012 710); Syracuse City School District, *Croton and Edward Smith Elementary School Pupils*, *supra* note 15; Schellenberg & Halteman, *supra* note 25; Harry Singer, *supra* note 38; Wolman, *supra* note 66; F. Aberdeen, *supra* note 15; Kurtz, *supra* note 2; Carolyn Thompson & Frances Dyke, *supra* note 39; and George Rentsch, Open-Enrollment: An Appraisal (1967) (unpublished Ed.D. dissertation, State University of New York at Buffalo).

79. M. INBAR, THE VULNERABLE AGE PHENOMENON (1976).

80. M. INBAR & C. ADLER, ETHNIC INTEGRATION IN ISRAEL: A COMPARATIVE CASE STUDY OF MOROCCAN BROTHERS WHO SETTLED IN FRANCE AND IN ISRAEL 57 (1977).

81. M. INBAR, *supra* note 79, at 6–8, 15.

82. R. CRAIN & C. WEISMAN, DISCRIMINATION, PERSONALITY, AND ACHIEVEMENT 12 (1972).

83. H. SULLIVAN, THE INTERPERSONAL THEORY OF PSYCHIATRY 241–42 (1953); M. INBAR, *supra* note 79, at 45.

84. N. ST. JOHN, *supra* note 2, at 119.

85. Clark School District, *supra* note 40; Dade County Evaluation, *supra* note 55; Charles Evans, Short-term Desegregation, and Integration Evaluation, *supra* note 15; Felice, *supra* note 48; James Fortenberry, *supra* note 53; R. MAYER, C. KING, A. BORDERS-PATTERSON, & J. McCULLOUGH, *supra* note 2; Prichard, *supra* note 40; B. Perry & N. Kopperman, *supra* note 36; Sacramento City Unified School District, Focus on Reading and Mathematics 1970–71: An Evaluation Report on a Program of Compensatory Education, ESEA Title I (July 1971) (Sacramento City Unified School District report, Sacramento, California); and Frank Williams, *supra* note 59.

86. R. MAYER, C. KING, A. BORDERS-PATTERSON, & J. McCULLOUGH, *supra* note 2; Mahan & Mahan, *supra* note 21; Herbert Walberg, *supra* note 15.

87. Zdep, *supra* note 23, at 181.

88. Zdep, *supra* note 23.

89. *Id.* at 181.

90. *Id.* Thus, the first graders attained a full standard deviation more than did their segregated control group while the desegregated second graders fell .15 standard deviations below the control group.

91. Frank Williams, *supra* note 59.

92. This amounts to 0.6 standard deviations.

93. This amounts to 0.9 standard deviations in English-langauage skills and 0.4 standard deviations in the other subjects.

94. James Fortenberry, *supra* note 53.

95. *See* discussion at text accompanying notes 91–93, *supra*.

96. Zdep, *supra* note 23; J. TEELE, *supra* note 40.

97. The positive results are from the studies by: Beers & Reardon, *supra* note 38; Clark County School District, *supra* note 40; Frank Dressler, *supra* note 77; Denmark, *supra* note 38; Mahan & Mahan, *supra* note 21; Syracuse City School District, *Washington Irving and Host Pupils*, *supra* note 15; Sacramento City Unified School District, *supra* note 85. Kurtz, *supra* note 2; and F. Aberdeen, *supra* note 15, present negative findings. Zero findings are by Arley Bondarin, *supra* note 78; Patricia Carrigan, *supra* note 15; Arthur Dambacher, *supra* note 40; H. GERARD & N. MILLER, *supra* note 40; Schellenberg & Halteman, *supra* note 25; and Harry Singer, *supra* note 38.

98. The nine studies of voluntary plans that obtained positive results are: David Archibald, Report on Change in Academic Achievement for a Sample of Elementary School Children: Progress Report on METCO (1967) (mimeographed report, Roxbury, Massachusetts); Ann Danahy, *supra* note 78; Mary Laird & Grace Weeks, The Effect of Bussing on Achievement in Reading and Arithmetic in Three Philadelphia Schools (1966) (mimeographed report, School District of Philadelphia Division of Research, Philadelphia, Pennsylvania); William Rock, *supra* note 77; Ronald Clinton, *supra* note 78; Barbara Heller, *supra* note 77; Joseph Samuels, *supra* note 77; Bruce Wood, *supra* note 78; and Wayne Scott, A Study of Bused and Non-Bused Children (June 1970) (Grand Rapids Public Schools report, Grand Rapids, Michigan). Among the studies of voluntary plans, the two zero-findings are by Bernice Brooks, A Study of Ninety-five Children Traveling by Bus to a K–5 School as Part of the Open Enrollment Program in a Large Urban School System (1969) (unpublished Ed.D. dissertation, Columbia University). A study of a voluntary plan that obtained negative results is Shaker Heights School Board, *supra* note 73. Of the studies of mandatory plans, the following show positive results: Harold Jonsson, *supra* note 78; Ronald Banks & Mary Di Pasquale, A Study of the Educational Effectiveness of Integration (January 1969) (Buffalo Public Schools report, Buffalo, N.Y.); Jayjia Hsia, *supra* note 15; Irene Slone, *supra* note 78; Orrin Bowman, Scholastic Development of Disadvantaged Negro Pupils; A Study of Pupils in Selected Segregated and Desegregated Elementary Classrooms (1973) (unpublished Ph.D. dissertation, State University of New York at Buffalo); Ivan Samuels, *supra* note 73; San Francisco Unified School District, Evaluation of San Francisco Unified School District Desegregation Data from Integration 1971–1972 (1972) (San Francisco Unified School District report, San Francisco, California). A zero finding for a mandatory plan is reported in Marian Graves & Frederick Bedell, A Three-Year Evaluation of the White Plains Racial Balance Plan (October 16, 1967) (mimeographed report of Board of Education, White Plains, N.Y.).

99. Zdep, *supra* note 23.

100. J. TEELE, *supra* note 40.

101. *See* J. TEELE, *supra* note 40, at 57–67. The account includes a description of the confrontation between the conservative school board and the black researcher who evaluated a black-run school program.

102. Zdep, *supra* note 23, at 181. The overall gain was 0.9 of a standard deviation, which took into account the .15 standard deviation loss in mathematics of the desegregated second graders compared to their segregated counterparts. *See* note 90 *supra* and accompanying text.

103. B. Perry & N. Kopperman, *supra* note 36.

104. Mahan & Mahan *supra* note 21, at 4.

105. Zdep, *supra* note 23, at 175.

106. *Id.*

107. J. TEELE, *supra* note 40, at 6–15.

108. David Fox, Colleen Stuart, and Vera Pitts, Services to Children in Open Enrollment Receiving Schools: Evaluation of ESEA Title I Projects in New York City, 1967–68 (mimeographed report, New York Center for Urban Education, N.Y., N.Y., December 1968) (ERIC Document No. 034 004).

109. Syracuse City School District, *Croton and Edward Smith Elementary School Pupils, supra* note 15 at 327–28; Syracuse City School District, *Washington Irving and Host Pupils, supra* note 15, at 323–326.

110. Herbert Walberg, *supra* note 15; Armor, *supra* note 15.

111. Wolman, *supra* note 66, at 30.

112. Carolyn Thompson & Frances Dyke, *supra* note 39.

113. B. Perry & N. Kopperman, *supra* note 36.

114. Burleigh Gardner, Benjamin Wright, and Sister Rita Dee, The Effect of Busing Black Ghetto Children into White Suburban Schools (report prepared for Chicago Catholic School Board, July 1970) (ERIC Document No. 048 389).

115. F. Aberdeen, *supra* note 15.

116. Patricia Carrigan, *supra* note 15. In analyzing Carrigan's study we used her cohort analysis. However, there are also weaknesses in cohort analyses. *See* discussion at pp. [12–13], *supra*.

117. *See* discussion at pp. [12–13], *supra*.

118. Harry Singer, *supra* note 38. H. GERARD & N. MILLER, *supra* note 40.

119. Kurtz, *supra* note 2.

120. Arthur Dambacher, *supra* note 40.

121. St. John cites positive findings by Harold Jonsson, *supra* note 78; Weinberg cites positive results in Frelow, *Minority Administrators and Desegregation*, 11 INTEGRATED EDUC. 27 (1973). *See* N. ST. JOHN, *supra* note 2, at 158; M. WEINBERG, *supra* note 17, at 117.

122. Arley Bondarin, *supra* note 78.

123. The cities are: Ann Arbor, Michigan, Riverside and Berkeley, California, White Plains, New York, and Evanston, Illinois.

124. Schellenberg & Halteman, *supra* note 25. The problems in the Bondarin study of White Plains are not as serious as those in the other studies mentioned previously (*see* text accompanying notes 115–120, *supra*); still, the Bondarin study is weaker than the Schellenberg and Halteman study.

125. Syracuse City School District, *Washington Irving and Host Pupils, supra* note 15; Frank Dressler, *supra* note 77; Sacramento City Unified School District, *supra* note 85; Mahan & Mahan, *supra* note 21; Denmark, *supra* note 38; Clark County School District, *supra* note 40; and Beers & Reardon, *supra* note 38.

126. Syracuse City School District, *Washington Irving and Host Pupils, supra* note 15.

127. Frank Dressler, *supra* note 77.

128. Sacramento City Unified School District, *supra* note 85.

129. Mahan & Mahan, *supra* note 21.

130. The evidence is internally consistent and statistically significant at the .10 level. When the twenty-six studies reviewed by the authors are combined with the studies reviewed by St. John and Weinberg, the correlation is .25.

131. *See* note 110, *supra*.

132. *See* B. Perry & N. Kopperman, *supra* note 36.

133. Zdep, *supra* note 23.

134. Wolman, *supra* note 66, at 30–31.

135. These studies are: Joseph Samuels, *supra* note 77; William Rock, *supra* note 77; N. ST. JOHN, *supra* note 2, at 154.

136. *See* notes 79–83, *supra*, and accompanying text.

137. Zdep, *supra* note 23.

138. Frank Williams, *supra* note 59.

139. The achievement gains found in the two studies are .5 to 1.0 standard deviations. Zdep, *supra* note 23, at 181; Frank Williams, *supra* note 59.

140. This amount of gain is approximately .2 standard deviations.

141. 20 U.S.C. § 241a (1976).

Section

IX

Crime Policy
and the
Criminal Justice System

40

THE EFFECT OF GUN AVAILABILITY
ON ROBBERY AND ROBBERY MURDER
A Cross-Section Study of Fifty Cities

Philip J. Cook

INTRODUCTION

Firearms are used in a large proportion of the violent crimes of robbery, assault, and murder. The widespread availability of firearms, particularly handguns, has frequently received part of the blame for the extraordinarily high rates of violent crimes in the United States, and the violent crime wave of the 1965-1975 decade may have been fueled in part by the growth in the availability of handguns in urban areas. Advocates of stringent gun control have long argued that the adoption of a program which made it more costly or time-consuming or legally risky for criminals to obtain guns would have the effect of reducing the amount and seriousness of violent crimes (see Newton and Zimring, 1969).

This chapter analyzes the relationship between gun availability and the crime of robbery, which is defined as theft or attempted theft through violence or the threat of violence. The importance of guns in robbery is indicated by the fact that 45 percent of robberies reported to the police are perpetrated with a gun (almost always a handgun), and that robberies with guns are much more likely to result in the death of the victim than robberies committed with other weapons. The major findings of this study, based on an extensive analysis of intercity differences in the rates of robbery and robbery murder, are that: (1) an increase in the density of guns in a city has no effect on the overall robbery rate but is associated with an increase in the fraction of robberies which involve a gun; (2) the per capita rates of gun and nongun robbery murder are nearly proportionate across cities to the rates of gun and nongun robbery, respectively; (3) these two findings, together with the fact that gun robberies are almost three times as likely to result in the death of the victim as nongun robberies, imply

AUTHOR'S NOTE: This research was supported by the U.S. Dept. of Justice and the Ford Foundation. I am indebted to Barbara Boland and Edward D. Jones III for providing some of the data on which this study is based, and to Philip Yen for programming assistance. Helpful comments on an earlier draft were received from Charles Clotfelter, Brian Forst, and Ann Witte.

that the per capita rate of robbery murder increases with the density of guns in a city—a result which also emerges from a direct analysis of the data. These findings are certainly relevant to the ongoing debate over the wisdom of adopting more stringent gun control measures, but do not yield predictions about the efficacy of adopting any particular gun control strategy. However, my results do suggest the prediction that, *if* a way could be found to reduce the density of handguns in a city, then this reduction would ameliorate the seriousness of the robbery problem.

The theoretical and empirical approach used in developing these results may be of interest as a contribution to the largely neglected study of how the availability of "inputs" into the crime production process influences the level and structure of crime rates. In robbery, the important inputs other than labor are weapons and "targets," and the terms on which these inputs are available appears to have a major influence on robbery patterns. Weapon availability is measured here by a new city gun density index, which should have applications in a number of other contexts.

This chapter is organized as follows:

— description of robbery and robbery data
— theoretical issues in gun availability and robbery
— construction of the gun density index
— determinants of intercity differences in robbery rate
— robbery murders
— conclusions

DESCRIPTION OF ROBBERY AND ROBBERY DATA

Definition

The Uniform Crime Reporting Handbook (U.S. Department of Justice, 1976: 14) defines robbery as "the taking or attempting to take anything of value from the care, custody, or control of a person or persons by force or threat of force or violence and/or by putting the victim in fear." This definition includes a wide variety of incidents, ranging from the strong-arm theft of a student's lunch money to bank holdups and truck hijackings. The distinction between robbery and "larceny from the person" rests on whether the victim resists—a purse-snatching becomes a robbery if the woman attempts to hold onto her purse and a struggle ensues. A burglary ("unlawful entry of a structure to commit a felony or a theft") is classified as a robbery if a resident of the building confronts the burglar and the burglar attempts to intimidate the resident. A large fraction of residential robberies are in fact interrupted burglaries (Repetto, 1972).

A robbery incident which results in the death of the victim or which includes a rape is counted by the FBI as a murder or a rape, not as a robbery.

Robbery Data

The most comprehensive source of data on robbery rates and patterns are the reports to the FBI made by cities participating in the Uniform Crime Reporting system. In recent years, a series of criminal victimization surveys has been conducted by the Census Bureau to supplement the Uniform Crime Reporting system.[1] A nationwide survey has been conducted every six months since 1973, and special surveys have been conducted in twenty-six large cities (see U.S. Department of Justice, LEAA, 1975, 1976a, 1976b). It remains an open question whether the crime surveys yield a more accurate representation of intertemporal and cross-section crime patterns than did the Uniform Crime Reports (see Skogan, 1975; Fienberg, 1977), but the question is moot for the analysis presented here: the twenty-six cities which have been surveyed do not constitute a large enough sample on which to base a comprehensive analysis of intercity robbery patterns. While I do use descriptive statistics from victimization survey data on occasion, most of the empirical work is based on 1975 UCR robbery data for the fifty largest cities.

There are serious doubts concerning the accuracy of the UCR data, as anyone who has even a nodding acquaintance with the criminology literature must know (Skogan, 1975). The robbery count published by the UCR for each city is the number reported to the FBI by the city police department. This number is suspect primarily because a large fraction of robberies (especially of the less serious incidents) are never reported to the police. Furthermore, the police departments may not classify incidents accurately (note the subtleties of classification described above), and in some cases may fail to report all known incidents to the FBI for political or other reasons. These problems of underreporting detract from the confidence which should be placed on any cross-section analysis of UCR statistics; if there are systematic intercity differences in the degree to which robbery rates are underreported, then the data will yield a biased impression of the importance of various city characteristics in influencing the true robbery rate.

Robbery Trends and Patterns

Robbery is predominantly a crime of the large cities: 65 percent of all robberies occur in cities with population exceeding 250,000 (which contain less than one-quarter of the U.S. population), and 18 percent of all U.S. robberies are committed in New York City alone.

A majority (56 percent) of big-city robberies reported to the FBI in 1975 occurred on the street, 14 percent in residences, and the remaining 30 percent involved commerical targets. An analysis of the victimization survey data for twenty-six cities conducted by Cook (1976) found that the typical street robbery was committed by two or more Negro male youths: 84 percent of these robberies involved nonwhite offenders, 53 percent involved youths aged less than twenty-one, 63 percent involved two or more offenders (though the victim was almost always alone at the time of the robbery). The typical victim was male (64%), white (62%), and aged twenty-five or more (62%).

Seriousness

The number of robberies reported to the FBI has more than tripled since 1965, and victimization rates in some of the most robbery-prone cities (Detroit,

Boston, Newark) are as high as 4 percent per year. The seriousness of the robbery problem is not the result of the direct economic loss to victims—72 percent of the street robberies reported in the victimization surveys resulted in the theft of less than $50 (Cook, 1976). Much more important is the high rate of injury and death which results from robbery incidents, and the mental anguish of even those robbery victims who are not injured. Furthermore, the widespread fear of "crime in the streets," endemic in most of the large cities, distorts the lifestyle of the city and has social costs far beyond the direct losses to actual robbery victims. That this fear is well founded is suggested by the fact that one out of every seven murders in the fifty largest cities was the result of a robbery incident.

The likelihood that a robbery will result in the injury or death of the victim is substantially influenced by the type of weapon used by the robber. The best data on the likelihood of injury are taken from the victimization surveys of the twenty-six cities. For street robberies reported in these surveys, gun robberies had the lowest injury rate (2.8 percent) while the highest injury rate occurred in robberies in which the robber used a club. Table 1 gives a complete breakdown on injury rates by weapon type. Directly comparable data for robbery murders are not available. However, calculations based on the 1975 UCR data for the fifty largest cities reveal a clear pattern which reverses the impression that guns are "safer" than other weapons in robbery. The fraction of gun robberies which result in the death of the victim is 2.8 times as high as the corresponding fraction for robberies with other weapons (including unarmed). Consequently, while less than half of robberies involved a gun, fully two-thirds of all robbery murders involved a gun. Table 2 summarizes these results.

Tables 1 and 2 give very different impressions of the relative dangerousness of guns in robberies. Could it be true that gun robbers are less likely to injure but much more likely to kill a victim than other robbers? The difference is almost certainly *not* the result of differences in the data sources. Indeed, since gun robberies are more likely to be reported to the police than nongun robberies (see Zimring, 1977), the true disparity between gun and nongun robbery murder rates/1000 robberies is *larger* than that reported in Table 2. I believe the correct explanation is the following: Nongun robberies are much more likely than gun robberies to be initiated by an assault on the victim (as connoted by the terms "mugging" and "yoking").[2] Such an attack is not needed in a gun robbery in most cases because the display of the gun is sufficient in itself to intimidate the victim. In the relatively few cases where the gun robber actually shoots the gun, however, it is much more likely to inflict deadly harm on the victim than an attack with some other sort of weapon. Some evidence for this explanation is found in Table 1, which indicates that the *serious* injury rate (medical costs exceeding $1000) in gun robberies is relatively high when compared with the overall injury rate. The weapon-linked *murder* pattern is a continuation of this "trend."

TABLE 1

Injury Rates in Street Robberies by Weapon Type

Weapon	Victims Incurring Medical Costs (%)	Victims Incurring Medical Costs Exceeding $1,000 (%)
Gun	2.8	0.3
Knife	6.6	0.4
Other weapon	12.0	0.7
Unarmed	5.2	0.2
All incidents	6.2	0.5

SOURCE: Table 10-8, P. J. Cook "A strategic choice analysis of robbery," in W. Skogan (ed.) *Sample Surveys of the Victims of Crime,* Ballinger, 1976.

TABLE 2

	Robbery Murders/ 1,000 Robberies with Stated Weapon Type	Robbery Murders/ 100,000 Population
Gun Robberies	7.66	2.29
Nongun Robberies	2.71	1.07
All Robberies	4.84	3.36

SOURCE: Unpublished UCR data on homicides and robberies in the 50 largest cities.

THEORETICAL ISSUES

The term "gun availability" appears frequently in the congressional hearings and scholarly literature dealing with gun control. Reducing gun availability, and particularly reducing the availability of handguns to potential criminals, is the proximate objective of the range of gun control policies which Bruce-Briggs (1976) has labeled the "interdiction" strategy: policies which include licensing and registration, mandatory waiting periods between purchase and transfer, bans on mail order sales, and even total bans on private possession.

Ideally, interdiction policies could be designed and implemented so as to discriminate between legitimate and criminal uses, preserving the public's access to the former while eliminating the latter. In practice, discrimination policies take the form of prohibiting certain categories of individuals from acquiring or possessing firearms. The current federal law, the Gun Control Act of 1968 (GCA), adopts this discrimination strategy; the GCA makes gun possession by a felon or ex-mental patient illegal, and furthermore makes it illegal for gun dealers to sell guns to anyone "they have reason to believe" is a felon, ex-mental patient, or minor (age less than twenty-one in the case of hand-guns).[3] In an effort to make the discrimination strategy more effective, and to facilitate the enforcement of state and local gun control ordinances, GCA bans mail order gun sales and requires that handguns be purchased in the buyer's state of residence. Dealers are required to be licensed by the federal government (Bureau of Alcohol, Tobacco, and Firearms) and to keep records of all sales; people who only sell a few guns per year are not required to be licensed and are not governed by the same restrictions as dealers.

A number of states and cities have adopted ordinances which strengthen the federal law in various ways. Table 3 summarizes the laws which apply in the thirty largest cities. With a few exceptions, state and local ordinances have adopted the discrimination strategy. For example, states and cities which require handgun buyers to be licensed have typically issued such licenses to almost all applicants after a brief effort to check criminal records, with no intent of inhibiting gun sales. States which have adopted a waiting period between purchase and transfer are in effect attempting to discriminate against buyers who might be in the middle of an argument and need a cooling-off period.

Discrimination policies are not intended to reduce the stock or the flow of new handguns into a jurisdiction. There are large differences in gun density among cities, with southern and mountain region cities tending to be relatively high and cities in the Northeast and far West relatively low (see Table 5). These differences surely reflect differences in demand rather than differences in supply or legal restrictions for the most part.

The alternatives to a discrimination strategy are any of a number of policies designed to reduce the density of handguns, which I will term "disarmament" policies. Examples of disarmament policies include restrictive licensing (Boston, New York City), a ban on cheap handguns or other means of raising the minimum price at which guns can be acquired (e.g., gun registration fees), a ban on the acquisition of handguns (recently adopted in Washington, D.C.), or a total ban on private possession. Such policies receive support from people who believe that effective gun control cannot be achieved through discrimination policies. The two main arguments are: (1) Discrimination policies are ineffective because it is impossible to prevent felons and minors from obtaining guns when guns are readily available to everyone else—the market is too "leaky"; and (2) many gun crimes (as well as gun accidents and gun suicides) are committed by adults who are neither ex-felons nor ex-mental patients, and hence can obtain a gun legally under GCA provisions. Recent scholarly studies which have attempted to assess the effectiveness of current state and local ordinances tend to support the claim that these ordinances have been ineffective at reducing crime (Magaddino, 1976; Murray, 1975). It is not clear whether these ordinances are ineffective as a result of a fundamental deficiency in their design, or rather because they have not been enforced adequately (Zimring, 1975; Bruce-Briggs, 1976).

Only a few evaluations of disarmament policies have been published. Since the first serious recent effort to disarm the public in a U.S. jurisdiction has just begun in Washington, D.C.,[4] published evaluations have been based on international comparisons or on analysis of the impact of adoption of a stringent gun control statute in a foreign nation. Naive international comparisons have virtually no value. For example, several authors have ascribed Japan's extra-

TABLE 3
State and Local Handgun Regulations, 1975[a]

A. STATE PERMIT TO BUY

Boston
Buffalo
Chicago
Detroit
Newark
New York
Baltimore[b]
St. Louis[c]

B. SOME STATE OR LOCAL REQUIREMENTS

1. Local permit required

Philadelphia
Cleveland
Milwaukee
District of Columbia

2. Local waiting time, possibility of investigation

New Orleans
Minneapolis
Miami

3. State waiting period required

Portland (5 days)
Oakland (5 days)
San Francisco (5 days)
San Diego (5 days)
Los Angeles (5 days)
Pittsburgh (2 days)

C. NO REGULATION

Atlanta
Dallas
Denver
Houston

a. Ordinances mandating that gun buyers obtain a permit from state or local authorities have been in effect in Massachusetts, New York, Illinois, Michigan, New Jersey, Maryland, Missouri, and North Carolina since 1968 or before.
b. Maryland law requires that an application for handgun purchase be sent to the state police seven days before the actual transaction, with at least the possibility that the state police will investigate the purchaser and disallow the purchase.
c. Missouri law requires that handgun purchasers have a permit from the county sheriff, but does not specify the categories of people who are ineligible to receive a permit (beyond the requirements that the applicant be of age and of "good" moral character).

ordinarily low murder rate to their stringent gun control statutes.[5] This explanation is completely inadequate, given that Japan's total murder rate is much lower than the U.S. *nongun* murder rate. In any event, cross-national comparisons always suffer from the difficulty of controlling for cultural and other differences, and should be interpreted with great caution.[6]

Of much greater interest is the possibility of evaluating the change in violent crime rates resulting from the adoption of a stringent disarmament statute,[7] although even with a valid study of this type it is difficult to extract lessons relevant to U.S. policy. In spite of the lack of experience with disarmament policies within the United States, analysis of available U.S. data can yield some insight into the potential effect of adopting such a policy at the national or local level. Since the main proximate objective for disarmament policies is to reduce gun density, one method of predicting the effects of adopting such a policy is to compare violent crime rates in jurisdictions which currently have high gun density with violent crime rates in low gun density jurisdictions. Such an analysis, based on 1975 data for fifty large cities, is presented in subsequent sections of this chapter for the crime of robbery. But first, it is necessary to discuss three preliminary questions: (1) How does gun density per se affect the availability of guns for robbery? (2) What effects should we expect a reduction in gun availability to have on robbery rates and patterns? (3) Is it valid to make inferences concerning the potential effects of a disarmament strategy from analysis of recent cross-section data on cities?

Gun Density and Gun Possession by Potential Robbers

The extent to which robbers are armed with guns in a particular city is the result of a number of factors which can be usefully classified in the usual supply and demand framework.

Supply. In a frictionless market, the notion of gun "availability" to an individual purchaser is equivalent to the money price of a gun (or vector of prices if there are a variety of types of guns for sale). The market for guns is far from frictionless, however. Transaction costs may be a particularly important consideration in analyzing supply conditions for the kinds of people who constitute the great majority of active robbers. The most visible and readily accessible gunsellers are presumably the federally licensed dealers, who advertise and are easily located by purchasers. However, licensed dealers are prohibited by federal law from selling handguns to minors or people with felony records, and furthermore are required to register every sale on a form which is subject to inspection by the police. While these requirements are no doubt widely violated in practice, they may be sufficient to deter a substantial fraction of potential robbers from buying from licensed dealers—especially in cities and states which require buyers to have a purchase permit. The alternative sources of supply are the informal "hand-to-hand" market, and fences of stolen merchandise.[8] (A black market for guns imported from less restrictive areas may be important in the few cities, such as New York, which have stringent regulations on gun purchase.)[9] These sources of supply are presumably characterized by significant transaction costs, due to the difficulty buyers and sellers encounter in finding each other and negotiating a deal in such markets. Potential buyers in these markets will ordinarily have to search, or simply postpone purchase for some length of time, before encountering an acceptable offer of sale. The result is that the typical robber will own a gun—if ever—during a smaller fraction of his active career than would be true if there were no transaction costs.

The crucial assertion for the present context is that transaction costs are directly related to the density of gun ownership in a city. The supply of guns by fences and in the hand-to-hand market will be relatively "thin" and erratic in cities with low gun ownership rates; the typical buyer will have to search (or wait) longer before finding an acceptable deal in Boston than in Dallas. Relatively high transaction costs in low density cities would be expected to reduce the gun ownership rate among robbers and other criminals.

Robbers can acquire guns by borrowing, renting, or stealing them as well as by purchase, but the effect of city gun density on the ease of negotiating these other types of transactions should be much the same as for purchasers. For example, a gun originally purchased by an adult member of the household may be "borrowed" by a teenage son. (More than one-quarter of all robberies are committed by youths aged less than eighteen years.) Obviously this possibility is more likely to be available to any one teenager in a high density city than a low density one.

It is impossible to assess directly the importance of these mechanisms by which gun density influences gun availability to robbers. It is no doubt true that anyone who is determined to obtain a gun will be able to so, given enough money and effort. The "professional" robber will not be deterred by the relatively low gun availability I have ascribed to low density cities. But the difference in availability between a low density city such as Boston and a high density city such as Dallas may be enough to deter a substantial fraction of potential robbers from obtaining guns.

In addition to the effects of gun density, supply conditions are potentially influenced by state and local ordinances governing gun transactions. States which require buyers to obtain a police-issued permit before acquiring a gun may thereby drive more buyers into the informal markets (supplied by unlicensed sellers) in which the purchase permit requirement is readily evaded in practice. The effect of this increase in demand in such markets will be to raise the average money price, thereby reducing the availability of guns to robbers. In the long run, a licensing requirement may also reduce availability to robbers by reducing the overall density of guns in an area.

Demand. The value of a gun to an active robber is the sum of two components. First, the robber may value the gun as a "tool of the trade"—an investment which will have some payoff in the form of increasing the profitability of robberies. If the robber views the acquisition of a gun as purely a business proposition, then he will buy if he encounters an offer to sell at a price less than the discounted present value of the prospective increase in net robbery earnings.[10] Robbers will of course differ in their perceptions of how much a gun is worth as an investment, depending on how active they plan to be, their time horizon, and other factors.

The second component of the value of a gun to a robber is derived from a gun's other uses. After all, most handgun owners in urban areas are not robbers;

they acquire guns for their value in self-defense, hunting, target-shooting, or simply as collector's items (Newton and Zimring, 1969: ch. 10). There is no reason to believe that robbers do not share these values to some extent, although once again we would expect robbers to be somewhat heterogeneous with respect to the value placed on the possession of a gun for these purposes.

Whether a robber actually acquires a gun depends on the *total* value he attaches to gun ownership, compared with the money price and transaction costs of acquiring a gun. I have argued above that the overall gun density in a city will influence the cost of acquisition; is there also reason to believe that gun density will influence robbers' *demand* for guns? In a sense, the answer is yes. Cities differ very widely with respect to gun density, for reasons which appear to have more to do with tradition and culture than with the residents' objective circumstances. How else can we explain why 50 percent of urban households in Texas and the mountain states report owning guns, compared with only 10 percent of urban households in New England and the mid-Atlantic states? To the extent that robbers tend to share their urban neighbors' taste for gun ownership, then it will be true that robbers in high gun density cities will have a greater demand for guns than robbers in low density cities. The argument is not so much that gun density has a direct causal effect on robbers' demand, but rather that the same cultural factors which influence overall gun density are also likely to influence robbers' demand.

There are several conclusions which follow from the discussion above. First, gun density in a city influences the "availability" (costs of acquisition) to actual or potential robbers. Second, robbers living in cities with a high density of gun ownership are likely to have a greater demand for guns than robbers in low density cities. Intercity differences in gun density do not directly *cause* these postulated differences in demand; both are the result of a shared culture or tradition which places widely differing values on gun ownership among different regions of the country. Third, these demand and supply considerations both suggest that a relatively high proportion of robbers in high density cities will possess guns.

What effect will these hypothesized differences in gun ownership rates among robbers have on the amount and composition of robbery rates in a city?

The Effect of Gun Possession on Robbery

The defining task of robbery is to overcome through intimidation or force the victim's natural resistance to parting with valuables. Several techniques of physical intimidation are commonly used in robbery, including actual attack (as in "muggings" and "yokings"), and the threatening display of a weapon such as a gun, knife, or club. The probability of success depends on quickly forestalling or overcoming resistance on the part of the victim. If we think of robbery as a production process with robbers, victim, and weapons as inputs, the marginal product of a gun in robbery can be defined as the increase in the probability of successful intimidation (compared with the most effective alternative weapon) due to the use of the gun. This marginal product will depend on the circumstances, but will presumably be positive in most cases. A plausible assertion is that the marginal product of a gun is directly related to the ability of victims to defend themselves—their strength, access to weapons and alarms, and the like. The marginal product tends to be especially high in a commercial or bank robbery, and close to zero when the victim is an elderly woman on the street. The *value* of a gun's marginal product (VMP) is equal to the marginal product multiplied by the amount of money and other valuables which can be stolen from the victim if the robbery is successful. Since better defended targets tend to have greater than average "loot," the gun's VMP increases a fortiori with the ability of a victim to defend.

The relative attractiveness of different robbery targets thus changes when a (potential) robber acquires a gun for some reason; well-defended high payoff targets become much more attractive, while weak targets become only slightly more attractive at best. Consider the possible effects of acquiring a gun: (1) choice of targets unaffected, robbery technique changes to include a gun (weapon substitution); (2) change target choice as well as technique (target substitution); and if he was not previously active; (3) entry into the robbery business. Given the postulated change in the relative attractiveness of targets, we would expect target substitution, if it occurs, to involve substitution of better-defended targets for weaker ones. Entry, if it occurs, would be likely to occur against well-defended targets.

This analysis of the individual robber's response to the acquisition of a gun is a useful basis for generating predictions about the effect of the adoption of a successful disarmament policy in a city. Policy-relevant concerns include the effect on the overall robbery rate, the effect on the relative frequency with which guns are used in robbery, and the effect on the relative frequency with which different target types are robbed.

Robbery rates. The effect of a change in gun availability on robbery rates is not clear. For example, an increase in gun availability may result in some potential robbers "entering" the business. But the average rate at which active robbers commit this crime may well *decrease* as a result of the increase in gun availability. The targets available to gun robbers tend to be more lucrative than those selected by nongun robbers,[11] and the likelihood that the robbery will be successful is also higher with a gun. The average "take" of a gun robbery is about two and one-half times as high as the average "take" of nongun street robberies. A robber who acquires a gun may substitute a few lucrative targets for many less lucrative targets, thereby maintaining his income while reducing his risk of arrest and punishment. It is possible that the average rate of robbery commission per active robber will fall enough to compensate for the postulated increase in the number of active robbers; if so, then an increase in gun availability will not cause an increase in the overall robbery rate.

This discussion can be formalized as follows. Suppose the individual robber maximizes the expected value of his utility for a period given by

$$pU[Y(p,G)] + (1 - p)V[Y(p,G)], \text{ where} \tag{1}$$

$1 - p$ = probability of being arrested and punished (assumed to occur at the end of the period)

G = indicator for the possession of a gun

Y = income from robbery, assumed to be a differentiable function of the risk level $(1 - p)$ chosen by the robber

U = utility of robbery income if the robber is not arrested and punished

V = utility of robbery income if the robber is arrested and punished

It is assumed that

$$U(Y) > V(Y) \tag{2}$$

$$U, V > 0 > U'', V'' \tag{3}$$

$$Y_p < 0 \tag{4}$$

These assumptions imply the following condition for a utility-maximizing choice of p (and hence Y):

$$Y_p = \frac{V - U}{pU' + (1 - p)V'} \tag{5}$$

It is crucial in interpreting this result to define the income locus $\dot{V} = Y(p, G)$ with some care. It is assumed that at the beginning of the period the robber perceives a variety of robbery opportunities, which differ according to the expected "take" and the probability of apprehension and punishment. Any given income level can be achieved in a variety of ways; for example, the robber might expect to take $200 either by robbing four people on the street or one liquor store. For each income level Y, the $Y - p$ locus reflects the minimum-p combination of robberies which will achieve at least that level of total income.

The solution for p will in general be different when the robber owns a gun $(G = 1)$ than when he does not $(G = 0)$. Figure 1 illustrates this shift, in the likely case in which acquisition of a gun increases the robber's illicit income. But this result does *not* imply that the *number* of robberies committed during the period increases as a result of the acquisition of a gun; the relationship between robbery income and the number of robberies is not clear, but it is plausible that the "gun"-solution involves fewer, more lucrative robberies than the nongun solution. The basic problem here is that a simple unweighted count of the number of robberies is not the theoretically appropriate index of robbery activity. However, appropriate adjustments to this count cannot be made from available data.

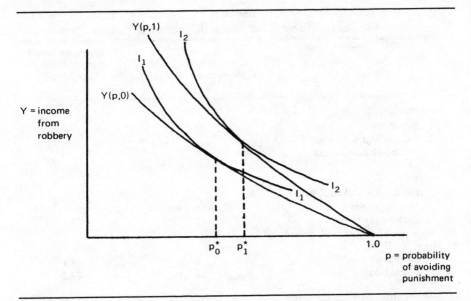

Figure 1

Another reason why an increase in gun availability (in the sense of gun density) may have a negative effect on the overall robbery rate is that potential robbery victims are more likely to be armed in cities where gun ownership is widespread. The probability that a robber will be killed or injured by his victim is small but not insignificant, particularly in the case of commercial robbery. Such justifiable homicides almost always are committed with a gun, so that potential victims in high gun density cities should pose a greater threat to robbers than in low density cities. Table 4 presents statistics on the likelihood that a robber will be killed by his victim or by an employee of a commercial enterprise. The probability is very low in the low gun density regions (the northeastern and Pacific coast cities), but much higher in the southern and midwestern cities where gun owner- ship is much more common. These death rates can be compared with the overall annual death rate for twenty-year-old Negro males of 340 per 100,000. In Atlanta, for example, a robber in this demographic group would double the likelihood of his death by committing seven robberies in a year. The likelihood of a robber being wounded by his victim is presumably some multiple of the likelihood that he will be killed. It should be noted that these data would have been much more informative if it had been possible to separate commercial and noncommercial justifiable homicides. It may be, for example, that justifiable homicide rates are a function of the fraction of robbery targets which hire armed guards, rather than a function of overall gun density in a city. Nevertheless, the statistics are adequate for demonstrating that the fear of some victims' ability to defend themselves should be considered when analyzing deterrents to robbery.

TABLE 4

Civilian Justifiable Homicides with Robbers as Victims

	Number of Civilian Justifiable Homicides in Robbery, 1973 and 1974	Estimated Death Rate of Robbers per 100,000 Robberies
A. Northeast		
1. New York	38	4.5
2. Boston, Buffalo, Newark, Pittsburgh (combined)	6	4.3
B. Pacific		
3. Los Angeles, Oakland, Portland, San Diego, San Francisco (combined)	11	3.1
C. Mid Atlantic		
4. Baltimore	9	8.1
5. Washington	11	27.2
D. Midwest—High Gun Density Cities		
6. Cincinnati	2	4.4
7. Cleveland	14	20.7
8. Detroit	50	25.6
9. St. Louis	10	23.1
E. South—High Gun Density Cities		
10. Atlanta	16	48.2
11. Houston	13	17.9
12. New Orleans	4	10.2

NOTE: The count of justifiable homicides of robbers was tabulated by hand from the Supplementary Homicide Reports submitted to the FBI by the city police departments. Most (though by no means all) reported justifiable homicides include some information on the circumstances, allowing the robbery justifiable homicides by civilians (including security guards) to be identified and distinguished from justifiable homicides in other contexts. It was not possible in many instances to distinguish between commercial and noncommercial robbery incidents.

The second column is the quotient of (1) one-half the two-year total of justifiable homicides, and (2) twice the number of robberies reported in the most recent victimization survey conducted in the city. (Surveys were conducted in 1974 or 1975.) The denominator is doubled to reflect the fact that the average robbery incident involves about two robbers.

Making Inferences from Analysis of Cross-Section Data

The empirical analysis which follows measures the intercity relationship between gun density and the rate and composition of robbery. There is also a preliminary attempt to measure the effect of a requirement that gun purchasers must possess a license issued by the state authorities.

These results can only be interpreted in the context of a causal framework such as that presented above. The central argument is that the fraction of active robbers who possess guns is closely related to the overall density of gun ownership in a city. To the extent that high gun density cities tend to have relatively undesirable patterns or levels of robbery, we can conclude that a program which was successful in reducing gun ownership among robbers would tend to improve this aspect of the crime program, other things being equal. One possible method of reducing gun ownership among robbers is to impose regulations, such as restrictive licensing, which have the effect of reducing overall gun density in a city. This strategy should be effective against robbery because it should reduce gun availability to robbers. The only caveat to this conclusion is that an overall reduction in gun ownership may undermine whatever deterrent effect that widespread gun ownership has on robbers (but this concern is unlikely to be important if shopkeepers are still permitted to own guns or hire guards). If high gun density cities do *not* differ with respect to robbery rates and patterns from low density cities, we can conclude that gun ownership by robbers is not of much concern to public policy.

Subsequent sections discuss the measurement of gun density, the issues involved in specifying appropriate robbery equations, and the results from estimating these equations using cross-section data on cities.

MEASURING GUN DENSITY

By "gun density" I mean either the fraction of households in a city who own guns or the number of guns per household. Ideally for my purposes, the measure would be limited to handguns and other concealable firearms (e.g., sawed-off shotguns), since almost all robberies are committed with such guns. In fact, 96 percent of robberies reported by police departments to the FBI were committed with handguns in 1967 (U.S. Department of Justice, FBI, 1967). A further desirable refinement would be to exclude guns which for one reason or another are not operational.[12]

Since data on gun sales by city are not available, and the many nationwide sample surveys of gun ownership have samples which are too thin to permit estimates for individual cities, it is necessary to measure gun density indirectly. Any measure which is highly correlated with gun density would be acceptable for my purpose here, since such a proxy would have essentially the same cardinal properties as a direct measure of density.[13]

Three possible proxies for gun density are the fraction of suicides committed with a gun, the fraction of homocides committed with a gun, and the number of fatal gun accidents per capita. Data on suicide and gun accidents for each of the fifty largest cities were calculated from unpublished vital statistics data. Homicide statistics were calculated from unpublished FBI data. The author can supply full statistics on request. Each of these measures is briefly discussed below.

The Fraction of Suicides Committed with a Gun

Assuming that most suicide attempts are made with weapons which are readily available to the victim, we would expect that the fraction of suicide attempts made with a gun in a city would reflect gun density in that city. The measure actually used here—the fraction of *successful* suicides committed with a gun—will presumably be larger than the fraction of attempts with a gun to the extent that guns tend to be more deadly than other suicide weapons.[14] However, this "instrumentality effect" of guns will not change the *ordering* which this statistic gives to the cities.

The Fraction of Murders Committed with a Gun[15]

Most murders are the direct result of arguments and fights. This lack of premeditation suggests, as in the case of suicide, that the weapon which is selected will be one readily at hand (and not acquired specifically for the purpose of committing the murder). The homicide statistics used exclude murders which were associated with an act of arson, robbery, or rape.

Since three-quarters of gun murders are committed with handguns, it would appear that this measure is more closely associated with handgun density than with the density of guns per se.

Fatal Accident Rate

The fatal firearms accident rate should reflect the density of guns which are actively in use in hunting, target shooting, and the like, rather than the overall density of guns. Hence it is not directly related to gun density, as are the preceding two measures. Indeed, the firearms fatal accident rate for the nation has fallen steadily over the last twenty-five years, in spite of the evident increase in gun ownership rates—this decrease may be the result of a decline in the amount of hunting in the United States during this period.

Besides this challenge to the validity of the fatal gun accident rate as an indicator of gun density, there is a practical problem in using it for this purpose: In many cities, the annual number of gun accidents is so low that relatively small inconsistencies in classification could result in a substantial change in the city's ranking. In any event, it is of some interest that the gun fatal accident rate is positively correlated across cities with each of the first two measures.

The gun density index which I have adopted for use in this study is the average of the percentage of suicides with gun and the percentage of homicides with gun. Besides the a priori arguments briefly presented above, there are two pieces of evidence which suggest very strongly that this measure is a valid indicator of gun density.

First, in spite of the fact that murder and suicide differ radically in terms of motivation, circumstances, and demographic patterns, the percentage of suicides with gun is highly correlated with the percentage of homicides with gun across cities ($p = .82$). Apparently both these measures are heavily influenced by the same underlying city characteristic.

A second test of the validity of the city gun density index was made by comparing it with the results of the gun ownership question on the NORC General Social Surveys conducted in 1973, 1974, and 1976 (no gun ownership question was included in the 1975 survey). By combining the three survey samples, I obtained a sample dense enough to estimate regional gun ownership patterns with a reasonable degree of accuracy. Table 5 gives the fraction of urban (population greater than 250,000) households which reported owning a firearm in each of eight regions. The fraction of households which reported owning a pistol is also given in this table. Both of these statistics can be compared with the population-weighted average of the city gun index for each of these regions. Figure 2 plots the NORC data against the gun density index across the eight regions, together with the corresponding regression line. Both pistol ownership and overall firearm ownership rates are linearly related to the gun density index across regions, with correlation coefficients of .83 and .94, respectively. Furthermore, the predicted values of gun and pistol ownership rates calculated from the regressions are within the 95 percent confidence interval of the survey point estimates in every case.

Taken together, these results demonstrate the validity of the gun density index. The comparison with the NORC survey results suggest that this index has interval scale properties, and the regression results provide a method for estimating the actual gun or pistol ownership rate for any one city from the gun density index number for that city.

DETERMINANTS OF THE INTERCITY DIFFERENCES IN ROBBERY RATE

Official (UCR) robbery rates differ tremendously among large cities; for 1975, the most robbery-prone city (Detroit) suffered from a reported robbery rate which was *nine times* as high as the lowest city (San Jose) with the range running from 1.6/1000 to 14.9/1000.

The criminology literature abounds with suggestions of city characteristics which should be considered in explaining intercity crime differences, and no single equation purporting to explain these differences could take more than a few of these explanatory variables into account. Since my objective is primarily to measure the effect of gun density on robbery rates, rather than to provide a complete explanation of intercity differences in robbery, there is no necessity to try all possibilities. It is well known that an unbiased estimate of the effect of an explanatory variable X can be generated by a multivariate regression analysis which includes only those explanatory variables which are correlated with X. In practice, the omission of explanatory variables from the regression equation will not seriously bias the coefficient estimate for X so long as these omitted variables are only weakly correlated with X or have only a weak causal effect on the dependent variable for the sample which is being used. Unfortunately, in a field such as criminology where theory gives so little direction to empirical work, it is difficult to know a priori which variables are important in the sense discussed above.

The procedure I have adopted for selecting a specification for the robbery equation is to map out several categories of explanatory variables which a priori

TABLE 5
Relationship Between Gun Density Index and Estimated Percentage of Households Owning Guns

Region	Gun Density Index	Urban Households Owning Pistol (%)	Predicted Pistol Owner-ship (%)	Residual	Urban Households Owning Firearm (%)	Predicted Firearm Ownership (%)	Residual	N
New England and Mid Atlantic	37.0	5.0	4.5	.5	10.0	11.1	-1.2	281
Pacific	46.8	11.6	10.7	.9	25.9	21.4	4.5	112
East North Central	57.4	14.6	17.4	-2.8	28.8	32.5	-3.7	205
South Atlantic	59.2	24.0	18.6	5.4	40.0	34.4	5.6	75
West North Central	60.5	11.1	19.4	-8.3	27.8	35.7	-7.9	54
West South Central	68.6	22.2	24.5	-2.3	41.7	44.2	-2.5	108
Mountain	69.0	33.8	24.8	9.0	48.5	44.6	3.9	68
East South Central	74.6	25.8	28.3	-2.5	51.7	50.5	1.2	58

considerations or previous research suggest are important. One or more variables which seem to capture the essential aspects of each category were then included in the equation, though in some cases they were dropped before being included in the final specification for reasons I explain below.

Each of these categories are briefly discussed below. For a definition of the variables actually used in the robbery equations and the data on which these equations were estimated, contact the author.

The Dependent Variables

For the regressions reported in Tables 6 and 8, the dependent variables are the total number of robberies of a particular type (gun, nongun, or total) which occurred in the central city in 1975, divided by the city's population. Each of these rates is distributed approximately log normally across cities. All regressions are run twice, once using a linear form and once using the log of the robbery rate as a dependent variable. In table 7, the dependent variable is the log of the ratio of gun and nongun robbery rates.

Since my focus is on conditions which influence the supply of robberies, the robbery rates are to be viewed as robbery commission rates rather than

---

NOTE TO TABLE 5:

NOTE: The regions include the following cities from the fifty cities sample: (1) Boston, Buffalo, Newark, New York, Philadelphia, Pittsburgh, Rochester; (2) San Francisco, San Diego, Long Beach, San Jose, Los Angeles, Seattle, Portland; (3) Milwaukee, Chicago, Toledo, Indianapolis, Cincinnati, Detroit, Cleveland, Columbus; (4) Washington, Baltimore, Miami, Norfolk, Charlotte, Atlanta, Jacksonville, Tampa; (5) Saint Paul, Minneapolis, Omaha, Kansas City, St. Louis; (6) Oklahoma City, Austin, Tulsa, El Paso, Houston, San Antonio, New Orleans, Fort Worth, Dallas, Baton Rouge; (7) Denver, Tucson, Phoenix; (8) Louisville, Memphis, Birmingham, Nashville.

The gun density index is the population weighted average for each region of the city gun density indexes in that region. The procedures used for constructing the city gun density indexes can be obtained from the author.

The "% owning pistol" and "% owning firearm" are calculated from the National Opinion Research Center's General Social Survey files for 1973, 1974, and 1976. The results for the three years were combined in order to yield more reliable estimates. "N" is the total number of respondents in these three years living in cities with population exceeding 250,000 in the relevant region. These surveys use a clustered sampling technique; the reliability of the estimates is about the same as the reliability which would be obtained by a pure random sample with two-thirds N respondents.

"Predicted % owning pistol" is calculated from a regression of the NORC estimates on the regional gun density indexes across the eight regions. The estimated equation is:

$$HG_r = -19.0 + .63\, I_r \qquad\qquad R^2 = .68$$
$$ (10.6) \quad (.18)$$

where the standard error of the coefficient estimates are given in parenthesis. The "residual" is the difference in the actual percentage owning a pistol and the percentage predicted from the equation.

"Predicted % owning firearm" is calculated similarly from this regression:

$$G_r = -27.5 + 1.05\, I_r \qquad\qquad R^2 = .88$$
$$ (9.3) \quad (.15)$$

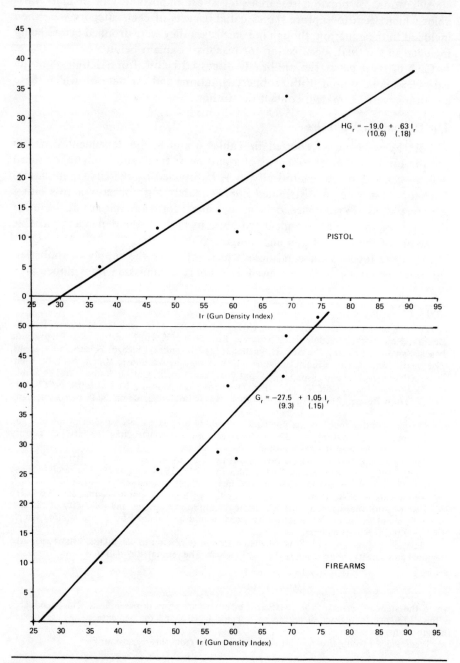

Figure 2

victimization rates. They are misleading as such to the extent that some robberies in each city are committed by people who are not residents of the city, and some residents of the city commit robberies outside the city limits. The few useful replies received in response to a questionnaire mailed to police chiefs in the sample of fifty central cities suggest that there is some difference among cities with respect to the fraction of robberies committed by nonresidents: Police estimates of the fraction of robbery arrestees who were nonresidents ranged from 1 percent to 20 percent. One possible proxy for the net flow of robbers into a city is the fraction of the metropolitan area's population which resides in the city.[16] Presumably the main city in a metropolitan area acts as a "magnet" for criminals, since in most cases it will be the center of commercial activity and night life in the area. The relative size of the inflow to the central city should be closely related to the relative size of the nearby population.

Errors in Measurement

It has been thoroughly documented that crime rates reported by the police understate the true crime rates in a city for every crime except murder. Of greater concern is that some cities underreport robberies to a greater degree than others. Intercity reporting differences are only of concern for our purposes if the fraction of robberies which are reported in official statistics happens to be correlated with the gun density index. There is no apparent method of controlling for reporting differences in the context of the robbery equation. However, it is possible to test the hypothesis that the degree of underreporting is uncorrelated with gun availability by using an alternative measure of the robbery rate.

Victimization surveys were conducted in twenty-six of the fifty cities during either 1974 or 1975. Reported robbery rates generated by these surveys are subject to various errors and are not strictly comparable to the published UCR data (the most important difference being the fact that nonresidents who are robbed in the central city are not counted in the victimization surveys; Skogan, 1975; Fienberg, 1977). In any event, the victimization survey results have been viewed by some scholars (though not all) as a more consistent representation of robbery rates than the UCR data.[17] If true, then the ratio of the UCR robbery rate to the victimization survey robbery rate should measure the degree of underreporting in a city. The correlation between this ratio and the gun availability index for cities for which data are available is small and statistically insignificant (-.13). The victimization survey measure of robbery rates is also used as a dependent variable in one of the regressions reported in Table 6. The primary problem with using this measure is the small sample size.

Demographic Characteristics

Almost all robberies are committed by youthful males, and about 70 percent of urban robberies are committed by blacks (Cook, 1976). These demographic patterns do not "explain" robbery in any sociological sense, but it is perhaps acceptable to include measures of the demographic characteristics of the cities' populations as proxies for whatever underlying factors *do* explain these patterns.

TABLE 6
Regression Results for Overall City Robbery Rates, 1975

Independent Variables	Dependent Variables								Means for 46 Cities[a]
	Log UCR Robbery Rate/1,000					UCR Robbery Rate/1,000		Log of Victim Survey Robbery Rate/1,000	
	(1)	(2)	(3)	(4)	(5)	(6)	(7)	(8)	
1. Constant	-.407 (1.332)	.870* (.472)	.837* (.450)	.847* (.486)	.784 (.471)	1.53 (2.92)	1.39 (2.84)	-4.73*** (.42)	
2. Gun density index	.140 (.706)	.341 (.667)	.230 (.637)	.508 (.682)	.411 (.661)	2.60 (4.09)	.95 (3.98)	.882 (.650)	.579
3. Gun regulation dummy	.256* (.142)	.252* (.135)	.254* (.126)						.196
4. Youthful Black males (%)	.128** (.052)	.114*** (.041)	.122*** (.044)	.108** (.042)	.116** (.046)	.467* (.255)	.637** (.278)	.0197 (.0328)	2.55
5. Population/Square mile (1,000s)	.0358* (.0210)	.0453** (.0170)	.0448*** (.0157)	.0577*** (.0161)	.0575*** (.0151)	.338*** (.097)	.315*** (.091)	.0480*** (.0150)	7.00
6. Fraction of SMSA in city	-.861** (.389)	-.972*** (.315)	-.971*** (.300)	-1.035*** (.323)	-1.027*** (.313)	-4.48** (1.94)	-3.87** (1.89)		.466
7. Crimes/Cop (1,000s)[a]			.855** (.360)		.913** (.376)	6.82*** (2.27)			.291

TABLE 6 (Continued)

	Dependent Variables								
	Log UCR Robbery Rate/1,000					UCR Robbery Rate/1,000		Log of Victim Survey Robbery Rate/1,000	Means for 46 Cities[a]
Independent Variables	(1)	(2)	(3)	(4)	(5)	(6)	(7)	(8)	
8. Retail stores/100 population	.635 (.451)	.418 (.398)	.178 (.373)	.215 (.396)	−.034 (.375)	−1.74 (2.37)	−3.09 (2.26)		.807
9. Fraction in relative poverty	.546 (1.753)	−.101 (1.583)	−.095 (1.573)	.345 (1.615)	.400 (1.629)	12.0 (9.7)	10.0 (9.8)		.219
10. NE region dummy	−.185 (.174)								.130
11. SE region dummy	−.118 (.143)								.370
12. W region dummy	.021 (.135)								.217
13. Log population	.0840 (.0951)								13.3
R^2	.825	.804	.858	.786	.839	.774	.830	.458	
N	46	46	39	46	39	46	39	25	

a. The mean for independent variable 7 (crimes/cop in 1,000s) is calculated for the thirty-nine cities for which these data were available.
*Significant at 10% level.
**Significant at 5% level.
***Significant at 1% level.

TABLE 7

Regression Results for City Robbery Rates, 1975: The Gun-Nongun Mix

Independent Variables	Dependent Variable	
	Log (Gun Robberies ÷ Nongun Robberies)	
	(1)	(2)
1. Constant	−.583 (.456)	−.876** (.364)
2. Gun density index	2.48*** (.64)	2.63*** (.52)
3. Gun regulation dummy	−.145 (.130)	−.102 (.102)
4. Youthful Black males (%)	.104** (.040)	.107*** (.036)
5. Population/Square mile (1,000s)	.00715 (.01639)	.00660 (.01270)
6. Fraction of SMSA in city	−.263 (.305)	−.235 (.242)
7. Crimes/Cop (1,000s)		.627** (.291)
8. Retail stores/100 population	−.508 (.385)	−.674** (.302)
9. Fraction in relative poverty	−3.30** (1.53)	−2.91** (1.27)
R^2	.701	.815
N	46	39

**Significant at 5% level.
***Significant at 1% level.

The variable used in the regression specification here is the percentage of the city's population in 1970 which was black males aged ten to twenty. (By 1975 this group would be aged fifteen to twenty-five, the peak ages for participation in robbery.)

Socioeconomic Characteristics of the Population

Robbers, like other violent criminals, are disproportionately drawn from poor neighborhoods. In part the relationship between poverty and violent crime may be the result of one aspect of the deterrence phenomenon; people with poor legitimate opportunities have less to lose from being arrested and punished. The variable actually used in the robbery regression is a measure of the fraction of the city population who are relatively poor; specifically, the per-

TABLE 8

Regression Results for City Robbery Rates, 1975: Separate Analyses for Gun and Nongun Rates

Dependent Variables

Independent Variables	Log Gun Robbery/1,000			Gun Robbery/1,000		Log Nongun Robbery/1,000			Nongun Robbery/1,000	
	(1)	*(2)*	*(3)*	*(4)*	*(5)*	*(6)*	*(7)*	*(8)*	*(9)*	*(10)*
1. Constant	−.101 (.542)	−.308 (.465)	−.268 (.455)	.425 (1.789)	−.052 (1.468)	.469 (.526)	.546 (.538)	.608 (.512)	1.10 (1.64)	1.45 (1.78)
2. Gun density index	1.74** (.76)	1.74** (.65)	1.60** (.64)	5.77** (2.51)	4.94** (2.06)	−.638 (.738)	−.816 (.755)	−1.030 (.724)	−3.17 (2.30)	−3.98 (2.50)
3. Gun regulation dummy			.197 (.127)					.299** (.143)		
4. Youthful Black males (%)	.160*** (.047)	.172*** (.046)	.176*** (.045)	.365** (.156)	.524*** (.144)	.0517 (.0458)	.0625 (.0527)	.0693 (.0502)	.102 (.143)	.113 (.174)
5. Population/Square mile (1,000s)	.0559*** (.0179)	.0563*** (.0149)	.0465*** (.0159)	.155*** (.059)	.139*** (.047)	.0559*** (.0174)	.0548*** (.0172)	.0399** (.0178)	.183*** (.054)	.175*** (.057)
6. Fraction of SMSA in city	−1.16*** (.36)	−1.13*** (.31)	−1.09*** (.30)	−3.01*** (1.19)	−2.45** (.98)	−.937** (.349)	−.922** (.358)	−.857** (.341)	−1.47 (1.09)	−1.42 (1.18)
7. Crimes/Cop (1,000s)		1.21*** (.37)	1.17*** (.36)		5.46*** (1.17)		.608 (.429)	.539 (.409)		1.36 (1.42)
8. Retail stores/100 population	−.048 (.441)	−.383 (.370)	−.219 (.378)	−2.12 (1.46)	−3.12** (1.17)	.344 (.428)	.206 (.429)	.455 (.424)	.379 (1.337)	.025 (1.417)
9. Fraction in relative poverty	−1.45 (1.80)	−1.28 (1.61)	−1.66 (1.59)	−.07 (5.94)	−2.21 (5.08)	2.11 (1.75)	1.83 (1.86)	1.25 (1.79)	12.1** (5.5)	12.2* (6.1)
R²	.738	.838	.850	.665	.814	.794	.823	.846	.810	.826
N	46	39	39	46	39	46	39	39	46	39

*Significant at 10% level.   **Significant at 5% level.   ***Significant at 1% level.

centage of the city's families with income less than one-half the median family income for the Standard Metropolitan Statistical Area.[18]

Robbery Inputs

Two inputs to the "production process" which characterizes robbery are weapons and targets.

The gun density index developed earlier is included in the robbery equation primarily as a measure of gun availability to robbers. One possible objection to including this variable as a determinant of the robbery rate is that the legitimate demand for guns (especially *handguns*) is in part motivated by a desire for self-protection against *criminals*.[19] It could therefore be argued that gun density and crime rates are *simultaneously* determined, with gun density influencing crime rates and vice versa. This problem, if present, would leave the proper interpretation of an estimated coefficient on gun density in a crime equation in doubt. However, this simultaneity argument is only a problem in the present context if guns are purchased for defense against *robbery*. This may be the case for store owners, but it is unlikely that the typical gun buyer who seeks protection for a home is concerned about robbery (most of which occurs on the street) so much as *burglary*—criminal intrusions into the home. If the threat of being robbed has little effect on the overall demand for guns, the simultaneity problem is not serious. It is certainly true that robbery is not the primary determinant of intercity differences in gun density, since the two are *negatively* correlated across cities ($\rho = -.38$; see Figure 3).

Ideally we would want to include a measure of the availability of attractive robbery targets in the robbery equation. The measure actually used—the number of stores per capita in the city—is not entirely satisfactory, but it can be justified. The extent to which store owners defend themselves against robbery (e.g., by minimizing the amount of cash kept on hand, hiring guards, and so on) depends in part on the probability that the store will be robbed. The robbery victimization rate *per store* will be lower in cities with a high density of stores, other things (including the robbery rate per capita) being equal. Thus, the arguable effect of an increase in store density is to dilute the robbery rate, thus reducing the incentive to self-protect and thereby increasing the attractiveness of stores as robbery targets.[20]

Criminal Justice System Effectiveness

The criminal justice system influences crime rates through a variety of mechanisms, the most important of which are associated with the threat and delivery of punishment. In particular, the deterrence mechanism has been widely studied in the context of explaining interjurisdictional differences in crime rates. A number of studies have reported that differences in the threat of punishment across jurisdictions (states, cities, counties, and even precincts have been used as units of observation in these studies) are negatively correlated with crime rates, and this negative correlation has been interpreted as a result of the deterrence process.[21] However, there are serious methodological problems with these studies. Furthermore, at least two carefully done empirical studies (both using cross-section data on states) have found no evidence that the deterrence effect explains a significant portion of interjurisdiction differences in crime rates (Forst, 1976; Nagin, 1977b). There are at least three possible explanations for the null result reported in these studies: (1) the deterrence effect is very weak; (2) states do not differ very much in the relative effectiveness of their CJSs; or, most likely, (3) the measures of CJS effectiveness used in these and other studies are very inadequate proxies for the underlying dimension of interest.

Because of the serious doubts I have concerning the usual measures of CJS effectiveness (see Cook, 1977b), I have used somewhat different variables in the robbery regressions which follow. The only such variable which appears in the final specification[22] is the ratio of FBI Index crimes to the average number of police officers who are actually on patrol at any one time in a city—an indicator of the workload of one sector of the CJS.[23] Presumably the police resources available for the solution of any one robbery, and hence police effectiveness, will decline as the overall crime workload increases. Because this CJS effectiveness measure was not available for all cities in the sample, all regressions were run both with and without this variable.

Population Density

Wilson and Boland (1976) give several possible justifications for including city population density in a regression analysis of robbery including the "opportunity" theory that potential victims are more readily available in dense cities and the "subculture" theory that "dense cities should make it easier for like minded individuals to find and associate with each other under conditions of weak social control and so, by their interaction, intensify any proclivities they may have for criminal activity" (1976: 224). Hoch's (1974) experiments with explaining inter-SMSA differences in crime rates found that the log of SMSA population performs better than population density as an explanatory variable, but such was not the case in the present context (see Table 6).

Regional Variables

I experimented with the common practice in cross-section studies of including regional indicators in the regression specification. In spite of the multitude of possible justifications for including these variables, coefficient estimates on regional variables were in all cases statistically insignificant and had little effect on estimates of the coefficients of other variables in the equation. For this reason, regression results for specifications which include regional indicators are not reported here, except for one example included in Table 6.

State Regulation

A dummy variable indicating relatively strong state regulation of gun purchasers is included in some of the regressions. In particular, the indicator takes the value one for cities located in states which require purchasers to obtain a permit, and zero otherwise. The cities so indicated are Boston, Buffalo, New York City, Chicago, Detroit, Newark, Baltimore, St. Louis, Kansas City, and Charlotte.

Regression Results for the Total Robbery Rate

Table 6 presents results for six alternative regression specifications for explaining intercity differences in the overall UCR robbery rate in 1975. A seventh regression is also included using as a dependent variable the National Crime Panel's survey-based measure of the robbery rate for each of twenty-six cities. The first six regressions differ with respect to functional form and which set of independent variables are included. Results for other regression specifications based on this same collection of variables (not reported here) are qualitatively similar.

The most important concern in the present context is the relationship between gun density and robbery rates. In every regression, the estimated coefficient is positive, but statistically insignificant. The conclusion that there is no demonstrable systematic relationship between these two variables could be anticipated from a glance at Figure 3; the scatter plot of robbery rates vs. the gun density index is diffuse and essentially patternless. Since the theoretical discussion earlier suggested that there is no strong a priori reason to expect either a positive or negative relationship between robbery rates and gun density, these results are not particularly troublesome.

The result which *is* surprising is that cities located in states which have the most stringent regulation on gun purchase have significantly *higher* robbery rates than other cities, ceteris paribus. The next section reports that this positive association obtains for both gun and nongun robbery (see Table 8). Since it is hard to believe that gun regulations cause increases in the robbery rate, one is forced to conclude that there are variables omitted from the regression specifications which influence robbery rates and which are systematically related to the presence of relatively stringent gun regulations.

Other coefficient estimates are for the most part in agreement with prior expectations, with the exception of "retail stores per capita" and the relative poverty measure. These two variables have weak and erratic estimated effects on the overall robbery rate.

Regression Results for Gun and Nongun Robbery Rates

Even if the gun density is not systematically related to the overall level of robbery in a city, the availability of guns to robbers is still of concern to policymakers if gun density influences robbers' choice of weapons or targets. Figure 4 presents the scatter diagram relating gun density to the fraction of robberies committed with a gun. This diagram illustrates a clear positive association between the two variables. The regression results in Table 7 demonstrate that this association persists when factors which are thought to influence the overall

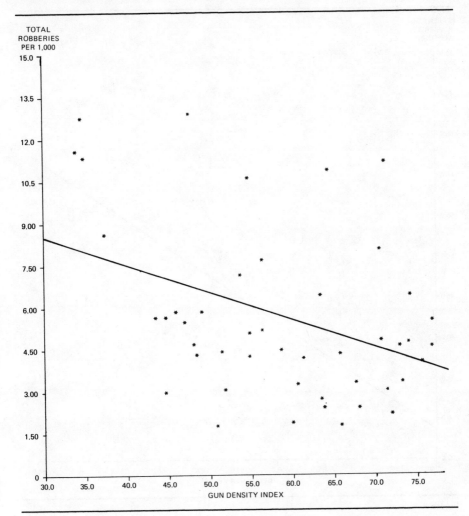

Figure 3

level of robbery are controlled for. Experiments with alternative functional forms, not reported here, yield similar results.

The estimated coefficient on the state gun regulation dummy variable requires some interpretation. Such regulations may affect weapon use in robbery indirectly by causing some reduction of overall gun density in a city. This indirect effect cannot be measured in the present context. The coefficient estimate on the dummy variable serves as a measure of the direct effect of these regulations, holding overall gun density constant. The negative coefficient estimate reported here is compatible with the existence of this direct effect, but the coefficient is not statistically significant.

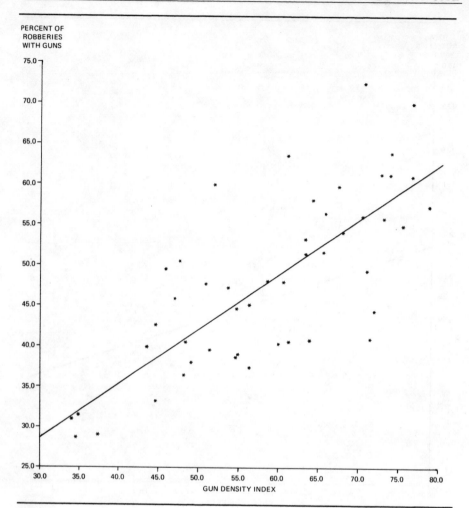

Figure 4

Table 8 presents regression results for a number of specifications utilizing gun or nongun robbery rates as the dependant variables. While there are no surprises here,[24] it is useful to make several more observations concerning the measured effect of gun density. First, the gun density coefficients in corresponding pairs of gun and nongun robbery regressions are measured with almost equal precision in every case. The estimated coefficients are significant in the gun robbery regressions and not in the nongun regressions because the estimated coefficients are larger (in absolute value) in the former.

Second, the elasticities associated with the gun density coefficient estimates for both the linear and log-dependant forms of the gun robbery regressions are all close to 1.0. This result can be transformed through a simple calculation to derive an estimate of the elasticity of gun robbery with respect to the percent of households owning a pistol—the answer in all cases is close to .5.[25] *In other words, a 10 percent reduction in the number of pistols in a city is associated with about a 5 percent reduction in the gun robbery rate.*

An analysis of the influence of gun availability on the distribution of robbery targets (commercial vs. noncommercial) did not yield any clear-cut results. The theoretical expectation that increasing gun availability should cause a relative increase in commercial robbery rates is not supported by the available data.

Conclusions from the findings presented in Tables 6, 7, and 8 can be briefly summarized. Both gun density and robbery rates differ widely among the cities in the sample, but there is little if any relationship between the two variables. The zero-order correlation is slightly negative and the partial correlations in a variety of multivariate specifications are all slightly positive. An increase in gun density is associated with some substitution of guns for other weapons in robbery. High gun density cities tend to have relatively high gun robbery rates and relatively low nongun robbery rates, whether or not other factors are controlled for in the analysis. The possible importance of this result is evaluated in the next section.

ROBBERY MURDERS

The evidence presented above suggests that the overall density of gun ownership in a city has little influence on the city's robbery rate, but a strong effect on the fraction of robberies which involve a gun. The propensity of robbers to use guns rather than other weapons is of concern to the extent that the type of weapon influences the outcome of the robbery. The weapon-related differences in outcome, documented above, include differences in the fractions of robberies which result in injury, and death of the victim. This section focuses on the issue of robbery murder. Is it true that the increase in gun robberies associated with an increase in gun density causes a concomitant increase in the robbery murder rate?

The relationship between the typical robbery and the relatively few events which are classified by UCR as "robbery murders" is not well understood.[26] Weapon use in robbery, and indeed the overall robbery rate, will only influence the robbery murder rate if robbery murders are closely related to the typical robbery in which the victim is not killed. The following hypothetical examples illustrate some of the possible relationships between robberies and robbery murders:

Example 1: A robber holds up a liquor store with a gun, demanding cash. When the clerk reaches under the counter as if to set off an alarm or pick up a gun, the robber panics and shoots and kills the clerk.

Example 2: A man enters a liquor store, shoots and kills the clerk without speaking, then empties the cash register.[27]

Example 3: One man shoots and kills another following a drunken argument. As an afterthought, the killer takes the victim's wallet.

All three of these cases would most likely be officially classified as robbery murders. The examples differ dramatically in terms of the relationship between the two elements of the crime: the theft, and the murder. If the robbery murder statistics are dominated by cases similar to example 3, then it is appropriate to view robbery murder as more murder than robbery; in this case, we would expect variations in robbery rates to have little relationship to variations in the robbery murder rate. At the other extreme, as in example 1, is the possibility of murder as an accidental outcome of the instrumental violence (or threat thereof) which is an element of every robbery. The rate of such "accidental" robbery murders may be influenced by the composition of robberies with respect to weapon use, circumstances, and the like. Holding such factors constant, we would expect the robbery murder rate to vary proportionately with the overall robbery rate.

The crucial distinction between examples 1 and 3 is in terms of whether the primary motive of the assailant is to injure or to steal from the victim. The criminal's behavior in example 2 can be viewed as the result of a combination of the two motives—the violent act may be an end in itself, as well as a means for completing the theft successfully. There is indirect evidence that a large proportion of robberies which result in the victim's serious injury do involve greater than "necessary" levels of violence, suggesting that violence in such cases is not simply a means for obtaining compliance from the robbery victim.[28] To the extent that the level of violence used in robbery is partially determined by the robber's personality, rather than by instrumental considerations alone, the relationship between the typical robbery and those robberies which result in the victim's death becomes rather complex. The robbery death rate will be influenced by the robbery rate, but also by the distribution of "violence proneness" among robbers.

Regression results reported in Table 9 suggest that there is a tight link between the rates of robbery and robbery murder across the fifty cities in the current sample. The correlation between the gun robbery murder rate and the gun robbery rate is .90, and the correlation for the nongun case is .76. These results are supported by Zimring's time-series analysis of Detroit data.[29] They are strong evidence for rejecting the scenario suggested by example 3 as typical of robbery murders.

Equation 4 includes the murder rate (net of felony murder) which can be viewed as a further test of the possibility that robbery murder is "more murder than robbery" in the sense discussed above. The coefficient estimate is positive but not significant at the 10 percent level, and the two robbery rate variables continue to be significant and important explanations of robbery murder.

The natural inference from these results is that robbery murders are the probabilistic result of robberies. The coefficient estimates in equations 1 and 2 suggest that an additional 1,000 gun robberies result in 6.6-8.8 additional robbery murders, whereas an additional 100 nongun murders result in 1.6-2.6 additional robbery murders. Since the constant terms are not significantly different from zero, the results are compatible with the simple model suggested by example 1: Every robbery involving a given type of weapon has the same probability of resulting in the victim's death. This probability is about three times as high for

TABLE 9
Robbery Murder Rate as a Function of the Robbery Rate
Regression Results

Dependent Variable	Constant	Gun Robbery Rate/1,000	Nongun Robbery Rate/1,000	Assault Murder Rate/1,000	R^2	N
1. Gun robbery murder rate/ 100,000[a]	−.239 (.174)	.773*** (.056)			.81	47
2. Nongun robbery murder rate/ 100,000[a]	.081 (.098)		.211*** (.027)		.58	47
3. Total robbery murder rate/ 100,000[a]	−.284 (.232)	.907*** (.089)	.136* (.072)		.82	47
4. Total robbery murder rate/ 100,000[a]	−.463* (.255)	.741*** (.138)	.138* (.071)	.359 (.230)	.83	47

NOTE: Standard errors in parentheses.
a. 1974-1975 average.
   *Significant at 10% level.
  **Significant at 5% level.
***Significant at 1% level.

gun robberies as for nongun robberies. An alternative view of the results—one which is more compatible with the evidence discussed above—is that the dangerousness of a robbery depends on the violence proneness of the robber, the robbery circumstances, and perhaps other factors, but that the distribution of these factors is independent of the robbery rates across cities.

An alternative approach to estimating weapons effects in robbery is to regress the fraction of robberies which result in death on the fraction of robberies which involve guns. If the number of murders is in fact strictly proportional to the number of robberies of each weapon type, then the constant in this regression term can be interpreted as the likelihood of death in a nongun murder, and the coefficient as the difference between the likelihood of death in gun and nongun robberies.[30] The results of this equation indicate that the fraction of robberies involving guns explains a small but significant percentage of the intercity variance in the robbery murder/robbery ratio. The point estimate for the likelihood of death in a gun robbery is 7.2/1000, which is close to the estimate generated by equation 1.

$$\frac{\text{Robbery murders}}{\text{1000 robberies}} = \underset{(1.16)}{1.52} + \underset{(2.38)}{5.68} \ \frac{\text{Gun robberies}}{\text{Robberies}} \quad R^2 = .113$$

We can infer the effect on the robbery murder rate of a reduction in city gun density by combining the results from Tables 8 and 9. For example, using gun density coefficient estimates from linear equations 5 and 10 in Table 8, and the coefficient estimates from equation 3 of Table 9, a straightforward calculation[31] yields the following result: *A 10 percent reduction in the number of pistols in a city is associated with about a 4.2 percent reduction in the number of robbery murders.*

An alternative approach to estimating the effect of gun availability on the robbery murder rate is to calculate the "reduced form" regressions, presented in Table 10. The results of these regressions are very similar to the gun robbery regression results in Table 8; this similarity is not surprising given the high correlation between the gun robbery rate and the robbery murder rate, and the fact that the two variables by coincidence have the same mean. Based on the regression results in Table 10, equation 3, a 10 percent reduction in the number of pistols is associated with a reduction in the robbery murder rate by about 5 percent.

CONCLUSIONS

The conclusions reached from the theoretical and empirical analysis in this chapter are of course tentative, and subject to a variety of possible sources of error. Some findings appear in my judgment to be more robust and more strongly supported by the data than others and hence deserving of greater confidence. These "strong" findings are summarized first, followed by a summary of the weaker findings and a discussion of the proper interpretation of the findings relating to the effects of gun density.

Strong Findings

1. The proxy measure of the density of gun ownership in the fifty largest cities, discussed earlier, has a strong claim to validity for cross-section studies. It is the first serious effort to develop such a measure, and should be valuable in a variety of research contexts.

2. The fraction of robberies which involve guns is closely (positively) related to the overall density of gun ownership in a city.

3. Murders which are classified as robbery murders by UCR occur at a rate that is closely linked to the robbery rate. Therefore, it would appear that robbery murder is an outcome (in a probabilistic sense) of encounters which were motivated in some important sense by theft; that is, robbery murders are similar in that respect to robberies. About three times as many gun robberies result in the victim's death as is true for nongun robberies. Gun robbery murders are roughly proportional to nongun robberies. There is a strong case, then, for the claim that an increase in the proportion of robberies with guns will increase the ratio of robbery murders to robberies. There is some evidence that a relative increase in the use of guns in robbery may *reduce* the victim injury rate, but this possibility could not be thoroughly analyzed.

Other Findings

4. The density of gun ownership among city residents is not an important determinant of the city's robbery rate. This finding is subject to doubt primarily because it is possible that an important relationship does exist but is being

TABLE 10
Robbery Murder Rate/1,000 Residents[a]

	Regression Results			
	Log Robbery Murder Rate		Robbery Murder Rate	
Independent Variables	(1)	(2)	(3)	(4)
1. Constant	−1.696*	−1.485	−.728	−.942
	(.849)	(.898)	(1.879)	(1.951)
2. Gun density index	2.08*	1.70	5.92**	4.90*
	(1.20)	(1.28)	(2.66)	(2.78)
3. Youthful Black males (%)	.229***	.292***	.462***	.689***
	(.076)	(.093)	(.169)	(.202)
4. Population/Square mile (1,000s)	.0736**	.0731**	.208***	.195***
	(.0282)	(.0288)	(.062)	(.063)
5. Fraction of SMSA in city	−.903	−.954	−2.49*	−1.90
	(.581)	(.619)	(1.29)	(1.35)
6. Crimes/Cop (1,000s)		.843		3.94**
		(.722)		(1.57)
7. Retail stores/100 population	.690	.716	−1.76	−1.82
	(.708)	(.734)	(1.57)	(1.59)
8. Fraction in relative poverty	−.510	−2.38	−1.05	−5.79
	(2.796)	(3.09)	(6.19)	(6.71)
R^2	.689	.730	.718	.767
N	45	38	45	38

NOTE: Standard errors in parentheses.
a. 1974-1975 average.
 *Significant at 10% level.
 **Significant at 5% level.
***Significant at 1% level.

obscured in the present sample by the effect of some unknown factors which have been excluded from the regression specifications. This possibility is of less concern in evaluating finding 2, to the extent that the unknown factors tend to have the same proportional effect on gun and nongun robbery. (The intercity correlation between gun and nongun robbery rates is .60, suggesting that the etiology of gun and nongun robbery is similar.)

5. An increase in the density of gun ownership is associated with an increase in the gun robbery rate, and a corresponding increase in the rate of robbery murder.

6. Differences in gun density have little measurable effect on robbers' choice of targets as between commercial and noncommercial alternatives. A number of other dimensions of target choice are of interest, but were not investigated here due to data limitations.

7. State regulations requiring purchase permits have little if any direct

effect on the robbers' choice of weapon. These regulations may have an indirect effect by reducing overall gun density, but this possibility was not explored here. One of several problems in evaluating this conclusion is that there was no attempt to take the quality of the state's implementation mechanisms into account in measuring the effect of a purchase permit requirement.

Interpretation

The extent of gun ownership in a city is reasonably viewed as an important determinant of whether actual and potential robbers will acquire guns. First, guns are arguably more readily available in the "grey" and black markets in cities where gun ownership is widespread. Second, there is no reason to believe that criminals acquire guns only for specifically criminal purposes. If robbers are similar to other residents of their city with respect to their valuation of a gun's uses in noncriminal activities, then robbers' demand for guns will be relatively high in high density cities. The net cost of a gun in noncriminal uses will hence be lower in high density cities. While it is not possible to sort out these supply and demand effects, they both point toward the conclusion that a relatively high fraction of robbers will be armed in high density cities. A policy which was successful in increasing the net cost of acquiring a gun for use in robbery will then reduce the fraction of robberies committed with a gun. Given the empirical results reported here, this reduction in gun use would have little effect on the overall robbery rate, but would reduce the robbery murder rate.

NOTES

1. Some of these data are published in *Crime in the United States.*
2. This claim is verified by results reported in Cook and Nagin (1978: table IV, 2). For robberies involving adult male offenders reported in the National Crime Panel household victimization surveys, the following results were obtained:

Robbery Weapon	With Attack (%)	Attacks Resulting in Victim Hospitalization (%)
Gun	23	26
Knife or other	40	22
Unarmed	73	9

It should be noted that "gun" robberies are those in which at least one of the offenders had a gun (most robberies are committed by two or more offenders). An attack in a gun robbery may therefore involve another weapon. If the attack does involve a gun, it may be in the form of clubbing or pistol-whipping, rather than shooting. Injury results in the second column should be interpreted accordingly.
3. For a comprehensive discussion of the legal antecedents, politics, and effects of the GCA, see Zimring (1975).
4. The ordinance in the District of Columbia, which went into effect in 1976, bans the acquisition or transfer of handguns by District residents. The Sullivan Law in New York State has imposed a restrictive licensing system throughout most of the twentieth century.
5. Etzioni (1973) makes the comparison with Japan and other nations which have strict gun control laws.
6. See Bruce-Briggs's (1976) humorous critique of international comparisons. Newton and Zimring (1969: 124-125) discuss difficulties with international comparisons.

7. Of particular interest are evaluations of the recent crackdown on gun ownership and use in Jamaica (see Gendreau and Surridge, 1976; Diener and Crandall [n.d.]).

8. Newton and Zimring (1969: ch. 3) report on the basis of a 1968 Harris poll that over half (54 percent) of handguns are acquired used. Over half of used firearms are acquired from friends or other private parties.

9. The Bureau of Alcohol, Tobacco, and Firearms traced over 2,500 handguns "received, recovered, or seized" by the New York Police Department during a six-month period. Only 4 percent of these guns were first sold retail in New York State. In cities with less stringent gun regulations, the percentage of traced guns originating in state was much higher—e.g., 80 percent in Atlanta (see *Project Identification*, ATF P 3310.1, 5/76).

10. This calculation may be quite complex in principle, since the acquisition of a gun may suggest changes in frequency of robbery, target selection, and number of accomplices; these changes will in turn cause a change in expected income coupled with changes in the threat of legal punishment and injury at the hands of a victim.

11. See Cook (1976) for statistics on the take and success rates in robbery.

12. See Zimring (1976) for an interesting categorization of guns according to their accessibility for immediate use.

13. See Zimring (1968) for a discussion of the use of hunting licenses as a gun density measure.

14. Newton and Zimring (1969: ch. 6) find that firearms suicide attempts are as likely to be successful as hanging, and much more likely to be successful than other common means.

15. Brill (1977: xv) constructs a firearm choice availability measure which consists of the percentage of murders, robberies, and aggravated assaults committed with a gun.

16. This measure was suggested by Wilson and Boland (1976: 230).

17. Wilson and Boland (1976) use a modification of the published results for victimization survey data for the twenty-six cities.

18. Ehrlich (1973) uses a similar measure in specifying a robbery regression on state data. His poverty measure is the percentage of households in the state with income less than half the median in the state.

19. Clotfelter (1977) finds that the demand for guns is influenced by the overall Index violent crime rate.

20. Cook (1977) presents this argument in greater detail.

21. See Nagin (1977a) for a review of these studies. A recent example is the paper by Mathieson and Passell (1976).

22. I experimented briefly with a variable indicating those states which give the juvenile court jurisdiction over defendants up to a relatively high age (eighteen), but without notable success.

23. Chaiken (1977) describes the intercity relationship between crime rates and the number of uniformed officers. The variable I use is based on the same data as is used in Wilson and Boland (1977). They report that there is a surprising amount of difference among cities with respect to the fraction of uniformed officers who are actually on patrol at any one time.

24. The sum of the coefficient estimates for each independent variable in the linear forms of the gun and nongun regressions is necessarily equal to the corresponding coefficient estimates for the linear form of the total robbery equation with the same specification (in Table 6).

25. The elasticity calculations are made using the means of the relevant variables. The gun density index has a mean of 57.8 over the forty cities in this sample, and the gun robbery rate has a mean of 2.60/1000 population.

The elasticity of gun robbery (GR) with respect to the fraction of households which own a pistol (HG) is given by the formula

$$E_{GR'HG} = \frac{\overline{HG}}{\overline{GR}} \cdot \frac{dGR}{dHG} = \frac{\overline{HG}}{\overline{GR}} \cdot \frac{dGR}{dI} \cdot \frac{dI}{dHG}$$

Now $\overline{GR}$ = 2.6

$\overline{HG}$ = $-19.0 + .63\ \overline{I}$ (from Table 5, notes)

where $\overline{I}$ = 57.8. therefore $\overline{HG}$ = 17.4

From equation 1 of Table 8, $dGR/dI = .049$ and, as noted above, the relationship between HG and I has slope .63. Therefore,

$$E_{GR'HR} = \frac{17.4}{2.6} \cdot \frac{.049}{.63} = .52$$

Using the log form (equation 1) the elasticity expression becomes

$$E_{GR'HG} = \frac{.017 \, (17.4)}{.63} = .47$$

26. Whether a murder involved a robbery or not must be inferred from the circumstances, if there are no eyewitnesses available. While robbery murders in commercial locations may be easily classified correctly in most cases, the problems are presumably much greater for street robberies.

27. This example is modelled on a real incident in Houston described by Lundsgaarde (1977: 138).

28. Cook and Nagin report a number of relevant findings from the National Crime Panel victimizations surveys in twenty-six cities. For example, only 25 percent of the victims who were seriously injured in gun robberies attempted any sort of physical resistance (fleeing or hitting the robber). The corresponding fraction is 33 percent for unarmed robberies.

29. Zimring (1977) finds that for Detroit the ratio of robbery murder to robberies by type of weapon is virtually constant from year to year during the 1960s. This finding reinforces my proportionality finding for cross-section data. However, Zimring finds that there was a tremendous jump in this ratio during 1971 and 1972 for each type of weapon. This change has not been explained as yet.

30. Suppose

$$M = aG + bN = aG + b\,(R - G)$$

where M = # of robbery murders
   G, N = # of gun (no gun) robberies
   R = # of robberies

Dividing through by R and rearranging terms yields

$$\frac{M}{R} = (a - b)\,\frac{G}{R} + b$$

31. The calculation of the elasticity here is similar to the procedure explained in note 25, above.

REFERENCES

BRILL, S. (1977) Firearm Abuse: A Research and Policy Report. Police Foundation.

BRUCE-BRIGGS, B. (1976) "The great American gun war." Public Interest 45 (Fall) 37-62.

CHAIKEN, J. (1977) "What's known about deterrent effects of police activities." Rand Corporation.

CLOTFELTER, C. (1977) "The demand for handguns: an empirical analysis." University of Maryland.

CONKLIN, J. E. (1972) Robbery and the Criminal Justice System. J. B. Lippincott.

COOK, P. J. (1976) "A strategic choice analysis of robbery," in W. Skogan (ed.) Sample Surveys of the Victims of Crime. Ballinger.

——— (1977a) "Punishment and crime: a critique of current findings on the preventive effects of punishment." Law & Contemporary Problems.

——— (1977b) "Problems in the interpretation of econometric results from deterrence research." Duke University.

——— and D. NAGIN (1978) Does the Weapon Matter? Institute for Law and Social Research.

DIENER, E. and E. CRANDALL (n.d.) "Impact of the Jamaica gun control laws." University of Illinois.

EHRLICH, I. (1973) "Participation in illegitimate activities: a theoretical and empirical investigation." Journal of Political Economy (March/April).

ERSKINE, H. (1972) "The polls: gun control." Public Opinion Quarterly: 455-469.

ETZIONI, A. (1973) "A technology whose removal 'works': gun control," pp. 103-151 in Technological Shortcuts to Social Change. Russell Sage Foundation.

FEENEY, F. and A. WEIR (1974) "The prevention and control of robbery: a summary." University of California, Davis.

FIENBERG, S. (1977) "Victimization and National Crime Survey: problems of design and analysis." University of Minnesota, Report 291.

FORST, B. (1976) "Participation in illegitimate activities: further empirical findings." Policy Analysis 2 (Summer): 477-492.

GEISEL, B., R. ROLL, and S. WETTICK (1969) "The effectiveness of state and local regulations of handguns: a statistical analysis." Duke Law Journal: 647-673.

GENDREAU, P. and C. T. SURRIDGE (1976) "Controlling gun crimes: the Jamaican experience." (unpublished)

HOCH, I. (1974) "Factors in urban crime." Journal of Urban Economics 1 (April): 184-229.

LUNDSGAARDE, H. P. (1977) Murder in Space City. Oxford University Press.

MAGADDINO, J. P. (1976) "Towards an economic evaluation of state gun control laws." California State University, Long Beach.

MATHIESON, D. and P. PASSELL (1976) "Homicide and robbery in New York City: an economic model." Journal of Legal Studies 5 (January): 83-98.

MURRAY, D. (1975) "Handguns, gun control laws and firearm violence." Journal of Social Problems.

NAGIN, D. (1977a) "General deterrence: a review of the empirical evidence." Management Science.

——— (1977b) "Crime rates and sanction levels in the context of an effective constraint on prison population." Duke University.

NEWTON, G. D. and F. E. ZIMRING (1969) Firearms and Violence in American Life. Government Printing Office.

PHILLIPS, L., H. VOTEY, and J. HOWELL (1976) "Handguns and homicide: minimizing losses and the costs of control." Journal of Legal Studies 5 (June): 463-478.

REPETTO, T. A. (1972) Residential Crime. Ballinger.

——— (1974) "The validity of official statistics: an empirical analysis." Social Science Quarterly 55: 25-38.

SKOGAN, W. (1975) "Measurement problems in official and survey crime rates." Journal of Criminal Justice 3: 17-32.

U.S. Department of Justice, FBI (1976) Uniform Crime Reporting Handbook.

——— (annual, esp. 1967) Crime in the United States.

U.S. Department of Justice, LEAA (1976a) Criminal Victimization Surveys in Chicago.

——— (1976b) Criminal Victimization Surveys in Eight American Cities.

——— (1975) Criminal Victimization Surveys in 13 American cities.

U.S. Treasury, Bureau of Alcohol, Tobacco, and Firearms (1976) Project Identification: A Study of Handguns Used in Crime.

WILSON, J. Q. and B. BOLAND (1977) The Effect of Police on Crime Rates. The Urban Institute.

——— (1976) "Crime," in W. Gorham and N. Glazer (eds.) The Urban Predicament. The Urban Institute.

WRIGHT, J. and L. MARSTON (1975) "The ownership of the means of destruction: weapons in the United States." Social Problems 23 (October).

ZIMRING, F. E. (1977) "Determinants of the death rate from robbery: a Detroit time study." Journal of Legal Studies 6 (June): 317-332.

——— (1976) "Street crime and new guns: some implications for firearms control." Journal of Criminal Justice 4: 95-107.

——— (1975) "Firearms and federal law: the Gun Control Act of 1968." Journal of Legal Studies 4 (January): 133-198.

——— (1968) "Games with guns and statistics." Wisconsin Law Review: 1113.

——— (1967) "Is gun control likely to reduce violent killings?" Chicago Law Review 35: 721-737.

41

BRINGING MANAGEMENT SCIENCE TO THE COURTS TO REDUCE DELAY

Stuart Nagel, Marian Neef, and Nancy Munshaw

Delay in processing is a serious problem in both civil and criminal court cases. Civil cases, for example, often take many years from filing to trial—if there is a trial at all. Such delay is harmful to the injured plaintiff, who must wait to be compensated for injuries, and to the judicial system because witnesses sometimes forget, disappear, or die before the case comes to trial.

Criminal cases generally do not take as long, but delay there may cause even greater harm. If the defendant is imprisoned while awaiting trial, he may be jailed for a longer period than the sentence he could receive if convicted, but he may not even be convicted. If the defendant is not confined while awaiting trial, long delay may increase his opportunity to commit further crimes or to fail to appear when his trial is scheduled.[1] Clearly, new techniques to reduce court delay are needed.

Management science seeks to develop

methods of determining policies for maximizing given goals under varying conditions, e.g., to maximize the speed at which work is done while holding constant the quality of the product.[2] Now, applications of management science are increasingly being made outside the realm of business administration and industrial management, and in the realm of government, including the legal process.[3] Such applications to the legal process have emphasized delay reduction, but have generally only dealt with flow chart models and queueing theory rather than the full range of management science methods.

What we want to do here is to explore the wider range of tools which management science now offers. Through these techniques, courts could not only find ways to

This article is based on a paper presented at the 1978 annual meeting of the American Society for Public Administration. The authors wish to thank the Ford Foundation Public Policy Committee, the Illinois Law Enforcement Commission, and the University of Illinois Research Board for financing various aspects of the legal policy research of which this is a part. None of them is responsible for these ideas.

For a further discussion of the management science models described here, see Nagel and Neef, *Time-Oriented Models and the Legal Process*, 1978 WASH. U. L. Q.

1. On the serious nature of the delay problem in the legal process, *see* Howard James, CRISIS IN THE COURTS. New York: David McKay, 1969; Harry Jones (ed.), THE COURTS, THE PUBLIC, AND THE LAW EXPLOSION. Englewood Cliffs, New Jersey: Prentice Hall, 1965; Walter E. Meyer Research Institute of Law, DOLLARS, DELAY AND THE AUTOMOBILE VICTIM: STUDIES IN REPARATION FOR HIGHWAY INJURIES AND RELATED COURT PROBLEMS. Indianapolis: Bobbs-Merrill, 1968; G. Winters, ed., SELECTED READINGS: COURT CONGESTION AND DELAY. Chicago: American Judicature Society, 1971; Hans Zeisel, Harry Kalven, Jr. & Bernard Buchholz, DELAY IN THE COURT. Boston: Little Brown, 1959.

2. General management science works include Samuel Richmond, OPERATIONS RESEARCH FOR MANAGEMENT DECISIONS. New York: Ronald Press, 1968; Robert Thierauf and Richard Grosse, DECISION MAKING THROUGH OPERATIONS RESEARCH. New York: John Wiley & Sons, 1970; Hamly Taha, OPERATIONS RESEARCH: AN INTRODUCTION. New York: Macmillan, 1971. Harvey Wagner, PRINCIPLES OF OPERATIONS RESEARCH WITH APPLICATIONS TO MANAGERIAL DECISIONS. Englewood Cliffs, New Jersey: Prentice-Hall, 1969; and David Anderson, Dennis Sweeney and Thomas Williams, AN INTRODUCTION TO MANAGEMENT SCIENCE: QUANTITATIVE APPROACHES TO DECISION MAKING. St. Paul: West, 1976. These works all include methods for delay reduction.

3. Management science and operations research as applied to governmental and legal problems include Saul Gass and Roger Sisson, A GUIDE TO MODELS IN GOVERNMENTAL PLANNING AND OPERATIONS. Washington, D.C.: Environmental Protection Agency, 1974; Edward Beltrami, MODELS FOR PUBLIC SYSTEMS ANALYSIS. New York: Academic Press, 1977; Michael White, Michael Radnor and David Tansik (eds.), MANAGEMENT AND POLICY SCIENCE IN AMERICAN GOVERNMENT. Lexington, Massachusetts: Lexington Books, D. C. Heath, 1975; Jack Byrd, Jr. OPERATIONS RESEARCH MODELS FOR PUBLIC ADMINISTRATION. Lexington, Massachusetts: Lexington Books, D. C. Heath, 1975; and Stuart Nagel and Marian Neef, THE LEGAL PROCESS: MODELING THE SYSTEM. Beverly Hills, California: Sage Publications, 1977.

reduce delay but they could also gain a better insight into how different aspects of the judicial system work together. Thus, a court could undertake significant changes confident that, for the most part, they would not produce unintended consequences.

In this article, we will discuss six ideas now popular in management science— queueing, optimum sequencing, critical path methods, optimum level and mix analysis, optimum choice analysis, and Markov chain analysis. The titles for these concepts make them sound far more complex than they really are. Actually, each of them will help us focus more sharply on aspects of court operations that now look confusing.

1. Queueing theory

In any program for reducing delay, a court will want to try to estimate what effects changes will have upon backlog and delay. Queueing formulas describe the relationships between the variables that affect backlog and delay—variables such as the rate at which cases arrive, the rate at which they are serviced, the number of judges and so on. Queueing theory also emphasizes that to reduce delay and backlogs, one must either increase the rate at which cases are disposed of or decrease the rate at which cases arrive into the system (i.e. increase the completions, decrease the arrivals, or favorably change the variables that affect completions and arrivals). In this section, we will discuss two of the basic queueing models.

Time: The first kind attempts to predict the amount of time needed (T) for various types of cases at various stages of the legal process. Those predictions are made from the average number of cases that arrive (A) per day (or other unit of time) in the system (or at the stage being considered), and from the average number of cases that are serviced (S) per day (or other unit of time). The basic prediction formula is $T = 1/(S-A)$, which indicates that time consumed relates inversely to the servicing rate of cases and directly to the arrival rate. Through this formula, we can predict how much time can be reduced by increasing the service rate or by decreasing the arrival rate.

Backlog: The other type of basic queueing formula estimates the number of cases (N) backed up in the system or at a given stage. Those predictions are also made from the arrival rate and the service rate. The basic prediction formula is $N = (A/S)/(1-A/S)$. In other words, the size of the backlog varies directly with how bad the arrival/service ratio is and inversely with the complement of that ratio. A bad arrival/service ratio is one in which the arrival rate approaches or exceeds the service ratio.

Instead of talking about total time in the system or at a stage (T), we can talk about waiting time to be serviced (T_w) and actual servicing time (T_s). The formula for waiting time is $T_w = T(A/S)$. In other words, waiting time equals the total time discounted or multiplied by the arrival/service ratio. It also follows that $T_s = T - T_w$, since total time is waiting time plus servicing time.

Likewise we can talk about the waiting backlog (N_w) which consists of the number of cases waiting to be serviced and the servicing backlog (N_s) which consists of the number of cases currently being serviced. The formula for the waiting backlog is $N = N(A/S)$, analogous to the formula for waiting time. It also follows that $N_s = N - N_w$, since total backlog is the waiting backlog plus the servicing backlog.

Other queueing formulas enable us to predict the probability of having a certain number of cases arrive or serviced given the average arrival and service rate. Still other formulas can be used to predict the time consumed and the size of backlogs when (1) the number of processors or judges is varied, (2) unusual arrival or service rates are present, and (3) the system operates under special rules concerning priority servicing of certain types of cases, judge shopping by lawyers, and maximum quotas on cases of certain types.

The formulas emphasize that the only way to reduce delay and backlog is through those variables. For example, we can reduce the initial arrival rate by diverting cases to other processors such as administrative agencies, and we can reduce the arrival rate at subsequent stages by encouraging pretrial settlement. Likewise, we can reduce the service time and thus increase the service rate by

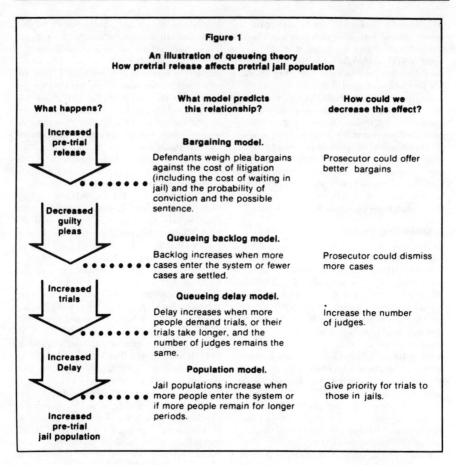

Figure 1

An illustration of queueing theory
How pretrial release affects pretrial jail population

What happens?	What model predicts this relationship?	How could we decrease this effect?
Increased pre-trial release	**Bargaining model.** Defendants weigh plea bargains against the cost of litigation (including the cost of waiting in jail) and the probability of conviction and the possible sentence.	Prosecutor could offer better bargains
Decreased guilty pleas	**Queueing backlog model.** Backlog increases when more cases enter the system or fewer cases are settled.	Prosecutor could dismiss more cases
Increased trials	**Queueing delay model.** Delay increases when more people demand trials, or their trials take longer, and the number of judges remains the same.	Increase the number of judges.
Increased Delay	**Population model.** Jail populations increase when more people enter the system or if more people remain for longer periods.	Give priority for trials to those in jails.
Increased pre-trial jail population		

having more judge-time (such as through delegation to quasi-judges), and by having fewer stages in the system (such as by eliminating grand juries for formal indictments). If an average two-day trial can be reduced one day, and there are 500 cases waiting, then queueing theory indicates that the 500th case will be heard 250 working days sooner.

An example

To illustrate how queueing analysis can help us to see things more clearly, we might look at the effect of increased pretrial release on the pretrial jail population (Figure 1).

Logically, increased pretrial release should result in a decreased pretrial jail population. But the opposite effect might occur because increased pretrial release decreases the vulnerability of many defendants to the prosecutor's offer to reduce the sentence to time served or probation in return for a guilty plea. If increased pretrial release thereby decreases guilty pleas, then our queueing backlog model tells us to expect increased trials, assuming all else remains constant.

Likewise, our queueing delay model tells us to expect increased delay from the increased trials. If there is increased delay, then defendants sitting in jail awaiting trial probably will be there longer. That, in turn, means the pretrial jail population may increase, even though fewer defendants are being sent to jail to await trial in view of the increased pretrial release.

Queueing and other models not only provide a better understanding of the causal relations but they also indicate ways of decreasing the occurrence of those relations. Thus, increased pretrial release need not result in decreased quilty pleas if the prosecutor offers better bargains (such as probation) to defendants out of jail who otherwise would receive jail sentences. Even if there are decreased quilty pleas, they need not result in increased trials if the prosecutor dismisses more cases to offset the decrease in cases settled. Likewise, increased trials need not result in increased delay if the system offsets the increased trials with more judges. Finally, increased delay need not result in an increased pretrial jail population if priority trials are provided for those defendants who are in jail, even though that might mean even greater delay for defendants out of jail.[4]

2. Optimum sequencing

Optimum sequencing emphasizes that delay can be reduced simply by the order in which cases are heard, even if there is no reduction

in arrivals, no acceleration in the servicing time per case, and no increase in judge time. For example, suppose we have only one judge and three cases, one of which takes 20 days to hear, one 10, and one 5. If the one judge hears those cases in the order of arrival, as is typical, then the first case will take 20 days to process, the second 30 days (10 days servicing time and 20 days waiting for the first case), and the third 35 days (5 days servicing time and 30 days waiting for the first two cases) (see Figure 2.)

The average time per case is thus 85 days divided by 3 cases, or 28 days. If, however, the judge hears those cases by taking the shortest first, then the first case will take 5 days, the second 15 days, and the third 40 days, for an average of only 60 days/3 cases, or 20 days per case. Thus, simply by reordering the way in which the cases are heard, we save an average of eight days per case, a time reduction of 8/28, or about 30 per cent.

One objection to a system of taking shorter cases first is that longer cases might either never get processed or their processing plus waiting time would exceed some maximum statutory, constitutional, or socially desirable limit. If we specify that every case should be concluded in, say, 30 days, then there is no way to order those three cases so that none will take as long as 30 days. To satisfy that constraint, we would have to change the problem by (1) specifying a shorter processing time for some or all the cases, or by (2) specifying that our one judge does not have to hear all three cases either because the arrivals have been reduced or, more likely, because a second judge has been added.

If we have two judges, with the first judge hearing the 5-day case and the second judge the 20-day case and the 10-day case, then those three cases will take 5, 20, and 30 days respectively for waiting and processing time, or an average of 55/3, or 18 days. If, on the other hand, the first judge hears the 20-day case and the second judge the 5-day and 10-day case, then those three cases will take 20, 5, and 15 days respectively, or an average of 40/3, or only 13 days.

However, we could also get the average down to 13 days by giving the first judge the

---

4. On queueing theory, see Jack Byrd, supra n. 3, at 198–208; Donald Gross and Carl Harris, FUNDAMENTALS OF QUEUEING THEORY. New York: Wiley, 1974; Alec Lee, APPLIED QUEUEING THEORY. New York: Macmillan, 1966; Samuel Richmond, supra n. 2, at 405–438; and Thomas Saaty, ELEMENTS OF QUEUEING THEORY WITH APPLICATIONS. New York: McGraw-Hill, 1961.

For other examples of queueing theory applied to the legal process, see Haig Bohigian, THE FOUNDATIONS AND MATHEMATICAL MODELS OF OPERATIONS RESEARCH WITH EXTENSIONS TO THE CRIMINAL JUSTICE SYSTEM 191-209. Yonkers, New York: Gazette Press, 1971; Jan Chaiken and P. Dormont, PATROL CAR ALLOCATION MODEL. Santa Monica, California: Rand, 1975; Jan Chaiken, Thomas Carbill, Leo Holliday, David Jaquette, Michael Lawless and Edward Quade, CRIMINAL JUSTICE MODELS: AN OVERVIEW. Santa Monica, California: Rand, 1975; and John Reed, THE APPLICATION OF OPERATIONS RESEARCH TO COURT DELAY. New York: Praeger, 1973.

See also Hans Zeisel, supra n. 1, since his book is organized in accordance with queueing concepts by being divided into parts on Reducing the Trial Time (i.e., increasing servicing rates), Increasing Settlements (i.e., decreasing arrival rates), and More Judge Time (i.e., increasing the channels or processors).

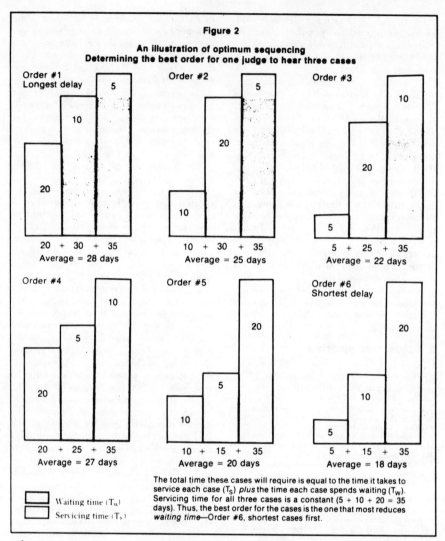

Figure 2

An illustration of optimum sequencing
Determining the best order for one judge to hear three cases

Order #1
Longest delay

20 + 30 + 35
Average = 28 days

Order #2

10 + 30 + 35
Average = 25 days

Order #3

5 + 25 + 35
Average = 22 days

Order #4

20 + 25 + 35
Average = 27 days

Order #5

10 + 15 + 35
Average = 20 days

Order #6
Shortest delay

5 + 15 + 35
Average = 18 days

Waiting time (T_w)
Servicing time (T_s)

The total time these cases will require is equal to the time it takes to service each case (T_s) *plus* the time each case spends waiting (T_w). Servicing time for all three cases is a constant (5 + 10 + 20 = 35 days). Thus, the best order for the cases is the one that most reduces *waiting time*—Order #6, shortest cases first.

10-day case and having the second judge hear the 5-and 20-day cases. Which of those two allocations and orders is best? If our only criterion is minimizing the average time per case, then they are tied for best. Logically, though, we could say that when two allocations and orders give the same minimum average time, pick the one in which the longest case also is minimized. This means our first 13-day example above would be best since its longest case takes only 20 days, whereas the longest case in the second 13-day example takes 25 days. The two general rules, within multiple courts, which could minimize both average time per case and the longest case are: (1) within each court the shorter cases should be taken first, and (2) the shortest case should be given to the court with the greater quantity of cases, where there is an uneven number of cases.

Predicting processing time

But how do we know what cases will last 5, 10, and 20 days? The best approach is probably to do a statistical prediction analysis for different sets of cases, such as criminal cases and personal injury cases, with time consumed always being the variable predicted. For criminal cases, the predictor variables might be the type of crime, its severity, the type of trial the defendant wants (jury or bench), and the type of counsel (private counsel or public defender). For personal injury cases, the predictor variables might be the plaintiff's latest settlement demand, the defendant's latest settlement offer, and the type of personal injury.

Knowing these variables, we can make reasonable predictions of the time that will be consumed by an incoming case. Many court systems are now using computers for calendaring purposes to avoid multiple court dates for the same lawyers or judges. Those computer programs could be supplemented to indicate the order in which a week's accumulation of new cases should be heard in light of sequencing principles.

Another type of optimum sequencing involves sequencing of stages within cases rather than sequencing of cases. One question, for example, is whether the court should hear pleadings for two cases before beginning the trial on the first case. The general rule in optimum sequencing of stages is to do all the stages for case 1 before starting any of the stages for case 2 in order to minimize the average time per case. As we said above, one also should order the cases by taking the shorter ones first. The rule of processing the stages of a given case in uninterrupted succession applies regardless of the relative length of the time of the stages within each case or across cases (so long as we are operating under the constraint that the pleadings must precede the trial in each case). The rule, however, assumes that the participants will be ready to begin the second stage immediately after the first. Otherwise it makes sense to start a new case so the court will not be idle during the preparation time for the first case.

A related problem concerns whether the liability verdict stage should be decided separately from the damages stage in personal injury cases by two juries or trials. Doing so saves time for three reasons: (1) personal injury cases in which the defendant is not found liable do not have to go to the damages stage, (2) personal injury cases in which the defendant is found liable can often be settled out of court after the liability stage *without* the damages stage since liability is usually more subjective and more difficult to settle than damages, and (3) by allowing the first jury to hear only the liability decision, they more frequently decide in favor of the defendant since they cannot offset the plaintiff's contributory negligence by reducing the damages.

This, however, is not truly a sequencing problem since under either the combined trial or the split trial, liability precedes damages. It is more an allocation problem with regard to whether one or two decision-makers (i.e., one or two trials) should decide damages and liability. It does, however, nicely illustrate the fact that any management science method for reducing delay should be analyzed carefully to determine if it will change the outcomes of cases, which we presumably do not want our delay reduction methods to do.[5]

---

5. On dynamic and sequential programming, see Jack Byrd, *supra* n. 3, at 139–156; Richard Conway, William Maxwell and Louis Miller, THEORY OF SCHEDULING. Reading, Massachusetts: Addison-Wesley, 1967; A. Kaufman, GRAPHS, DYNAMIC PROGRAMMING, AND FINITE GAMES. New York: Academic Press, 1967; Kenneth Baker, INTRODUCTION TO SEQUENCING AND SCHEDULING. New York: Wiley, 1974; Samuel Richmond, *supra* n. 2 at 461–480; George Newhauser, INTRODUCTION TO DYNAMIC PROGRAMMING. New York: Wiley, 1966; and Brian Gliess, AN ELEMENTARY INTRODUCTION TO DYNAMIC PROGRAMMING. Boston: Allyn and Bacon, 1972.

For additional examples of dynamic and sequential programming applied to the legal process, see Haig Bohigian, *supra* n. 4, at 171–190; John Jennings, EVALUATION OF THE MANHATTAN CRIMINAL COURTS MASTER CALENDAR PROJECT. Santa Monica, California: Rand, 1971; Raymond Nimmer, THE SYSTEM IMPACT OF CRIMINAL JUSTICE REFORMS: JUDICIAL DELAY AS A CASE STUDY 62–96. Chicago: American Bar Foundation, 1974; Programming Methods Incorporated, JUSTICE: JUDICIAL SYSTEM TO INCREASE COURT EFFECTIVENESS. New York: Programming Methods, Inc., 1971; Hans Zeisel, *supra* n. 1, at 201–205; and Jack Hausner, Thomas Cane and Gary Oleson, *Automated Scheduling in the Courts,* in Sidney Brounstein and Murray Kamrass, eds., OPERATIONS RESEARCH IN LAW ENFORCEMENT: JUSTICE, AND SOCIETAL SECURITY 217. Lexington, Mass.: Lexington Books, 1976.

3. Critical path methods

Critical path method (CPM), or Program Evaluation and Review Technique (PERT), emphasizes that if total time is going to be reduced, we should not concentrate on reducing all the stages, but only those stages that are especially influential on the total time. Influential in this context means two things. First, the stage is essential to some subsequent stage which cannot be started until the first is completed. Second, the stage takes longer than other stages that are also essential to the subsequent stage.

For example, preparation by the public defender and preparation by the prosecutor are normally both essential for going to trial (Figure 3). If, however, the public defender on the average takes three weeks to prepare for trial and the prosecutor only two weeks, then the critical path from pleading to trial is through the lower arrow of preparation by the public defender. Reducing the *prosecutor's* preparation time would not make trials occur any sooner. Reducing the *public defender's* preparation time (by providing him or her with additional resources, for example) would enable trials to occur sooner. If the public defender's preparation time is reduced to less than two weeks, then preparation by the prosecutor becomes a critical path.

This kind of analysis could be expanded to include the total criminal justice process from arrest to parole or the civil process from complaint to collecting the judgment. Many of the stages in either process, however, do not involve two or more procedures coming together as prerequisites to a subsequent stage. Rather, the legal process tends to be more like an assembly line in which each stage follows the preceding one.

But the critical path method could help speed up other converging stages, including the bringing together of information by the defense and prosecutor on the matter of pretrial release, and the bringing together of information by the defense, prosecutor, and probation department on post-conviction sentencing. Normally, the probation department prepares its presentence report after the conviction of the defendant, but the

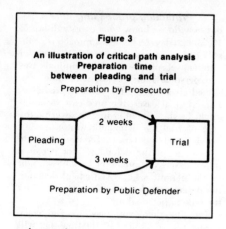

Figure 3

**An illustration of critical path analysis
Preparation time
between pleading and trial**
Preparation by Prosecutor

Pleading   2 weeks   Trial

3 weeks

Preparation by Public Defender

probation department could save time if it prepared presentence reports on all defendants *before* they are convicted, rather than just for the 70 per cent who are convicted. The extra cost of preparing reports for the 30 per cent of defendants who are not convicted may be more than offset by the time wasted waiting for reports whose preparation does not begin until conviction. More specifically, the extra cost of reporting on all defendants would be .30 times the number of defendants times the average cost per report, whereas the extra cost of not reporting on all the defendants equals (1) the extra cost of storing a defendant in the county jail when he could be free if he were given probation, and (2) the extra cost to the county if the defendant could be transported sooner to the state prison when he is sentenced to prison.

Estimating preparation times

In Figure 3, we indicated that preparation by the prosecutor would be two weeks by averaging the prosecutor's preparation time over a set of cases and then doing likewise for the public defender. Often that kind of data is not available. A common substitute is to ask the prosecutor for a subjective estimate or better yet, three subjective estimates. One would be the most likely or most common time (comparable to the mode in statistical analysis), the second would be an optimistic time (which occurs about once in 100 cases), and the third would be a pessimistic time (which also occurs about once in 100 cases).

From these three estimates an average or mean time is computed by the formula: T_E (for expected time) equals the optimistic time plus four times the most likely time plus the pessimistic time, with the sum divided by six. That formula is based on (1) the idea that people cannot directly estimate averages, but they can more easily estimate optimistic, most likely, and pessimistic figures as above defined, (2) assumptions concerning how averages tend to relate to those figures, and (3) the usefulness of those input figures in PERT-CPM outputs.

By inputting into a PERT or CPM computer program information concerning the ordering of the stages and the optimistic, modal, and pessimistic estimates for each, we can obtain a variety of useful outputs. These include (1) estimates of the date by which each stage is likely to be completed, (2) estimates of how much time will have accumulated as of each stage, (3) the stages that constitute the critical path from start to finish, (4) the amount of slack or dead time at the end of each stage that has to wait for an adjacent stage to be completed in order to bring the results from the two together at the next stage, and (5) the probability that a subsequent stage will have to wait for a previous stage that is not on the critical path.

These informational outputs can be helpful in better planning of both big and routine cases. Such planning should not emphasize equally all stages that are on the critical path, but rather (1) those that consume the most time and (2) those that are most subject to time reduction as indicated by the amount of spread between the optimistic, most likely, and pessimistic estimates. The more spread or diversity between the amount of time consumed at a given stage, the more that stage may be subject to time reduction if one can determine what correlates with that variance or spread across cases, over time, or across courts.

Flow chart models

Closely related to critical path analysis are flow chart models. They consist of a series of rectangles or other geometric shapes which represent the beginnings or endings of stages in the legal process, and a series of arrows connecting the rectangles. On the arrows are generally written the quantity of time needed to go from the beginning to the end of each stage. The arrows also show how the stages flow into each other or how the stages represent either-or possibilities, including the possibility or probability of dropping out rather than going ahead.

Flow chart models are a useful aid for seeing general case processing more clearly.[6] This, in turn, can suggest ideas for reducing time. Models can also be computerized to show the output effects of changes in the times, case quantities, stages, or other inputs. More complicated variations of flow chart models include showing in one or more flow charts average time consumption for each passage, measures of spread or distribution, optimistic or desired time consumption as determined by asking experts, the proportion of cases that move from one event to another where there is provision for branching or dropping out, and the dollar

6. On critical path method and flow chart modeling, *see* Russell Archibald and Richard Villoria, NETWORK-BASED MANAGEMENT SYSTEMS (PERT/CPM). New York: Wiley, 1967; Jack Byrd, *supra* n. 3, at 115–138; H. F. Evarts, INTRODUCTION TO PERT. Boston: Allyn & Bacon, 1964; B. J. Hansen, PRACTICAL PERT. Washington, D.C.: America House, 1964; Samuel Richmond, *supra* n. 2, at 481–500; and Gary Whitehouse, SYSTEM ANALYSIS AND SYSTEMS DESIGN. Englewood Cliffs, New Jersey: Prentice-Hall, 1973.

Other examples of flow chart modeling applied to the legal process include Jan Chaiken, Thomas Carbill, Lee Holliday, David Jaquette, Michael Lawless, and Edward Quade, *supra* n. 4; Alfred Blumstein, *A Model to Aid in Planning for the Total Criminal Justice System*, in Leonard Oberlander, ed., QUANTITATIVE TOOLS FOR CRIMINAL JUSTICE PLANNING 129. Washington, D.C.: LEAA, 1975; Joseph Navarro and Jean Taylor, *Data Analyses and Simulation of a Court System for the Processing of Criminal Cases*, in THE PRESIDENT'S COMMISSION ON LAW ENFORCEMENT AND ADMINISTRATION OF JUSTICE, TASK FORCE REPORT: SCIENCE AND TECHNOLOGY. Washington, D.C.: Government Printing Office, 1967; R. Gordon Cassidy, *A Systems Approach to Planning and Evaluation in Criminal Justice Systems*, 9 SOCIO-ECON. PLAN. SCI. 301 (1975).

See also, William Biles, "A Simulation Study of Delay Mechanisms in Criminal Courts" (unpublished paper presented at the 1972 meeting of the Operations Research Society of America at New Orleans, Louisiana); and Gary Hogg, Richard DeVor and Michael Handwerker, "Analysis of Criminal Justice Systems via Stochastic Network Simulation" (unpublished paper presented at the Workshop on the Criminal Justice System at San Diego, California, 1973).

cost of each event or time passage to the legal system or the parties.

In addition to rectangles and arrows, one can also develop a variety of geometric forms to show events or nodes that begin the process, end the process, or that are both beginning and ending points within the process, and to show time passages that always occur or that occur with given probabilities, and to provide queueing, critical path, and other information. That mass of information can then be used as input into a computerized simulation program which provides a variety of outputs showing how all the numbers change if there is a change in such variables as the number of cases entering the system or the proportion of cases which take one turn rather than another at a branching point.

4. Optimum level and mix analysis

Queueing theory tells us cases can be processed faster if we decrease arrivals, increase the servicing rate, and increase the number of processors. This does not mean we should strive to reduce arrivals to zero, or increase the servicing rate or number of processors to the point where time consumption becomes virtually zero. On the contrary, speed-up costs may be greater than the delay costs.

Optimum level analysis,[7] in the context of

7. On optimum level analysis, *see* Michael Brennan, PREFACE TO ECONOMETRICS: AN INTRODUCTION TO QUANTITATIVE METHODS IN ECONOMICS 111–192. Cincinnati: Southwestern, 1973; Jack Byrd, *supra* n. 3, at 183–198; Samuel Richmond, *supra* n. 2, at 87–126; and James Shockley, THE BRIEF CALCULUS: WITH APPLICATIONS IN THE SOCIAL SCIENCES, New York: Holt, Rinehart, and Winston, 1971.

For other examples of optimum level analysis applied to reducing delay and other aspects of the legal process, *see* Stuart Nagel and Marian Neef LEGAL POLICY ANALYSIS: FINDING AN OPTIMUM LEVEL OR MIX. Lexington, Massachusetts: Lexington Books, D.C. Heath, 1977; Nagel, Neef and Paul Wice, TOO MUCH OR TOO LITTLE POLICY: THE EXAMPLE OF PRETRIAL RELEASE. Beverly Hills, California, Sage Publications, 1977; Hans Zeisel, *supra* n. 1, at 169–220; Llad Phillips and Harold Votey, *An Economic Basis for the Definition and Control of Crime* in Stuart Nagel, ed., MODELING THE CRIMINAL JUSTICE SYSTEM 89. Beverly Hills, California: Sage Publications, 1977; Fredric Merrill and Linus Schrage, *Efficient Use of Jurors: A Field Study and Simulation Model of a Court System*, 2 WASH.U.L.Q. 151, 1969; and G. Thomas Munsterman and William Pabst, "Operating an Efficient Jury System" (unpublished paper at the International Meeting of the Institute of Management Sciences, 1975).

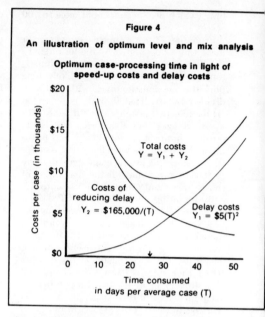

Figure 4

An illustration of optimum level and mix analysis

Optimum case-processing time in light of speed-up costs and delay costs

optimum time consumption, is designed to tell us the optimum level of delay in the sense of minimizing the sum of the delay costs (Y_1) and the speed-up costs (Y_2). Figure 4 shows what is involved in optimum level analysis for a hypothetical metropolitan court system. It consists of three curves.

The delay cost curve shows that as time consumed increases, a set of costs referred to as delay costs also increase and at an increasing rate. To be more exact the relation between delay costs and time consumed is indicated by the equation $Y_1 = \$5(T)^2$. The equation tells us is that if there are zero days consumed, there will be no delay costs. The $5 tells us that if only one day is consumed, there will be $5 in delay costs.

Of that $5 figure, $7 represents wasted cost per day per jailed defendant (discounted by the fact that only 50 per cent of the defendants are jailed) and $3 represents wasted cost per day per released non-jailed defendant (discounted by the fact that only 50 per cent of the defendants are released). That $7 figure can be broken into $2 wasted jail maintenance costs and $5 unnecessarily lost national income. The $2 figure reflects the fact that it costs $6 per day to maintain a defendant in jail, and one third of them have their case dismissed or acquitted when they come to trial. The $5 figure reflects the fact that defendants could be earning about $15 a day if they were out of jail and one-third of them will be out when their trials occur.

The $3 figure per released defendant is determined by calculating the crime-committing cost or the rearresting cost for the average released defendant, multiplied by the low probability of crime or rearrest, multiplied by the middling probability of being convicted and jailed if the case were to come to disposition, and divided by the number of days released. The hypothetical 2 in the exponent of the equation tells us that as time consumed goes up 1 per cent, delay costs go up 2 per cent.

The speed-up cost curve shows that time consumed can be reduced toward zero by spending money to speed up the legal process. More specifically, the money of which we speak is money for hiring additional judges at $40,000 per year or $110 per day, figuring 365 days to a year. The exact relation between speed-up costs and time consumed is indicated by the equation $Y_2 = \$165,000/(T)$. The $165,000 represents $110 per day multiplied by a 1500 figure, which was arrived at by statistically analyzing a set of data showing the average time consumed per case and the number of working judges for various years in the court system.

Computing total costs

The total costs curve is simply the sum of the first two. Where that total cost curve bottoms out is the point where we are minimizing the sum of the delay costs and the speed-up costs. We can visually see that point in Figure 4 is at approximately 25 days, and we could prove it algebraically given our equations. This means that 25 days or about one month is the optimum level of time consumption in order to minimize the sum of the relevant costs. We could also say that the optimum level of judges is 60, since we previously noted that the relation between number of judges (J) and days consumed (T) is about J = 1500/T, or 60

judges equals 1500 divided by 25 days.

We could make this optimum level analysis more realistic by taking into consideration that speed-up costs (Y_2) may only be accurately indicated as a combination of the cost of judges, prosecutors, public defenders, other personnel, courtrooms, and other costs, rather than just judges. An equation to determine the cost of prosecutors might be T = 98,400/$P, where T is time consumed in days and $P is dollars allocated to the prosecutor's office. That equation would follow if prosecutors get paid $30,000 a year or $82 a day over 365 days, and previous annual data show a relation between time consumed and the number of prosecutors of the form T = 1200/P. Likewise, a cost equation for defenders might be T = 55,000/$D, where $D is dollars allocated to the public defender's office. That equation would follow if defenders get paid an average of $20,000 a year or $55 a day, and previous annual data show a relation between T and D of the form T = 1000/D.

With equations such as these for judges, prosecutors, and defenders, we can calculate the marginal rate of return in terms of time reduction for an extra dollar spent for each of these three types of court personnel. These three figures enable us to determine the optimum mix of our total court budget between those three types of personnel in order to minimize the average time consumed per case.[8] We may have to supplement those figures, however, with some notion as to what minimum amount is required for each type of personnel. Instead of finding the mix that will minimize time con-

---

8. On optimum mix analysis, *see* Jack Byrd, *supra* n. 3, at 85–114; Philip Kotler, MARKETING DECISION MAKING: A MODEL BUILDING APPROACH. New York: Holt, Rinehart and Winston, 1971; Robert Llewellyn, LINEAR PROGRAMMING. New York: Holt, Rinehart and Winston, 1963; Claude McMillan, MATHEMATICAL PROGRAMMING. New York: Wiley, 1970; and Samuel Richmond, *supra* n. 2, at 314–404. For additional examples of optimum mix analysis applied to the legal process, *see* Werner Hirsch, THE ECONOMICS OF STATE AND LOCAL GOVERNMENT 217–254. New York: McGraw-Hill, 1970; Stuart Nagel, MINIMIZING COSTS AND MAXIMIZING BENEFITS IN PROVIDING LEGAL SERVICES TO THE POOR. Beverly Hills, California: Sage Publications, 1973; and Donald Schoup and Stephen Mehay, PROGRAM BUDGETING FOR URBAN POLICE SERVICE. New York: Praeger, 1971.

sumption, we might also decide what *maximum* time consumption we are willing to tolerate, and then determine what minimum total expenditures (in light of those figures) will enable us to reach that *maximum* time consumption.

5. Optimum choice analysis

In both optimum level and optimum mix analysis we try to maximize a variable such as dollars, which we can increase little by little. In optimum choice analysis, on the other hand, we work with a variable which gives only one of two results like yes/no, or do it/don't do it. That type of analysis might be especially valuable in analyzing how to get judicial personnel like judges, prosecutors, and defense counsel to do the things that are most likely to lead to settlements, a reduction in servicing time, or other activities that will reduce the average time consumed per case.

Optimum choice analysis operates on the assumption that when individuals choose one activity over another, they are indicating that the expected benefits minus costs of the chosen activity are greater than the expected benefits minus costs of the rejected activity.[9] The expected benefits equal the benefits to be received from an action discounted or multiplied by the probability of the occurrence of whatever events those benefits depend upon. Likewise, the expected costs equal the costs to be incurred by an action discounted by the probability of whatever

events those costs depend upon. The general decision theory involved in optimum choice analysis is shown in Figure 5.

Figure 5 specifically applies optimum choice analysis to the problem of how to get prosecutors and assistant states attorneys to make decisions to accelerate the slow and difficult cases so they do not exceed a maximum time. Doing that could involve (1) increasing the benefits and decreasing the costs from making time-saving decisions, (2) decreasing the benefits and increasing the costs from making time-lengthening decisions, and (3) increasing or decreasing the probabilities of relevant contingent events.

To encourage favorable time consumption decisions, assistant states attorneys can be given monetary rewards (to increase the benefits) and be given work-saving resources (to decrease the costs). Likewise, to discourage unfavorable time consumption decisions, states attorneys can in effect be punished by providing for an absolute discharge not subject to re-prosecution of excessively delayed defendants, and they can be deprived of the plea bargaining benefits of lengthy pretrial incarceration by providing more release on recognizance. These devices may cost more than delay itself costs, as we said under optimum level analysis. Optimum choices analysis, however, does stimulate thinking with regard to how decision-makers can be influenced to make time-saving decisions if one is, at least for the moment, primarily concerned with time-saving.

Making delay costly

A similar optimum choice analysis could be applied to the decisions made in the public defender's office or the offices of private defense attorneys. The suggestions there for encouraging time-saving decisions may, however, conflict with the decisions applicable to the states' attorney. For example, one might recommend more pretrial release to decrease the delay benefit the prosecutor receives from the increased willingness to plead guilty by defendants held in jail. On the other hand, one might recommend less pretrial release in order to make the defendant and indirectly his attorney suffer more

---

9. On optimum choice analysis, *see* Robert Behn and James Vaupel, ANALYTICAL THINKING FOR BUSY DECISION MAKERS. New York: Basic Books, 1979; Ruth Mack, PLANNING ON UNCERTAINTY: DECISION MAKING IN BUSINESS AND GOVERNMENT ADMINISTRATION. New York: Wiley, 1971; Howard Raiffa, DECISION ANALYSIS: INTRODUCTORY LECTURES ON CHOICES UNDER UNCERTAINTY. Reading, Massachusetts: Addison-Wesley, 1968; and Samuel Richmond, *supra* n. 2, at 301–60.

For additional examples of choice theory applied to the legal process, *see* Stuart Nagel and Marian Neef, DECISION THEORY AND THE LEGAL PROCESS, Lexington, Massachusetts: Lexington Books, D.C. Heath, 1978; Stuart Nagel and Marian Neef, *Decision Theory and the Pretrial Release Decision in Criminal Cases*, U. MIAMI L. REV., 1977; and Robert Stover and Don Brown, *Reducing Rule Violations by Police, Judges, and Corrections Officials* in Stuart Nagel, ed., MODELING THE CRIMINAL JUSTICE SYSTEM 297. Beverly Hills, California: Sage Publications, 1977.

Figure 5
An illustration of optimum choice analysis
Encouraging prosecutors to reach time-saving decisions

Alternative occurrences

Alternative decisions		Being penalized for lengthening time (P)	Not being penalized for lengthening time (1-P)
Time-saving decision (S)		B_S Benefits from S	C_S Costs from S
Time-lengthening decision (L)		C_L Costs from L	B_L Benefits from L

Benefits *minus* costs *equals profits*

The object of this optimum choice analysis is to make time-saving decisions more *profitable* than time-lengthening decisions. (In the equation, *P* represents the probability that the procecutor will be penalized.)

$$B_S - C_S > (B_L)(1-P) - (C_L)(P)$$

How can we encourage prosecutors to make time-saving decisions?

1. *Increase the benefits from making time-saving decision (increase B_S).*

For example, reward assistant states attorneys with salary increase and promotions for reducing the average time per case.

2. *Decrease the costs of making time saving decisions (decrease C_S).*

For example, establish a computerized system to inform assistant states attorneys about actual and predicted times at various stages for all cases to minimize the trouble of keeping track of cases. Provide more investigative and preparation resources.

3. *Increase the costs of making time-lengthening decisions (increase C_L).*

For example, provide under the speedy trial rules for absolute discharge of the defendant whose case extends beyond the time limit rather than just release on recognizance.

4. *Decrease the benefits from making time-lengthening decisions (decrease B_L).*

For example, increase release on recognizance so that lengthening the pretrial time will not make the jailed defendant more vulnerable to pleading guilty.

5. *Raise the probability of the decision-maker being penalized for lengthening time (i.e. increase P).*

For example, allow fewer exceptions to the speedy trial rules such as suspending their application "for good cause" or "exceptional circumstances."

from delaying the case. In such conflicting situations, we must decide which side is more responsible for the delay, or decide on the basis of criteria other than saving time.

There are also benefit-cost suggestions stimulated by this analysis applicable to the defense side that do not conflict with the previous suggestions applicable to the prosecution. For example, providing monetary rewards to assistant public defenders and more resources does not conflict with the prosecutor suggestions unless one assumes there is a fixed quantity of resources available to the criminal justice system, and whatever the prosecutor gets must be taken away from the public defender or other parts of the system.

A similar optimum choice analysis could also be applied to judicial decisions that affect delay. For example, judges now incur virtually no personal costs from granting repeated continuances or making other delaying decisions. If, however, records were publicized showing how long, on the average, each judge takes to process cases of various types, that visibility might cause slower judges to change their ways. That kind of record-keeping can also be done for making comparisons across assistant states attorneys and assistant public defenders in a given court system, or across court systems if one calculates separate averages for cases of different types of severity and different expected time consumptions.

6. Markov chain analysis

By Markov chain analysis, we can predict subsequent events by knowing the probability of one event leading to another.[10] Here is an example, greatly oversimplified. If we know that 60 per cent of the convicted defendants in a court system go to prison and 40 per cent receive probation, we know something about what would happen if convictions increased from 200 to 300 per year. Before the increase, the prison caseload would be 120 cases per year (.60 times 200) and the probation caseload would be 80 cases. After the increase, the prison caseload will probably be 180 cases per year (.60 times 300) and the probation caseload 120 cases. That simple example could be made substantially more interesting if it were part of a chain of branching events, where the ultimate effects are not so readily predictable without a Markov chain analysis.

Figure 6 predicts the effect on the public defender's caseload of a change in the probability of being held in jail pending trial. Suppose 100 cases enter the system and 10 per cent were released on their own recognizance, 30 per cent were released on bond, and 60 per cent were held in jail pending trial. What would happen to the public de-

10. On Markov chain analysis, *see* Dean Isaacson and Richard Madsen, MARKOV CHAINS THEORY AND APPLICATIONS. New York: Wiley, 1975; John Kemeny and J. Laurie Snell, FINITE MARKOV CHAINS. Englewood Cliffs, New Jersey: Prentice-Hall, 1960; Samuel Richmond, *supra* n. 2, at 439–460; and Sidney Ulmer, *Stochastic Process Models in Political Analysis,* in James Herndon and Joseph Bernd, eds., MATH APPLICATIONS IN POLITICAL SCIENCE. Blacksburg, Virginia: Virginia Polytechnic Institute, 1965.

For other examples of Markov chain analysis applied to the legal process, *see* Ronald Rardin and Paul Gray, *Analysis of Crime Control Strategies,* 1 J. OF CRIM. JUSTICE 339, 1973; Ronald Slivka and Frank Cannavale, Jr., *An Analytical Model of the Passage of Defendants through a Court System,* J. OF RESEARCH IN CRIME AND DELINQUENCY 132, 1973.

See also S. J. Deutsch, J. J. Jarvis and R. G. Parker, "A Network Flow Model for Predicting Criminal Displacement and Deterrence" (unpublished paper, 1975); Thomas Schelling and Richard Zeckhauser, "Law and Public Policy: Policy Analysis" (unpublished course materials, 1975); David White, Soo Hong Uh and Kim Andriano, *Juvenile Court Records and Markov Chains: Their Use as Aids in Identification and Treatment of Delinquent Youth,* 1 L. AND HUMAN BEHAVIOR 217, (1977); and J. Belkin, A. Blumstein and W. Glass, *Recidivism as Feedback Process: An Analytical Model and Empirical Validation,* 1 J. CRIM. JUSTICE 7 (1973).

fender's caseload if those probabilities were to change to .40, .20, and .40 respectively as the result of a bail reform movement?

To answer that question, we need to know for each of those categories of pretrial release their probability of pleading not guilty rather than guilty, and of those who plead not guilty, the probability of having the public defender appointed to represent them.

The data indicate that those in jail pending trial are more likely to plead guilty than those released. The data also indicate that, of those defendants who plead not guilty, the ones most likely to be indigent and thus eligible for the public defender are the defendants who have been kept in jail pending trial unable to make bond. Of those released, the defendants who put up bond money are possibly less likely to be indigent enough to have the public defender appointed than those who are released on their own recognizance (ROR). The hypothetical data assume that about one-half of the ROR cases are middle-class defendants who are considered good risks for ROR but are not eligible for the public defender, and the other half are poor defendants who are also considered good risks for ROR but who are eligible for the public defender.

The analysis simply involves allocating the entering 100 cases in accordance with the first tier of probabilities to the second column of events; allocating those allocations in accordance with the second tier of probabilities to the third column of events; and then allocating those allocations in accordance with the third tier of probabilities to the fourth column of events. The last step in the analysis involves summing the number of cases probabilistically allocated to the public defender in various rows of the fourth column of events to determine the total public defender caseload.

The same is done both with the "before" and "after" probabilities. Doing so indicates that the predicted "before" caseload for 100 cases is 25½ cases to the public defender and the predicted "after" caseload for 100 cases is 30½ cases. This means an increase of 19 per cent in the public defender's caseload. Thus, if the public defender's of-

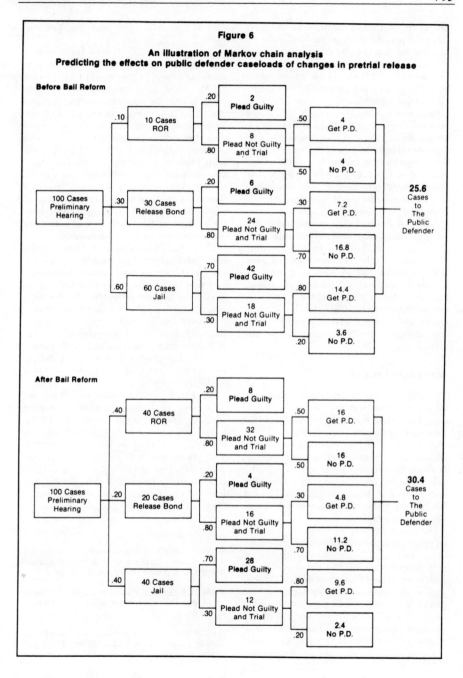

Figure 6

An illustration of Markov chain analysis
Predicting the effects on public defender caseloads of changes in pretrial release

fice is to continue to operate at the same caseload per assistant public defender, 19 per cent more assistants should be hired.

Legal process literature shows a number of examples of Markov chain reasoning for trying to predict the probability that a convict will commit another crime within a certain number of time periods after being released from prison. David White, for example, finds that a released juvenile who was not referred to the court during the first three months after release has a .978 probability of not being referred in the fourth month, a .019 probability of committing a minor crime in the fourth month, and a .003 probability of committing a major crime. Other probabilities can be calculated for subsequent months (either empirically from direct data or deductively from probability formulas) for other combinations of non-referrals, minor crimes, and major crimes in the preceding months. That kind of analysis can be useful in predicting behavior, comparing different types of convicts or treatments, and developing recommendations for special supervision of certain types of convicts.

Some conclusions

The time-oriented models presented here are all useful for saving time in the legal process. Queueing theory is especially useful for deducing the implications of arrival rates and servicing rates with regard to the amount of delay and backlog likely to occur. It also points up the importance in reducing delay and backlog of (1) decreasing the arrival rate and the number of stages, and of (2) increasing the service rate and the number of processors.

Optimum sequencing helps us arrive at an optimum ordering of cases and case stages as part of a scientific calendaring of judicial and other legal procedures. Critical path analysis and flow chart models emphasize what stages in the legal process are particularly important for concentrating one's time reduction efforts, and the effects of input and parameter changes on those stages. Optimum level analysis as a time-oriented model emphasizes minimizing the

sum of the delay costs and the speed-up costs.

Optimum mix analysis is useful in allocating scarce resources among different programs or groups of personnel in order to get (1) the most time reduction for a given budget or (2) the least expenditures under a maximum time constraint. Optimum choice analysis can be helpful in developing incentives for getting judges, prosecutors, and defense counsel to do the things that are most likely to lead to delay reduction. Markov chain analysis emphasizes how a given change can produce a chain reaction through a series of branching or successive probabilities and relations, especially where the change or the reaction relates to time consumed or arrivals in the system.

This article has summarized some of the basic principles and purposes with regard to each modeling approach. It has also provided a number of examples where the models have been or can be applied to the legal process. The number of past applications, however, is quite small relative to the potentiality of these useful perspectives. The applications have also been mainly by people who are skilled in the methods of modeling, but not necessarily skilled in the substance of the legal process.

What may be particularly needed is more awareness of these management science ideas by lawyers, judges, judicial administrators, legal researchers, and others who are constantly involved with the legal process. That awareness will not make them into professional modelers, but it will give them a better understanding of the potential and limits of management science approaches so they can use them more constructively. □

STUART NAGEL is a professor of political science at the University of Illinois, Champaign-Urbana, and a member of the Illinois bar.

MARIAN NEEF is a Ph.D. candidate in political science at the University of Illinois, Champaign-Urbana.

NANCY MUNSHAW is a master's degree candidate in urban and regional planning at the University of Illinois, Champaign-Urbana.

MANAGEMENT SCIENCE IN
THE REAL WORLD OF COURTS
Orange County's Experience with Optimum Sequencing

John Paul Ryan

Management science characteristically focuses on efficiency. In courts, the central target is the reduction of delay in processing cases. Yet *how* courts choose to attack this problem critically affects the allocation of justice. Do courts send a message to prosecutors by dismissing "stale" cases for lack of prosecution? Or do judges refuse to grant continuances to defense counsel? Do courts establish pretrial conference programs to expedite settlements? Or do judges limit the scope of discovery?

Procrastination by litigants and their counsel is only one face of delay. Some litigants seek to be heard, to have their problems adjudicated, even to have their names cleared. It is this tension between delay and access which subtly envelops the management science models whose applications for the legal process Nagel, Neef and Munshaw ably discuss in this issue.

Their descriptions of queuing theory, optimum sequencing of cases, critical path analysis, optimum levels and mixes, optimum choice, and Markov chain analysis—in the context of delay—offer courts ways of theorizing about case processing time. Of course, translating management theories into practice in specific courts is by no means a simple or straightforward task.[1] But at least one court is trying to do just that.

The Orange county court

The Orange County (California) Superior Court actively utilizes one of these models, optimum sequencing of cases. We came across this phenomenon during the course of field observations of trial judges in that court, as part of a larger national study of the tasks which trial judges perform.[2] We believe we gained sufficient insight into this practice in the Orange county court to use information from it for illustrative purposes. In particular, I wish to discuss three key issues which arise when a court utilizes optimum sequencing of cases:

(1) How able is a court to collect accurate data to implement optimum sequencing?

(2) How likely is a court to consider establishing maximum time limits for processing cases?

(3) How will equity be affected—i.e., will certain classes of citizens have greater access to court adjudications?

At the time of our observations, the Orange County Superior Court had 32 judges serving in a unified master calendar. Most of these judges heard criminal and civil trials in the general trial division. Criminal cases take place within the context of a state speedy trial provision, but no such restriction exists for civil cases.[3] It is here that the court has implemented a version of the optimum sequencing principle.

---

1. The most recent writings on courts seem to suggest that the court is not an organization *per se*, but rather a place where a number of organizations and their representatives meet. *See* James Eisenstein and Herbert Jacob, FELONY JUSTICE: AN ORGANIZATIONAL ANALYSIS OF CRIMINAL COURTS. Boston: Little, Brown, 1977; Austin Sarat, *Understanding Trial Courts: A Critique of Social Science Approaches*, 61 JUDICATURE 318 (1978). Thus, the introduction of innovations must take into account the disparate, as well as shared, goals of these actors and their sponsoring organizations.

2. *See* John Paul Ryan, Allan Ashman, Bruce Dennis Sales, and Sandra Shane-DuBow, AMERICA'S TRIAL JUDGES AT WORK: THE ROLE OF ORGANIZATIONAL INFLUENCES, in preparation. (Supported by a grant to the American Judicature Society from the National Science Foundation, Division of Research Applied to National Needs, #76-14964.)

3. CAL. PEN. CODE §1381.

From John Paul Ryan, "Management Science in the Real World of Courts: Orange County's Experience with Optimum Sequencing," 62(3) *Judicature* 144-146 (September 1978). Copyright 1978 by the American Judicature Society.

Once a civil case is certified to be "at issue," it is assigned a trial date by the presiding judge of the court in "Department 1." This date depends upon two factors: (1) the presence of a jury trial request, and (2) the estimated time needed for actually trying the case. In December, 1976, jury trial requests with a three day or longer estimate were being assigned a date 17 months later (May, 1978). Jury requests with a shorter trial time estimate were assigned dates 10 months later. The assignment of non-jury cases was even more refined. Trials which were estimated at three days or longer received a date 11 months into the future; for two days, 10 months; and for one day, seven months later. "Short cause" matters (requiring two hours or less) were assigned dates within two months. Thus, the request for a jury trial, particularly one with a trial time estimate of three days or longer, resulted in potentially long waits for litigants.

Determining trial time

But how can a court know, in advance, the likely trial time of a particular case? Nagel *et al.* suggest "statistical prediction analysis," utilizing such variables, in civil cases, as plaintiff/defendant monetary demands and

If 'short cause' matters go to the head of the line, do affluent litigants battling for possession of boats, silverware and the family dog have greater access to justice than, say, workmen who fall off scaffolds?

offers, and the type of personal injury involved. Whether courts, even those currently using computers, could easily collect and incorporate this kind of data into their trial-setting calculus is problematic. Further, there is little empirical evidence to suggest that these factors are related to trial time to a degree large enough to be of predictive value.

In fact, the Orange county court, which does utilize computers for certain scheduling functions, uses a much simpler formula to determine likely trial time: the presiding judge asks each side's counsel to estimate how long the trial will take. Where the attorneys disagree, the judge accepts the longer estimate. This might seem to be uneventful but sound administrative practice, but invariably the *defense* made the longer estimate. Just as defendants often want to put off the day of reckoning as far as possible, many plaintiffs want to get to trial as soon as possible. These differences in perspective as to the "value" of delay are predictable enough in personal injury-type cases, but the determination of which perspective is more accurate—either in individual cases (as Nagel *et al.* propose) or across many cases—is not immediately clear.[4]

A second issue in the use of optimum sequencing is whether there will be a limit to the time which a case could, or should, spend waiting in the queue. Such a limit could be imposed externally (e.g., a speedy trial statute) or by local court practice. Optimum sequencing makes such limits more critical because it sends cases with long trial time estimates to the back of the line. In order to reduce delay in most cases (i.e., average delay), delay in some cases will actually have to be increased.

Because the Orange county court has not established outer limits for the processing of civil cases, it faces precisely this problem.

4. Survey responses, from Orange county judges, to a question asking about the time needed to try a typical "personal injury/auto accident" case before a jury indicated an average (mean) of 24.2 hours. Thus, if individual judges' estimates are reasonably accurate, the typical personal injury jury case would consume five court days, based upon data nationally (and from Orange County) indicating that the judge who hears a (civil) jury trial on a given day spends five hours on that day presiding at trial. Unpublished data, *supra* note 2.

Divorce settlements may quickly be obtained, but the relatively small proportion of litigants in search of an available courtroom for a jury trial were waiting 28 months at the time of our observations.[5] While Nagel *et al.* suggest that (arbitrary) limits can easily enough be established, they also acknowledge that additional resources might be needed to accomplish simultaneously optimum sequencing and acceptable maximum case processing time limits. Thus, the *likelihood* that a court can control the unwanted or undesirable consequences of "optimum" sequencing of cases is, perhaps, slim. Additional resources are not within the court's control, and the Orange county court for one has been locked in a political struggle for new judgeships.[6]

Access to justice

Finally, both optimum sequencing and its applications in real world settings affect the delivery of court services. Optimum sequencing, on its face, requires a preference, or value judgment, that cases should not necessarily be heard in the order in which they enter the system. In order to reduce overall delay, cases requiring longer trial times are penalized. This may be a desirable practice from a utilitarian philosophy (the greatest good for the most litigants) but not from other political or philosophical perspectives. We need more empirical information about whether classifying *cases* for scheduling purposes also results in classifying *litigants.* Are plaintiffs in personal injury cases different, for example, from litigants in divorce cases, with respect to social class, life-situation, etc.? More bluntly stated, do

affluent litigants battling for possession of boats, silverware and family dogs have greater access to the courts than, say, workmen who fall off scaffolds? "Short cause" matters may bring together not only different legal interests, but different social interests, compared with lengthy jury trial cases. It is these kinds of questions which need to be asked, and researched, when criteria *other than* simple queuing are applied to determine who is to be heard first.

Then, too, the application of the principle may result in biases. If courts rely on attorney estimates to determine trial time, *systematic* distortions may occur, particularly if the court does not have the time or other resources to ferret out actual causes of discrepancies in estimates.[7] The absence of maximum time limits for the processing of cases, so difficult to establish (especially on the civil side), further exacerbates the equity questions raised by a re-ordering of cases to achieve minimum average delay.

It has been fashionable in the literature of judicial administration to remove from easy purview questions focusing on the equity, or the distribution of, and access to, justice. Management practices are often spoken of in the context of science or "operations research." Competence of personnel is often appraised on narrow "technical" grounds. Nevertheless, policy questions are resilient, not easily buried even by a slew of management jargon.

Optimum sequencing of cases, on first blush seeming to be an obscure, value-free management precept, is integrally related to larger questions of citizen access to courts. In the administration of their internal affairs (as well as in their actual decisions), trial courts make policy which affects, however indirectly, the lives of those who seek justice in their courtrooms. □

---

5. Jeffrey Perlman, "Marathon Sessions Planned to Reduce Backlog of Civil Suits," *Los Angeles Times,* Orange County ed., December 10, 1976, Part II, p. 1. The disparity between the 28 months cited here and the 17 month figure noted earlier is probably a function of relatively few trials taking place on the date initially set for trial. Subsequent continuances, no doubt, stretch that 17 month period considerably.

6. California Governor Edmund G. Brown, Jr. has been a critic of his state's courts, including judges. His belief that judges work too short hours, exemplified by his delay in filling some 50 or more interim vacancy appointments, had a chilling effect on legislative approval of new judgeships in California. In addition, the county supplement required to fund new judgeships created a wave of local political controversy.

7. One way for a court like Orange County to determine the accuracy of attorney estimates is to "follow" cases retrospectively—e.g., to examine what percentage of cases, initially set for trial on a three day or longer estimate, actually consumed three days or longer when tried.

JOHN PAUL RYAN is senior research associate of AJS and project director of the Evaluation of Court Delay-Reduction Programs.

ABOUT THE EDITORS

Robert H. Haveman is Professor of Economics and Fellow, Institute for Research on Poverty, University of Wisconsin, Madison. From 1970 to 1975 he was Director of the Institute for Research on Poverty and a member of the Department of Economics. Prior to 1970, he was Professor of Economics at Grinnell College (1963-1975), Senior Economist on the Joint Economic Committee of the U.S. Congress (1968-1970), and Research Professor at the Brookings Institution. Professor Haveman's primary fields of interest are public finance and human resources economics. His publications include: with J. V. Krutilla, *Unemployment, Excess Capacity, and the Evaluation of Public Expenditures* (Baltimore: Johns Hopkins Press, 1968), *The Economics of the Public Sector* (New York: John Wiley, 1970), and with I. Garfinkel, *Earnings Capacity, Poverty, and Inequality* (New York: Academic Press, 1978). From 1971 to 1974 he was the editor of the Aldine *Benefit-Cost and Policy Analysis Annuals.* Professor Haveman has also published in *The American Economic Review, The Review of Economics and Statistics,* and the *Quarterly Journal of Economics.*

B. Bruce Zellner is a doctoral candidate in economics at the University of Wisconsin, Madison. He received the A.B. in 1963 from the City College of New York and attended Columbia University, Graduate Department of Economics, from 1963 to 1965. Mr. Zellner has also served as a consultant to the State of Wisconsin and the City of New York.